Machine Translation Summit XVIII

Volume 1: MT Research Track

Online
16 – 20 August 2021

Editors:

Kevin Duh
Francisco Guzman
Stephen Richardson

ISBN: 978-1-7138-3919-4

Printed from e-media with permission by:

Curran Associates, Inc.
57 Morehouse Lane
Red Hook, NY 12571

CURRAN ASSOCIATES INC.
proceedings
.com

Some format issues inherent in the e-media version may also appear in this print version.

Printed with permission by Curran Associates, Inc. (2022)

For permission requests, please contact the Association for Computational Linguistics at the address below.

Association for Computational Linguistics
209 N. Eighth Street
Stroudsburg, Pennsylvania 18360

Phone: 1-570-476-8006
Fax: 1-570-476-0860

acl@aclweb.org

Additional copies of this publication are available from:

Curran Associates, Inc.
57 Morehouse Lane
Red Hook, NY 12571 USA
Phone: 845-758-0400
Fax: 845-758-2633
Email: curran@proceedings.com
Web: www.proceedings.com

MT SUMMIT 20
VIRTUAL 21

Proceedings of Machine Translation Summit XVIII

https://mtsummit2021.amtaweb.org

Volume 1: MT Research Track

Editors:
Kevin Duh and Francisco Guzmán (Research Track Co-chairs)
Stephen Richardson (General Conference Chair)

Welcome to the 18th biennial conference of the International Association of Machine Translation (IAMT) – MT Summit 2021 Virtual!

Dear MT Colleagues and Friends,

This year's MT Summit is hosted by the Association for Machine Translation in the Americas (AMTA). Every two years, the Summit is hosted on a rotating basis by one of the three sister organizations comprising IAMT: the European Association for Machine Translation (EAMT), the Asian-Pacific Association for Machine Translation (AAMT), and of course, AMTA. While each of these organizations holds its own conferences annually or biennially, the Summit is always held in odd-numbered years, and this year, AMTA is grateful to have that honor.

After a tremendously successful MT Summit XVII held in Dublin in 2019, we anticipated an equally successfully Summit in 2021 given the rapidly accelerating interest in and research and development of neural machine translation (NMT) in both academia and industry. But as you all know, the year 2020 brought a major surprise that no one anticipated. Our biennial AMTA conference, scheduled for the fall of 2020 in Orlando, Florida was transformed into a completely virtual conference after much consternation followed by a great deal of effort. We successfully rescheduled the MT Summit 2021 conference at the same venue for the following year, thinking that it would at least be a "hybrid" conference, but alas, here we are once again with a completely virtual conference. This decision was made late in the game last April when, based on the results of a survey of likely participants, it become obvious that the vast majority would not be attending in person. Recent spikes in the cases of COVID throughout the world have further justified our decision to go completely virtual.

There have been some silver linings to this COVID cloud, however, the main one being that our AMTA 2020 virtual attendance was double that of previous years, and we anticipate that attendance for the virtual Summit will be at least double what it was in Dublin. We are also grateful that once again, we were able to reschedule our intended venue in Orlando, Florida for AMTA 2022. We hope that many of you will join us there in person! And yes, we will still add a virtual component to the conference for those who are yet unable to travel.

But enough of this COVID-related confusion! We are very pleased with the response we have had to our calls for papers, presentations, workshops, tutorials, and exhibitions for MT Summit 2021 and we are sure you'll agree that the program is brimming with relevant, exciting, and useful information, not to mention the many opportunities to view the latest technology demonstrations and opportunities to network with colleagues both old and new from across the MT spectrum. The most unique aspect of these conferences is that they are truly global gatherings of MT researchers, developers, providers, and users. Academics, students, and commercial researchers and developers are able to share their latest results and offerings with colleagues, in addition to receiving and understanding real-world user requirements. Individual MT users, as well as those from language services providers, enterprises, and governments, benefit from updates on leading-edge R&D in machine translation and have a chance to present and discuss their use cases.

At this point, I need to give some serious thanks to many organizations and individuals who have made this conference possible. First, we have received amazing support from our sponsors, for which we are tremendously grateful! Our visionary sponsor, Microsoft, made it possible for the first 150 students to register for the conference at a very significant discount, and those students quickly took advantage of this generous offer. Our Leader-level sponsors, who will be sponsoring our conference tracks, include: Apple, Intento, Lilt, Pangeanic, (RWS) Language Weaver, Systran, Vistatec, and Yandex Cloud. Our Patron-level sponsors are: Amazon (AWS), Facebook AI, Google, Kudo, Lengoo, Logrus Global, Star, and Welocalize. To all these companies we express our most sincere gratitude for their support of MT Summit 2021. Many of them will also give demonstrations of their systems and software during our Technology Exhibition Fair, and we hope that all our attendees will take advantage of this great opportunity to see the very latest commercial offerings and advancements in the world of MT. We are grateful to have three additional exhibitors in the Fair as well: CustomMT, KantanMT, and XTM.

Finally, I need to give special thanks and recognition to the members of our organizing committee, all of whom have worked very hard and given many hours and days of their time, for the most part voluntarily, to make MT Summit 2021 a success. Listing their names and official positions doesn't really seem to be an adequate reflection of their work and sacrifice, but it's the best I can do here, and I trust they know how much their efforts are truly appreciated.

Patti O'Neill-Brown, AMTA VP, Networking chair
Natalia Levitina, AMTA Secretary
Jen Doyon, AMTA Treasurer
Kevin Duh, Research Track Co-chair
Paco Guzman, Research Track Co-chair
Janice Campbell, Users and Providers Track Co-chair
Jay Marciano, Users and Providers Track Co-chair, Workshops and Tutorials Chair
Konstantin Savenkov, Users and Providers Track Co-chair
Alex Yanishevsky, Users and Providers Track Co-chair, Conference Online Platform Chair
Ben Huyck, Government Track Co-chair
Steve La Rocca, Government Track Co-chair
Ray Flournoy, Sponsorships Chair
Kenton Murray, Student Mentoring Chair
Elaine O'Curran, AMTA Counselor, Publications Chair
Alon Lavie, AMTA Consultant
Konstantin Dranch, Communications Chair
Kate Ozerova, Marketing Lead
Darius Hughes, Webmaster

Again, welcome one and all to MT Summit XVIII 2021! I look forward to "seeing" you online and hopefully, too, in person in the future.

Steve Richardson
IAMT President and MT Summit 2021 General Conference Chair

Introduction

The research track at MTSummit 2021 continues the tradition of bringing MT practitioners together from academia, industry and government from around the world.

This year we have a very rich program with 24 papers from a variety of topics. The most popular subject this year is low-resource machine translation, with papers spanning unsupervised MT, bilingual lexicon induction and curriculum learning. In addition, we have many works discussing modeling (e.g. transfer learning, domain adaptation and reinforcement learning); others discussing morphology (e.g. target-side inflection, subword tokenization); domain-specific translation (e.g. user-generated content translation, product-reviews); and papers performing error analyses of modern NMT systems and understanding their limitations. We are also excited about our invited keynote speakers for the research track: Lucia Specia (Imperial College London) will talk about Multimodal Simultaneous MT, while Graham Neubig (Carnegie Mellon University) will discuss Context-aware MT.

We hope that this conference brings many productive exchanges of ideas and sparks future collaborations.

We would like to thank the hard work of individuals that made this happen: the authors, the reviewers, the MT Summit organizing committee. We would also like to thank Michael Denkowski for numerous pieces of advice on organizing the research track.

Sincerely,

Kevin Duh and Francisco Guzmán (Research Track Co-Chairs)

Program Committee

Yuki Arase (Osaka University)
Nguyen Bach (Alibaba US)
Pushpak Bhattacharya (IIT Bombay)
Alexandra Birch (University of Edinburgh)
Marine Carpuat (University of Maryland)
Francisco Casacuberta (UPV)
Daniel Cer (Google Research; UC Berkeley)
Vishrav Chaudhary (Facebook)
Boxing Chen (Alibaba Group)
Colin Cherry (Google)
Raj Dabre (NICT)
Asif Ekbal (IIT Patna)
Akiko Eriguchi (Microsoft)
Angela Fan (Facebook)
Atsushi Fujita (NICT)
Hongyu Gong (Facebook)
Matthias Huck (SAP SE)
Katharina Kann (Univ. of Colorado Boulder)
Rebecca Knowles (NRC)
Philipp Koehn (Johns Hopkins University)
Shankar Kumar (Google)
Anoop Kunchukuttan (Microsoft)
Alon Lavie (Unbabel)
Gurpreet Lehal (PU)
Yang Liu (Tsinghua University)
Kelly Marchisio (Johns Hopkins University)
Daniel Marcu (Amazon)
Josep Maria Crego (Systran)
Benjamin Marie (NICT)
Marianna Martindale (University of Maryland)
Haitao Mi (Ant Group)
Tetsuji Nakagawa (Google)
Toshiaki Nakazawa (The University of Tokyo)
Jan Niehues (Maastricht University)
Vassilina Nikoulina (Naver Labs Europe)
Atul Ojha (National Univ. of Ireland Galway)
Shantipriya Parida (Idiap Research Institute)
Stephan Peitz (Apple Inc.)
Juan Pino (Facebook)
Maja Popovic (ADAPT Centre @ DCU)
Jean Senellart (Systran)
Rico Sennrich (University of Zurich)
Christophe Servan (Qwant)
Patrick Simianer (Lilt)
Matthias Sperber (Apple)
Katsuhito Sudoh (NAIST)
Christoph Tillmann (IBM Research)
Marco Turchi (FBK)
Josef van Genabith (Saarland University)
Yogarshi Vyas (Amazon AI)
Xinyi Wang (Carnegie Mellon University)
Taro Watanabe (NAIST)
Derek F. Wong (University of Macau)
François YVON (CNRS)
Jiajun Zhang (Institute of Automation, CAS)
Bing Zhao (SRI International)

Contents

Learning Curricula for Multilingual Neural Machine Translation Training

Gaurav Kumar gkumar@cs.jhu.edu
Philipp Koehn phi@jhu.edu
Sanjeev Khudanpur khudanpur@jhu.edu
CLSP, Johns Hopkins University, Baltimore, 21218, USA

Abstract

Low-resource Multilingual Neural Machine Translation (MNMT) is typically tasked with improving the translation performance on one or more language pairs with the aid of high-resource language pairs. In this paper, we propose two simple search based curricula – orderings of the multilingual training data – which help improve translation performance in conjunction with existing techniques such as fine-tuning. Additionally, we attempt to learn a curriculum for MNMT from scratch jointly with the training of the translation system using contextual multi-arm bandits. We show on the FLORES low-resource translation dataset that these learned curricula can provide better starting points for fine tuning and improve overall performance of the translation system.

1 Introduction

Curriculum learning (Bengio et al., 2009; Elman, 1993; Rohde and Plaut, 1994) hypothesizes that presenting training samples in a meaningful order to machine learners during training may help improve model quality and convergence speed. In the field of Neural Machine Translation (NMT) most curricula are hand designed e.g., fine-tuning (Luong and Manning, 2015; Freitag and Al-Onaizan, 2016) and data selection (Moore and Lewis, 2010; Axelrod et al., 2011; Duh et al., 2013; Durrani et al., 2016). Another common curriculum is one based on ordering samples from *easy* to *hard* using linguistic features and auxiliary model scores (Zhang et al., 2018, 2019) but these are hard to tune, relying to extensive trial and error to find the right hyperparameters. Attempts to learn a curriculum jointly with the NMT training setup (Kumar et al., 2019) can suffer from observation sparsity, where a single training run does not provide enough training samples for an external agent to learn a good curriculum policy.

Our NMT task of choice in this paper is *low-resource multi-lingual NMT* (MNMT). While standard NMT systems typically deal with a language pair, the source and the target, an MNMT model may have multiple languages as source and/or target. Most large-scale MNMT models are trained using some form of model parameter sharing (Johnson et al., 2017; Aharoni et al., 2019; Arivazhagan et al., 2019; Bapna and Firat, 2019). The notion of how input data should be presented to the MNMT system during training only finds prominence in the case of low-resource MNMT. A typical low-resource task will try to leverage a high-resource language pair to aid the training of an NMT system for a low-resource (very small or no parallel data available) and related language-pair of interest. Typical approaches for low resource MNMT involve pivoting and zero-shot training (Lakew et al., 2018; Johnson et al., 2017) and transfer learning via fine-tuning (Zoph et al., 2016; Dabre et al., 2019). Finn et al. (2017) attempt to meta-learn parameter initialization for child models using trained-high resource parent models for this task.

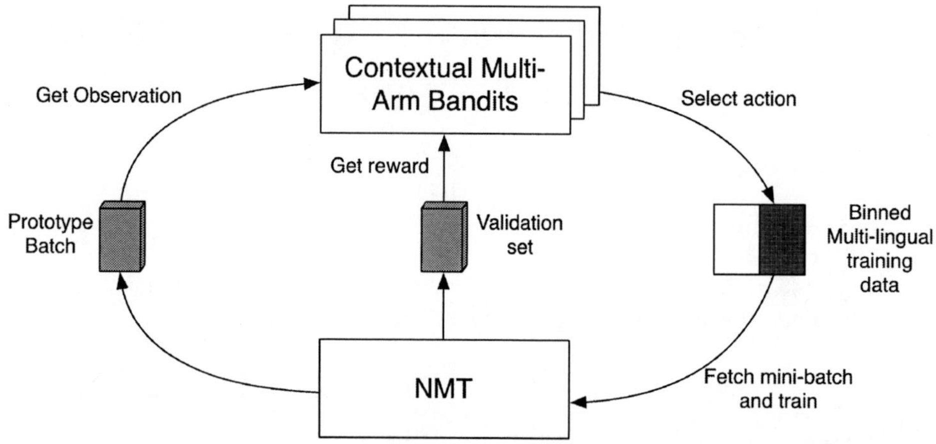

Figure 1: The multi-arm bandit agents' (MAB) interface with the NMT system.

In this paper, we build upon the framework for learning curricula introduced in Kumar et al. (2019) and attempt to alleviate the problem of observation sparsity by learning more robust policies from multiple training runs. We use contextual multi-arm bandits for our agents which learn multilingual data sampling policies jointly with the training of the NMT system. Additionally, we explore some simple policy search methods to our list of baselines; specifically, we try and find the best policies using the expensive grid search and pruned-tree search methods. We use state-of-the-art hand-designed curricula as our baselines to beat. Building upon the task and datasets established by Guzmán et al. (2019), in this paper, we will attempt to learn a curriculum to train an NMT system for the Nepali-English language pair while leveraging the high resource Hindi-English pair. The agent will learn to choose between mini-batches containing either Hindi-English or Nepali-English data at each time step during NMT training to maximize the expected reward (improvement in validation set performance). The learned curriculum will hence condition on the state of the NMT system during training and determine whether to expose it to a batch of Nepali-English or Hindi-English data. We start by presenting our methods for obtaining search-based and learned curricula in section 2. We present our experiment setup in section 3 and results in section 4.

2 Methods

The procedure for learning a multi-lingual training curriculum uses multiple multi-arm bandits as agents which explore independent of each other in randomly initialized environments (NMT systems) and effectively learn their own policies. The stochastic nature of their exploration policy ensures that they explore different action-reward spaces (the agent executes an action on the NMT environment and receives a reward associated with this action). Figure 1 shows an overview of this interface. The training data for all agents is pooled at the end of the training of individual agents and one final agent is trained using this data which determines the final policy we use as our multi-lingual curriculum. We provide more details about this method of learning and the associated baselines below.

2.1 Data Binning

Instead of mixing together all the language pairs into one single dataset, we create separate *bins* for each language pair. Hence, with respect to the agent, this is a two bin problem, where its

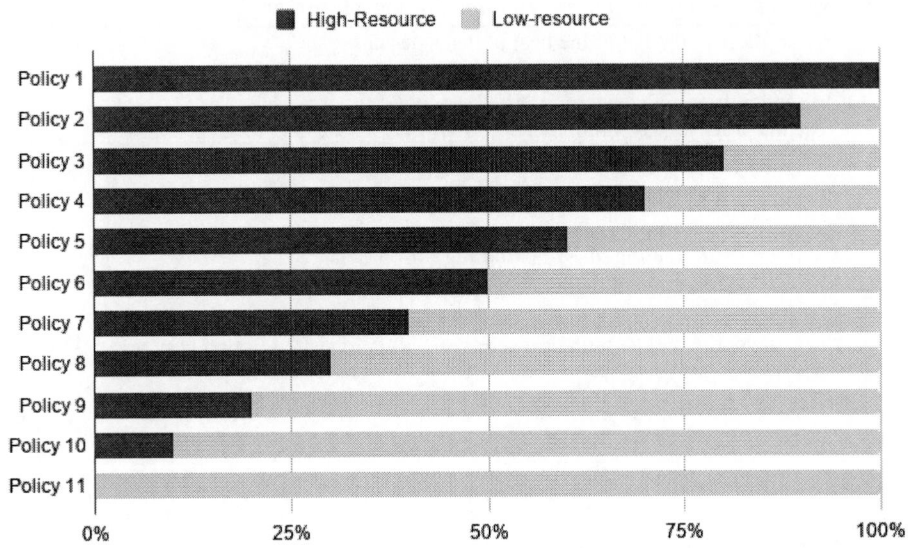

Figure 2: A line search for a fixed curriculum baseline which samples from one language pair (high resource, Hindi-English) with a fixed probability or else samples from the other (low resource, Nepali-English).

action is the choice of the bin to draw the next mini-batch for NMT training. As a result of this design decision, each batch will only contain a single language pair and will hence we relatively homogeneous (with respect the the feature of interest, language id). More generally, this can be extended to an arbitrary number of bins, one per language-pair being used to train the MNMT system.

2.2 Grid-search baselines

The simplest (albeit expensive to find) search-based learn-able curriculum to consider in this case is one where we sample batches from one language with a fixed probability or else sample from the other bin during training. Since there is only one degree of freedom (the probability of sampling from one language-pair) in this search problem, we perform a simple line-search over the range of possible values for this probability. Note that, although this curriculum is 'learned' it remains fixed during each training run and does not change based on the state of the NMT system. Figure 2 shows a visual representation of this search method.

2.3 Pruned Tree search

A variation of the previous search method involves one which uses a technique similar to beam search. We divide training into a finite number of *phases* and then starting from the beginning of training, we search for the best fixed sampling probability. At the end of this *phase*, we discard all but the best model and the policy (sampling probability) which led to it, and continue the search for the best policy in the next phase from this model checkpoint. The result is a tree-search which prunes all but the best node after each phase. The final policy is the culmination of all phase-wise best fixed sampling ratios. This procedure appears in Algorithm 1.

Algorithm 1: Pruned tree-search for multi-lingual curricula search

Result: P^*, the list of the best policies per phase
$\hat{p} = \{0.0, 0.1, \cdots, 1.0\}$ // Policies to explore;
Randomly initialize starting NMT model Θ^*;
while *NMT next training phase t exists* **do**
  for p *in* $\hat{p}$ **do**
    Bin sampling probablity = p;
    Training start checkpoint = Θ^*;
    Run training of NMT training for phase t;
    Store trained model checkpoint θ
  end
  Select model θ^* with best score on validation set with policy p^*;
  $P^* = P^* + [(t, p^*)]$;
  $\Theta^* = \theta^*$;
end

2.4 Observation Engineering

The observations provided to the multi-arm bandit agents are identical in structure to the ones introduced in Kumar et al. (2019). A *prototype* batch – a finite number of sentences from each language pair – is randomly sampled per bin (language-pair) and concatenated together. At each time step, the observation is the vector containing sentence-level log-likelihoods produced by the NMT system for this prototype batch. We exclude observations from the initial portion of NMT interaction to counteract the naturally decaying property of log-likelihood scores during NMT training.

2.5 Contextual Multi-arm Bandits

Multi-arm bandit (MAB) based agents are typically trained to learn policies which maximize the expected reward received (minimize regret). Contextual multi-arm bandits (Pandey et al., 2007; Chih-Chun Wang et al., 2005; Langford and Zhang, 2008) allows the use of state based information to determine this policy. In our case the contextual MABs condition on the *observation* received from the NMT system to determine an *action*, the choice of bin to sample a mini-batch. The *reward* obtained for this action is the *delta-validation perplexity* post update, the improvement in perplexity on the validation set in a finite window. The exploration strategy is the linearly-decaying *epsilon-greedy* strategy (Kuleshov and Precup, 2014). The contextual MABs are implemented as simple feed-forward neural networks which take the *observation* vector as input and produce a distribution over two states representing the bins. If we choose to *exploit* this learned policy, the bin with maximum probability mass is selected for sampling.

3 Experiment Setup

We use Fairseq (Ott et al., 2019) for all our NMT experiments and the our NMT systems are configured to replicate the setup described in Guzmán et al. (2019). The grid search experiments search over the the range $[0, 1]$ for sampling in increments of 0.1. The pruned tree-search uses a beam width of 1. The phase duration for tree-search is set to one epoch of NMT training. We use either 5 or 10 concurrent contextual MABs which are implemented as two 256-dimensional feed forward neural networks trained using RMSProp with a learning rate of 0.00025 and a decay of 0.95. Rewards for the agent (validation delta-perplexity) are provided every ten training steps. To create the observations, we sample 32 prototype sentences from each bin to create a *prototype*

Dataset	Sentences	Tokens
Nepali-English	563K	6.8M
Hindi-English	1.6M	16.7M

Table 1: Statistics of the training data for the Nepali-Hindi-English multilingual NMT system.

	valid	test
Baselines		
ne-en: Random Baseline	6.35	7.71
hi-en: Random baseline (with ne valid)	2.71	3.9
ne-hi-en: Random Baseline	**12.24**	**14.88**
ne-hi-en: Multi-lingual Transformer	12.01	14.78
ne-hi-en: Continued training from hi-en	12.2	14.3
Searched Curricula		
Grid Search (best = 50/50)	12.01	14.78
Grid Search (best = 50/50) + Continued training	**12.33**	**15.1**
Pruned Tree-search	12.3	14.8
Pruned Tree-search + Continued training	12.41	14.92
Agent Learned Curricula		
MAB2 (best = 10 concurrent, 500 updates)	12.21	14.87
MAB4 (best = 5 concurrent, 2 epochs)	12.18	14.67
MAB2 + Continued Training	**12.4**	**15.45**
MAB4 + Continued Training	12.27	15.2

Table 2: BLEU scores for the Nepali-English test set using the fixed, searched and learned multilingual curricula. The values in bold are the best results per section. Continued training from the models learned using multi-arm bandits provides the best results overall.

batch of 64 sentences and measure sentence level log-likelihood after each update. We use an NMT warmup of 5000 steps (no training data for the agent from this period is recorded). For the exploration strategy we use a linearly decaying epsilon function with decay period set to 25k steps. The decay floor was set to 0.01. The window for the delta-perplexity reward was 1.

We use the datasets provided as part of the FLORES task (Guzmán et al., 2019) for our experiments. The statistics of the training dataset for the multi-lingual task appear in table 1. The Hindi-English dataset comes from the IIT Bombay corpus[1]. The validation and test sets for Nepali-English (the low resource language-pair of interest) contain 2500 and 3000 sentences respectively.

4 Results

Our results are presented in Table 2. Our baselines consist of:

- ne-en random baseline: This is the NMT setup which is only trained on the Nepali-English corpus. The data is randomly shuffled to form mini-batches.
- hi-en random baseline: The NMT system trained on the high-resource Hindi-English dataset with the Nepali-English validation and test sets.

[1] `http://www.cfilt.iitb.ac.in/iitb_parallel`

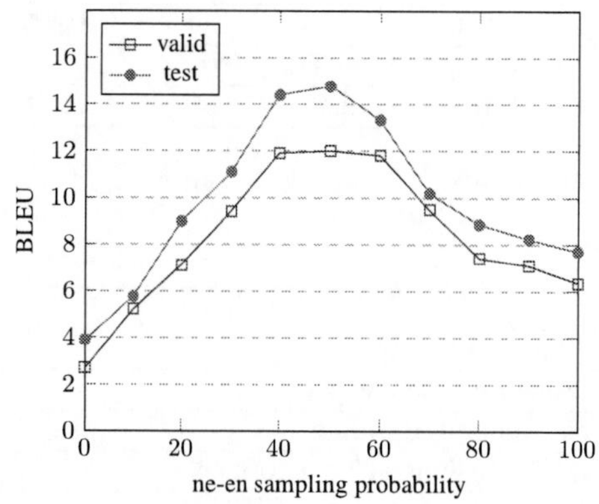

Figure 3: BLEU scores for the Nepali-English validation and test set at various values of the ne-en sampling probability.

- ne-hi-en random baseline: The Hindi-English and Nepali-English data is mixed together to train the NMT system. The Nepali-English data is upsampled to match the size of the the Hindi-English corpus.
- Multilingual transformer: Replicates the setup from Guzmán et al. (2019).
- Continued training baseline: Uses the hi-en random baseline as a starting point to fine tune using the Nepali-English validation and test sets.

Our non-MAB search-based curriculum baselines are:

- Grid search: A static curriculum is learned by searching over the space of sampling probabilities for the bins.
- Grid Search + Continued training: The previous model is fine tuned using the Nepali-English validation and test sets.
- Pruned tree-search: Epoch-dependent curriculum searched using the pruned tree-search method.
- Pruned tree-search + Continued training: The previous model is fine tuned using the Nepali-English validation and test sets.

From Table 2, we see that the ne-en and hi-en baselines are very weak, with the latter lagging behind despite having access to more data. This indicates that with these language pairs, even though adding the high-resource dataset may help, in isolation it is not a good proxy for the low-resource pair. The random baseline with the combination of the two datasets (upsampled low-resource) is the strongest amongst the fixed baselines marginally beating the multi-lingual transformer and (surprisingly) the continued training baselines. While the grid search and pruned-tree search baselines are close in performance to the best fixed baselines, continued training with them provides much stronger results where the 50/50 configuration for the grid search[2] provides the best result at 15.1 BLEU and the tree search slightly behind at 14.92 BLEU. Figure 3 shows the BLEU scores for the grid search experiments over the chosen search points in the probability space (the probability of sampling from the low resource language pair).

[2]Note that the grid search method has access to the binned data and can only ever select data from one language

	valid	test
MAB1 (5 conc., 500 updates)	12.2	14.11
MAB2 (10 conc., 500 updates)	**12.21**	**14.87**
MAB3 (5 conc., 1 epoch)	11.44	13.98
MAB4 (5 conc., 2 epoch)	12.18	14.67
With continued training		
MAB2 + Continued Training	**12.4**	**15.45**
MAB4 + Continued Training	12.27	15.2

Table 3: BLEU scores for the Nepali-English test set using various configurations (number of concurrent agents, policy update interval) of the contextual MABs to learn the multilingual sampling curriculum.

For the contextual MABs, we use either 5 or 10 concurrent agents; training data is gathered from all concurrent bandits to train the final curriculum. In addition, we choose to update the bandit policy only once every 500 updates, 1 epoch or 2 epochs of NMT training. The results of all our experiments appear in table 3 and the best configurations are in table 2. While the curricula learned using the contextual MABs are able to match the performance of the strongest fixed policy (ne-hi-en random baseline), it performs slightly worse than the curriculum obtained using the (expensive) grid search combined with continued training, by about 0.2 BLEU points. Interestingly, continuing training from the models trained using the curricula learned by the MABs leads to the strongest results. Specifically, using the model trained using the curriculum learned by the strongest MAB (MAB2 in Table 2) results in a BLEU score of 15.45 on this task, a gain of 0.6 on the strongest baseline.

5 Conclusion

In this paper, we present techniques which learn curricula for multilingual NMT training from multiple training runs and agents. On the task of low-resource multilingual NMT training, we use conditional multi-arm bandits which condition on the state of the NMT system and learn policies which determine whether to train on a batch of a high-resource (Hindi-English) or the low-resource (Nepali-Hindi) language pair per step in training. In addition, we introduce some simple search-based methods for policy search (grid search and pruned tree search) for this task. We show that both these simple *learned* curricula and the ones derived from the MABs can match the state-of-the-art hand-designed multilingual baselines. However, continued training on models trained using these *learned* curricula yields better results, indicating that they may serve as good starting models for fine-tuning.

References

Aharoni, R., Johnson, M., and Firat, O. (2019). Massively multilingual neural machine translation. In *Proceedings of the 2019 Conference of the North American Chapter of the Association for Computational Linguistics: Human Language Technologies, Volume 1 (Long and Short Papers)*, pages 3874–3884, Minneapolis, Minnesota. Association for Computational Linguistics.

Arivazhagan, N., Bapna, A., Firat, O., Lepikhin, D., Johnson, M., Krikun, M., Chen, M. X., Cao, Y., Foster, G. F., Cherry, C., Macherey, W., Chen, Z., and Wu, Y. (2019). Massively multilingual neural machine translation in the wild: Findings and challenges. *CoRR*, abs/1907.05019.

pair or the other, resulting in relatively homogeneous training batches. This is in contrast to the truly random baseline, (ne-hi-en) random, which can have mixed data in mini-batches.

Axelrod, A., He, X., and Gao, J. (2011). Domain adaptation via pseudo in-domain data selection. In *Proceedings of the Conference on Empirical Methods in Natural Language Processing*, EMNLP '11, pages 355–362. Association for Computational Linguistics.

Bapna, A. and Firat, O. (2019). Simple, scalable adaptation for neural machine translation. In *Proceedings of the 2019 Conference on Empirical Methods in Natural Language Processing and the 9th International Joint Conference on Natural Language Processing (EMNLP-IJCNLP)*, pages 1538–1548, Hong Kong, China. Association for Computational Linguistics.

Bengio, Y., Louradour, J., Collobert, R., and Weston, J. (2009). Curriculum Learning. In *Proceedings of the 26th Annual International Conference on Machine Learning*, ICML '09, pages 41–48, Montreal, Quebec, Canada. ACM.

Chih-Chun Wang, Kulkarni, S. R., and Poor, H. V. (2005). Bandit problems with side observations. *IEEE Transactions on Automatic Control*, 50(3):338–355.

Dabre, R., Fujita, A., and Chu, C. (2019). Exploiting multilingualism through multistage fine-tuning for low-resource neural machine translation. In *Proceedings of the 2019 Conference on Empirical Methods in Natural Language Processing and the 9th International Joint Conference on Natural Language Processing (EMNLP-IJCNLP)*, pages 1410–1416, Hong Kong, China. Association for Computational Linguistics.

Duh, K., Neubig, G., Sudoh, K., and Tsukada, H. (2013). Adaptation data selection using neural language models: Experiments in machine translation. In *The 51st Annual Meeting of the Association for Computational Linguistics (ACL)*, pages 678–683, Sofia, Bulgaria.

Durrani, N., Sajjad, H., Joty, S. R., and Abdelali, A. (2016). A deep fusion model for domain adaptation in phrase-based MT. In *COLING*, pages 3177–3187. ACL.

Elman, J. L. (1993). Learning and development in neural networks: the importance of starting small. *Cognition*, 48(1):71 – 99.

Finn, C., Abbeel, P., and Levine, S. (2017). Model-agnostic meta-learning for fast adaptation of deep networks. *CoRR*, abs/1703.03400.

Freitag, M. and Al-Onaizan, Y. (2016). Fast domain adaptation for neural machine translation. *CoRR*, abs/1612.06897.

Guzmán, F., Chen, P.-J., Ott, M., Pino, J., Lample, G., Koehn, P., Chaudhary, V., and Ranzato, M. (2019). The FLORES evaluation datasets for low-resource machine translation: Nepali–English and Sinhala–English. In *Proceedings of the 2019 Conference on Empirical Methods in Natural Language Processing and the 9th International Joint Conference on Natural Language Processing (EMNLP-IJCNLP)*, pages 6098–6111, Hong Kong, China. Association for Computational Linguistics.

Johnson, M., Schuster, M., Le, Q. V., Krikun, M., Wu, Y., Chen, Z., Thorat, N., Viegas, F., Wattenberg, M., Corrado, G., Hughes, M., and Dean, J. (2017). Google's multilingual neural machine translation system: Enabling zero-shot translation. *Transactions of the Association for Computational Linguistics*, 5:339–351.

Kuleshov, V. and Precup, D. (2014). Algorithms for multi-armed bandit problems. *CoRR*, abs/1402.6028.

Kumar, G., Foster, G., Cherry, C., and Krikun, M. (2019). Reinforcement learning based curriculum optimization for neural machine translation. In *Proceedings of the 2019 Conference of the North American Chapter of the Association for Computational Linguistics: Human Language Technologies, Volume 1*

(Long and Short Papers), pages 2054–2061, Minneapolis, Minnesota. Association for Computational Linguistics.

Lakew, S. M., Lotito, Q. F., Negri, M., Turchi, M., and Federico, M. (2018). Improving zero-shot translation of low-resource languages. *CoRR*, abs/1811.01389.

Langford, J. and Zhang, T. (2008). The epoch-greedy algorithm for multi-armed bandits with side information. In Platt, J., Koller, D., Singer, Y., and Roweis, S., editors, *Advances in Neural Information Processing Systems*, volume 20. Curran Associates, Inc.

Luong, M.-T. and Manning, C. D. (2015). Stanford neural machine translation systems for spoken language domain. In *International Workshop on Spoken Language Translation*, Da Nang, Vietnam.

Moore, R. C. and Lewis, W. (2010). Intelligent selection of language model training data. In *Proceedings of the ACL 2010 Conference Short Papers*, ACLShort '10, pages 220–224. Association for Computational Linguistics.

Ott, M., Edunov, S., Baevski, A., Fan, A., Gross, S., Ng, N., Grangier, D., and Auli, M. (2019). fairseq: A fast, extensible toolkit for sequence modeling. In *Proceedings of NAACL-HLT 2019: Demonstrations*.

Pandey, S., Agarwal, D., Chakrabarti, D., and Josifovski, V. (2007). Bandits for taxonomies: a model-based approach. In *SIAM Data Mining Conference*.

Rohde, D. L. and Plaut, D. C. (1994). Language acquisition in the absence of explicit negative evidence: how important is starting small? In *Cognition*, volume 72, pages 67–109.

Zhang, X., Kumar, G., Khayrallah, H., Murray, K., Gwinnup, J., Martindale, M. J., McNamee, P., Duh, K., and Carpuat, M. (2018). An empirical exploration of curriculum learning for neural machine translation. *CoRR*, abs/1811.00739.

Zhang, X., Shapiro, P., Kumar, G., McNamee, P., Carpuat, M., and Duh, K. (2019). Curriculum learning for domain adaptation in neural machine translation. In *Proceedings of the 2019 Conference of the North American Chapter of the Association for Computational Linguistics: Human Language Technologies, Volume 1 (Long Papers)*. Association for Computational Linguistics.

Zoph, B., Yuret, D., May, J., and Knight, K. (2016). Transfer learning for low-resource neural machine translation. In *Proceedings of the 2016 Conference on Empirical Methods in Natural Language Processing*, pages 1568–1575, Austin, Texas. Association for Computational Linguistics.

Investigating Active Learning in Interactive Neural Machine Translation

Kamal Kumar Gupta, Dhanvanth Boppana, Rejwanul Haque,[†] Asif Ekbal and Pushpak Bhattacharyya

Department of Computer Science and Engineering, Indian Institute of Technology Patna, Patna, India
[†]ADAPT Centre, School of Computing, Dublin City University, Dublin, Ireland
kamal.pcs17, boppana.cs17, asif, pb@iitp.ac.in
[†]rejwanul.haque@adaptcentre.ie

Abstract

Interactive-predictive translation is a collaborative iterative process, where human translators produce translations with the help of machine translation (MT) systems interactively. Various sampling techniques in active learning (AL) exist to update the neural MT (NMT) model in the interactive-predictive scenario. In this paper, we explore term based (named entity count (NEC)) and quality based (quality estimation (QE), sentence similarity (Sim)) sampling techniques – which are used to find the ideal candidates from the incoming data – for human supervision and MT model's weight updation. We carried out experiments with three language pairs, *viz.* German-English, Spanish-English and Hindi-English. Our proposed sampling technique yields 1.82, 0.77 and 0.81 BLEU points improvements for German-English, Spanish-English and Hindi-English, respectively, over random sampling based baseline. It also improves the present state-of-the-art by 0.35 and 0.12 BLEU points for German-English and Spanish-English, respectively. Human editing effort in terms of number-of-words-changed also improves by 5 and 4 points for German-English and Spanish-English, respectively, compared to the state-of-the-art.

1 Introduction

Neural machine translation (NMT) requires a significantly large amount of in-domain data for building the robust systems. Absence of sufficient training samples often result in the generation of erroneous output samples. Post-editing could be an effective solution in this situation, where human interference may help to rectify the errors in the output samples. However, there are two problems, *viz. (i)* post-editing a large number of output samples is time consuming and not very efficient in terms of productivity *and (ii)* not including all the post-edited examples might pose the risk of encountering the same mistakes in future. Hence, there is a necessity that instead of post-editing all the output samples, we explore effective sampling techniques for selecting important samples for post-editing, and further these post-edited samples are used to update the model's parameter following an active learning technique that makes the translation model learns from these (new) samples.

Interactive MT (IMT) is viewed as an effective mean to increase the productivity in the translation industry. In principle, IMT aims to reduce human effort in automatic translation workflows by employing an iterative collaborative strategy with its two most important

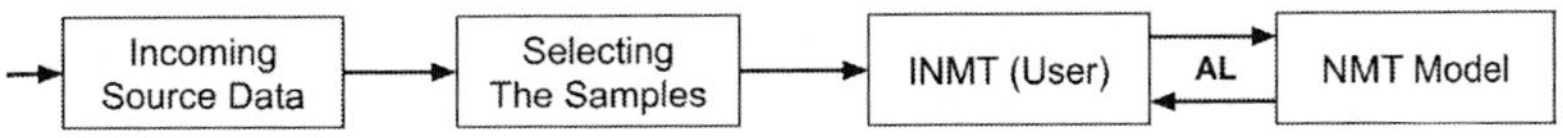

Figure 1: A pipeline showing the flow of data through sampling module, model updation through active learning.

components, the human agent and the MT engine. As of today, NMT models (Bahdanau et al., 2015; Vaswani et al., 2017) represent state-of-the-art in MT research. This has led researchers to test interactive-predictive protocol on NMT too. Papers (Knowles and Koehn, 2016; Peris et al., 2017) that pursued this line of research suggest that NMT is superior than phrase-based statistical MT (Koehn et al., 2003). So use of interactive NMT (INMT) for output sample correction can significantly reduce the overall translation time and active learning strategy can use human corrected samples for adapting the underlying NMT model so that in future, the model does not repeat previous errors and improves the translation quality.

The contributions of our current work are stated as follows:

- We propose term based (NEC) and quality based (QE and Sim) sampling techniques that provide us with the ideal source samples which are first post-edited using interactive NMT (INMT) and then used to update the Transformer (Vaswani et al., 2017) based NMT model.
- With the help of the proposed sampling techniques, we significantly reduce human efforts in correcting the hypothesis in terms of token replacements using this proposed INMT model.

2 Related Work

In a case, where an MT model is not providing high quality translation due to low resource or out-of-domain scenarios, it could be beneficial to update the model with new samples while preserving the previous knowledge too. There has been some works which deal with the large input data streams but generally adopt the incremental learning approaches (e.g. updating the model as the labelled data become available) rather than the active learning approach (where labelled data stream is not guaranteed). In the literature (Levenberg et al., 2010; Denkowski et al., 2014), authors used incremental learning to update the translation model but these were with respect to the statistical machine translation (SMT) model. Turchi et al. (2017) applied incremental learning over the NMT model where they used the human post-edited data to update the initially trained models which make it very costly and time consuming due to human-edited data. Nepveu et al. (2004); Ortiz-Martínez (2016) used an interactive paradigm for updating the SMT model on the iteratively corrected outputs.

As for active learning, it has also been well adopted for model learning. The unbounded and unlabelled large data streams is well suited to the objective of active learning (Olsson, 2009; Settles, 2009). This unbounded data stream scenario was explored by Haffari et al. (2009); Bloodgood and Callison-Burch (2010), where a pool of data was edited and the SMT model was updated using this data. González-Rubio et al. (2011) used the stream data to update the SMT model. Further, *interactive paradigm* of *SMT* was introduced in González-Rubio et al. (2012); González-Rubio and Casacuberta (2014).

Later, the NMT became more prominent and efficient in the interactive paradigm of *MT* (Knowles and Koehn, 2016; Peris et al., 2017). Peris and Casacuberta (2018) explored the application of active learning and IMT on the NMT model. They performed the experiments over the attention based encoder-decoder NMT model (Bahdanau et al., 2015). To handle the

Source	aunque nunca jugué un juego de beber basado en el tema nazi .
Reference	never played a Nazi themed drinking game though .
Initial Hypothesis	never played a Nazi drinking play there .
Hypo-1	never played a Nazi themed play though .
Hypo-2	never played a Nazi themed drinking though .
Hypo-3	never played a Nazi themed drinking game though .

Table 1: Hypothesis correction and translation in INMT process. Here, **Hypo-** shows the step by step correction by user to achieve reference/desired sentence

incoming and unlabelled data stream, they introduced the sampling techniques which are majorly attention and alignment based. We explore the sampling criteria on the basis of lexical properties (term-based) and semantic properties (quality-based). We observe the impact of the proposed sampling techniques over the Transformer based NMT.

3 Interactive Neural Machine Translation

In INMT (Knowles and Koehn, 2016; Peris et al., 2017), human translators correct errors in automatic translations in collaboration with the MT systems. Here, users read tokens of the generated hypothesis from left to right and modifies (insert/replace) his/her choice of words in the hypothesis generated by the NMT model. From the start index to the right most token position where the user make change is considered as the 'validated prefix'. After the user makes any change, the model regenerates a new hypothesis by preserving the validated prefix and new tokens next to it. Multiple attempts of token replacements may be required by a user to get the desired output as shown by an example in Table 1.

For an input-output sentence pair [x, y], where $x = (x_1, x_2, ..., x_m)$ being a sequence of input tokens and $y = (y_1, y_2, ..., y_n)$ being a sequence of output tokens, the probability of the ith translated word y_i is calculated as in Eq. (1):

$$p(y_i|y_1, ..., y_{i-1}, x) = f(y_{i-1}, s_i, c_i) \tag{1}$$

Here, s_i and c_i are the i^{th}decoder hidden state and context vector, respectively. As shown in Eq. (1), in NMT, during decoding, next predicted output y_i depends on model's previous output $y_1, ..., y_{i-1}$. In INMT, y_i will be generated by considering $y_1^*, ..., y_{i-1}^*$ as the previous tokens, where y_{i-1}^* is actually the token of user's choice at sequence position $i-1$. Eq. (2) shows the conditional probability of generating y_i in the INMT scenario.

$$p(y_i|y_1^*, ..., y_{i-1}^*, x) = f(y_{i-1}^*, s_i, c_i) \tag{2}$$

4 Sampling Techniques

From Figure 1, we see that the sampling module selects and recommends the incoming inference samples to the INMT for supervision. The purpose of a sampling technique is to filter out the ideal candidate from the incoming inference samples for which the trained NMT model is most uncertain and by supervising that sample it should increase the NMT performance using the technique of AL. Let *S* be the input sentences for inference, *B* be the block of sentences that are taken from *S* iteratively. From the block *B*, *C* a chunk, the size of which depends on the percentage (%) of the samples from *B* are taken, is used to be supervised from the human. We take the size of *B* as 10,000 samples and the chunk size from *B* can be 20, 40, 60 and 80%. The amount of samples is measured by the count of sentence pairs. The sampling techniques which are implemented are pool based, and basically belong to two categories, namely uncertainty

	English-German	English-Spanish	English-Hindi
Train	1.26m (Europarl)	1.9m (Europarl)	1.6m (IITB corpus)
Dev	1,057 (Europarl)	2000 (Europarl)	599 (IITB corpus)
Testset	59,975 (newscommentary)	51,613 (newscommentary)	47,999 (ILCI corpus)

Table 2: Size of the corpora used for the experiments

sampling (which labels those instances for which the model is least certain about the correct output to be generated) and query-by-committee (QbC) (where a variety of models are trained on the labeled data, and vote on the outputs of unlabeled data; label those instances which the committee disagrees the most). Hence, the objective of the sampling techniques as mentioned below is to select from the unbounded data stream S, those sentences $S'(\subset S)$ which are worth to be used to update the parameters p of the *NMT* model.

4.1 Random Sampling (RS)

In RS, samples from the unlabelled block are taken without any criteria or uncertainty metric. Even though random sampling has no logically involved concept still it is expected to produce good and diverse samples from this sampling. We consider random sampling as the baseline for the proposed sampling techniques.

4.2 Quality Estimation (QE)

Quality estimation (QE) is the process of evaluating the MT outputs without using gold-standard references. This requires some kind of uncertainty measure which indicates the confidence that the model has in translating the sentence. It uses human translation edit rate (HTER) score evaluation metric. The HTER score is generally used to measure human effort in editing (insert/replace/delete) the generated hypothesis (Specia et al., 2018). we use this as a confidence score of the translation model. A high HTER scored translation can be seen as a bad translation which requires more human effort for editing and a low HTER scored translation can be seen as a good translation which requires less human effort for editing. We did QE sampling using the *Openkiwi* toolkit (Kepler et al., 2019). Openkiwi provides the pre-trained QE models for language pairs (like English-German). We use one of the pre-trained models to obtain the HTER (uncertainty measure or score s_i) for every sentence S_i in the S data stream. In our case, the high HTER score is the sampling criteria. For every input sentence, this tool takes two inputs which are source sentence and translation of the source sentence generated by the initial *NMT* model and gives us the estimated *HTER* score. For a test sentence S_i in S where $(1 \leq i \leq |S|)$ $(|S| =$ number of sentences in $S)$, quality estimation (QE) pre-trained model takes S_i and its generated translation T_i, and returns the corresponding HTER score $HTER_i$.

4.3 Sentence Similarity (SS)

Here, we calculate the similarity between the source sentence and its round trip translation (source-to-target and again target-to-source translation) (Moon et al., 2020). We explore the similarity based sampling criteria since the quality of the round trip translation depends on the two intermediate translations i.e. forward translation (source-to-target) and back-translation (target-to-source). In case of a weak NMT model (i.e. MT system that does not generate high quality translations; e.g. say in low resource scenario or translating out-of-domain data), it is unlikely that a generated round-trip translation would be closer to the source sentence. As for the *RTT* setup, we had to train forward- and back-translation models. In this case, a low similarity score is the criteria for sampling. We calculated similarity between sentences in the following manner: (1). similarity between the semantic form of the sentences and (2). similarity between the lexical (surface) form of the sentences.

4.3.1 Similarity Based on Nearest Sentence Embedding (Sim_{emb})

On completion of RTT, the RTT-ed sentence may be different from the original source sentence but semantically similar to it, which is not captured by surface level metrics such as *BLEU*. In fact, we need information about the semantics of both source and back translation. 'Similarity based on sentence embedding' (Sim_{emb}) as the name itself suggests, this sampling technique uses a cosine similarity measure based on sentence embeddings. For every input sentence, two embeddings are generated: *1)* embedding of the source sentence and *2)* embedding of the RTT-ed sentence of the source sentence. These embeddings are generated using *S-BERT*[1] Reimers and Gurevych (2019). Sentences having the least similarity scores in the block are sampled and supervised by the user.

4.3.2 Similarity based on Edit distance between sentences (Sim_{fuzzy})

This similarity is a surface level similarity method and it does not take into account the semantics of the source and back translated sentences. In this sampling technique the similarity measure/score is based on the 'levenshtein-distance' between the source sentence and the round-trip translation of the source sentence. For every test sentence the similarity score (Sim_{fuzzy}) between the sentence and round-trip translation is calculated using 'fuzzywuzzy' toolkit[2] which is based on the levenshtein-distance and generates a score between 0-100 (0 and 100 are the lowest and highest similarity level). The sentences having the least score in the block are considered for supervision.

4.4 Named Entity Counting (NEC)

The NMT model suffers with the vocabulary restriction problem due to the limitation over the decoder side vocabulary size (Sennrich et al., 2016). Named entities (NEs) are open vocabularies and it is not possible for the NMT model to have all the NEs in the decoder vocabulary. Therefore, we considered presence of NEs as one of the sampling criteria. In other words, we took inability of the NMT model to translate the NEs perfectly into account for sampling. We count the NE tokens in each source sample of the incoming inference data and the sentences having the most number of NE tokens in the block are considered as "difficult to translate" by the NMT model, and hence filtered for supervision. We use Spacy[3] named entity recognizer (NER) for marking NEs in sentences from English, German and Spanish languages.

4.5 Query-by-committee (QbC)

Here, we combine the opinions of the random and the proposed sampling techniques to filter out the input samples for human supervision. Like Peris and Casacuberta (2018), we use a voted entropy function as in Eq. (3) to calculate the highest disagreement among the sampling techniques for a sample x. In the given Eq. (3), *#V(x)* is the number of sampling techniques voted for x to be supervised. *C* denotes the number of all the sampling techniques participating in the voting process.

$$C_{QbC}(x) = \frac{-\#V(x)}{|C|} + log\frac{\#V(x)}{|C|} \tag{3}$$

[1]https://github.com/BinWang28/SBERT-WK-Sentence-Embedding

[2]https://github.com/seatgeek/fuzzywuzzy

[3]https://spacy.io/usage/linguistic-features#named-entities

4.6 Attention Distraction Sampling (ADS)

Attention distraction sampling (ADS) is introduced by Peris and Casacuberta (2018). Attention based NMT distributes the weights over the source tokens based on their contribution in generating a target token. If the system finds the translation of a sample uncertain then the attention probability distribution features like the uniform distribution. It shows that NMT model is having difficulty in distributing weights over the source tokens based on their contribution in target generation. The samples having highest distraction are selected for active learning. The kurtosis of weights given by the attention model while generating y_i is calculated to measure the attention distraction.

$$Kurt(y_i) = \frac{\frac{1}{|x|}\sum_{j=1}^{|x|}(\alpha_{i,j} - \frac{1}{|x|})^4}{(\frac{1}{|x|}\sum_{j=1}^{|x|}(\alpha_{i,j} - \frac{1}{|x|})^2)^2} \tag{4}$$

Here, $\alpha_{i,j}$ is the attention weight between the j-th source word and i-th target word. Note that, the fraction $\frac{1}{|x|}$is equivalent to the mean of the attention weights of the word y_i. Finally, The kurtosis values for all the target words are used to obtain the attention distraction score.

5 Dataset

We carried out experiments on three language pairs using three benchmark datasets. Table 2 shows the statistics of training, development and test sets used for our experiments. In order to measure performance of the proposed sampling techniques, we use different domain datasets for training and testing. For German-English and Spanish-English, we use Europarl corpus (Koehn, 2005) for training and News-Commentary (NC) corpus for testing. This gives us a clear indication whether the translation models trained over Europarl corpus are able to adapt over the sampled examples from NC corpus using active learning. Similarly, for English-Hindi translation, we use the IITB corpus (Kunchukuttan et al., 2018) for training which is a combination of sentences from government sites, ted talks, administration books etc. As for evaluation, we use the ILCI corpus (Jha, 2010) which is a combination of sentences from the health and tourism domain.

6 Experimental Setup

Our experiments were based on the Transformer NMT model Vaswani et al. (2017). We used 6 layered Encoder-Decoder stacks with 8 attention heads. Embedding size and hidden sizes were set to 512, dropout rate was set to 0.1. Feed-forward layer consists of 2,048 cells. Adam optimizer (Kingma and Ba, 2015) was used for training with 8,000 warm up steps. We used the BPE (Sennrich et al., 2016) with a vocabulary size of 40K. Models were trained with OpenNMT toolkit[4] (Klein et al., 2020) with batch size of 2,048 tokens till convergence and checkpoints were created after every 10,000 steps. During inference, beam size is set to 5. We measured BLEU (calculated with *multi-bleu.pl* script) (Papineni et al., 2002) of the trained models on the test sets.

7 Results and Analysis

We evaluate the impact of the proposed sampling techniques for active learning in NMT in two different ways. Firstly, we test whether the proposed techniques help the NMT model to improve its translation performance in terms of the BLEU score. Secondly, in order to see whether the proposed techniques are able to reduce the human efforts (number of token correction required) in correcting the hypothesis, we compare the performance of the proposed

[4]https://opennmt.net/

En-to-De	20%	40%	60%	80%
Random	23.88	24.26	24.67	25.31
ADS	24.36	25.69	26.24	26.78
Quality estimation	24.02	24.98	25.61	26.17
Fuzzy	24.55	25.66	26.21	26.68
Sentence Similarity	24.35	25.73	26.47	26.9
NE Counting	25.22	26.14	26.31	26.84
QbC	25.51	26.08	26.69	27.13

En-to-Hi	20%	40%	60%	80%
Random	25.84	26.08	26.41	26.83
ADS	25.90	26.81	27.1	27.58
Fuzzy	25.97	26.67	27.03	27.52
Sentence Similarity	25.88	26.44	26.91	27.28
NE Counting	25.92	26.75	27.2	27.64
QbC	26.18	26.87	27.15	27.42

De-to-En	20%	40%	60%	80%
Random	25.19	26.32	27.11	27.05
ADS	25.80	26.58	27.39	27.98
Fuzzy	25.98	26.64	27.29	27.85
Sentence Similarity	26.18	26.73	27.52	28.11
NE Counting	25.50	26.38	27.26	27.48
QbC	26.53	26.83	27.62	28.13

Es-to-En	20%	40%	60%	80%
Random	39.16	39.52	40.19	40.87
ADS	39.50	39.85	40.51	41.52
Fuzzy	39.28	40.25	40.85	41.27
Sentence Similarity	39.74	39.91	40.75	41.64
NE Counting	39.43	39.74	40.36	41.38
QbC	39.78	40.26	40.97	41.68

Table 3: BLEU scores of the hypothesis generated by NMT model based on samples selected by different sampling techniques and % of data used to adapt it. For each translation direction, the initial BLEU score before applying the sampling techniques is: *En-to-De:* 23.28, *De-to-En:* 24.08, *En-to-Hi:* 25.76 and *Es-to-En:* 38.76

sampling techniques with the baseline i.e random sampling and the state-of-the-art sampling *i.e. attention distraction sampling (ADS)* (Peris and Casacuberta, 2018) methods.

7.1 Effect on Translation Quality

We consider the random sampling-based method as a baseline model. By increasing the amount of the supervised samples of the block recommended by the proposed sampling techniques with 20, 40, 60 and 80%, we observed changes in the BLEU score. The BLEU scores presented are calculated based on a single block of 10,000 sentences. Table 3 shows the BLEU scores for different translation directions. We also present the charts (see Figure 2) to illustrate the effect of the sampling techniques on the translation quality of the NMT model for the specific translation directions using AL. As can be seen from Figure 2, for English-to-German translation, the initial BLEU score of the trained NMT model before active learning was 23.28. By adapting the trained NMT to the new samples recommended by the random sampling, the BLEU score increases upto 25.31 (when 80% of the samples of block are supervised) which is 2.03 BLEU points improvement over the initial score. Compared to the random sampling, the proposed sampling techniques QE, Sim_{emb}, Sim_{fuzzy} and NEC yield 26.17, 26.90, 26.68 and 26.84 BLEU scores, respectively, by supervising 80% of the samples in the block. Here, we can see that Sim_{emb} performs the best and achieves 26.90 which is 1.59 BLEU more than that we obtain with the random sampling method (baseline). We also tested a combined opinion of sampling techniques (i.e. QbC) and it outperformed the other methods and produced 27.13 BLEU points, which is a 1.82 BLEU improvement over the one that we obtained after applying the random sampling method.

For German-to-English translation, we observed the BLEU score of 24.08 without using any active learning. The baseline INMT system (i.e. based on random sampling method) brought about 27.05 BLEU points on the test set. The INMT system with sentence-similarity sampling feature (i.e. Sim_{emb}) surpassed the baseline by 0.94 BLEU points. Furthermore, the QbC method outperforms all the other sampling methods, and with this, we achieve 28.13 BLEU points (an improvement of 1.08 points over the random sampling technique) on the test set.

In case of English-to-Hindi translation, the initial BLEU score was observed to be 25.76. Here, NEC was found to be the best performing sampling method. The INMT system setup

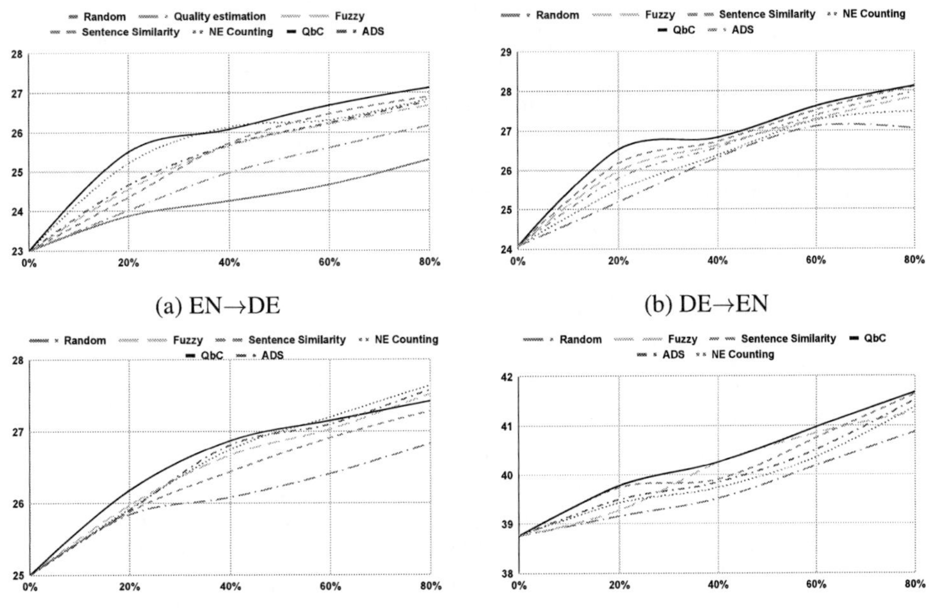

(a) EN→DE

(b) DE→EN

(c) EN→HI

(d) ES→EN

Figure 2: Presenting the BLEU score improvements of NMT model based on the new learned samples chosen by different sampling techniques and data size used to adapt it.

with this method statistically significantly outperforms the baseline INMT system (built on the random sampling method), and we obtain an improvement of 0.81 BLEU points over the baseline. The statistical significance test is performed using the bootstrap resampling method Koehn (2004).

For Spanish-to-English translation, the initial BLEU score was found to be 38.76. The baseline sampling strategy provided us with 40.87 BLEU points on the test set. As in English-to-German, QbC is found to be the best performing sampling method, and provides us a gain of 0.81 BLEU points over the baseline. It is to be noted that for Spanish-to-English translation, Sim_{emb} also yields the comparable score to that of one by QbC.

Furthermore, in Figure 2, we demonstrate the performance of different sampling techniques in AL for the German-to-English, English-to-German, English-to-Hindi and Spanish-to-English translation. The x-axis of the graphs in Figure 2 represents the amount (%) of the samples supervised in the block and the y-axis represents the BLEU scores. For English-to-Hindi, the baseline INMT model (i.e. random sampling) produces 26.83 BLEU points on the test set, which corresponds to an absolute improvement of 1.07 BLEU points over the vanilla NMT system (i.e. 25.76 BLEU points). NEC is found to be the best-performing sampling technique, and yields 27.64 BLEU points with an absolute improvement of 0.82 BLEU points over the baseline (random sampling).

As for Spanish-to-English translation, we see that Sim_{emb} significantly outperforms the random sampling by 0.77 BLEU points. Furthermore, for English-to-German, English-to-Hindi and Spanish-to-English, the respective best-performing sampling techniques, which are our proposed methods, bring about gains over ADS (Peris and Casacuberta, 2018) by 0.35, 0.06 and 0.12 BLEU scores. These improvements are very small and except English-to-German, the re-

	Random Sampling	QbC
En-to-De	52.06	57.73
De-to-En	45.60	50.45
En-to-Hi	37.82	46.14
Es-to-En	49.37	53.61

Table 4: Word prediction accuracy (WPA) of the NMT models for different translation directions with 80% samples supervised.

maining two improvements are not statistically significant[5]. However, in the next section, we will see that our proposed sampling techniques outperform ADS significantly in terms of human effort reduction.

7.2 Effect on Human Effort

We check if the proposed sampling techniques in AL are helpful to reduce the human effort in correcting (supervising) the generated hypothesis. For interaction between the user and the MT system, we used an INMT system which generates the hypothesis based on the NMT models adapted over the samples recommended by the sampling techniques in AL. Due to the high cost of involving humans in the performance evaluation, we measure the human effort in a reference-simulated environment, where the reference sentences are considered as the user's choice of sentences. The idea is to correct the hypothesis until it matches the reference sentence. Using different sampling techniques, we aimed at improving the translation quality of the NMT system. We recorded performance of the INMT system in terms of the model's ability to predict the next word at decoding. Every time the *user modified hypothesis* is fed to the NMT model, the model predicts next correct token based on the modifications made by the user. We calculate the model's accuracy in predicting the next words using a commonly-used metric: word prediction accuracy (WPA) metric. WPA is the ratio of the number of correct tokens predicted and the total number of tokens in the reference sentences Peris et al. (2017). Higher the WPA scores of the NMT model means the lesser human efforts in correcting the hypothesis. We also calculated human efforts using another metric: word stroke ratio (WSR). WSR is the ratio of the number of tokens corrected by the user and the total number of tokens present in the reference sentences Knowles and Koehn (2016). In our case, we investigated whether the proposed sampling techniques are able to reduce human efforts in translation (i.e. lower WSR and higher WPA scores are better).

Table 4 shows WPA scores of our INMT systems in different translation tasks. Here, we showed the WPA scores only when 80% of the samples in the block are supervised. We considered random sampling as the baseline and compared it with the QbC since we found that it is the best performing approach out of all proposed sampling techniques (i.e. Sim, NEC, Fuzzy) as far as WPA is concerned. In sum, the interactive-predictive translation setup with QbC surpassed the baseline setup by 5.67%, 4.85%, 8.32% and 4.24% accuracies in terms of WPA for the English-to-German, German-to-English, English-to-Hindi and Spanish-to-English translation tasks, respectively.

In Figure 3, we show WSR scores obtained by the different sampling techniques. As above, we considered varying sizes of sentences for supervision, i.e. 20, 40, 60 and 80% of the samples are supervised in a block. We calculated average number of total tokens replaced in the hypotheses generated by the NMT models adapted over the samples recommended by the sampling techniques. The x-axis of the graphs shows the % of samples supervised and y-axis shows

[5]https://github.com/moses-smt/mosesdecoder/blob/master/scripts/analysis/bootstrap-hypothesis-difference-significance.pl

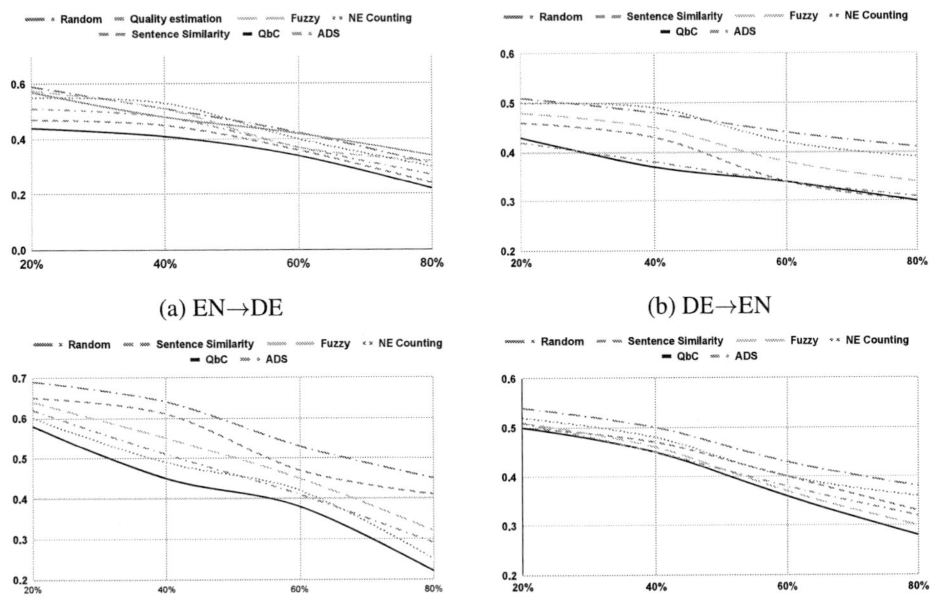

(a) EN→DE (b) DE→EN

(c) EN→HI (d) ES→EN

Figure 3: Human effort reduction in terms of token replacement in Interactive NMT

the average number of tokens replaced. As can be seen from the graphs, for English-to-German translation, QbC achieves statistically significantly absolute improvement of 1.82 BLEU points over the baseline. As for English-to-Hindi and Spanish-to-English, NEC and Sim_{emb} yield 0.81 and 0.77 BLEU improvements over the baseline. We also observed the reduction of human efforts in terms of word stroke ratio (WSR). For English-to-German, English-to-Hindi and Spanish-to-English, we achieve a reduction in WSR of 9%, 23% and 10% over the baseline. We also present the scores that were shown in graphs in Table 3. We see that for English-to-German translation, QbC performs the best with respect to WSR reduction. For German-to-English, QbC and Sim_{emb} are found to be the best-performing strategies. For English-to-Hindi and Spanish-to-English, along with the QbC, the second best-performing sampling techniques are NEC and Sim_{emb}, respectively. Unlike German-to-English and Spanish-to-English, for English-to-Hindi, Sim_{emb} is not the best-performing method. We observed that there may be some reasons for this: (i) morphological richness of Hindi, and (ii) syntactic divergence of English and Hindi languages. These might introduce more challenges in RTT in case of Sim_{emb}. We also compared the amount of human effort reduction by the proposed techniques and ADS. For English-to-German, English-to-Hindi and Spanish-to-English translation, we observed the reduction in WSR by 5, 7 and 4 points, respectively, over the ADS.

8 Conclusion

In this paper, we have explored the applicability of various sampling techniques in active learning to update the NMT models. We select the incoming source samples using the sampling techniques, correct them in an interactive NMT scenario and subsequently update the trained NMT model using the corrected parallel samples. It helps the model to adapt over the new parallel samples which results in improving the translation quality and reducing the human effort for further hypothesis correction. We proposed term based (NEC) and quality based (QE, Sim_{emb}, Sim_{fuzzy}) sampling techniques to pick the source samples from a large block of input sentences for correction and subsequently updating the NMT models. Since it is not feasible for a human to supervise (modify) a large set of input data coming for the translation, the proposed sampling techniques help to pick and recommend the suitable samples from large input data to the user for supervision. We measure the impact of sampling techniques by two criteria: *first*, improvement in translation quality in terms of BLEU score and *second*, reduction in human effort (i.e. number of tokens in generated outputs needed to correct).

We performed experiments over three language pairs i.e. English-German, English-Spanish and English-Hindi. We use different domain data for training and testing the NMT model to see if the NMT model trained over the data from one domain can successfully adapt to the different domain data. We empirically showed that the proposed term and quality based sampling techniques outperform the random sampling and outperformed the *attention distraction sampling (ADS)* method

9 Acknowledgement

The research reported in this paper is an outcome of the generous support received from the project "Hindi to English Machine Aided Translation for the Judicial Domain (HEMAT)", sponsored by the Technology Development in Indian Language (TDIL), MeiTy, Government of India.

References

Bahdanau, D., Cho, K., and Bengio, Y. (2015). Neural machine translation by jointly learning to align and translate. In *3rd International Conference on Learning Representations (ICLR 2015)*, San Diego, CA.

Bloodgood, M. and Callison-Burch, C. (2010). Bucking the trend: Large-scale cost-focused active learning for statistical machine translation. In *Proceedings of the 48th Annual Meeting of the Association for Computational Linguistics*, pages 854–864, Uppsala, Sweden. Association for Computational Linguistics.

Denkowski, M., Dyer, C., and Lavie, A. (2014). Learning from post-editing: Online model adaptation for statistical machine translation. In *Proceedings of the 14th Conference of the European Chapter of the Association for Computational Linguistics*, pages 395–404, Gothenburg, Sweden. Association for Computational Linguistics.

González-Rubio, J. and Casacuberta, F. (2014). Cost-sensitive active learning for computer-assisted translation. *Pattern Recognition Letters*, 37:124–134.

González-Rubio, J., Ortiz-Martínez, D., and Casacuberta, F. (2011). An active learning scenario for interactive machine translation. In *Proceedings of the 13th international conference on multimodal interfaces - ICMI '11*. ACM Press.

González-Rubio, J., Ortiz-Martínez, D., and Casacuberta, F. (2012). Active learning for interactive machine translation. In *Proceedings of the 13th Conference of the European Chapter of the Association for Computational Linguistics*, pages 245–254, Avignon, France. Association for Computational Linguistics.

Haffari, G., Roy, M., and Sarkar, A. (2009). Active learning for statistical phrase-based machine translation. In *Proceedings of Human Language Technologies: The 2009 Annual Conference of the North American Chapter of the Association for Computational Linguistics on - NAACL '09*. Association for Computational Linguistics.

Jha, G. N. (2010). The tdil program and the indian langauge corpora intitiative (ilci). In *LREC*.

Kepler, F., Trénous, J., Treviso, M., Vera, M., and Martins, A. F. T. (2019). OpenKiwi: An open source framework for quality estimation. In *Proceedings of the 57th Annual Meeting of the Association for Computational Linguistics–System Demonstrations*, pages 117–122, Florence, Italy. Association for Computational Linguistics.

Kingma, D. P. and Ba, J. (2015). Adam: A method for stochastic optimization. In Bengio, Y. and LeCun, Y., editors, *3rd International Conference on Learning Representations, ICLR 2015, San Diego, CA, USA, May 7-9, 2015, Conference Track Proceedings*.

Klein, G., Hernandez, F., Nguyen, V., and Senellart, J. (2020). The opennmt neural machine translation toolkit: 2020 edition. In *Proceedings of the 14th Conference of the Association for Machine Translation in the Americas (AMTA 2020)*, pages 102–109.

Knowles, R. and Koehn, P. (2016). Neural interactive translation prediction. In *Proceedings of AMTA 2016, vol. 1: MT Researchers' Track*, pages 107–120. Association for Machine Translation in the Americas, AMTA. Twelfth Conference of The Association for Machine Translation in the Americas, AMTA 2016 ; Conference date: 28-10-2016 Through 01-11-2016.

Koehn, P. (2004). Statistical significance tests for machine translation evaluation. In *Proceedings of the 2004 Conference on Empirical Methods in Natural Language Processing*, pages 388–395, Barcelona, Spain. Association for Computational Linguistics.

Koehn, P. (2005). Europarl: A parallel corpus for statistical machine translation. In *MT summit*, volume 5, pages 79–86. Citeseer.

Koehn, P., Och, F. J., and Marcu, D. (2003). Statistical phrase-based translation. In *HLT-NAACL 2003: conference combining Human Language Technology conference series and the North American Chapter of the Association for Computational Linguistics conference series*, pages 48–54, Edmonton, AB.

Kunchukuttan, A., Mehta, P., and Bhattacharyya, P. (2018). The IIT Bombay English-Hindi parallel corpus. In *Proceedings of the Eleventh International Conference on Language Resources and Evaluation (LREC 2018)*, Miyazaki, Japan.

Levenberg, A., Callison-burch, C., and Osborne, M. (2010). Stream-based translation models for statistical machine translation. In *In Proceedings of the 11th Annual Conference of the North American Chapter of the Association for Computational Linguistics (NAACL HLT 2010*.

Moon, J., Cho, H., and Park, E. L. (2020). Revisiting round-trip translation for quality estimation. In *Proceedings of the 22nd Annual Conference of the European Association for Machine Translation*, pages 91–104, Lisboa, Portugal. European Association for Machine Translation.

Nepveu, L., Lapalme, G., and Foster, G. (2004). Adaptive language and translation models for interactive machine translation. In *In Proc. of EMNLP*, pages 190–197.

Olsson, F. (2009). A literature survey of active machine learning in the context of natural language processing.

Ortiz-Martínez, D. (2016). Online learning for statistical machine translation. *Computational Linguistics*, 42(1):121–161.

Papineni, K., Roukos, S., Ward, T., and Zhu, W.-J. (2002). Bleu: a method for automatic evaluation of machine translation. In *Proceedings of the 40th annual meeting of the Association for Computational Linguistics*, pages 311–318.

Peris, Á. and Casacuberta, F. (2018). Active learning for interactive neural machine translation of data streams. In *Proceedings of the 22nd Conference on Computational Natural Language Learning*, pages 151–160, Brussels, Belgium. Association for Computational Linguistics.

Peris, Á., Domingo, M., and Casacuberta, F. (2017). Interactive neural machine translation. *Computer Speech & Language*, 45:201–220.

Reimers, N. and Gurevych, I. (2019). Sentence-bert: Sentence embeddings using siamese bert-networks. In *Proceedings of the 2019 Conference on Empirical Methods in Natural Language Processing*. Association for Computational Linguistics.

Sennrich, R., Haddow, B., and Birch, A. (2016). Neural machine translation of rare words with subword units. In *Proceedings of the 54th Annual Meeting of the Association for Computational Linguistics (Volume 1: Long Papers)*, pages 1715–1725, Berlin, Germany. Association for Computational Linguistics.

Settles, B. (2009). Active learning literature survey. Computer Sciences Technical Report 1648, University of Wisconsin–Madison.

Specia, L., Scarton, C., and Paetzold, G. H. (2018). Quality estimation for machine translation. *Synthesis Lectures on Human Language Technologies*, 11(1):1–162.

Turchi, M., Negri, M., Farajian, M. A., and Federico, M. (2017). Continuous learning from human post-edits for neural machine translation. *The Prague Bulletin of Mathematical Linguistics*, 108(1):233–244.

Vaswani, A., Shazeer, N., Parmar, N., Uszkoreit, J., Jones, L., Gomez, A. N., Kaiser, Ł., and Polosukhin, I. (2017). Attention is all you need. In *Advances in neural information processing systems*, pages 5998–6008.

Crosslingual Embeddings are Essential in UNMT for Distant Languages: An English to IndoAryan Case Study

Tamali Banerjee ⋆ tamali@cse.iitb.ac.in
Department of Computer Science and Engineering, IIT Bombay, India.

Rudra Murthy V ⋆ rmurthyv@in.ibm.com
IBM Research Lab, India.

Pushpak Bhattacharyya pb@cse.iitb.ac.in
Department of Computer Science and Engineering, IIT Bombay, India.

Abstract

Recent advances in Unsupervised Neural Machine Translation (UNMT) have minimized the gap between supervised and unsupervised machine translation performance for closely related language-pairs. However, the situation is very different for distant language pairs. Lack of lexical overlap and low syntactic similarities such as between English and Indo-Aryan languages lead to poor translation quality in existing UNMT systems. In this paper, we show that initialising the embedding layer of UNMT models with cross-lingual embeddings shows significant improvements in BLEU score over existing approaches with embeddings randomly initialized. Further, static embeddings (freezing the embedding layer weights) lead to better gains compared to updating the embedding layer weights during training (non-static). We experimented using Masked Sequence to Sequence (MASS) and Denoising Autoencoder (DAE) UNMT approaches for three distant language pairs. The proposed cross-lingual embedding initialization yields BLEU score improvement of as much as ten times over the baseline for English-Hindi, English-Bengali, and English-Gujarati. Our analysis shows the importance of cross-lingual embedding, comparisons between approaches, and the scope of improvements in these systems.

1 Introduction

Unsupervised approaches to training a neural machine translation (NMT) system typically involve two stages: (i) Language Model (LM) pre-training and (ii) finetuning of NMT model using Back-Translated (BT) sentences. Training a shared encoder-decoder model on combined monolingual data of multiple languages helps the model learn better cross-lingual representations (Conneau et al., 2020; Wang et al., 2019). Fine-tuning the pre-trained model iteratively using Back-translated sentences helps further align the two languages closer in latent space and also trains an NMT system in an unsupervised manner.

Unsupervised MT has been successful for closely related languages (Conneau and Lample, 2019; Song et al., 2019). On the other hand, very poor translation performance has been reported

*The two authors contributed equally to this paper.

for distant language pairs (Kim et al., 2020a; Marchisio et al., 2020). Lack of vocabulary overlap and syntactic differences between the source and the target languages make the model fail to align the two language representations together. Recently, few approaches (Kulshreshtha et al., 2020; Wu and Dredze, 2020) take advantage of resources in the form of bilingual dictionary, parallel corpora, *etc.* to better align the language representations together during LM pre-training.

In this paper, we explore the effect of initialising the embedding layer with cross-lingual embeddings for training UNMT systems for distant languages. We also explore the effect of static cross-lingual embeddings (embedding are not updated during training) *v/s* non-static cross-lingual embeddings (embedding are updated during training). We experiment with two existing UNMT approaches namely, MAsked Sequence-to-Sequence (MASS) (Song et al., 2019) and a variation of Denoising Auto-Encoder (DAE) based UNMT approach (Artetxe et al., 2018c; Lample et al., 2018) for English to IndoAryan language pairs *i.e.* English-Hindi, English-Bengali, English-Gujarati.

The contribution of the paper is as follows:

1. We show that approaches initialized with cross-lingual embeddings significantly outperform approaches with randomly initialized embeddings.

2. We observe that the use of *static cross-lingual embeddings* leads to better gains compared to the use of *non-static* cross-lingual embeddings for these language-pairs.

3. We did a case study of UNMT for English-IndoAryan language pairs. For these language-pairs SOTA UNMT approaches perform very poorly.

4. We observed that DAE-based UNMT with crosslingual embeddings performs better than MASS-based UNMT with crosslingual embeddings for these language-pairs.

The rest of the paper is organized as follows. In Section 2, we discuss the related work in detail. Then, we present our approach in Section 3. In Section 4, we outline the experimental setup and present the results of our experiments in Section 5. Finally, we conclude the paper and discuss future work in Section 6.

2 Related Work

Neural machine translation (NMT) (Cho et al., 2014; Sutskever et al., 2014; Bahdanau et al., 2015) typically needs a lot of parallel data to be trained on. However, parallel data is expensive and rare for many language pairs. To solve this problem, unsupervised approaches to train machine translation (Artetxe et al., 2018d; Lample et al., 2018; Yang et al., 2018) was proposed in the literature which uses only monolingual data to train a translation system.

Artetxe et al. (2018c) and Lample et al. (2018) introduced Denoising Auto-Encoder-iterative (DAE-iterative) UNMT which utilizes cross-lingual embeddings and trains a RNN-based encoder-decoder model (Bahdanau et al., 2015). Architecture proposed by Artetxe et al. (2018d) contains a shared encoder and two language-specific decoders while architecture proposed by Lample et al. (2018) contains a shared encoder and a shared decoder. In the approach by Lample et al. (2018), the training starts with word-by-word translation followed by denoising and backtranslation (BT). Here, noise in the input sentences in the form of shuffling of words and deletion of random words from sentences was performed.

Conneau and Lample (2019) (XLM) proposed a two-stage approach for training a UNMT system. The pre-training phase involves training of the model on the combined monolingual corpora of the two languages using Masked Language Modelling (MLM) objective (Devlin et al., 2019). The pre-trained model is later fine-tuned using denoising auto-encoding objective and backtranslated sentences. Song et al. (2019) proposed a sequence to sequence pre-training strategy. Unlike XLM, the pre-training is performed via MAsked Sequence to Sequence (MASS) objective. Here, random n-grams in the input are masked and the decoder is trained to generate the missing n-grams in the pre-training phase. The pre-trained model is later fine-tuned using backtranslated sentences.

Recently, Kim et al. (2020b) demonstrated that the performance of current SOTA UNMT systems is severely affected by language divergence and domain difference. The authors demonstrated that increasing the corpus size does not lead to improved translation performance. The authors hypothesized that existing UNMT approaches fail for distant languages due to lack of mechanism to bootstrap out of a poor initialization.

Recently, Chronopoulou et al. (2021) trained UNMT systems with 2 language pairs English-Macedonian (En-Mk) and English-Albanian (En-Sq) in low resource settings. These pairs achieved BLEU scores ranging from 23 to 33 using UNMT baseline XLM (Conneau and Lample, 2019) and RE-LM (Chronopoulou et al., 2020) systems. They showed further improvement up to 4.5 BLEU score when initialised embedding layer with crosslingual embedding. However, they did not explore the effect of initialising embedding layers on MASS, DAE-pretrained, and DAE-iterative approaches. Moreover, they did not experiment with language-pairs for which UNMT approaches with randomly initialised embedding layers fail completely even after training with a sufficient amount of monolingual data.

Additionally, there is some work on understanding multilingual language models and their effectiveness on zero-shot performance on downstream tasks (Pires et al., 2019; Kulshreshtha et al., 2020; Liu et al., 2020; Wang et al., 2020; Wu and Dredze, 2020). Here, the pre-trained multilingual language model is fine-tuned for the downstream NLP task in one language and tested on an unseen language (unseen during fine-tuning stage). While multilingual models have shown promising results on zero-shot transfer, the gains are limited for distant languages unless additional resources in the form of dictionary and corpora are used (Kulshreshtha et al., 2020; Wu and Dredze, 2020). Also, training a single model on unrelated languages might lead to negative interference (Wang et al., 2020).

3 Approaches

In this section, we explain different approaches used in our experiments. We use MASS (Song et al., 2019) and DAE based iterative approach similar to Lample et al. (2018) as our baseline models.

3.1 MASS UNMT

In MASS (Song et al., 2019), random n-grams in the input are masked and the model is trained to generate the missing n-grams in the pre-training phase. The pre-trained model is later fine-tuned using back-translated sentences. For every token, the input to the model is the summation of randomly initialised word embedding, positional encoding, and language code.

3.2 DAE UNMT

DAE UNMT approach is similar to the MASS UNMT approach with the difference being the pre-training objective. Here, we add random noise to the input sentence before giving it as input and the model is trained to generate the entire original sentence. Here, noise in the input sentences in the form of shuffling of words and deletion of random words from sentences was performed.

3.3 Cross-lingual Embedding Initialization

In both MASS and DAE UNMT approaches, the embedding layer is randomly initialized before the pre-training phase. We use Vecmap (Artetxe et al., 2018a) approach as a black-box to

Language	# train sentences
English (en)	54.3 M
Hindi (hi)	63.1 M
Bengali (bn)	39.9 M
Gujarati (gu)	41.1 M

Table 1: Monolingual Corpus Statistics in Million

Language-pair	# valid sentences	# test sentences
En - Hi	2000	3169
En - Bn	2000	3522
En - Gu	2000	4463

Table 2: Validation and Test Data Statistics

obtain cross-lingual embeddings. We then initialize the word-embedding layer with the cross-lingual embeddings obtained. During pre-training and fine-tuning, we have the opportunity to either *freeze* the embedding layer (static embeddings) or update them during training (non-static embeddings). We experiment with these two variations on both MASS and DAE approaches. We refer to MASS UNMT approach using static cross-lingual embeddings as *MASS + Static* and *MASS + Non-Static* for non-static cross-lingual embeddings. Similarly, We refer to DAE UNMT approach using static cross-lingual embeddings as *DAE + Static* and *DAE + Non-Static* for non-static cross-lingual embeddings.

3.4 DAE-iterative UNMT

Artetxe et al. (2018c) and Lample et al. (2018) proposed an approach based on Denoising Auto-Encoder and Back-Translation. Their approach trained the UNMT in one stage. During training, they alternated between denoising and back translation objectives iteratively. They initialised the embedding layer with cross-lingual embeddings and trained an RNN-based encoder-decoder model (Bahdanau et al., 2015). Architecture proposed by Artetxe et al. (2018d) contains a shared encoder and two language-specific decoders while architecture proposed by Lample et al. (2018) contains a shared encoder and a shared decoder, where all the modules are bi-LSTMs. We use Transformer-based architecture instead of bi-LSTM. In input, we do not add language code here. Similar to MASS and DAE, we experiment with using static and non-static cross-lingual embeddings.

4 Experimental Setup

We trained the models using 8 approaches for all language-pair out of which 3 approaches use DAE as LM pretraining, 3 approaches use MASS as LM pretraining, and the other two train DAE and BT simultaneously.

4.1 Dataset and Languages used

We use monolingual data of 4 languages *i.e.* English (en), Hindi (hi), Bengali (bn), Gujarati (gu). While English is of European language family, the other three languages are of Indo-Aryan language family. These three Indian languages follow Subject-Object-Verb word order. However, for English the word order is Subject-Verb-Object. We organise this experiment for distant language pairs with word-order divergence. Therefore, we pair English language with one of these three Indic languages resulting in three language-pairs, *i.e.* en-hi, en-bn, en-gu.

We use monolingual data provided by AI4Bharat (Kunchukuttan et al., 2020) dataset as training data. We use English-Indic validation and test data provided in WAT 2020 Shared task (Nakazawa et al., 2020) [*]. Details of our dataset used in this experiment are in Table 2.

[*] `http://www.statmt.org/wmt20/translation-task.html`

Language-pair	en → x		x → en	
	NN	CSLS	NN	CSLS
En - Hi	52.16 %	55.46 %	43.51 %	46.82 %
En - Bn	36.76 %	41.39 %	33.77 %	39.17 %
En - Gu	43.35 %	46.47 %	46.07 %	50.38 %

Table 3: Word-to-word translation accuracy using our crosslingual embeddings

4.2 Preprocessing

We have preprocessed the English corpus for normalization, tokenization, and lowercasing using the scripts available in *Moses* (Koehn et al., 2007) and the Indo-Aryan corpora for tokenization using *Indic NLP Library* (Kunchukuttan, 2020). For BPE segmentation we use *FastBPE*[†] jointly on the source and target data with number of merge operations set to 100k.

4.3 Word Embeddings

We use the BPE-segmented monolingual corpora to independently train the embeddings for each language using skip-gram model of *Fasttext*[‡] (Bojanowski et al., 2017). To map embeddings of the two languages to a shared space, we use *Vecmap*[§] to obtain cross-lingual embedding proposed by Artetxe et al. (2018b). We report the quality of the cross-lingual embeddings in Table 3 w.r.t. word-translation quality on MUSE data (Conneau et al., 2018) by nearest-neighbour and Cross-Domain Similarity Local Scaling (CSLS) approaches.

4.4 Network Parameters

We use MASS code-base [¶] and to tun our experiments. We train all the models with a 6 layer 8-headed transformer encoder-decoder architecture of dimension 1024. The model is trained using an epoch size of $0.2M$ steps and a batch size of 64 sentences (token per batch $3K$)). We use Adam optimizer with $beta_1$ set to 0.9, and $beta_2$ to 0.98, with learning rate to 0.0001. We pre-training for a total of 100 epochs and fine-tune for a maximum of 50. However, we stop the training if the model converges before the max-epoch is reached. The input to the model is a summation of word embedding and positional encoding of dimension 1024. In all our models, we drop the language code at the encoder side. For MASS pre-training we use word-mass of 0.5. Other parameters are default parameters given in the code-base. We do not search for optimised parameters, instead, we are looking for approaches that give decent results on most hyperparameters as hyperparameter tuning is very expensive.

4.5 Evaluation and Analysis

We report both BLEU scores as translation accuracy metric for these approaches. We additionally plot perplexity, accuracy, and BLEU scores for intermediate results of each model.

5 Result and Analysis

In this section, we present the results from our experiments and present a detailed analysis of the same.

[†] `https://github.com/glample/fastBPE`
[‡] `https://github.com/facebookresearch/fastText`
[§] `https://github.com/artetxem/vecmap`
[¶] `https://github.com/microsoft/MASS`

5.1 Results

The translation performance from our experiments is as shown in Table 4. We compared BLEU scores between models where embedding layers were initialised with cross-lingual embeddings and models where embedding layers were randomly initialised.

Initialising embedding layer with static cross-lingual embedding helps both MASS-based and DAE-based UNMT systems to learn better translations as seen from the table. Our results suggest that, freezing cross-lingual embeddings (static) during UNMT training results in better translation quality compared to the approach where cross-lingual embeddings are updated (non-static).

BLEU scores suggest that DAE objective based models surpass MASS objective based models for these language pairs. Though DAE-iterative models produce lower BLEU scores than *DAE Static* or *DAE Non-Static* models, the former approach gives better BLEU scores in less number of iterations as shown in Fig. 3.

For completeness, we compare the BLEU scores of the best UNMT model, *i.e. DAE Static*, with the best reported BLEU scores in WAT 2020 Shared Task (Nakazawa et al., 2020) reported by Yu et al. (2020) on the same test data in the supervised setting. The supervised approach uses parallel data in a multilingual setting. Their models reached high accuracy by improving baseline multilingual NMT models with Fast-align, Domain transfer, ensemble, and Adapter fine-tuning methods.

While our en-hi and en-gu models produce decent values of BLEU score, en-bn models produce low BLEU score. Intuitively, we assume language characteristics to be the reason behind it.

UNMT approaches	en → hi	hi → en	en → bn	bn → en	en → gu	gu → en
MASS	1.15	1.61	0.11	0.27	0.62	0.79
DAE	0.63	0.95	0.06	0.31	0.39	0.61
DAE-iterative Non-Static	5.37	6.63	1.66	4.19	3.12	5.98
MASS Non-Static	5.49	6.06	1.86	3.5	3.47	4.82
DAE Non-Static	7.65	8.85	2.35	4.67	4.55	6.84
DAE-iterative Static	7.96	9.09	2.88	5.54	5.63	8.64
MASS Static	5.5	6.49	2.09	4.7	4.13	6.09
DAE Static	**10.3**	**11.57**	**3.3**	**6.91**	**7.39**	**10.88**

Table 4: UNMT translation performance on distant languages, i.e. en-hi, en-bn, en-gu test sets (BLEU scores reported). The values marked in bold indicate the best score for a language pair.

System	en → hi	hi → en	en → bn	bn → en	en → gu	gu → en
Our best UNMT	10.3	11.57	3.3	6.91	7.39	10.88
SOTA Supervised NMT	24.48	28.51	19.24	23.38	14.16	30.26

Table 5: Comparison of results between our best unsupervised NMT models and SOTA supervised NMT models on WAT20 test data. Supervised NMT results are reported from Yu et al. (2020)

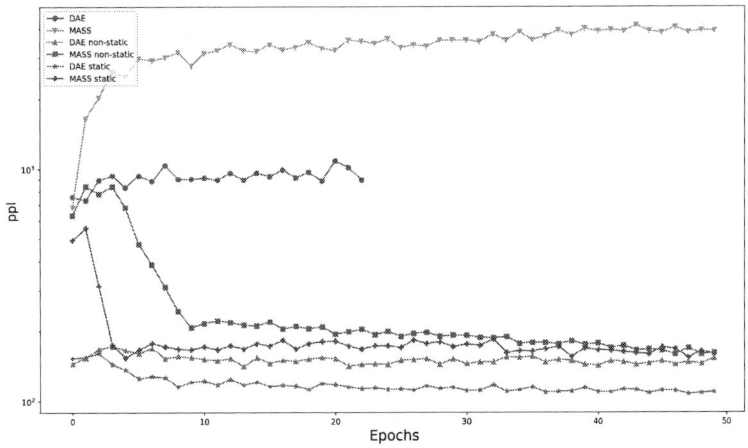

Figure 1: Change in Validation Set Translation Perplexity during Fine-tuning for English to Hindi Language pair

Hindi Source Word translation	आत्मनिर्भर बन रही है self-reliant becoming
English reference	it is becoming self reliant .
DAE	the same show is
MASS	employment back to the world
DAE Non-Static	it has become self - reliant
MASS Non-Static	resilient to the world
DAE Static	it is becoming self - sufficient
MASS Static	empowering the people

Figure 2: Example of a Hindi to English translation using various approaches

5.2 Analysis

We analyse the performance of our models by plotting translation perplexities on the validation set. Moreover, we manually analyse translation outputs and discuss them in this section.

5.2.1 Quantitative Analysis

In Fig. 1, we observe that for both MASS (baseline MASS) and DAE (baseline DAE) the plot of translation perplexity over epoch of finetuning stage increases rather than decreasing. On the other hand, when cross-lingual word embeddings are used the validation set translation perplexity decreases.

Among these embedding initialised models, we observe better convergence for models where embedding layers are frozen (static) than the models where embedding layers are updated (non-static). We also observe that the DAE-UNMT models converge better than MASS-UNMT models when initialized with cross-lingual embeddings.

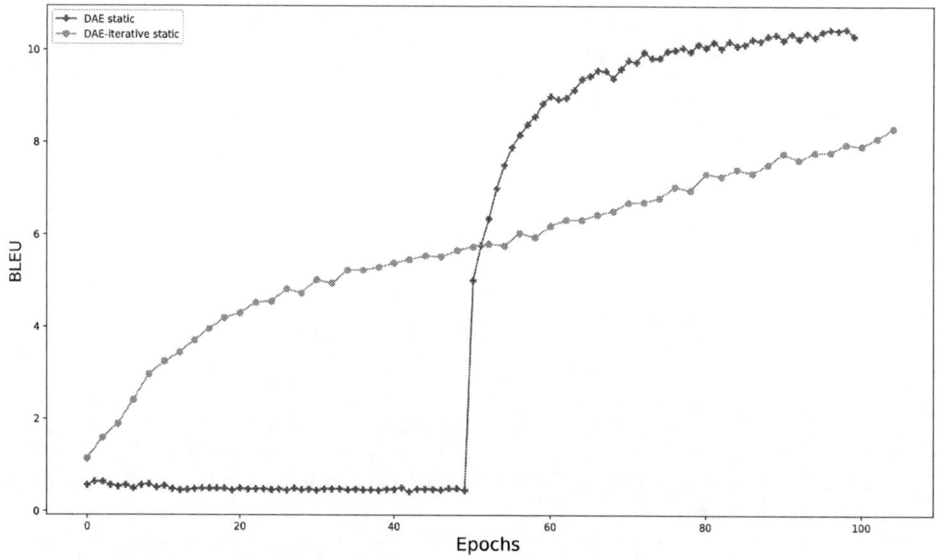

Figure 3: Comparison of Test Set BLEU Score for every epoch between DAE Static (DAE-pretrained UNMT) (both Pre-training and Fine-tuning) and DAE-iterative Static approach. Embedding layers of both the approaches are initialised with cross-lingual embedding and frozen during training. Language-pair: English-Hindi.

5.2.2 Qualitative Analysis

An example of a Hindi → English translation produced by various approaches is presented in Fig. 2. We observe the translation to be capturing the meaning of the source sentence when cross-lingual embeddings are used. However, we report some observations we found while analysing the translation outputs.

Lose of Phrasal Meaning We observe some translations where word meanings are prioritised over phrasal meaning. Fig. 4 shows such an example where dis-fluent translation is generated because of ignoring the phrasal meaning. Here, the model is unable to get the conceptual meaning of the sentence, instead translates words of the sentence literally.

Word Sense Ambiguity In Fig. 5 model fails to disambiguate word sense resulting in wrong translation. English word *'fine'* have different sense, *i.e.* beautiful and penalty. In this example, the model selects wrong sense of the word.

Scrambled Translation For many instances like Fig. 6, though the reference sentence and its corresponding generated sentences are formed with almost the same set of words, the sequence of words is different making the sentence lose its meaning. The error looks similar to the error addressed in Banerjee et al. (2019).

6 Conclusion

We show that existing UNMT methods such as DAE-based and MASS-based UNMT models fail for distant languages such as English to IndoAryan language pairs (*i.e.* en-hi, en-bn, en-gu). However, initialising the embedding layer with cross-lingual embeddings before Language Model (LM) pre-training helps the model train better UNMT systems for distant language pairs.

English Source	their hearts and my heart beat to the same rhythm .
Bengali reference	তাদের মনই আমার মন ।
English transliteration	tAdera manai AmAra mana |
Word translation	their mind my mind
System translation	তাঁদের হৃদয় এবং আমার হৃদয়ও একই ছন্দ মারিল ।
English transliteration	tA.Ndera hRRidaya ebaM AmAra hRRidayao ekai Chanda mArila |
Word translation	their heart and my heart same rhythm beat
English meaning	their hearts and my heart too beat to the same rhythm .

Figure 4: Example of a English to Bengali translation using DAE Static model

English Source	what a fine , purposeful message
Bengali reference	কত সুন্দর বার্তা ।
English transliteration	kata sundara bArtA |
Word translation	what a beautiful message .
System translation	কী একটা জরিমানা , purposeful বার্তা
English transliteration	kI ekaTA jarimAnA , purposeful bArtA
Word translation	what a penalty , purposeful message
English meaning	what a penalty/fine , purposeful message

Figure 5: Example of a English to Bengali translation using DAE Static model

English Source	they live in a parking shed with their family .
Bengali reference	তাঁরা সপরিবারে গাড়ি রাখার শেডের মধ্যে থাকেন ।
English transliteration	tA.NrA saparibAre gADai rAkhAra sheDera madhye thAkena |
Word translation	they with family parking shed inside lives
System translation	পার্কিং শেডের সঙ্গে বসবাস করে তাদের পরিবার ।
English transliteration	pArkiM sheDera sa Nge basabAsa kare tAdera paribAra |
Word translation	parking shed with live their family
English meaning	Their family live with parking shed

Figure 6: Example of a English to Bengali translation using DAE Static model

We also observe that static cross-lingual embedding gives better translation quality compared to non-static cross-lingual embeddings. For these distant language pairs, DAE objective based UNMT approaches produce better translation quality and converges better than MASS-based UNMT.

7 acknowledgements

The authors acknowledge the *IBM Research Cognitive Computing Cluster* service for providing resources that have contributed to the research results reported within this paper.

References

Artetxe, M., Labaka, G., and Agirre, E. (2018a). A robust self-learning method for fully unsupervised cross-lingual mappings of word embeddings. In *Proceedings of the 56th Annual Meeting of the Association for Computational Linguistics (Volume 1: Long Papers)*, pages 789–798.

Artetxe, M., Labaka, G., and Agirre, E. (2018b). A robust self-learning method for fully unsupervised cross-lingual mappings of word embeddings. In *Proceedings of the 56th Annual Meeting of the Association for Computational Linguistics (Volume 1: Long Papers)*, volume 1, pages 789–798.

Artetxe, M., Labaka, G., and Agirre, E. (2018c). Unsupervised statistical machine translation. In *Proceedings of the 2018 Conference on Empirical Methods in Natural Language Processing*, pages 3632–3642.

Artetxe, M., Labaka, G., Agirre, E., and Cho, K. (2018d). Unsupervised neural machine translation. *Proceedings of the International Conference on Learning Representations (ICLR)*.

Bahdanau, D., Cho, K., and Bengio, Y. (2015). Neural machine translation by jointly learning to align and translate. In *Proceedings of the International Conference on Learning Representations (ICLR)*.

Banerjee, T., Murthy, V. R., and Bhattacharyya, P. (2019). Ordering matters: Word ordering aware unsupervised NMT. *CoRR*, abs/1911.01212.

Bojanowski, P., Grave, E., Joulin, A., and Mikolov, T. (2017). Enriching word vectors with subword information. *Transactions of the Association for Computational Linguistics*, 5:135–146.

Cho, K., van Merrienboer, B., Gulcehre, C., Bahdanau, D., Bougares, F., Schwenk, H., and Bengio, Y. (2014). Learning phrase representations using rnn encoder–decoder for statistical machine translation. In *Proceedings of the 2014 Conference on Empirical Methods in Natural Language Processing (EMNLP)*, pages 1724–1734.

Chronopoulou, A., Stojanovski, D., and Fraser, A. (2020). Reusing a pretrained language model on languages with limited corpora for unsupervised nmt. In *Proceedings of the 2020 Conference on Empirical Methods in Natural Language Processing (EMNLP)*, pages 2703–2711.

Chronopoulou, A., Stojanovski, D., and Fraser, A. (2021). Improving the lexical ability of pretrained language models for unsupervised neural machine translation.

Conneau, A. and Lample, G. (2019). Cross-lingual language model pretraining. In *Advances in Neural Information Processing Systems*, pages 7057–7067.

Conneau, A., Lample, G., Ranzato, M., Denoyer, L., and Jégou, H. (2018). Word translation without parallel data. *Proceedings of the International Conference on Learning Representations (ICLR)*.

Conneau, A., Wu, S., Li, H., Zettlemoyer, L., and Stoyanov, V. (2020). Emerging cross-lingual structure in pretrained language models. In *Proceedings of the 58th Annual Meeting of the Association for Computational Linguistics*, pages 6022–6034, Online. Association for Computational Linguistics.

Devlin, J., Chang, M.-W., Lee, K., and Toutanova, K. (2019). Bert: Pre-training of deep bidirectional transformers for language understanding. In *Proceedings of the 2019 Conference of the North American Chapter of the Association for Computational Linguistics: Human Language Technologies, Volume 1 (Long and Short Papers)*, pages 4171–4186.

Kim, Y., Graça, M., and Ney, H. (2020a). When and why is unsupervised neural machine translation useless? In *Proceedings of the 22nd Annual Conference of the European Association for Machine Translation*, pages 35–44, Lisboa, Portugal. European Association for Machine Translation.

Kim, Y., Graça, M., and Ney, H. (2020b). When and why is unsupervised neural machine translation useless? In *Proceedings of the 22nd Annual Conference of the European Association for Machine Translation*, pages 35–44.

Koehn, P., Hoang, H., Birch, A., Callison-Burch, C., Federico, M., Bertoldi, N., Cowan, B., Shen, W., Moran, C., Zens, R., et al. (2007). Moses: Open source toolkit for statistical machine translation. In *Proceedings of the 45th annual meeting of the ACL on interactive poster and demonstration sessions*, pages 177–180. Association for Computational Linguistics.

Kulshreshtha, S., Garcia, J. L. R., and Chang, C. Y. (2020). Cross-lingual alignment methods for multilingual bert: A comparative study. In *Proceedings of the 2020 Conference on Empirical Methods in Natural Language Processing: Findings*, pages 933–942.

Kunchukuttan, A. (2020). The IndicNLP Library. `https://github.com/anoopkunchukuttan/indic_nlp_library/blob/master/docs/indicnlp.pdf`.

Kunchukuttan, A., Kakwani, D., Golla, S., N.C., G., Bhattacharyya, A., Khapra, M. M., and Kumar, P. (2020). Ai4bharat-indicnlp corpus: Monolingual corpora and word embeddings for indic languages. *arXiv preprint arXiv:2005.00085*.

Lample, G., Conneau, A., Denoyer, L., and Ranzato, M. (2018). Unsupervised machine translation using monolingual corpora only. *Proceedings of the International Conference on Learning Representations (ICLR)*.

Liu, Y., Gu, J., Goyal, N., Li, X., Edunov, S., Ghazvininejad, M., Lewis, M., and Zettlemoyer, L. (2020). Multilingual denoising pre-training for neural machine translation. *Transactions of the Association for Computational Linguistics*, 8:726–742.

Marchisio, K., Duh, K., and Koehn, P. (2020). When does unsupervised machine translation work? In *Proceedings of the Fifth Conference on Machine Translation*, pages 571–583, Online. Association for Computational Linguistics.

Nakazawa, T., Nakayama, H., Ding, C., Dabre, R., Higashiyama, S., Mino, H., Goto, I., Pa, W. P., Kunchukuttan, A., Parida, S., et al. (2020). Overview of the 7th workshop on asian translation. In *Proceedings of the 7th Workshop on Asian Translation*, pages 1–44.

Pires, T., Schlinger, E., and Garrette, D. (2019). How multilingual is multilingual BERT? In *Proceedings of the 57th Annual Meeting of the Association for Computational Linguistics*, pages 4996–5001, Florence, Italy. Association for Computational Linguistics.

Song, K., Tan, X., Qin, T., Lu, J., and Liu, T.-Y. (2019). Mass: Masked sequence to sequence pre-training for language generation. In *International Conference on Machine Learning*, pages 5926–5936.

Sutskever, I., Vinyals, O., and Le, Q. V. (2014). Sequence to sequence learning with neural networks. In *Advances in neural information processing systems*, pages 3104–3112.

Wang, Z., Lipton, Z. C., and Tsvetkov, Y. (2020). On negative interference in multilingual models: Findings and a meta-learning treatment. In *Proceedings of the 2020 Conference on Empirical Methods in Natural Language Processing (EMNLP)*, pages 4438–4450, Online. Association for Computational Linguistics.

Wang, Z., Xie, J., Xu, R., Yang, Y., Neubig, G., and Carbonell, J. G. (2019). Cross-lingual alignment vs joint training: A comparative study and A simple unified framework. *CoRR*, abs/1910.04708.

Wu, S. and Dredze, M. (2020). Do explicit alignments robustly improve multilingual encoders? In *Proceedings of the 2020 Conference on Empirical Methods in Natural Language Processing (EMNLP)*, pages 4471–4482, Online. Association for Computational Linguistics.

Yang, Z., Chen, W., Wang, F., and Xu, B. (2018). Unsupervised neural machine translation with weight sharing. In *Proceedings of the 56th Annual Meeting of the Association for Computational Linguistics (Volume 1: Long Papers)*, pages 46–55.

Yu, Z., Wu, Z., Chen, X., Wei, D., Shang, H., Guo, J., Li, Z., Wang, M., Li, L., Lei, L., et al. (2020). Hw-tsc's participation in the wat 2020 indic languages multilingual task. In *Proceedings of the 7th Workshop on Asian Translation*, pages 92–97.

Neural Machine Translation in Low-Resource Setting: a Case Study in English-Marathi Pair

Aakash Banerjee abanerjee@cse.iitb.ac.in
Aditya Jain adityajainiitb@cse.iitb.ac.in
Shivam Mhaskar shivammhaskar@cse.iitb.ac.in
Sourabh Deoghare sourabhdeoghare@cse.iitb.ac.in
Aman Sehgal aman.sehgal@iiml.org
Pushpak Bhattacharyya pb@cse.iitb.ac.in
Department of Computer Science and Engineering, IIT Bombay, India.

Abstract

In this paper, we explore different techniques of overcoming the challenges of low-resource in Neural Machine Translation (NMT), specifically focusing on the case of English-Marathi NMT. NMT systems require a large amount of parallel corpora to obtain good quality translations. We try to mitigate the low-resource problem by augmenting parallel corpora or by using transfer learning. Techniques such as Phrase Table Injection (PTI), back-translation and mixing of language corpora are used for enhancing the parallel data; whereas pivoting and multilingual embeddings are used to leverage transfer learning. For pivoting, Hindi comes in as assisting language for English-Marathi translation. Compared to baseline transformer model, a significant improvement trend in BLEU score is observed across various techniques. We have done extensive manual, automatic and qualitative evaluation of our systems. Since the trend in Machine Translation (MT) today is post-editing and measuring of Human Effort Reduction (HER), we have given our preliminary observations on Translation Edit Rate (TER) vs. BLEU score study, where TER is regarded as a measure of HER.

1 Introduction

The aim of this work is to improve the quality of Machine Translation (MT) for the English-Marathi language pair for which less amount of parallel corpora is available. One of the major requirements for good performance of the Neural Machine Translation (NMT) models is the availability of a large parallel corpora. As a result, there is a need to come up with additional resources by augmenting parallel corpora or by using knowledge from other tasks using transfer learning.

Kunchukuttan and Bhattacharyya (2020) have shown that the lexical and orthographic similarities among languages can be utilized to improve translation quality between Indic languages when limited parallel corpora is available. English and Marathi does not have common ancestry and hence are not related languages, whereas Hindi and Marathi are related languages. Also, among the various English to Indic language corpora, English-Hindi corpus is comparatively larger. In our pivot based transfer learning, combined corpus, and multilingual experiments we try to utilize this high resource English-Hindi language pair in various ways to assist in English-Marathi translation. In our Phrase Table Injection (PTI) experiment, we explore how the phrases generated during Statistical Machine Translation (SMT) model training can be further utilized in NMT. We also explore how the monolingual corpus of the target language can be leveraged to create additional pseudo-parallel sentences using back-translation. We also try to understand the correlation between the BLEU and Translation Edit Rate (TER) scores by fitting a linear regression line on the TER vs BLEU graph, where TER is regarded as a measure of Human Effort Reduction (HER).

2 Related Work

Transformer model (Vaswani et al., 2017) was introduced in 2017 and gave significant improvements in the quality of translation as compared to the previous Recurrent Neural Network (RNN) based approaches (Bahdanau et al., 2014; Cho et al., 2014; Sutskever et al., 2014). Self-Attention and absence of recurrent layers enabled models to train faster and get better performance. However, this did not help improve the translation quality in the low-resource setting.

Various methods have been proposed over the years to deal with the low-resource NMT problem. Some methods which use monolingual data involve integrating a separately trained language model (Gülçehre et al., 2015) into the decoder, using an autoencoding objective (Luong et al., 2015) or augmenting pseudo-parallel data using back-translation (Sennrich et al., 2016). Sen et al. (2018) introduced a method for combining SMT and NMT by taking phrases from SMT training and augmenting them to NMT. Zoph et al. (2016) introduced a transfer learning approach where a parent model trained on a high resource language pair is used to initialize some parameters of the child model, which is then trained on a low-resource language pair. Kim et al. (2019) also uses a transfer learning approach with the help of a pivot language to learn parameters initially which are then transferred. Multi-lingual NMT (Zoph and Knight, 2016; Firat et al., 2016; Johnson et al., 2017) is another approach which uses knowledge transfer among various languages to improve the performance of all the language pairs involved.

3 Our Approaches

In this section, we discuss the details of the various techniques that we have explored to deal with the problem of low-resource English-Marathi language pair.

3.1 Phrase Table Injection (PTI)

Sen et al. (2018) and Dewangan et al. (2021) used this technique, shown in Figure 1, to combine both SMT and NMT. We know that the phrase table, generated during training of a SMT model, plays a key role in the SMT translation process. It contains a probabilistic mapping of phrases from the source language to the target language. The phrases present in the phrase table are combined with the available parallel corpora; thereby increasing the data available to train the NMT model. This also helps the model to learn translation of short correct phrases along with long sentences.

3.2 Expansion of data using Back-Translation

Back-translation (Sennrich et al., 2016) is a technique that uses monolingual data of the target language to improve the translation performance of low-resource language

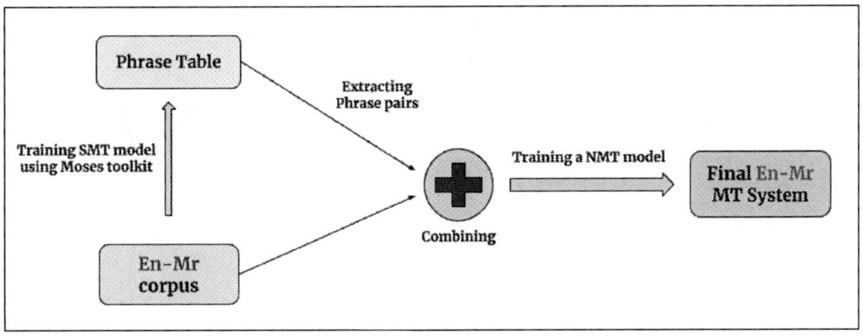

Figure 1: Phrase Table Injection

pairs. The amount of available monolingual data in the target language typically far exceeds the amount of parallel data. In SMT, this monolingual data can be used to train a language model, which accounts for fluent translations in SMT. This ability of leveraging the monolingual data for training can be incorporated in NMT by the process of back-translation.

Initially, the available parallel corpora is used to train a Marathi-English NMT model. This model is then used to translate the Marathi monolingual data to create a pseudo-parallel corpus, which in turn is combined with the available parallel corpora to train the NMT model. The ratio of parallel corpora to pseudo-parallel corpora is tuned depending on various factors like quality of target to source model, languages involved in translation, to name a few.

3.3 Combined Corpus

In this technique we exploit the knowledge from similar languages on the target side. As shown in Figure 2, we first train a NMT model using combined corpora from English-Marathi and English-Hindi (EnglishEnglish-HindiMarathi) language pairs. This model is then fine-tuned with the English-Marathi parallel corpora only, using the same vocabulary as that used while training. The intuition is that a model which at the start of training knows how to translate mixed languages is better than a model initialized with random weights.

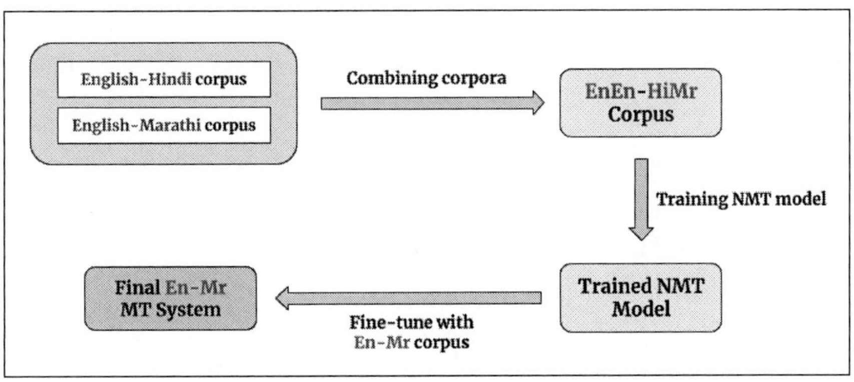

Figure 2: Combined Corpus

This technique will be more effective if the languages at the target side are similar as this will potentially lead to a partial overlap in the target side vocabulary. Here Hindi and Marathi are the target languages which are similar as both belong to the same language family (Indo-Aryan) and have an overlap in their alphabet set.

3.4 Transfer Learning Approach

The transfer learning approach we used utilizes a pivot language. For the task of English to Marathi translation we use Hindi as a pivot language which assists this task. We chose Hindi as the pivot language because Hindi and Marathi are linguistically close languages. Also English-Hindi parallel corpus is larger as compared to other English to Indic language pairs. We use two pivot based transfer learning techniques proposed by Kim et al. (2019), both of which are discussed below.

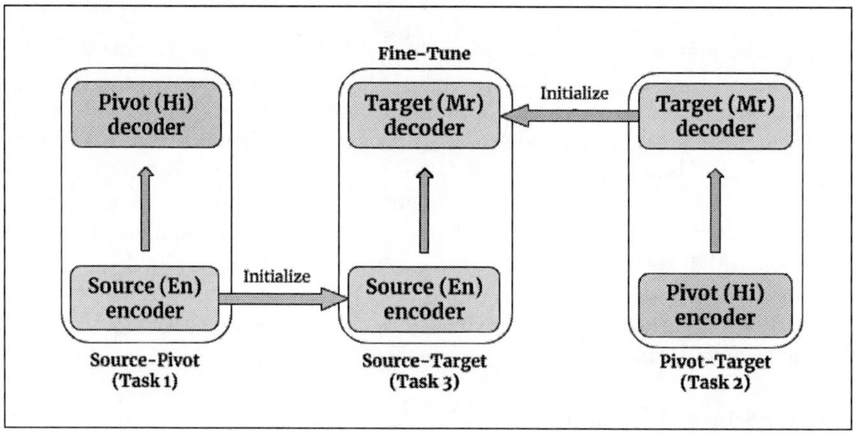

Figure 3: Direct Pivoting (En:English, Hi:Hindi, Mr:Marathi)

3.4.1 Direct Pivoting

In this technique we train two separate NMT models, a source-pivot model and a pivot-target model. As demonstrated in Figure 3, we first separately train an English-Hindi (source-pivot) model (task 1) and a Hindi-Marathi (pivot-target) model (task 2) on their respective parallel corpus. We then use the encoder of the English-Hindi (source-pivot) model and the decoder of Hindi-Marathi (pivot-target) model to initialize the encoder and decoder of the English-Marathi (source-target) model, respectively. Finally, we fine-tune this English-Marathi (source-target) model using the available English-Marathi parallel corpus.

The problem with this approach is that the final English-Marathi (source-target) model is built by combining the encoder trained to produce outputs for the pivot decoder instead of the target decoder; and the decoder trained on the outputs of the pivot encoder instead of the source encoder.

3.4.2 Step-wise Pivoting

As shown in Figure 4, here we first train an English-Hindi (source-pivot) model. Then we use the encoder of the English-Hindi (source-pivot) model to initialize the encoder of the Hindi-Marathi (pivot-target) model. After this, we train the Hindi-Marathi (pivot-target) model on the Hindi-Marathi corpus by freezing the encoder parameters. Then

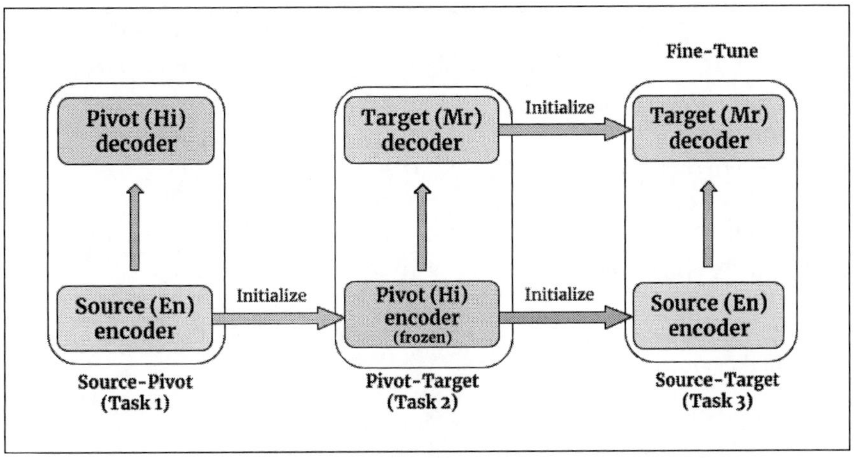

Figure 4: Step-wise Pivoting (En:English, Hi:Hindi, Mr:Marathi)

the encoder and decoder from this Hindi-Marathi (pivot-target) model are used to initialize the encoder and decoder of the English-Marathi (source-target) model. Finally, we fine-tune the English-Marathi (source-target) model using the available English-Marathi corpus.

3.5 Multi-Lingual MT System

The various types of multilingual models are one-to-many, many-to-one and many-to-many. Among these, we use the one-to-many multilingual model with source language as English and target languages as Hindi and Marathi. One of the ways to achieve this is by making use of a single encoder for the source language and two separate decoders for the target languages. The disadvantage with this method is that, as there are multiple decoders, the size of the model increases. Another way to achieve this is to use a single encoder and a single shared decoder. An advantage of this method is that the representations learnt by English-Hindi task can further be utilized by the English-Marathi task. Also, Hindi and Marathi being similar languages, the overlap between their vocabulary is large resulting in a smaller shared vocabulary.

4 Experiments

In this section, we discuss the details of the various experiments that we have carried out to improve the quality of the English-Marathi translation.

4.1 Dataset Preparation

The NMT models were trained using a corpus formed by combining the Indian Languages Corpora Initiative (ILCI) Phase 1 corpus (Jha, 2010), Bible corpus (Christodouloupoulos and Steedman, 2015; Jha, 2010), CVIT-Press Information Bureau (CVIT-PIB) corpus (Philip et al., 2021), IIT Bombay English-Hindi corpus (Kunchukuttan et al., 2017) and PMIndia (PMI) corpus (Haddow and Kirefu, 2020). The English-Marathi corpus, English-Hindi corpus and Hindi-Marathi corpus consisted of 0.25M, 2M and 0.24M parallel sentences, respectively. Barring the ILCI corpus, the remaining Hindi-Marathi data was synthetically generated by translating the English sentences

	Number of Sentences		
	English-Marathi	**English-Hindi**	**Hindi-Marathi**
ILCI	46,277	46,277	46,277
Bible corpus	60,876	62,073	58,375
IITB corpus	—	1,603,080	—
CVIT-PIB	114,220	266,545	108,220
PMIndia	28,974	50,349	28,973
Total Corpus Size	250,347	2,028,324	241,845

Table 1: Corpora statistics of the three language pairs: English-Marathi, English-Hindi and Hindi-Marathi

of the English-Marathi corpus to Hindi using the Google Cloud Translation API[1]. The detailed corpus statistics are mentioned in Table 1.

For reporting the results, the test set introduced in WAT 2021[2] MultiIndicMT: An Indic Language Multilingual Task[3] and the test set from ILCI corpus are used. The test set from WAT 2021 contains 2,390 sentences and is a part of the PMIndia corpus. The PMIndia corpus from WAT 2021 task is used for training to avoid any overlap between the train and test sets. The test set from ILCI corpus consists of 2000 sentences.

The English sentences are tokenized and lowercased using Moses[4] (Koehn et al., 2007) toolkit. The Hindi and Marathi sentences are lowercased and normalized using Indic NLP Library (Kunchukuttan, 2020). Byte Pair Encoding (BPE) (Sennrich et al., 2015) is used as a segmentation technique; as breaking up words into subwords has become standard now and is especially helpful for morphologically rich languages like Marathi and Hindi.

4.2 Training Setup

The Transformer architecture was used to train the NMT models. The PyTorch version of OpenNMT (Klein et al., 2017) was used to carry out the PTI, combined corpus and back-translation experiments. For the pivot language based transfer learning and multilingual NMT experiments, the fairseq (Ott et al., 2019) library was used. The SMT model for PTI was trained using the Moses toolkit.

For the baseline model, a vanilla transformer model was trained using the default parameters[5] for 200K training steps. In the experiment with PTI, Moses toolkit was used to train the model to get phrases from the phrase table. The grow-diag-final-and method was used for symmetrization and msd-bidirectional-fe method was used for lexicalized reordering. While making batches for training, the parallel data and parallel phrases were selected in the ratio 4:1, as giving less weightage to phrases enhances the performance. For back-translation experiment, the amount of pseudo-parallel sentences used is same as that of the available corpus. Both the corpus were combined and a model was trained with the default parameters. In the combined corpus experiment, the model was trained for 200k training steps and then was further fine-tuned for 100k training steps.

[1] https://cloud.google.com/translate

[2] http://lotus.kuee.kyoto-u.ac.jp/WAT/WAT2021/index.html

[3] http://lotus.kuee.kyoto-u.ac.jp/WAT/indic-multilingual/

[4] https://github.com/moses-smt/mosesdecoder

[5] https://opennmt.net/OpenNMT-py/FAQ.html

For the pivot language based transfer learning experiments, a transformer model from the fairseq library was used. The optimizer used was adam with betas (0.9, 0.98). The initial learning rate used was 5e-4 with the inverse square root learning rate scheduler and 4000 warm-up updates. The dropout probability value used was 0.3 and the criterion used was label smoothed cross entropy with label smoothing of 0.1. All the models were trained for 400 epochs. Same training setup was used for the multilingual NMT experiments as well. A one (English) to many (Hindi, Marathi) multilingual model was used. As the multilingual model we used had a shared decoder, the source sentence was prepended with a target language token, both at the training and the inference time, to specify the target language during translation.

5 Results and Analysis

We use the BLEU evaluation metric (Papineni et al., 2002) to report our results. Sacrebleu (Post, 2018) python library was used to calculate the BLEU scores. We detokenize the translated sentences before calculating the BLEU scores. The results of all our experiments are summarized in Table 2.

Model	ILCI	WAT 2021
Baseline	16.03	16.26
Phrase Table Injection (PTI)	15.81	17.15
Combined Corpus (CC)	17.69	18.02
Backtranslation (BT)	15.90	15.78
BT + PTI	15.83	16.34
CC + BT	17.51	17.45
CC + PTI	17.75	17.97
CC + PTI + BT	17.47	17.43
Direct Pivoting	18.32	16.68
Step-wise Pivoting	17.94	16.74
Multi-Lingual	18.83	17.09

Table 2: BLEU scores of English-Marathi language pair using various techniques (CC: Combined Corpus, BT: Backtranslation, PTI: Phrase Table Injection).

In PTI experiment we observe an increase in BLEU score on WAT 2021 test set while the BLEU score on ILCI test set decreases. For combined corpus there is improvement of more than 1.5 BLEU score on both the test sets, indicating that English-Hindi corpus helped during the training. We observe that using back-translation, the BLEU score decreases. This can be attributed to the fact that the Marathi-English model used for back-translating the Marathi monolingual corpora was not of good quality. This Marathi-English model was trained using 0.25M parallel sentences which affects the quality of back-translated data. We also tried out experiments by combining the above mentioned methods, among which, the combination of phrase table injection and combined corpus methods give the best results.

The results of the direct pivoting technique show an improvement of 2.29 BLEU score over the baseline model on the ILCI test set and of 0.42 on the WAT 2021 test set. The results of step-wise pivoting show an improvement of 1.91 BLEU score over the baseline on the ILCI test set and of 0.74 on the WAT 2021 test set. The reason for this BLEU score increase is that, the encoder and decoder used to initialize the English-Marathi model before training have already learned some representations. This is because the encoder and decoder are initialized from the encoder and decoder of the trained English-Hindi (source-pivot) and Hindi-Marathi (pivot-target) models, respectively. We observe that this initialization of encoder and decoder performs better than a random initialization.

The results of the multilingual model on English-Marathi translation task show a BLEU score increase of 2.8 on the ILCI test set and 0.83 on the WAT 2021 test set over the baseline model. In a multilingual model, we use a shared decoder for both the target languages, due to which, the representations learnt by the model for the task of English-Hindi translation helps in the English-Marathi task as well. This leads to a better performance of the multilingual model over the baseline model. For direct pivoting, step-wise pivoting and multilingual model we observe that the BLEU score increase on ILCI test set is more than that on the WAT 2021 test set. Our conjecture is that as the size of the ILCI corpus used in training is larger than that of the PMIndia corpus(from which WAT 2021 test set is derived), the BLEU score increase for ILCI test set is more.

6 Extensive Evaluation

In this section, we discuss the analysis that we have carried out to compare our models with baseline; and also understand the correlation of BLEU score with TER, where TER is regarded as a measure of HER.

6.1 Qualitative Analysis

In this sub-section, we present the analysis of few sentences to demonstrate how our model performs better than the baseline. In each of the below given examples, **En-Source** represents source English sentences, **Mr-xx** represents translated Marathi sentence using "**xx**" model, **Mr-xx-Transliterate** represents translated Marathi sentence transliterated in English, and **Mr-xx-Gloss** represents word-to-word English translations of the translated Marathi sentence.

- **Example 1: Translation of named entity**

  En-Source: The toy train from Kalka to Shimla is considered as the most beautiful rail line in India.

  Mr-Baseline: कालका ते सिमलापर्यंत धावणारी रेल्वे भारतात सर्वात सुंदर रेल्वे लाईन मानली जाते.

  Mr-Baseline-Transliterate: kalka te shimlaa dhavanari railway bharatat cervat sunder railway laiin maanli jate.

  Mr-Baseline-Gloss: Kalka to up-to-Shimla running railway in-India most beautiful railway line considered is.

  Mr-DirectPivoting: कालकापासून सिमला पर्यंतची टॉय ट्रेन भारतातील सर्वात सुंदर रेल्वे लाइन मानली जाते .

  Mr-DirectPivoting-Transliterate: kalkaapasun shimla paryantachi toy train bharatatil sarvat sundar railway laiin maanli jate.

  Mr-DirectPivoting-Gloss: From-Kalka Shimla up-to toy train in-India most beautiful railway line considered is.

The English source sentence contains a named entity "***toy train***". The baseline translated "***toy train***" incorrectly as "रेल्वे" (which means "***railway***"), whereas our model was able to translate "***toy train***" correctly as "टॉय ट्रेन" (which means"**toy train**").

- **Example 2: Translation of long sentences**

  En-Source: The Prime Minister expressed happiness that on this occasion, the devotional hymn Vaishnav Jan To, which was so dear to Bapu, had been rendered by artistes in about 150 countries across the world.

  Mr-Baseline: यावेळी पंतप्रधानांनी आनंद व्यक्त केला की, पूज्य बापूंच्या देशांचे निष्ठावंत भजन असणाऱ्या वैष्णव जन यांना जगातील सुमारे 150 देशांमध्ये पारितोषिके देण्यात आली होती.

  Mr-Baseline-Transliterate: yawelii pantpradhanani anand vyakt kela kii, pujy bapunchyaa deshanche nithavant bhajan assnaryaa vaishnav jan yaannaa jagaatil sumaare 150 deshaanmadhye paaritoshik deanyaat aali hoti .

  Mr-Baseline-Gloss: This-time Prime-Minister happiness expressed did that, reverend Bapu's of-countries loyal hymn is vaishnav jan to in-world around 150 in-countries awards given came was.

  Mr-PTI: सुमारे 150 देशांमध्ये बापूंना प्रिय असलेले वैष्णव जन तो भक्तीगीत जगभरातल्या 150 देशातल्या कलाकारांनी सादर केल्याबद्दल पंतप्रधानांनी आनंद व्यक्त केला.

  Mr-PTI-Translitarate: sumaare 150 deshaanmadhye baapunnaa priya aslele vaishnav jan to bhaktigeet jagbharatlyaa 150 deshatlyaa kalakaranii saadar kelyaabaddadal pantprdhaanaanii aanand vyakt kelaa .

  Mr-PTI-Gloss: Around 150 in-countries to-Bapu loved vaishnav jan to devotional-song around-world 150 in-countries artists performed for-doing Prime-Minister happiness express did.

  The baseline model was not able to completely translate the long source English sentence adequately. The model was able to translate the entire long source English sentence adequately.

- **Example 3: Translation of low readability sentences**

  En-Source: The Union Cabinet chaired by the Prime Minister Shri Narendra Modi has given its ex post-facto approval to the MoU between India and Singapore on cooperation in the field of urban planning and development.

  Mr-CombinedCorpus: पंतप्रधान नरेंद्र मोदी यांच्या अध्यक्षतेखाली केंद्रीय मंत्रिमंडळाने भारत आणि सिंगापूर दरम्यान शहर नियोजन आणि विकास क्षेत्रातील सहकार्याबाबतच्या सामंजस्य कराराला कार्योत्तर मंजुरी दिली.

  Mr-CombinedCorpus-Transliterate: pantprdhaan narendra modi yaanchyaa adhyakshatekhali kendriya mantrimandalaane bharat aani singapore darmyaan shahar niyojan aani vikas kshetraatiil sahakaaryaabaabatchyaa saamanjsy karaaraalaa kaaryottar manjurii dilii .

  Mr-CombinedCorpus-Gloss: Prime-Minister Narendra Modi his chaired-under central cabinet India and Singapore during city planning and development in-field regarding-cooperation Memorandum-of understanding after-work approval given.

  The above example shows the performance of our model on sentences with low readability i.e. sentences with high Automated Readability Index (ARI) (Senter and Smith, 1967). Our model was able to translate the low readability sentence adequately and fluently.

6.2 Understanding the Correlation between BLEU and TER

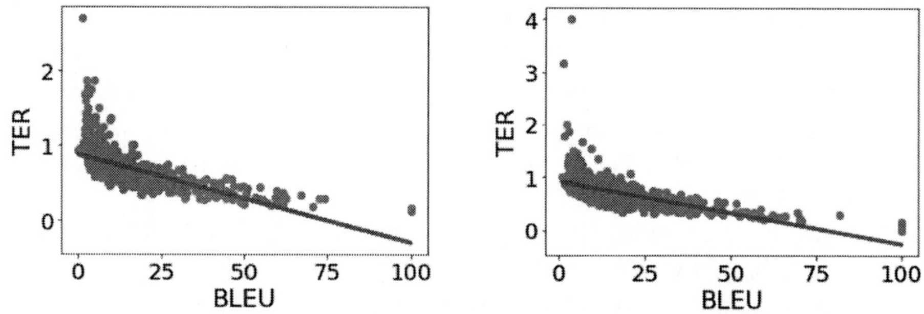

(a) ILCI (b) WAT 2021

Figure 5: TER vs BLEU for ILCI and WAT 2021 test sets

The trend in machine translation these days is to perform post-editing on the output of the MT system. When post-editing is performed by humans on a large amount of sentences, it is very important to measure the reduction in human effort by the MT system. This can be achieved by calculating the HER which can be an important MT evaluation metric. In this paper, we use TER (Snover et al., 2006) as a measure of HER. TER measures the amount of editing that is required by a human to convert a system output to a reference translation.

In order to understand the correlation between BLEU and TER scores, we plot sentencewise TER vs BLEU score graphs for the ILCI and WAT 2021 test sets. Figure 5 shows that as the BLEU score increases the TER decreases. A linear regression line was fitted on TER vs BLEU graph for both the ILCI and WAT 2021 test sets.

$$y = -0.0117x + 0.8805 \tag{1}$$

$$y = -0.0117x + 0.9124 \tag{2}$$

Equation 1 represents the linear regression line on the ILCI test set having slope of -0.0117 and the y-intercept as 0.8805. Equation 2 represents the linear regression line on the WAT 2021 test set having a slope of -0.0117 and the y-intercept as 0.9124. We observe that the slope of the line is negative for both the equations indicating that BLEU and TER are negatively correlated. This is expected as BLEU is a measure of how *good* the sentence got translated, whereas TER is a measure of how *bad* the sentence got translated. This supports the use of TER as a metric of HER.

7 Conclusion and Future Work

In this work, we have implemented and compared various techniques to improve the task of translation involving a low-resource English-Marathi language pair. We have shown that the pivot based transfer learning approach can significantly improve the quality of the English-Marathi translations over the baseline by using Hindi as an assisting language. We also observe that the phrases from the SMT training can help the NMT model perform better. The one (English) to many (Hindi, Marathi) multilingual model is able to improve the English-Marathi translations by leveraging the English-Hindi parallel corpus. Combined corpus experiment also uses the English-Hindi parallel corpus to improve the English-Marathi translation quality.

In future, we plan to further extend these approaches to a variety of languages to understand how the phenomenon of language relatedness can help improve the translation quality in low resource setting. We also plan to explore how multiple pivot languages can be used while translating from some source to target language pair.

Acknowledgement

We would like to thank all the members of CFILT lab of IIT Bombay for their valuable inputs. The authors would like to specially thank Girishkumar Ponkiya, Lata Popale and Jyotsana Khatri for their support and feedback. We would like to thank Ministry of Electronics and Information Technology(MeitY) TDIL program for their support towards this work.

References

Bahdanau, D., Cho, K., and Bengio, Y. (2014). Neural machine translation by jointly learning to align and translate. *arXiv preprint arXiv:1409.0473.*

Cho, K., van Merrienboer, B., Bahdanau, D., and Bengio, Y. (2014). On the properties of neural machine translation: Encoder-decoder approaches. *CoRR*, abs/1409.1259.

Christodouloupoulos, C. and Steedman, M. (2015). A massively parallel corpus: the bible in 100 languages. *Language resources and evaluation*, 49(2):375–395.

Dewangan, S., Alva, S., Joshi, N., and Bhattacharyya, P. (2021). Experience of neural machine translation between indian languages. *Machine Translation*, pages 1–29.

Firat, O., Cho, K., and Bengio, Y. (2016). Multi-way, multilingual neural machine translation with a shared attention mechanism. In *Proceedings of the 2016 Conference of the North American Chapter of the Association for Computational Linguistics: Human Language Technologies*, pages 866–875, San Diego, California. Association for Computational Linguistics.

Gülçehre, Ç., Firat, O., Xu, K., Cho, K., Barrault, L., Lin, H., Bougares, F., Schwenk, H., and Bengio, Y. (2015). On using monolingual corpora in neural machine translation. *CoRR*, abs/1503.03535.

Haddow, B. and Kirefu, F. (2020). Pmindia - A collection of parallel corpora of languages of india. *CoRR*, abs/2001.09907.

Jha, G. N. (2010). The TDIL program and the Indian langauge corpora intitiative (ILCI). In *Proceedings of the Seventh International Conference on Language Resources and Evaluation (LREC'10)*, Valletta, Malta. European Language Resources Association (ELRA).

Johnson, M., Schuster, M., Le, Q. V., Krikun, M., Wu, Y., Chen, Z., Thorat, N., Viégas, F., Wattenberg, M., Corrado, G., Hughes, M., and Dean, J. (2017). Google's multilingual neural machine translation system: Enabling zero-shot translation. *Transactions of the Association for Computational Linguistics*, 5:339–351.

Kim, Y., Petrov, P., Petrushkov, P., Khadivi, S., and Ney, H. (2019). Pivot-based transfer learning for neural machine translation between non-English languages. In *Proceedings of the 2019 Conference on Empirical Methods in Natural Language Processing and the 9th International Joint Conference on Natural Language Processing*

(EMNLP-IJCNLP), pages 866–876, Hong Kong, China. Association for Computational Linguistics.

Klein, G., Kim, Y., Deng, Y., Senellart, J., and Rush, A. (2017). OpenNMT: Open-source toolkit for neural machine translation. In *Proceedings of ACL 2017, System Demonstrations*, pages 67–72, Vancouver, Canada. Association for Computational Linguistics.

Koehn, P., Hoang, H., Birch, A., Callison-Burch, C., Federico, M., Bertoldi, N., Cowan, B., Shen, W., Moran, C., Zens, R., Dyer, C., Bojar, O., Constantin, A., and Herbst, E. (2007). Moses: Open source toolkit for statistical machine translation. In *Proceedings of the 45th Annual Meeting of the Association for Computational Linguistics Companion Volume Proceedings of the Demo and Poster Sessions*, pages 177–180, Prague, Czech Republic. Association for Computational Linguistics.

Kunchukuttan, A. (2020). The IndicNLP Library. `https://github.com/anoopkunchukuttan/indic_nlp_library/blob/master/docs/indicnlp.pdf`.

Kunchukuttan, A. and Bhattacharyya, P. (2020). Utilizing language relatedness to improve machine translation: A case study on languages of the indian subcontinent. *arXiv preprint arXiv:2003.08925*.

Kunchukuttan, A., Mehta, P., and Bhattacharyya, P. (2017). The iit bombay english-hindi parallel corpus. *arXiv preprint arXiv:1710.02855*.

Luong, M.-T., Le, Q. V., Sutskever, I., Vinyals, O., and Kaiser, L. (2015). Multi-task sequence to sequence learning. *arXiv preprint arXiv:1511.06114*.

Ott, M., Edunov, S., Baevski, A., Fan, A., Gross, S., Ng, N., Grangier, D., and Auli, M. (2019). fairseq: A fast, extensible toolkit for sequence modeling. *arXiv preprint arXiv:1904.01038*.

Papineni, K., Roukos, S., Ward, T., and Zhu, W.-J. (2002). Bleu: a method for automatic evaluation of machine translation. In *Proceedings of the 40th annual meeting of the Association for Computational Linguistics*, pages 311–318.

Philip, J., Siripragada, S., Namboodiri, V. P., and Jawahar, C. (2021). Revisiting low resource status of indian languages in machine translation. In *8th ACM IKDD CODS and 26th COMAD*, pages 178–187.

Post, M. (2018). A call for clarity in reporting BLEU scores. In *Proceedings of the Third Conference on Machine Translation: Research Papers*, pages 186–191, Belgium, Brussels. Association for Computational Linguistics.

Sen, S., Hasanuzzaman, M., Ekbal, A., Bhattacharyya, P., and Way, A. (2018). Neural machine translation of low-resource languages using smt phrase pair injection. *Natural Language Engineering*, pages 1–22.

Sennrich, R., Haddow, B., and Birch, A. (2015). Neural machine translation of rare words with subword units. *arXiv preprint arXiv:1508.07909*.

Sennrich, R., Haddow, B., and Birch, A. (2016). Improving neural machine translation models with monolingual data. In *Proceedings of the 54th Annual Meeting of the Association for Computational Linguistics (Volume 1: Long Papers)*, pages 86–96, Berlin, Germany. Association for Computational Linguistics.

Senter, R. and Smith, E. A. (1967). Automated readability index. Technical report, CINCINNATI UNIV OH.

Snover, M., Dorr, B., Schwartz, R., Micciulla, L., and Makhoul, J. (2006). A study of translation edit rate with targeted human annotation. In *Proceedings of association for machine translation in the Americas*, volume 200. Citeseer.

Sutskever, I., Vinyals, O., and Le, Q. V. (2014). Sequence to sequence learning with neural networks. *CoRR*, abs/1409.3215.

Vaswani, A., Shazeer, N., Parmar, N., Uszkoreit, J., Jones, L., Gomez, A. N., Kaiser, L., and Polosukhin, I. (2017). Attention is all you need. *CoRR*, abs/1706.03762.

Zoph, B. and Knight, K. (2016). Multi-source neural translation. In *Proceedings of the 2016 Conference of the North American Chapter of the Association for Computational Linguistics: Human Language Technologies*, pages 30–34, San Diego, California. Association for Computational Linguistics.

Zoph, B., Yuret, D., May, J., and Knight, K. (2016). Transfer learning for low-resource neural machine translation. In *Proceedings of the 2016 Conference on Empirical Methods in Natural Language Processing*, pages 1568–1575, Austin, Texas. Association for Computational Linguistics.

Transformers for Low-Resource Languages: Is Féidir Linn!

Séamus Lankford seamus.lankford@adaptcentre.ie
ADAPT Centre, Department of Computing, Dublin City University, Dublin, Ireland.
Haithem Afli haithem.afli@adaptcentre.ie
ADAPT Centre, Department of Computer Science, Munster Technological University, Ireland.
Andy Way andy.way@adaptcentre.ie
ADAPT Centre, School of Computing, Dublin City University, Dublin, Ireland.

Abstract

The Transformer model is the state-of-the-art in Machine Translation. However, in general, neural translation models often under perform on language pairs with insufficient training data. As a consequence, relatively few experiments have been carried out using this architecture on low-resource language pairs. In this study, hyperparameter optimization of Transformer models in translating the low-resource English-Irish language pair is evaluated. We demonstrate that choosing appropriate parameters leads to considerable performance improvements. Most importantly, the correct choice of subword model is shown to be the biggest driver of translation performance. SentencePiece models using both unigram and BPE approaches were appraised. Variations on model architectures included modifying the number of layers, testing various regularisation techniques and evaluating the optimal number of heads for attention. A generic 55k DGT corpus and an in-domain 88k public admin corpus were used for evaluation. A Transformer optimized model demonstrated a BLEU score improvement of 7.8 points when compared with a baseline RNN model. Improvements were observed across a range of metrics, including TER, indicating a substantially reduced post editing effort for Transformer optimized models with 16k BPE subword models. Bench-marked against Google Translate, our translation engines demonstrated significant improvements. The question of whether or not Transformers can be used effectively in a low-resource setting of English-Irish translation has been addressed. Is féidir linn - yes we can.

1 Introduction

The advent of Neural Machine Translation (NMT) has heralded an era of high-quality translations. However, these improvements have not been manifested in the translation of all languages. Large datasets are a prerequisite for high quality NMT. This works well in the context of well-resourced languages where there is an abundance of data. In the context of low-resource languages which suffer from a sparsity of data, alternative approaches must be adopted.

An important part of this research involves developing applications and models to address the challenges of low-resource language technology. Such technology incorporates methods to address the data scarcity affecting deep learning for digital engagement of low-resource languages.

It has been shown that an out-of-the-box NMT system, trained on English-Irish data, achieves a lower translation quality compared with using a tailored SMT system (Dowling et al, 2018). It is in this context that further research is required in the development of NMT for low-resource languages and the Irish language in particular.

Most research on choosing subword models has focused on high resource languages (Ding et al., 2019; Gowda and May, 2020). In the context of developing models for English to Irish translation, there are no clear recommendations on the choice of subword model types. One of the objectives in this study is to identify which type of subword model performs best in this low resource scenario.

2 Background

Native speakers of low-resource languages are often excluded from useful content since, more often than not, online content is not available to them in their language of choice. Such a digital divide and the resulting social exclusion experienced by second language speakers, such as refugees living in developed countries, has been well documented in the research literature (MacFarlane et al., 2008; Alam and Imran, 2015).

Research on Machine Translation (MT) in low-resource scenarios directly addresses this challenge of exclusion via pivot languages (Liu et al., 2018), and indirectly, via domain adaptation of models (Ghifary et al., 2016). Breakthrough performance improvements in the area of MT have been achieved through research efforts focusing on NMT (Bahdanau et al., 2014; Cho et al., 2014). Consequently, state-of-the-art (SOA) performance has been attained on multiple language pairs (Bojar et al., 2017, 2018).

2.1 Irish Language

The Irish language is a primary example of such a low-resource language that will benefit from this research. NMT involving Transformer model development will improve the performance in specific domains of low-resource languages. Such research will address the end of the Irish language derogation in the European Commission in 2021 [1] (Way, 2020) helping to deliver parity in support for Irish in online digital engagement.

2.2 Hyperparameter Optimization

Hyperparameters are employed in order to customize machine learning models such as translation models. It has been shown that machine learning performance may be improved through hyperparameter optimization (HPO) rather than just using default settings (Sanders and Giraud-Carrier, 2017).

The principle methods of HPO are Grid Search (Montgomery, 2017) and Random Search (Bergstra and Bengio, 2012)]. Grid search is an exhaustive technique which evaluates all parameter permutations. However, as the number of features grows, the amount of data permutations grows exponentially making optimization expensive in the context of developing long running translation models.

An effective, and less computationally intensive, alternative is to use random search which samples random configurations.

2.2.1 Recurrent Neural Networks

Recurrent neural networks are often used for the tasks of natural language processing, speech recognition and MT. RNN models enable previous outputs to be used as inputs while having hidden states. In the context of MT, such neural networks were ideal due to their ability to process inputs of any length. Furthermore, the model sizes do not necessarily increase with the size of its input. Commonly used variants of RNN include Bidirectional (BRNN) and Deep (DRNN)

[1] amtaweb.org/wp-content/uploads/2020/11/MT-in-EU-Overview-with-Voiceover-Andy-Way-KEYNOTE-K1.pdf

Hyperparameter	**Values**
Learning rate	0.1, 0.01, 0.001, **2**
Batch size	1024, **2048**, 4096, 8192
Attention heads	**2**, 4, **8**
Number of layers	5, **6**
Feed-forward dimension	**2048**
Embedding dimension	128, **256**, 512
Label smoothing	**0.1**, 0.3
Dropout	0.1, **0.3**
Attention dropout	**0.1**
Average Decay	0, **0.0001**

Table 1: Hyperparameter Optimization for Transformer models. Optimal parameters are highlighted in bold. The highest performing model trained on the 55k DGT corpus uses 2 attention heads whereas the best model trained with the larger 88k PA dataset uses 8 attention heads.

architectures. However, the problem of vanishing gradients coupled with the development of attention-based algorithms often leads to Transformer models performing better than RNNs.

2.2.2 Transformer

The greatest improvements have been demonstrated when either the RNN or the CNN architecture is abandoned completely and replaced with an attention mechanism creating a much simpler and faster architecture known as Transformer (Vaswani et al., 2017). Transformer models use attention to focus on previously generated tokens. The approach allows models to develop a long memory which is particularly useful in the domain of language translation. Performance improvements to both RNN and CNN approaches may be achieved through the introduction of such attention layers in the translation architecture.

Experiments in MT tasks show such models are better in quality due to greater parallelization while requiring significantly less time to train.

2.3 Subword Models

Translation, by its nature, requires an open vocabulary and the use of subword models aims to address the fixed vocabulary problem associated with NMT. Rare and unknown words are encoded as sequences of subword units. By adapting the original Byte Pair Encoding (BPE) algorithm (Gage, 1994), the use of BPE submodels can improve translation performance (Sennrich et al., 2015; Kudo, 2018).

Designed for NMT, SentencePiece, is a language-independent subword tokenizer that provides an open-source C++ and a Python implementation for subword units. An attractive feature of the tokenizer is that SentencePiece trains subword models directly from raw sentences (Kudo and Richardson, 2018).

2.3.1 Byte Pair Encoding compared with Unigram

BPE and unigram language models are similar in that both encode text using fewer bits but each uses a different data compression principle (dictionary vs. entropy). In principle, we would expect the same benefits with the unigram language model as with BPE. However, unigram models are often more flexible since they are probabilistic models that output multiple segmentations with their probabilities.

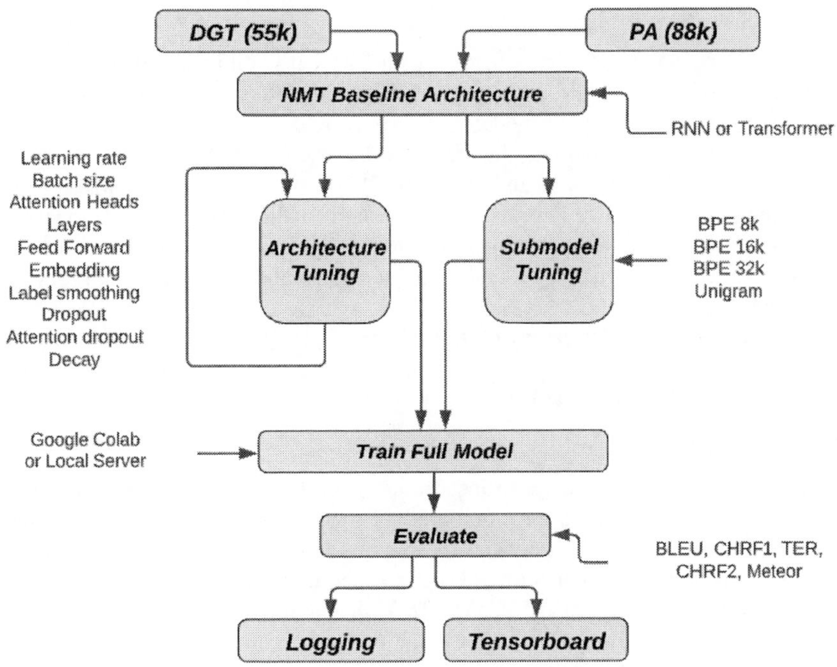

Figure 1: Proposed Approach

3 Proposed Approach

HPO of RNN models in low-resource settings has previously demonstrated considerable performance improvements. The extent to which such optimization techniques may be applied to Transformer models in similar low-resource scenarios is evaluated as part of this study. Evaluations included modifying the number of attention heads, the number of layers and experimenting with regularization techniques such as dropout and label smoothing. Most importantly, the choice of subword model type and the vocabulary size are evaluated.

In order to test the effectiveness of our approaches, optimization was carried out on two English-Irish parallel datasets: a general corpus of 52k lines from the Directorate General for Translation (DGT) and an in-domain corpus of 88k lines of Public Administration (PA) data. With DGT, the test set used 1.3k lines and the development set comprised of 2.6k lines. In the case of the PA dataset, there were 1.5k lines of test data and 3k lines of validation. All experiments involved concatenating source and target corpora to create a shared vocabulary and a shared SentencePiece subword model. The impact of using separate source and target subword models was not explored.

The approach adopted is illustrated in Figure 1. Two baseline architectures, RNN and Transformer, are evaluated. On evaluating the hyperparameter choices for Transformer models, the values outlined in Table 1 were tested using a random search approach. A range of values for each parameter was tested using short cycles of 5k training steps. Once an optimal value, within the sampled range was identified, it was locked in for tests on subsequent parameters.

3.1 Architecture Tuning

Given the long training times associated with NMT, it is difficult and costly to tune systems using a conventional Grid Search approach. Therefore a Random Search approach was adopted in the HPO of our transformer models.

With low-resource datasets, the use of smaller and fewer layers has previously been shown to improve performance (Araabi and Monz, 2020). Performance of low-resource NMT has also been demonstrated to improve in cases where shallow Transformer models are adopted (Van Biljon et al., 2020). Guided by these findings, configurations were tested which varied the number of neurons in each layer and modified the number of layers used in the Transformer architecture.

The impact of regularization, by applying varying degrees of dropout to Transformer models, was evaluated. Configurations using smaller (0.1) and larger values (0.3) were applied to the output of each feed forward layer.

3.2 Subword Models

It has become standard practise to incorporate word segmentation approaches, such as Byte-Pair-Encoding (BPE), when developing NMT models. Previous work shows that subword models may be particularly beneficial for low-resource languages since rare words are often a problem. Reducing the number of BPE merge operations resulted in substantial improvements of 5 BLEU points (Sennrich and Zhang 2019) when tested on RNN models.

In the context of English to Irish translation, there is no clear agreement as to what constituted the best approach. Consequently, as part of this study, subword regularization techniques, involving BPE and unigram models were evaluated to determining the optimal parameters for maximising translation performance. BPE models with varying vocabulary sizes of 4k, 8k, 16k and 32k were tested.

4 Empirical Evaluation

4.1 Experimental Setup

4.1.1 Datasets

The performance of the Transformer and RNN approaches is evaluated on English to Irish parallel datasets. Two datasets were used in the evaluation of our models namely the publicly available DGT dataset which may be broadly categorised as generic and an in-domain dataset which focuses on public administration data.

The DGT, and its Joint Research Centre, has made available all Translation Memory (TM; i.e. sentences and their professionally produced translations) which cover all official European Union languages (Steinberger et al., 2013).

Data provided by the Department of Tourism, Culture, Arts, Gaeltacht, Sport and Media in Ireland formed the majority of the data in the public administration dataset. This includes staff notices, annual reports, website content, press releases and official correspondence.

Parallel texts from the Digital Corpus of the European Parliament (DCEP) and the DGT are included in the training data. Crawled data, from sites of a similar domain are included. Furthermore a parallel corpus collected from Conradh na Gaeilge (CnaG), an Irish language organisation that promotes the Irish language, was included. The dataset was compiled as part of a previous study which carried out a preliminary comparison of SMT and NMT models for the Irish language (Dowling et al., 2018).

4.1.2 Infrastructure

Models were developed using a lab of machines each of which has an AMD Ryzen 7 2700X processor, 16 GB memory, a 256 SSD and an NVIDIA GeForce GTX 1080 Ti. Rapid prototype

Architecture	BLEU ↑	TER ↓	ChrF3 ↑	Steps	Runtime (hours)	$kgCO_2$
dgt-rnn-base	52.7	0.42	0.71	75k	4.47	0
dgt-rnn-bpe8k	54.6	0.40	0.73	85k	5.07	0
dgt-rnn-bpe16k	55.6	0.39	0.74	100k	5.58	0
dgt-rnn-bpe32k	55.3	0.39	0.74	95k	4.67	0
dgt-rnn-unigram	**55.6**	**0.39**	**0.74**	105k	5.07	0

Table 2: RNN performance on DGT dataset of 52k lines

Architecture	BLEU ↑	TER ↓	ChrF3 ↑	Steps	Runtime (hours)	$kgCO_2$
pa-rnn-base	40.4	0.47	0.63	60k	2.13	0
pa-rnn-bpe8k	41.5	0.46	0.64	110k	4.16	0
pa-rnn-bpe16k	41.5	0.46	0.64	105k	3.78	0
pa-rnn-bpe32k	41.9	0.47	0.64	100k	2.88	0
pa-rnn-unigram	**41.9**	**0.46**	**0.64**	95k	2.75	0

Table 3: RNN performance on PA dataset of 88k lines

development was enabled through a Google Colab Pro subscription using NVIDIA Tesla P100 PCIe 16 GB graphic cards and up to 27GB of memory when available (Bisong, 2019).

Our MT models were trained using the Pytorch implementation of OpenNMT 2.0, an open-source toolkit for NMT (Klein et al., 2017).

4.1.3 Metrics

As part of this study, several automated metrics were used to determine the translation quality. All models were trained and evaluated on both the DGT and PA datasets using the BLEU (Papineni et al., 2002), TER (Snover et al., 2006) and ChrF (Popović, 2015) evaluation metrics. Case-insensitive BLEU scores, at the corpus level, are reported. Model training was stopped once an early stopping criteria of no improvement in validation accuracy for 4 consecutive iterations was recorded.

4.2 Results

4.2.1 Performance of subword models

The impact on translation accuracy when choosing a subword model is highlighted in Tables 2 - 5. In training both RNN and Transformer architectures, incorporating any submodel type led to improvements in model accuracy. This finding is evident when training either the smaller generic DGT dataset or the larger in-domain PA dataset.

Using an RNN architecture on DGT, as illustrated in Table 2, the best performing model with a 32k unigram submodel, achieved a BLEU score 7.4% higher than the baseline. With the PA dataset using an RNN, as shown in Table 3, the model with the best BLEU, TER and ChrF3 scores again used a unigram submodel.

There are small improvements in BLEU scores when the RNN baseline is compared with models using a BPE submodel of either 8k, 16k or 32k words, as illustrated in Tables 2 and 3. The maximum BLEU score improvement of 1.5 points (2.5%) is quite modest in the case of the public admin corpus. However, there are larger gains with the DGT corpus. A baseline RNN model, trained on DGT, achieved a BLEU score of 52.7 whereas the highest-performing BPE variant, using a 16k vocab, recorded an improvement of nearly 3 points with a score of 55.6.

In the context of Transformer architectures, highlighted in Table 4 and Table 5, the use

Architecture	BLEU ↑	TER ↓	ChrF3 ↑	Steps	Runtime (hours)	$kgCO_2$
dgt-trans-base	53.4	0.41	0.72	55k	14.43	0.81
dgt-trans-bpe8k	59.5	0.34	0.77	200k	24.48	1.38
dgt-trans-bpe16k	**60.5**	**0.33**	**0.78**	180k	26.90	1.52
dgt-trans-bpe32k	59.3	0.35	0.77	100k	18.03	1.02
dgt-trans-unigram	59.3	0.35	0.77	125k	21.95	1.24

Table 4: Transformer performance on 52k DGT dataset. Highest performing model uses 2 attention heads. All other models use 8 attention heads.

Architecture	BLEU ↑	TER ↓	ChrF3 ↑	Steps	Runtime (hours)	$kgCO_2$
pa-trans-base	44.1	0.44	0.66	20k	5.97	0.34
pa-trans-bpe8k	46.6	**0.40**	0.68	160k	20.1	1.13
pa-trans-bpe16k	**47.1**	0.41	**0.68**	100k	14.22	0.80
pa-trans-bpe32k	46.8	0.41	0.68	70k	12.7	0.72
pa-trans-unigram	46.6	0.42	0.68	75k	13.34	0.75

Table 5: Transformer performance on 88k PA dataset. All models use 8 attention heads.

of subword models delivers significant performance improvements for both the DGT and public admin corpora. The performance gains for Transformer models are far greater than RNN models. Baseline DGT Transformer models achieve a BLEU score of 53.4 while a Transformer model, with a 16k BPE submodel, has a score of 60.5 representing a BLEU score improvement of 13% at 7.1 BLEU points.

For translating into a morphologically rich language, such as Irish, the ChrF metric has proven successful in showing strong correlation with human translation (Stanojević et al., 2015). In the context of our experiments, it worked well in highlighting the performance differences between RNN and Transformer architectures.

4.2.2 Transformer performance compared with RNN

The performance of RNN models is contrasted with the Transformer approach in Figure 2 and Figure 3. Transformer models, as anticipated, outperform all their RNN counterparts. It is interesting to note the impact of choosing the optimal vocabulary size for BPE submodels.

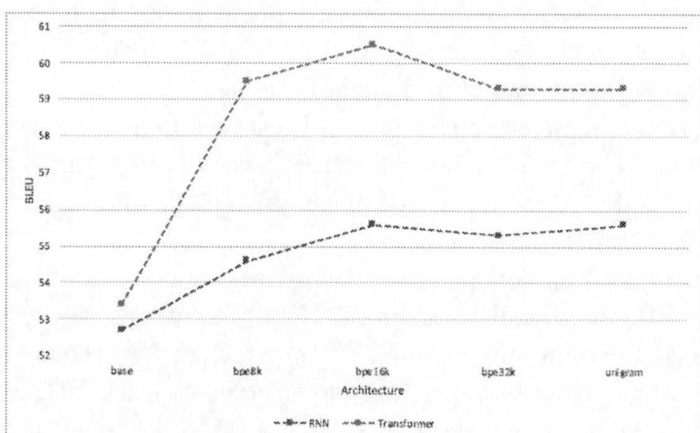

Figure 2: BLEU performance for all model architectures

Both datasets demonstrate that choosing a BPE vocabulary of 16k words yields the highest performance.

Furthermore, the TER scores highlighted in Figure 3 reinforce the findings that using 16k BPE submodels on Transformer architectures leads to better translation performance. The TER score for the DGT Transformer 16k BPE model is significantly better (0.33) when compared with the baseline performance (0.41).

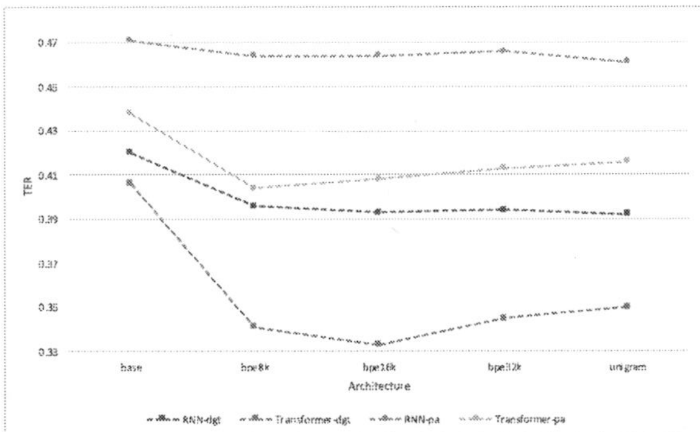

Figure 3: TER performance for all model architectures

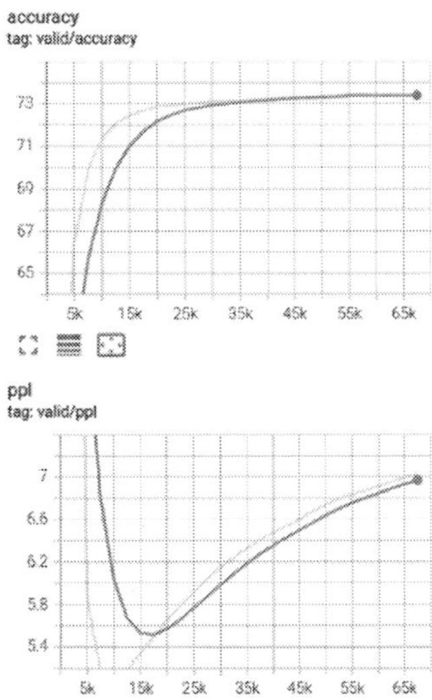

Figure 4: Training DGT Transformer baseline

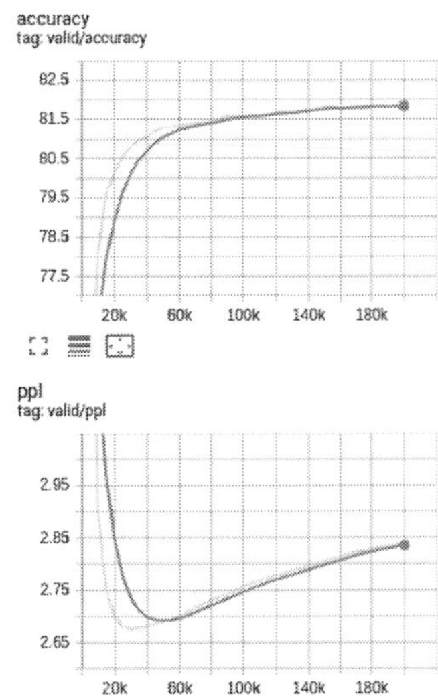

Figure 5: Training DGT Transformer 16k BPE

5 Environmental Impact

Motivated by the findings of Stochastic Parrots (Bender et al., 2021), energy consumption during model development was tracked. Prototype model development used Colab Pro, which as part of Google Cloud is carbon neutral (Lacoste et al., 2019). However, longer running Transformer experiments were conducted on local servers using 324 gCO_2 per kWh [2](SEAI, 2020).

[2]https://www.seai.ie/publications/Energy-in-Ireland-2020.pdf

The net result was just under 10 $kgCO_2$ created for a full run of model development. Models developed during this study, will be reused for ensemble experiments in future work.

6 Discussion

Validation accuracy, and model perplexity, in developing the baseline and optimal models for the DGT corpus are illustrated in Figure 4 and Figure 5. Rapid convergence was observed while training the baseline model such that little accuracy improvement occurs after 20k steps. Including a subword model led to much slower convergence and there were only marginal gains after 60k steps. Furthermore, it is observed that training the DGT model, with a 16k BPE submodel, boosted validation accuracy by over 8% compared with its baseline.

With regard to the key metric of perplexity, it is shown to rise after training for 15k steps in the baseline models. PPL was observed to rise at later stages, typically after 40k steps in models developed using subword models. Perplexity (PPL), shows how many different, equally probable words can be produced during translation. As a metric for translation performance, it is important to keep low scores so the number of alternative translations is reduced. Therefore, for future model development it may be worthwhile to set PPL as an early stopping parameter.

On examining the PPL graphs of Figure 4 and Figure 5, it is clear that a lower global minimum is achieved when the Transformer approach is used with a 16k BPE submodel. The PPL global minimum (2.7) is over 50% lower than the corresponding PPL for the Transformer base model (5.5). Such a finding illustrates that choosing an optimal submodel delivers significant performance gains.

Translation engine performance was bench-marked against Google Translate's [3] English to Irish translation service which is freely available on the internet. Four random samples were selected from the English source test file and are presented in Table 6. Translation of these samples was carried out on the optimal DGT Transformer model and using Google Translate. Case insensitive, sentence level BLEU scores were recorded and are presented in Table 7. The results are encouraging and indicate well-performing translation models on the DGT dataset.

The optimal parameters selected in this discovery process are identified in bold in Table 2. A higher initial learning rate of 2 coupled with an average decay of 0.0001 led to longer training times but more accurate models. Despite setting an early stopping parameter, many of the Transformer builds continued for the full cycle of 200k steps over periods of 20+ hours.

Training transformer models with a reduced number of attention heads led to a marginal improvement in translation accuracy with a smaller corpus. Our best performing model on a 55k DGT corpus, with 2 heads and a 16k BPE submodel, achieved a BLEU score of 60.5 and a TER score of 0.33. By comparison, using 8 heads with the same architecture and dataset yielded 60.3 for the BLEU and 0.34 for the TER. In the case of a larger 88k PA corpus, all transformer models using 8 heads performed better than equivalent models using just 2 heads.

[3] https://translate.google.com/

Source Language (English)	Reference Human Translation (Irish)
A clear harmonised procedure, including the necessary criteria for disease–free status, should be established for that purpose.	Ba cheart nós imeachta comhchuibhithe soiléir, lena n-áirítear na critéir is gá do stádas saor ó ghalar, a bhunú chun na críche sin.
the mark is applied anew, as appropriate.	déanfar an mharcáil arís, mar is iomchuí.
If the court decides that a review is justified on any of the grounds set out in paragraph 1, the judgment given in the European Small Claims Procedure shall be null and void.	Má chinneann an chúirt go bhfuil bonn cirt le hathbhreithniú de bharr aon cheann de na forais a leagtar amach i mír 1, beidh an breithiúnas a tugadh sa Nós Imeachta Eorpach um Éilimh Bheaga ar neamhní go hiomlán.
households where pet animals are kept;	teaghlaigh ina gcoimeádtar peataí;

Table 6: Samples of human reference translations

Transformer (16 kBPE)	BLEU ↑	Google Translate	BLEU ↑
Ba cheart nós imeachta soiléir comhchuibhithe, lena n-áirítear na critéir is gá maidir le stádas saor ó ghalair, a bhunú chun na críche sin.	61.6	Ba cheart nós imeachta comhchuibhithe soiléir, lena n-áirítear na critéir riachtanacha maidir le stádas saor ó ghalair, a bhunú chun na críche sin.	70.2
go gcuirtear an marc i bhfeidhme, de réir mar is iomchuí.	21.4	cuirtear an marc i bhfeidhm as an nua, de réir mar is cuí.	6.6
Má chinneann an chúirt go bhfuil bonn cirt le hathbhreithniú ar aon cheann de na forais a leagtar amach i mír 1, beidh an breithiúnas a thugtar sa Nós Imeachta Eorpach um Éilimh Bheaga ar neamhní.	77.3	Má chinneann an chúirt go bhfuil údar le hathbhreithniú ar aon cheann de na forais atá leagtha amach i mír 1, beidh an breithiúnas a thugtar sa Nós Imeachta Eorpach um Éilimh Bheaga ar neamhní	59.1
teaghlaigh ina gcoimeádtar peataí;	100	teaghlaigh ina gcoinnítear peataí;	30.2

Table 7: Transformer model compared with Google Translate using random samples from the DGT corpus. Full evaluation of Google Translate on the DGT test set, with 1.3k lines, generated a BLEU score of 46.3 and a TER score of 0.44. Comparative scores on the test set using our Transformer model, with 2 attention heads and 16k BPE submodel realised 60.5 for BLEU and 0.33 for TER.

Standard Transformer parameters for batch size (2048) and the number of encoder / decoder layers (6) were all observed to perform well on the DGT and PA corpora. Reducing hidden neurons to 256 and increasing regularization dropout to 0.3 improved translation performance and were chosen when building all Transformer models.

7 Conclusion

In our paper, we demonstrated that a random search approach to hyperparameter optimization leads to the development of high-performing translation models.

We have shown that choosing subword models, in our low-resource scenarios, is an important driver for the performance of MT engines. Moreover, the choice of vocabulary size leads to varying degrees of performance. Within the context of low-resource English to Irish translation, we achieved optimal performance, on a 55k generic corpus and an 88k in-domain corpus, when a Transformer architecture with a 16k BPE submodel was used. The importance of selecting hyperparameters in training low-resource Transformer models was also demonstrated. By reducing the number of hidden layer neurons and increasing dropout, our models performed significantly better than baseline models and Google Translate.

Performance improvement of our optimized Transformer models, with subword segmentation, was observed across all key indicators namely a higher validation accuracy, a PPL achieved at a lower global minimum, a lower post editing effort and a higher translation accuracy.

Acknowledgements

This work was supported by ADAPT, which is funded under the SFI Research Centres Programme (Grant 13/RC/2016) and is co-funded by the European Regional Development Fund. This research was also funded by the Munster Technological University.

References

Alam, K. and Imran, S. (2015). The digital divide and social inclusion among refugee migrants. *Information Technology & People*.

Araabi, A. and Monz, C. (2020). Optimizing transformer for low-resource neural machine translation. *arXiv preprint arXiv:2011.02266*.

Bahdanau, D., Cho, K., and Bengio, Y. (2014). Neural machine translation by jointly learning to align and translate. *arXiv preprint arXiv:1409.0473*.

Bender, E. M., Gebru, T., McMillan-Major, A., and Shmitchell, S. (2021). On the dangers of stochastic parrots: Can language models be too big?. In *Proceedings of the 2021 ACM Conference on Fairness, Accountability, and Transparency*, pages 610–623.

Bergstra, J. and Bengio, Y. (2012). Random search for hyper-parameter optimization. *Journal of machine learning research*, 13(2).

Bisong, E. (2019). Google colaboratory. In *Building Machine Learning and Deep Learning Models on Google Cloud Platform*, pages 59–64. Springer.

Bojar, O., Chatterjee, R., Federmann, C., Graham, Y., Haddow, B., Huang, S., Huck, M., Koehn, P., Liu, Q., Logacheva, V., Monz, C., Negri, M., Post, M., Rubino, R., Specia, L., and Turchi, M. (2017). Findings of the 2017 conference on machine translation (WMT17). In *Proceedings of the Second Conference on Machine Translation*, pages 169–214, Copenhagen, Denmark. Association for Computational Linguistics.

Bojar, O., Federmann, C., Fishel, M., Graham, Y., Haddow, B., Koehn, P., and Monz, C. (2018). Findings of the 2018 conference on machine translation (WMT18). In *Proceedings of the Third Conference on Machine Translation: Shared Task Papers*, pages 272–303, Belgium, Brussels. Association for Computational Linguistics.

Cho, K., Van Merriënboer, B., Bahdanau, D., and Bengio, Y. (2014). On the properties of neural machine translation: Encoder-decoder approaches. *arXiv preprint arXiv:1409.1259.*

Ding, S., Renduchintala, A., and Duh, K. (2019). A call for prudent choice of subword merge operations in neural machine translation. *arXiv preprint arXiv:1905.10453.*

Dowling, M., Lynn, T., Poncelas, A., and Way, A. (2018). Smt versus nmt: Preliminary comparisons for irish.

Gage, P. (1994). A new algorithm for data compression. *C Users Journal*, 12(2):23–38.

Ghifary, M., Kleijn, W. B., Zhang, M., Balduzzi, D., and Li, W. (2016). Deep reconstruction-classification networks for unsupervised domain adaptation. In *European Conference on Computer Vision*, pages 597–613. Springer.

Gowda, T. and May, J. (2020). Finding the optimal vocabulary size for neural machine translation. *arXiv preprint arXiv:2004.02334.*

Klein, G., Kim, Y., Deng, Y., Senellart, J., and Rush, A. M. (2017). Opennmt: Open-source toolkit for neural machine translation. *arXiv preprint arXiv:1701.02810.*

Kudo, T. (2018). Subword regularization: Improving neural network translation models with multiple subword candidates. *arXiv preprint arXiv:1804.10959.*

Kudo, T. and Richardson, J. (2018). Sentencepiece: A simple and language independent subword tokenizer and detokenizer for neural text processing. *arXiv preprint arXiv:1808.06226.*

Lacoste, A., Luccioni, A., Schmidt, V., and Dandres, T. (2019). Quantifying the carbon emissions of machine learning. *arXiv preprint arXiv:1910.09700.*

Liu, C.-H., Silva, C. C., Wang, L., and Way, A. (2018). Pivot machine translation using chinese as pivot language. In *China Workshop on Machine Translation*, pages 74–85. Springer.

MacFarlane, A., Glynn, L. G., Mosinkie, P. I., and Murphy, A. W. (2008). Responses to language barriers in consultations with refugees and asylum seekers: a telephone survey of irish general practitioners. *BMC Family Practice*, 9(1):1–6.

Montgomery, D. C. (2017). *Design and analysis of experiments.* John wiley & sons.

Papineni, K., Roukos, S., Ward, T., and Zhu, W.-J. (2002). Bleu: a method for automatic evaluation of machine translation. In *Proceedings of the 40th annual meeting of the Association for Computational Linguistics*, pages 311–318.

Popović, M. (2015). chrf: character n-gram f-score for automatic mt evaluation. In *Proceedings of the Tenth Workshop on Statistical Machine Translation*, pages 392–395.

Sanders, S. and Giraud-Carrier, C. (2017). Informing the use of hyperparameter optimization through metalearning. In *2017 IEEE International Conference on Data Mining (ICDM)*, pages 1051–1056. IEEE.

SEAI (2020). Sustainable Energy in Ireland.

Sennrich, R., Haddow, B., and Birch, A. (2015). Neural machine translation of rare words with subword units. *arXiv preprint arXiv:1508.07909.*

Snover, M., Dorr, B., Schwartz, R., Micciulla, L., and Makhoul, J. (2006). A study of translation edit rate with targeted human annotation. In *Proceedings of association for machine translation in the Americas*, volume 200. Citeseer.

Stanojević, M., Kamran, A., Koehn, P., and Bojar, O. (2015). Results of the wmt15 metrics shared task. In *Proceedings of the Tenth Workshop on Statistical Machine Translation*, pages 256–273.

Steinberger, R., Eisele, A., Klocek, S., Pilos, S., and Schlüter, P. (2013). Dgt-tm: A freely available translation memory in 22 languages. *arXiv preprint arXiv:1309.5226*.

Van Biljon, E., Pretorius, A., and Kreutzer, J. (2020). On optimal transformer depth for low-resource language translation. *arXiv preprint arXiv:2004.04418*.

Vaswani, A., Shazeer, N., Parmar, N., Uszkoreit, J., Jones, L., Gomez, A. N., Kaiser, L., and Polosukhin, I. (2017). Attention is all you need. *arXiv preprint arXiv:1706.03762*.

Way, A. (2020). MT Developments in the EU: Keynote AMTA 2020.

The Effect of Domain and Diacritics in Yorùbá–English Neural Machine Translation

David Ifeoluwa Adelani* didelani@lsv.uni-saarland.de
Spoken Language Systems Group (LSV), Saarland University, Germany & Masakhane NLP

Dana Ruiter* druiter@lsv.uni-saarland.de
Spoken Language Systems Group (LSV), Saarland University, Germany

Jesujoba O. Alabi* jalabi@mpi-inf.mpg.de
Max Planck Institute for Informatics, Saarbrücken, Germany & Masakhane NLP

Damilola Adebonojo iyayorubagidi@gmail.com
Alamoja Yoruba & Masakhane NLP

Adesina Ayeni info@yobamoodua.org
Yobamoodua Cultural Heritage (YMCH)

Mofe Adeyemi mofetoluwa@outlook.com
Defence Space Administration, Abuja, Nigeria & Masakhane NLP

Ayodele Awokoya ayodeleawokoya@gmail.com
University of Ibadan, Nigeria & Masakhane NLP

Cristina España-Bonet cristinae@dfki.de
DFKI GmbH, Saarland Informatics Campus, Saarbrücken, Germany

Abstract

Massively multilingual machine translation (MT) has shown impressive capabilities, including zero and few-shot translation between low-resource language pairs. However, these models are often evaluated on high-resource languages with the assumption that they generalize to low-resource ones. The difficulty of evaluating MT models on low-resource pairs is often due to lack of standardized evaluation datasets. In this paper, we present MENYO-20k, the first multi-domain parallel corpus with a special focus on clean orthography for Yorùbá–English with standardized train-test splits for benchmarking. We provide several neural MT benchmarks and compare them to the performance of popular pre-trained (massively multilingual) MT models both for the heterogeneous test set and its subdomains. Since these pre-trained models use huge amounts of data with uncertain quality, we also analyze the effect of diacritics, a major characteristic of Yorùbá, in the training data. We investigate how and when this training condition affects the final quality and intelligibility of a translation. Our models outperform massively multilingual models such as Google (+8.7 BLEU) and Facebook M2M (+9.1 BLEU) when translating to Yorùbá, setting a high quality benchmark for future research.

* Equal contribution to the work

1 Introduction

Neural machine translation (NMT) achieves high quality performance when large amounts of parallel sentences are available (Barrault et al., 2020). Large and freely-available parallel corpora do exist for a small number of high-resource pairs and domains. However, for low-resource languages such as Yorùbá (*yo*), one can only find few thousands of parallel sentences online[1]. In the best-case scenario, i.e. some amount of parallel data exists, one can use the Bible — the Bible is the most available resource for low-resource languages (Resnik et al., 1999)— and JW300 (Agić and Vulić, 2019). Notice that both corpora belong to the religious domain and they do not generalize well to popular domains such as news and daily conversations.

In this paper, we address this problem for the Yorùbá–English (*yo–en*) language pair by creating a multi-domain parallel dataset, MENYO-20k, which we make publicly available[2] with CC BY-NC 4.0 licence. It is a heterogeneous dataset that comprises texts obtained from news articles, TED talks, movie and radio transcripts, science and technology texts, and other short articles curated from the web and translated by professional translators. Based on the resulting train-development-test split, we provide a benchmark for the *yo–en* translation task for future research on this language pair. This allows us to properly evaluate the generalization of MT models trained on JW300 and the Bible on new domains. We further explore transfer learning approaches that can make use of a few thousand sentence pairs for domain adaptation. Finally, we analyze the effect of Yorùbá diacritics on the translation quality of pre-trained MT models, discussing in details how this affects the understanding of the translated text especially in the *en–yo* direction. We show the benefit of automatic diacritic restoration in addressing the problem of noisy diacritics.

2 The Yorùbá Language

The Yorùbá language is the third most spoken language in Africa, and it is native to south-western Nigeria and the Republic of Benin. It is one of the national languages in Nigeria, Benin and Togo, and spoken across the West African regions. The language belongs to the Niger-Congo family, and it is spoken by over 40 million native speakers (Eberhard et al., 2019).

Yorùbá has 25 letters without the Latin characters c, q, v, x and z, and with additional characters ẹ, gb, ṣ , ọ. Yorùbá is a tonal language with three tones: low, middle and high. These tones are represented by the grave (e.g. "à "), optional macron (e.g. "ā") and acute (e.g. "á") accents respectively. These tones are applied on vowels and syllabic nasals, but the mid tone is usually ignored in writings. The tone information and underdots are important for the correct pronunciation of words. Often, articles written online, including news articles such as BBC[3] ignore diacritics. Ignoring diacritics makes it difficult to identify or pronounce words except when they are embedded in context. For example, *èdè* (language), *edé* (crayfish), *ẹdẹ* (a town in Nigeria), *ẹ̀dẹ* (trap) and *ẹ̀dẹ̀* (balcony) will be mapped to *ede* without diacritics.

Machine translation might be able to learn to disambiguate the meaning of words and generate correct English even with un-diacriticized Yorùbá. However, one cannot generate correct Yorùbá if the training data is un-diacriticized. One of the purposes of our work is to build a corpus with correct and complete diacritization in several domains.

3 MENYO-20k

The dataset collection was motivated by the inability of machine translation models trained on JW300 to generalize to new domains (∀ et al., 2020). Although ∀ et al. (2020) evaluated this

[1]http://opus.nlpl.eu

[2]https://github.com/uds-lsv/menyo-20k_MT

[3]https://www.bbc.com/yoruba

Data name	Source	No. Sent.
source language: en-yo		
JW News	`jw.org/yo/iroyin`	3,508
VON News	`von.gov.ng`	3,048
GV News	`globalvoices.org`	2,932
Yorùbá Proverbs	`@yoruba_proverbs`	2,700
Movie Transcript	"Unsane" on YouTube	774
UDHR	`ohchr.org`	100
ICT localization	from Yorùbá translators	941
Short texts	from Yorùbá translators	687
source language: en		
TED talks	`ted.com/talks`	2,945
Out of His Mind	from the book author	2,014
Radio Broadcast	from Bond FM Radio	258
CC License	Creative Commons	193
Total		20,100

Domain	Number of Sentences Train. Set	Dev. Set	Test Set
MENYO-20k			
News	4,995	1,391	3,102
TED Talks	507	438	2,000
Book	-	1,006	1,008
IT	356	312	273
Yorùbá Proverbs	2,200	250	250
Others	2,012	250	250
Standard (religious) corpora			
Bible	30,760	–	–
JW300	459,871	–	–
TOTAL	500,701	3,397	6,633

Table 1: **Left:** Data collection. **Right:** MENYO-20k domains and training, development and test splits (top); figures for standard corpora used in this work (bottom).

for Yorùbá with surprisingly high BLEU scores, the evaluation was done on very few examples from the COVID-19 and TED Talks domains with 39 and 80 sentences respectively. Inspired by the FLoRes dataset for Nepali and Sinhala (Guzmán et al., 2019), we create a high quality test set for Yorùbá-English with few thousands of sentences in different domains to check the quality of industry MT models, pre-trained MT models, and MT models based on popular corpora such as JW300 and the Bible.

3.1 Dataset Collection for MENYO-20k

Table 1 summarizes the texts collected, their source, the original language of the texts and the number of sentences from each source. We collected both parallel corpora freely available on the web (e.g JW News) and monolingual corpora we are interested in translating (e.g. the TED talks) to build the MENYO-20k corpus. The JW News is different from the JW300 since they contain only news reports, and we manually verified that they are not in JW300. Some few sentences were donated by professional translators such as "short texts" in Table 1. Our curation followed two steps: (1) translation of monolingual texts crawled from the web by professional translators; (2) verification of translation, orthography and diacritics for parallel texts obtained online and translated. Texts obtained from the web that were judged by native speakers being high quality were verified once, the others were verified twice. The verification of translation and diacritics was done by professional translators and volunteers who are native speakers.

Table 1 on the right (top) summarizes the figures for the MENYO-20k dataset with 20,100 parallel sentences split into 10,070 training sentences, 3,397 development sentences, and 6,633 test sentences. The test split contains 6 domains, 3 of them have more than 1000 sentences and can be used as domain test sets by themselves.

3.2 Other Corpora for Yorùbá and English

Parallel corpora For our experiments, we use two widely available parallel corpora from the religion domain, Bible and JW300 (Table 1, bottom). The parallel version of the Bible is not available, so we align the verses from the New International Version (NIV) for English and the Bible Society of Nigeria version (BSN) for Yorùbá. After aligning the verses, we obtain

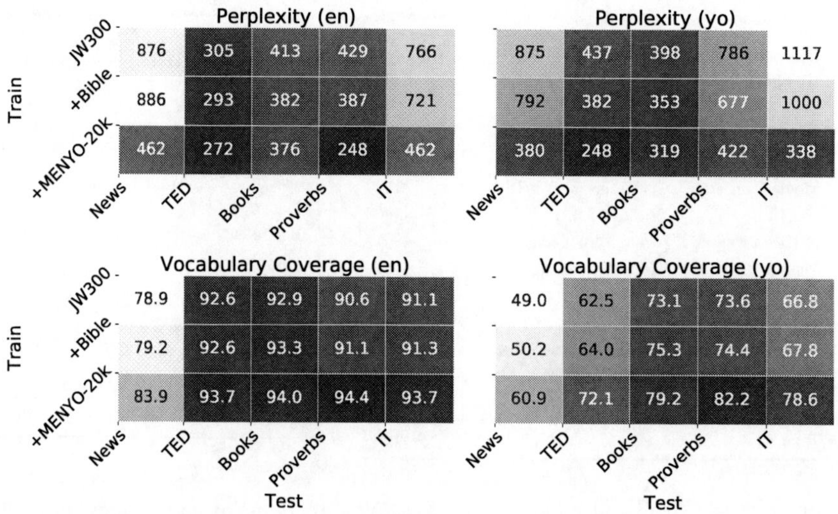

Figure 1: **Top:** Perplexities of KenLM 5-gram language model learned on different training corpora and tested on subsets of MENYO-20k for English (left) and Yorùbá (right) respectively. **Bottom:** Vocabulary coverage (%) of different subsets of the MENYO-20k test set per training sets for English (left) and Yorùbá (right).

30,760 parallel sentences. Also, we download the JW300 parallel corpus which is available for a large variety of low-resource language pairs. It has parallel corpora from English to 343 languages containing religion-related texts. From the JW300 corpus, we get 459, 871 sentence pairs already tokenized with *Polyglot*[4] (Al-Rfou, 2015).

Monolingual Corpora We make use of additional monolingual data to train the semi-supervised MT model using back-translation. The Yorùbá monolingual texts are from the Yorùbá embedding corpus (Alabi et al., 2020), one additional book ("Ojowu") with permission from the author, JW300-*yo*, and Bible-*yo*. We only use Yorùbá texts that are properly diacritized. In order to keep the topics in the Yorùbá and English monolingual corpora close, we choose two Nigerian news websites (The Punch Newspaper[5] and Voice of Nigeria [6]) for the English monolingual corpus. The news scraped covered categories such as politics, business, sports and entertainment. Overall, we gather 475,763 monolingual sentences from the website.

3.3 Dataset Domain Analysis

MENYO-20k is, on purpose, highly heterogeneous. In this section we analyze the differences and how its (sub)domains depart from the characteristics of the commonly used Yorùbá–English corpora for MT.

Characterizing the domain of a dataset is a difficult task. Some metrics previously used need either large corpora or a characteristic vocabulary of the domain (Beyer et al., 2020; España-Bonet et al., 2020). Here, we do not have these resources and we report the overlapping vocabulary between training and test sets and the perplexity observed in the test sets when a language model (LM) is trained on the MT training corpora.

[4] https://github.com/aboSamoor/polyglot

[5] https://punchng.com

[6] https://von.gov.ng

In order to estimate the perplexities, we train a language model of order 5 with KenLM (Heafield, 2011) on each of the 3 training data subsets: JW300 (named C2 for short in tables), JW300+Bible (C3), JW300+Bible+MENYO-20k (C4). Following NMT standard processing pipelines (see subsection 4.2), we perform byte-pair encoding (BPE) (Sennrich et al., 2016) on the corpora to avoid a large number of out-of-vocabulary tokens which, for small corpora, could alter the LM probabilities. For each of the resulting language models, we evaluate their average **perplexity** on the different domains of the test set to evaluate *compositional* domain differences (Figure 1, top). As expected, the average perplexity drops when adding more training data. Due to the limited domain of both JW300 and Bible, a literary style close to the Books domain, the decrease in perplexity is small when adding additional Bible data to JW300, namely -8% (*en*) and -11% (*yo*). Interestingly, both JW300 and Bible also seem to be close to the TED domain (1st and 2nd lowest perplexities for *en* and *yo* respectively), which may be due to discourse/monologue content in both training corpora. Adding the domain-diverse MENYO-20k corpus largely decreases the perplexity across all domains with a major decrease of -66% on IT (*yo*) and smallest decrease of -1% on Books (*en*). The perplexity scores correlate negatively with the resulting BLEU scores in Table 3, with a Pearson's r (r) of -0.367 (*en*) and -0.461 (*yo*), underlining that compositional domain differences between training and test subsets is the main factor of differences in translation quality.

Further, to evaluate *lexical* domain differences, we calculate the **vocabulary coverage** (tokenized, not byte-pair encoded[7]) of the different domains of the test set by each of the training subsets (Figure 1, bottom). The vocabulary coverage increases to a large extend when MENYO-20k is added. However, while vocabulary coverage and average perplexities have a strong (negative) correlation, $r = -0.756$ (*en*) and $r = -0.689$ (*yo*), a high perplexity does not necessarily mean low vocabulary coverage. E.g., the vocabulary coverage of the IT domain by JW300 is high (91% for *en*) despite leading to high perplexities (765 for *en*). In general, vocabulary coverage of the test sets is less indicative of the resulting translation performance than perplexity, showing only a weak correlation between vocabulary coverage and BLEU, with $r = 0.150$ and $r = 0.281$ for *en* and *yo* respectively.

4 Neural Machine Translation for Yorùbá–English

4.1 Systems

Supervised NMT We use the transformer-base architecture proposed by Vaswani et al. (2017) as implemented in Fairseq[8] (Ott et al., 2019). We set the drop-out at 0.3 and batch size at 10,240 tokens. For optimization, we use *adam* (Kingma and Ba, 2015) with $\beta_1 = 0.9$ and $\beta_2 = 0.98$ and a learning rate of 0.0005. The learning rate has a warmup update of 4000, using label smoothed cross-entropy loss function with label-smoothing value of 0.1.

Semi-supervision via iterative back-translation We use the best performing supervised system to translate the monolingual corpora described in section 3 yielding to $476k$ back-translations. This data is used together with the original corpus to train a new system. The process is repeated until convergence.

Fine-tuning mT5 We examine a transfer learning approach by fine-tuning a massively multilingual model mT5 (Xue et al., 2021). mT5 had been pre-trained on 6.3T tokens originating from Common Crawl in 101 languages (including Yorùbá). The approach has already shown competitive results on other languages (Tang et al., 2020). In our experiments, we use mT5-

[7]We do not use byte-pair encoded data here, since, due to the nature of BPE, the vocabulary overlap would be close to 1 between all training and test sets.

[8]https://github.com/pytorch/fairseq

base, a model with 580M parameters. We transferred all the parameters of the model including the sub-word vocabulary.

Publicly Available NMT Models We further evaluate the performance of three multilingual NMT systems: OPUS-MT (Tiedemann and Thottingal, 2020), Google Multilingual NMT (GMNMT) (Arivazhagan et al., 2019) and Facebook's M2M-100 (Fan et al., 2020) with 1.2B parameters. All the three pre-trained models are trained on over 100 languages. While GMNMT and M2M-100 are a single multilingual model, OPUS-MT models are for each translation direction, e.g *yo–en*. We generate the translations of the test set using the *Google Translate* interface,[9] and OPUS-MT using *Easy-NMT*.[10] For M2M-100, we make use of *Fairseq* to translate the test set.

4.2 Experimental Settings

Data and Preprocessing For the MT experiments, we use the training part of our MENYO-20k corpus and two other parallel corpora, Bible and JW300 (section 3). For tuning the hyper-parameters, we use the development split of the multi-domain data which has $3,397$ sentence pairs and for testing the test split with $6,633$ parallel sentences. To ensure that all the parallel corpora are in the same format, we convert the Yorùbá texts in the JW300 dataset to Unicode Normalization Form Composition (NFC), the format of the Yorùbá texts in the Bible and multi-domain dataset. Our preprocessing pipeline includes punctuation normalization, tokenization, and truecasing. For punctuation normalization and truecasing, we use the *Moses* toolkit (Koehn et al., 2007) while for tokenization, we use *Polyglot*, since it is the tokenizer used in JW300. We apply joint BPE, with a vocabulary threshold of 20 and 40k merge operations.

Evaluation Metrics To evaluate the models, we use tokenized BLEU (Papineni et al., 2002) score implemented in *multi-bleu.perl* and confidence intervals ($p = 95\%$) in the scoring package[11]. Since diacritics are applied on individual characters, we also use chrF, a character n-gram F1-score (Popović, 2015), for *en–yo* translations.

Automatic Diacritization In order to automatically diacritize Google MNMT and M2M-100 outputs for comparison, we train an automatic diacritization system using the supervised NMT setup. We use the Yorùbá side of MENYO-20k and JW300, which use consistent diacritization. We split the resulting corpus into train ($458k$ sentences), test (517 sentences) and development (500 sentences) portions. We apply a small BPE of 2k merge operations to the data. We apply noise on the diacritics by i) randomly removing a diacritic with probability $p = 0.3$ and ii) randomly replacing a diacritic with $p = 0.3$. The corrupted version of the corpus is used as the source data, and the NMT model is trained to reconstruct the original diacritics. On the test set, where the corrupted source has a BLEU (precision) of 19.0 (29.8), reconstructing the diacritics using our system lead to a BLEU (precision) of 87.0 (97.1), thus a major increase of $+68.0$ ($+67.3$) respectively.

4.3 Automatic Evaluation

Internal Comparison We train four basic NMT engines on different subsets of the training data: Bible (C1), JW300 (C2), JW300+Bible (C3) and JW300+Bible+MENYO-20k (C4). Further, we analyse the effect of fine-tuning for in-domain translation. For this, we fine-tune the converged model trained on JW300+Bible on MENYO-20k (C3+Transfer) and, similarly, we fine-tune the converged model trained on JW300+Bible+MENYO-20k on MENYO-20k (C4+Transfer). This yields six NMT models in total for *en–yo* and *yo–en* each. Their transla-

[9]`https://translate.google.com/`

[10]`https://github.com/UKPLab/EasyNMT`

[11]`https://github.com/lvapeab/confidence_intervals`

Model	*en–yo*		*en–yo*^{p}		*yo–en*	*yo–en*^{u}
	chrF	BLEU	chrF	BLEU	BLEU	BLEU
Internal Comparison						
C1: Bible	16.9	2.2±0.1	–	–	1.4±0.1	1.6±0.1
C2: JW300	29.1	7.5±0.2	–	–	9.6±0.3	9.3±0.3
C3: JW300+Bible	29.8	8.1±0.2	–	–	10.8±0.3	10.5±0.3
+Transfer	33.8	12.3±0.3	–	–	13.2±0.3	13.9±0.3
C4: JW300+Bible+MENYO-20k	32.5	10.9±0.3	–	–	14.0±0.3	14.0±0.3
+Transfer	34.3	**12.4**±0.3	–	–	14.6±0.3	–
+ BT	34.6	12.0±0.3	–	–	18.2±0.4	–
mT5: mT5-base+Transfer	32.9	11.5±0.3	–	–	16.3±0.4	16.3±0.4
External Comparison						
OPUS-MT	–	–	–	–	5.9±0.2	–
Google GMNMT	18.5	3.7±0.2	34.4	10.6±0.3	**22.4**±0.5	–
Facebook M2M-100	15.8	3.3±0.2	25.7	6.8±0.3	4.6±0.3	–

Table 2: Tokenized BLEU with confidence intervals ($p = 95\%$) and chrF scores over the full test for NMT models trained on different subsets of the training data C_i (top) and performance of external systems (bottom). For Yorùbá, we analyse the effect of diacritization: *en–yo*^{p} applies an in-house diacritizer on the translations obtained from **pre**-trained models and *yo–en*^{u} reports results using **u**ndiacritized Yorùbá texts as source sentences for training (see text). Top-scoring results per block are underlined and globally boldfaced.

tion performance is evaluated on the complete MENYO-20k test set (Table 2, top) and later we analyze in-domain translation in Table 3.

As expected, the BLEU scores obtained after training on Bible only (C1) are low, with BLEU 2.2 and 1.4 for *en–yo* and *yo–en* respectively, which is due to its small amount of training data. Training on the larger JW300 corpus (C2) leads to higher scores of BLEU 7.5 (*en–yo*) and 9.6 (*yo–en*), while combining it with Bible (C3) only leads to a small increase of BLEU +0.6 and +1.2 for *en–yo* and *yo–en* respectively. When further adding MENYO-20k (C4) to the training data, the translation quality increases by +2.8 (*en–yo*) and +3.2 (*yo–en*). When, instead of adding MENYO-20k to the training pool, it is used to fine-tune the converged JW300+Bible model, (C3+Transfer) the increase in BLEU over JW300+Bible is even larger for *en–yo* (BLEU +4.2), which results in an overall top-scoring model with BLEU 12.3. For *yo–en* fine-tuning is slightly less effective (BLEU 13.2) than simply adding MENYO-20k to the training data (BLEU 14.0). As seen in subsection 3.3, perplexities and vocabulary coverage in English are not as distant among training/test sets as in Yorùbá, so the fine-tuning step resulted less efficient.

When we use the MENYO-20k dataset to fine-tune the converged JW300+Bible+ MENYO-20k model (C4+Transfer) we observe an increase in BLEU over JW300+Bible for both translation directions: +4.3 for *en–yo* and +3.8 for *yo–en*. This is the best performing system and the one we use for back-translation. Table 2 also shows the performance of the semi-supervised system (C4+Transfer+BT). After two iterations of BT, we obtain an improvement of +3.6 BLEU points on *yo–en*. There is, however, no improvement in the *en–yo* direction probably because a significant portion of our monolingual data is based on JW300. Finally, fine-tuning mT5 with MENYO-20k does not improve over fine-tuning only the JW300+Bible system on *en–yo*, but it does for *yo–en*. Again, multilingual systems are stronger when used for English, and we need the contribution of back-translation to outperform the generic mT5.

External Comparison We evaluate the performance of the open source multilingual engines introduced in the previous section on the full test set (Table 2, bottom). **OPUS-MT**, while having no model available for *en–yo*, achieves a BLEU of 5.9 for *yo–en*. Thus, despite being trained on JW300 and other available *yo–en* corpora on OPUS, it is largely outperformed by our NMT model trained on JW300 only (BLEU +3.7). This may be caused by some of the noisy corpora included in OPUS (like CCaligned), which can depreciate the translation quality.

Facebook's **M2M-100**, is also largely outperformed even by our simple JW300 baseline by 5 BLEU points in both translation directions. A manual examination of the *en–yo* LASER extractions used to train M2M-100 shows that these are very noisy similar to the findings of Caswell et al. (2021), which explains the poor translation performance.

Google, on the other hand, obtains impressive results with **GMNMT** for the *yo–en* direction, with BLEU 22.4. The opposite direction *en–yo*, however, shows a significantly lower performance (BLEU 3.7), being outperformed even by our simple JW300 baseline (BLEU +3.8). The difference in performance for English can be attributed to the highly multilingual but English-centric nature of the Google MNMT model. As already noticed by Arivazhagan et al. (2019), low-resourced language pairs benefit from multilinguality when translated into English, but improvements are minor when translating into the non-English language. For the other translation direction, *en–yo*, we notice that lots of diacritics are lost in Google translations, damaging the BLEU scores. Whether this drop in BLEU scores really affects understanding or not is analyzed via a human evaluation (Section 4.4).

Diacritization Diacritics are important for Yorùbá embeddings (Alabi et al., 2020). However, they are often ignored in popular multilingual models (e.g. multilingual BERT (Devlin et al., 2019)), and not consistently available in training corpora and even test sets. In order to investigate whether the diacritics in Yorùbá MT can help to disambiguate translation choices, we additionally train *yo–en*^{u} equivalent models on **un**diacritized JW300, JW300+Bible and JW300+Bible+MENYO-20k (Table 2, indicated as *yo–en*^{u} in comparison to the ones with diacritics *yo–en*). Since one cannot generate correct Yorùbá text when training without diacritics, *en–yo*^{u} systems are not trained. Alternatively, we restore diacritics using our in-house diacritizer in the output of open source models that produce undiacritized text.

Results for *yo–en* are not conclusive. Diacritization is useful when only out-of-domain data is used in training (JW300, JW300+Bible[12] for testing on MENYO-20k). In this case, the domain of the training data is very different from the domain of the test set, and disambiguation is needed not to bias all the lexicon towards the religious domain. When we include in-domain data (JW300+Bible+MENYO-20k), both models perform equally well, with BLEU 14.0 for both diacritized and undiacritized versions. Diacritization is not needed when we fine-tune the model with data that shares the domain with the test set (JW300+Bible+Transfer), BLEU is 13.2 for the diacritized version vs. BLEU 13.9 for the undiacritized one.

In practice, this means that, when training data is far from the desired domain, investing work for a clean diacritized Yorùbá source input can help improve the translation performance. When more data is present, the diacritization becomes less important, since context is enough for disambiguation.

When Yorùbá is the target language, diacritization is always needed. An example is the low automatic scores GMNMT (BLEU 3.7, chrF 18.5) and M2M-100 (BLEU 3.3, chrF 15.8) reach for *en–yo* translation. Table 2-bottom (indicated as *en–yo*^{p}) show the improvements after automatically restoring the diacritics, namely $BLEU + 6.9$ points, chrF +15.9 for GMNMT; and +3.5 and +9.9 for M2M-100. Even if the diacritizer is not perfect, diacritics do not seem enough to get state-of-the-art results according to automatic metrics: fine-tuning with high

[12] We do not consider Bible alone. Due to its small data size, the BLEU scores are less indicative.

	en–yo					*yo–en*				
	Prov.	**News**	**TED**	**Book**	**IT**	**Prov.**	**News**	**TED**	**Book**	**IT**
C1	0.8	1.7	3.1	3.4	1.5	1.1	0.9	2.1	2.4	0.9
C2	2.2	6.4	9.8	9.8	4.8	2.6	8.4	13.1	9.6	7.0
C3	3.5	6.7	10.7	11.3	4.9	4.8	9.5	14.4	10.9	7.8
+Transfer	9.0	10.2	**16.1**	**15.0**	11.8	8.6	12.5	16.8	10.8	9.7
C4	7.0	10.0	12.3	11.5	10.5	8.7	13.5	16.7	11.6	12.4
+Transfer	**10.3**	10.9	15.1	13.2	**13.6**	**9.3**	14.0	17.8	11.9	13.7
+BT	7.5	11.4	12.9	14.5	9.7	7.9	**18.6**	**20.6**	**13.3**	**16.4**
mT5+Transfer	3.8	**11.2**	13.1	11.8	7.9	6.0	16.4	18.9	13.1	15.1

Table 3: Tokenized BLEU over different domains of the test set for NMT models trained on different subsets of the training data, with top-scoring results per domain in bold.

	en–yo			*yo–en*		
Task	**C4+Trf**	**C4+Trf+BT**	**GMNMT**	**mT5+Trf**	**C4+Trf+BT**	**GMNMT**
Adequacy	3.12*	3.58	**3.69**	3.42*	3.41*	**4.02**
Fluency	**4.57***	4.49*	3.74	4.39*	4.18*	**4.71**
Diacritics acc.	**4.91***	4.90*	1.74	-	-	-

Table 4: Human evaluation for *en–yo* and *yo–en* MT models (C4+Transfer (C4+Trf), C4+Trf+BT, mT5+Trf, and GMNMT) in terms of Adequacy, Fluency and Diacritics prediction accuracy. The rating that is significantly different from GMNMT is indicated by * (T-test $p < 0.05$)

quality data (C4+Transfer+BT, chrF 34.6) is still better than using huge but unadapted systems.

Domain Differences In order to analyze the domain-specific performance of the different NMT models, we evaluate each model on the different domain subsets of the test set (Table 3). The Proverb subset is especially difficult in both directions, as it shows the lowest translation performance across all domains, i.e. maximum BLEU of 9.04 (*en–yo*) and 8.74 (*yo–en*). This is due to the fact that proverbs often do not have literal counterparts in the target language, thus making them especially difficult to translate. The TED domain is the best performing test domain, with maximum BLEU of 16.1 (*en–yo*) and 16.8 (*yo–en*). This can be attributed to the decent base coverage of the TED domain by JW300 and Bible together (monologues) with the additional TED domain data included in the MENYO-20k training split (507 sentence pairs). Also, most BLEU results are on line with the LM perplexity results and conclusions drawn in subsection 3.3. Due to the closeness of Bible and JW300 to the book domain, we see only small improvements of BLEU on this domain, i.e. +0.2 (*en–yo*) and +0.7 (*yo–en*), when adding MENYO-20k (C4) to the JW300+Bible (C3) training data pool. On the other hand, the IT domain benefits the most from the additional MENYO-20k data, with major gains of BLEU +5.5 (*en–yo*) and 4.6 (*yo–en*), owing to the introduction of IT domain content in the MENYO-20k training data ($\sim 1k$ sentence pairs), which is completely lacking in JW300 and Bible.

4.4 Human Evaluation

To have a better understanding of the quality of the translation models and the intelligibility of the translations, we compare three top performing models in *en–yo* and *yo–en*. For *en–yo*, we use **C4+Transfer**, **C4+Transfer+BT** and **GMNMT**. Although GMNMT is not the third best system according to BLEU (Table 2), we are interested in the study of diacritics in translation quality and intelligibility. For the *yo–en*, we choose **C4+Transfer+BT**, **mT5+Transfer** and **GMNMT** being the 3 models with the highest BLEU scores on Table 2.

We ask 7 native speakers of Yorùbá that are fluent in English to rate the adequacy, fluency and diacritic accuracy in a subset of test sentences. Four of them rated the *en–yo* translation direction and the others rated the opposite direction *yo–en*. We randomly select 100 sentences within the outputs of the six systems and duplicate 5 of them to check the intra-agreement consistency of our raters. Each annotator is then asked to rate 105 sentences per system on a $1-5$ Likert scale for each of the features (for English, diacritic accuracy cannot be evaluated). We calculate the agreement among raters using Krippendorff's α. The inter-agreement per task is 0.44 (adequacy), 0.40 (fluency) and 0.87 (diacritics) for Yorùbá, and 0.71 (adequacy), 0.55 (fluency) for English language. We observe that a lot of raters often rate the fluency score for many sentences with the same values (e.g 4 or 5), which results to a lower Krippendorff's α for fluency. The intra-agreement for the four Yorùbá raters are 0.75, 0.91, 0.66, and 0.87, while the intra-agreement for the three English raters across all evaluation tasks are 0.92, 0.71, and 0.81.

For *yo–en*, our evaluators rated on average GMNMT to be the best in terms of adequacy (4.02 out of 5) and fluency (4.71), followed by mT5+Transfer, which shows that fine-tuning massively multilingual models also benefits low resource languages MT especially in terms of fluency (4.39). This contradicts the results of the automatic evaluation which prefers C4+Transfer+BT over mT5+Transfer.

For *en–yo*, GMNMT is still the best in terms of adequacy (3.69) followed by C4+Transfer+BT, but performs the worst in terms of fluency and diacritics prediction accuracy. So, the bad quality of the diacritics affects fluency and drastically penalises automatic metrics such as BLEU, but does not interfere with the intelligibility of the translations as shown by the good average adequacy rating. Automatic diacritic restoration for Yorùbá (Orife, 2018; Orife et al., 2020) can therefore be very useful to improve translation quality. C4+Transfer and C4+Transfer+BT perform similarly with high scores in terms of fluency and near perfect score in diacritics prediction accuracy (4.91 ± 0.1) as a result of being trained on cleaned corpora.

5 Related Work

In order to make MT available for a broader range of linguistic communities, recent years have seen an effort in creating new **parallel corpora** for low-resource language pairs. Recently, Guzmán et al. (2019) provided novel supervised, semi-supervised and unsupervised benchmarks for Indo-Aryan languages {Sinhala,Nepali}–English on an evaluation set of professionally translated sentences sourced from the Sinhala, Nepali and English Wikipedias.

Novel parallel corpora focusing on **African languages** cover South African languages ({Afrikaans, isiZulu, Northern Sotho, Setswana, Xitsonga}–English) (Groenewald and Fourie, 2009) with MT benchmarks evaluated in Martinus and Abbott (2019), as well as multidomain (News, Wikipedia, Twitter, Conversational) Amharic–English (Hadgu et al., 2020) and multidomain (Government, Wikipedia, News etc.) Igbo–English (Ezeani et al., 2020). Further, the LORELEI project (Strassel and Tracey, 2016) has created parallel corpora for a variety of low-resource language pairs, including a number of Niger-Congo languages such as {isiZulu, Twi, Wolof, Yorùbá }–English. However, these are not open-access. On the contrary, Masakhane (∀ et al., 2020) is an ongoing participatory project focusing on creating new freely-available parallel corpora and MT benchmark models for a large variety of African languages.

While creating parallel resources for low-resource language pairs is one approach to increase the number of linguistic communities covered by MT, this does not scale to the sheer amount of possible language combinations. Another research line focuses on **low-resource**

MT from the modeling side, developing methods which allow a MT system to learn the translation task with smaller amounts of supervisory signals. This is done by exploiting the weaker supervisory signals in larger amounts of available monolingual data, e.g. by identifying additional parallel data in monolingual corpora (Artetxe and Schwenk, 2019; Schwenk et al., 2021, 2020), comparable corpora (Ruiter et al., 2019, 2021), or by including auto-encoding (Currey et al., 2017) or language modeling tasks (Gulcehre et al., 2015; Ramachandran et al., 2017) during training. Low-resource language pairs can benefit from high-resource languages through transfer learning (Zoph et al., 2016), e.g. in a zero-shot setting (Johnson et al., 2017), by using pre-trained language models (Lample and Conneau, 2019), or finding an optimal path of pivoting through related languages (Leng et al., 2019). By adapting the model hyperparameters to the low-resource scenario, Sennrich and Zhang (2019) were able to achieve impressive improvements over a standard NMT system.

6 Conclusion

We present MENYO-20k, a novel *en–yo* multi-domain parallel corpus for machine translation and domain adaptation. By defining a standardized train-development-test split of this corpus, we provide several NMT benchmarks for future research on the *en–yo* MT task. Further, we analyze the domain differences on the MENYO-20k corpus and the translation performance of NMT models trained on religion corpora, such as JW300 and Bible, across the different domains. We show that, despite consisting of only $10k$ parallel sentences, adding the MENYO-20k corpus train split to JW300 and Bible largely improves the translation performance over all domains. Further, we train a variety of supervised, semi-supervised and fine-tuned MT benchmarks on available *en–yo* corpora, creating a high quality baseline that outperforms current massively multilingual models, e.g. Google MNMT by BLEU $+18.8$ (*en–yo*). This shows the positive impact of using smaller amounts of high-quality data (e.g. C4+Transfer, BLEU 12.4) that takes into account language-specific characteristics, i.e. diacritics, over massive amounts of noisy data (Facebook M2M-100, BLEU 3.3). Apart from having low BLEU scores, our human evaluation reveals that models trained on low-quality diacritics (Google MNMT) suffer especially in fluency, while still being intelligible to the reader. While correctly diacritized data is vital for translating *en–yo*, it only has an impact on the quality of *yo–en* translation quality when there is a domain mismatch between training and testing data.

Acknowledgements

We would like to thank Adebayo O. Adeojo, Babunde O. Popoola, Olumide Awokoya, Modupe Olaniyi, Princess Folasade, Akinade Idris, Tolulope Adelani, Oluyemisi Olaose, and Benjamin Ajibade for their support in translating English sentences to Yorùbá, verification of Yorùbá diacritics, and human evaluation. We thank Bayo Adebowale and 'Dele 'Adelani for donating their books ("Out of His Mind", and "Ojowu"). We thank Iroro Orife for providing the Bible corpus and Yorùbá Proverbs corpus. We thank Marine Carpuat, Mathias Müller, and the entire Masakhane NLP community for their feedback. We are also thankful to Damyana Gateva for evaluations with open-source models. This project was funded by the AI4D language dataset fellowship (Siminyu et al., 2021)[13]. DIA acknowledges the support of the EU-funded H2020 project COMPRISE under grant agreement No. 3081705. CEB is partially funded by the German Federal Ministry of Education and Research under the funding code 01IW20010. The authors are responsible for the content of this publication.

[13]`https://www.k4all.org/project/language-dataset-fellowship/`

References

Agić, Ž. and Vulić, I. (2019). JW300: A wide-coverage parallel corpus for low-resource languages. In *Proceedings of the 57th Annual Meeting of the Association for Computational Linguistics*, pages 3204–3210, Florence, Italy. Association for Computational Linguistics.

Al-Rfou, R. (2015). *Polyglot: A massive multilingual natural language processing pipeline*. PhD thesis, Stony Brook University.

Alabi, J., Amponsah-Kaakyire, K., Adelani, D., and España-Bonet, C. (2020). Massive vs. curated embeddings for low-resourced languages: the case of Yorùbá and Twi. In *Proceedings of the 12th Language Resources and Evaluation Conference*, pages 2754–2762, Marseille, France. European Language Resources Association.

Arivazhagan, N., Bapna, A., Firat, O., Lepikhin, D., Johnson, M., Krikun, M., Chen, M. X., Cao, Y., Foster, G. F., Cherry, C., Macherey, W., Chen, Z., and Wu, Y. (2019). Massively multilingual neural machine translation in the wild: Findings and challenges. *arXiv e-prints 1907.05019*.

Artetxe, M. and Schwenk, H. (2019). Margin-based parallel corpus mining with multilingual sentence embeddings. In *Proceedings of the 58th Annual Meeting of the Association for Computational Linguistics*, pages 3197–3203, Florence, Italy. Association for Computational Linguistics.

Barrault, L., Bojar, O., Bougares, F., Chatterjee, R., Costa-jussà, M. R., Federmann, C., Fishel, M., Fraser, A., Graham, Y., Guzman, P., Haddow, B., Huck, M., Yepes, A. J., Koehn, P., Martins, A., Morishita, M., Monz, C., Nagata, M., Nakazawa, T., and Negri, M., editors (2020). *Proceedings of the Fifth Conference on Machine Translation*. Association for Computational Linguistics, Online.

Beyer, A., Kauermann, G., and Schütze, H. (2020). Embedding space correlation as a measure of domain similarity. In *Proceedings of the 12th Language Resources and Evaluation Conference*, pages 2431–2439, Marseille, France. European Language Resources Association.

Caswell, I., Kreutzer, J., Wang, L., Wahab, A., van Esch, D., Ulzii-Orshikh, N., Tapo, A., Subramani, N., Sokolov, A., Sikasote, C., Setyawan, M., Sarin, S., Samb, S., Sagot, B., Rivera, C., Rios, A., Papadimitriou, I., Osei, S., Ortiz Suárez, P. J., Orife, I., Ogueji, K., Niyongabo, R. A., Nguyen, T. Q., Müller, M., Müller, A., Hassan Muhammad, S., Muhammad, N., Mnyakeni, A., Mirzakhalov, J., Matangira, T., Leong, C., Lawson, N., Kudugunta, S., Jernite, Y., Jenny, M., Firat, O., Dossou, B. F. P., Dlamini, S., de Silva, N., Çabuk Ballı, S., Biderman, S., Battisti, A., Baruwa, A., Bapna, A., Baljekar, P., Abebe Azime, I., Awokoya, A., Ataman, D., Ahia, O., Ahia, O., Agrawal, S., and Adeyemi, M. (2021). Quality at a Glance: An Audit of Web-Crawled Multilingual Datasets. *arXiv e-prints*, page arXiv:2103.12028.

Currey, A., Miceli Barone, A. V., and Heafield, K. (2017). Copied monolingual data improves low-resource neural machine translation. In *Proceedings of the Second Conference on Machine Translation*, pages 148–156, Copenhagen, Denmark. Association for Computational Linguistics.

Devlin, J., Chang, M.-W., Lee, K., and Toutanova, K. (2019). BERT: Pre-training of deep bidirectional transformers for language understanding. In *Proceedings of the 2019 Conference of the North American Chapter of the Association for Computational Linguistics: Human Language Technologies, Volume 1 (Long and Short Papers)*, pages 4171–4186, Minneapolis, Minnesota. Association for Computational Linguistics.

Eberhard, D. M., Simons, G. F., and (eds.), C. D. F. (2019). Ethnologue: Languages of the world. twenty-second edition.

España-Bonet, C., Barrón-Cedeño, A., and Màrquez, L. (2020). Tailoring and Evaluating the Wikipedia for in-Domain Comparable Corpora Extraction. *arXiv e-prints 2005.01177*, pages 1–26.

Ezeani, I., Rayson, P., Onyenwe, I., Chinedu, U., and Hepple, M. (2020). Igbo-english machine translation: An evaluation benchmark. In *Eighth International Conference on Learning Representations: ICLR 2020*.

Fan, A., Bhosale, S., Schwenk, H., Ma, Z., El-Kishky, A., Goyal, S., Baines, M., Celebi, O., Wenzek, G., Chaudhary, V., Goyal, N., Birch, T., Liptchinsky, V., Edunov, S., Grave, E., Auli, M., and Joulin, A. (2020). Beyond english–centric multilingual machine translation. *arXiv e-prints 2010.11125*.

∀, Nekoto, W., Marivate, V., Matsila, T., Fasubaa, T., Fagbohungbe, T., Akinola, S. O., Muhammad, S., Kabongo Kabenamualu, S., Osei, S., Sackey, F., Niyongabo, R. A., ..., Ogueji, K., Siminyu, K., Kreutzer, J., .., and Bashir, A. (2020). Participatory research for low-resourced machine translation: A case study in african languages. In *Findings of the Association for Computational Linguistics: EMNLP 2020*, pages 2144–2160, Online. Association for Computational Linguistics.

Groenewald, H. J. and Fourie, W. (2009). Introducing the autshumato integrated translation environment. In *Proceedings of the 13th Annual conference of the European Association for Machine Translation*, pages 190–196, Barcelona, Spain. European Association for Machine Translation.

Gulcehre, C., Firat, O., Xu, K., Cho, K., Barrault, L., Lin, H.-C., Bougares, F., Schwenk, H., and Bengio, Y. (2015). On using monolingual corpora in neural machine translation. *arXiv preprint arXiv:1503.03535*.

Guzmán, F., Chen, P.-J., Ott, M., Pino, J., Lample, G., Koehn, P., Chaudhary, V., and Ranzato, M. (2019). The FLORES evaluation datasets for low-resource machine translation: Nepali–English and Sinhala–English. In *Proceedings of the 2019 Conference on Empirical Methods in Natural Language Processing and the 9th International Joint Conference on Natural Language Processing (EMNLP-IJCNLP)*, pages 6098–6111, Hong Kong, China. Association for Computational Linguistics.

Hadgu, A. T., Beaudoin, A., and Aregawi, A. (2020). Evaluating Amharic Machine Translation. *arXiv e-prints 2003.14386*.

Heafield, K. (2011). KenLM: Faster and smaller language model queries. In *Proceedings of the Sixth Workshop on Statistical Machine Translation*, pages 187–197, Edinburgh, Scotland. Association for Computational Linguistics.

Johnson, M., Schuster, M., Le, Q. V., Krikun, M., Wu, Y., Chen, Z., Thorat, N., Viégas, F. B., Wattenberg, M., Corrado, G., Hughes, M., and Dean, J. (2017). Google's Multilingual Neural Machine Translation System: Enabling Zero-Shot Translation. *Transactions of the Association for Computational Linguist*, 5:339–351.

Kingma, D. P. and Ba, J. (2015). Adam: A method for stochastic optimization. In *International Conference for Learning Representations (ICLR)*.

Koehn, P., Hoang, H., Birch, A., Callison-Burch, C., Federico, M., Bertoldi, N., Cowan, B., Shen, W., Moran, C., Zens, R., Dyer, C., Bojar, O., Constantin, A., and Herbst, E. (2007). Moses: Open source toolkit for statistical machine translation. In *Proceedings of the 45th Annual Meeting of the Association for Computational Linguistics Companion Volume Proceedings of the Demo and Poster Sessions*, pages 177–180, Prague, Czech Republic. Association for Computational Linguistics.

Lample, G. and Conneau, A. (2019). Cross-lingual language model pretraining. In Wallach, H., Larochelle, H., Beygelzimer, A., d'Alché-Buc, F., Fox, E., and Garnett, R., editors, *Advances in Neural Information Processing Systems*, volume 32, pages 7059–7069. Curran Associates, Inc.

Leng, Y., Tan, X., Qin, T., Li, X.-Y., and Liu, T.-Y. (2019). Unsupervised pivot translation for distant languages. In *Proceedings of the 57th Annual Meeting of the Association for Computational Linguistics*, pages 175–183.

Martinus, L. and Abbott, J. Z. (2019). A focus on neural machine translation for african languages. *arXiv e-prints 1906.05685.*

Orife, I., Adelani, D., Fasubaa, T. E., Williamson, V., Oyewusi, W. F., Wahab, O., and Túbosún, K. (2020). Improving Yorùbá Diacritic Restoration. *ArXiv*, abs/2003.10564.

Orife, I. F. d. (2018). Sequence-to-Sequence Learning for Automatic Yorùbá Diacritic Restoration. In *Proceedings of the Interspeech*, pages 27–35.

Ott, M., Edunov, S., Baevski, A., Fan, A., Gross, S., Ng, N., Grangier, D., and Auli, M. (2019). Fairseq: A fast, extensible toolkit for sequence modeling. In *Proceedings of the 2019 Conference of the North American Chapter of the Association for Computational Linguistics (Demonstrations)*, pages 48–53, Minneapolis, Minnesota. Association for Computational Linguistics.

Papineni, K., Roukos, S., Ward, T., and Zhu, W.-J. (2002). Bleu: a method for automatic evaluation of machine translation. In *Proceedings of the 40th Annual Meeting of the Association for Computational Linguistics*, pages 311–318, Philadelphia, Pennsylvania, USA. Association for Computational Linguistics.

Popović, M. (2015). chrF: character n-gram F-score for automatic MT evaluation. In *Proceedings of the Tenth Workshop on Statistical Machine Translation*, pages 392–395, Lisbon, Portugal. Association for Computational Linguistics.

Ramachandran, P., Liu, P., and Le, Q. (2017). Unsupervised pretraining for sequence to sequence learning. In *Proceedings of the 2017 Conference on Empirical Methods in Natural Language Processing*, pages 383–391, Copenhagen, Denmark. Association for Computational Linguistics.

Resnik, P., Olsen, M. B., and Diab, M. T. (1999). The Bible as a Parallel Corpus: Annotating the 'Book of 2000 Tongues'. *Computers and the Humanities*, 33:129–153.

Ruiter, D., España-Bonet, C., and van Genabith, J. (2019). Self-supervised neural machine translation. In *Proceedings of the 57th Annual Meeting of the Association for Computational Linguistics*, pages 1828–1834, Florence, Italy. Association for Computational Linguistics.

Ruiter, D., Klakow, D., van Genabith, J., and España-Bonet, C. (2021). Integrating Unsupervised Data Generation into Self-Supervised Neural Machine Translation for Low-Resource Languages. In *Proceedings of Machine Translation Summit (Research Track)*. European Association for Machine Translation.

Schwenk, H., Chaudhary, V., Sun, S., Gong, H., and Guzmán, F. (2021). WikiMatrix: Mining 135M Parallel Sentences in 1620 Language Pairs from Wikipedia. In Merlo, P., Tiedemann, J., and Tsarfaty, R., editors, *Proceedings of the 16th Conference of the European Chapter of the Association for Computational Linguistics: Main Volume, EACL 2021, Online, April 19 - 23, 2021*, pages 1351–1361. Association for Computational Linguistics.

Schwenk, H., Wenzek, G., Edunov, S., Grave, E., and Joulin, A. (2020). Ccmatrix: Mining billions of high-quality parallel sentences on the web. *arXiv e-prints arXiv:1911.04944.*

Sennrich, R., Haddow, B., and Birch, A. (2016). Neural machine translation of rare words with subword units. In *Proceedings of the 54th Annual Meeting of the Association for Computational Linguistics (Volume 1: Long Papers)*, pages 1715–1725.

Sennrich, R. and Zhang, B. (2019). Revisiting low-resource neural machine translation: A case study. In *Proceedings of the 57th Annual Meeting of the Association for Computational Linguistics*, pages 211–221, Florence, Italy. Association for Computational Linguistics.

Siminyu, K., Kalipe, G., Orlic, D., Abbott, J., Marivate, V., Freshia, S., Sibal, P., Neupane, B., Adelani, D., Taylor, A., Ali, J. T., Degila, K., Balogoun, M., Diop, T. I., David, D., Fourati, C., Haddad, H., and Naski, M. (2021). Ai4d - african language program. *ArXiv*, abs/2104.02516.

Strassel, S. and Tracey, J. (2016). LORELEI language packs: Data, tools, and resources for technology development in low resource languages. In *Proceedings of the Tenth International Conference on Language Resources and Evaluation (LREC 2016)*, pages 3273–3280, Portorož, Slovenia. European Language Resources Association (ELRA).

Tang, Y., Tran, C., Li, X., Chen, P., Goyal, N., Chaudhary, V., Gu, J., and Fan, A. (2020). Multilingual translation with extensible multilingual pretraining and finetuning. *ArXiv*, abs/2008.00401.

Tiedemann, J. and Thottingal, S. (2020). OPUS-MT – building open translation services for the world. In *Proceedings of the 22nd Annual Conference of the European Association for Machine Translation*, pages 479–480, Lisboa, Portugal. European Association for Machine Translation.

Vaswani, A., Shazeer, N., Parmar, N., Uszkoreit, J., Jones, L., Gomez, A. N., Kaiser, L. u., and Polosukhin, I. (2017). Attention is all you need. In *Advances in Neural Information Processing Systems*, pages 5998–6008.

Xue, L., Constant, N., Roberts, A., Kale, M., Al-Rfou, R., Siddhant, A., Barua, A., and Raffel, C. (2021). mT5: A massively multilingual pre-trained text-to-text transformer. In *Proceedings of the 2021 Conference of the North American Chapter of the Association for Computational Linguistics: Human Language Technologies*, pages 483–498, Online. Association for Computational Linguistics.

Zoph, B., Yuret, D., May, J., and Knight, K. (2016). Transfer learning for low-resource neural machine translation. In *Proceedings of the 2016 Conference on Empirical Methods in Natural Language Processing*, pages 1568–1575, Austin, Texas. Association for Computational Linguistics.

Integrating Unsupervised Data Generation into Self-Supervised Neural Machine Translation for Low-Resource Languages

Dana Ruiter druiter@lsv.uni-saarland.de
Dietrich Klakow dietrich.klakow@lsv.uni-saarland.de
Spoken Language Systems Group, Saarland University, Germany

Josef van Genabith josef.van_genabith@dfki.de
DFKI GmbH & Saarland University, Saarland Informatics Campus, Saarbrücken, Germany

Cristina España-Bonet cristinae@dfki.de
DFKI GmbH, Saarland Informatics Campus, Saarbrücken, Germany

Abstract

For most language combinations, parallel data is either scarce or simply unavailable. To address this, unsupervised machine translation (UMT) exploits large amounts of monolingual data by using synthetic data generation techniques such as back-translation and noising, while self-supervised NMT (SSNMT) identifies parallel sentences in smaller comparable data and trains on them. To date, the inclusion of UMT data generation techniques in SSNMT has not been investigated. We show that including UMT techniques into SSNMT significantly outperforms SSNMT and UMT on all tested language pairs, with improvements of up to $+4.3$ BLEU, $+50.8$ BLEU, $+51.5$ over SSNMT, statistical UMT and hybrid UMT, respectively, on Afrikaans to English. We further show that the combination of multilingual denoising autoencoding, SSNMT with backtranslation and bilingual finetuning enables us to learn machine translation even for distant language pairs for which only small amounts of monolingual data are available, e.g. yielding BLEU scores of 11.6 (English to Swahili).

1 Introduction

Neural machine translation (NMT) achieves high quality translations when large amounts of parallel data are available (Barrault et al., 2020). Unfortunately, for most language combinations, parallel data is non-existent, scarce or low-quality. To overcome this, unsupervised MT (UMT) (Lample et al., 2018b; Ren et al., 2019; Artetxe et al., 2019) focuses on exploiting large amounts of monolingual data, which are used to generate synthetic bitext training data via various techniques such as back-translation or denoising. Self-supervised NMT (SSNMT) (Ruiter et al., 2019) learns from smaller amounts of *comparable* data –i.e. topic-aligned data such as Wikipedia articles– by learning to discover and exploit similar sentence pairs. However, both UMT and SSNMT approaches often do not scale to low-resource languages, for which neither monolingual nor comparable data are available in sufficient quantity (Guzmán et al., 2019; España-Bonet et al., 2019; Marchisio et al., 2020). To date, UMT data augmentation techniques have not been explored in SSNMT. However, both approaches can benefit from each other, as i) SSNMT has strong internal quality checks on the data it admits for training, which can be of use to filter low-quality synthetic data, and ii) UMT data augmentation makes monolingual data available for SSNMT.

In this paper we explore and test the effect of combining UMT data augmentation with SSNMT on different data sizes, ranging from very low-resource ($\sim 66k$ non-parallel sentences) to high-resource ($\sim 20M$ sentences). We do this using a common high-resource language pair (en–fr), which we downsample while keeping all other parameters identical. We then proceed to evaluate the augmentation techniques on different truly low-resource similar and distant language pairs, i.e. English (en)–{Afrikaans (af), Kannada (kn), Burmese (my), Nepali (ne), Swahili (sw), Yorùbá (yo)}, chosen based on their differences in typology (*analytic, fusional, agglutinative*), word order (*SVO, SOV*) and writing system (*Latin, Brahmic*). We also explore the effect of different initialization techniques for SSNMT in combination with finetuning.

2 Related Work

Substantial effort has been devoted to muster training data for **low-resource NMT**, e.g. by identifying parallel sentences in monolingual or noisy corpora in a pre-processing step (Artetxe and Schwenk, 2019a; Chaudhary et al., 2019; Schwenk et al., 2021) and also by leveraging monolingual data into supervised NMT e.g. by including autoencoding (Currey et al., 2017) or language modeling tasks (Gulcehre et al., 2015; Ramachandran et al., 2017). Low-resource NMT models can benefit from high-resource languages through transfer learning (Zoph et al., 2016), e.g. in a zero-shot setting (Johnson et al., 2017), by using pre-trained language models (Conneau and Lample, 2019; Kuwanto et al., 2021), or finding an optimal path for pivoting through related languages (Leng et al., 2019).

Back-translation often works well in high-resource settings (Bojar and Tamchyna, 2011; Sennrich et al., 2016a; Karakanta et al., 2018). NMT training and back-translation have been used in an incremental fashion in both unidirectional (Hoang et al., 2018) and bidirectional systems (Zhang et al., 2018; Niu et al., 2018).

Unsupervised NMT (Lample et al., 2018a; Artetxe et al., 2018; Yang et al., 2018) applies bi-directional back-translation in combination with denoising and multilingual shared encoders to learn MT on very large monolingual data. This can be done multilingually across several languages by using language-specific decoders (Sen et al., 2019), or by using additional parallel data for a related pivot language pair (Li et al., 2020). Further combining unsupervised neural MT with phrase tables from statistical MT leads to top results (Lample et al., 2018b; Ren et al., 2019; Artetxe et al., 2019). However, unsupervised systems fail to learn when trained on small amounts of monolingual data (Guzmán et al., 2019), when there is a domain mismatch between the two datasets (Kim et al., 2020) or when the languages in a pair are distant (Koneru et al., 2021). Unfortunately, all of this is the case for most truly low-resource language pairs.

Self-supervised NMT (Ruiter et al., 2019) jointly learns to extract data and translate from comparable data and works best on 100s of thousands of documents per language, well beyond what is available in true low-resource settings.

3 UMT-Enhanced SSNMT

SSNMT jointly learns MT and extracting similar sentences for training from comparable corpora in a loop on-line. Sentence pairs from documents in languages $L1$ and $L2$ are fed as input to a bidirectional NMT system $\{L1, L2\} \rightarrow \{L1, L2\}$, which filters out non-similar sentences after scoring them with a similarity measure calculated from the internal embeddings.

Sentence Pair Extraction (SPE): Input sentences $s_{L1} \in L1$, $s_{L2} \in L2$, are represented by the sum of their word embeddings and by the sum of the encoder outputs, and scored using the margin-based measure introduced by Artetxe and Schwenk (2019a). If a pair (s_{L1}, s_{L2}) is top

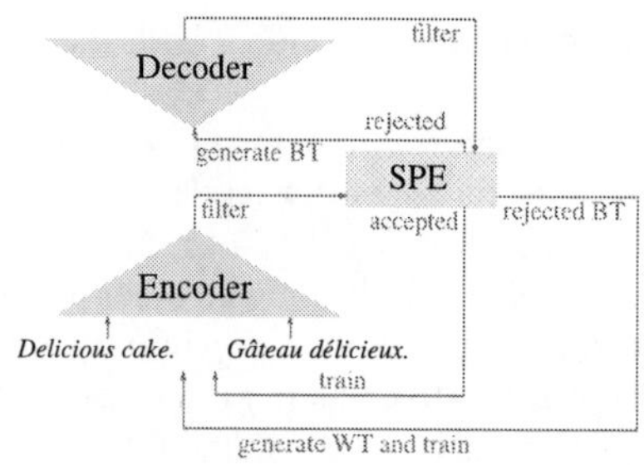

Figure 1: UMT-Enhanced SSNMT architecture (Section 3).

scoring for both language directions *and* for both sentence representations, it is accepted for training, otherwise it is filtered out. This is a strong quality check and equivalent to *system P* in Ruiter et al. (2019). A SSNMT model with SPE is our **baseline (B)** model.

Since most possible sentence pairs from comparable corpora are non-similar, they are simply discarded. In a low-resource setting, this potentially constitutes a major loss of usable monolingual information. To exploit sentences that have been rejected by the SSNMT filtering process, we integrate the following UMT synthetic data creation techniques *on-line* (Figure 1):

Back-translation (BT): Given a rejected sentence s_{L1}, we use the current state of the SSNMT system to back-translate it into s_{L2}^{BT}. The synthetic pair in the opposite direction $s_{L2}^{BT} \rightarrow s_{L1}$ is added to the batch for further training. We perform the same filtering process as for SPE so that only good quality back-translations are added. We apply the same to source sentences in $L2$.

Word-translation (WT): For synthetic sentence pairs rejected by BT filtering, we perform word-by-word translation. Given a rejected sentence s_{L1} with tokens $w_{L1} \in L1$, we replace each token with its nearest neighbor $w_{L2} \in L2$ in the bilingual word embedding layer of the model to obtain s_{L2}^{WT}. We then train on the synthetic pair in the opposite direction $s_{L2}^{WT} \rightarrow s_{L1}$. As with BT, this is applied to both language directions. To ensure sufficient volume of synthetic data (Figure 2, right), WT data is trained on without filtering.

Noise (N): To increase robustness and variance in the training data, we add noise, i.e. token deletion, substitution and permutation, to copies of source sentences (Edunov et al., 2018) in parallel pairs identified via SPE, back-translations and word-translated sentences and, as with WT, we use these without additional filtering.

Initialization: When languages are related and large amounts of training data is available, the initialization of SSNMT is not important. However, similarly to UMT, initialization becomes crucial in the low-resource setting (Edman et al., 2020). We explore four different initialization techniques: i) no initialization (*none*), i.e. random initialization for all model parameters, ii) initialization of tied source and target side word embedding layers only via pre-trained cross-lingual word-embeddings (WE) while randomly initializing all other layers and iii) initialization of all layers via denoising autoencoding (DAE) in a bilingual and iv) multilingual (MDAE) setting.

Finetuning (F): When using MDAE initialization only, the following SSNMT is multilingual, otherwise it is bilingual. Due to the multilingual nature of the SSNMT with MDAE initialization, the performance of the individual languages can be limited by the *curse of multilinguality* (Conneau et al., 2020), where multilingual training leads to improvements on low-resource languages up to a certain point after which it decays. To alleviate this, we finetune converged

	Comparable						Monolingual		
	# Art (k)	VO (%)	# Sent (k)		# Tok (k)		# Sent (k)	# Tok (k)	
en–L			en	L	en	L	en/L	en	L
en–af	73	7.1	4,589	780	189,990	27,640	1,034	34,759	31,858
en–kn	18	1.4	1,739	764	95,481	30,003	1,058	47,136	35,534
en–my	19	2.1	1,505	477	82,537	15,313	997	43,752	24,094
en–ne	20	0.6	1,526	207	83,524	7,518	296	13,149	9,229
en–sw	34	6.5	2,375	244	122,593	8,774	329	13,957	9,937
en–yo	19	5.7	1,314	34	82,674	1,536	547	17,953	19,370

Table 1: Number of sentences (Sent) and tokens (Tok) in the comparable and monolingual datasets. For comparable datasets, we report the number of articles (Art) and percentage of vocabulary overlap (VO) between the two languages in a pair. # Sent of monolingual data (en/L) is the same for en and its corresponding L due to downsampling of en to match L.

multilingual SSNMT models bilingually on a given language pair $L1$–$L2$.

4 Experimental Setting

4.1 Data

MT Training For training, we use Wikipedia (WP) as a comparable corpus and download the dumps[1] and extract comparable articles per language pair (*Comparable* in Table 1) using WikiExtractor[2]. For validation and testing, we use the test and development data from McKellar and Puttkammer (2020) (en–af), WAT2021[3] (en–kn), WAT2020 (en–my) (ShweSin et al., 2018), FLoRes (en–ne) (Guzmán et al., 2019), Lakew et al. (2021) (en–sw), and MENYO-20k (en–yo) (Adelani et al., 2021a). For en–fr we use *newstest2012* for development and *newstest2014* for testing. As the en–af data does not have a development split, we additionally sample 1 k sentences from CCAligned (El-Kishky et al., 2020) to use as en–af development data. The en–sw test set is divided into several sub-domains, and we only evaluate on the TED talks domain, since the other domains are noisy, e.g. localization or religious corpora.

MT Initialization We use the monolingual Wikipedias to initialize SSNMT. As the monolingual Wikipedia for Yorùbá is especially small (65 k sentences), we use the Yorùbá side of JW300 (Agić and Vulić, 2019) as additional monolingual initialization data. For each monolingual data pair en–$\{af$,...,$yo\}$, the large English monolingual corpus is downsampled to its low(er)-resource counterpart before using the data (*Monolingual* in Table 1).

For the word-embedding-based initialization, we learn CBOW word embeddings using `word2vec` (Mikolov et al., 2013), which are then projected into a common multilingual space via `vecmap` (Artetxe et al., 2017) to attain bilingual embeddings between en–$\{af$,...,$yo\}$. For the weak-supervision of the bilingual mapping process, we use a list of numbers (en–fr only) which is augmented with 200 Swadesh list[4] entries for the low-resource experiments.

For DAE initialization, we do not use external, highly-multilingual pre-trained language models, since in practical terms these may not cover the language combination of interest[5]. We therefore use the monolingual data to train a bilingual (en+$\{af$,...$yo\}$) DAE using BART-style

[1]Dumps were downloaded on February 2021 from `dumps.wikimedia.org/`

[2]`github.com/attardi/wikiextractor`

[3]`lotus.kuee.kyoto-u.ac.jp/WAT/indic-multilingual/index.html`

[4]`https://en.wiktionary.org/wiki/Appendix:Swadesh_lists`

[5]This is the case here: `MBart-50` (Tang et al., 2020) does not cover Kannada, Swahili and Yorùbá.

noise (Liu et al., 2020). We set aside 5 k sentences for testing and development each. We use BART-style noise ($\lambda = 3.5$, $p = 0.35$) for word sequence masking. We add one random mask insertion per sequence and perform a sequence permutation. For the multilingual DAE (MDAE) setting, we train a single denoising autoencoder on the monolingual data of all languages, where en is downsampled to match the largest non-English monolingual dataset (kn).

In all cases SSNMT training is bidirectional between two languages en–$\{af,...,yo\}$, except for MDAE, where SSNMT is trained multilingually between all language combinations in $\{af,en,...,yo\}$.

4.2 Preprocessing

On the Wikipedia corpora, we perform sentence tokenization using NLTK (Bird, 2006). For languages using Latin scripts (af,en,sw,yo) we perform punctuation normalization and truecasing using standard Moses (Koehn et al., 2007) scripts on all datasets. For Yorùbá only, we follow Adelani et al. (2021b) and perform automatic diacritic restoration. Lastly, we perform language identification on all Wikipedia corpora using `polyglot`.[6] After exploring different byte-pair encoding (BPE) (Sennrich et al., 2016b) vocabulary sizes of 2 k, 4 k, 8 k, 16 k and 32 k, we choose 2 k (en–yo), 4 k (en–$\{kn,my,ne,sw\}$) and 16 k (en–af) merge operations using `sentence-piece`[7] (Kudo and Richardson, 2018). We prepend a source and a target language token to each sentence. For the en–fr experiments only, we use the data processing by Ruiter et al. (2020) in order to minimize experimental differences for later comparison.

4.3 Model Specifications and Evaluation

Systems are either not initialized, initialized via bilingual word embeddings, or via pre-training using (M)DAE. Our implementation of SSNMT is a transformer base with default parameters. We use a batch size of 50 sentences and a maximum sequence length of 100 tokens. For evaluation, we use BLEU (Papineni et al., 2002) calculated using `SacreBLEU`[8,9] (Post, 2018) and all confidence intervals ($p = 95\%$) are calculated using bootstrap resampling (Koehn, 2004) as implemented in `multeval`[10] (Clark et al., 2011).

5 Exploration of Corpus Sizes (en–fr)

To explore which technique works best with varying data sizes, and to compare with the high-resource SSNMT setting in Ruiter et al. (2020), we train SSNMT on en–fr, with different combinations of techniques (+BT, +WT, +N) over decreasingly small corpus sizes. The base (B) model is a simple SSNMT model with SPE.

Figure 2 (left) shows that translation quality as measured by BLEU is very low in the low-resource setting. For experiments with only 4 k comparable articles (similar to the corpus size available for en–yo), BLEU is close to zero with base (B) and B+BT models. Only when WT is applied to rejected back-translated pairs does training become possible, and is further improved by adding noise, yielding BLEUs of 3.38[11] ($en2fr$) and 3.58 ($fr2en$). The maximum gain in performance obtained by WT is at 31 k comparable articles, where it adds $\sim$ 9 BLEU over the B+BT performance. While the additional supervisory signal provided by WT is useful in the low and medium resource settings, up until $\sim$ 125 k articles, its benefits are overcome by

[6] `https://github.com/aboSamoor/polyglot`

[7] `https://github.com/google/sentencepiece`

[8] `https://github.com/mjpost/sacrebleu`

[9] `BLEU+case.mixed+numrefs.4+smooth.exp+tok.intl+version.1.4.9`

[10] `https://github.com/jhclark/multeval`

[11] Note that such low BLEU scores should be taken with a grain of salt: While there is an automatically measurable improvement in translation quality, a human judge would not see a meaningful improvement between different systems with low BLEU scores.

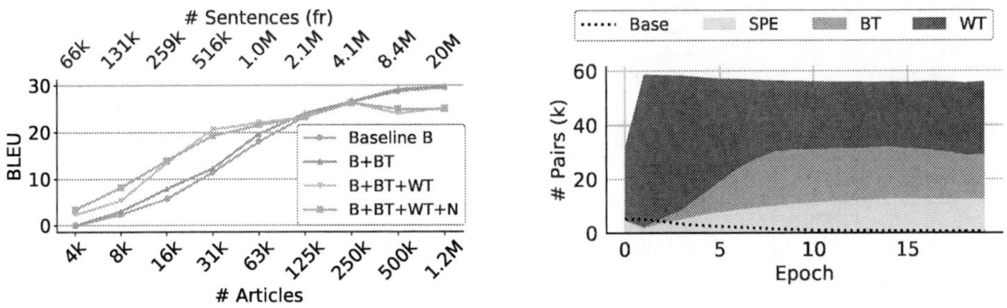

Figure 2: **Left**: BLEU scores ($en2fr$) of different techniques (+BT,+WT,+N) added to the base (B) SSNMT model when trained on increasingly large numbers $en–fr$ WP articles (# Articles). **Right**: Number of extracted (SPE) or generated (BT,WT) sentence pairs (k) per technique of the B+BT+WT model trained on 4 k comparable WP articles. Number of extracted sentence pairs by the base model is shown for comparison as a dotted line.

the noise it introduces in the high-resource scenario, leading to a drop in translation quality. Similarly, the utility of adding noise varies with corpus size. Only BT constantly adds a slight gain in performance of ~1–2 over all base models, where training is possible. In the high resource case, the difference between B and B+BT is not significant, with BLEU 29.64 ($en2fr$) and 28.56 ($fr2en$) for B+BT, which also leads to a small, yet statistically insignificant gain over the $en–fr$ SSNMT model in Ruiter et al. (2020), i.e. $+0.1$ ($en2fr$) and $+0.9$ ($fr2en$) BLEU.

At the beginning of training, the number of **extracted sentence pairs** (SPE) of the B+BT+WT+N model trained on the most extreme low-resource setting (4 k articles), is low (Figure 2, right), with 4 k sentence pairs extracted in the first epoch. This number drops further to 2 k extracted pairs in the second epoch, but then continually rises up to 13 k extracted pairs in the final epoch. This is not the case for the base (B) model, which starts with a similar amount of extracted parallel data but then continually extracts less as training progresses. The difference between the two models is due to the added BT and WT techniques. At the beginning of training B+BT+WT is not able to generate backtranslations of decent quality, with only few (196) backtranslations accepted for training. Rejected backtranslations are passed into WT, which leads to large numbers of WT sentence pairs up to the second epoch (56 k). These make all the difference: through WT, the system is able to gain noisy supervisory signals from the data, which leads to the internal representations to become more informative for SPE, thus leading to more and better extractions. Then, BT and SPE enhance each other, as SPE ensures original (clean) parallel sentences to be extracted, which improves translation accuracy, and hence more and better backtranslations (e.g. up to 20 k around epoch 15) are accepted.

6 Exploration of Language Distance

BT, WT and N data augmentation techniques are especially useful for the low- and mid-resource settings of related language pairs such as English and French (both *Indo-European*). To apply the approach to truly low-resource language pairs, and to verify which language-specific characteristics impact the effectiveness of the different augmentation techniques, we train and test our model on a selected number of languages (Table 2) based on their typological and graphemic distance from English (*fusional→analytic*[12], SVO, Latin script). Focusing on similarities on

[12]English and Afrikaans are traditionally categorized as fusional languages. However, due to their small morpheme-word ratio, both English and Afrikaans are nowadays often categorized as analytic languages.

	English	Afrikaans	Nepali	Kannada	Yorùbá	Swahili	Burmese
Typology	fusional[9]	fusional[9]	fusional	agglutinative	analytic	agglutinative	analytic
Word Order	SVO	SOV,SVO	SOV	SOV	SOV,SVO	SVO	SOV
Script	Latin	Latin	Brahmic	Brahmic	Latin	Latin	Brahmic
sim(L–en)	1.000	0.822	0.605	0.602	0.599	0.456	0.419

Table 2: Classification (typology, word order, script) of the languages L together with their cosine similarity (sim) to English based on lexical and syntactic URIEL features.

the lexical and syntactic level,[13] we retrieve the URIEL (Littell et al., 2017) representations of the languages using `lang2vec`[14] and calculate their cosine similarity to English. Afrikaans is the most similar language to English, with a similarity of 0.822, and pre-BPE vocabulary (token) overlap of 7.1% (Table 1), which is due to its similar typology (*fusional→analytic*) and comparatively large vocabulary overlap (both languages belong to the West-Germanic language branch). The most distant language is Burmese (sim 0.419, vocabulary overlap 2.1%), which belongs to the Sino-Tibetan language family and uses its own (Brahmic) script.

We train SSNMT with combinations of BT, WT, N on the language combinations en–$\{af,kn,my,ne,sw,yo\}$ using the four different types of model initialization (none, WE, DAE, MDAE).

Intrinsic Parameter Analysis We focus on the intrinsic *initialization* and *data augmentation technique* parameters. The difference between no (*none*) and word-embedding (*WE*) **initialization** is barely significant across all language pairs and techniques (Figure 3). For all language pairs, except en–af, MDAE initialization tends to be the best choice, with major gains of +4.2 BLEU ($yo2en$, B+BT) and +5.3 BLEU ($kn2en$, B+BT) over their WE-initialized counterparts. This is natural, since pre-training on (M)DAE allows the SSNMT model to learn how to generate fluent sentences. By performing (M)DAE, the model also learns to denoise noisy inputs, resulting in a big improvement in translation performance (e.g. +37.3 BLEU, $af2en$ DAE) on the en–af and en–sw B+BT+WT models in comparison to their WE-initialized counterparts. Without (M)DAE pre-training, the noisy word-translations lead to very low BLEU scores. Adding an additional denoising task, either via (M)DAE initialization or via adding the +N data augmentation technique, lets the model also learn from noisy word-translations with improved results. For en–af only, the WE initialization generally performs best, with BLEU scores of 52.2 ($af2en$) and 51.2 ($en2af$). For language pairs using different scripts, i.e. Latin–Brahmic (en–$\{kn,my,ne\}$), the gain by performing bilingual DAE pre-training is negligible, as results are generally low. These languages also have a different word order (SOV) than English (SVO), which may further increase the difficulty of the translation task (Banerjee et al., 2019; Kim et al., 2020). However, once the pre-training and MT learning is multilingual (MDAE), the different language directions benefit from another and an internal mapping of the languages into a shared space is achieved. This leads to BLEU scores of 1.7 ($my2en$), 3.3 ($ne2en$) and 5.3 ($kn2en$) using the B+BT technique. The method is also beneficial when translating into the low-resource languages, with $en2kn$ reaching BLEU 3.3 (B).

B+BT+WT seems to be the best **data augmentation technique** when the amount of data is very small, as is the case for en–yo, with gains of +2.4 BLEU on $en2yo$ over the baseline B. This underlines the findings in Section 5, that WT serves as a crutch to start the extraction and training of SSNMT. Further adding noise (+N) tends to adversely impact on results on this

[13]This corresponds to `lang2vec` features `syntax_average` and `inventory_average`.

[14]`https://pypi.org/project/lang2vec/`

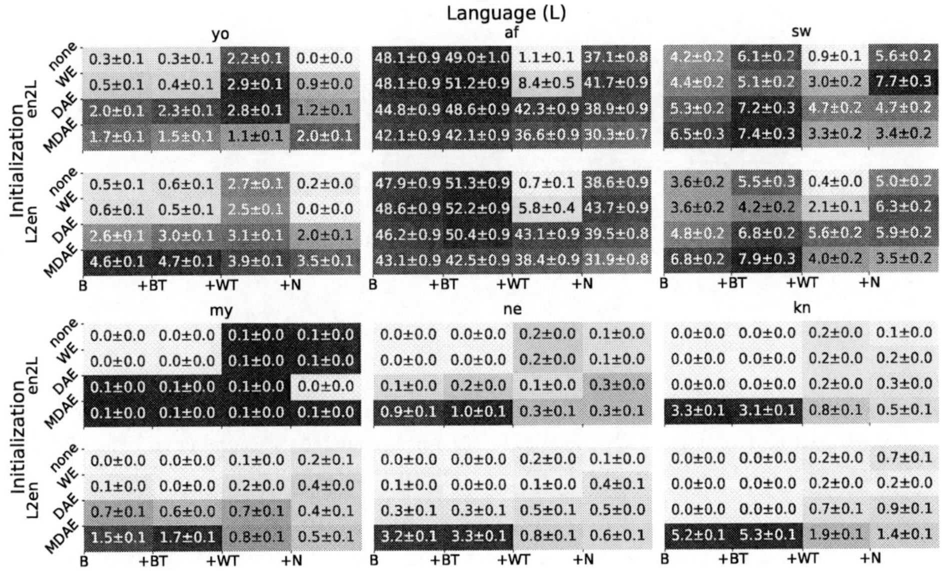

Figure 3: BLEU scores of SSNMT Base (B) with added techniques (+BT,+WT,+N) on low-resource language combinations $en2L$ and $L2en$, with $L = \{af, kn, my, ne, sw, yo\}$.

language pair. On languages with more data available (en–$\{af$,kn,my,ne,$sw\}$), +BT tends to be the best choice, with top BLEUs on en–sw of 7.4 ($en2sw$, MDAE) and 7.9 ($sw2en$, MDAE). This is due to these models being able to sufficiently learn on B (+BT) only (Figure 4), thus not needing +WT as a crutch to start the extraction and MT learning process. Adding +WT to the system only adds additional noise and thus makes results worse.

Extrinsic Parameter Analysis We focus on the extrinsic parameters *linguistic distance* and *data size*. Our model is able to learn MT also on **distant language pairs** such as en–sw (sim 0.456), with top BLEUs of 7.7 ($en2sw$, B+BT+W+N) and 7.9 ($sw2en$, B+BT). Despite being typologically closer, training SSNMT on en–ne (sim 0.605) only yields BLEUs above 1 in the multilingual setting (BLEU 3.3 $ne2en$). This is the case for all languages using a different script than English (kn,my,ne), underlining the fact that achieving a cross-lingual representation, i.e. via multilingual (pre-)training or a decent overlap in the (BPE) vocabulary (as in en–$\{af$,sw,$yo\}$) of the two languages, is vital for identifying good similar sentence pairs at the beginning of training and thus makes training possible. For en–my the MDAE approach was only beneficial in the $my2en$ direction, but had no effect on $en2my$, which may be due to the fact that my is the most distant language from en (sim 0.419) and, contrary to the other low-resource languages we explore, does not have any related language[15] in our experimental setup, which makes it difficult to leverage supervisory signals from a related language.

When the **amount of data** is small (en–yo), the model does not achieve BLEUs above 1 without the WT technique or without (M)DAE initialization, since the extraction recall of a simple SSNMT system is low at the beginning of training (Ruiter et al., 2020) and thus SPE fails to identify sufficient parallel sentences to improve the internal representations, which would then improve SPE recall. This is analogous to the observations on the en-fr base model B

[15]Both Nepali and Kannada share influences from Sanskrit. Swahili and Yorùbá are both Niger-Congo languages, while English and Afrikaans are both Indo-European.

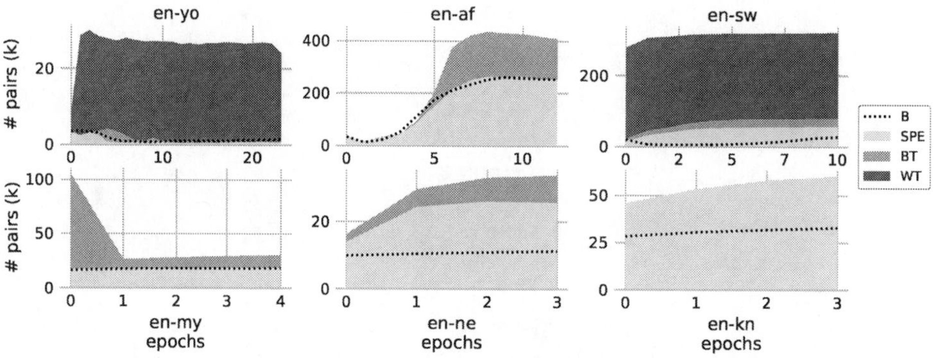

Figure 4: Number of extracted (SPE) or generated (BT,WT) sentence pairs (k) per technique of the best performing SSNMT model ($en2L$) per language L. Number of extracted sentence pairs by the base model (B) are shown for comparison as a dotted line.

trained on $4\,k$ WP articles (Figure 2). Interestingly, the differences between no/WE and DAE initialization are minimized when using WT as a data augmentation technique, showing that it is an effective method that makes pre-training unnecessary when only small amounts of data are available. For larger data sizes (en–$\{af,sw\}$), the opposite is the case: the models sufficiently learn SPE and MT without WT, and thus WT just adds additional noise.

Extraction and Generation The SPE extraction and BT/WT generation curves (Figure 4) for en–af (B+BT, WE) are similar to those on en–fr (Figure 2, right). At the beginning of training, not many pairs ($32\,k$) are extracted, but as training progresses, the model internal representations are improved and it starts extracting more and more parallel data, up to $252\,k$ in the last epoch. Simultaneously, translation quality improves and the number of backtranslations generated increases drastically from $2\,k$ up to $156\,k$ per epoch. However, as the amount of data for en–af is large, the base model B has a similar extraction curve. Nevertheless, translation quality is improved by the additional backtranslations (+3.1 BLEU). For en–sw (B+BT+WT+N, WE), the curves are similar to those of en–fr, where the added word-translations serve as a crutch to make SPE and BT possible, thus showing a gap between the number of extracted sentences (SPE) ($\sim 5.5\,k$) of the best model and those of the baseline (B) ($\sim$1–2 k). For en–yo (B+BT+WT, WE), the amount of extracted data is very small ($\sim 0.5\,k$) for both the baseline and the best model. Here, WT fails to serve as a crutch as the number of extractions does not increase, but instead is overwhelmed by the number of word translations. For en–$\{kn,ne\}$ (MDAE), the extraction and BT curves also rise over time. For en–my, where all training setups show similar translation performance in the $en2my$ direction, we show the extraction and BT curves for B+BT with WE initialization. We observe that, as opposed to all other models, both lines are flat, underlining the fact that due to the lack of sufficiently cross-lingual model-internal representations, the model does not enter the self-supervisory cycle common to SSNMT.

Bilingual Finetuning The overall trend shows that MDAE pre-training with multilingual SSNMT training in combination with back-translation (B+BT) leads to top results for low-resource similar and distant language combinations. For en–afonly, which has more comparable data available for training and is a very similar language pair, the multilingual setup is less beneficial. The model attains enough supervisory signals when training bilingually on en–af, thus the additional languages in the multilingual setup are simply noise for the system. While the MDAE setup with multilingual MT training makes it possible to map distant languages into a

	en–af		*en–kn*		*en–my*		*en–ne*		*en–sw*		*en–yo*	
	→	←	→	←	→	←	→	←	→	←	→	←
Best*	**51.2**	**52.2**	0.3	0.9	0.1	0.7	0.3	0.5	7.7	6.8	**2.9**	3.1
MDAE	42.5	42.5	3.1	5.3	0.1	1.7	1.0	3.3	7.4	7.9	1.5	4.7
MDAE+F	46.3	50.2	**5.0**	**9.0**	**0.2**	**2.8**	**2.3**	**5.7**	**11.6**	**11.2**	**2.9**	**5.8**

Table 3: BLEU scores on the $en2L$ (→) and $L2en$ (←) directions of top performing SSNMT model without finetuning and without MDAE (Best*) and SSNMT using MDAE initialization and B+BT technique with (MDAE+F) and without finetuning (MDAE).

Pair	Init.	Config.	Best	Base	UMT	UMT+NMT	Laser	TSS	#P (k)
en2af	WE	B+BT	**51.2±.9**	48.1±.9	27.9±.8	44.2±.9	**52.1±1.0**	35.3	37
af2en	WE	B+BT	**52.2±.9**	47.9±.9	1.4±.1	0.7±.1	**52.9±.9**	–	–
en2kn	MDAE	B+BT+F	**5.0±.2**	0.0±.0	0.0±.0	0.0±.0	–	21.3	397
kn2en	MDAE	B+BT+F	**9.0±.2**	0.0±.0	0.0±.0	0.0±.0	–	40.3	397
en2my	MDAE	B+BT+F	**0.2±.0**	0.0±.0	0.1±.0	0.0±.0	0.0±.0	39.3	223
my2en	MDAE	B+BT+F	**2.8±.1**	0.0±.0	0.0±.0	0.0±.0	0.1±.0	38.6	223
en2ne	MDAE	B+BT+F	**2.3±.1**	0.0±.0	0.1±.0	0.0±.0	0.5±.1	8.8	–
ne2en	MDAE	B+BT+F	**5.7±.2**	0.0±.0	0.0±.0	0.0±.0	0.2±.0	21.5	–
en2sw	MDAE	B+BT+F	**11.6±.3**	4.2±.2	3.6±.2	0.2±.0	10.0±.3	14.8	995
sw2en	MDAE	B+BT+F	**11.2±.3**	3.6±.2	0.3±.0	0.0±.0	8.4±.3	19.7	995
en2yo	MDAE	B+BT+F	**2.9±.1**	0.3±.1	1.0±.1	0.3±.1	–	12.3	501
yo2en	MDAE	B+BT+F	**5.8±.1**	0.5±.1	0.6±.0	0.0±.0	–	22.4	501

Table 4: BLEU scores of the best SSNMT configuration (columns 2-4) compared with SSNMT base, USMT(+UNMT) and a supervised NMT system trained on Laser extractions (columns 5-8). Top scoring systems (TSS) per test set and the amount of parallel training sentences (#P) available for reference (columns 9-10).

shared space and learn MT, we suspect that the final MT performance on the individual language directions is ultimately being held back due to the multilingual noise of other language combinations. To verify this, we use the converged MDAE B+BT model and fine-tune it using the B+BT approach on the different en–$\{af,...,yo\}$ combinations individually (Table 3).

In all cases, the bilingual finetuning improves the multilingual model, with a major increase of $+4.2$ BLEU for en–sw resulting in a BLEU score of 11.6. The finetuned models almost always produce the best performing model, showing that the process of i) multilingual pre-training (MDAE) to achieve a cross-lingual representation, ii) SSNMT online data extraction (SPE) with online back-translation (B+BT) to obtain increasing quantities of supervisory signals from the data, followed by iii) focused bilingual fine-tuning to remove multilingual noise is key to learning low-resource MT also on distant languages without the need of any parallel data.

7 Comparison to other NMT Architectures

We compare the best SSNMT model configuration per language pair with the SSNMT **baseline** system, and with Monoses (Artetxe et al., 2019), an **unsupervised** machine translation model in its statistical (USMT) and hybrid (USMT+UNMT) version (Table 4). Over all languages,

SSNMT with data augmentation outperforms both the SSNMT baseline and UMT models.

We also compare our results with a **supervised** NMT system trained on WP parallel sentences **extracted** by Laser[16] (Artetxe and Schwenk, 2019b) (en–$\{af,my\}$) in a preprocessing data extraction step with the recommended extraction threshold of 1.04. We use the pre-extracted and similarity-ranked WikiMatrix (Schwenk et al., 2021) corpus, which uses Laser to extract parallel sentences, for en–$\{ne,sw\}$. Laser is not trained on kn and yo, thus these languages are not included in the analysis. For en–af, our model and the supervised model trained on Laser extractions perform equally well. In all other cases, our model statistically significantly outperforms the supervised LASER model, which is surprising, given the fact that the underlying LASER model was trained on parallel data in a highly multilingual setup (93 languages), while our MDAE setup does not use any parallel data and was trained on the monolingual data of much fewer language directions (7 languages) only. This again underlines the effectiveness of joining SSNMT with BT, multilingual pre-training and bilingual finetuning.

For reference, we also report the **top-scoring system** (TSS) per language direction based on top results reported on the relevant test sets together with the amount of parallel training data available to TSS systems. In case of language pairs whose test set is part of ongoing shared tasks (en–$\{kn,my\}$), we report the most recent results reported on the shared task web-pages (Section 4). The amount of parallel data available for these TSS varies greatly across languages, from 37 k (en–af) to 995 k (often noisy) sentences. In general, TSS systems perform much better than any of the SSNMT configurations or unsupervised models. This is natural, as TSS systems are mostly supervised (Martinus and Abbott, 2019; Adelani et al., 2021a), semi-supervised (Lakew et al., 2021) or multilingual models with parallel pivot language pairs (Guzmán et al., 2019), none of which is used in the UMT and SSNMT models. For $en2af$ only, our best configuration and the supervised NMT model trained on Laser extractions outperform the current TSS, with a gain in BLEU of $+16.9$ (B+BT), which may be due to the small amount of parallel data the TSS was trained on (37 k parallel sentences).

8 Discussion and Conclusion

Across all tested low-resource language pairs, joining SSNMT-style online sentence pair extraction with UMT-style online back-translation significantly outperforms the SSNMT baseline and unsupervised MT models, indicating that the small amount of available supervisory signals in the data is exploited more efficiently. Our models also outperform supervised NMT systems trained on Laser extractions, which is remarkable given that our systems are trained on non-parallel data only, while Laser has been trained on massive amounts of parallel data.

While SSNMT with data augmentation and MDAE pre-training is able to learn MT even on a low-resource distant language pair such as en–kn, it can fail when a language does not have any relation to other languages included in the multilingual pre-training, which was the case for my in our setup. This can be overcome by being conscientious of the importance of language distance and including related languages during MDAE pre-training and SSNMT training. We make our code and data publicly available.[17]

Acknowledgements

We thank David Adelani and Jesujoba Alabi for their insights on Yorùbá. Part of this research was made possible through a research award from Facebook AI. Partially funded by the German Federal Ministry of Education and Research under the funding code 01IW20010 (Cora4NLP). The authors are responsible for the content of this publication.

[16] `https://github.com/facebookresearch/LASER`

[17] `https://github.com/ruitedk6/comparableNMT`

References

Adelani, D. I., Ruiter, D., Alabi, J. O., Adebonojo, D., Ayeni, A., Adeyemi, M., Awokoya, A., and España-Bonet, C. (2021a). MENYO-20k: A Multi-domain English-Yorùbá Corpus for Machine Translation and Domain Adaptation. *AfricaNLP Workshop, CoRR*, abs/2103.08647.

Adelani, D. I., Ruiter, D., Alabi, J. O., Adebonojo, D., Ayeni, A., Adeyemi, M., Awokoya, A., and España-Bonet, C. (2021b). The Effect of Domain and Diacritics in Yorùbá–English Neural Machine Translation. In *Proceedings of Machine Translation Summit (Research Track)*. European Association for Machine Translation.

Agić, Ž. and Vulić, I. (2019). JW300: A wide-coverage parallel corpus for low-resource languages. In *Proceedings of the 57th Annual Meeting of the Association for Computational Linguistics*, pages 3204–3210, Florence, Italy. Association for Computational Linguistics.

Artetxe, M., Labaka, G., and Agirre, E. (2017). Learning bilingual word embeddings with (almost) no bilingual data. In *Proceedings of the 55th Annual Meeting of the Association for Computational Linguistics (Volume 1: Long Papers)*, pages 451–462.

Artetxe, M., Labaka, G., and Agirre, E. (2019). An effective approach to unsupervised machine translation. In *Proceedings of the 57th Annual Meeting of the Association for Computational Linguistics*, pages 194–203, Florence, Italy. Association for Computational Linguistics.

Artetxe, M., Labaka, G., Agirre, E., and Cho, K. (2018). Unsupervised neural machine translation. In *Proceedings of the Sixth International Conference on Learning Representations, ICLR.*

Artetxe, M. and Schwenk, H. (2019a). Margin-based parallel corpus mining with multilingual sentence embeddings. In *Proceedings of the 58th Annual Meeting of the Association for Computational Linguistics*, pages 3197–3203, Florence, Italy. Association for Computational Linguistics.

Artetxe, M. and Schwenk, H. (2019b). Massively multilingual sentence embeddings for zero-shot cross-lingual transfer and beyond. *Transactions of the Association for Computational Linguistics*, 7:597–610.

Banerjee, T., Murthy, V. R., and Bhattacharyya, P. (2019). Ordering matters: Word ordering aware unsupervised NMT. *CoRR*, abs/1911.01212.

Barrault, L., Bojar, O., Bougares, F., Chatterjee, R., Costa-jussà, M. R., Federmann, C., Fishel, M., Fraser, A., Graham, Y., Guzman, P., Haddow, B., Huck, M., Yepes, A. J., Koehn, P., Martins, A., Morishita, M., Monz, C., Nagata, M., Nakazawa, T., and Negri, M., editors (2020). *Proceedings of the Fifth Conference on Machine Translation.* Association for Computational Linguistics, Online.

Bird, S. (2006). NLTK: The Natural Language Toolkit. In *Proceedings of the COLING/ACL 2006 Interactive Presentation Sessions*, pages 69–72, Sydney, Australia. Association for Computational Linguistics.

Bojar, O. and Tamchyna, A. (2011). Improving translation model by monolingual data. In *Proceedings of the Sixth Workshop on Statistical Machine Translation*, pages 330–336, Edinburgh, Scotland. Association for Computational Linguistics.

Chaudhary, V., Tang, Y., Guzmán, F., Schwenk, H., and Koehn, P. (2019). Low-resource corpus filtering using multilingual sentence embeddings. In *Proceedings of the Fourth Conference on Machine Translation (Volume 3: Shared Task Papers, Day 2)*, pages 263–268, Florence, Italy. Association for Computational Linguistics.

Clark, J. H., Dyer, C., Lavie, A., and Smith, N. A. (2011). Better hypothesis testing for statistical machine translation: Controlling for optimizer instability. In *Proceedings of the 49th Annual Meeting of the Association for Computational Linguistics: Human Language Technologies*, pages 176–181, Portland, Oregon, USA. Association for Computational Linguistics.

Conneau, A., Khandelwal, K., Goyal, N., Chaudhary, V., Wenzek, G., Guzmán, F., Grave, E., Ott, M., Zettlemoyer, L., and Stoyanov, V. (2020). Unsupervised cross-lingual representation learning at scale. In *Proceedings of the 58th Annual Meeting of the Association for Computational Linguistics*, pages 8440–8451, Online. Association for Computational Linguistics.

Conneau, A. and Lample, G. (2019). Cross-lingual language model pretraining. In Wallach, H., Larochelle, H., Beygelzimer, A., d'Alché-Buc, F., Fox, E., and Garnett, R., editors, *Advances in Neural Information Processing Systems*, volume 32. Curran Associates, Inc.

Currey, A., Miceli Barone, A. V., and Heafield, K. (2017). Copied monolingual data improves low-resource neural machine translation. In *Proceedings of the Second Conference on Machine Translation*, pages 148–156, Copenhagen, Denmark. Association for Computational Linguistics.

Edman, L., Toral, A., and van Noord, G. (2020). Low-resource unsupervised NMT: Diagnosing the problem and providing a linguistically motivated solution. In *Proceedings of the 22nd Annual Conference of the European Association for Machine Translation*, pages 81–90, Lisboa, Portugal. European Association for Machine Translation.

Edunov, S., Ott, M., Auli, M., and Grangier, D. (2018). Understanding back-translation at scale. In *Proceedings of the 2018 Conference on Empirical Methods in Natural Language Processing*, pages 489–500, Brussels, Belgium. Association for Computational Linguistics.

El-Kishky, A., Chaudhary, V., Guzmán, F., and Koehn, P. (2020). CCAligned: A massive collection of cross-lingual web-document pairs. In *Proceedings of the 2020 Conference on Empirical Methods in Natural Language Processing (EMNLP 2020)*, pages 5960–5969, Online. Association for Computational Linguistics.

España-Bonet, C., Ruiter, D., and van Genabith, J. (2019). UdS-DFKI Participation at WMT 2019: Low-Resource (*en–gu*) and Coreference-Aware (*en–de*) Systems. In *Proceedings of the Fourth Conference on Machine Translation*, pages 382–389, Florence, Italy. Association for Computational Linguistics.

Gulcehre, C., Firat, O., Xu, K., Cho, K., Barrault, L., Lin, H.-C., Bougares, F., Schwenk, H., and Bengio, Y. (2015). On using monolingual corpora in neural machine translation. *arXiv preprint arXiv:1503.03535*.

Guzmán, F., Chen, P.-J., Ott, M., Pino, J., Lample, G., Koehn, P., Chaudhary, V., and Ranzato, M. (2019). The FLORES evaluation datasets for low-resource machine translation: Nepali–English and Sinhala–English. In *Proceedings of the 2019 Conference on Empirical Methods in Natural Language Processing and the 9th International Joint Conference on Natural Language Processing (EMNLP-IJCNLP)*, pages 6098–6111, Hong Kong, China. Association for Computational Linguistics.

Hoang, V. C. D., Koehn, P., Haffari, G., and Cohn, T. (2018). Iterative back-translation for neural machine translation. In *Proceedings of the 2nd Workshop on Neural Machine Translation and Generation*, pages 18–24, Melbourne, Australia. Association for Computational Linguistics.

Johnson, M., Schuster, M., Le, Q. V., Krikun, M., Wu, Y., Chen, Z., Thorat, N., Viégas, F. B., Wattenberg, M., Corrado, G., Hughes, M., and Dean, J. (2017). Google's Multilingual Neural Machine Translation System: Enabling Zero-Shot Translation. *Transactions of the Association for Computational Linguist*, 5:339–351.

Karakanta, A., Dehdari, J., and van Genabith, J. (2018). Neural machine translation for low-resource languages without parallel corpora. *Machine Translation*, 32(1):167–189.

Kim, Y., Graça, M., and Ney, H. (2020). When and why is unsupervised neural machine translation useless? In *Proceedings of the 22nd Annual Conference of the European Association for Machine Translation*, pages 35–44, Lisboa, Portugal. European Association for Machine Translation.

Koehn, P. (2004). Statistical significance tests for machine translation evaluation. In *Proceedings of the 2004 Conference on Empirical Methods in Natural Language Processing*, pages 388–395, Barcelona, Spain. Association for Computational Linguistics.

Koehn, P., Hoang, H., Birch, A., Callison-Burch, C., Federico, M., Bertoldi, N., Cowan, B., Shen, W., Moran, C., Zens, R., Dyer, C., Bojar, O., Constantin, A., and Herbst, E. (2007). Moses: Open source toolkit for statistical machine translation. In *Proceedings of the 45th Annual Meeting of the Association for Computational Linguistics Companion Volume Proceedings of the Demo and Poster Sessions*, pages 177–180, Prague, Czech Republic. Association for Computational Linguistics.

Koneru, S., Liu, D., and Niehues, J. (2021). Unsupervised machine translation on Dravidian languages. In *Proceedings of the First Workshop on Speech and Language Technologies for Dravidian Languages*, pages 55–64, Kyiv. Association for Computational Linguistics.

Kudo, T. and Richardson, J. (2018). SentencePiece: A simple and language independent subword tokenizer and detokenizer for neural text processing. In *Proceedings of the 2018 Conference on Empirical Methods in Natural Language Processing: System Demonstrations*, pages 66–71, Brussels, Belgium. Association for Computational Linguistics.

Kuwanto, G., Akyürek, A. F., Tourni, I. C., Li, S., and Wijaya, D. (2021). Low-resource machine translation for low-resource languages: Leveraging comparable data, code-switching and compute resources. *CoRR*, abs/2103.13272.

Lakew, S. M., Negri, M., and Turchi, M. (2021). Low Resource Neural Machine Translation: A Benchmark for Five African Languages. *AfricaNLP Workshop, CoRR*, abs/2003.14402.

Lample, G., Conneau, A., Denoyer, L., and Ranzato, M. (2018a). Unsupervised machine translation using monolingual corpora only. In *Proceedings of the Sixth International Conference on Learning Representations, ICLR*.

Lample, G., Ott, M., Conneau, A., Denoyer, L., and Ranzato, M. (2018b). Phrase-based & neural unsupervised machine translation. In *Proceedings of the 2018 Conference on Empirical Methods in Natural Language Processing*, pages 5039–5049. Association for Computational Linguistics.

Leng, Y., Tan, X., Qin, T., Li, X.-Y., and Liu, T.-Y. (2019). Unsupervised Pivot Translation for Distant Languages. In *Proceedings of the 57th Annual Meeting of the Association for Computational Linguistics*, pages 175–183.

Li, Z., Zhao, H., Wang, R., Utiyama, M., and Sumita, E. (2020). Reference language based unsupervised neural machine translation. In *Findings of the Association for Computational Linguistics: EMNLP 2020*, pages 4151–4162, Online. Association for Computational Linguistics.

Littell, P., Mortensen, D. R., Lin, K., Kairis, K., Turner, C., and Levin, L. (2017). URIEL and lang2vec: Representing languages as typological, geographical, and phylogenetic vectors. In *Proceedings of the 15th Conference of the European Chapter of the Association for Computational Linguistics: Volume 2, Short Papers*, pages 8–14, Valencia, Spain. Association for Computational Linguistics.

Liu, Y., Gu, J., Goyal, N., Li, X., Edunov, S., Ghazvininejad, M., Lewis, M., and Zettlemoyer, L. (2020). Multilingual Denoising Pre-training for Neural Machine Translation. *Transactions of the Association for Computational Linguistics*, 8:726–742.

Marchisio, K., Duh, K., and Koehn, P. (2020). When does unsupervised machine translation work? In *Proceedings of the Fifth Conference on Machine Translation*, pages 571–583, Online. Association for Computational Linguistics.

Martinus, L. and Abbott, J. Z. (2019). A Focus on Neural Machine Translation for African Languages. *CoRR*, abs/1906.05685.

McKellar, C. A. and Puttkammer, M. J. (2020). Dataset for comparable evaluation of machine translation between 11 South African languages. *Data in Brief*, 29:105146.

Mikolov, T., Sutskever, I., Chen, K., Corrado, G., and Dean, J. (2013). Distributed representations of words and phrases and their compositionality. In *Proceedings of the 26th International Conference on Neural Information Processing Systems - Volume 2*, NIPS'13, page 3111–3119, Red Hook, NY, USA. Curran Associates Inc.

Niu, X., Denkowski, M., and Carpuat, M. (2018). Bi-directional neural machine translation with synthetic parallel data. In *Proceedings of the 2nd Workshop on Neural Machine Translation and Generation*, pages 84–91, Melbourne, Australia. Association for Computational Linguistics.

Papineni, K., Roukos, S., Ward, T., and Zhu, W.-J. (2002). BLEU: A Method for Automatic Evaluation of Machine Translation. In *Proceedings of the 40th Annual Meeting on Association for Computational Linguistics*, pages 311–318, Stroudsburg, PA, USA. Association for Computational Linguistics.

Post, M. (2018). A call for clarity in reporting BLEU scores. In *Proceedings of the Third Conference on Machine Translation: Research Papers*, pages 186–191, Belgium, Brussels. Association for Computational Linguistics.

Ramachandran, P., Liu, P., and Le, Q. (2017). Unsupervised pretraining for sequence to sequence learning. In *Proceedings of the 2017 Conference on Empirical Methods in Natural Language Processing*, pages 383–391, Copenhagen, Denmark. Association for Computational Linguistics.

Ren, S., Zhang, Z., Liu, S., Zhou, M., and Ma, S. (2019). Unsupervised Neural Machine Translation with SMT as Posterior Regularization. In *The Thirty-Third AAAI Conference on Artificial Intelligence, AAAI 2019, Honolulu, Hawaii, USA*, pages 241–248. AAAI Press.

Ruiter, D., España-Bonet, C., and van Genabith, J. (2019). Self-supervised neural machine translation. In *Proceedings of the 57th Annual Meeting of the Association for Computational Linguistics*, pages 1828–1834, Florence, Italy. Association for Computational Linguistics.

Ruiter, D., van Genabith, J., and España-Bonet, C. (2020). Self-Induced Curriculum Learning in Self-Supervised Neural Machine Translation. In *Proceedings of the 2020 Conference on Empirical Methods in Natural Language Processing (EMNLP)*, pages 2560–2571, Online. Association for Computational Linguistics.

Schwenk, H., Chaudhary, V., Sun, S., Gong, H., and Guzmán, F. (2021). WikiMatrix: Mining 135M Parallel Sentences in 1620 Language Pairs from Wikipedia. In Merlo, P., Tiedemann, J., and Tsarfaty, R., editors, *Proceedings of the 16th Conference of the European Chapter of the Association for Computational Linguistics: Main Volume, EACL 2021, Online, April 19 - 23, 2021*, pages 1351–1361. Association for Computational Linguistics.

Sen, S., Gupta, K. K., Ekbal, A., and Bhattacharyya, P. (2019). Multilingual unsupervised NMT using shared encoder and language-specific decoders. In *Proceedings of the 57th Annual Meeting of the Association for Computational Linguistics*, pages 3083–3089, Florence, Italy. Association for Computational Linguistics.

Sennrich, R., Haddow, B., and Birch, A. (2016a). Improving neural machine translation models with monolingual data. In *Proceedings of the 54th Annual Meeting of the Association for Computational Linguistics (Volume 1: Long Papers)*, pages 86–96, Berlin, Germany. Association for Computational Linguistics.

Sennrich, R., Haddow, B., and Birch, A. (2016b). Neural machine translation of rare words with subword units. In *Proceedings of the 54th Annual Meeting of the Association for Computational Linguistics (Volume 1: Long Papers)*, pages 1715–1725, Berlin, Germany. Association for Computational Linguistics.

ShweSin, Y. M., Soe, K. M., and Htwe, K. Y. (2018). Large Scale Myanmar to English Neural Machine Translation System. In *2018 IEEE 7th Global Conference on Consumer Electronics (GCCE)*, pages 464–465.

Tang, Y., Tran, C., Li, X., Chen, P.-J., Goyal, N., Chaudhary, V., Gu, J., and Fan, A. (2020). Multilingual translation with extensible multilingual pretraining and finetuning. *CoRR*, abs/2008.00401.

Yang, Z., Chen, W., Wang, F., and Xu, B. (2018). Unsupervised neural machine translation with weight sharing. In *Proceedings of the 56th Annual Meeting of the Association for Computational Linguistics (Volume 1: Long Papers)*, pages 46–55. Association for Computational Linguistics.

Zhang, Z., Liu, S., Li, M., Zhou, M., and Chen, E. (2018). Joint training for neural machine translation models with monolingual data. In McIlraith, S. A. and Weinberger, K. Q., editors, *Proceedings of the Thirty-Second AAAI Conference on Artificial Intelligence, (AAAI-18), New Orleans, Louisiana, USA*, pages 555–562. AAAI Press.

Zoph, B., Yuret, D., May, J., and Knight, K. (2016). Transfer learning for low-resource neural machine translation. In *Proceedings of the 2016 Conference on Empirical Methods in Natural Language Processing*, pages 1568–1575, Austin, Texas. Association for Computational Linguistics.

Surprise Language Challenge: Developing a Neural Machine Translation System between Pashto and English in Two Months

Alexandra Birch,[1] Barry Haddow,[1] Antonio Valerio Miceli Barone,[1]
Jindřich Helcl,[1] Jonas Waldendorf,[1] Felipe Sánchez-Martínez,[2]
Mikel L. Forcada,[2] Miquel Esplà-Gomis,[2] Víctor M. Sánchez-Cartagena,[2]
Juan Antonio Pérez-Ortiz,[2] Wilker Aziz,[3] Lina Murady,[3] Sevi Sariisik,[4]
Peggy van der Kreeft,[5] Kay MacQuarrie[5]

[1]University of Edinburgh, [2]Universitat d'Alacant, [3]Universiteit van Amsterdam,
[4]BBC , [5]Deutsche Welle

Abstract

In the media industry, the focus of global reporting can shift overnight. There is a compelling need to be able to develop new machine translation systems in a short period of time, in order to more efficiently cover quickly developing stories. As part of the low-resource machine translation project GoURMET, we selected a surprise language for which a system had to be built and evaluated in two months (February and March 2021). The language selected was Pashto, an Indo-Iranian language spoken in Afghanistan, Pakistan and India. In this period we completed the full pipeline of development of a neural machine translation system: data crawling, cleaning, aligning, creating test sets, developing and testing models, and delivering them to the user partners. In this paper we describe the rapid data creation process, and experiments with transfer learning and pretraining for Pashto-English. We find that starting from an existing large model pre-trained on 50 languages leads to far better BLEU scores than pretraining on one high-resource language pair with a smaller model. We also present human evaluation of our systems, which indicates that the resulting systems perform better than a freely available commercial system when translating from English into Pashto direction, and similarly when translating from Pashto into English.

1 Introduction

The Horizon 2020 European-Union-funded project GoURMET[1] (Global Under-Resourced MEdia Translation) aims to improve neural machine translation for under-resourced language pairs with a special emphasis on the news domain. The two media partners in the GoURMET project, the BBC in the UK and Deutsche Welle (DW) in Germany, publish news content in 40 and 30 different languages, respectively, and gather news in over 100 languages. In such a global information scenario, machine translation technologies become an important element in the everyday workflow of these media organisations.

[1]https://GoURMET-project.eu/

Surprise language exercises (Oard et al., 2019) started in March 2003, when the US Defense Advanced Research Projects Agency (DARPA) designated Cebuano, the second most widely spoken indigenous language in the Philippines, as the focus of an exercise. Teams were given only ten days to assemble language resources and to create whatever human language technology they could in that time. These events have been running annually ever since.

The GoURMET project undertook its surprise language evaluation as an exercise to bring together the whole consortium to focus on a language pair of particular interest to the BBC and DW for a short period of time. Given the impact of the COVID-19 pandemic, a two-month period was considered realistic. On 1 February 2021, BBC and DW revealed the chosen language to be Pashto. By completing and documenting how this challenge was addressed, we prove we are able to bootstrap a new high quality neural machine translation task within a very limited window of time.

There has also been a considerable amount of recent interest in using pretrained language models for improving performance on downstream natural language processing tasks, especially in a low resource setting (Liu et al., 2020; Brown et al., 2020; Qiu et al., 2020), but how best to do this is still an open question. A key question in this work is how best to use training data which is not English (`en`) to Pashto (`ps`) translations. We experimented, on the one hand, with pretraining models on a high-resource language pair (German–English, one of the most studied high-resource language pairs) and, on the other hand, with fine-tuning an existing large pretrained translation model (mBART50) trained on parallel data involving English and 49 languages including Pashto (Tang et al., 2020). We show that both approaches perform comparably or better than commercial machine translation systems especially when Pashto is the output language, with the large multilingual model achieving the highest translation quality between our two approaches.

The paper is organised as follows. Section 2 motivates the choice of Pashto and presents a brief analysis of the social and technical context of the language. Section 3 describes the efforts behind the crawling of additional monolingual and parallel data in addition to the linguistic resources already available for English–Pashto. Section 4 introduces the twofold approach we followed in order to build our neural machine translation systems: on the one hand, we developed a system from scratch by combining mBART-like pretraining, German–English translation pretraining and fine-tuning; on the other hand, we also explored fine-tuning on the existing pretrained multilingual model mBART50. We present automatic results and preliminary human evaluation of the systems in Section 5.

2 The Case for Pashto

The primary goal, when selecting which low-resource language pair to work on, was to provide a tool that would be useful to both the BBC and Deutsche Welle. It had to be an under-resourced language with high news value and audience growth potential, and one that could pose a satisfactory research challenge to complement the wider goals of the project. Pashto ticked all of these boxes.

Pashto is one of the two official languages of Afghanistan along with Dari. Almost half of the country's 37.5 million people, up to 10 percent of the population in neighbouring Pakistan, and smaller communities in India and Tajikistan speak Pashto, bringing estimates of Pashto speakers worldwide around 45–50 million (Brown, 2005). Europe hosts a growing number of Pashto speakers, too. As of the end of 2020, there were over 270,000 Afghans living in Germany[2] and 79,000 in the UK[3]. Projecting from Afghanistan's national linguistic breakdown,[4] up to half of these could be Pashto speakers.

Pashto (also spelled *Pukhto* and *Pakhto* is an Iranian language of the Indo-European family and is grouped with other Iranian languages such as Persian, Dari, Tajiki, in spite of major linguistic diferences among them. Pashto is written with a unique enriched Perso-Arabic script with 45 letters and four diacritics.

Translating between English and Pashto poses interesting challenges. Pashto has a richer morphology than that of English; the induced data sparseness may partly be remedied with segmentation in subword units tokenization models such as SentencePiece (Kudo and Richardson, 2018), as used in mBART50. There are Pashto categories in Pashto that do not overtly exist in English (such as verb aspect or the oblique case in general nouns) and categories in English that do not overtly exist in Pashto (such as definite and indefinite articles), which may pose a certain challenge when having to generate correct text in machine translation output.

Due to the chronic political and social instability and conflict that Afghanistan has experienced in its recent history, the country features prominently in global news coverage. Closely following the developments there remains a key priority for international policy makers, multilateral institutions, observers, researchers and the media, alongside the wider array of individual news consumers. Pashto features in BBC Monitoring's language portfolio. Enhancing the means to better follow and understand Pashto resources first hand through machine translation offers a valuable contribution.

The interest of commercial providers of machine translation solutions in Pashto is recent and there is room for improvement for existing solutions. Google Translate integrated Pashto in 2016, ten years after its launch.[5] Amazon followed suit in November 2019 and Microsoft Translator added Pashto into its portfolio in August 2020.[6] Nevertheless, Pashto has been of interest to the GoURMET Media Partners long before that. Deutsche Welle started its Pashto broadcasts in 1970 and BBC World Service in 1981. Both partners are currently producing multimedia content (digital, TV, radio) in Pashto. BBC Pashto reaches 10.4 million people per week, with significant further growth potential.

3 Data Creation

The process of data collection and curation is divided into two clearly different processes to obtain: (a) training data, and (b) development and test data. This section describes these two proceses. Note that our neural systems were trained with additional training data which will be described in Section 4.

3.1 Training Data

Traning data consists of English–Pashto parallel data and Pashto monolingual data, and was obtained by two means: directly crawling websites likely to contain parallel data, and crawling the top-level domain (TLD) of Afganistan (`.af`), where Pashto is an official language.

Direct crawling was run using the tool Bitextor (Espla-Gomis and Forcada, 2010) on a collection of web domains that were identified as likely to contain English–Pashto parallel data.

[2]German Federal Statistical Office, `https://bit.ly/3fg5LGr`

[3]ONS statistics, `https://bit.ly/3oh92cS`

[4]World Factbook, `https://www.cia.gov/the-world-factbook/field/languages/`

[5]`https://blog.google/products/translate/google-translate-now-speaks-pashto`

[6]`https://bit.ly/3w4WMPi`

This list was complemented by adding the web domains used to build the data sets released for the parallel corpus filtering shared task at WMT2020 (Koehn et al., 2020). A total of 427 websites were partially crawled during three weeks following this strategy, from which only 50 provided any English–Pashto parallel data.

Crawling the Afganistan TLD was carried out by using the tool LinguaCrawl.[7] An initial set of 30 web domains was manually identified, mostly belonging to national authorities, universities and news sites. Starting from this collection, a total of 150 new websites were discovered containing documents in Pashto. After document and sentence alignment (using the tool Bitextor), 138 of them were identified to contain any English–Pashto parallel data.

3.2 Test and Development Data

The development and test sets were extracted from a large collection of news articles in Pashto and English, both from the BBC and the DW websites. In both cases, documents in English and documents in Pashto were aligned using the URIs of the images included in each of them, as, in both cases, these elements are language-independent. Given the collection of image URLs in a document in English (I_{en}) and that collection in a document in Pashto (I_{ps}), the similarity score between these two documents was computed as:

$$\mathrm{score}(I_{\mathrm{en}}, I_{\mathrm{ps}}) = \frac{1}{|I_{\mathrm{en}} \cup I_{\mathrm{ps}}|} \sum_{i \in I_{\mathrm{en}} \cap I_{\mathrm{ps}}} \mathrm{IDF}(i)$$

where $\mathrm{IDF}(i)$ is the inverse document frequency (Robertson, 2004) of a given image. English–Pashto pairs of documents were ranked using this score, and document pairs with a score under 0.1 were discarded.

After document alignment, documents were split into sentences and all the Pashto segments were translated into English using Google Translate.[8] English segments and machine-translated Pashto segments in each pair of documents were compared using the metric `chrF++` (Popović, 2017), and the best 4,000 segment pairs were taken as candidate segments for human validation.

Finally, a team of validators from BBC and DW manually checked the candidate segments. Through human validation, 2,000 valid segment pairs were obtained from the BBC dataset, and 815 for the DW dataset. The BBC dataset whas then divided into two sub-sets: 1,350 segment pairs for testing and 1,000 segment pairs for development; for the DW data, the whole set of 815 segment pairs was used as a test set.

3.3 Final Data Set Statistics

Table 1 shows the number of segment pairs, the number of tokens both in Pashto and English, and the average number of tokens per segment for the corpus obtained.

4 Training of Neural Machine Translation Systems

We developed two different neural models: a *from-scratch* system, and a larger and slower system based on an existing pretrained model. The development of the former starts with a mediun-size randomly-initialized transformer (Vaswani et al., 2017), whereas the latter is obtained by fine-tuning the larger downloadable mBART50 pretrained system (Tang et al., 2020).

[7] `https://github.com/transducens/linguacrawl`

[8] `https://translate.google.com`

Corpus name	# segm. pairs	Pastho # tokens	Pastho tokens/segm.	English # tokens	English tokens/segm.
Crawled	59,512	759,352	12.8	709,630	11.9
BBC Test	1,350	25,453	18.8	30,417	22.5
BBC Dev	1,000	18,793	18.8	22,438	22.4
DW Test	813	14,956	18.3	20,797	25.5

Table 1: Crawled and in-house parallel corpora statistics.

Remarkably, mBART50 has been pretrained with some Pashto (and English) data which makes it a very convenient model to explore.

The size of pretrained models make them poor candidates for production environments, especially where they are required to run on CPU-only servers as it is the case in the GoURMET project, yet translations have to be available at a fast rate. In those scenarios, the from-scratch system may be considered a more efficient alternative. Our mBART50 systems can still be useful in those scenarios to generate synthetic data with which to train smaller models.

4.1 From-scratch Model

This has been trained "from scratch" in the sense that it does not exploit third-party pretrained models. It was built by using a combination of mBART-like pretraining (Liu et al., 2020), German–English translation pretraining and fine-tuning. We used the Marian toolkit (Junczys-Dowmunt et al., 2018) to implement this model.

Data preparation. We use different version of training data in different rounds, starting from a small and relatively high-quality dataset and adding more data as it becomes available in parallel to our model training efforts.

Initial data. For our initial English-Pashto parallel training corpus we use the WMT 2020 data excluding ParaCrawl. This dataset consists mostly of OPUS data.[9] We did not use existing data from the ParaCrawl project[10] at this point because it requires filtering to be used effectively and we first wanted to build initial models on relatively clean data. For our initial monolingual corpus we use all the released Pashto NewsCrawl[11] and the 2019 version of the English NewsCrawl[12]. Finally, we also use the Pashto-English corpus that was submitted by the Bytedance team to the WMT 2020 cleaning shared task (Koehn et al., 2020).

For pretraining the German–English model we use exisiting WMT data (Europarl, Common Crawl and News Commentary). We use WMT dev and test sets[13] for early stopping and evaluation, and the BBC development and test sets (see Section 3) for additional evaluation. We process these data with standard Moses cleaning and punctuation normalization scripts[14]. For Pashto we also filter the training data with a language detector based on Fasttext word embeddings to remove the sentences in incorrect languages, and we apply an external character

[9] http://opus.nlpl.eu
[10] https://paracrawl.eu/
[11] http://data.statmt.org/news-crawl/ps/
[12] http://data.statmt.org/news-crawl/en/news.2019.en.shuffled.deduped.gz
[13] http://www.statmt.org/wmt20/translation-task.html
[14] https://github.com/marian-nmt/moses-scripts

normalization script[15].

We generate a shared SentencePiece vocabulary (BPE mode) on a merged corpus obtained by concatenating the German–English training data, the first 6,000,000 English monolingual sentences, and all the Pashto monolingual and Pashto–English parallel data each upsampled to approximately match the size of the English monolingual data. We reserve a small number of special tokens for language id and mBART masking. The total vocabulary size is $32,000$ token types.

mBART-like pretraining. We pretrain a standard Marian transformer-based model (Junczys-Dowmunt et al., 2018) with a reproduction of the mBART (Liu et al., 2020) pretraining objective with our English and Pashto monolingual data. We use only the masking distortion, but not the consecutive sentences shuffling distortion, as our monolingual data is already shuffled and therefore the original ordering of the sentences is not available. We also did not use online backtranslation as it is not available in Marian. We upsample the Pashto data so that each batch contains an equal amount of English and Pashto sentences. The output language is specified by a language identification token at the beginning of the source sentence. We perform early stopping on cross-entropy evaluated on a monolingual validation set obtained in the same way as the training data.

Exploitation of German–English data. We pretrain a bidirectional German–English model with the same architecture as the mBART-like model defined above (see Section 4.1 above). As in the mBART model, we use a language id token prepended to the source sentence to specify the output language. We use WMT data (see Section 4.1) for training and early stopping.

Training of the from-scratch system. Training consists of fine-tuning a pretrained model with Pashto–English parallel data, using it to generate initial backtranslations which are combined with the parallel data and used to train another round of the model, starting again from a pretrained model. At this point, we include the first 220,000 sentence pairs of "Bytedance" filtered parallel data, sorted by filtering rank.

Following similar work with English–Tamil (Bawden et al., 2020), we start with our mBART-like model and we fine-tune it in the Pashto→English direction with our parallel data. Then we use this model to backtranslate the Pashto monolingual data, generating a pseudo-parallel corpus which we combine with our true parallel corpus and use to train a English→Pashto model again starting from mBART. We use this model to backtranslate the first 5,000,000 monolingual English sentences (we also experimented with the full corpus, but found minimal difference), and we train another round of Pashto→English followed by another round of English→Pashto, both initialized from mBART pretraining.

After this phase we switch to German–English pretraining. Due to the limited available time, we did not experiment on the optimal switching point between the two pretraining schemes; we based this decision instead on our previous experience with English–Tamil (Bawden et al., 2020). We perform four rounds (counting each translation direction as one round) of iterative backtranslation with initialization from German–English pretraining.

On the last round we evaluate multiple variants of training data as more data became available. We found that including additional targeted crawls on news websites (see Section 3) improved translation quality. Adding synthetic English paraphrases or distillation data from the large mBART50 model however did not provide improvements.

[15]https://github.com/rnd2110/SCRIPTS_Normalization

4.2 mBART50-Based Model

The experiments in this section try to show how far we can get by building our English–Pashto NMT systems starting from the recently released (January 2021) pretrained multilingual model mBART50 (Tang et al., 2020).[16] mBART50 is an extension of mBART (Liu et al., 2020) additionally trained on collections of parallel data with a focus on English as source (*one-to-many* system or mBART50 1–to–n for short) or target (*many-to-one* system). As of March 12th 2021 the n–to–1 system is not available for download; therefore, we used the *many-to-many* (mBART50 n–to–n for short) version as a replacement. As regards mBART50 1–to–n, our preliminary experiments showed that the bare model without further fine-tuning gave in the English→Pashto direction results similar to mBART50 n–to–n. We also confirmed that mBART50 1–to–n gives very bad results on Pashto→English as the system has not been exposed to English during pretraining. Consequently, our experiments focus on mBART50 n–to–n for both translation directions; being a multilingual model, this will also reduce the number of experiments to consider as the same system is trained at the same time in both directions. As already mentioned, mBART50 was pretrained with Pashto and English data which makes it a very convenient model to start with.

Experimental set-up. Although these models have already processed English and Pashto texts (not necessarily mutual translations) during pretraining, fine-tuning them on English–Pashto parallel data may improve the results. Therefore, apart from evaluating the plain non-fine-tuned mBART50 n–to–n system, we *incrementally* fine-tuned it in three consecutive steps:

1. First, we fine-tuned the model with a very small parallel corpus of 1,400 sentences made of the TED Talks and Wikimedia files in the clean parallel data set provided for the WMT 2020 shared task on parallel corpus filtering and allignment for low-resource conditions.[17] Validation-based early stopping was used and training stopped after 20 epochs (this took around 20 minutes on one NVIDIA A100 GPU). This scenario may be considered as a few-shot adaptation of the pretrained model.
2. Then, we further fine-tuned the model obtained in the first step with a much larger parallel corpus of 343,198 sentences made of the complete WMT 2020 clean dataset and the first 220,000 sentences in the corpus resulting from the system submitted by Bytedance to the same shared task (Koehn et al., 2020). Training stopped after 7 epochs (around 2 hours and 20 minutes on one A100 GPU).
3. Finally, we additionally fine-tuned the model previously obtained with a synthetic English–Pashto parallel corpus built by translating 674,839 Pashto sentences[18] into English with the model resulting from the second step. The Pashto→English model in the second step gave a BLEU score of 25.27 with the BBC test set, allowing us to assume that the synthetic English generated has reasonable quality. Note that we carried out a multilingual fine-tuning process and therefore the synthetic corpus is used to fine-tune the system in both directions, which yields giving a system which will be probably worse than the initial one in the Pashto→English direction. Training stopped after 7 epochs (around 4 hours on one A100 GPU). Only sentences in the original Pashto monolingual corpus with lengths between 40 and 400 characters were included the synthetic corpus.

Fine-tuning configuration. Validation-based early stopping was applied with a patience value of 10 epochs. The development set evaluated by the stopping criterion was the in-house

[16] `https://github.com/pytorch/fairseq/blob/master/examples/multilingual`

[17] `http://www.statmt.org/wmt20/parallel-corpus-filtering.html`

[18] Concatenation of all files available at `http://data.statmt.org/news-crawl/ps` on March 2021 except for `news.2020.Q1.ps.shuffled.deduped.gz`.

	BBC test	DW test	FLORES devtest
Google	12.84	10.19	9.16
from-scratch	15.00	10.41	9.73
mBART50	2.47	1.53	7.56
+ small	9.93	7.67	8.24
+ small, large	11.85	10.31	**10.82**
+ small, large, synthetic	**18.55**	**12.54**	8.61

Table 2: BLEU scores of the English→Pashto systems. Each column represents a different test set used to compute the score. The first row contains the results for a commercial general-purpose system. The second row contains the scores for the model trained from scratch. The results for mBART50 correspond, from top to bottom, to a non-fine-tuned mBART50 n–to–n system, and this system incrementally fine-tuned with a small parallel corpus of 1,400 sentences, a larger parallel corpus of 343,198 sentences, and a synthetic corpus of 674,839 sentences obtained from Pashto monolingual text.

	BBC test	DW test	FLORES devtest
Google	0.413	**0.374**	**0.345**
from-scratch	0.411	0.336	0.331
mBART50	0.170	0.147	0.284
+ small	0.351	0.301	0.314
+ small, large	0.389	0.341	0.343
+ small, large, synthetic	**0.463**	**0.374**	0.330

Table 3: chrF2 scores of the English→Pashto systems. See table 2 for details.

validation set made of 1,000 sentences curated by the BBC presented in Section 3. Note that no hyper-parameter tuning was performed and, therefore, better results could be attained after a careful grid search hyper-parameter optimization.

Embedding table filtering. As already shown, these models may have strong memory requirements. As a way to verifying whether these requirements could be relaxed, we ran a script to reduce the embedding tables by removing those entries corresponding to tokens not found in a collection of English and Pashto texts. The original vocabulary size of 250,054 tokens of the mBART50 model was reduced to 16,576. This resulted in a relatively small decrease in memory consumption: for example, the GPU memory requirements of mBART n–to–n at inference time (setting the maximum number of tokens per mini-batch to 100) moved from around 4 GB to around 3 GB.

5 Results and Discussion

Tables 2 and 3 show BLEU and chrF2 scores, respectively, for the English to Pashto systems with different test sets. The evaluation metrics for the Google MT system are also included for reference purposes. Similarly, tables 4 and 5 show BLEU and chrF2 scores, respectively, for the Pashto to English systems. All the scores were computed with `sacrebleu` (Post, 2018).

The test sets considered are the two in-house parallel sets created by BBC and DW (see Section 3) and the devtest set provided in the FLORES[19] benchmark (2,698 sentences).

[19]`https://github.com/facebookresearch/flores`

	BBC test	DW test	FLORES devtest
Google	**35.03**	**24.65**	**21.54**
from-scratch	20.00	15.06	14.90
mBART50	19.42	15.30	14.59
+ small	22.55	17.50	14.77
+ small, large	25.27	19.13	17.71
+ small, large, synthetic	25.38	17.88	17.08

Table 4: BLEU scores of the Pashto→English systems. See table 2 for details.

	BBC test	DW test	FLORES devtest
Google	**0.628**	**0.532**	**0.506**
from-scratch	0.482	0.445	0.411
mBART50	0.456	0.431	0.423
+ small	0.512	0.471	0.420
+ small, large	0.527	0.481	0.451
+ small, large, synthetic	0.535	0.477	0.448

Table 5: chrF2 scores of the Pashto→English systems. See table 2 for details.

As can be seen, the from-scratch system provides worse results than the mBART50-based model obtained after the three-step fine-tuning procedure, which may be easily explained by the smaller number of parameters and the lack of initial knowledge.

Regarding the mBART50-based models, for the English→Pashto direction, the scores obtained with the non-fine-tuned models for the FLORES test set are considerably higher than those corresponding to the BBC and DW test sets, which suggests that either they belong to different domains, or they contain very different grammatical or lexical structures, or the FLORES corpus was used to pretrain mBART50. This indicates that fine-tuning could provide a twofold benefit: on the one hand, it may allow the model to focus on our two languages of interest, partially forgetting what it learned for other languages; on the other hand, it may allow the model to perform domain adaptation. In the English→Pashto direction each successive fine-tuning step improves the scores, except when the last model is evaluated against the FLORES devtest set, which makes sense as the development set belongs to the domain of the BBC and DW test sets. Notably, the system resulting from the three-step fine-tuning process improves Google's scores as of April 2021. In the Pashto→English direction, the same trend can be observed, although in this case the best mBART50-based system is noticeably behind the scores of Google's system, yet it still provides scores higher than those for the other translation direction.

5.1 Human Evaluation

Four senior editors from BBC Pashto were asked to score translations in a blind exercise from 1 to 100, with 100 indicating top quality. The evaluators were provided with four outputs for both English→Pashto and Pashto→English samples; these outputs were obtained from the mBART50-based models with beam widths of 1 and 5, from the from-scratch system and from Google Translate. Table 6 demonstrates the average scores by human evaluators for 20 selected sentences. This small sample means that the scores are indicative of the model performance, but together with the BLEU scores gives the user partners confidence in the translation quality.

	Pashto→English	English→Pashto
Google	83.80	68.50
from-scratch	63.50	67.65
mBART50 (beam width 1)	**85.15**	83.60
mBART50 (beam width 5)	83.15	**92.30**

Table 6: Average human scores for 20 translations generated by 3 of our models and a commercial general-purpose system.

Both mBART50-based models performed very strongly, with outcomes significantly better than Google or from-scratch models into Pashto. The model will be made available for further utilization for monitoring and content creation purposes of the media partners as well as the API's public-facing site.[20] The confidence derived from the human evaluation has encouraged the BBC and DW to adopt Pashto↔English machine translation solutions.

6 Conclusion

We present a description of our rapid Pashto↔English machine translation system building exercise. We performed extensive crawling and data cleaning and alignment, combined with pretraining experiments to deliver a strong translation system for a low-resource language. We test different transfer learning approaches and show that large, multilingual models perform better than smaller models from a high-resource language pair. The data [21], models [22] and tools [23] are shared publically.

Acknowledgments

Work funded by the European Union's Horizon 2020 research and innovation programme under grant agreement number 825299, project Global Under-Resourced Media Translation (GoURMET). Some of the computational resources used in the experiments have been funded by the European Regional Development Fund (ERDF) through project IDIFEDER/2020/003.

References

Bawden, R., Birch, A., Dobreva, R., Oncevay, A., Miceli Barone, A. V., and Williams, P. (2020). The university of edinburgh's english-tamil and english-inuktitut submissions to the wmt20 news translation task. In *Proceedings of the Fifth Conference on Machine Translation*, pages 92–99, Online. Association for Computational Linguistics.

Brown, K. (2005). *Encyclopedia of language and linguistics*, volume 1. Elsevier.

Brown, T. B., Mann, B., Ryder, N., Subbiah, M., Kaplan, J., Dhariwal, P., Neelakantan, A., Shyam, P., Sastry, G., Askell, A., Agarwal, S., Herbert-Voss, A., Krueger, G., Henighan, T., Child, R., Ramesh, A., Ziegler, D. M., Wu, J., Winter, C., Hesse, C., Chen, M., Sigler, E., Litwin, M., Gray, S., Chess, B., Clark, J., Berner, C., McCandlish, S., Radford, A., Sutskever, I., and Amodei, D. (2020). Language models are Few-Shot learners.

[20] https://translate.GoURMET.newslabs.co/

[21] http://data.statmt.org/gourmet/models/en-ps

[22] http://data.statmt.org/gourmet/models/en-ps

[23] https://gourmet-project.eu/data-model-releases/

Espla-Gomis, M. and Forcada, M. (2010). Combining content-based and url-based heuristics to harvest aligned bitexts from multilingual sites with bitextor. *The Prague Bulletin of Mathematical Linguistics*, 93(2010):77–86.

Junczys-Dowmunt, M., Heafield, K., Hoang, H., Grundkiewicz, R., and Aue, A. (2018). Marian: Cost-effective high-quality neural machine translation in C++. In *Proceedings of the 2nd Workshop on Neural Machine Translation and Generation*, pages 129–135.

Koehn, P., Chaudhary, V., El-Kishky, A., Goyal, N., Chen, P.-J., and Guzmán, F. (2020). Findings of the WMT 2020 shared task on parallel corpus filtering and alignment. In *Proceedings of the Fifth Conference on Machine Translation*, pages 726–742. Association for Computational Linguistics.

Kudo, T. and Richardson, J. (2018). SentencePiece: A simple and language independent subword tokenizer and detokenizer for neural text processing. In *Proceedings of the 2018 Conference on Empirical Methods in Natural Language Processing: System Demonstrations*, pages 66–71.

Liu, Y., Gu, J., Goyal, N., Li, X., Edunov, S., Ghazvininejad, M., Lewis, M., and Zettlemoyer, L. (2020). Multilingual denoising pre-training for neural machine translation.

Oard, D. W., Carpuat, M., Galuscakova, P., Barrow, J., Nair, S., Niu, X., Shing, H.-C., Xu, W., Zotkina, E., McKeown, K., Muresan, S., Kayi, E. S., Eskander, R., Kedzie, C., Virin, Y., Radev, D. R., Zhang, R., Gales, M. J. F., Ragni, A., and Heafield, K. (2019). Surprise languages: Rapid-response cross-language IR. In *Proceedings of the Ninth International Workshop on Evaluating Information Access, EVIA 2019*.

Popović, M. (2017). chrF++: words helping character n-grams. In *Proceedings of the Second Conference on Machine Translation*, pages 612–618.

Post, M. (2018). A call for clarity in reporting BLEU scores. In *Proceedings of the Third Conference on Machine Translation: Research Papers*, pages 186–191, Belgium, Brussels. Association for Computational Linguistics.

Qiu, X., Sun, T., Xu, Y., Shao, Y., Dai, N., and Huang, X. (2020). Pre-trained models for natural language processing: A survey.

Robertson, S. (2004). Understanding inverse document frequency: On theoretical arguments for IDF. *Journal of Documentation*, 60.

Tang, Y., Tran, C., Li, X., Chen, P.-J., Goyal, N., Chaudhary, V., Gu, J., and Fan, A. (2020). Multilingual translation with extensible multilingual pretraining and finetuning. *arXiv preprint.*

Vaswani, A., Shazeer, N., Parmar, N., Uszkoreit, J., Jones, L., Gomez, A. N., Kaiser, L. u., and Polosukhin, I. (2017). Attention is all you need. In Guyon, I., Luxburg, U. V., Bengio, S., Wallach, H., Fergus, R., Vishwanathan, S., and Garnett, R., editors, *Advances in Neural Information Processing Systems*, volume 30. Curran Associates, Inc.

Like Chalk and Cheese?
On the Effects of Translationese in MT Training

Samuel Larkin Samuel.Larkin@nrc-cnrc.gc.ca
Michel Simard Michel.Simard@nrc-cnrc.gc.ca
Rebecca Knowles Rebecca.Knowles@nrc-cnrc.gc.ca
National Research Council Canada, Ottawa, Ontario, Canada

Abstract

We revisit the topic of translation direction in the data used for training neural machine translation systems, focusing on a real-world scenario with known translation direction and imbalances in translation direction: the Canadian Hansard. According to automatic metrics, we observe that using parallel data that was produced in the "matching" translation direction (authentic source, translationese target) improves translation quality. In cases of data imbalance in terms of translation direction, we find that tagging the translation direction of training data can close the performance gap. We perform a human evaluation that differs slightly from the automatic metrics, but nevertheless confirms that for this French–English dataset that is known to contain high-quality translations, authentic or tagged mixed source improves over translationese source for training.

1 Introduction

Prior work in statistical machine translation (SMT) highlighted potential benefits of making use of information about the translation direction of training data (Kurokawa et al., 2009). When text is translated, there is an *authentic source* (the language in which the text was originally produced), and its translation, which in contrast can be described as *translationese.* Thus when considering translation direction in machine translation, training data can be described as consisting of *authentic source*, *translationese source*, or a mix.[1] Backtranslated data produced by machine translation may be thought of as an extreme case of translationese source (Marie et al., 2020), but because the quality and types of errors that occur in machine translation are quite different from those that occur in human translation, it is worth examining translation direction of human translation separately from MT-based data augmentation. In Figure 1 we show a fairly dramatic example of the kinds of translation quality differences that can occur when building MT systems using authentic source as opposed to translationese source.

Recent work in neural machine translation (NMT) has revisited this issue, motivating the automatic detection of (human) translationese by showing improved performance on several metrics when training translation direction matches the testing translation direction (Sominsky and Wintner, 2019), examining domain and backtranslation along with the translation direction of test sets (Bogoychev and Sennrich, 2019), and evaluating the treatment of predicted translation direction as separate languages in a multilingual-style NMT system through human and automatic metrics (Riley et al., 2020).

[1]For the purposes of this paper, we will set aside the situation where both sides of the text consist of translationese, translated from one or more other pivot languages.

Source	Les producteurs de fromage au Québec sont des fleurons dont on est fiers.
Reference	We are proud of our exceptional Quebec cheese producers.
MT (Authentic Src.)	We are proud of the success of cheese producers in Quebec.
MT (Translationese Src.)	The cheese producers in Quebec are proud flowers.

Figure 1: Example output of French-English MT trained on Authentic-source (authentic French, translationese English) and Translationese-source (translationese French, authentic English).

We focus this work on a particular real-world scenario, where translation direction is known, and translation (whether human, machine, or computer aided) is expected to be performed from authentic source language text. This is, in fact, a fairly common scenario (i.e., parliamentary, legal, medical, patent, etc. translation), and we highlight one such case as an example: the Canadian Hansard (House of Commons), which consists of transcripts of parliamentary speech, alongside their translations. These proceedings are published in French and English, and it is indicated whether the authentic source was French or English.[2] There is also an imbalance in translation direction; most of the text of the Hansard was originally spoken in English and transcribed and then translated into French. Given that the text is formal and falls within the parliamentary domain, it is appropriate to build or adapt translation systems using the existing Hansard as training data, for use in translating future Hansard text (i.e., in a computer aided translation setting), which raises questions about how to make the best use of the available text and the metadata regarding source language.

In this work, we focus on translating original (authentic) source language text. We examine the following questions:

Q1: What effect does translation direction of training data have on system output?

Q2: Can tagging source side translationese in the training data (i.e., adding a special token like "<translationese>" to the start of translationese source sentences) improve translation of authentic source language test data?

Q3: In a moderate resource setting (approx. 3.7 million sentence pairs), what effect does the proportion of source side translationese (from 0% to 100%) in the training data have?

We experiment and evaluate these using automatic metrics and a small human judgment task, looking at both French–English and English–French translation directions. With regard to **Q1**, we find that systems trained exclusively with Authentic source data outperform by a large margin those trained exclusively with Translationese source data, even with twice as much training data. Combining Authentic and Translationese source does not always produce significantly better systems, compared to using Authentic source only, but tagging Translationese source in the training and tuning data (**Q2**) can improve performance, especially in situations where there is more Translationese source than Authentic source data. In general, translation quality increases as the percentage of Authentic source training data increases (**Q3**): below 50%, tagging Translation source data can help bridge the gap, but the importance of tagging decreases as the percentage of Authentic source training data increases.

2 Data

We use parallel English–French (EN-FR) text from the Canadian Hansard, House of Commons. Our corpus contains transcripts of debates from 1986 to 2016. Earlier parts of this dataset are

[2]Other languages are spoken in the House of Commons, notably Indigenous languages, but in those cases, English and French translations are provided in the Hansard. (`https://www.ourcommons.ca/DocumentViewer/en/42-1/PROC/report-66/`)

available from LDC (Ma, 1999), more recent transcripts are publicly available from the Canadian Parliament website.[3] This data is known to have high translation quality. It is annotated with direction of translation (the original language, FR or EN, as spoken in the House is known); we omit all lines marked as unspecified.[4]

The question of domain is always intertwined with the question of translation direction. Here we hope to minimize that by confining our work to the parliamentary domain; we expect that the level of formality and style of parliamentary speech is relatively consistent, even across languages (certainly more so than it would be if compared between news data and parliamentary speech). Nevertheless, we acknowledge that there will remain differences within this domain; i.e., Members of Parliament may speak more frequently about topics related to their own constituencies or about different topics over time. We also sample our data with an eye toward temporal aspects for this reason.

The full dataset (from which we select our training, development, and test data) is unbalanced in terms of original language: 10,091,250 lines (68.5%) were originally spoken in English, while 3,699,822 lines (25.1%) were originally spoken in French (the remaining 933,996 lines, 6.3%, were labeled as unspecified). In order to run experiments on the proportion of source-side translationese used, we are limited by the size of the smaller sub-corpus, the Authentic-FR language data.

We sample data for validation and testing (2k and 8k lines, respectively), with Authentic-EN source data used for translation into FR and vice versa. The validation and testing data are randomly sampled sentences from recent data (Nov. 1 to Dec. 15, 2016), while training contains older data. This mimics a real-world scenario, where translators (potentially using computer aided translation) might post-edit or interactively translate new text using the output of machine translation systems build on older text. By drawing the test sentences from a separate portion of the Hansard as the training data, we guarantee that test sentence performance is not inflated due to having included neighboring context in the training data; rather, the test data performance should be representative of realistic performance on new and previously unseen Hansard data.

For Q3, we subsample Authentic-EN parallel text once, to match the Authentic-FR training data in size, also attempting to match it in date distribution (which we expect may also serve as a proxy for matching topic distributions).[5] For the experiments that consider between 0% and 100% source side Translationese, we then subsample this Authentic-EN subsample and the Authentic-FR data.

We preprocess the data using open-source normalization and tokenization scripts from `PortageTextProcessing`.[6] Specifically, we applied `clean-utf8-text.pl` (removing control characters, standardization, etc.), followed by `fix-slashes.pl` (heuristically adding whitespace around slashes), and tokenization with `utokenize.pl -noss -lang=$lang`. We then train joint 32k byte-pair encoding (BPE) subword vocabularies on the training data (Sennrich et al., 2016),[7] and apply them to train, development, and test.

3 Models

We build Transformer (Vaswani et al., 2017) models using Sockeye-1.18.115 (Hieber et al., 2018), with 6 layers, 8 attention heads, network size of 512 units, and feedforward size of 2048 units. We have changed the default gradient clipping type to *absolute*, used source-target soft-

[3] `https://www.ourcommons.ca/`

[4] This includes both boilerplate text and full sentences.

[5] We read in the corpus chronologically, maintaining counts of Authentic-EN and FR and sampling from a Gaussian to determine whether to keep or discard incoming original-EN sentences to maintain similar counts.

[6] `https://github.com/nrc-cnrc/PortageTextProcessing`

[7] `https://github.com/rsennrich/subword-nmt`

max weight tying, an initial learning rate of 0.0002, batches of ~8192 tokens/words, maximum sentence length of 200 tokens, optimizing for BLEU, checkpoint intervals of 4000, and early stopping after 32 checkpoints without improvement. Decoding used beam size 5. Training used 4 NVIDIA V100 GPUs.

4 Experiments

4.1 Challenges and Evaluation

We measure system quality through automatic metrics: BLEU (Papineni et al., 2002) and chrF (Popović, 2015), both of which we computed using SacreBLEU (Post, 2018). We show BLEU score 95% confidence intervals using bootstrap resampling (Koehn, 2004) with 1000 iterations of sampling the full test set (with replacement). When the confidence intervals are non-overlapping, we can claim statistically significant differences between the systems, but when they overlap we cannot directly make claims about statistical significance or the lack thereof. We also perform *pairwise* bootstrap resampling, again with 1000 iterations, in order to evaluate whether improvements from one system to another are statistically significant (Koehn, 2004). Recent work has noted that BLEU score can effectively be gamed by producing more translationese-like text (Riley et al., 2020), improving automatic metric scores while decreasing quality according to human ratings. Mathur et al. (2020) observe that small improvements in metric scores may not always result in corresponding improvements in human judgments. We address this by complementing BLEU with another metric (chrF) and doing a manual (human) analysis of translation quality.

For the human evaluation, we asked annotators to perform two sets of three-way ranking tasks on a sample of test sentences produced by three different systems. We then computed average rankings of the three systems based on the human judgments.[8] Annotators viewed a source sentence, its reference translation, and were asked to rank three translations of it based on which output they found to be the best translation (semantically, grammatically, and fluency-wise).[9] There was also a free text box for optional comments. The ranking was performed using LimeSurvey,[10] and the three sentences were displayed in a random order. All annotators first completed 100 annotations for interannotator agreement; we expected this to be quite low.

We measured interannotator agreement using Cohen's kappa coefficient (κ), as in Bojar et al. (2013):

$$\kappa = \frac{P(A) - P(E)}{1 - P(E)}$$

where P(A) is the proportion of times that pairs of annotators agree on the relative ranking of pairs of systems, and P(E) is the proportion of times that they would agree by chance.[11] We find overall $\kappa = 0.25$ for EN-FR translations and $\kappa = 0.28$ for FR-EN. Such values of κ are typically interpreted as indicating "fair" agreement (Landis and Koch, 1977). If we convert the rankings into the task of labeling the *best* system, annotator agreement increases: $\kappa = 0.31$ (EN-FR) and $\kappa = 0.31$ (FR-EN). The agreement on which is the *worst* system is even stronger: $\kappa = 0.34$

[8]Annotators were adult L1/fluent speakers of the target language with knowledge (ranging from conversational to fluent) of the source language, including the authors and colleagues, five for French, four for English; all volunteer. No personally identifying information was collected.

[9]Annotators were only asked to judge sentence tuples where there were at least two unique translations of the sentence; exact matches ranked consecutively were scored as ties (such that the final ranking could be either: 1-2-3, 1-1-2, or 1-2-2). This explains why average ranks don't always sum to 6, as would be expected if all ranks were exclusive. 21 annotations where exact matches were ranked non-consecutively were dropped (out of a total of 1800 annotations, this is approximately 1%).

[10]`https://www.limesurvey.org/`

[11]κ is calculated excluding comparison of identical system outputs.

(EN-FR) and $\kappa = 0.39$ (FR-EN). The example sentence pair in Figure 1 is an extreme one, showing the worst effects of translationese training. In their qualitative assessments, annotators noted that this was a challenging ranking task, as the sentences they were judging often differed by only a few tokens; several annotators expressed a wish for a mechanism for marking ties. In many cases this was an issue of three high-quality outputs, though there were also examples of three equally-poor outputs.

As with BLEU scores, we compute 95% confidence intervals around the average rankings using bootstrap resampling of the human ranking data (Koehn, 2004) with 1000 iterations of sampling the full annotated sets with replacement. We also perform pairwise bootstrap resampling for significance.

In the following sections, we discuss both the automatic and the human rankings in greater detail, including the matter of statistical significance (via confidence intervals and pairwise bootstrap resampling), where the human and automatic metrics agree and disagree, and what trends we observe that do not rise to the level of statistical significance but which may still merit future work.

4.2 Q1: Translation Direction

We first examine the effects of translation direction in our realistic setting, considering three systems built with three different training sets: Authentic source only, Translationese source only, and finally their combination (Mixed; all available data). As we evaluate by translating Authentic source data, we expect that training on Authentic source data should be better than training on Translationese source data.

	EN→FR				FR→EN			
	Lines	BLEU ↑	chrF ↑	Human ↓	Lines	BLEU	chrF	Human
Auth. Src.	10.0M	42.8 ± 0.6	0.651	1.57	3.7M	52.0 ± 0.7	0.716	1.74
Transl. S.	3.7M	38.0 ± 0.6	0.616	2.03	10.0M	48.0 ± 0.7	0.689	1.97
Mixed	13.7M	43.0 ± 0.6	0.652	1.64	13.7M	52.0 ± 0.7	0.715	1.70

Table 1: Comparison of translation quality of systems trained on Authentic source only, Translationese source only, or the combination of the two, measured in terms of BLEU (with 95% confidence intervals) and chrF on the test data. The *Human* column reports the average ranking of the system (1 is the best, 3 is the worst). The *Lines* column shows the number of lines used in training the system.

Table 1 shows the results. As expected, in both translation directions, using Authentic source data for training outperforms using Translationese source data (by a difference of 4.8 BLEU in the EN-FR direction and by a difference of 4.0 in the FR-EN direction). This is particularly striking in the FR-EN direction: despite using more than twice as much training data (10.0M lines as compared to 3.7M), the Translationese source condition lags well behind the Authentic source condition by all metrics. We conclude that the Translationese source system is significantly worse than the Authentic source and Mixed source systems, as evidenced by the non-overlapping 95% confidence intervals and the fact that 100% of pairwise bootstrap resampling iterations found the Translationese to be worse than either system it was paired with.

The performance of training with the Mixed data is very comparable to training with only Authentic data. In the EN-FR direction, there is a difference of 0.2 BLEU in favor of the Mixed training data, while in the FR-EN direction there is a very small difference of 0.08 BLEU. According to pairwise bootstrap resampling of BLEU scores, the EN-FR Mixed system is significantly better than the Authentic only system ($p < 0.05$, with the Mixed system performing better in 95.7% of resampling instances). In the FR-EN direction, the BLEU difference between

Mixed and Authentic is not statistically significant. In the EN-FR direction, chrF also shows a small gain for the Mixed training data, while in the FR-EN direction, the Authentic source has a very small advantage.

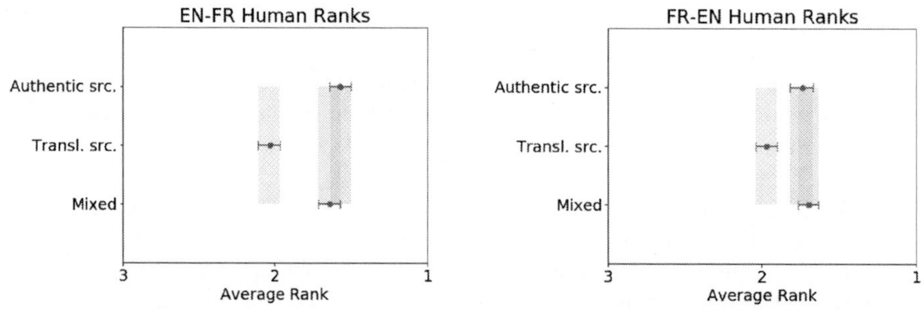

(a) English–French

(b) French–English

Figure 2: Confidence intervals (shaded for visibility) for average human-annotated rank (rank 3 is worst and rank 1 is best) for systems corresponding to Table 1.

We turn to human evaluation, where for systems in Table 1, we have 395 (EN-FR) and 498 (FR-EN) annotations respectively. We found that the human rankings agreed with the automatic metrics in terms of which system was consistently worst: the Translationese source system. As evidenced by the distinctly non-overlapping 95% confidence intervals in Figure 2 and via pairwise bootstrap resampling with $p = 0.05$, human judgments (like automatic metrics) judge the Translationese source model to be significantly worse than each of the other two. This result contrasts with Riley et al. (2020).

Annotators disagreed slightly with automatic metrics in terms of ranking Authentic source and Mixed source, but we note that the differences between those scores (both automatic and human) were quite small. For EN-FR, automatic scores scored the Mixed source best by 0.2 BLEU and 0.001 chrF, while human judgments scored Authentic source systems as best by an average rank difference of 0.07. For FR-EN, BLEU had Authentic and Mixed source tied, while chrF had Authentic source edging out Mixed by a difference of 0.001; human rankings favored the Mixed by 0.04. While these results are not *statistically* significant (for human rankings), they do raise questions about the effects of the ratio of Authentic and Translationese source data, which we examine in more detail in Section 4.4.

When testing the above systems on Translationese source test data, we observe results similar to the ones discussed here: in that setting, systems trained on Translationese source perform better than systems trained on Authentic or Mixed data. However, since our primary interest is in the more realistic task setting of translating Authentic source data, we do not further discuss these results here.

We note that the data is unbalanced, with much more Authentic English source than Authentic French source, due to the distribution of language as spoken in the House of Commons. The fact that using Authentic source training data performs better when translating Authentic source test data than Translationese source data (even when there is *much* more Translationese source data) indicates that translation direction does matter.

4.3 Q2: Tagging Translation Direction

Having observed through automatic and human metrics that the translation direction does matter, we turn to the question of tagging translation direction (with a special "<translationese>" tag at the start of the source sentence for source-Translationese sentences), to see if this will enable the Mixed data systems to make better use of all available information. Tagging has been shown to be effective in multilingual (Johnson et al., 2017; Rikters et al., 2018) and multi-domain (Kobus et al., 2017) systems, as well as when using backtranslated data (Caswell et al., 2019). All of these systems for Q2 make use of the full 13.7M line training set.

	EN→FR			FR→EN		
	BLEU ↑	chrF ↑	Human ↓	BLEU	chrF	Human
Mixed	43.0 ±0.6	0.652	1.81	52.0 ±0.7	0.715	1.85
Tagged Mixed	43.0 ±0.6	0.653	1.72	52.6 ±0.7	0.720	1.67
Tagged Mixed+mixdev	43.1 ±0.6	0.653	1.78	52.9 ±0.7	0.722	1.75

Table 2: BLEU and chrF scores for training with Mixed data, untagged and tagged (the latter with Authentic source validation or Mixed validation). We indicate if a system is tagged through the addition of "Tagged" in the system name, while untagged systems are unmarked. The untagged systems here are the same Mixed systems shown in Table 1.

Table 2 shows our results. The effect of tagging is stronger in the FR-EN translation direction, where simply adding tags results in a BLEU score increase of 0.6 (chrF increase of 0.005). We recall that the Authentic FR source data is much smaller than the Authentic EN source, so we hypothesize that tagging allows the system to take better advantage of the two types of data. In the other translation direction, where Authentic EN source already comprises the majority of the training data, we observe minimal changes when applying tagging.

The Mixed (untagged) and initial Tagged Mixed experiments are performed with a validation set that consists only of Authentic source data. This raises the question of whether that is adequate to make the most of the information contained in the tags, or whether using a Tagged Mixed validation set (with 1461 lines Authentic-EN source, and 539 lines Authentic-FR source) might be better. We refer to this system that uses the Tagged Mixed validation set as "Tagged Mixed+mixdev" in Table 2. In the FR-EN direction, we see an additional 0.3 BLEU improvement when using the Tagged Mixed+mixdev (0.002 chrF improvement). In the other direction, we see a small 0.1 BLEU improvement and no corresponding change in chrF. In the EN-FR direction, where Authentic data was already the majority, we do not find any significant BLEU score differences between the various tagged and untagged systems. However, in the FR-EN direction, both the Tagged Mixed and Tagged Mixed+mixdev systems are found to be significantly better in terms of BLEU than the Mixed (untagged) system, according to pairwise bootstrap resampling (with 100% of samples showing this to be the case). Paired bootstrap resampling also finds that in the FR-EN direction the Tagged Mixed+mixdev system is significantly better in terms of BLEU than the Tagged Mixed system ($p < 0.05$, with 98.6% of the samples showing this result).

Human evaluation provides additional insight. For Table 2 systems, we collected rankings for 391 (EN-FR) and 495 (FR-EN) source sentences and their translation triplets, respectively. We first note that in both translation systems, we observe the same pattern: Tagged Mixed is ranked best, followed by Tagged Mixed+mixdev, with Mixed (untagged) ranked worst. In the English–French direction, none of the average human system rankings differ significantly, which is unsurprising given how close they are to one another, as shown in Figure 3a. This matches the automatic metrics and our intuitions: Authentic English source makes up the majority of the Mixed training data, and we already observed that Authentic and Mixed translation systems performed quite similarly in this direction. In the French–English direction, shown in Figure 3b, we do not find a significant difference in human rankings between the the two tagged systems (Tagged Mixed and Tagged Mixed+mixdev). However, based on pairwise bootstrap resampling, the human annotators rank both tagged systems (Tagged Mixed and Tagged

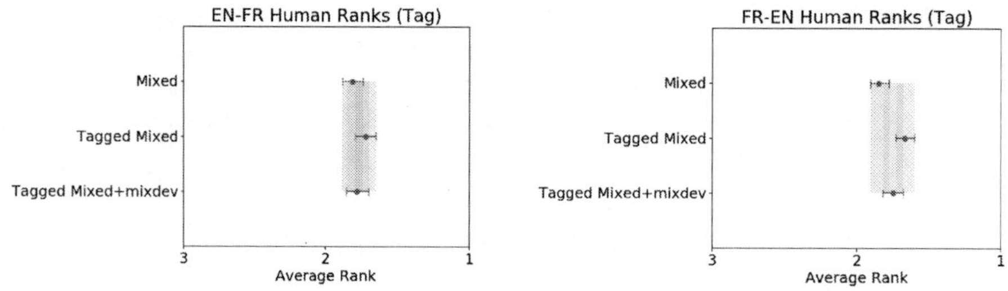

(a) English–French (b) French–English

Figure 3: Confidence intervals (shaded for visibility) for average human-annotated rank (rank 3 is worst and rank 1 is best) for systems corresponding to Table 2 (effects of tagging).

Mixed+mixdev) significantly higher than the (untagged) Mixed system. This is partially in agreement with the results on BLEU, but may merit more exploration.

The significant improvement in human ranking by adding tagging (FR-EN) suggests that in a scenario where the Authentic source data makes up a minority of the training data, it is beneficial to add direction tags. When Authentic data makes up the majority of the training data, it does not *hurt* to add direction tags, but it does not appear to significantly help. We examine this in a controlled experiment in Section 4.4.

4.4 Q3: Proportion of Source Translationese

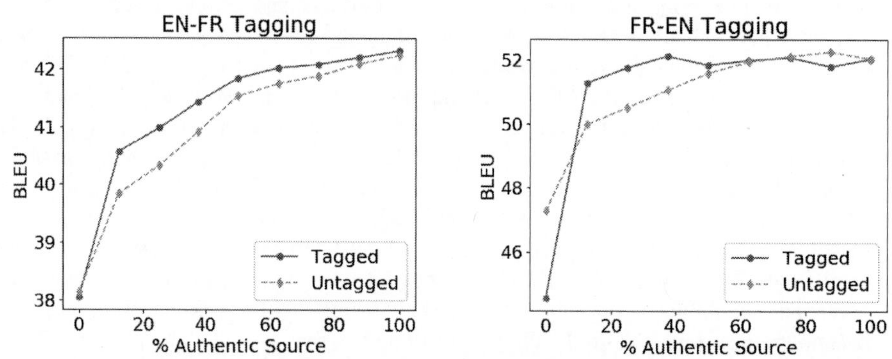

(a) English–French (b) French–English

Figure 4: Effect of tagging and percentage of Authentic source data.

In our previous experiments, we maintained a fixed ratio of Authentic and source Translationese, matching the true distribution of our dataset. We now examine what happens when we vary the ratio of Authentic to Translationese source data, maintaining a fixed corpus size. This is a moderate resource setting with 3.7M lines.[12] We vary the proportion of Authentic training data from 0% to 100% (by steps of 12.5%) and build translation systems in both directions, both tagged and untagged, using Authentic source validation sets. As we see in Figure 4, translation quality on Authentic source test data increases as the percentage of Authentic source training

[12]As described in Section 2, this consists of all Authentic French source and a sample of Authentic English source, subsampled to vary proportions.

data increases. Below 50%, tagging clearly helps bridge the gap, but the importance of tagging decreases as the percentage of Authentic source training data increases. This trend matches our earlier intuitions. In the English–French direction (Figure 4a), the gap is greatest at 12.5% (i.e., tagging provides the most additional benefit), and shrinks as it approaches in 100%. In the French–English direction (Figure 4b), the story is similar, though the two approaches appear to converge around 50%.[13] Thus we would argue that tagging translation direction is worth considering in situations where the "matching" translation direction (Authentic source) makes up the minority of the data, though it may still have some benefits at higher percentages.

5 Conclusion

We have shown that in a moderate-resource setting with high-quality translations in training data, training on Authentic-source data or Tagged Mixed-source data is preferred over training on Translationese-source or Mixed (untagged) source data, by both automatic metrics and human judgments. This is in contrast with the findings of Riley et al. (2020), who found that BLEU scores could be "gamed" to produce higher scores with translationese-like output, while being judged to be worse by human annotators. This raises questions for future work, such as whether Translationese training effects may vary depending on the quality of the parallel text, the proportion of Translationese data, and the size of the training data, or whether differences in experimental setup and human annotation may also come into play. Future work could examine these issues across a wider range of language pairs and domains, as well as directly comparing known translation direction with automatically predicted translation direction.

Acknowledgments

We thank the anonymous reviewers for their comments and suggestions and Gabriel Bernier-Colborne and Cyril Goutte for feedback and discussion. We thank the volunteer annotators for their time and assistance. This work was done as part of a collaboration with the Canadian Translation Bureau and was funded in part by Public Services and Procurement Canada.

References

Bogoychev, N. and Sennrich, R. (2019). Domain, translationese and noise in synthetic data for neural machine translation. *CoRR*, abs/1911.03362.

Bojar, O., Buck, C., Callison-Burch, C., Federmann, C., Haddow, B., Koehn, P., Monz, C., Post, M., Soricut, R., and Specia, L. (2013). Findings of the 2013 Workshop on Statistical Machine Translation. In *Proceedings of the Eighth Workshop on Statistical Machine Translation*, pages 1–44, Sofia, Bulgaria. Association for Computational Linguistics.

Caswell, I., Chelba, C., and Grangier, D. (2019). Tagged back-translation. In *Proceedings of the Fourth Conference on Machine Translation (Volume 1: Research Papers)*, pages 53–63, Florence, Italy. Association for Computational Linguistics.

Hieber, F., Domhan, T., Denkowski, M., Vilar, D., Sokolov, A., Clifton, A., and Post, M. (2018). The sockeye neural machine translation toolkit at AMTA 2018. In *Proceedings of the 13th Conference of the Association for Machine Translation in the Americas (Volume 1: Research Papers)*, pages 200–207, Boston, MA. Association for Machine Translation in the Americas.

[13] We do note, in the French–English direction, that the tagged 0% system performs surprisingly poorly; we expect this is due to chance initialization issues, rather than anything specifically to do with the tags, which *should* have no effect in that scenario.

Johnson, M., Schuster, M., Le, Q. V., Krikun, M., Wu, Y., Chen, Z., Thorat, N., Viégas, F., Wattenberg, M., Corrado, G., Hughes, M., and Dean, J. (2017). Google's multilingual neural machine translation system: Enabling zero-shot translation. *Transactions of the Association for Computational Linguistics*, 5:339–351.

Kobus, C., Crego, J., and Senellart, J. (2017). Domain control for neural machine translation. In *Proceedings of the International Conference Recent Advances in Natural Language Processing, RANLP 2017*, pages 372–378, Varna, Bulgaria. INCOMA Ltd.

Koehn, P. (2004). Statistical significance tests for machine translation evaluation. In *Proceedings of the 2004 Conference on Empirical Methods in Natural Language Processing*, pages 388–395, Barcelona, Spain. Association for Computational Linguistics.

Kurokawa, D., Goutte, C., and Isabelle, P. (2009). Automatic detection of translated text and its impact on machine translation. In *In Proceedings of MT-Summit XII*, pages 81–88.

Landis, J. R. and Koch, G. G. (1977). The measurement of observer agreement for categorical data. *Biometrics*, 33(1):159–174.

Ma, X. (1999). Parallel text collections at linguistic data consortium. In *Machine Translation Summit VII, Singapore*.

Marie, B., Rubino, R., and Fujita, A. (2020). Tagged back-translation revisited: Why does it really work? In *Proceedings of the 58th Annual Meeting of the Association for Computational Linguistics*, pages 5990–5997, Online. Association for Computational Linguistics.

Mathur, N., Baldwin, T., and Cohn, T. (2020). Tangled up in BLEU: Reevaluating the evaluation of automatic machine translation evaluation metrics. In *Proceedings of the 58th Annual Meeting of the Association for Computational Linguistics*, pages 4984–4997, Online. Association for Computational Linguistics.

Papineni, K., Roukos, S., Ward, T., and Zhu, W.-J. (2002). Bleu: a method for automatic evaluation of machine translation. In *Proceedings of the 40th Annual Meeting of the Association for Computational Linguistics*, pages 311–318, Philadelphia, Pennsylvania, USA. Association for Computational Linguistics.

Popović, M. (2015). chrF: character n-gram f-score for automatic MT evaluation. In *Proceedings of the Tenth Workshop on Statistical Machine Translation*, pages 392–395, Lisbon, Portugal. Association for Computational Linguistics.

Post, M. (2018). A call for clarity in reporting BLEU scores. In *Proceedings of the Third Conference on Machine Translation: Research Papers*, pages 186–191, Belgium, Brussels. Association for Computational Linguistics.

Rikters, M., Pinnis, M., and Krišlauks, R. (2018). Training and adapting multilingual NMT for less-resourced and morphologically rich languages. In *Proceedings of the Eleventh International Conference on Language Resources and Evaluation (LREC-2018)*, Miyazaki, Japan. European Languages Resources Association (ELRA).

Riley, P., Caswell, I., Freitag, M., and Grangier, D. (2020). Translationese as a language in "multilingual" NMT. In *Proceedings of the 58th Annual Meeting of the Association for Computational Linguistics*, pages 7737–7746, Online. Association for Computational Linguistics.

Sennrich, R., Haddow, B., and Birch, A. (2016). Improving neural machine translation models with monolingual data. In *Proceedings of the 54th Annual Meeting of the Association for Computational Linguistics (Volume 1: Long Papers)*, pages 86–96, Berlin, Germany. Association for Computational Linguistics.

Sominsky, I. and Wintner, S. (2019). Automatic detection of translation direction. In *Proceedings of the International Conference on Recent Advances in Natural Language Processing (RANLP 2019)*, pages 1131–1140, Varna, Bulgaria. INCOMA Ltd.

Vaswani, A., Shazeer, N., Parmar, N., Uszkoreit, J., Jones, L., Gomez, A. N., Kaiser, L. u., and Polosukhin, I. (2017). Attention is all you need. In Guyon, I., Luxburg, U. V., Bengio, S., Wallach, H., Fergus, R., Vishwanathan, S., and Garnett, R., editors, *Advances in Neural Information Processing Systems 30*, pages 5998–6008. Curran Associates, Inc.

Investigating Softmax Tempering for Training Neural Machine Translation Models

Raj Dabre raj.dabre@nict.go.jp
Atsushi Fujita atsushi.fujita@nict.go.jp
National Institute of Information and Communications Technology,
3-5 Hikaridai, Seika-cho, Soraku-gun, Kyoto, 619-0289, Japan

Abstract

Neural machine translation (NMT) models are typically trained using a softmax cross-entropy loss where the softmax distribution is compared against the gold labels. In low-resource scenarios, NMT models tend to perform poorly because the model training quickly converges to a point where the softmax distribution computed using logits approaches the gold label distribution. Although label smoothing is a well-known solution to address this issue, we further propose to divide the logits by a temperature coefficient greater than one, forcing the softmax distribution to be smoother during training. This makes it harder for the model to quickly over-fit. In our experiments on 11 language pairs in the low-resource Asian Language Treebank dataset, we observed significant improvements in translation quality. Our analysis focuses on finding the right balance of label smoothing and softmax tempering which indicates that they are orthogonal methods. Finally, a study of softmax entropies and gradients reveals the impact of our method on the internal behavior of our NMT models.

1 Introduction

Neural machine translation (NMT) (Sutskever et al., 2014; Bahdanau et al., 2015) enables end-to-end training of translation models and is known to give state-of-the-art results for a large variety of language pairs. NMT for high-resource language pairs is straightforward: choose an NMT architecture and implementation, and train a model on all existing data by minimizing the softmax cross-entropy loss, i.e., cross-entropy between the softmax distribution and the label distribution typically represented with a one-hot vector. In contrast, for low-resource language pairs, this does not work well due to the inability of neural networks to generalize from small amounts of data. One reason for this is over-fitting (Zoph et al., 2016; Koehn and Knowles, 2017), where the softmax distribution (sparse vector) ends up resembling the label distribution (one-hot vector).

There are several solutions that address this issue, of which the two most effective ones are transfer learning and model regularization. Transfer learning can sometimes be considered as data regularization and comes in the form of monolingual or cross-lingual (multilingual) fashion (Zoph et al., 2016; Song et al., 2019), pseudo-parallel data generation (back-translation) (Sennrich et al., 2016), or multi-task learning (Eriguchi et al., 2017). On the other hand, model regularization techniques place constraints on the learning of model parameters in order to aid the model to learn robust representations that positively impact model performance. Among existing model regularization methods, dropout (Srivastava et al., 2014) is most commonly used and is known to be effective regardless of the size of data. Label smoothing (Szegedy et al., 2016) is another effective approach that uses smoothed label vectors as opposed to one-hot label vectors. Previous work on NMT has shown that label smoothing is very effective in low-resource settings (Sennrich and Zhang, 2019) and we believe that this deserves further study. We thus focus on a technique that does not need additional data and can complement dropout and label smoothing in an extremely low-resource situation.

In this paper, we propose to apply *softmax tempering* (Hinton et al., 2015) to the training of NMT models. Softmax tempering is realized by dividing the pre-softmax logits with a positive real number greater than 1.0. This leads to a smoother softmax probability distribution, which is then used to compute the cross-entropy loss. Softmax tempering has been devised and used regularly in knowledge distillation (Hinton et al., 2015; Kim and Rush, 2016) and model calibration (Guo et al., 2017) albeit for different purposes. We regard softmax tempering as a means of deliberately making the softmax distribution noisy during training with the expectation that this will have a positive impact on the final translation quality. It is especially important to note that calibration involves tempering after a model has been trained whereas we perform tempering during training.

We primarily evaluate the utility of softmax tempering on extremely low-resource settings involving English and 11 languages in the Asian Languages Treebank (ALT) (Riza et al., 2016). Our experiments reveal that softmax tempering with a reasonably high temperature improves the translation quality. Furthermore, greedy-search performance of models trained with softmax tempering becomes comparable to or better than the beam-search performance of models that are trained without softmax tempering. Our analysis focuses on the orthogonality of softmax tempering and label smoothing. We additionally compare these methods with the related softmax entropy maximization method (Pereyra et al., 2017). Finally, we analyze the impact of softmax tempering on the softmax distributions and on the gradient flows during training.

2 Related Work

The method presented in this paper is a training technique aimed to improve the quality of NMT models in low-resource scenarios.

Work on knowledge distillation (Hinton et al., 2015) for training compact models is highly related to our application of softmax tempering. However, the purpose of softmax tempering for knowledge distillation is to smooth the student and teacher distributions which is known to have a positive impact on the quality of student models. In our case, we use softmax tempering to make softmax distributions noisy during training a model from scratch to avoid over-fitting. In the context of NMT, Kim and Rush (2016) conducted experiments with softmax tempering. However, their focus was on model compression and they did not experiment with low-resource settings. Softmax tempering is also used in model calibration (Guo et al., 2017; Kumar and Sarawagi, 2019), where the temperature coefficient is optimized on the development set in order to penalize overconfident predictions, which is a common practice in low-resource settings. While model calibration is performed after a model is trained, we use softmax tempering during training.

We regard softmax tempering as a regularization technique, since it adds noise to NMT model training. Thus, it is related to techniques, such as L_N regularization (Ng, 2004), dropout (Srivastava et al., 2014), and tuneout (Miceli Barone et al., 2017). The most important aspect of our method is that it is only applied at the softmax layer whereas other regularization techniques add noise to several parts of the entire model. Label smoothing (Szegedy et al., 2016), which is known to help low-resource NMT (Sennrich and Zhang, 2019), is highly related to our idea, where the key difference is that label smoothing affects the label distributions whereas softmax tempering affects the softmax distributions. On a related note, softmax entropy maximization (Pereyra et al., 2017) seeks to mitigate overconfident predictions but is not known to work well for NMT. Our method is intended to complement these techniques, i.e., label smoothing and softmax entropy maximization, and not necessarily replace them.

Existing methods effective for low-resource language pairs include data augmentation via back-translating additional monolingual data (Sennrich et al., 2016), exploitation of multilingualism (Firat et al., 2016; Zoph et al., 2016; Dabre et al., 2019), and pre-training on monolingual data (Devlin et al., 2019; Song et al., 2019; Mao et al., 2020). These require more training time and resources, while ours does not.

3 Softmax Tempering

Softmax tempering (Hinton et al., 2015) consists of two tiny changes in the implementation of the training phase of any neural model used for classification.

Assume that $D_i \in \mathbb{R}^V$ is the logit output of the decoder for the i-th word prediction in the target language sentence, Y_i, where V stands for the target vocabulary size, and that $P_i = P(Y_i|Y_{<i}, X) = softmax(D_i)$ represents the softmax function producing the probability distribution, where X and $Y_{<i}$ indicate the given source sentence and the past decoder output, respectively. Let $R_i \in \mathbb{R}^V$ be the label-smoothed reference label for the i-th prediction. Then, the cross-entropy loss for the prediction is computed as $\mathcal{L}_i = -\langle \log(P_i), R_i \rangle$, where $\langle \cdot, \cdot \rangle$ is the inner product of two vectors.

Let $T \in \mathbb{R}_+$ be the temperature hyper-parameter. Then, the prediction with softmax tempering (P_i^{temp}) and the corresponding cross-entropy loss ($\mathcal{L}_i^{temp}$) are formalized as follows.

$$P_i^{temp} = P^{temp}(Y_i|Y_{<i}, X) = softmax(D_i/T), \quad (1)$$

$$\mathcal{L}_i^{temp} = -\langle \log(P_i^{temp}), R_i \rangle \cdot T \quad (2)$$

By referring to Equation (1), when T is greater than 1.0, the logits, D_i, are down-scaled which leads to a smoother probability distribution before loss is computed. The smoother the distribution becomes, the higher its entropy is and hence the more uncertain the prediction is. Because loss is to be minimized, back-propagation will force the model to generate logits to counter the smoothing effect of temperature. During decoding with a model trained in this way, the temperature coefficient is also used which mitigates overconfident predictions[1] stemming from tempering during training.

The gradients are altered by tempering, and we thus re-scale the loss by the temperature as shown in Equation (2). This is inspired by the loss scaling method used in knowledge distillation (Hinton et al., 2015), where both the student and teacher's softmax distributions are tempered and the loss is multiplied by the square of the temperature.

4 Experiments

To evaluate the effectiveness of softmax tempering, we conducted experiments on both low-resource and high-resource settings.

4.1 Datasets

We experimented with the Asian Languages Treebank (ALT),[2] comprising English (En) news articles consisting of 18,088 training, 1,000 development, and 1,018 test sentences manually translated into 11 Asian languages: Bengali (Bn), Filipino (Fil), Indonesian (Id), Japanese (Ja), Khmer (Km), Lao (Lo), Malay (Ms), Burmese (My), Thai (Th), Vietnamese (Vi), and Chinese

[1] This is characterized by sharp probability distributions where the most probable word has an extremely high probability value approaching 1.0.

[2] http://www2.nict.go.jp/astrec-att/member/mutiyama/ALT/ALT-Parallel-Corpus-20190531.zip

(Zh). We focused on translation to and from English to each of these 11 languages. As a high-resource setting, we also experimented with the WMT 2019 English-to-German (En→De) translation task.[3] For training, we used the Europarl and the ParaCrawl corpora containing 1.8M and 37M sentence pairs, respectively. For evaluation, we used the WMT 2019 development and test sets consisting of 2,998 and 1,997 lines, respectively.

4.2 Implementation Details

We evaluated softmax tempering on top of the Transformer model (Vaswani et al., 2017), which gives the state-of-the-art results for NMT. More specifically, we employed the following models.

- En→XX and XX→En "Transformer Base" models where XX is an Asian language.
- En→De "Transformer Base" and "Transformer Big" models.

We modified the code of the Transformer model in the tensor2tensor v1.14.[4] For "Transformer Base" and "Transformer Big" models, we used the hyper-parameter settings in *transformer_base_single_gpu* and *transformer_big_single_gpu*, respectively. Label smoothing of 0.1 was used. We used the internal sub-word tokenization mechanism of tensor2tensor with separate source and target language vocabularies of size 8,192 and 32,768 for low-resource and high-resource settings, respectively.

We trained our models for each of the softmax temperature values, 1.0 (default softmax), 1.2, 1.4, 1.6, 1.8, 2.0, 3.0, 4.0, 5.0, and 10.0. We used early-stopping on the BLEU score (Papineni et al., 2002) for the development set which was evaluated every 1k iterations. Our early-stopping mechanism halts training when the BLEU score does not improve over 10 consecutive evaluation steps. For decoding, we averaged the final 10 checkpoints, and evaluated beam search and greedy search. Note that the training time temperature coefficient was used during decoding as well. If this is not done then the softmax distributions will be extremely sharp and beam search will collapse to greedy search.

4.3 Evaluation Criteria

We evaluated translation quality of each model using BLEU (Papineni et al., 2002) provided by *SacreBLEU* (Post, 2018).[5] The optimal temperature (T_{opt}) for the tempered model was determined based on greedy-search BLEU score on the development set, given that beam- and greedy-search score improvements are almost always correlated. We therefore used these optimal temperature models to perform beam search, where the beam width (among 2, 4, 6, 8, 10, and 12) and length penalty (among 0.6, 0.7, 0.8, 0.9, 1.0, 1.1, 1.2, 1.3, and 1.4) were tuned on the development set. We performed statistical significance testing[6] to determine if differences in BLEU are significant.

4.4 Results in Low-Resource Settings

Table 1 shows the greedy- and beam-search BLEU scores along with the optimal temperature (T_{opt}) for translation to and from Asian languages and compare them against those obtained by non-tempered models. In most cases, the greedy-search BLEU scores of the best performing tempered models are higher than the beam-search BLEU scores of non-tempered models.

Figure 1 shows how the greedy- and beam-search results vary with the temperature, taking Ms→En and Id→En translation tasks as examples. As the temperature is raised, both the greedy- and beam-search BLEU scores increase peaking between a temperature of 3.0 and 5.0.

[3] http://www.statmt.org/wmt19/translation-task.html

[4] https://github.com/tensorflow/tensor2tensor

[5] https://github.com/mjpost/sacrebleu, BLEU+case.mixed+numrefs.1+smooth.exp+tok.13a+version.1.5.0

[6] https://github.com/moses-smt/mosesdecoder/blob/master/scripts/analysis/bootstrap-hypothesis-difference-significance.pl

T	Decoding	En→XX										
		Bn	Fil	Id	Ja	Km	Lo	Ms	My	Th	Vi	Zh
1.0	Greedy	3.5	24.3	27.4	13.4	19.3	11.5	31.5	8.3	13.7	24.0	10.4
1.0	Beam	4.1	25.8	28.7	15.0	21.3	13.0	32.6	9.1	15.9	26.5	12.1
T_{opt}	Greedy	4.5	25.7	29.5†	15.5	20.7	11.8	33.7†	9.3	15.6	25.8	12.9†
T_{opt}	Beam	**4.7**	**27.0**†	**30.2**†	**17.5**†	**22.3**†	**13.3**†	**34.7**†	**10.6**†	**17.4**†	**27.5**†	**15.1**†
Value for T_{opt}		5.0	3.0	4.0	4.0	5.0	5.0	4.0	5.0	5.0	3.0	5.0
T	Decoding	XX→En										
		Bn	Fil	Id	Ja	Km	Lo	Ms	My	Th	Vi	Zh
1.0	Greedy	7.1	22.2	25.1	8.7	14.9	9.8	27.4	7.8	10.5	19.4	9.4
1.0	Beam	8.5	24.0	26.3	9.9	16.4	11.9	28.5	9.3	12.4	20.9	10.8
T_{opt}	Greedy	9.1	24.7	27.5†	11.0†	16.8	11.4	29.7†	11.7†	12.2	21.3	11.5
T_{opt}	Beam	**10.4**†	**26.3**†	**28.2**†	**12.9**†	**18.0**†	**12.9**†	**30.3**†	**13.3**†	**13.7**†	**22.1**†	**12.9**†
Value for T_{opt}		5.0	5.0	3.0	5.0	4.0	5.0	4.0	4.0	4.0	4.0	5.0

Table 1: BLEU scores for the ALT En→XX and XX→En tasks, where XX is one of the Asian languages in the ALT dataset, obtained by non-tempered ($T = 1.0$) and tempered ($T = T_{opt}$) NMT models with greedy and beam search. Best BLEU scores are in bold. "†" marks scores that are significantly ($p < 0.05$) better than non-tempered model's beam-search scores.

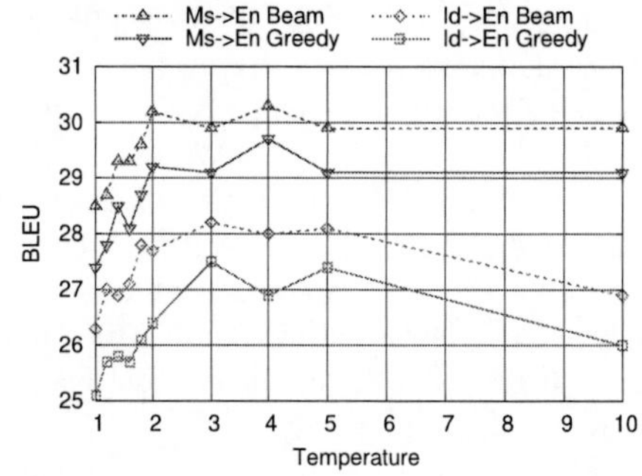

Figure 1: Improvement of greedy- and beam-search BLEU scores with temperature for the Ms→En and Id→En translation tasks.

While the gap between greedy- and beam-search scores was around 1.3 for a temperature of 1.0 (non-tempered), it narrows down to about 0.8 for temperatures which give the best greedy-search score. Furthermore, the best beam-search score almost always corresponds with the best greedy-search score which justifies our choice of the optimal temperature based on greedy-search performance. However, increasing the temperature beyond 10.0 always has a negative effect on the translation quality, because it leads to an excessively smoothed distribution, quantified by high entropy, that does not seem to be useful for NMT training. Consequently, we conclude that training with reasonably high temperature (between 3.0 and 5.0), softmax tempering has a positive impact on translation quality for extremely low-resource settings.

4.5 Results in High-Resource Settings

Table 2 gives the BLEU scores for the high-resource En→De translation task. The results indicate that compared to the low-resource settings, relatively lower temperature values are effective for improving translation quality. Greedy and beam search respectively improve by 0.8 to 2.3 BLEU points for temperature values around 1.2 to 1.4. For the models trained only on the Europarl corpus (EP), the greedy- and beam-search performances of the Transformer Base model starts approaching those of the Transformer Big model. However, when the very large ParaCrawl corpus is used (PC), the gains are around 1.0 BLEU and thus the impact of tempering

Model	Training	T	BLEU	
			Greedy	Beam
Base	EP	1.0	23.6	25.8
		1.4	25.5	**27.6**†
	PC	1.0	28.2	29.2
		1.2	29.1	**30.3**†
Big	EP	1.0	26.8	29.4
		1.2	29.1	**30.2**†
	PC	1.0	32.7	33.7
		1.2	33.6	**34.7**†

Table 2: BLEU scores for the En→De task obtained by non-tempered ($T = 1.0$) and tempered ($T = T_{opt}$) NMT models exclusively trained on Europarl (EP) and ParaCrawl (PC) corpora.

appears to reduce as corpora sizes increase. Using higher temperature values deteriorates translation quality and thus we do not recommend using high temperature values in high-resource settings. This happens presumably because the larger corpora sizes (cf. ALT corpora) enable data regularization and do not need model regularization. Overall, these experiments show that softmax tempering is very important in low-resource settings but not that important in high-resource settings. Note that we did not use any advanced methods, such as back-translation or ensembling, since our focus here was to examine the effectiveness of softmax tempering. In the future, we will explore the impact of softmax tempering on these advanced methods along with a study of how optimal temperatures vary with corpora sizes.

4.6 Impact on Training and Decoding Speed

Although training with softmax tempering makes it difficult for a model to over-fit the label distributions, we did not notice any large impact on the training time. This indicates that the improvements are unrelated to longer training times. With regard to decoding, in low-latency settings, we can safely use greedy search with tempered models given that it is as good as, if not better than, beam search using non-tempered models. Thus, by comparing the greedy- and beam-search decoding speeds, we can determine the benefits that softmax tempering brings in low-latency settings. Greedy-search decoding of the Vi→En[7] test set requires 37.6s on average, whereas beam search with beam sizes of 4 and 10 require 56.4s and 138.2s, respectively. For non-tempered models, where beam-search scores are higher than greedy-search scores by over 2.0 BLEU points, and the best BLEU scores are obtained using beam sizes between 4 and 10. Given the improved performance with greedy search, we can decode anywhere from 1.5 to 3.5 times faster. This also justifies our decision to choose optimal temperature using greedy-search scores. Subjecting softmax tempering to model compression methods, such as weight pruning, might further reduce decoding time.

5 Analysis and Further Exploration

Softmax tempering directly manipulates the softmax distribution making it noisy (smoother). In this section, we explore the relationship between softmax tempering and its closest related methods that directly affect the softmax distribution, i.e., label smoothing and entropy maximization. We also study the internal working of the softmax-tempered models during training. For these analyses, we focus on extremely low-resource settings, since our results in Section 4.5 demonstrate that softmax tempering is less impactful in high-resource settings. We especially take Bn→En, Ja→En, Ms→En, and Vi→En as examples due to lack of space. We focus on the models with optimal hyper-parameters determined via a grid search on greedy-search BLEU scores on the development set, and report on greedy-search BLEU scores on the test set.

[7] For ALT tasks, decoding times are very similar when translating into English due to it being a multi-parallel corpus.

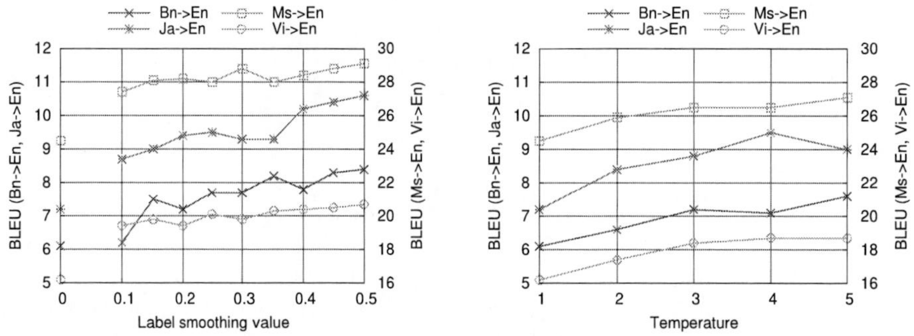

Figure 2: Independent investigation of impact of label smoothing and softmax tempering. On the left, label smoothing value, S, is varied from 0.1 to 0.5 in increments of 0.05 without softmax tempering (i.e., $T = 1.0$). In contrast, on the right, temperature value for softmax tempering, T, is varied from 1 to 5 in increments of 1 without label smoothing (i.e., $S = 0$).

Config.	Bn→En		Ja→En		Ms→En		Vi→En	
	BLEU	(T, S)	BLEU	(T, S)	BLEU	(T, S)	BLEU	(T, S)
Default	7.1	(1.0, 0.1)	8.7	(1.0, 0.1)	27.4	(1.0, 0.1)	19.4	(1.0, 0.1)
LS	8.4	(1.0, 0.5)	10.6	(1.0, 0.5)	29.1	(1.0, 0.5)	20.7	(1.0, 0.5)
Temp.	9.1	(5.0, 0.1)	11.0	(5.0, 0.1)	29.7	(4.0, 0.1)	21.3	(4.0, 0.1)
Temp. & LS	**9.4**	(5.0, 0.5)	**11.8**	(5.0, 0.5)	**30.1**	(5.0, 0.45)	**22.1**	(4.0, 0.45)

Table 3: Results of empirically searching the optimal values of softmax tempering and label smoothing. For each configuration, we present the greedy-search BLEU score and the hyper-parameter set (T for softmax tempering and S for label smoothing) that gives the score.

5.1 Softmax Tempering vs. Label Smoothing

Label smoothing (LS) involves using a smoothed reference label vector instead of a one-hot vector. Let S $(0 \leq S \leq 1)$ be the amount of smoothing, where 0 indicates no smoothing. Then the label-smoothed vector contains a value of $(1 - S) + \frac{S}{V}$ in the position corresponding to the correct word and a value of $\frac{S}{V}$ elsewhere, where V is the size of the vocabulary. This prevents the softmax from being sharp which is known to have a strong impact on the final performance (Szegedy et al., 2016; Sennrich and Zhang, 2019). To this end, we first show how the individual impacts of LS and softmax tempering and then we show how they can be effectively combined for the best translation quality. Note that the results in the previous section were obtained using LS of 0.1 which is the default value in tensor2tensor.

The left figure in Figure 2 shows the effect of increasing the LS value (S) from 0.1 to 0.5 in increments of 0.05 for models trained without softmax tempering. BLEU scores for $S = 0.1$ are those in Table 1. We also give scores for $S = 0$ for reference. It is clear that $S = 0$ gives the worst BLEU scores indicating the fundamental importance of LS. Increasing the LS value leads to a general improvement in BLEU which peaks for an LS value of 0.5. Even though we did not test, LS values greater than 0.5 may give better results. On the other hand, the right figure in Figure 2 shows the effect of increasing the temperature with LS value (S) of 0, where translation quality improves with softmax tempering even without any LS. Earlier in Figure 1, we have also shown that increasing temperature while keeping $S = 0.1$ leads to an improvement in BLEU. As this may indicate complementarity between LS and softmax tempering, we examined their combination in further detail.

Table 3 shows that the best BLEU scores are obtained by combining softmax tempering and LS ("Temp. & LS"), along with the temperature and LS values. It also shows the scores of

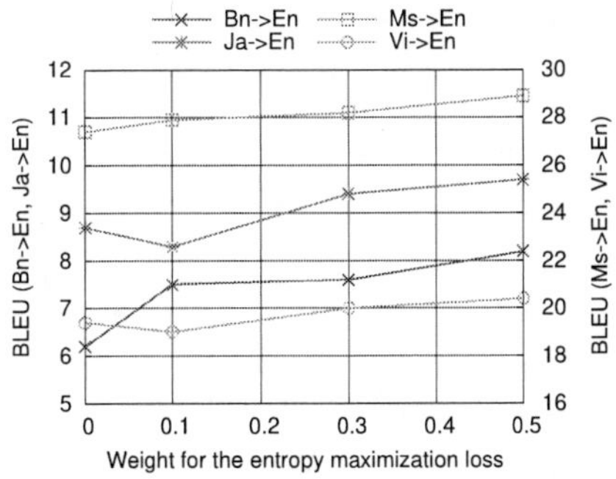

Figure 3: Effect of softmax entropy maximization on models trained without either softmax tempering (default temperature of 1.0) or fixed label smoothing (default value of 0.1).

the models with default LS value ($S = 0.1$) and no tempering ("Default"), best label-smoothed models ("LS") without softmax tempering, and the best softmax tempered models with a fixed LS value of $S = 0.1$ ("Temp.") for reference. Consistently with the results in Figure 2, using high values of temperatures and LS individually lead to better results compared to using no tempering and low values of LS. High values of LS, e.g., $[0.4, 0.5]$, can also lead to translations whose quality approaches those of the best tempered models with a low value of LS ($S = 0.1$). However, softmax tempering is often slightly, if not significantly, better than LS. Ultimately, their combination gives a further improvement in translation quality ranging from 0.3 to 1.0 BLEU points. Even when combining, the best temperature and LS values are between 3.0 to 5.0 and 0.4 to 0.5, respectively. These results show that while increased LS can significantly improve translation quality, softmax tempering is what pushes the translation quality to its limit. Nevertheless, the importance of LS should not be discounted because the combination of softmax tempering and LS is consistenty better than softmax tempering, even if by a small amount, for all translation directions we experimented with.

5.2 Softmax Tempering vs. Softmax Entropy Maximization

Softmax entropy maximization (SEM) is a method to penalize overconfident predictions by producing smoother softmax distributions (Pereyra et al., 2017) which should help in mitigating over-fitting issues prevalent in NMT. As this method directly affects the softmax and has the opposite impact of tempering, we consider its comparison with tempering to be important. SEM can be done by an additional loss which can be combined with the cross-entropy loss. Let P_i be the softmax distribution (regardless of tempering). Then the negative softmax entropy, $\mathcal{L}_{\text{NSE}} = \langle \log(P_i), \log(P_i) \rangle$, is regarded as a loss, which is combined with the cross-entropy loss, $\mathcal{L}_{\mathcal{X}}$. For instance, one can define the final loss to be minimized by linearly interpolating them with a weight w ($0 \leq w \leq 1$) as $\mathcal{L} = w \cdot \mathcal{L}_{\text{NSE}} + (1 - w) \cdot \mathcal{L}_{\mathcal{X}}$.

First, we determined whether SEM really helps or not with SEM loss weights 0.0, 0.1, 0.3, and 0.5.[8] Here, softmax tempering is not applied whereas label smoothing is performed with the default value of 0.1. As shown in Figure 3, in the absence of strong label smoothing and softmax tempering, SEM is important in these low-resource settings: improvements of 1.0 to 2.0 BLEU points can be observed. Previous research on high-resource NMT showed that SEM is not very useful (Pereyra et al., 2017) and, to the best of our knowledge, ours is the first work that confirms its importance in a low-resource setting.

Encouraged by these results, we further experimented with SEM in addition to the com-

[8]In our preliminary experiments, we observed drops in translation quality when $w > 0.5$.

Config.	Bn→En		Ja→En		Ms→En		Vi→En	
	BLEU	(T, S, w)	BLEU	(T, S, w)	BLEU	(T, S, w)	BLEU	(T, S, w)
SEM	8.2	(1.0, 0.1, 0.5)	9.7	(1.0, 0.1, 0.5)	28.9	(1.0, 0.1, 0.5)	20.4	(1.0, 0.1, 0.5)
LS & SEM	8.8	(1.0, 0.5, 0.1)	11.2	(1.0, 0.5, 0.3)	28.9	(1.0, 0.5, 0.3)	20.7	(1.0, 0.3, 0.3)
Temp. & SEM	8.8	(5.0, 0.1, 0.5)	11.5	(5.0, 0.1, 0.5)	**30.1**	(5.0, 0.1, 0.5)	21.6	(5.0, 0.1, 0.1)
Temp. & LS & SEM	**9.4**	(5.0, 0.5, 0.0)	**11.8**	(5.0, 0.5, 0.0)	**30.1**	(5.0, 0.45, 0.0)	**22.1**	(4.0, 0.45, 0.0)

Table 4: Results of empirically searching the optimal values of softmax tempering, label smoothing, and softmax entropy maximization. For each configuration, we present the greedy-search BLEU score and the hyper-parameter set (T for softmax tempering, S for label smoothing, and w for softmax entropy maximization) that gives the score.

bination of softmax tempering with T ranging from 1.0 to 5.0 (increments of 1.0) and label smoothing with S ranging from 0.1 to 0.5 (increments of 0.05). We compared four training configurations: SEM is done for default values of tempering and label smoothing ("SEM"), SEM and label smoothing is done without tempering ("LS & SEM"), tempering and SEM is done for the default label smoothing ("Temp & SEM"), and when tempering, label smoothing, and SEM are performed jointly (last row). Table 4 shows the results. When label smoothing and temperature are kept to their default values, giving a high weight to the SEM loss gives improvements of over 1.0 BLEU points as observed in Figure 3. This shows that in low-resource settings, mitigating overconfident predictions by controlling softmax predictions is crucial even if mild label smoothing is already applied. When label smoothing and SEM are combined, without tempering, the translation quality improves but the SEM loss seems to matter less as lower values for SEM loss are preferred. This indicates that these two methods might cause the model to have similar behavior and thus are not strongly complementary. In contrast, tempering and SEM seem to be complementary as high temperatures and high weights for SEM loss lead to better results. This behavior can be explained by a visualization of softmax entropy in Section 5.3. The final row shows that when tempering and label smoothing are already used, SEM is more often than not useless, i.e., the optimal SEM loss weight is 0.0. This is partially observed in Pereyra et al. (2017) where SEM was not seen to be useful in high-resource settings. Regardless of our observations, we encourage readers to duly experiment with a combination of tempering, label smoothing, and SEM when working in low-resource scenarios.

5.3 Temperature and Model Learning

We expected that tempering leads to a smoother softmax distribution and that loss minimization using such a softmax makes it sharper as training progresses. With softmax tempering, the model will continue to receive strong gradient updates even during later training stages due to the deliberate perturbation of the softmax distribution. We examined whether our model truly behaves this way through visualizing the softmax entropies and gradient values.

Figure 4 visualizes the variation of softmax entropy averaged over all tokens in a batch during training. The left-hand side shows the entropy of tempered softmax distribution in Equation (1), where there is no visible differences between charts with different values for temperature, i.e., T. Considering that the distribution is tempered with T, this indicates that the distribution of logits, D_i, is sharper when tempered with a higher T. The right-hand side plots the entropy of softmax distribution derived from the logits without dividing them by T. The lower entropies confirm that the distribution of logits is indeed sharper with higher T and that division by T as in Equation (1) counters the effect of sharpening. This means that the distribution of logits is forced to become sharper and thus confidently produce exactly one word that the model believes is the best. Pereyra et al. (2017) discouraged overconfident predictions and given that tempering does not reduce translation quality, we suspect that non-tempered models in low-

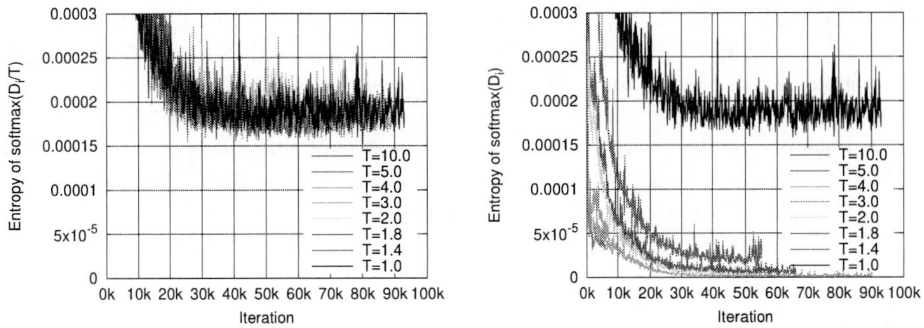

Figure 4: Variation of entropy: the left-hand side shows $softmax(D_i/T)$ in Equation (1) actually used for computing the loss during training, whereas the right-hand side shows $softmax(D_i)$ drawn for this analysis.

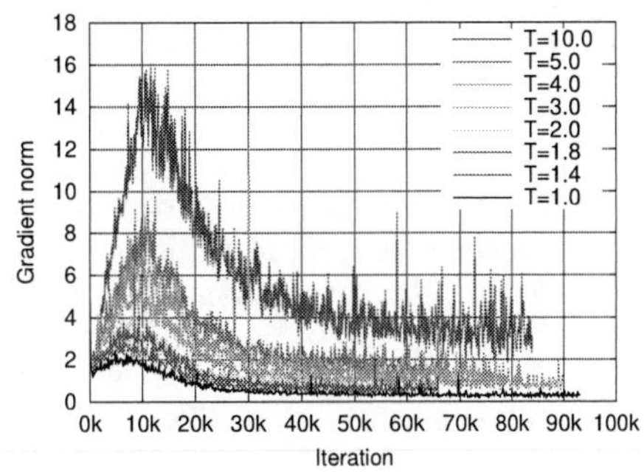

Figure 5: Global gradient norms during training models with softmax tempering.

resource settings are not confident enough. Tempering and softmax entropy maximization have opposite effects on the softmax but they combine together to give better translation quality than when they are used individually as seen in Section 5.2. The same applies for tempering and label smoothing in Section 5.1. Consequently, future efforts should focus on methods that automatically determine the appropriate levels of confidence, especially in low-resource settings.

Figure 5 shows the gradient norms during training with softmax tempering. This revealed that, similarly to ordinary non-tempered training, gradient norms in softmax tempering first increase during the warm-up phase of training and then gradually decrease. However, the major difference is that the norm values significantly decrease for the non-tempered training, whereas they are much higher for training with softmax tempering. Note that we re-scaled the loss for softmax tempering as in Equation (2), which is one reason why the gradient norms are higher. Larger gradient norms indicate that strong learning signals are being back-propagated and this will continue as long as the softmax is forced to make erroneous decisions because of higher temperature values. We can thus conclude that the noise introduced by softmax tempering and subsequent loss re-scaling strongly affect the translation quality of NMT models.

6 Conclusion

In this paper, we explored the utility of softmax tempering for training NMT models. Our experiments in low-resource and high-resource settings revealed that softmax tempering leads to an improvement in the greedy- and beam-search decoding quality. As an indirect consequence, in latency sensitive scenarios, we can use greedy search while achieving better translation quality than non-tempered models leading to 1.5 to 3.5 times faster decoding. We also explored the compatibility of softmax tempering with label smoothing and softmax entropy maximization where we showed that the combination of tempering and label smoothing is very important. We also identified settings where each method works best. Furthermore, our analysis of the softmax entropies and gradients during training confirms that tempering gives precise softmaxes while enabling the model to learn with strong gradient signals even during late training stages. In the future, we will explore the effectiveness of softmax tempering in other natural language processing tasks.

Acknowledgments

A part of this work was conducted under the commissioned research program "Research and Development of Advanced Multilingual Translation Technology" in the "R&D Project for Information and Communications Technology (JPMI00316)" of the Ministry of Internal Affairs and Communications (MIC), Japan. Atsushi Fujita was partly supported by JSPS KAKENHI Grant Number 19H05660.

References

Bahdanau, D., Cho, K., and Bengio, Y. (2015). Neural machine translation by jointly learning to align and translate. In *Proceedings of the 3rd International Conference on Learning Representations (ICLR)*, San Diego, USA. International Conference on Learning Representations.

Dabre, R., Fujita, A., and Chu, C. (2019). Exploiting multilingualism through multistage fine-tuning for low-resource neural machine translation. In *Proceedings of the 2019 Conference on Empirical Methods in Natural Language Processing and the 9th International Joint Conference on Natural Language Processing (EMNLP-IJCNLP)*, pages 1410–1416, Hong Kong, China. Association for Computational Linguistics.

Devlin, J., Chang, M.-W., Lee, K., and Toutanova, K. (2019). BERT: Pre-training of deep bidirectional transformers for language understanding. In *Proceedings of the 2019 Conference of the North American Chapter of the Association for Computational Linguistics: Human Language Technologies, Volume 1 (Long and Short Papers)*, pages 4171–4186, Minneapolis, USA. Association for Computational Linguistics.

Eriguchi, A., Tsuruoka, Y., and Cho, K. (2017). Learning to parse and translate improves neural machine translation. In *Proceedings of the 55th Annual Meeting of the Association for Computational Linguistics (Volume 2: Short Papers)*, pages 72–78, Vancouver, Canada. Association for Computational Linguistics.

Firat, O., Cho, K., and Bengio, Y. (2016). Multi-way, multilingual neural machine translation with a shared attention mechanism. In *Proceedings of the 2016 Conference of the North American Chapter of the Association for Computational Linguistics: Human Language Technologies*, pages 866–875, San Diego, USA. Association for Computational Linguistics.

Guo, C., Pleiss, G., Sun, Y., and Weinberger, K. Q. (2017). On calibration of modern neural networks. In *Proceedings of the 34th International Conference on Machine Learning*, pages 1321–1330, Sydney, Australia. JMLR.org.

Hinton, G., Vinyals, O., and Dean, J. (2015). Distilling the knowledge in a neural network. *CoRR*, abs/1503.02531.

Kim, Y. and Rush, A. M. (2016). Sequence-level knowledge distillation. In *Proceedings of the 2016 Conference on Empirical Methods in Natural Language Processing*, pages 1317–1327, Austin, USA. Association for Computational Linguistics.

Koehn, P. and Knowles, R. (2017). Six challenges for neural machine translation. In *Proceedings of the First Workshop on Neural Machine Translation*, pages 28–39, Vancouver, Canada. Association for Computational Linguistics.

Kumar, A. and Sarawagi, S. (2019). Calibration of encoder decoder models for neural machine translation. *CoRR*, abs/1903.00802.

Mao, Z., Cromieres, F., Dabre, R., Song, H., and Kurohashi, S. (2020). JASS: Japanese-specific sequence to sequence pre-training for neural machine translation. In *Proceedings of the 12th Language Resources and Evaluation Conference*, pages 3683–3691, Marseille, France. European Language Resources Association.

Miceli Barone, A. V., Haddow, B., Germann, U., and Sennrich, R. (2017). Regularization techniques for fine-tuning in neural machine translation. In *Proceedings of the 2017 Conference on Empirical Methods in Natural Language Processing*, pages 1489–1494, Copenhagen, Denmark. Association for Computational Linguistics.

Ng, A. Y. (2004). Feature selection, L1 vs. L2 regularization, and rotational invariance. In *Proceedings of the 21st International Conference on Machine Learning*, Banff, Canada. Association for Computing Machinery.

Papineni, K., Roukos, S., Ward, T., and Zhu, W.-J. (2002). BLEU: A method for automatic evaluation of machine translation. In *Proceedings of the 40th Annual Meeting on Association for Computational Linguistics (ACL)*, pages 311–318, Philadelphia, USA. Association for Computational Linguistics.

Pereyra, G., Tucker, G., Chorowski, J., Kaiser, Ł., and Hinton, G. (2017). Regularizing neural networks by penalizing confident output distributions. *CoRR*, abs/1701.06548.

Post, M. (2018). A call for clarity in reporting BLEU scores. In *Proceedings of the Third Conference on Machine Translation: Research Papers*, pages 186–191, Belgium, Brussels. Association for Computational Linguistics.

Riza, H., Purwoadi, M., Gunarso, Uliniansyah, T., Ti, A. A., Aljunied, S. M., Mai, L. C., Thang, V. T., Thai, N. P., Chea, V., Sun, R., Sam, S., Seng, S., Soe, K. M., Nwet, K. T., Utiyama, M., and Ding, C. (2016). Introduction of the Asian Language Treebank. In *Proceedings of the 2016 Conference of the Oriental Chapter of International Committee for Coordination and Standardization of Speech Databases and Assessment Technique (O-COCOSDA)*, pages 1–6, Bali, Indonesia.

Sennrich, R., Haddow, B., and Birch, A. (2016). Improving neural machine translation models with monolingual data. In *Proceedings of the 54th Annual Meeting of the Association for Computational Linguistics (ACL), Volume 1: Long Papers*, pages 86–96, Berlin, Germany. Association for Computational Linguistics.

Sennrich, R. and Zhang, B. (2019). Revisiting low-resource neural machine translation: A case study. In *Proceedings of the 57th Annual Meeting of the Association for Computational Linguistics*, pages 211–221, Florence, Italy. Association for Computational Linguistics.

Song, K., Tan, X., Qin, T., Lu, J., and Liu, T. (2019). MASS: masked sequence to sequence pre-training for language generation. In Chaudhuri, K. and Salakhutdinov, R., editors, *Proceedings of the 36th International Conference on Machine Learning*, pages 5926–5936, Long Beach, USA.

Srivastava, N., Hinton, G., Krizhevsky, A., Sutskever, I., and Salakhutdinov, R. (2014). Dropout: A simple way to prevent neural networks from overfitting. *Journal of Machine Learning Research*, 15(56):1929–1958.

Sutskever, I., Vinyals, O., and Le, Q. V. (2014). Sequence to sequence learning with neural networks. In *Proceedings of the 27th Neural Information Processing Systems Conference (NIPS)*, pages 3104–3112, Montréal, Canada. Curran Associates, Inc.

Szegedy, C., Vanhoucke, V., Ioffe, S., Shlens, J., and Wojna, Z. (2016). Rethinking the inception architecture for computer vision. In *Proceedings of IEEE Conference on Computer Vision and Pattern Recognition*, pages 2818–2826, Las Vegas, USA. Institute of Electrical and Electronics Engineers.

Vaswani, A., Shazeer, N., Parmar, N., Uszkoreit, J., Jones, L., Gomez, A. N., Kaiser, Ł., and Polosukhin, I. (2017). Attention is all you need. In *Proceedings of the 30th Neural Information Processing Systems Conference (NIPS)*, pages 5998–6008, Long Beach, USA. Curran Associates, Inc.

Zoph, B., Yuret, D., May, J., and Knight, K. (2016). Transfer learning for low-resource neural machine translation. In *Proceedings of the 2016 Conference on Empirical Methods in Natural Language Processing (EMNLP)*, pages 1568–1575, Austin, USA. Association for Computational Linguistics.

Scrambled Translation Problem: A Problem of Denoising UNMT

Tamali Banerjee tamali@cse.iitb.ac.in
Department of Computer Science and Engineering, IIT Bombay, India.

Rudra Murthy V rmurthyv@in.ibm.com
IBM Research Lab, India.

Pushpak Bhattacharyya pb@cse.iitb.ac.in
Department of Computer Science and Engineering, IIT Bombay, India.

Abstract

In this paper, we identify an interesting kind of error in the output of Unsupervised Neural Machine Translation (UNMT) systems like *Undreamt*[1]. We refer to this error type as *Scrambled Translation problem.* We observe that UNMT models which use *word shuffle* noise (as in case of Undreamt) can generate correct words, but fail to stitch them together to form phrases. As a result, words of the translated sentence look *scrambled*, resulting in decreased BLEU. We hypothesise that the reason behind *scrambled translation problem* is 'shuffling noise' which is introduced in every input sentence as a denoising strategy. To test our hypothesis, we experiment by retraining UNMT models with a simple *retraining* strategy. We stop the training of the Denoising UNMT model after a pre-decided number of iterations and resume the training for the remaining iterations- which number is also pre-decided- using original sentence as input without adding any noise. Our proposed solution achieves significant performance improvement UNMT models that train conventionally. We demonstrate these performance gains on four language pairs, *viz.*, English-French, English-German, English-Spanish, Hindi-Punjabi. Our qualitative and quantitative analysis shows that the retraining strategy helps achieve better alignment as observed by attention heatmap and better phrasal translation, leading to statistically significant improvement in BLEU scores.

1 Introduction

Training a machine translation system using only the monolingual corpora of the two languages was successfully demonstrated by (Artetxe et al., 2018c; Lample et al., 2018). They train the machine translation system using denoising auto-encoder (DAE) and backtranslation (BT) iteratively. Recently, pre-training of large language models (Conneau and Lample, 2019; Song et al., 2019; Liu et al., 2020) using monolingual corpus is used to initialize the weights of the encoder-decoder models. These encoder-decoder models are later fine-tuned using backtranslated sentences for the task of Unsupervised Neural Machine Translation (UNMT). While we appreciate language model (LM) pre-training to better initialise the models, it is important to understand the shortcomings of earlier approaches. In this paper, we explore in this direction.

[1] `https://github.com/artetxem/undreamt`

We observe that the translation quality of undreamt models (Artetxe et al., 2018c) suffers partially due to wrong positioning of the target words in the translated sentence. For many instances, though the reference sentence and its corresponding generated sentence are formed with almost the same set of words, the sequence of words is different resulting in the sentence being ungrammatical and/or loss of meaning. This results in a difference in syntax and semantic rules. We define such generated sentences as **scrambled sentences** and the problem as **scramble translation problem**. Scrambled sentences can be either **disfluent** or **fluent-but-inadequate**. Here, if the LM decoder is not learnt well, we observe disfluent translations. If the LM decoder is learnt well, we observe fluent-but-inadequate translations. An example of fluent-but-inadequate translation will be *'leaving better kids for our planet'* instead of *'leaving better planet for our kids'*. Due to this phenomenon, during BLEU computation n-gram matching lessens, for $n > 1$. However, this error is absent in translation generated from recent state-of-the-art systems (Conneau and Lample, 2019; Song et al., 2019; Liu et al., 2020).

We hypothesise, DAE introduces uncertainty to the previous UNMT (Lample et al., 2018; Artetxe et al., 2018c, 2019; Wu et al., 2019) models, specifically to the encoders. It has been observed that encoders are sensitive to the exact ordering of the input sequence (Michel and Neubig, 2018; Murthy V et al., 2019; Ahmad et al., 2019). By performing random word-shuffle in all the source sentences, encoder may lose important information about the sentence composition. The DAE fails to learn informative representation which affects the decoder resulting in wrong translations generated.

If our hypothesis is true, retraining these previous UNMT system models with noise-free sentences as input should resolve the problem for previous systems (Artetxe et al., 2018c; Lample et al., 2018). Moreover, using this retraining strategy will not benefit recent approaches (Conneau and Lample, 2019; Song et al., 2019) as they do not shuffle words of input sentence while training with back-translated data.

In this paper, we prove our hypothesis by showing that a simple **retraining strategy** mitigates the 'scrambled translation problem'. We observe consistent improvements in BLEU score and word-alignment over the denoising UNMT approach by Artetxe et al. (2018c) for four language pairs. We do not wish to beat the state-of-the-art UNMT systems with pre-training, instead, we demonstrate a limitation of previous denoising UNMT (Artetxe et al., 2018c; Lample et al., 2018) systems and prove why it happens.

2 Related Work

Neural machine translation (NMT) (Cho et al., 2014; Sutskever et al., 2014; Bahdanau et al., 2015) typically needs lot of parallel data to be trained on. However, parallel data is expensive and rare for many language-pairs. To solve this problem, unsupervised approaches to train machine translation (Artetxe et al., 2018c; Lample et al., 2018; Yang et al., 2018) was proposed in the literature which uses only monolingual data to train a translation system.

Artetxe et al. (2018b) and Lample et al. (2018) introduced denoising-based U-NMT which utilizes cross-lingual embeddings and trains a RNN-based encoder-decoder model (Bahdanau et al., 2015). Architecture proposed by Artetxe et al. (2018c) contains a shared encoder and two language-specific decoders while architecture proposed by Lample et al. (2018) contains a shared encoder and a shared decoder. In the approach by Lample et al. (2018), the training starts with word-by-word translation followed by denoising and backtranslation. Here, noise in the input sentences in the form of shuffling of words and deletion of random words from sentences was performed.

Conneau and Lample (2019) (XLM) proposed a two-stage approach for training a UNMT system. The pre-training phase involves training of the model on the combined monolingual corpora of the two languages using Masked Language Modelling (MLM) objective (Devlin et al., 2019). The pre-trained model is later fine-tuned using denoising auto-encoding objective and backtranslated sentences. Song et al. (2019) proposed a sequence to sequence pre-training strategy. Unlike XLM, the pre-training is performed via MAsked Sequence to Sequence (MASS) objective. Here, random ngrams in the input is masked and the decoder is trained to generate the missing ngrams in the pre-training phase. The pre-trained model is later fine-tuned using backtranslated sentences.

Murthy et al. (2019) demonstrated that LSTM encoders of the NMT system are sensitive to the word-ordering of the source language. They considered the scenario of zero-shot translation from language l_3 to l_2. They train a NMT system for $l_1 \rightarrow l_2$ languages and use l_1 - l_3 languages bilingual embeddings. This enables the trained model to perform zero-shot translation from $l_3 \rightarrow l_2$. However, if the word-order of the languages l_1 and l_3 are different, the translation quality from l_1 - l_3 is hampered.

Michel and Neubig (2018) have also made a similar observation albeit in the monolingual setting. They observe that accuracy of the machine translation system gets adversely affected due to noise in the input sentences. They discuss various sources of noise with one of them being word emission/insertion/repetition or grammatical errors. The lack of robustness to such errors could be attributed to the sequential processing of LSTM or Transformer encoders. As the encoder processes the input as a sequence and generates encoder representation at each time-step, such errors would lead to bad encoder representations resulting in bad translations generated. Similar observations have also been made by Ahmad et al. (2019) for cross-lingual transfer of dependency parsing. They observe that self-attention encoder with relative position representations is more robust to word-order divergence and enable better cross-lingual transfer for dependency parsing task compared to RNN encoders.

3 Baseline Approach

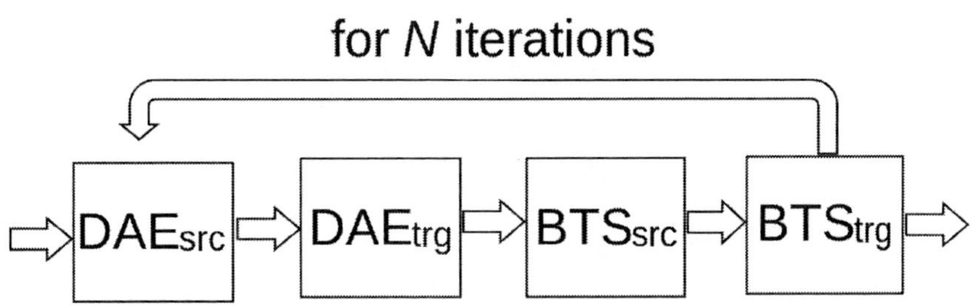

Figure 1: Our baseline training procedure: Undreamt. DAE_{src}: Denoising of source sentences; DAE_{trg}: Denoising of target sentences; BTS_{src}: Training with shuffled back-translated source sentences; BTS_{trg}: Training with shuffled back-translated target sentences.

We use Undreamt (Artetxe et al., 2018c) which is one of the previous UNMT approaches as the baseline for experimentation. Artetxe et al. (2018c) introduced denoising-based U-NMT which utilize cross-lingual embeddings and train a RNN-based encoder-decoder architecture Bahdanau et al. (2015). This architecture contains a shared encoder and two language-specific decoders. Training is a combination of denoising and back translation iteratively as shown in Fig. 1. By adding noise Artetxe et al. (2018c) meant shuffling of words of a sentence. Here, shuffling is performed by swapping neighboring words *l/2* times, where *l* is the number of words in the sentence. 4 sub-tasks of the training mechanism are listed below. (i) DAE_{src}: Denoising of source sentences in which we train shared-encoder, source-decoder, and attention with noisy source sentence as input and original source sentence as output. (ii) DAE_{trg}: Denoising of target sentences which trains shared-encoder, target-decoder and attention with noisy target sentence as input and original target sentence as output. (iii) BTS_{src}: Training shared-encoder, target-decoder, and attention with shuffled back-translated source sentences as input and actual target sentences as output. (iv) BTS_{trg}: Training shared-encoder, source-decoder, and attention with shuffled back-translated target sentences as input and actual source sentences as output. Here, shuffling is performed by swapping neighboring words *l/2* times, where *l* is the number of words in the sentence.

For completeness, we also experimented with XLM UNMT (Conneau and Lample, 2019) with initialise the model with MLM objective followed by finetuning it with DAE and BT iteratively. In this approach, they do not add noise with the input sentence while training with backtranslated data.

4 Proposed Retraining Strategy

Our proposed strategy to train a denoising-based UNMT system consists of two phases. In the first phase, we proceed with training using denoised sentences similar to the baseline system (Artetxe et al., 2018c) for *M* number of iterations. Adding random shuffling in the input side, however, could introduce uncertainty to the model leading to inconsistent encoder representations. To overcome this, in the second phase, we retrain the model with simple AE and on-the-fly BT using sentences with the correct ordering of words for *(N-M)* iterations as shown in Fig. 2. Here, N is the total number of iterations and $M < N$. More concretely, this training approach consists of 4 more sub-processes other than the 4 subprocesses of the baseline system. These are: (v) AE_{src}: Auto-encoding of source sentences in which we train shared-encoder, source-decoder, and attention. (vi) AE_{trg}: Auto-encoding of target sentences in which we train shared-encoder, target-decoder, and attention. (vii) BT_{src}: Training shared-encoder, target-decoder, and attention with back-translated source sentences as input and actual target sentences as output. (viii) BT_{trg}: Training shared-encoder, source-decoder, and attention with back-translated target sentences as input and actual source sentences as output. The second phase ensures that the encoder learns to generate context representation with information about the correct ordering of words. For XLM (Conneau and Lample, 2019), we add these 4 subprocesses only with fine-tuning step. We do not change anything in LM pretraining step.

5 Experimental Setup

We test our hypothesis with undreamt as a previous approach and XLM as a SOTA approach. We applied our *retraining strategy* on both the approaches and observed the result.

For undreamt, we have used monolingual data of six languages, *i.e.* English (en), French (fr), German (de), Spanish (es), Hindi (hi), and Punjabi (pa). Among these languages, Hindi and Punjabi are of SOV word-order where the other four languages are of SVO word order. In our experiments, we choose language-pairs such that the word-order of source language matches with that of target language. We have used the NewsCrawl corpora for en, fr, de of WMT14, and for es of WMT13. For hi-pa, we use Wikipedia dumps of the august 2019 snapshot for training. The en-fr and en-de models are tested using WMT14 test-data and en-es models using WMT13 test-data, and hi-pa models using ILCI test data (Jha, 2010).

We have preprocessed the corpus for normalization, tokenization and lowercasing using the scripts available in *Moses* (Koehn et al., 2007) and *Indic NLP Library* (Kunchukuttan, 2020), for BPE segmentation using *subword-NMT* (Sennrich et al., 2016) with number of merge operations set to 50k.

We use the monolingual corpora to independently train the embeddings for each language using skip-gram model of *word2vec* (Mikolov et al., 2013). To map embeddings of two languages

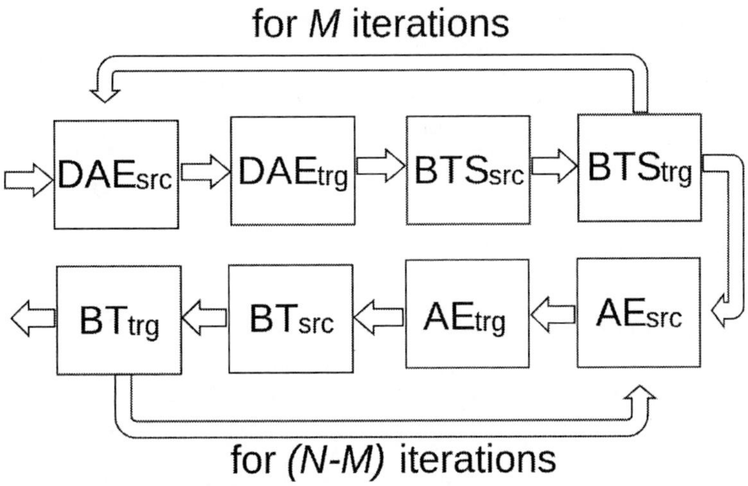

Figure 2: Workflow of Proposed training procedure. DAE_{src}: Denoising of source sentences; DAE_{trg}: Denoising of target sentences; BTS_{src}: Training with shuffled back-translated source sentences; BTS_{trg}: Training with shuffled back-translated target sentences; AE_{src}: Autoencoding of source sentences; AE_{trg}: Autoencoding of target sentences; BT_{src}: Training with shuffled back-translated source sentences; BT_{trg}: Training with shuffled back-translated target sentences.

to a shared space, we use *Vecmap*[2] by Artetxe et al. (2018a).

We use *undreamt*[3] tool to train the UNMT system proposed by Artetxe et al. (2018c). We train the baseline model untill convergence and noted the number of steps N required to reach convergence. We now train our proposed system for $N/2$ steps and re-train the model after removing denoising noise for the remaining $N/2$ steps. They converge between 500k to 600k steps depending on the language pairs. Further details of dataset and network parameters are available in Appendix.

We also report results on *XLM*[4] approach (Conneau and Lample, 2019). XLM employs two-stage training of UNMT model. The pre-training stage trains encoder and decoder with masked language modeling objective. The retraining stage employs denoising along with iterative back-translation. However, XLM uses a different denoising (word shuffle) mechanism compared to Artetxe et al. (2018c). We replace the denoising mechanism by Conneau and Lample (2019) with the denoising mechanism used by Artetxe et al. (2018c). We use the pre-trained models for English-French, English-German, and English-Romanian provided by Conneau and Lample (2019). We retrain the XLM model until convergence using the denoising approach which makes the baseline system. We later retrain the pre-trained XLM model using our proposed approach where we remove the denoising component after $N/2$ steps.

We report both BLEU scores and n-gram BLEU scores using *multi-bleu.perl* of Moses. We have tested statistical significance of BLEU improvements (Koehn, 2004). To analyse the systems, we have produced heatmaps of attention generated by the models.

[2]https://github.com/artetxem/vecmap

[3]https://github.com/artetxem/undreamt

[4]https://github.com/facebookresearch/XLM

Language Pairs	Baseline (Undreamt)	Retrain with AE+BT†
en→fr	15.23	**17.05**
fr→en	15.99	**16.94**
en→de	6.69	**8.03**
de→en	10.67	**11.66**
en→es	15.09	**16.97**
es→en	15.33	**17.12**
hi→pa	22.39	**28.61**
pa→hi	28.38	**33.59**

(a) The translation performance using Undreamt-baseline and Undreamt-retraining on en-fr, en-de, en-es, hi-pa test sets (BLEU scores reported).

Language Pairs	Baseline (XLM)	Retrain with AE+BT
en→fr	**33.24**	31.94
fr→en	**31.34†**	30.79
en→de	25.06	25.02
de→en	30.53	30.34
en→ro	31.37	**31.72**
ro→en	29.01	**29.96†**

(b) The translation performance using XLM-baseline and XLM-retraining on en-fr, en-de, en-ro test sets (BLEU scores reported).

Table 1: The Translation performance using the Baseline approach and our Approach. Trained for a total of N iterations for all approaches. *Undreamt* and *XLM* results are results from our replication using the code provided by the authors. † indicates statistically significant improvements using paired bootstrap re-sampling (Koehn, 2004) for a p-value less than 0.05 .

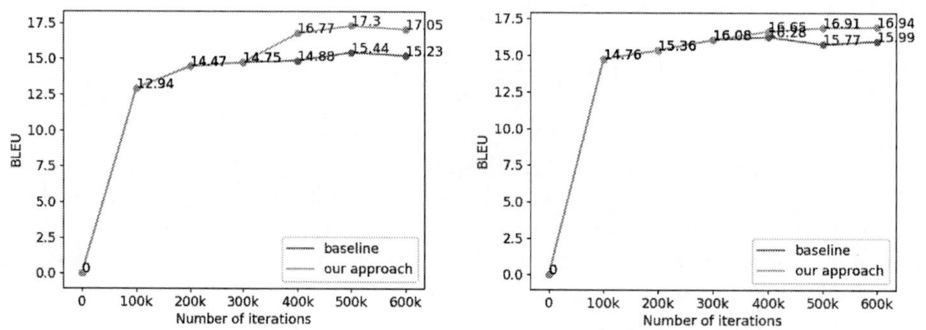

(a) English → French

(b) French → English

Figure 3: Change in translation accuracy using undreamt-baseline vs. our approach with increasing number of iterations for English-French (BLEU scores reported).

6 Results and Analysis

Table 1 reports BLEU score of the trained models using the undreamt (Artetxe et al., 2018c) and XLM (Conneau and Lample, 2019) and retraining them with our approach. *Undreamt* and *XLM* results are results from our replication using the code provided by the authors. In Table 1a we observe that the proposed re-training strategy of AE used in conjunction with BT results in statistically significant improvements (p-value < 0.05) across all language pairs when compared to the undreamt baseline approach (Artetxe et al., 2018c).

We report results on XLM (Conneau and Lample, 2019) with our *retraining* approach in Table 1b. XLM is one of the state-of-the-art (SOTA) UNMT approaches for these language pairs. The approach by XLM (Conneau and Lample, 2019) does not add noise to the input backtranslated sentence during training. Therefore, our retraining strategy does not benefit here.

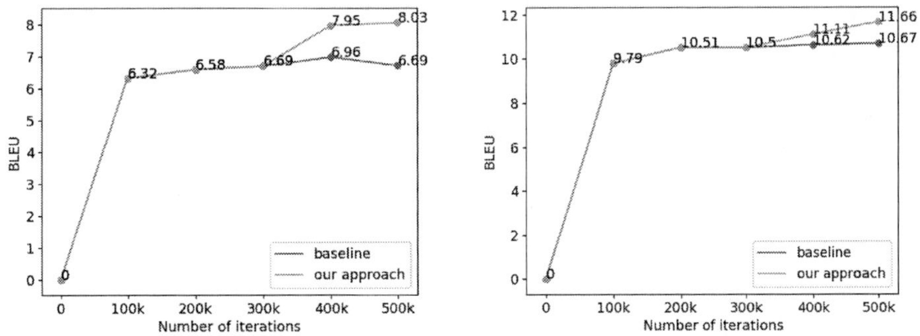

(a) English → German

(b) German → English

Figure 4: Change in translation accuracy using undreamt-baseline vs. our approach with increasing number of iterations for English-German (BLEU scores reported).

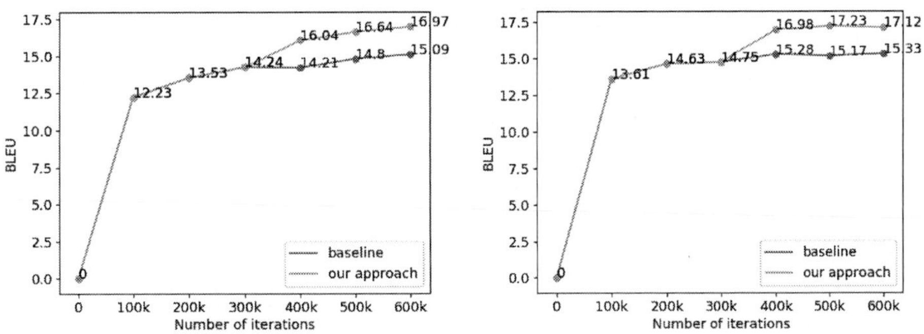

(a) English → Spanish

(b) Spanish → English

Figure 5: Change in translation accuracy using undreamt-baseline vs. our approach with increasing number of iterations for English-Spanish (BLEU scores reported).

Language Pairs	Δ **BLEU-1**	Δ **BLEU-2**	Δ **BLEU-3**	Δ **BLEU-4**
en→fr	0.00	4.50	8.85	11.67
fr→en	2.17	5.53	7.48	10.90
en→de	17.44	11.71	17.07	25.00
de→en	1.75	6.87	12.12	13.33
en→es	1.75	6.88	12.04	20
es→en	3.20	9.13	14.85	21.15
hi→pa	7.49	24.48	32.71	46.39
pa→hi	4.30	15.89	24.12	30.56

Table 2: Improvements in n-BLEU (represented in %) on using our approach over baseline for en-fr, en-de, en-es, hi-pa test sets.

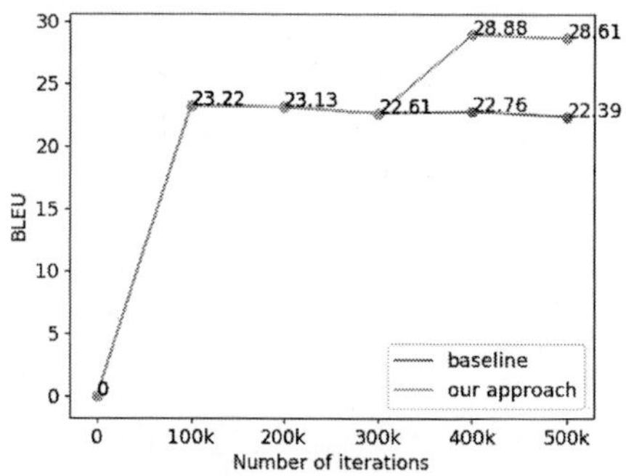

(a) Hindi → Punjabi

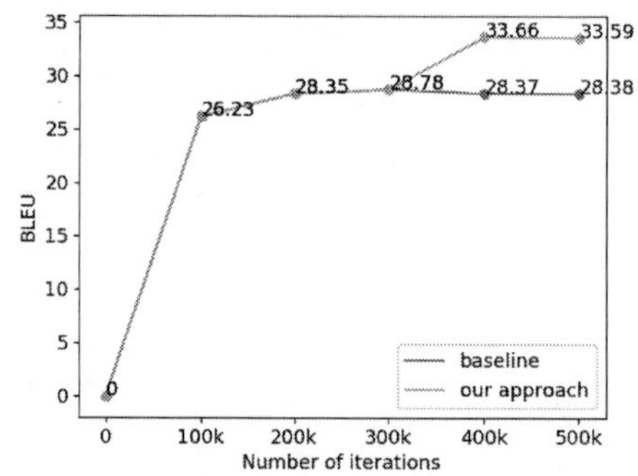

(b) Punjabi → Hindi

Figure 6: Change in translation accuracy using undreamt-baseline vs. our approach with increasing number of iterations for Hindi-Punjabi (BLEU scores reported).

German	der us-senat genehmigte letztes jahr ein 90 millionen dollar teures pilotprojekt , das 10.000 autos umfasst hätte .
English reference	the u . s . senate approved a $ 90 - million pilot project last year that would have involved about 10,000 cars .
Artetxe et al. 2018	the u . s . district of the last $ 90 million a year , it would have 10,000 cars .
Our approach	the u . s . district last year approved 90 million initiative that would have included 10,000 cars .

Figure 7: Sample translation of German → English translation models.

Punjabi	ਸੁੱਕੇ	ਅੰਗੂਰ	ਜਾਂ ਫਿਰ	ਕਿਸ਼ਮਿਸ਼	ਵਿਚ	ਪਾਣੀ	ਦੀ	ਮਾਤਰਾ	੧੫	ਪ੍ਰਤੀਸ਼ਤ	ਹੁੰਦੀ ਹੈ	।
(Word transliteration)	suke	agUra	jAM phira	kisamisa	vicha	pANI	dI	mAtarA	15	pratIsata	hudI hai	|
(Word-to-word translation)	dry	grapes	or	raisins	in	water	of	quantity	15	percent	is	.
(Sentence translation)	Dried grapes or raisins have 15 percent water content .											
Hindi reference	सूखे	अंगूर	या फिर	किशमिश	में	पानी	की	मात्रा	15	प्रतिशत	होती है	।
(Word transliteration)	sUkhe	aMgUra	yA phira	kishamisha	meM	pAnI	kI	mAtrA	15	pratishata	hotI hai	|
(Word-to-word translation)	dry	grapes	or	raisins	in	water	of	quantity	15	percent	is	.
Artetxe et al. 2018	अंगूर	या फिर	अंगूर	में	फिर से	पानी	की	मात्रा	१२	प्रतिशत	होती है	।
(Word transliteration)	aMgUra	yA phira	aMgUra	meM	phira se	pAnI	kI	mAtrA	12	pratishata	hotI hai	|
(Word-to-word translation)	grapes	or	grapes	in	again	water	of	quantity	12	percent	is	.
(Sentence translation)	The amount of water in the grape or grape again is 12 percent .											
Our approach	सूखे	अंगूर	या फिर	मालवण	में	पानी	की	मात्रा	१२	प्रतिशत	होती है	।
(Word transliteration)	sUkhe	aMgUra	yA phira	mAlavaNa	meM	pAnI	kI	mAtrA	12	pratishata	hotI hai	|
(Word-to-word translation)	dry	grapes	or	Malavan	in	water	of	quantity	12	percent	is	.
(Sentence translation)	Dried grapes or Malavan have 12 percent water content .											

Figure 8: Sample translation of Punjabi→Hindi translation models.

Spanish	el anuncio del probable descubrimiento del bosón de higgs generó una gran conmoción el verano pasado , y con razón .
English reference	the announcement of the probable discovery of the higgs boson created quite a stir last summer , and with good reason .
Artetxe et al. 2018	the likely announcement of the discovery of the higgs boson triggered a major shock last summer , and with reason .
Our approach	the announcement of the likely discovery of the higgs boson generated a major shock last summer , and with reason .

Figure 9: Sample translation of Spanish → English translation models.

We also observe robustness of the pre-trained language models to the scrambled translation problem.

Fig. 3, 4, 5 and 6 show changes in BLEU scores of intermediate UNMT models with

English	in india , china and many other countries , people work ten to twelve hours a day .
French reference	en inde , en chine et dans plein d' autres pays , on travaille dix à douze heures par jour .
Artetxe et al. 2018 (Google translation)	en inde , chine et autres pays , les autres gens travaillent à quinze heures à un jour . In India, China and other countries, other people work from fifteen to one.
Our approach (Google translation)	en inde , en chine et de nombreux autres pays , les gens travaillent quinze à douze heures un jour . In India, China and many other countries, people work fifteen to twelve hours a day .

Figure 10: Sample translation of English → French translation models.

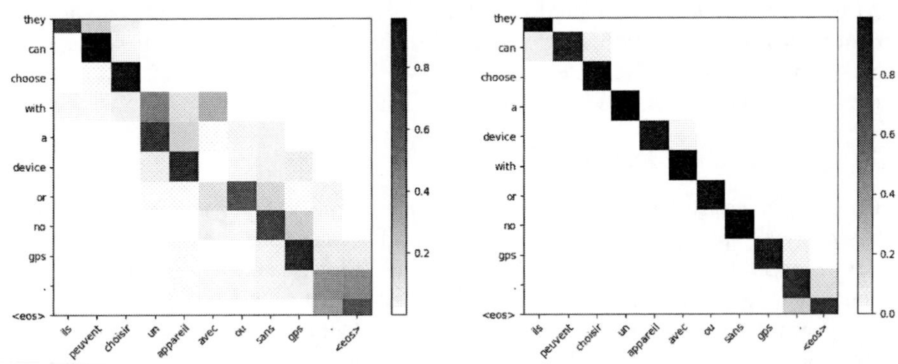

(a) Using baseline approach

(b) Using our approach

Figure 11: Attention heatmaps of a French→English translation.

increasing number of iterations on test-data. We observe that our proposed approach leads to increase in BLEU score in the re-training phase as the denoising strategy is removed. The baseline system suffers from drop in BLEU score due to denoising strategy introducing ambiguity into the model.

6.1 Quantitative analysis

We hypothesize that the baseline UNMT model using DAE is able to generate correct word translation but fails to stitch them together to generate phrases. To validate the hypothesis, we calculate the percentage improvement on using our approach over the baseline system in terms of individual n-gram (n=1,2,3,4) specific BLEU scores for each language-pair and a particular value of *n*. The results presented in Table 2 indicate that our method achieves higher improvements in n-gram BLEU for higher $n-$grams $(n > 1)$ compared to the improvement in n-gram BLEU for lower values of *n*, indicating better phrasal matching. This could be attributed to the proposed approach not suffering from the *scrambled translation problem* introduced by the DAE.

6.2 Qualitative analysis

We observe several instances where our proposed approach results in better translations compared to the baseline. On manual analysis of translation outputs generated by the baseline system, we have found out some instances of *scrambled translation problem*.

Due to uncertainty introduced by shuffling of words before training, the baseline model chooses to generate sentences that are more acceptable by a language model. Fig 7 shows such an example in our test data. Here, two German phrases *'ein 90 millionen'* (*'a 90 million'*) and *'letztes jahr'* (*'last year'*) are mixed up and translated as *'last $ 90 million a year'* in English. However, our approach handled the issue correctly.

Fig 8 shows an example of a situation where the baseline model prefers to generate a word in multiple probable positions. Here, the source Punjabi sentence consists of a phrase *'jAM phira'* (*'or'*) meaning *'yA phira'*(*'or'*) in Hindi. In the translation produced by the baseline model, the correct phrase is generated along with the word *'phira'* wrongly occurring again forming another phrase *'phira se'* (*'again'*). Note that, both the phrases are commonly used in Hindi. In Fig 9, the model trained on baseline system produced the word *'likely'*, which is a synonym of 'probably', in the wrong position. In Fig 10, the model trained on baseline system produced the word *'autres'*(*'other'*) in the multiple positions.

Attention Analysis: Attention distributions generated by our proposed systems have lesser confusion when compared with the attention distribution generated by baseline systems, as shown in Heatmaps of Fig. 11. Production of word-aligned attention distribution was easy for the attention models, which we retrained on sentences without noise.

7 Conclusion and Future work

In this paper, we addressed 'scrambled translation problem', a shortcoming of previous denoising-based UNMT approaches like *UndreaMT* approach (Artetxe et al., 2018c; Lample et al., 2018). We demonstrated that adding shuffling noise to all input sentences is the reason behind it. Our simple *retraining* strategy, *i.e.* retraining the trained models by removing the denoising component from auto-encoder objective (AE), results in significant improvements in BLEU scores for four language pairs. We observe larger improvements in n-gram specific BLEU scores for higher value of *n* indicating better phrasal translations. We also observe robustness of the pre-trained language models to the scrambled translation problem. We would also like to explore applicability of our approach in other ordering-sensitive DAE-based tasks.

References

Ahmad, W., Zhang, Z., Ma, X., Hovy, E., Chang, K.-W., and Peng, N. (2019). On difficulties of cross-lingual transfer with order differences: A case study on dependency parsing. In *Proceedings of the 2019 Conference of the North American Chapter of the Association for Computational Linguistics: Human Language Technologies, Volume 1 (Long and Short Papers)*, pages 2440–2452, Minneapolis, Minnesota. Association for Computational Linguistics.

Artetxe, M., Labaka, G., and Agirre, E. (2018a). A robust self-learning method for fully unsupervised cross-lingual mappings of word embeddings. In *Proceedings of the 56th Annual Meeting of the Association for Computational Linguistics (Volume 1: Long Papers)*, volume 1, pages 789–798.

Artetxe, M., Labaka, G., and Agirre, E. (2018b). Unsupervised statistical machine translation. In *Proceedings of the 2018 Conference on Empirical Methods in Natural Language Processing*, pages 3632–3642.

Artetxe, M., Labaka, G., and Agirre, E. (2019). An effective approach to unsupervised machine translation. In *Proceedings of the 57th Annual Meeting of the Association for Computational Linguistics*.

Artetxe, M., Labaka, G., Agirre, E., and Cho, K. (2018c). Unsupervised neural machine translation. *Proceedings of the International Conference on Learning Representations (ICLR)*.

Bahdanau, D., Cho, K., and Bengio, Y. (2015). Neural machine translation by jointly learning to align and translate. In *Proceedings of the International Conference on Learning Representations (ICLR).*

Cho, K., van Merrienboer, B., Gulcehre, C., Bahdanau, D., Bougares, F., Schwenk, H., and Bengio, Y. (2014). Learning phrase representations using rnn encoder–decoder for statistical machine translation. In *Proceedings of the 2014 Conference on Empirical Methods in Natural Language Processing (EMNLP)*, pages 1724–1734.

Conneau, A. and Lample, G. (2019). Cross-lingual language model pretraining. In *Advances in Neural Information Processing Systems*, pages 7057–7067.

Devlin, J., Chang, M.-W., Lee, K., and Toutanova, K. (2019). Bert: Pre-training of deep bidirectional transformers for language understanding. In *Proceedings of the 2019 Conference of the North American Chapter of the Association for Computational Linguistics: Human Language Technologies, Volume 1 (Long and Short Papers)*, pages 4171–4186.

Jha, G. N. (2010). The tdil program and the indian langauge corpora intitiative (ilci). In *LREC*.

Koehn, P. (2004). Statistical Significance Tests for Machine Translation Evaluation. In *Proceedings of the 2004 Conference on Empirical Methods in Natural Language Processing, EMNLP 2004.*

Koehn, P., Hoang, H., Birch, A., Callison-Burch, C., Federico, M., Bertoldi, N., Cowan, B., Shen, W., Moran, C., Zens, R., et al. (2007). Moses: Open source toolkit for statistical machine translation. In *Proceedings of the 45th annual meeting of the ACL on interactive poster and demonstration sessions*, pages 177–180. Association for Computational Linguistics.

Kunchukuttan, A. (2020). The IndicNLP Library. `https://github.com/anoopkunchukuttan/indic_nlp_library/blob/master/docs/indicnlp.pdf`.

Lample, G., Conneau, A., Denoyer, L., and Ranzato, M. (2018). Unsupervised machine translation using monolingual corpora only. *Proceedings of the International Conference on Learning Representations (ICLR).*

Liu, Y., Gu, J., Goyal, N., Li, X., Edunov, S., Ghazvininejad, M., Lewis, M., and Zettlemoyer, L. (2020). Multilingual denoising pre-training for neural machine translation. *Transactions of the Association for Computational Linguistics*, 8:726–742.

Michel, P. and Neubig, G. (2018). MTNT: A testbed for machine translation of noisy text. In *Proceedings of the 2018 Conference on Empirical Methods in Natural Language Processing*, pages 543–553, Brussels, Belgium. Association for Computational Linguistics.

Mikolov, T., Sutskever, I., Chen, K., Corrado, G. S., and Dean, J. (2013). Distributed representations of words and phrases and their compositionality. In *Advances in neural information processing systems*, pages 3111–3119.

Murthy, R., Kunchukuttan, A., and Bhattacharyya, P. (2019). Addressing word-order divergence in multilingual neural machine translation for extremely low resource languages. In *Proceedings of the 2019 Conference of the North American Chapter of the Association for Computational Linguistics: Human Language Technologies, Volume 1 (Long and Short Papers)*, pages 3868–3873, Minneapolis, Minnesota. Association for Computational Linguistics.

Murthy V, R., Kunchukuttan, A., Bhattacharyya, P., et al. (2019). Addressing word-order divergence in multilingual neural machine translation for extremely low resource languages. In *Annual Conference of the North American Chapter of the Association for Computational Linguistics*.

Sennrich, R., Haddow, B., and Birch, A. (2016). Neural machine translation of rare words with subword units. In *Proceedings of the 54th Annual Meeting of the Association for Computational Linguistics (Volume 1: Long Papers)*, volume 1, pages 1715–1725.

Song, K., Tan, X., Qin, T., Lu, J., and Liu, T.-Y. (2019). Mass: Masked sequence to sequence pre-training for language generation. In *International Conference on Machine Learning*, pages 5926–5936.

Sutskever, I., Vinyals, O., and Le, Q. V. (2014). Sequence to sequence learning with neural networks. In *Advances in neural information processing systems*, pages 3104–3112.

Wu, J., Wang, X., and Wang, W. Y. (2019). Extract and edit: An alternative to back-translation for unsupervised neural machine translation. *Proceedings of the 57th Annual Meeting of the Association for Computational Linguistics*.

Yang, Z., Chen, W., Wang, F., and Xu, B. (2018). Unsupervised neural machine translation with weight sharing. In *Proceedings of the 56th Annual Meeting of the Association for Computational Linguistics (Volume 1: Long Papers)*, pages 46–55.

Make the Blind Translator See The World: A Novel Transfer Learning Solution for Multimodal Machine Translation

Minghan Wang wangminghan@huawei.com
Jiaxin Guo guojiaxin1@huawei.com
Yimeng Chen chenyimeng@huawei.com
Chang Su suchang8@huawei.com
Min Zhang zhangmin186@huawei.com
Shimin Tao taoshimin@huawei.com
Hao Yang yanghao30@huawei.com
Huawei Translation Service Center, Beijing, China

Abstract

Based on large-scale pretrained networks, the liability to be easily overfitting with limited labelled training data of multimodal translation (MMT) is a critical issue in MMT. To this end, we propose a transfer learning solution. Specifically, 1) A vanilla Transformer is pre-trained on massive bilingual text-only corpus to obtain prior knowledge; 2) A multimodal Transformer named VLTransformer is proposed with several components incorporated visual contexts; and 3) The parameters of VLTransformer are initialized with the pre-trained vanilla Transformer, then being fine-tuned on MMT tasks with a newly proposed method named cross-modal masking which forces the model to learn from both modalities. We evaluated on the Multi30k en-de and en-fr dataset, improving up to 8% BLEU score compared with the SOTA performance. The experimental result demonstrates that performing transfer learning with monomodal pre-trained NMT model on multimodal NMT tasks can obtain considerable boosts.

1 Introduction

Transformer-based models using large-scale parallel corpora have significantly improved the performance of neural machine translation (NMT), marking an important milestone (Vaswani et al., 2017). Additionally, multimodal machine translation (MMT) incorporating image signals into RNN-based encoder-decoder shows improvements on translation quality due to the forceful disambiguation (Specia et al., 2016a). In this paper, we aim to investigate, on top of Transformer, whether the paradigm of first pretraining and then fine-tuning can be effectively applied to MMT, concretely transferring from monomodal to multimodal tasks.

Constant attention has been paid on MMT task (Specia et al., 2016a) in the Conference of Machine Translation (WMT) in recent years (2016-2018). Formally, it aims to learn a function mapping: $\mathcal{X} \times \mathcal{I} \rightarrow \mathcal{Y}$, which takes source text and an image as input and translate them into the target text as shown in Figure 1. Additional modality is to disambiguate the source sentence, with the reference of image. However, the effectiveness of the visual context has been questioned by prior work (Specia et al., 2016b; Elliott et al., 2017; Barrault et al., 2018; Caglayan et al., 2019). They show that visual context is not convincingly useful and the marginal gain is pretty modest, which is speculated to be resulted from the limitation of available datasets — the

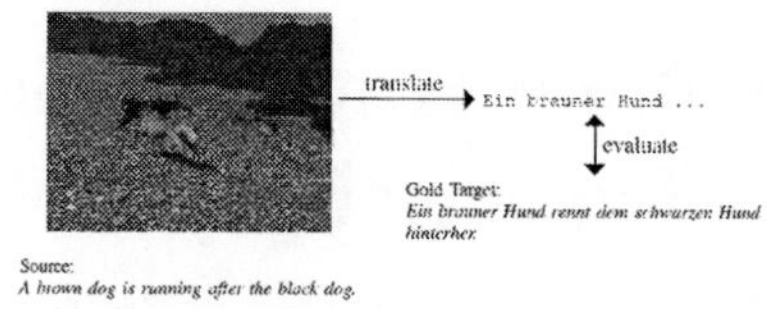

Figure 1: An example of the multimodal translation. (Specia et al., 2016b)

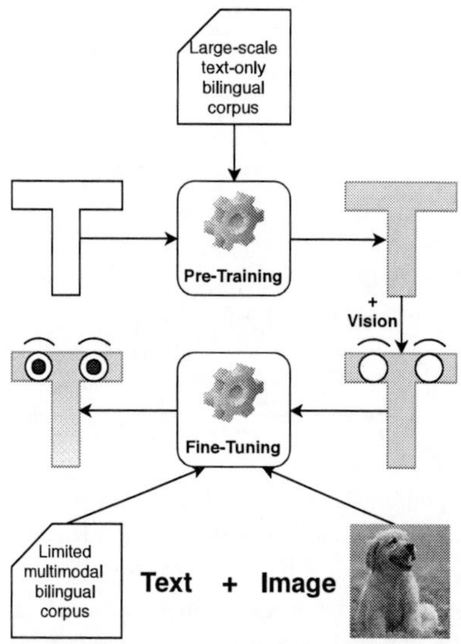

Figure 2: The multimodal transfer learning solution. 1) Initialize a vanilla Transformer. 2) Train the model with large-scale parallel corpus. 3) Add visual related components. 4) Fine-tune the model on limited multimodal corpus.

scale of parallel dataset of MMT task is not enough to train a robust MMT model. Compared with the translation corpus on news such as Common Crawl and UN corpus, commonly-used MMT dataset Multi30k (Elliott et al., 2016) is too small to train large-capacity models with millions of parameters. Therefore, it is imperative to put efforts on methods in low-resource MMT.

For the text-only NMT tasks, the Transformer (Vaswani et al., 2017) provides a novel architecture on language generation which supersedes RNN architectures rapidly with enhanced parallelizability. Meanwhile, the framework of pre-training and fine-tuning becomes a standard pipeline since BERT (Devlin et al., 2019) achieved the SOTA performances over a bunch of natural language understanding tasks. This to some extent suggests that transfer learning could effectively solve NLP tasks which requires deep understanding on the semantics but have limited size of in-domain data.

Therefore, in this paper, we will investigate whether it's feasible to apply transfer learning to MMT task, i.e. transferring the prior knowledge learned from monomodal task into a multimodal task, as shown in Figure 2. The contribution of our work can be summarized as follows:

- We propose the Visual Language Transformer (VLTransformer) which is compatible for both monomodal and multimodal inputs. The model achieves competitive results on

Multi30k En-De and En-Fr tasks.

- We present a method of fine-tuning a pretrained monomodal MT model in the multimodal MT task, which is implemented by appropriately masking elements in both modalities to encourage the model to make full use of the input information.

2 Related Work

There are a spectrum of prior works investigating MMT. (Caglayan et al., 2016; Calixto and Liu, 2017) used standard RNN encoder-decoder with attention (Bahdanau et al., 2015) to fuse textual and visual features. Both of them employed pretrained image classification models like VGG and ResNet to extract visual features and combine with textual features with different schemes of attentions. Imaginet is proposed to predict the visual feature conditioned on textual inputs, which is used to improve the quality of the representation of contexts (Elliott and Kádár, 2017), where they decompose the MMT task into two sub-tasks where each can be trained separately with large external corpus. Hirasawa et al. (2019) extends the work of Imagination by converting the decoding process into a similarity based searching between the predicted embedding and the embedding of the vocabulary, which is achieved by optimizing a marginal loss on pre-trained word embeddings with predicted word embeddings.

Besides, (Specia et al., 2016b; Elliott et al., 2017; Barrault et al., 2018) make comprehensive summaries on the MMT tasks from MMT 2016 to 2018, which shows two major findings from the task: 1). The effectiveness of the additional modality is still questionable or limited, which encourages researchers to go further on the usage of visual information. 2). Fine-grained evaluation metrics have to be adopted to evaluate the true impact of the multimodality.

There are still some impressive works built upon Transformer-based architecture. MeMAD (Grönroos et al., 2018) achieves the best performance on flickr16 and flickr17 test sets with a multimodal Transformer model, which is pre-trained on massive out of domain data including OpenSubtitles and MS-COCO captions. They perform comprehensive experiments on the model with different data and model settings. (Zhang et al., 2020) proposes the method named universal visual retrieval which builds a look up table from topic word and image with TF-IDF. Before translation, m images are retrieved from the image set. Then, visual features will be aggregated with textual features to produce the hidden states. The UMNMT proposed in (Su et al., 2019) makes it possible to train a MMT model with bilingual but non-paired corpus and images. In their work, each language has an encoder and a decoder but shares one image encoder. They use the cycle-consistency loss to train the model by translating the text into target language, then, recover it back.

In summary, many approaches are proposed to tackle the MMT task from following two direction:

- Improve the architecture of the model to make better use of visual modality.
- Leveraging external resources, monolingual or monomodal resources to enhance the performance.

However, we find that the pre-training and fine-tuning framework is under-investigated for MMT tasks, especially the cross-modal pre-training, which motivates us to explore in this work.

3 VLTransformer

First of all, we briefly review the architecture of Transformer (Vaswani et al., 2017). In the transformer, source texts are fed into the encoder and transformed into vectors with the word embedding and positional embedding, then, N layers of multi-head attention blocks are applied

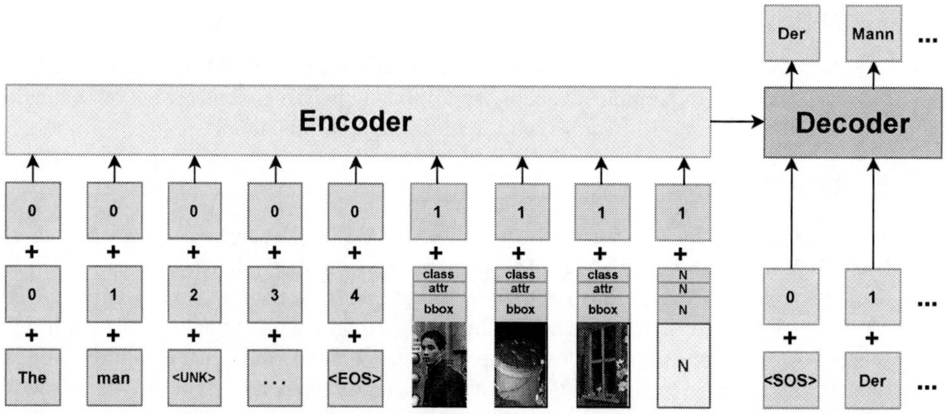

Figure 3: This figure shows the architecture of the proposed VLTransformer. For the textual inputs, three rows (from bottom to top) represent for word embedding, positional encoding and type embedding, respectively. For image inputs, two rows represent for the summation of 4 groups of transformed visual features (pooled ROI, bounding box, attributes and class) and the type embedding respectively. The decoder remains unchanged comparing with original Transformer. The $<$ unk $>$ and the N feature vector are cross-modal masks, being exclusively appears in one modality and are controlled by τ and p.

to produce the hidden states $\mathbf{H}$. For the decoder, the previously generated tokens until step t will be fed into the decoder to interact with the context $\mathbf{H}$ to predict the token of step $t+1$. More formally, the encoding and decoding process is denoted as follows:

$$\mathbf{E}_S = \text{We}_S(\mathbf{X}) + \text{Pe}_S(\mathbf{X}) \tag{1}$$

$$\mathbf{H}_S = \text{MHA}_{\text{encoder}}(\mathbf{E}_S) \tag{2}$$

$$\mathbf{E}_T = \text{We}_T(\mathbf{Y}_{[:t]}) + \text{Pe}_T(\mathbf{Y}_{[:t]}) \tag{3}$$

$$\mathbf{H}_T = \text{MHA}_{\text{decoder}}(\mathbf{E}_T, \mathbf{H}_S) \tag{4}$$

$$y_{t+1} = g(h_{T,t}) \tag{5}$$

where $\mathbf{X}$ and $\mathbf{Y}$ are source and target tokens, $\mathbf{E}_S, \mathbf{H}_S$ and $\mathbf{E}_T, \mathbf{H}_T$ represent for embeddings and hidden states of source and target texts respectively. We and Pe are word embeddings and positional embeddings. MHA represents for the Multi-head Attention blocks. y_{t+1} is the predicted token comes from the transformation of the last hidden state $h_{T,t}$.

3.1 Image Embedding

To create high quality visual features, we use the Bottom-Up and Top-Down Attention (BUTD) (Anderson et al., 2018) to extract image features. Specifically, the Bottom Up attention of BUTD is based on Faster R-CNN (Ren et al., 2015) for object detection. They pre-train the model on the Visual Genome (Krishna et al., 2017) dataset which has fine-grained labels of objects with 1600 object classes and 400 object attributes. The extracted features are used as follows in the MMT model:

$$\mathbf{V} = \phi_{\text{ROI}}(\mathbf{V}_{\text{ROI}}) + \phi_c(\mathbf{V}_c) + \phi_a(\mathbf{V}_a) + \phi_{\text{bbox}}(\mathbf{V}_{\text{bbox}}) \tag{6}$$

where the pooled ROI features are represented by $\mathbf{V}_{\text{ROI}} \in \mathbb{R}^{m \times d_{\text{ROI}}}$, $d_{\text{ROI}} = 2048$ in the experiment, m is the number of detected objects. $\mathbf{V}_c \in \mathbb{R}^{m \times 1600}$ are predicted class one-hot vectors which will be multiplied with an embedding matrix in the experiment. $\mathbf{V}_a \in \mathbb{R}^{m\times 400}$ are attribute class one-hot vectors, and the bounding boxes $\mathbf{V}_{\text{bbox}} \in \mathbb{R}^{m\times 4}$ represents for normalized coordinates (x_0, y_0, x_1, y_1) of detected objects. Coordinates are normalized into $[0, 1]$ with the size of the image, i.e. $x/x_{\text{img}}, y/y_{\text{img}}$. ϕ represents for linear transformations to scale the dimensionality along with the original Transformer d_{model}. The summation of 4 types of features simultaneously encodes most of necessary visual information, which is more fine-grained and informative comparing with previous works (Elliott and Kádár, 2017; Zhou et al., 2018; Caglayan et al., 2016) which only uses pooled ResNet (He et al., 2016) features or pooled object embeddings (Grönroos et al., 2018).

3.2 Fusion of Image and Text

In order to take the advantage of pre-trained NMT models and avoid overfitting using large-capacity network with limited multimodal labelled training data, we introduce parameters that needs to be trained from scratch as few as possible into the model. Therefore, instead of using architectures like LXMERT (Tan and Bansal, 2019) and the model proposed in (Zhang et al., 2020), where large sets of newly initialized parameters will be introduced into an independent image encoder, we share the original encoder layers of the Transformer to encode both modalities by directly concatenating the visual and the textual features. More specifically:

$$\mathbf{E}_S = \text{We}_S(\mathbf{X}) + \text{Pe}_S(\mathbf{X}) + \text{Te}(\mathbf{X}) \tag{7}$$

$$\mathbf{V} = \mathbf{V} + \text{Te}(\mathbf{V}) \tag{8}$$

$$\mathbf{E}_{S,V} = [\mathbf{E}_S; \mathbf{V}] \tag{9}$$

where the Te represents for newly introduced type embedding inspired by the Next sentence prediction (NSP) of BERT (Devlin et al., 2019), which uses 0 for text and 1 for vision. $\mathbf{E}_S$ is the replacement of Eq. 1. Finally, we concatenate embeddings of tokens and objects along the length dimension, as described in Figure 3. The sequence length becomes the summation of token number and detected objects number, $|\mathbf{E}_{S,V}| = |\mathbf{V}| + |\mathbf{E}_S|$.

In such case, we only introduce a few amount of parameters to incorporate vision features, which reduces the perturbation on the Transformer Encoder and Decoder. In the experiment, we find that this can significantly improve the training efficiency on the small dataset. In addition, compared with the cross-attention method (i.e. H=SelfAttn(Token, Vision, Vision) which maps visual information onto token representations), concatenation reserves complete contexts in both modalities for the decoder, which is not limited by the length of source sentence.

3.3 Cross Modal Masking

In experiment, compared to using text-only inputs, we find that directly fine-tuning the pre-trained transformer on multimodality inputs can't obtain extra performance boosts, which motivates us to investigate the reason behind that. Observing the attention map of encoder-decoder attention weights, we find that the model only assigns weights to text representations and entirely ignores visual information.

To force the model fully exploit both two modalities: text and image, we propose a cross modal masking (CMM) method to train the model with complementary information by partially masking out some inputs in one of any modality. Specifically, we randomly choose a modality to mask following the Bernoulli distribution, and then, randomly mask q tokens or q objects within specific modality. The masked token will be replaced by special token "¡unk¿" and the masked image region will be replaced by a noisy vector sampled from the standard normal distribution. This method is inspired by the masked language model (Devlin et al., 2019) and (Chen et al., 2020). Differently, they use the masking for unsupervised pre-training, while we use it directly in the translation task without predicting the masked place. Thus, masking here

Method	test 2016				test 2017			
	En-De		En-Fr		En-De		En-Fr	
	B	M	B	M	B	M	B	M
WMT16_MMT_Winner (Specia et al., 2016b)	34.2	53.2	-	-	-	-	-	-
WMT17_MMT_Winner (Elliott et al., 2017)	-	-	-	-	33.4	54	55.9	72.1
Imagination (Elliott and Kádár, 2017)	36.8	55.8	-	-	-	-	-	-
NMTUVR (Zhang et al., 2020)	36.94	-	57.53	-	28.63	-	48.46	-
UMONS (Delbrouck and Dupont, 2018)	40.34	59.58	62.49	76.83	32.57	53.6	55.13	71.52
MeMAD (Grönroos et al., 2018)	45.09	-	68.30	-	40.81	-	62.45	-
Pretrained Trans (baseline)	41.2	59.69	46.3	65.9	37.9	56.3	48.3	65.8
Fine-tuned Trans	45.6	62.9	65.7	79.2	42.7	60.1	60.8	75.9
VLTransformer (ours)	46.2	63.5	65.4	78.8	43.6	60.4	62.0	76.3
VLTransformer + CMM (ours)	**48.1**	**64.7**	**68.7**	**81.5**	**44.0**	**61.3**	**63.5**	**77.3**

Table 1: The experimental result of the Multi30k dataset on test-2016 and test-2017 En-De and En-Fr tasks. First six rows are results of previous works including the 2016 and 2017 winner, widely used Imagination, the 2018 MMT task participants MeMAD and UMONS, as well as the newly proposed Transformer based model NMTUVR. Last four rows are our ablation studies including the un-fine-tuned Transformer, fine-tuned Transformer and the VLTransformer with and without cross-modal masking (CMM). We can see that on 4 test sets, the VLTransformer with CMM is consistently better than the text-only model and the model trained without CMM. Note that B and M represents for BLEU and METEOR, Trans represents for Transformer.

only acts like the noise introduced in denoising autoencoder, it forces the model to learn by predicting unknown tokens and recover the corrupted vectors. We find it effectively prevents the model from neglecting visual contexts by CMM in training. See Figure 3 for more intuitive details.

4 Experiment

4.1 Dataset

In the experiment, we use the Multi30k (Elliott et al., 2016) dataset to evaluate our method. The sizes of the dataset are 29000:1014:1000:1000 for training, validation, test2016 and test2017 set, each instance in form of triples (source, target, image). English descriptions are provided as source texts, German and French corpus are provided as target texts. All corresponding images are from Flickr30k (Young et al., 2014) dataset. We use the Moses toolkit (Hoang and Koehn, 2008) to pre-process the data with lowercasing, tokenizing and punctuation normalization.

For image features, we use BUTD (Anderson et al., 2018) to extract 4 groups of features for each object, including pooled ROI feature vector, object class, object attribute and bounding box. Maximum of 36 detected objects are reserved with the prediction probability higher than 0.5. The BUTD model is not fine-tuned in the translation task.

4.2 Setup

We use the pre-trained transformer model provided by fairseq (Ott et al., 2019) which is implemented with PyTorch (Paszke et al., 2019). The En-De model (Transformer-Large) is trained on WMT'19 corpus and En-Fr (Transformer-Big) model is trained on WMT'14 corpus. Both models share the vocabulary between source and target language, resulting in sizes of 42020 and 44508 for En-De and En-Fr vocabularies. The parameters of the embedding layer as well as the output projection layer are also shared for the encoder and the decoder in both models. The BPE (Sennrich et al., 2016) is applied to create the vocabulary. The model of En-De is slightly larger (270M) than the En-Fr (222M) model, because of the difference of the dimen-

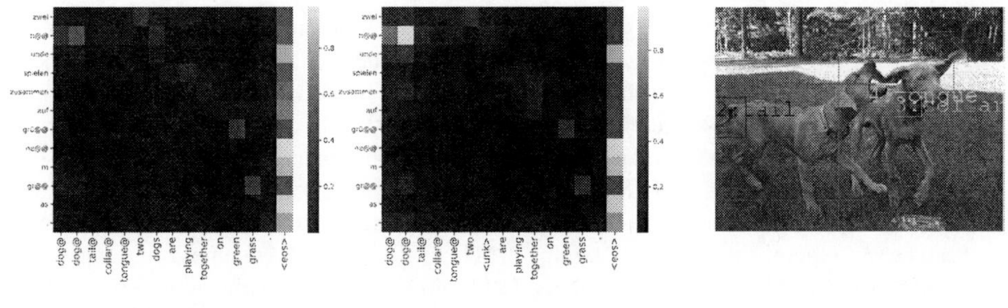

Figure 4: This figure shows an example of the attention map between source inputs and target tokens in En-De MMT translation. The X axis for left 2 plots are source inputs, where visual features are represented by the object class (token with an @ in the end, only 5 high score objects are preserved as shown in the right plot. The order for visual and text inputs are changed for more clearance). The difference between the left and the middle plot is that the **cross-modal masking is performed on the middle one** where "dog" is deliberated replaced by $<$ unk $>$. We can see that when the "dog" is masked, the model pays more attention on the visual features of two detected dogs.

sionality of the FFN block (8192 for En-De and 4096 for En-Fr). Apart from that, the En-De and En-Fr model have exactly same architectures with hidden size of 1024, 6 $\times$ encoders and 6 $\times$ decoders. The parameter size of the vision related components are 6M for both model, thereby makes the VLTransformer to have 276M and 228M parameters for En-De and En-Fr, respectively.

During fine-tuning, we use the learning-rate of 1e-4 with 4000 steps of warm-up and inverse-sqrt warm-up strategy. We use 0.3 for dropout probability, 0.1 for label smoothing (Pereyra et al., 2017), Adam (Kingma and Ba, 2015) is used as the optimizer. For the VL-Transformer, we use the parameter of fairseq pre-trained Transformer to initialize the backbone and text related embeddings, vision related parameters are initialized randomly. The model is fine-tuned on a Tesla V100 GPU with fp16 enabled and converges in less than 20 minutes for 10 epochs.

The baseline method is the pre-trained Transformer without fine-tuning. We use BLEU (Papineni et al., 2002) and METEOR (Banerjee and Lavie, 2005) as evaluation metrics with lowercased text.

5 Analysis

We compare our results with another six latest methods in Table 1. As the goal of newly-proposed NMTUVR (Zhang et al., 2020) is to improve universal NMT with multimodality, direct comparison with ours is unfair. As expectation, the pre-trained Transformer set a very strong baseline, which demonstrate that a well-trained text-only NMT model has been able to produce satisfying translations in the absence of word and phrase ambiguitity. At the same time, the profit of fine-tuning the Transformer is significant, even with only textual inputs. For the VLTransformer, the model trained without CMM is already better than the text-only method, which could demonstrates the effectiveness of visual contexts, in addition, the model trained with CMM is consistently better than the model without CMM, which demonstrates that CMM is a key point to improve the cross-modal interaction. Comparing with the MeMAD (Grönroos et al., 2018) which uses massive of external multimodal corpus (OpenSubtitles and MS-COCO), we only use the officially published training set for fine-tuning which is more efficiency.

Figure 4 is an example of the En-De translation from a VLTransformer model trained with

CMM. We filter 5 high score objects to investigate the alignment between target tokens and source inputs. There is evidence showing that the model is able to attend correct objects (i.e. two dogs) no matter the word "dog" is appeared in source texts or not (replaced by the $< \text{unk} >$ or not), which means it could translate the sentence with both modality.

Although the attention map looks good, we actually manually amplify the score of visual features, in the experiment, we find that the model is more inclined to get contextual information from text instead of image although we have already used cross-modal masking. Some reasons can be speculated: 1) The size of training data is relatively small which means the newly initialized visual related parameters can not be fully trained. 2) We investigate the extracted detected objects and find out that there are mistakes in the detection which actually leads noise into the model.

6 Conclusion

We propose a cross-modal transfer learning solution to take full advantage of pre-trained monomodal model in the multimodal task. The approach of CMM to incorporate visual information into translation achieves remarkable results in the MMT tasks evaluated on Multi30k dataset, which reveals that prior knowledge of monomodal data can be transferred in a multimodal model even if fine-tuning on limited multimodal data. Furthermore, the shared encoder demonstrates perfect compatibility with the newly introduced visual features, which encourages us to dig into methods for visual and textual alignment with Transformer architectures. To sum, we show the evidence that our model is able to decode from both modalities after fine-tuning with the cross-modal masking method.

References

Anderson, P., He, X., Buehler, C., Teney, D., Johnson, M., Gould, S., and Zhang, L. (2018). Bottom-up and top-down attention for image captioning and visual question answering. In *2018 IEEE Conference on Computer Vision and Pattern Recognition, CVPR 2018, Salt Lake City, UT, USA, June 18-22, 2018*, pages 6077–6086.

Bahdanau, D., Cho, K., and Bengio, Y. (2015). Neural machine translation by jointly learning to align and translate. In *3rd International Conference on Learning Representations, ICLR 2015, San Diego, CA, USA, May 7-9, 2015, Conference Track Proceedings*.

Banerjee, S. and Lavie, A. (2005). METEOR: an automatic metric for MT evaluation with improved correlation with human judgments. In *Proceedings of the Workshop on Intrinsic and Extrinsic Evaluation Measures for Machine Translation and/or Summarization@ACL 2005, Ann Arbor, Michigan, USA, June 29, 2005*, pages 65–72.

Barrault, L., Bougares, F., Specia, L., Lala, C., Elliott, D., and Frank, S. (2018). Findings of the third shared task on multimodal machine translation. In *Proceedings of the Third Conference on Machine Translation: Shared Task Papers, WMT 2018, Belgium, Brussels, October 31 - November 1, 2018*, pages 304–323.

Caglayan, O., Barrault, L., and Bougares, F. (2016). Multimodal attention for neural machine translation. *CoRR*, abs/1609.03976.

Caglayan, O., Madhyastha, P., Specia, L., and Barrault, L. (2019). Probing the need for visual context in multimodal machine translation. In *Proceedings of the 2019 Conference of the North American Chapter of the Association for Computational Linguistics: Human Language Technologies, NAACL-HLT 2019, Minneapolis, MN, USA, June 2-7, 2019, Volume 1 (Long and Short Papers)*, pages 4159–4170.

Calixto, I. and Liu, Q. (2017). Incorporating global visual features into attention-based neural machine translation. In *Proceedings of the 2017 Conference on Empirical Methods in Natural Language Processing, EMNLP 2017, Copenhagen, Denmark, September 9-11, 2017*, pages 992–1003.

Chen, Y., Li, L., Yu, L., Kholy, A. E., Ahmed, F., Gan, Z., Cheng, Y., and Liu, J. (2020). UNITER: universal image-text representation learning. In Vedaldi, A., Bischof, H., Brox, T., and Frahm, J., editors, *Computer Vision - ECCV 2020 - 16th European Conference, Glasgow, UK, August 23-28, 2020, Proceedings, Part XXX*, volume 12375 of *Lecture Notes in Computer Science*, pages 104–120. Springer.

Delbrouck, J. and Dupont, S. (2018). UMONS submission for WMT18 multimodal translation task. *CoRR*, abs/1810.06233.

Devlin, J., Chang, M., Lee, K., and Toutanova, K. (2019). BERT: pre-training of deep bidirectional transformers for language understanding. In *Proceedings of the 2019 Conference of the North American Chapter of the Association for Computational Linguistics: Human Language Technologies, NAACL-HLT 2019, Minneapolis, MN, USA, June 2-7, 2019, Volume 1 (Long and Short Papers)*, pages 4171–4186.

Elliott, D., Frank, S., Barrault, L., Bougares, F., and Specia, L. (2017). Findings of the second shared task on multimodal machine translation and multilingual image description. In *Proceedings of the Second Conference on Machine Translation, WMT 2017, Copenhagen, Denmark, September 7-8, 2017*, pages 215–233.

Elliott, D., Frank, S., Sima'an, K., and Specia, L. (2016). Multi30k: Multilingual english-german image descriptions. In *Proceedings of the 5th Workshop on Vision and Language*, pages 70–74.

Elliott, D. and Kádár, Á. (2017). Imagination improves multimodal translation. In *Proceedings of the Eighth International Joint Conference on Natural Language Processing, IJCNLP 2017, Taipei, Taiwan, November 27 - December 1, 2017 - Volume 1: Long Papers*, pages 130–141.

Grönroos, S., Huet, B., Kurimo, M., Laaksonen, J., Mérialdo, B., Pham, P., Sjöberg, M., Sulubacak, U., Tiedemann, J., Troncy, R., and Vázquez, R. (2018). The memad submission to the WMT18 multimodal translation task. In *Proceedings of the Third Conference on Machine Translation: Shared Task Papers, WMT 2018, Belgium, Brussels, October 31 - November 1, 2018*, pages 603–611.

He, K., Zhang, X., Ren, S., and Sun, J. (2016). Deep residual learning for image recognition. In *2016 IEEE Conference on Computer Vision and Pattern Recognition, CVPR 2016, Las Vegas, NV, USA, June 27-30, 2016*, pages 770–778.

Hirasawa, T., Yamagishi, H., Matsumura, Y., and Komachi, M. (2019). Multimodal machine translation with embedding prediction. In *Proceedings of the 2019 Conference of the North American Chapter of the Association for Computational Linguistics: Human Language Technologies, NAACL-HLT 2019, Minneapolis, MN, USA, June 3-5, 2019, Student Research Workshop*, pages 86–91.

Hoang, H. and Koehn, P. (2008). Design of the moses decoder for statistical machine translation. In *Software Engineering, Testing, and Quality Assurance for Natural Language Processing@ACL 2008, Columbus, Ohio, USA, June 20, 2008*, pages 58–65.

Kingma, D. P. and Ba, J. (2015). Adam: A method for stochastic optimization. In *3rd International Conference on Learning Representations, ICLR 2015, San Diego, CA, USA, May 7-9, 2015, Conference Track Proceedings*.

Krishna, R., Zhu, Y., Groth, O., Johnson, J., Hata, K., Kravitz, J., Chen, S., Kalantidis, Y., Li, L., Shamma, D. A., Bernstein, M. S., and Fei-Fei, L. (2017). Visual genome: Connecting language and vision using crowdsourced dense image annotations. *International Journal of Computer Vision*, 123(1):32–73.

Ott, M., Edunov, S., Baevski, A., Fan, A., Gross, S., Ng, N., Grangier, D., and Auli, M. (2019). fairseq: A fast, extensible toolkit for sequence modeling. In *Proceedings of NAACL-HLT 2019: Demonstrations*.

Papineni, K., Roukos, S., Ward, T., and Zhu, W. (2002). Bleu: a method for automatic evaluation of machine translation. In *Proceedings of the 40th Annual Meeting of the Association for Computational Linguistics, July 6-12, 2002, Philadelphia, PA, USA*, pages 311–318.

Paszke, A., Gross, S., Massa, F., Lerer, A., Bradbury, J., Chanan, G., Killeen, T., Lin, Z., Gimelshein, N., Antiga, L., Desmaison, A., Kopf, A., Yang, E., DeVito, Z., Raison, M., Tejani, A., Chilamkurthy, S., Steiner, B., Fang, L., Bai, J., and Chintala, S. (2019). Pytorch: An imperative style, high-performance deep learning library. In Wallach, H., Larochelle, H., Beygelzimer, A., d' Alché-Buc, F., Fox, E., and Garnett, R., editors, *Advances in Neural Information Processing Systems 32*, pages 8024–8035. Curran Associates, Inc.

Pereyra, G., Tucker, G., Chorowski, J., Kaiser, L., and Hinton, G. E. (2017). Regularizing neural networks by penalizing confident output distributions. In *5th International Conference on Learning Representations, ICLR 2017, Toulon, France, April 24-26, 2017, Workshop Track Proceedings*.

Ren, S., He, K., Girshick, R. B., and Sun, J. (2015). Faster R-CNN: towards real-time object detection with region proposal networks. In *Advances in Neural Information Processing Systems 28: Annual Conference on Neural Information Processing Systems 2015, December 7-12, 2015, Montreal, Quebec, Canada*, pages 91–99.

Sennrich, R., Haddow, B., and Birch, A. (2016). Neural machine translation of rare words with subword units. In *Proceedings of the 54th Annual Meeting of the Association for Computational Linguistics, ACL 2016, August 7-12, 2016, Berlin, Germany, Volume 1: Long Papers*. The Association for Computer Linguistics.

Specia, L., Frank, S., Sima'an, K., and Elliott, D. (2016a). A shared task on multimodal machine translation and crosslingual image description. In *First Conference on Machine Translation, Volume 2: Shared Task Papers*, WMT, pages 540–550, Berlin, Germany.

Specia, L., Frank, S., Sima'an, K., and Elliott, D. (2016b). A shared task on multimodal machine translation and crosslingual image description. In *Proceedings of the First Conference on Machine Translation, WMT 2016, colocated with ACL 2016, August 11-12, Berlin, Germany*, pages 543–553.

Su, Y., Fan, K., Bach, N., Kuo, C. J., and Huang, F. (2019). Unsupervised multi-modal neural machine translation. In *IEEE Conference on Computer Vision and Pattern Recognition, CVPR 2019, Long Beach, CA, USA, June 16-20, 2019*, pages 10482–10491.

Tan, H. and Bansal, M. (2019). LXMERT: learning cross-modality encoder representations from transformers. In *Proceedings of the 2019 Conference on Empirical Methods in Natural Language Processing and the 9th International Joint Conference on Natural Language Processing, EMNLP-IJCNLP 2019, Hong Kong, China, November 3-7, 2019*, pages 5099–5110.

Vaswani, A., Shazeer, N., Parmar, N., Uszkoreit, J., Jones, L., Gomez, A. N., Kaiser, L., and Polosukhin, I. (2017). Attention is all you need. In *Advances in Neural Information Processing Systems 30: Annual Conference on Neural Information Processing Systems 2017, 4-9 December 2017, Long Beach, CA, USA*, pages 5998–6008.

Young, P., Lai, A., Hodosh, M., and Hockenmaier, J. (2014). From image descriptions to visual denotations: New similarity metrics for semantic inference over event descriptions. *TACL*, 2:67–78.

Zhang, Z., Chen, K., Wang, R., Utiyama, M., Sumita, E., Li, Z., and Zhao, H. (2020). Neural machine translation with universal visual representation. In *International Conference on Learning Representations*.

Zhou, M., Cheng, R., Lee, Y. J., and Yu, Z. (2018). A visual attention grounding neural model for multimodal machine translation. In *Proceedings of the 2018 Conference on Empirical Methods in Natural Language Processing, Brussels, Belgium, October 31 - November 4, 2018*, pages 3643–3653.

Sentiment Preservation in Review Translation using Curriculum-based Re-inforcement Framework

Divya Kumari*, Soumya Chennabasavraj**, Nikesh Garera** and Asif Ekbal*
*Department of Computer Science and Engineering, Indian Institute of Technology Patna, Patna, India
**Flipkart, India
*divya_1921cs10, asif@iitp.ac.in
**soumya.cb, nikesh.garera@flipkart.com

Abstract

Machine Translation (MT) is a common approach to feed humans or machines in a cross-lingual context. However, there are some expected drawbacks. Studies suggest that in the cross-lingual context, MT system often fails to preserve different stylistic and pragmatic properties of the source text (e.g. sentiment, emotion, gender traits, etc.) to the target translation. These disadvantages can degrade the performance of any downstream Natural Language Processing (NLP) applications, such as sentiment analyser, that heavily relies on the output of the MT systems (especially in a low-resource setting). The susceptibility to sentiment polarity loss becomes even more severe when an MT system is employed for translating a source content that lacks a legitimate language structure (e.g. review text). Therefore, while improving the general quality of the Neural Machine Translation (NMT) output (e.g. adequacy), we must also find ways to minimize the sentiment loss in translation. In our current work, we present a deep re-inforcement learning (RL) framework in conjunction with the curriculum learning to fine-tune the parameters of a full-fledged NMT system so that the generated translation successfully encodes the underlying sentiment of the source without compromising the adequacy, unlike the previous method. We evaluate our proposed method on the English–Hindi (product domain) and French–English (restaurant domain) review datasets, and found that our method (*further*) brings a significant improvement over a full-fledged supervised baseline for the machine translation and sentiment classification tasks.

1 Introduction

Product and/or service reviews available in the e-commerce portals are predominantly in the English language, and hence a large number of population can not understand these. Machine Translation (MT) system can play a crucial role in bridging this gap by translating the user-generated contents, and directly displaying them, or making these available for the downstream Natural Language Processing (NLP) tasks e.g. sentiment classification[1] (Araújo et al., 2020; Barnes et al., 2016; Mohammad et al., 2016; Kanayama et al., 2004). However, numerous studies (Poncelas et al., 2020a; Afli et al., 2017; Mohammad et al., 2016; Sennrich et al., 2016a) have found a significant loss of sentiment during the automatic translation of the source text.

The susceptibility to sentiment loss aggravates when the MT system is translating a noisy review that lacks a legitimate language structure at the origin. For example, a noisy review contains several peculiarities and informal structures, such as shortening of words (e.g. "awesome" as "awsm"), acronyms (e.g. "Oh My God" as "OMG"), phonetic substitution of numbers (e.g. "before" as "b4"), emphasis on characters to define extremity of the emotion (e.g. "good" as "gooooooood"), spelling mistakes, etc. Unfortunately, even a pervasively used commercial neural

[1] Please note that our current work is limited to cross-lingual sentiment analysis [CLSA] via MT based approach.

machine translation (NMT) system, Google Translate, is very brittle and easily falters when presented with such noisy text, as illustrated through the following example.
Review Text (English): I found an awsome product. (Positive)
Google Transliteration (Hindi): mujhe ek ajeeb utpaad mila. (Neutral)
The example shows how the misspelling of a sentiment bearing word "awesome" gets this positive expression translated to a neutral expression. In the above context, if an unedited raw MT output is directly fed to the downstream sentiment classifier, it might not get the expected classification accuracy. Thus, in this work we propose a deep-reinforcement-based framework to adapt the parameters of a pre-trained neural MT system such that the generated translation improves the performance of a cross-lingual multi-class sentiment classifier (without compromising the adequacy).

More specifically, we propose a deep *actor-critic (AC)* reinforcement learning framework in the ambit of *curriculum learning* (CL) to alleviate the issue of sentiment loss while improving the quality of translation in a cross-lingual setup. The idea of actor-critic is to have two neural networks, *viz.* (i). an actor (i.e. a pre-trained NMT) that takes an action (policy-based), and (ii). a critic that observes how good the action taken is and provides feedback (value-based). This feedback acts as a guiding signal to train the actor. Further, to better utilize the data, we also integrate curriculum learning into our framework.

Recently, Tebbifakhr et al. (2019) demonstrated that an MT system (actor) can be customised to produce a controlled translation that essentially improves the performance of a cross-lingual (binary) sentiment classifier. They achieved this task-specific customisation of a "generic-MT" system via a policy-based method that optimizes a task-specific metric, i.e. $F1$ score (see Section 2). However, this often miserably fails to encode the semantics of the source sentence.

Recent studies (Xu et al., 2018) demonstrated that the non-opinionated semantic content improves the quality of a sentiment classifier. Accordingly, the transfer of such information from the source to the target can be pivotal for the quality of the sentiment classifier in a cross-lingual setup. Towards this, we investigate the optimization of a harmonic-score-based reward function in our proposed RL-based framework that ensures to preserve both sentiment and semantics. This function operates by taking a weighted harmonic mean of two rewards: (i). content preservation score measured through Sentence-level BLEU or SBLEU; and (ii). sentiment preservation score measured through a function that performs element-wise dot product between a predicted sentiment distribution and the gold sentiment distribution.

Empirical results, unlike Tebbifakhr et al. (2019), suggest that our RL-based fine-tuning framework, tailored to optimize the harmonic reward, preserves both sentiment and semantics in a given NMT context. Additionally, we also found that the above fine-tuning method in the ambit of curriculum learning achieves an additional performance gain of the MT system over a setting where curriculum based fine-tuning is not employed. The core of *curriculum learning* (CL) (Bengio et al., 2009) is to design a metric that scores the difficulty of training samples, which is then used to guide the order of presentation of samples to the learner (NMT) in an easy-to-hard fashion. To the best of our knowledge, this is the very first work that studies the curriculum learning (CL) for NMT from a new perspective, i.e. given a pre-trained MT model, the dataset to fine-tune, and the two tasks *viz.* sentiment and content preservation; we utilize a reward-based metric (i.e. harmonic score) to define the difficulty of the tasks and use it to score the data points. The use of harmonic reward based scoring/ranking function implicitly covers the tasks' overall difficulty through a single metric.

Moreover, understanding that obtaining a gold-standard polarity annotated data is costlier, the fine-tuning of pre-trained NMT model is performed by re-using only a small subset of the supervised training samples that we annotated with respect to (w.r.t) their sentiment. Empirical results suggest that additionally enriching a random small subset of the training data with extra sentiment information, and later re-using them for the fine-tuning of the referenced model via our proposed framework (c.f. Section 3) observes an additional gain in BLEU and $F1$ score over a supervised baseline. We summarize the main contributions and/or the key attributes of our current work as follows:
(i). create a new domain-specific (i.e. product review) parallel corpus, a subset of which is annotated for their sentiment;
(ii). propose an AC-based fine-tuning framework that utilizes a novel harmonic mean-based reward function to meet our two-fold objectives, *viz.* enabling our NMT model to preserve; (a).

the non-opinionated semantic content; and (b). the source sentiment during translation.
(iii). Additionally, we utilize the idea of CL during the RL fine-tuning of the pre-trained model and try to learn from easy to hard data, where hard corresponds to the instances with lower harmonic reward. To the best of our knowledge, this is the first work in NMT that studies CL in the ambit of RL fine-tuning.

2 Related Work

The use of translation-based solution for cross-lingual sentiment classification is successfully leveraged in the literature (Wu et al., 2021; Tebbifakhr et al., 2020; Araújo et al., 2020; Poncelas et al., 2020b; Fei and Li, 2020; Tebbifakhr et al., 2019; Akhtar et al., 2018; Barnes et al., 2016; Balahur and Turchi, 2012; Kanayama et al., 2004) which suggest an inspiring use-case of the MT system, and brings motivation for this piece of work.

Given the context of this work, we look at the pieces of works that address the preservation of sentiment in the automatic translation. In one of the early works, Chen and Zhu (2014) used a lexicon-based consistency approach to design a list of sentiment-based features and used it to rank the candidates of *t*-table in a Phrase based MT system. Lohar et al. (2017, 2018) prepared the positive, negative and neutral sentiment-specific translation systems to ensure the cross-lingual sentiment consistency.

Recently, Tebbifakhr et al. (2019) proposed Machine-Oriented (MO) Reinforce, a policy-based method to pursue a machine-oriented objective[2] in a sentiment classification task unlike the traditional human-oriented objective [3]. It gives a new perspective for a use-case of the MT system (i.e. machine translation for machine). To perform this task-specific adaption (i.e. produce output to feed a machine), Tebbifakhr et al. (2019) adapted the REINFORCE of Williams (1992) by incorporating an exploration-oriented sampling strategy. As opposed to one sampling of REINFORCE, MO Reinforce samples k times, $(k = 5)$, and obtains a reward for each sample from the sentiment classifier. A final update of the model parameters are done w.r.t the highest rewarding sample. Although they achieved a performance boost in the sentiment classification task, they had to greatly compromise with the translation quality. In contrast to Tebbifakhr et al. (2019), we focus on performing a task-specific customisation of a pre-trained MT system via a harmonic reward based deep reinforcement framework that uses an AC method in conjunction with the CL. The adapted NMT system, thus obtained, is expected to produce a more accurate (high-quality) translation as well as improve the performance of a sentiment analyser. Bahdanau et al. (2017); Nguyen et al. (2017), unlike us, used the popular AC method, and focused only on preserving the semantics (translation quality) of a text. Additionally, we develop a CL based strategy to guide the training. Recently, Zhao et al. (2020) also studied AC method in the context of NMT. However, they used this method to learn the curriculum for re-selecting influential data samples from the existing training set that can further improve the performance (translation quality) of a pre-trained NMT system.

3 Methodology

Firstly, we perform the pre-training of a NMT model until the convergence using the standard log-likelihood (LL) training on the supervised dataset (c.f. Table 1: (A)). The model, thus obtained, acts as our referenced MT system/actor. To demonstrate the improvements brought by the proposed curriculum-based AC fine-tuning over the above LL-based baseline in the sentiment preservation and machine translation tasks, we carry out the task-specific adaption of the pre-trained LL-based MT model (actor) by re-using a subset of the supervised training samples. It is worth mentioning here that, in the fine-tuning stage, the actor does not observe any new sentence, rather re-visit (randomly) a few of the supervised training samples which are now additionally annotated with their sentiment (c.f. Section 4).
Actor-critic Overview : Here, we present a brief overview of our AC framework which is discussed at length in the subsequent section. In the AC training, the actor (NMT) receives an input sequence, s, and produces a sample translation, $\hat{t}$, which is evaluated by the critic model.

[2]Where the MT objective is to feed a machine.
[3]Where the MT objective is to feed the human.

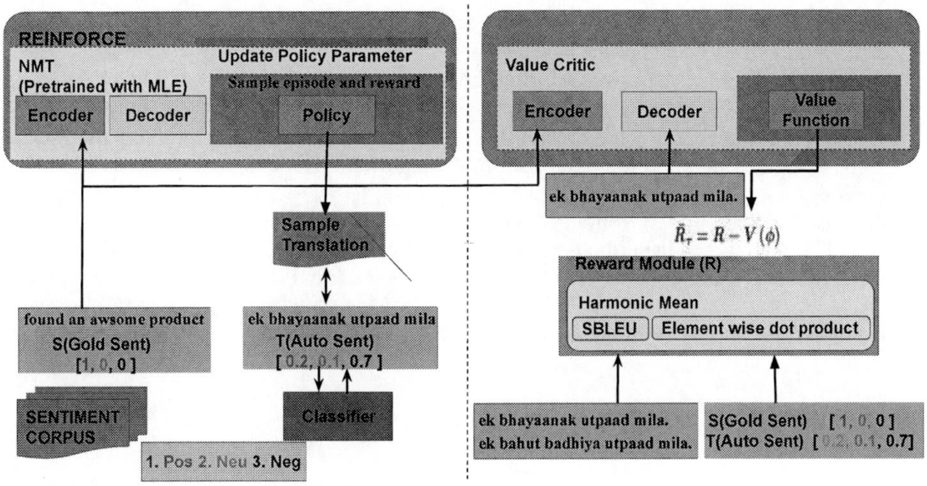

Figure 1: An illustration of the Actor-Critic Method

The critic feedback is used by the actor to identify those actions that bring it a better than the average reward. In the above context, a feedback of a random critic would be useless for training the actor. Hence, similar to the actor we warm up the critic for one epoch by feeding it samples from the pre-trained actor, while the actor's parameters are frozen. We then fine-tune these models jointly so that - as the actor gets better w.r.t its action, the critic gets better at giving feedback (see Section 4.2 for the dataset and reward used in the pre-training and fine-tuning stages). The details of the loss functions that the actor and critic minimizes are discussed in Section 3.1.

Furthermore, to better utilize the data, we finally integrate CL into our AC framework (our proposed approach). Empirical results (Section 5.1) show that during fine-tuning, presenting the data in an easy-to-hard fashion yields a better learned actor model over the one obtained via *vanilla* (no-curriculum based) fine-tuning. Our proposed framework brought improvements over several baselines without using any additional new training data in the two translation tasks, i.e. (i). English–Hindi[4] and (ii). French–English [5]. Since our proposed framework is a combination of RL via AC method and CL, we first present the details of the main components of the AC model alongside their training procedure in Section 3.1. The details of the reward model are presented in Section 3.2, and then introduce the plausibility of CL in Section 3.3. Finally, we describe our proposed CL-based AC framework in Algorithm 1.

3.1 Proposed Fine-tuning Method

The architecture of our AC-based framework is illustrated in Figure 1. It has three main components *viz.* (i). an actor : the pre-trained neural agent (NMT) whose parameters define the policy and the agent takes action, i.e. sample translations according to the policy (ii). a reward model : a score function used to evaluate the policy. It provides the actual (true) estimated reward to the translations sampled from the model's policy. To ensure the preservation of sentiment and content in translation, the chosen reward model gives two constituent rewards - a classifier-based score and a SBLEU score (Section 3.2), respectively, and (iii). a critic : a deep neural function approximator that predicts an expected value (reward) for the sampled action. This is then used to center the true reward (step (ii)) from the environment (see Equation 2). Subtracting critic estimated reward from the true reward helps the actor to identify action that yields extra reward beyond the expected return. We employ a critic with the same architecture as of the actor.

We see from the lower-left side of Figure 1 that, for each input sentence (s), we draw a

[4]Trained using a new parallel dataset created as a part of this work, a subset of which is polarity annotated.

[5]Trained using publicly available dataset, a part of it is additionally annotated with sentiment.

single sample ($\hat{t}$) from the actor, which is used for both estimating gradients of the actor and the critic model as explained in the subsequent section.

Critic Network training: During the RL training, we feed a batch of source sentences, $B_j(s)$, to the critic encoder and the corresponding sampled translations obtained from the actor, $B_j(\hat{t})$, to the decoder of the critic model. The critic decoder then predicts the rewards (i.e. value estimates, V_ϕ, predicted for each time step of the decoder), and accordingly updates its parameters supervised by the actual (or true) rewards, $\mathrm{R}(\hat{t}, s)$ [6] (steps to obtain this reward is discussed in Section 3.2) from the environment.

The objective of the critic network is, thus, to find its parameter value ϕ that minimizes the *mean square error* (MSE) between the *true reward* (see R in Figure 1) from the environment, and the critic *estimated reward* (i.e. values predicted by the critic, see V_ϕ in Figure 1). Accordingly, the MSE loss that the critic minimizes is as in Equation (1), where τ' being the critic decoding step.

$$\nabla_\phi \mathrm{L}_{crt}(\phi) \approx \sum_{\tau'=1}^{n} \left[\mathrm{V}(\hat{t}_{<\tau'}, s) - \mathrm{R}(\hat{t}, s)\right] \nabla_\phi \mathrm{V} \tag{1}$$

Note that in this work we explore the setting, where the reward, R, is observable only at time step $\tau = n$ of the actor (a scalar for each complete sentence). Thus, to calculate the difference terms in Equation 1 for n steps, we use the same terminal reward, R, in all the intermediate time steps of the critic decoder.

Actor Network training: To update the actor (G) parameters, θ, we use the policy gradient loss; weighted by a reward which is centered via the critic estimated value (i.e. the critic estimated value, V, is subtracted from the true reward, R, from the environment), as in equation (2). The updated reward is finally used to weigh the policy gradient loss, as shown in (3), where τ being the decoding step of the actor.

$$\bar{\mathrm{R}}_\tau(\hat{t}, s) = \mathrm{R}(\hat{t}, s) - \mathrm{V}(\hat{t}_{<\tau'}, s) \tag{2}$$

$$\nabla_\theta \mathrm{L}^{\mathrm{pg}}_{\mathrm{actor}}(\theta) \approx \sum_{\tau=1}^{n} \bar{\mathrm{R}}_\tau \nabla_\theta \log \mathrm{G}_\theta(\hat{t}_\tau | \hat{t}_{<\tau}) \tag{3}$$

The actor and the critic both are global-attention based recurrent neural networks (RNN). Algorithm 1 summarizes the overall update framework. We run this algorithm for mini-batches.

3.2 Defining Rewards

As our primary goal is to optimize the performance of the pre-trained NMT system towards sentiment classification and machine translation tasks, accordingly we investigate the utility of the following three reward functions (i.e. true reward, R in Equation 1 as R_1, R_2, R_3) for optimization through our *vanilla* AC method. Please note, for brevity we only choose the reward that serves the best to our purpose (i.e. harmonic reward as it ensures both, an improved cross-lingual sentiment projection, and a high quality translation with our *vanilla* AC approach, as discussed in Section 5.1) for our subsequently proposed curriculum-based experiment. The three types of feedbacks we explored are: (i). Sentence-level BLEU as a reward to ensure the content preservation, also referred as R_1, is calculated following the Equation (4)

$$\mathrm{R}_1 = \mathrm{SBLEU}(\hat{t}, t) \tag{4}$$

(ii). Element-wise dot product between the gold sentiment distribution and predicted sentiment distribution (e.g. $[1, 0, 0]$ and $[0.2, 0.1, 0.7]$ in Figure 1 evaluates to scalar value 0.2) taken from the softmax layer of the target language classifier to ensure sentiment preservation, also referred

[6] Although shown like this, it only means true reward corresponding to a given source sentence and the corresponding sampled action, not as a function.

as R_2. To simulate the target language classifier, we fine-tune the pre-trained BERT model (Devlin et al., 2019). The tuned classifier (preparation steps discussed in Section 4.1) is used to obtain the reward R_2 as in Equation (5).

$$\mathrm{R}_2 = \mathrm{P}(s)_{gold} \bullet \mathrm{P}(\hat{t})_{bert} \tag{5}$$

and,
(iii). Harmonic mean of (i) and (ii) as a reward, also referred to as R_3 to ensure the preservation of both sentiment and semantic during the translation, as in Equation (6).

$$\mathrm{R}_3 = (1 + \beta^2)\frac{(2 \cdot \mathrm{R}_1 \cdot \mathrm{R}_2)}{(\beta^2 \cdot \mathrm{R}_1) + \mathrm{R}_2} \tag{6}$$

where β is the harmonic weight which is set to 0.5.

3.3 Curriculum Construction

The core of CL is (i). to design an evaluation metric for difficulty, and (ii). to provide the model with easy samples first before the hard ones.

In this work, the notion of difficulty is derived from the harmonic reward, R_3, as follows. Let, $X = \{x_i\}_{i=1}^{N} = \{(s^i, t^i)\}_{i=1}^{N}$ denotes the RL training data points. To measure the difficulty of say, i^{th} data point, (s^i, t^i), we calculate the reward, R_3 using $(\hat{t^i}, s^i)$. In order to obtain the corresponding sample translation, $\hat{t^i}$, we use the LL-based model (pre-trained actor). We do this for the N data points. Finally, we sort the RL training data points from easy, i.e., with high harmonic reward, to hard as recorded on their translations. In the fine-tuning step, the entire sorted training data points are divided into mini-batches, $B = [B_1, ..., B_M]$, and the actor processes a mini-batch sequentially from B. Hence, at the start of each epoch of training, the actor will learn from the easiest examples first followed by the hard examples in a sequential manner until all the M batches exhaust. Another alternative is the use of pacing function $f_{pace}(s)$, which helps to decide the fraction of training data available for sampling at a given time step s, i.e. $f_{pace}(s)|D_{train}|$. However, we leave it to explore in our future work. The Pseudo-code for the proposed CL-based AC framework including pre-training is described by Algorithm 1.

4 Datasets and Experimental Setup

In this section, we first discuss the datasets used in different stages of experiments followed by the steps involved in the creation of datasets, the baselines used for comparison, and the model implementation details.

Dataset: Our NMT adaptation experiments are performed across two language pairs from different families with different typological properties, i.e. English to Hindi (henceforth, En–Hi) and French–English (henceforth, Fr–En). We use the following supervised datasets for the pre-training and validation of LL-based NMT in En–Hi and Fr–En tasks,
(i). For En–Hi task, we use a newly created domain-specific parallel corpus (see section 4.1) whose sources were selected from an e-commerce site. This corpus is released as a part of this work. Statistics of the dataset is shown in Table 1 : (A), row(ii).
(ii). For Fr–En task, we concatenate a recently released domain-specific parallel corpus, namely Foursquare (4SQ) corpus [7] (Berard et al., 2019) with first $60K$ sentences from $OpenSubtitles$ [8] corpus to simulate a low-resource setting. The basic statistics of this dataset are shown in Table 1 : (A), row(i). For RL fine-tuning of the LL-based NMT(s), we use the corresponding RL datasets from Table 1: (B). In each task, the RL trainset sentences are a subset of human translated sentences drawn from the supervised training samples and additionally annotated with respect to sentiment. For En–Hi task, these sentences are randomly sampled from the supervised training corpus (c.f. Table 1: (A), row(ii)), and for Fr–En we use 4SQ-HT dataset (c.f. Table 1:

[7] A small parallel restaurant reviews dataset released as a part of the review translation task.

[8] We choose this dataset as it is made of spoken-language sentences which are noisy, sentiment-rich and is closest to 4SQ corpus as suggested by the author.

Algorithm 1 Proposed algorithm (Curriculum based fine-tuning process). In the *vanilla* (i.e. no curriculum-based) approach, we skip steps 5 to 7.

```
1: Initialize the actor model G_θ with uniform weights θ ∈ [−0.1, 0.1].
2: Pre-train the actor (G_θ) with LL loss until convergence.
3: Initialize the critic model V_φ with uniform weights φ ∈ [−0.1, 0.1].
4: Pre-train the critic for one epoch with SBLEU as a reward on the same LL training data by feeding it
   samples from the pre-trained actor, while the actor's parameters are frozen.
5: Use the actor model to translate all the data points in X.
6: Obtain rewards R_3 corresponding to N data points.
7: Rank {X_i}_{i=1}^N = {(s^i, t^i)}_{i=1}^N based on R_3.
8: for K epochs do
9:     for mini-batches, B = [B_1, ..., B_M] do
10:        Obtain the sample translations B_m(t̂) from the actor for the given source sentences, B_m(s).
11:        Obtain R_1, R_2 and finally observe the rewards R_3.
12:        Feed the source sentences, B_m(s) to the critic encoder and sampled translations, B_m(t̂) to the
           decoder.
13:        Obtain the predicted rewards, V_φ, using the critic model.
14:        Update the critic's parameter using (1).
15:        Obtain final reward R̄ using (2).
16:        Update the actor's parameter using (2) in (3).
17:    end for
18: end for
```

(A), row(i)). To evaluate the performance of all the NMT system(s) we use the corresponding RL testsets from Table 1.

4.1 Data Creation

To the best of our knowledge, there is no existing (freely available) sentiment annotated parallel data for English–Hindi in the review domain. Hence, we crawl the electronic products reviews from a popular e-commerce portal (i.e. Flipkart). These reviews were translated into Hindi using the Google Translate API. A significant part of this automated translation is then verified by a human translator with a post-graduate qualification and proficient in English and Hindi language skills. One more translator was asked to verify the translation. The detailed statistics of new in-domain parallel corpus are shown in Table 1: (A), row(ii). Further, a subset of human translated product reviews is selected randomly for sentiment annotation. Three annotators who are bilingual and experts in both Hindi and English took part in the annotation task. Details of the instructions given to the annotators and translators are mentioned below.

Instructions to the Translators:

For translation, following were the instructions: (i). experts were asked to read the Hindi sentence carefully; (ii). source and target sentences should carry the same semantic and syntactic structure; (iii). they were instructed to carefully read the translated sentences, and see whether the fluency (grammatical correctness) and adequacy are preserved; (iv). they made the correction in the sentences, if required; (v). vocabulary selection at Hindi (target) side should be user friendly; (vi). transliteration of an English can also be used, especially if this is a named entity (NE).

Instructions to the Annotators:

The annotators have post-graduate qualification in linguistics, possessing good knowledge of English and Hindi both. They have prior experience in judging the quality of machine translation and sentiment annotation.

For sentiment labeling, annotators were asked to follow the guidelines as below:

(i). they were instructed to look into the sentiment class of the source sentence (Tebbifakhr et al., 2019) (English), locate its sentiment bearing tokens; (ii). they were asked to observe both of these properties in the translated sentences; (iii). they were asked to annotate the source sentences into the four classes, namely positive, negative, neutral and others.

The further detailed instructions for sentiment annotation are given as below:
(i). Select the option that best captures the sentiment being conveyed in the sentences:- positive- negative- neutral- others- (ii). Select positive if the sentence shows a positive attitude (possibly toward an object or event). e.g. great performance and value for money. (iii). Select negative if the sentence shows a negative attitude (possibly toward an object or event). e.g. please do not exchange your phone on flipkart they fool you . (iv.) Select neutral if the sentence shows a neutral attitude (possibly toward an object or event) or is an objective sentence. Objective sentences are sentences that do not carry any opinion, e.g. facts are objective expressions about entities, events and their properties. e.g. (a). the selfie camera is 32 mp .(objective), (b). after doing research on the latest phones, i bought this phone . (neutral). (iv) Select others for sentences that do not fall in above three categories, e.g. (a). if the sentence is highly ungrammatical and hard to understand. (b). if the sentence expresses both positive and negative sentiment, i.e. mixed polarity.

These annotation guidelines were decided after thorough discussions among ourselves. After we had drafted our initial guidelines, the annotators were asked to perform the verification of the translated sentences, and sentiment annotation for the 100 sentences. The disagreement cases were thereafter discussed and resolved through discussions among the experts and annotators. Finally, we came up with the set of instructions as discussed above to minimize the number of disagreement cases. Class-wise statistics of the sentiment-annotated dataset for En–Hi task are shown in Table 1: (B). Additionally, the same annotators also annotated a part of the 4SQ corpus (i.e. target [9] (English) sentences from the 4SQ-HT training and 4SQ-test set) to obtain the sentiment annotated RL dataset for the Fr–En task (c.f. Table 1: (B)). For sentiment classification, the inter-annotator agreement ratio (Fleiss, 1971) is 0.72 for En–Hi, and 0.76 for Fr–En. We manually filtered the RL datasets to only include the positive, negative and neutral sentences as per the the manual annotations. We refer these sentiment-annotated corpora as the RL dataset(s).

Classifier training: In order to build the target language sentiment analyser, we use the BERT-based [10] language model. The classifier is first pre-trained using the target-side sentences of the supervised training corpus. Classifier pre-training is followed by the task-specific fine-tuning using the target-side sentences of the RL training set. For example, to build the target language English classifier for the Fr–En task, the classifier is first pre-trained using the English sentences from the supervised dataset (c.f. Table 1: (A), row(i)) followed by fine-tuning by using polarity-labelled English sentences from the RL training corpus (c.f. Table 1: (B), row(i)).

Baselines: Other than the supervised baseline, we also compare our CL-based AC fine-tuning framework with the following state-of-the-art RL-based fine-tuning frameworks, i.e. (1). *REINFORCE*, and (2). *Machine-Oriented Reinforce*. Additionally, we also conduct the ablation study to better analyse the utility of harmonic reward in the task through our *vanilla* AC method as follows: (3). $\mathbf{MT^{ac}_{bert}}$: AC fine-tuning with sentiment reward only; (4). $\mathbf{MT^{ac}_{bleu}}$: AC fine-tuning with content reward only; (5). $\mathbf{MT^{ac}_{har}}$: AC fine-tuning with both the rewards. Finally, for brevity we choose the best performing AC-reward model for the proposed curriculum-based learning.

4.2 Hyper-parameters Setting

In all our experiments, we use an NMT system based on Luong et al. (2015), using a single layer bi-directional RNN for the encoder. All the encoder-decoder parameters are uniformly initialized in the range of [-0.1,0.1]. The sizes of embedding and hidden layers are set to 256 and 512, respectively. The Adam optimizer (Abdalla and Hirst, 2017) with $\beta1 = 0.9, \beta2 = 0.99$ is used and the gradient vector is clipped to magnitude 5. We set the dropout to 0.2 and use the input feeding with learning rate (lr) and batch size (bs) set to $1e-3$ and 64. We first perform supervised pre-training of the NMT using the parallel corpora from Table 1: (A), and select the best model parameters according to the perplexity on the development set (c.f. Table 1: (A)). We refer the actor- thus obtained- as $\mathbf{MT_{LL}}$, that acts as a trained policy in the RL training (refer to the upper left side of Figure 1). Then, we keep the actor fixed and warm-up the critic for one epoch with SBLEU reward on the supervised training samples (c.f. Table 1: (A)) with the lr

[9]This is different from En–Hi task setting where we annotate source sentence. We do so due to resource constraint.

[10]We used BERT-Base multilingual uncased model for Hindi and monolingual uncased BERT for English language.

(A)

Task(s)	**Corpus**		**#Sentences**
(i). Fr–En	60K-OPUS	(training)	60,000
	4SQ-PE	(training)	12,080
	4SQ-HT	(training)	2,784
	4SQ-valid	(validation)	1,243
(ii). En–Hi		(training)	75,821
		(validation)	700
	Vocabulary	(En-Hi)	(22,031-27,229)
	Avg. Length	(En-Hi)	(16.04-17.30)

(B)

Task(s)	**RL trainset**			**RL devset**			**RL testset**		
	Pos	Neu	Neg	Pos	Neu	Neg	Pos	Neu	Neg
(i). Fr–En	1,469	1,049	241	1,469	1,049	241	870	769	184
(ii). En–Hi	1,147	1,147	1,147	1,147	1,147	1,147	800	800	800

(C)

Task(s)	**Metrics**	$\mathbf{M_{LL}}$	$\mathbf{M^{mo}_{bert}}$	$\mathbf{M^{r}_{bleu}}$	$\mathbf{M^{ac}_{bert}}$	$\mathbf{M^{ac}_{bleu}}$	$\mathbf{M^{ac}_{har}}$
(i). Fr–En	BLEU	25.02	24.99	25.15	25.04	25.14	**25.18**
	$F1$ score	75.31	75.33	75.65	75.43	75.35	75.39
(ii). En–Hi	BLEU	27.87	28.01	27.75	27.97	28.14	28.13
	$F1$ score	73.14	73.42	73.12	73.12	72.77	73.29

(D)

Models	**Fr–En**		**En–Hi**	
	BLEU	$\mathbf{F_1}$ **score**	**BLEU**	$\mathbf{F_1}$ **score**
$\mathbf{M_{LL}}$	25.02	75.31	27.87	73.14
$\mathbf{M^{mo}_{bert}}$	24.99(−0.03)	75.33(+0.02)	28.01(+0.14)	73.42(+0.28)
$\mathbf{M^{r}_{bleu}}$	25.15(+0.13)	75.65(+0.34)	27.75(−0.12)	73.12(−0.02)
$\mathbf{M^{ac}_{har}}$	25.18*(+0.16)	75.39**(+0.08)	28.13*(+0.26)	73.29* (+0.15)
$\mathbf{M^{ac}_{har}}+CL$	**25.26***(+0.24)	75.38**(+0.07)	**28.18***(+0.31)	73.22*(+0.08)

Table 1: (A). Supervised parallel corpora for LL training. **(B).** Class-wise distribution of the polarity-tagged RL dataset(s) used to fine-tune the LL-based (En–Hi and Fr–En) pre-trained NMT(s). For the Fr–En task, we annotate a part of the 4SQ corpora (i.e. training: 4SQ-HT and testing: 4SQ-test). We do not keep a separate development set for the fine-tuning of the LL model. **(C).** Results of the fine-tuned *vanilla* reinforcement-based NMT(s). Here, superscripts **mo, r** and **ac** refers to the Machine-Oriented Reinforce, REINFORCE and actor-critic approach, respectively to fine-tune the LL-based model(s) ($\mathbf{M_{LL}}$, column (iii); En–Hi: row (i), Fr–En: row (ii)), and the subscripts **bleu, bert** and **har** refers to the corresponding rewards (i.e. SBLEU (R_1), classifier (R_2), and harmonic mean (R_3)) optimized via the policy gradient method. **(D).** Results of curriculum-based fine-tuning and other baselines. Proposed approach is $\mathbf{M^{ac}_{har}}+CL$. * significant at $p < .05$, ** significant at $p < .01$

of $1e-3$ and bs of 64. We employ the same encoder-decoder configuration as of the actor for the critic. In the RL training, we jointly train the actor and the critic model with lr of:- $1e-6$ (Fr–En); $1e-5$ (En–Hi), respectively and bs of 4 on the RL datasets with harmonic reward. For sampling the candidate translation in the RL training, we use multinomial sampling, with a sampling length of 50 tokens. We run the experiments three times with different seed values, and record the $F1$ and BLEU scores (c.f. Table 1: (C)) to evaluate the performance of the sentiment analysers and customised MT systems on the RL testset and report the average of the runs in Section 5. For all the RL-based models, the fine-tuning steps maximize the chosen average reward discussed in Section 3.2 on the RL devset. The fine-tuning continues for a maximum of 20 epochs (including the baselines). The best epoch is chosen based on the performance observed on the RL devset (i.e. the best average rewarding epoch). All the sentences are tokenized. As an extra pre-processing step, we lowercase all the English, French, and normalize all the Hindi sentences. Tokens in the training sets are segmented into sub-word units using the Byte-Pair Encoding (BPE) technique (Sennrich et al., 2016b) with 4,000 merge operations.

For evaluating our customised MT systems over all the baselines, we use the relevant RL testsets.

5 Results and Analysis

We first present the results of fine-tuning the pre-trained MT through different RL-based methods, i.e. (i). REINFORCE (ii). MO Reinforce, and (iii). *vanilla* AC (ours) in Section 5.1. Further, to better analyse the utility of harmonic reward (R_3) in sentiment and content preservation task over the previously studied rewards (i.e. SBLEU: R_1 or BERT: R_2) in the context of NMT (Tebbifakhr et al., 2020, 2019; Nguyen et al., 2017; Bahdanau et al., 2017; Wu et al., 2018; Ranzato et al., 2016), we additionally present the fine-tuning results of the *vanilla* AC method with the following two types of rewards: (i). only content, i.e. R_1 and (ii). only sentiment, i.e. R_2 as a reward.

We choose the best performing reward model (i.e. R_3) among the AC-based NMT(s). At last, we discuss the results in the context of our curriculum-based AC framework. To evaluate the translation quality we record the BLEU score of the RL testset when translated from the relevant models. To validate our claim that the translations obtained by our proposed MT system can further improve the performance of the sentiment classifier in a cross-lingual setup over the baselines, we do the following. We apply the target language sentiment classifier to the translations obtained by the LL-based NMT system vs. all the customised RL-based NMT systems, and record their F_1 scores.

5.1 Evaluation Results

As shown in Table 1: (C), the full-fledged LL-based NMT(s) (trained until convergence as observed on the development sets, column (iii).) obtain the following BLEU points (25.02, 27.87) and F_1 scores (75.31, 73.14) for the Fr–En, En–Hi tasks, respectively. We then perform fine-tuning of the pre-trained models through our *vanilla* AC harmonic approach (by re-visiting only a subset of samples from the existing supervised training sets which are now additionally annotated with their sentiment). We see for both Fr–En and En–Hi that our harmonic-reward-based models can obtain a significant performance boost (further) over the pre-trained baselines in both the optimized (targeted) metrics, i.e. BLEU improved to 25.18 ($+0.16$), 28.13 ($+0.26$) and F_1 scores reached to 75.39 ($+0.08$), 73.29 ($+0.15$) in both the language pairs. This is not the case with other reinforcement-based fine-tuned models - MO Reinforce [11] and REINFORCE that optimizes a single reward for which we observe non-optimized reward drop in at least one language-pair. For example, if we consider the MO Reinforce for the Fr–En task, the non-optimized metric - BLEU drops by -0.03 point (despite an improvement of $+0.02$ point in the optimized metric, F_1 score), and for the REINFORCE in En–Hi task both BLEU and F_1 score drop by -0.12 and -0.02 points, respectively. This establishes the efficacy of our reinforcement method. Further, when we see the results form critic-based fine-tuning of the LL model via two commonly used reward routines (R_1, R_2 - column (vi). and (vii).). As expected, we see an improvement in the targeted metric (e.g. for R_1-based model the optimized reward is BLEU. We can see improvement in BLEU). However, to our surprise, we found that the improvement in BLEU score does not have a high correlation with the performance in the sentiment classification task. For example, in the En–Hi task, the critic model with R_1 as a reward (columns (vii).) observed the highest BLEU score (28.14) but the highest F_1 score (73.29) is observed from the R_3 based model (column (viii).). This suggests the effectiveness of the harmonic reward which successfully improves both BLEU and F_1 score over the supervised baselines for both the language pairs. For the sake of brevity, we choose the harmonic model for our curriculum experiment.

When comparing the performance in the context of our proposed curriculum-based AC framework, the results from Table 1:(D) show that our method is better at producing coherent as well as sentiment-rich translation. By comparing row (i). and row (vi)., we can see that in both Fr–En and En–Hi task, merely learning in an easy-to-hard fashion brings the highest improvement in BLEU scores over the supervised baselines, i.e. $+0.24$, $+0.31$ point for the Fr–En and En–Hi tasks, respectively. F_1 scores are also improved by $+0.07$ and $+0.08$ point, respectively. All these improvement are statistically significant[12]. Furthermore, we also observe

[11]Please note unlike Tebbifakhr et al. (2019) "out-of-domain" MT-adaption approach ours' LL-based MT is trained using in-domain data.

[12]To test significance, we use bootstrap resampling method (Koehn, 2004) for BLEU and student's t-test for sentiment

that the CL-based fine-tuning observes a faster convergence over the *vanilla* approach.

5.2 Error Analysis for English–Hindi task

Although our proposed method outperforms the LL-based baseline in the sentiment classification task, we also observe several failure cases. To investigate this, we observe the sentiment-conflicting cases, i.e. selected those samples from ours' model where there is an observed disagreement between the predicted and the gold sentiment. From these samples, we filter those examples where the source (English) sentences have an explicit presence of the positive or the negative sentiment expression. Unsurprisingly, we found the main reason for sentiment loss was still the low-translation quality. Secondly, to better understand what policy is learned by our-proposed NMT that brings the observed improvement in the sentiment-classifier performance, we investigate those translations where the LL model has a predicted (by the classifier) sentiment-disagreement, whereas ours' shows an agreement, both with the gold sentiment. We present below one such example.
Review Text (Source): satisfy with overall working. *(positive)* || **Transliteration(Ref.)**: kul meelaakar kaam se santusht hoon. *(positive)* || **Transliteration(Auto.)**: kul milaakar kaam ke saath santusht. *(positive)* ($\mathrm{MT}^{ac}_{har} + CL$) || **Transliteration(Auto.):** kul milaakar kaam kar rahe hain . *(neutral)* (MT_{LL}) . We can see that our proposed model indeed learned to translate the sentiment expressions to their preferred variant (positive sentiment bearing expression *satisfy* translated as *santusht*).

6 Conclusion

In this paper, we have proposed a curriculum-based deep re-inforcement learning framework that successfully encodes both the underlying sentiment and semantics of the text during translation. In contrast to the REINFORCE-based frameworks (Williams, 1992; Tebbifakhr et al., 2019) (actor only models), ours is a critic-based approach that helps the actor learns an efficient policy to select the actions, yielding a high return from the critic. Besides, with the support of curriculum learning, it can be more efficient. This is also established (empirically) through the observed additional boost (significant at $p < .05$) in BLEU score over the baselines. Further, we have manually created a domain-specific (product reviews) polarity-labelled balanced bilingual corpus for English–Hindi, that could be a useful resource for research in the similar areas. We shall make the data and our codes available to the community.

7 Acknowledgement

Authors gratefully acknowledge the unrestricted research grant received from the Flipkart Internet Private Limited to carry out the research. Authors thank Muthusamy Chelliah for his continuous feedbacks and suggestions to improve the quality of work; and to Anubhav Tripathee for gold standard parallel corpus creation and translation quality evaluation.

References

Abdalla, M. and Hirst, G. (2017). Cross-lingual sentiment analysis without (good) translation. In *Proceedings of the Eighth International Joint Conference on Natural Language Processing (Volume 1: Long Papers)*, pages 506–515, Taiwan. Asian Federation of Natural Language Processing.

Afli, H., Maguire, S., and Way, A. (2017). Sentiment translation for low resourced languages: Experiments on Irish general election tweets. In *18th International Conference on Computational Linguistics and Intelligent Text Processing*, Budapest, Hungry.

Akhtar, M. S., Sawant, P., Sen, S., Ekbal, A., and Bhattacharyya, P. (2018). Solving data sparsity for aspect based sentiment analysis using cross-linguality and multi-linguality. In *Proceedings of the 2018 Conference of the North American Chapter of the Association for Computational Linguistics: Human Language Technologies, Volume 1 (Long Papers)*, pages 572–582, New Orleans, Louisiana. Association for Computational Linguistics.

classification.

Araújo, M., Pereira, A., and Benevenuto, F. (2020). A comparative study of machine translation for multilingual sentence-level sentiment analysis. *Information Sciences*, 512:1078–1102.

Bahdanau, D., Brakel, P., Xu, K., Goyal, A., Lowe, R., Pineau, J., Courville, A., and Bengio, Y. (2017). An actor-critic algorithm for sequence prediction. In *5th International Conference on Learning Representations*, Toulon, France.

Balahur, A. and Turchi, M. (2012). Multilingual sentiment analysis using machine translation? In *Proceedings of the 3rd Workshop in Computational Approaches to Subjectivity and Sentiment Analysis*, pages 52–60, Jeju, Korea. Association for Computational Linguistics.

Barnes, J., Lambert, P., and Badia, T. (2016). Exploring distributional representations and machine translation for aspect-based cross-lingual sentiment classification. In *Proceedings of COLING 2016, the 26th International Conference on Computational Linguistics: Technical Papers*, pages 1613–1623.

Bengio, Y., Louradour, J., Collobert, R., and Weston, J. (2009). Curriculum learning. In *Proceedings of the 26th annual international conference on machine learning*, pages 41–48.

Berard, A., Calapodescu, I., Dymetman, M., Roux, C., Meunier, J.-L., and Nikoulina, V. (2019). Machine translation of restaurant reviews: New corpus for domain adaptation and robustness. In *Proceedings of the 3rd Workshop on Neural Generation and Translation*, pages 168–176, Hong Kong. Association for Computational Linguistics.

Chen, B. and Zhu, X. (2014). Bilingual sentiment consistency for statistical machine translation. In *Proceedings of the 14th Conference of the European Chapter of the Association for Computational Linguistics*, pages 607–615.

Devlin, J., Chang, M.-W., Lee, K., and Toutanova, K. (2019). BERT: Pre-training of deep bidirectional transformers for language understanding. In *Proceedings of the 2019 Conference of the North American Chapter of the Association for Computational Linguistics: Human Language Technologies, Volume 1 (Long and Short Papers)*, pages 4171–4186, Minneapolis, Minnesota.

Fei, H. and Li, P. (2020). Cross-lingual unsupervised sentiment classification with multi-view transfer learning. In *Proceedings of the 58th Annual Meeting of the Association for Computational Linguistics*, pages 5759–5771, Online. Association for Computational Linguistics.

Fleiss, J. L. (1971). Measuring nominal scale agreement among many raters. *Psychological bulletin*, 76(5):378.

Kanayama, H., Nasukawa, T., and Watanabe, H. (2004). Deeper sentiment analysis using machine translation technology. In *COLING 2004: Proceedings of the 20th International Conference on Computational Linguistics*, pages 494–500, Geneva, Switzerland. COLING.

Koehn, P. (2004). Statistical significance tests for machine translation evaluation. In *Proceedings of the 2004 Conference on Empirical Methods in Natural Language Processing*, pages 388–395, Barcelona, Spain.

Lohar, P., Afli, H., and Way, A. (2017). Maintaining sentiment polarity in translation of user-generated content. *The Prague Bulletin of Mathematical Linguistics*, 108(1):73–84.

Lohar, P., Afli, H., and Way, A. (2018). Balancing translation quality and sentiment preservation. In *Proceedings of the 13th Conference of the Association for Machine Translation in the Americas (Volume 1: Research Papers)*, pages 81–88, Boston, MA.

Luong, T., Pham, H., and Manning, C. D. (2015). Effective approaches to attention-based neural machine translation. In *Proceedings of the 2015 Conference on Empirical Methods in Natural Language Processing*, pages 1412–1421, Lisbon, Portugal.

Mohammad, S. M., Salameh, M., and Kiritchenko, S. (2016). How translation alters sentiment. *Journal of Artificial Intelligence Research*, 55:95–130.

Nguyen, K., Daumé III, H., and Boyd-Graber, J. (2017). Reinforcement learning for bandit neural machine translation with simulated human feedback. In *Proceedings of the 2017 Conference on Empirical Methods in Natural Language Processing*, pages 1464–1474, Copenhagen, Denmark.

Poncelas, A., Lohar, P., Hadley, J., and Way, A. (2020a). The impact of indirect machine translation on sentiment classification. In *Proceedings of the 14th Conference of the Association for Machine Translation in the Americas (Volume 1: Research Track)*, pages 78–88, Virtual. Association for Machine Translation in the Americas.

Poncelas, A., Lohar, P., Way, A., and Hadley, J. (2020b). The impact of indirect machine translation on sentiment classification. *arXiv preprint arXiv:2008.11257*.

Ranzato, M., Chopra, S., Auli, M., and Zaremba, W. (2016). Sequence level training with recurrent neural networks. In *4th International Conference on Learning Representations*, San Juan, Puerto Rico.

Sennrich, R., Haddow, B., and Birch, A. (2016a). Controlling politeness in neural machine translation via side constraints. In *Proceedings of the 2016 Conference of the North American Chapter of the Association for Computational Linguistics: Human Language Technologies*, pages 35–40.

Sennrich, R., Haddow, B., and Birch, A. (2016b). Neural machine translation of rare words with subword units. In *Proceedings of the 54th Annual Meeting of the Association for Computational Linguistics (Volume 1: Long Papers)*, pages 1715–1725, Berlin, Germany.

Tebbifakhr, A., Bentivogli, L., Negri, M., and Turchi, M. (2019). Machine translation for machines: the sentiment classification use case. In *Proceedings of the 2019 Conference on Empirical Methods in Natural Language Processing and the 9th International Joint Conference on Natural Language Processing (EMNLP-IJCNLP)*, pages 1368–1374, Hong Kong, China.

Tebbifakhr, A., Negri, M., and Turchi, M. (2020). Automatic translation for multiple nlp tasks: a multi-task approach to machine-oriented nmt adaptation. In *Proceedings of the 22nd Annual Conference of the European Association for Machine Translation*, pages 235–244.

Williams, R. J. (1992). Simple statistical gradient-following algorithms for connectionist reinforcement learning. *Mach. Learn.*, 8(3–4):229–256.

Wu, H., Wang, Z., Qing, F., and Li, S. (2021). Reinforced transformer with cross-lingual distillation for cross-lingual aspect sentiment classification. *Electronics*, 10(3):270.

Wu, L., Tian, F., Qin, T., Lai, J., and Liu, T.-Y. (2018). A study of reinforcement learning for neural machine translation. In *Proceedings of the 2018 Conference on Empirical Methods in Natural Language Processing*, pages 3612–3621, Brussels, Belgium.

Xu, J., Sun, X., Zeng, Q., Zhang, X., Ren, X., Wang, H., and Li, W. (2018). Unpaired sentiment-to-sentiment translation: A cycled reinforcement learning approach. In *Proceedings of the 56th Annual Meeting of the Association for Computational Linguistics (Volume 1: Long Papers)*, pages 979–988, Melbourne, Australia.

Zhao, M., Wu, H., Niu, D., and Wang, X. (2020). Reinforced curriculum learning on pre-trained neural machine translation models. In *The Thirty-Fourth AAAI Conference on Artificial Intelligence, AAAI 2020, The Thirty-Second Innovative Applications of Artificial Intelligence Conference, IAAI 2020, The Tenth AAAI Symposium on Educational Advances in Artificial Intelligence, EAAI 2020, New York, NY, USA, February 7-12, 2020*, pages 9652–9659. AAAI Press.

On nature and causes of observed MT errors

Maja Popović maja.popovic@adaptcentre.ie
ADAPT Centre, School of Computing, Dublin City University, Ireland

Abstract

This work describes analysis of nature and causes of MT errors observed by different evaluators under guidance of different quality criteria: adequacy, comprehension, and a not specified generic mixture of adequacy and fluency. We report results for three language pairs, two domains and eleven MT systems. Our findings indicate that, despite the fact that some of the identified phenomena depend on domain and/or language, the following set of phenomena can be considered as generally challenging for modern MT systems: rephrasing groups of words, translation of ambiguous source words, translating noun phrases, and mistranslations. Furthermore, we show that the quality criterion also has impact on error perception. Our findings indicate that comprehension and adequacy can be assessed simultaneously by different evaluators, so that comprehension, as an important quality criterion, can be included more often in human evaluations.

1 Introduction and related work

Machine translation (MT), like many other natural language generation tasks, is difficult to evaluate because there is no single correct output for a given input: for each source text, there is a large set of possible correct translations. Therefore, while costly both in time and resources, human evaluation is required to provide a reliable feedback for measuring MT quality and progress, as well as to serve as a gold standard for development of automatic evaluation metrics. While better and better automatic metrics are constantly emerging (Mathur et al., 2020; Ma et al., 2019), many of them being based on semantic word representations (embeddings), all of them represent only an approximate substitution for human assessment of translation quality. Various methods have been proposed and used for the human evaluation of MT output from the beginning of MT until now (ALPAC, 1966; White et al., 1994; Koehn and Monz, 2006; Vilar et al., 2007; Graham et al., 2013; Forcada et al., 2018; Barrault et al., 2020; Kreutzer et al., 2020; Popović, 2020a), and all of them are essentially based on some of the following three quality criteria: adequacy (how much meaning is preserved), comprehensibility (how comprehensible/readable the translation is) and fluency (grammar of the target language).

The evaluators are usually asked to assign an overall quality score for the given MT output (ALPAC, 1966; White et al., 1994; Koehn and Monz, 2006; Roturier and Bensadoun, 2011; Graham et al., 2013; Barrault et al., 2020) or to rank two or more competing outputs from best to worst (Vilar et al., 2007; Callison-Burch et al., 2008; Bojar et al., 2015). For assessing comprehension, question answering (Scarton and Specia, 2016) and filling gaps (Forcada et al., 2018) were explored, too. Recently, evaluators have been asked to highlight the observed translation errors (Kreutzer et al., 2020; Popović, 2020a).

In order to get more details about the actual errors, error classification according to a predefined error scheme is often performed. The mostly applied schemes have been the one proposed by Vilar et al. (2006), and the MQM scheme[1] (Lommel et al., 2014) in recent years (Klubička et al., 2018; Freitag et al., 2021).

Another method to better understand particular strengths and weaknesses of MT systems is to identify nature and causes of the errors in form of linguistically motivated phenomena which, although related, often go beyond the usual error types. This type of analysis is being increasingly employed in the last years in order to better understand the ocurring errors (Popović, 2018; Arnejšek and Unk, 2020) and also to create specialised test sets ("challenge test sets" or "test suites") in order to perform more focussed evaluation procedures on identified phenomena (Isabelle et al., 2017; Šoštarić et al., 2018; Voita et al., 2019).

This work goes in this direction, but in a slightly different way: we do not try to identify the phenomena from scratch, but from translation errors already observed and highlighted by several evaluators (Kreutzer et al., 2020; Popović, 2020a). The error marking was not guided by any pre-defined error scheme, so that the evaluators had more freedom in annotating errors than in typical error classification tasks such as MQM.

We analysed the nature of these errors by tagging them with possible causes and/or plausible explanations of their origin (referred to as "phenomena"). The definition of these phenomena is based both on general linguistic knowledge as well as on phenomena related to the (machine) translation process. We did not have any pre-defined scheme for the phenomena, but we started by looking into errors and identifying the phenomena on the fly.

It is worth noting that we did not create any test suite – we do not know how many instances of each of the identified phenomena exists in the data in total, nor how many of them are correctly translated. We only analyse the observed translation errors. Nevertheless, our findings can be inspiring and useful for future work on creation of test suites.

The main goal of this work is to identify nature and causes of translation errors perceived by a set of evaluators and to get a better insight about the underlying phenomena and their impact on translation quality. In addition, we investigate the perception of major and minor errors, and also explore perception of errors for two different quality criteria: adequacy and comprehension.

We used two publicly available data sets containing English→Croatian, English→Serbian and English→German MT outputs with highligted translation errors. We first identified a set of 26 underlying phenomena around these errors and then analysed them.

2 Data sets

We worked on two publicly available data sets with highlighted MT errors: one provided by Dublin City University (*DCU*)[2] and one provided by Heidelberg University (*HU*).[3] While both data sets contain MT outputs with highlighted translation errors, there are several important differences between them.

***DCU* data set** This data set was created for purposes of MT evaluation (Popović, 2020a). The set consists of English user reviews translated into Croatian and Serbian. For each of the target languages, five different MT systems were used: three online systems (Amazon, Bing and Google) and two in-house systems based on the Sockeye[4] (Hieber et al., 2018) implementation. In total, the data set contains outputs of ten different MT systems.

Two quality criteria were used for highlighting errors: adequacy and comprehension. An important difference between the two (apart from the definition) which can lead to differences

[1] `http://www.qt21.eu/mqm-definition/definition-2015-12-30.html`

[2] `https://github.com/m-popovic/QRev-annotations`

[3] `https://www.cl.uni-heidelberg.de/statnlpgroup/humanmt/`

[4] `https://github.com/awslabs/sockeye`

in perception of errors is that seeing the source text was *required* for adequacy while seeing the source text was *forbidden* for comprehension. For both quality aspects, the evaluators were asked to concentrate on problematic parts of the text and to highlight them. They were also asked to distinguish between major and minor errors. All translations were evaluated in context – the evaluators were seeing entire reviews.

In total, 15 evaluators participated in the annotation. The largest part of the text is annotated by two evaluators, while a small part of the text (about 40 sentences) is annotated by three or four evaluators. Nothing is annotated by a single evaluator. Inter-annotator agreement in terms of Krippendorf's α is 0.61 for adequacy errors and 0.51 for comprehension errors.

***HU* data set** This data set was not created for purposes of MT evaluation, but for improving an NMT system by giving it feedback about errors (Kreutzer et al., 2020). The set consists of English TED talks translated into German by one MT system, an in-house system based on the Joey NMT[5] (Kreutzer et al., 2019) implementation.

A very important difference in comparison to the *DCU* data set is that no specific quality criterion was used: the evaluators were only asked to "highlight the errors". Usually, such "generic" criterion represents a mixture of adequacy and fluency. Also, they were not asked to distinguish between major and minor errors. Another very important fact is, since the data set is created in order to improve a system, and the used loss function did not support omissions and reordering errros, the evaluators are specifically asked not to highlight these two types of errors. As for context, translated sentences were judged in isolation, however in consecutive order as they appeared in the original documents so that a reasonable amount of context was provided.

Ten evaluators participated in this annotation, although the largest part of the text is annotated by a single evaluator. Eleven sentences are, however, annotated by all ten evaluators and the reported Krippendorf's α is 0.201.

data set	language pairs	domain	# of segments	# of MT systems	quality criterion	% of marked errors
DCU	en→sr,hr	user	3334	10	adequacy	20.9
		reviews	3334	10	comprehension	24.1
HU	en→de	TED talks	302	1	not specified	13.7

Table 1: Statistics of the two analysed data sets containing MT outputs with highlighted errors.

An overview of the two data sets together with the overal percentage of highlighted words is presented in Table 1. The number of errors in the *HU* data set might be underrated due to unmarked reordering errors and omissions.

3 Identified phenomena

The errors in the described data sets were analysed in the following way: they were tagged as a particular phenomenon if 1) they were marked by at least one evaluator 2) it was possible to define a plausible cause and/or explanation for their origin. In order to motivate and facilitate future work of creating test suites and getting ideas for potential improvements of MT systems, we also tagged all corresponding English words. The analysed data sets with phenomena tags are available together with the original *DCU*[6] data set.

The identified phenomena are different by their nature: some of them are equivalent to the typical error classes (such as "mistranslation", "tense/aspect/mood") while some are going

[5]https://github.com/joeynmt/joeynmt

[6]https://github.com/m-popovic/QRev-annotations

far beyond that, often bringing on several different interwining types of errors. Some of them involve single words, while others might involve a large group of words, even entire sentences. For the phenomena with larger spans, we tagged all consecutive words although not necessarily all those words are marked as errors. A typical example is negation where all words within the negation span were considered as "negation" although the evaluators might perceive only some of the words as problematic. In total, we identified 26 phenomena which will now be described and explained in alphabetical order.

ambiguity Ambiguous source words are identified as one of the most frequent causes for observed errors.
An ambiguous word is a word which can have multiple meanings, depending on the context. The translation of such word is in principle correct, but not in the given context. For example, the English verb "play" has different meanings in sentences "The children are playing in the park" and "The children are playing piano".

case Morphological form of a word (inflection) denotes incorrect case.

conjunction If a conjunction in the source language is omitted (typical for English), it can result in incorrect translation with different types of errors (lexical, morphological, order). For example, "Did you know I bought a new bike?" vs "Did you know *that* I bought a new bike?", the first sentence can provoke errors in all investigated target languages because they require a conjunction. The phenomenon involves several words around the conjunction.

determiner Incorrect or added determiner.

extra word Word(s) is/are added in the translation.

gender Morphological form of a word (inflection) denotes incorrect gender.

hallucination Translation is absolutely unrelated to the source text. For example, if the source text "Hi, how are you" is translated into "Hi, how it's going, shall we meet tomorrow?", "shall we meet tomorrow" is considered as hallucination.

"ing"-word English words with the suffix "ing" can denote present continous tense, gerund, or a noun, which might be difficult to translate properly.

mistranslation Mistranslation is one of the most frequent causes for the highlighted translation errors. It refers to an incorrect translation of the given word or phrase.

named entity A named entity generated in the target language is incorrect for some of the following reasons or a combination of them: 1) incorrectly translated 2) untranslated 3) unnecessarily translated 4) incorrectly transcribed 5) incorrect case/gender/number.
Errors related to named entities are quite frequent in user reviews, however very rare in TED talks. Also, named entities are generally easier to handle in German than in Croatian and Serbian.

negation Missing negation marker(s), added negation marker(s), or incorrectly formed negation structure involving different types of errors. The phenomenon involves all words within the negation span, possibly entire sentence.

non-existing word A word in translation does not exist either in the source or in the target language. Includes non-existing morphological variants as well as completely invented words.

noun phrase Noun phrases also belong to the most frequent causes of the highlighted translation errors. An English noun phrase consists of a head noun and additional nouns and adjectives.

Its translation can result in different types of often interwined errors (lexical, morphological, omissions, order) because formation rules for Serbian and Croatian are rather different than for English and there is often no unique solution. And even though formation rules in German are similar to the English ones, translation errors are still occurring. The examples in Table 2 represent four English noun phrases and their correct translations into Serbian, Croatian or German, together with some of the observed erroneous translations.

domain	language	noun phrase
user reviews	EN source	grill cover
	SR/HR correct	poklopac za roštilj
	MT outputs	roštilj poklopac, roštilj
	EN source	bird feeder
	SR/HR correct	hranilica za ptice
	MT outputs	hranilica ptica, ptica hranilica
TED talks	EN source	traveling salesman problem
	DE correct	Problem des Handlungsreisenden
	MT output	Reisen Verkäufer Problem
	EN source	slime mold
	DE correct	Schleimpilz
	MT output	Schlamm, Schlamm mold

Table 2: Examples of noun phrases.

number Morphological form of a word (inflection) denotes incorrect number.

omission Word(s) is/are missing in the translation: either a part of the source text is omitted, or something is not complete in the target language. This type of error cannot been found in the *HU* corpus because the evaluators were specifically instructed not to highlight it.

order Word(s) in the translation is/are at incorrect position(s). Although the evaluators of the *HU* corpus were instructed not to highlight this type of errors, a small amount of marked errors could be related to order.

passive Passive voice appears in the translation where active voice should be used, or other way round.

person (subject-verb agreement) Morphological form of a verb (inflection) denoting person does not correspond to the subject.

POS ambiguity A source word which can be interpreted as different POS tags. For example, the English word "works" can be plural of the noun "work" or third person singular of the verb "to work".

preposition Incorrect or added preposition.

pronoun Incorrect or added pronoun.

repetition Word(s) is/are unnecessarily repeated in the translation.

rephrasing Rephrasing is ranked as the most frequent cause for observed errors in all analysed data sets. It always affects more than one word, and sometimes spans over the entire sentence.
Rephrasing refers to a sequence of source words which is not translated properly for some of the following reasons or their combination: 1) the choice of each target language word looks random, both lexically and morphologically, without taking any context into account 2) rephrasing is needed in the target language but the translation follows the structure of the source language 3) rephrasing is not needed in the target language but is applied 4) rephrasing is needed in the target language but it is incorrectly applied. The phenomenon also comprises incorrect translation of multi-word expressions and collocations. It is usually manifested by several consecutive different but interwined types of errors, such as morphological (case, gender, person/tense/mood/aspect, etc.), lexical (ambiguity, mistranslation, multi-word expression), word order, etc.

Table 3 shows six groups of English source words which had to be rephrased in the given target language. Even non-speakers of the target languages can note that the correct version and the generated MT output are significantly different in several ways (order, words, endings).

In all examples except the fourth one, the translation output is rather literal, namely the system failed to apply rephrasing and the output follows the structure of the source text. In the fourth example, however, the system rephrased the source text, but the applied rephrasing was incorrect and changed the meaning.

domain	language	group of words to be rephrased
user reviews	EN source	tries really hard in this one
	SR/HR correct	baš se trudi u ovom
	MT output	pokušava stvarno jako teško u ovom jednom
	EN source	it does a good job of protecting
	SR/HR correct	dobro štiti
	MT output	to radi dobar posao štititi
	EN source	nowhere close
	SR/HR correct	ni približno
	MT output	nigde nije blizu
	EN source	gets his little gray cells working
	SR/HR correct	aktivira svoje male sive ćelije
	MT output	radi na svojim malim sivim ćelijama
	EN gloss	works on his little gray cells
TED talks	EN source	you name it
	DE correct	was (auch immer) Sie wollen
	MT output	Sie bennenen es
	EN source	and so am I
	DE correct	und ich auch
	MT output	und so bin ich

Table 3: Examples of rephrasing.

source error A word in the original text in the source language has spelling or grammar errors which resulted in incorrect translation. This type of issue has been found in user reviews but not in TED talks.

tense/aspect/mood Morpho-syntactic form of a verb (inflection, derivation, auxiliary verb) denotes incorrect tense, aspect or mood.

untranslated A word in the source language is simply copied into the translation.

4 Distribution of the observed errors over the identified phenomena

Once the phenomena were identified and tagged, for each of them the contribution was calculated as percentage of observed errors related to it. Due to the differences between the two data sets described in Section 2 as well as the two different quality criteria in the *DCU* data set, the results in Table 4 are presented separately for each of these three texts.

The numbers should be interpreted as follows: the first number in the first column means that from all highlighted adequacy errors in the *DCU* set, 17.6% are related to rephrasing, 11.2% are related to an ambiguous source word, 7.67% are related to a noun phrase, etc. The other columns are to be interpreted in the same way (second column: "from all highlighted comprehension errors in the *DCU* set", third column: "from all highlighted errors in the *HU* set"). Phenomena contributing with at least 2% of highlighted words are shown in bold.

To errors which could not be interpreted by any particular phenomenon, a tag "None" was assigned. A number of these errors is related to individual preferences of different annotators, and therefore is less frequent in the *HU* corpus which was mainly annotated by a single evaluator. Some of these words are marked due to "error propagation", when several consecutive words are marked although only one of them is actually an errors. This effect is much stronger for comprehension, because adequacy is guided by the source text.

Table 4 presents phenomena with a contribution of at least 2% of errors in at least one of the three texts. Those with at least 2% in all three texts are presented in bold. The phenomena are sorted according to their contribution to adequacy errors in the *DCU* set, but it can be noted that the contributions are very similar for comprehension errros, and also for the *HU* set.

Rephrasing, **ambiguous words**, **noun phrases** and **mistranslations** have very similar (high) influence on error perception in all data sets, strongly indicating that they represent challenging phenomena for modern MT systems.

data set:	*DCU*		*HU*
domain:	user reviews		TED talks
language pair:	en→sr, hr		en→de
quality criterion:	adequacy	comprehension	not specified
rephrasing	**17.6**	**16.6**	**21.7**
ambiguity	**11.2**	**8.98**	**13.3**
noun phrase	**7.67**	**6.65**	**7.10**
named entity	**4.63**	**4.38**	0.07
mistranslation	**4.37**	**3.10**	**13.7**
omission	**2.94**	1.38	0 (!)
gender	**2.84**	**2.41**	1.53
case	**2.45**	**2.30**	0.66
untranslated	**2.05**	1.86	**4.11**
preposition	1.02	0.90	**3.25**
extra word	0.05	0.36	**3.25**
none	27.6	38.3	21.0

Table 4: Percentages of perceived errors related to the identified phenomena: adequacy errors in *DCU* corpus (left), comprehension errors in *DCU* corpus (middle), errors in *HU* corpus (right).

Rephrasing errors seem to be partly dependent on MT system: some systems tend to stay close to the source text (generating overly literal translations) while others tend to diverge from the source (generating incorrect rephrasings). These effects should be investigated further in more details, also by creating appropriate test suites.

As for ambiguous source words, our analysis confirmed that they represent a challenge for modern NMT systems. Several test suites have already been developed (Rios Gonzales et al., 2018; Müller et al., 2018; Raganato et al., 2019), but creating more test suites covering different types of ambiguous words and various language pairs would be certainly beneficial. It should be noted that, while translation of ambiguous words can be improved by context-aware ("document-level") NMT systems, incorporating external context often could be more helpful than extending context to more sentences. For example, if a source text is a product review, it can indicate that "I will get this part" most probably means "I will buy this part of some object", while for a movie or book review "I don't get this part" probably means "I don't understand this part of a movie/book".

Mistranslations mostly consist of simply incorrect lexical choices, however a number of them looks as "false friends". Sub-word units are the most probably reason for this type of errors, but it should be investigated further in more details.

Untranslated words contribute to errors, too, although to lesser extent. The same can be observed for **omissions**, however it has to be noted that the contribution of omissions is underrated in both analysed data sets; they are not at all marked in the *HU* corpus, and even though they are marked in the *DCU* corpus by omission mark, the evaluators mostly added one single omission mark for missing phrases. Furthermore, the nature of omissions should be investigated more, for example how many of them are related to the source text and how many to the target text. Another difference between the two data sets can be seen for **named entites**: they seem to be rather problematic only in the *DCU* corpus. Therefore, errors related to named entities are probably domain and/or language dependent.

The largest difference between the two corpora can be observed for **prepositions** and **extra words**, which resulted in much more errors in the *HU* corpus. This indicates possible dependance on domain and language, but also on MT system (since only one MT system was annotated in this corpus) and on quality criterion (because it was not specified for this corpus).

Also, contribution of **gender** and especially **case** is larger in morphologically rich(er) Slavic languages than in German. It should be noted that these two phenomena include only single-word errors *exclusively* related to gender and/or case: there are more gender and case errors, but within other phenomena with larger spans: rephrasing, noun phrase, conjunction.

4.1 Major vs minor errors

As mentioned in Section 2, the evaluators of the *DCU* data set were asked to distinguish between major and minor errors. While some of the phenomena are found to be much more frequent than others, frequency of errors is not necessarily related to their importance/severity (Federico et al., 2014; Kirchhoff et al., 2014). Therefore, we further analysed *all* identified phenomena in order to determine whether they are more related to major or to minor errors. We have, however, to take into account that for the less frequent phenomena, the results of this analysis might not be sufficiently reliable.

Perceptions of each of the phenomena in the form of percentage are shown in Table 5. The numbers are to be interpreted as follows (first row, first three columns): from all words belonging to the "rephrasing" phenomenon, 32.0% are perceived as major adequacy errors, 37.6% as minor adequacy errors, and 30.3% are not perceived as errors. These correct words are often related to the phenomena with larger word spans where not all words were perceived as errors, but also to the individual preferences of different annotators.

	adequacy			comprehension		
phenomenon	major	minor	correct	major	minor	correct
rephrasing	32.0	37.6	30.3	33.6	38.0	28.4
ambiguity	**48.2**	31.5	20.3	39.2	39.2	21.6
noun phrase	35.5	34.2	30.2	33.1	35.6	31.3
named entity	27.5	**44.3**	28.2	26.6	**44.8**	28.5
mistranslation	**68.5**	18.6	13.0	**53.2**	28.0	18.8
omission	**53.7**	46.3	0	21.6	**78.1**	0.31
gender	10.6	**69.9**	19.5	13.8	**64.1**	22.1
case	15.4	**66.7**	17.9	25.2	**59.4**	15.4
untranslated	**73.2**	13.1	13.7	**64.8**	22.7	12.5
person	27.5	**57.8**	14.6	23.1	**58.5**	18.4
tense/aspect/mood	18.7	**56.9**	24.4	25.2	**50.9**	23.4
pronoun	21.1	**53.9**	24.9	21.4	**47.9**	30.6
non-existing word	**58.9**	28.7	12.3	**57.1**	33.3	9.6
source error	**68.3**	18.5	13.2	**56.6**	27.8	15.6
negation	22.1	22.9	**55.0**	25.8	28.3	**45.8**
"-ing" word	33.9	37.6	28.5	35.0	38.3	26.7
preposition	39.1	38.8	22.1	30.4	**47.8**	21.8
POS ambiguity	**46.2**	36.6	17.2	**49.1**	32.2	18.7
order	12.7	**56.9**	30.4	18.6	**54.2**	27.1
conjunction	24.8	33.1	**42.1**	**44.1**	25.8	30.1
passive	23.5	**54.9**	21.6	21.0	**58.6**	20.4
number	11.3	**72.2**	16.5	13.3	**68.1**	18.6
repetition	39.7	40.9	19.4	21.7	**69.6**	8.7
extra word	34.9	**42.9**	22.2	26.5	**55.9**	17.6
determiner	27.8	**44.4**	27.8	18.2	**45.4**	36.4
hallucination	**87.5**	0	12.5	**50.0**	0	**50.0**
none	2.00	5.60	**92.4**	4.63	7.37	**88.0**

Table 5: Percentages of words related to each of the identified phenomena perceived as major errors, minor errors or as correct.

The phenomena are again ordered according to their overall contribution to observed adequacy errors. It can be seen that ambiguity, mistranslation and untranslated words are mostly perceived as major errors, while named entitites, gender and case as minor errors. For phenomena with larger spans, namely rephrasing and noun phrase, words are equally often perceived as major errors, minor errors or as correct. Generally, for phenomena with larger spans, a number of words is perceived as correct, especially for negation and conjunction. Interestingly, perception of conjunction-related errors is rather different for comprehension: most of the words are perceived as major errors. It indicates that many of those words are hard to read although their meaning did not change.

As for omissions, they are also perceived differently for adequacy and for comprehension: mainly as major adequacy errors, but as minor comprehension errors. The main reason for this discrepance is that many omissions are not possible to perceive without access to the source text.

As for less frequent phenomena, the following tendencies can be observed: verb forms (person, tense/aspect/mood, passive), pronouns, determiners, word order, number and extra words are mainly perceived as minor errors, while non-existing words, errors in the source text, POS ambiguity and hallucinations are mainly perceived as major errors. Repetitions and prepositions are mostly perceived as minor comprehension errors, but equally often as major and as minor adequacy errors.

The presented results indicate not only that severity of errors is perceived differently for different phenomena, but also that perception of some phenomena depends on the quality criterion. Previous work has already shown that adequacy errors are often "masked" by good fluency (Martindale and Carpuat, 2018), and also by good comprehension (Popović, 2020b). All that motivated us to investigate the differences between quality criteria for each of the identified phenomena.

4.2 Adequacy vs comprehension

Table 6 presents discrepances between the two quality criteria: *inadequate comprehensible words* are the words which changed the meaning of the source text but are perceived as comprehensible when reading the translation. On the other hand, *adequate incomprehensible words* are the words which are perceived as incomprehensible although their meaning is preserved. The results are presented only for the most prominent and most interesting phenomena.

Apart from exploring discrepancies between adequacy and comprehension errors observed by one evaluator, we also explored these discrepancies for two different evaluators. The motivation is that evaluating both criteria can be made easier if different evaluators are working on different criteria. If one single evaluator works on both criteria (as was the case with the *DCU* corpus), they have first to finish comprehension (in order not to see the source text), and then to start with adequacy. On the other hand, different evaluators could work simultaneously, thus saving time. Furthermore, while adequacy requires high proficiency in both the source and the target language, comprehension can be evaluated by fully monolingual evaluators. The results in Table 6 show that for two different evaluators all discrepances become higher (as intuitively expected), but the tendencies remain the same.

	same evaluator for A and C		different evaluators for A and C	
phenomenon	inadequate comprehensible words	adequate incomprehensible words	inadequate comprehensible words	adequate incomprehensible words
all	33.6	42.4	45.0	51.6
non-existing word	*4.31*	*9.76*	*10.0*	*15.4*
untranslated	*11.1*	*13.8*	*16.0*	*16.9*
source error	*16.2*	*14.1*	*22.9*	*19.8*
omission	**81.7**	**65.6**	**88.2**	**77.3**
hallucination	**42.8**	0	**57.1**	25.0
mistranslation	29.3	*12.4*	31.9	*16.1*
conjunction	**44.8**	**48.5**	**52.6**	**55.8**
negation	31.7	**40.5**	40.4	**48.0**
rephrasing	24.3	29.3	33.0	36.3
ambiguity	27.8	21.2	34.6	27.6
noun phrase	24.1	23.2	32.7	32.7

Table 6: Percentages of discrepances between adequacy and comprehension for the most interesting and the most prominent phenomena.

It can be seen that overall, 33% of all adequacy errors is comprehensible and more than 40% of all incomprehensible words are adequate translations. This confirms the previous findings that good comprehensibility often "masks" adequacy errors, but also shows a tendency in the opposite direction, namely "forgiving" incomprehensible errors after seeing the source text. Some of these "forgiven" errors were result of error propagation (as explained in Section 4), though, but not all of them.

For the majority of phenomena (most of them not presented in Table 6), the percentage of discrepances for the same evaluator is ranging from 20-35% (30-45% for different evaluators).

For some phenomena, however, a much lowe discrepancy can be seen in Table 6: source errors, non-existing and untranslated words result in similar perception of errors for both quality aspects.

On the other hand, there is a large number of comprehensible omissions, over 80%. This can be intuitively expected, because evaluators cannot perceive any omission related to the source text without access to it. Also, more than 65% omissions related to comprehension are "forgiven" or perceived as different error types when looking at the source text. Another phenomenon with a high discrepancy is hallucination: this type of errors is inadequate by its definition, but is often perceived as comprehensible. An opposite effect can be observed for mistranslations which are rarely observed as comprehensible.

A high discrepancy, although much smaller than for omissions, can be seen for phenomena with large spans. For missing English conjunctions and negation, there are more incomprehensible adequate words than "masked" adequacy errors. As previously mentioned, this is partly due to error propagation, but also indicates that the reader tends to "forgive" some incomprehensible parts after seeing the source text. The same tendency can be seen for the predominant phenomenon, rephrasing, although to much less extent.

5 Summary and outlook

We have carried out an extensive analysis of MT errors observed and highlighted by different evaluators according to different quality criteria. The analysis includes three language pairs, two domains and eleven NMT systems. Our main findings show that the majority of perceived errors are caused by rephrasing, ambiguous words, noun phrases and mistranslations, followed by untranslated words and omissions.

Furthermore, it is shown that perception of errors is dependent on the pre-defined quality criterion. For example, non-existing and untranslated words, as well as errors in the source text are perceived similarly for different quality aspects, but there is a large discrepance between adequacy and comprehension errors caused by negation, hallucinations and missing English conjunctions. Therefore, the ideal evaluation would include both quality criteria. However, comprehension cannot be properly assessed if the source text is seen, so that it cannot be evaluated together with adequacy, but has to be performed beforehand as a separated task. This is time and resource-consuming, so that usually a (often unspecified) combination of adequacy and fluency is used, while comprehension, although more important than fluency, is rarely included. Our findings indicate that evaluating both adequacy and comprehension can be facilitated, because it is not necessary that the same evaluators work on both quality criteria.

The findings also open several directions for future work. For some phenomena, further analysis is recommended, for example the type of rephrasing (literal translation or not), more details about the negation (span, type of negation marker(s), etc.), source vs target omissions, etc. Test suites should also be created for some of the phenomena, in order to provide more information about errors and give ideas for potential improvements of the current systems.

Acknowledgments

This project was partially funded by the European Association for Machine Translation through its 2019 sponsorship of activities programme. The ADAPT Centre for Digital Content Technology (www.adaptcentre.ie) at Dublin City University is funded by the Science Foundation Ireland Research Centres Programme (Grant13/RC/2106) and is co-funded by the European Regional Development Fund.

References

ALPAC (1966). Language and machines. Computers in translation and linguistics.

Arnejšek, M. and Unk, A. (2020). Multidimensional assessment of the eTranslation output for English–Slovene. In *Proceedings of the 22nd Annual Conference of the European Association for Machine Translation (EAMT 20)*, pages 383–392, Lisboa, Portugal.

Barrault, L., Biesialska, M., Bojar, O., Costa-juss, M. R., Federmann, C., Graham, Y., Grundkiewicz, R., Haddow, B., Huck, M., Joanis, E., Kocmi, T., Koehn, P., Lo, C.-k., Ljubei, N., Monz, C., Morishita, M., Nagata, M., Nakazawa, T., Pal, S., Post, M., and Zampieri, M. (2020). Findings of the 2020 conference on machine translation. In *Proceedings of the Fifth Conference on Machine Translation (WMT 20)*, pages 1–55, Online.

Bojar, O., Chatterjee, R., Federmann, C., Haddow, B., Huck, M., Hokamp, C., Koehn, P., Logacheva, V., Monz, C., Negri, M., Post, M., Scarton, C., Specia, L., and Turchi, M. (2015). Findings of the 2015 workshop on statistical machine translation. In *Proceedings of the Tenth Workshop on Statistical Machine Translation (WMT 15)*, pages 1–46, Lisbon, Portugal.

Callison-Burch, C., Fordyce, C., Koehn, P., Monz, C., and Schroeder, J. (2008). Further meta-evaluation of machine translation. In *Proceedings of the Third Workshop on Statistical Machine Translation (WMT 08)*, pages 70–106, Columbus, Ohio.

Federico, M., Negri, M., Bentivogli, L., and Turchi, M. (2014). Assessing the impact of translation errors on machine translation quality with mixed-effects models. In *Proceedings of the 2014 Conference on Empirical Methods in Natural Language Processing (EMNLP 14)*, pages 1643–1653, Doha, Qatar.

Forcada, M. L., Scarton, C., Specia, L., Haddow, B., and Birch, A. (2018). Exploring gap filling as a cheaper alternative to reading comprehen sion questionnaires when evaluating machine translation for gisting. In *Proceedings of the Third Conference on Machine Translation (WMT 18)*, pages 192–203, Brussels, Belgium.

Freitag, M., Foster, G., Grangier, D., Ratnakar, V., Tan, Q., and Macherey, W. (2021). Experts, errors, and context:a large-scale study of human evaluation for machine translation.

Graham, Y., Baldwin, T., Moffat, A., and Zobel, J. (2013). Continuous measurement scales in human evaluation of machine translation. In *Proceedings of the 7th Linguistic Annotation Workshop and Interoperability with Discourse*, pages 33–41, Sofia, Bulgaria.

Hieber, F., Domhan, T., Denkowski, M., Vilar, D., Sokolov, A., Clifton, A., and Post, M. (2018). The sockeye neural machine translation toolkit at AMTA 2018. In *Proceedings of the 13th Conference of the Association for Machine Translation in the Americas (AMTA 18)*, pages 200–207, Boston, MA.

Isabelle, P., Cherry, C., and Foster, G. (2017). A Challenge Set Approach to Evaluating Machine Translation. In *Proceedings of the 2017 Conference on Empirical Methods in Natural Language Processing (EMNLP 17)*, pages 2486–2496, Copenhagen, Denmark.

Kirchhoff, K., Capurro, D., and Turner, A. M. (2014). A conjoint analysis framework for evaluating user preferences in machine translation. *Machine Translation*, 28(1):117.

Klubička, F., Toral, A., and Sánchez-Cartagena, V. M. (2018). Quantitative Fine-grained Human Evaluation of Machine Translation Systems: A Case Study on English to Croatian. *Machine Translation*, 32(3):195–215.

Koehn, P. and Monz, C. (2006). Manual and automatic evaluation of machine translation between European languages. In *Proceedings on the Workshop on Statistical Machine Translation (WMT 06)*, pages 102–121, New York City.

Kreutzer, J., Bastings, J., and Riezler, S. (2019). Joey NMT: A minimalist NMT toolkit for novices. In *Proceedings of the 2019 Conference on Empirical Methods in Natural Language Processing and the 9th International Joint Conference on Natural Language Processing (EMNLP-IJCNLP 19)*, pages 109–114, Hong Kong, China.

Kreutzer, J., Berger, N., and Riezler, S. (2020). Correct Me If You Can: Learning from Error Corrections and Markings. *Proceedings of the 22nd Annual Conference of the European Association for Machine Translation (EAMT 20)*.

Lommel, A., Burchardt, A., Popović, M., Harris, K., and Avramidis, Eleftherios, a. d. U. H. (2014). Using a new analytic measure for the annotation and analysis of MT errors on real data. In *Proceedings of the 17th Annual Conference of the European Association for Machine Translation (EAMT 14)*, pages 165–172.

Ma, Q., Wei, J., Bojar, O., and Graham, Y. (2019). Results of the wmt19 metrics shared task: Segment-level and strong mt systems pose big challenges. In *Proceedings of the Fourth Conference on Machine Translation (WMT 19)*, pages 62–90, Florence, Italy.

Martindale, M. and Carpuat, M. (2018). Fluency over adequacy: A pilot study in measuring user trust in imperfect MT. In *Proceedings of the 13th Conference of the Association for Machine Translation in the Americas (AMTA 18)*, pages 13–25, Boston, MA.

Mathur, N., Wei, J., Freitag, M., Ma, Q., and Bojar, O. (2020). Results of the wmt20 metrics shared task. In *Proceedings of the Fifth Conference on Machine Translation (WMT 20)*, pages 688–725, Online.

Müller, M., Rios Gonzales, A., Voita, E., and Sennr ich, R. (2018). A Large-Scale Test Set for the Evaluation of Context-Aware Pronoun Translation in Neural Machine Translation. In *Proceedings of the 3rd Conference on Machine Translation (WMT 18)*, pages 61–72, Belgium, Brussels.

Popović, M. (2018). Language-related issues for NMT and PBMT for English–German and English–Serbian. *Machine Translation*, 32(3):237–253.

Popović, M. (2020a). Informative manual evaluation of machine translation output. In *Proceedings of the 28th International Conference on Computational Linguistics (COLING 20)*, Online.

Popović, M. (2020b). Relations between comprehensibility and adequacy errors in machine translation output. In *Proceedings of the Conference on Computational Natural Language Learning (CoNLL 20)*, Online.

Raganato, A., Scherrer, Y., and Tiedemann, J. (2019). The MuCoW Test Suite at WMT 2019: Automatically Harvested Multilingual Contrastive Word Sense Disambiguation Test Sets for Machine Translation. In *Proceedings of the 4th Conference on Machine Translation (WMT 19)*, Florence, Italy.

Rios Gonzales, A., Müller, M., and Sennrich, R. (2018). The Word Sense Disambiguation Test Suite at WMT18. In *Proceedings of the 3rd Conference on Machine Translation (WMT 18)*, pages 594–602, Belgium, Brussels.

Roturier, J. and Bensadoun, A. (2011). Evaluation of MT Systems to Translate User Generated Content. In *Proceedings of the MT Summit XIII*, Xiamen, China.

Scarton, C. and Specia, L. (2016). A reading comprehension corpus for machine translation evaluation. In *Proceedings of the Tenth International Conference on Language Resources and Evaluation (LREC 16)*, pages 3652–3658, Portorož, Slovenia. European Language Resources Association (ELRA).

Šoštarić, M., Hardmeier, C., and Stymne, S. (2018). Discourse-related language contrasts in English-Croatian human and machine translation. In *Proceedings of the Third Conference on Machine Translation (WMT 18)*, pages 36–48, Brussels, Belgium.

Vilar, D., Leusch, G., Ney, H., and Banchs, R. E. (2007). Human evaluation of machine translation through binary system comparisons. In *Proceedings of the Second Workshop on Statistical Machine Translation (WMT 07)*, pages 96–103, Prague, Czech Republic.

Vilar, D., Xu, J., D'Haro, L. F., and Ney, H. (2006). Error analysis of statistical machine translation output. In *Proceedings of the Fifth International Conference on Language Resources and Evaluation (LREC 06)*, Genoa, Italy.

Voita, E., Sennrich, R., and Titov, I. (2019). When a good translation is wrong in context: Context-aware machine translation improves on deixis, ell ipsis, and lexical cohesion. In *Proceedings of the 57th Annual Meeting of the Association for Computational Linguistics (ACL 19)*, Florence, Italy.

White, J., O'Connell, T., and O'Mara, F. (1994). The ARPA MT evaluation methodologies: evolution, lessons, and future approaches. In *Proceedings of the 1994 Conference of Association for Machine Translation in the Americas (AMTA 94)*, pages 193–205.

A Comparison of Sentence-Weighting Techniques for NMT

Simon Riess simon@tiger-bytez.com
Matthias Huck mhuck@cis.uni-muenchen.de
Work done while the author was employed at
Center for Information and Language Processing, LMU Munich, Germany

Alexander Fraser fraser@cis.uni-muenchen.de
Center for Information and Language Processing, LMU Munich, Germany

Abstract

Sentence weighting is a simple and powerful domain adaptation technique. We carry out domain classification for computing sentence weights with 1) language model cross entropy difference 2) a convolutional neural network 3) a Recursive Neural Tensor Network. We compare these approaches with regard to domain classification accuracy, and study the posterior probability distributions. Then we carry out NMT experiments in the scenario where we have no in-domain parallel corpora, and only very limited in-domain monolingual corpora. Here, we use the domain classifier to reweight the sentences of our out-of-domain training corpus. This leads to improvements of up to 2.1 BLEU for German to English translation.

1 Introduction

Neural Machine Translation (NMT) outperforms phrase based SMT for settings with large amounts of parallel data. However, in general adding out-of-domain data during training does not particularly improve NMT translation quality and is sometimes even harmful. For SMT domain adaptation is well understood and can be classified into two main approaches: 1) model centric techniques adapt the training objective on instance level (e.g., sentence weighting or regularization) or model level (e.g., ensembling or language models), and 2) data centric techniques perform a sentence selection based on a score indicating the similarity between the sentence to be translated and in-domain data.

We combine ideas from model centric and data centric approaches. We apply CNNs and Recursive Neural Tensor Networks (RNTNs) to compute domain scores for sentence weighting in NMT. We compare with a Cross-Entropy classifier (XenC) as a well established baseline. Our approach modifies the training objective so that every sentence pair is scaled by its individual weight, with sentences most similar to the in-domain data having most impact during training.

Our classifier is trained on small amounts of in-domain and out-of-domain monolingual data. We then use the classifier to find useful sentences within the out-of-domain data, i.e., sentences which are similar to the in-domain data.

We carry out intrinsic (classification) and extrinsic (MT) experiments applying sentence classification for domain adaptation. The scores obtained by the CNN and RNTN are strongly peaked in comparison to the cross-entropy classifier, which is important for the NMT sentence weighting. As the neural classifiers showed rather extreme probability score distributions in the intrinsic experiments, we studied various transformations of the scores which we use to find less peaked distributions. The resulting distributions showed less extreme behavior while preserving the strong classification ability. Applying our transformed scores to the task of sentence weighting for domain adaptation outperformed cross-entropy classifiers.

In summary, the contributions of this paper are as follows: 1) Neural classifiers show high confidence separating in- and out-of-domain data, higher than a cross-entropy classifier, hence posterior probabilities are distributed closely around the extremes 0 and 1. 2) The CNN and RNTN classifiers don't differ much from each other with respect to their score distributions, both are strongly peaked. 3) The extreme scores need to be transformed in order to be applied as weights in NMT, and we show how to do this effectively. 4) We show that using transformed CNN scores as weights during NMT training is better than a cross-entropy based classifier, which was the previous state-of-the-art solution.

2 Sentence-Weighting Techniques

In order to apply sentence weighting to the translation process, one first needs to come up with a method for scoring sentences with respect to how similar they are to in-domain data. Here we carry out a comparison between an established baseline (cross entropy) to the two different techniques based on neural networks that we have discussed (CNN and RNTN).

2.1 XenC: LM Cross-Entropy Difference

Language model (LM) cross-entropy difference scoring is a widely used technique for MT domain adaptation. The approach is implemented in the tool XenC Rousseau (2013). Here the difference between cross-entropy scores of sentences from the entire training corpus and the sentences of an in-domain corpus is computed. We applied monolingual cross-entropy difference as proposed by (Moore and Lewis, 2010), which is defined as

$$H(P_{LM}) = -\frac{1}{n}\sum_{i=1}^{n} logP_{LM}(w_i \mid w_i, \ldots, w_{i-1}) \quad (1)$$

where P_{LM} is the probability of the word w_i given the words w_1 to w_{i-1} for the language model LM. LM is estimated from the specified in-domain corpus. The formula is applied to all sentences in the training data for the NMT system, and is then interpreted as the sentence weight. XenC is not a neural system. It applies statistical computation of cross-entropy given an LM. The language model is a 4-gram model and Kneser-Ney smoothing is applied Ney et al. (1994).

This approach is widely used throughout various papers and systems with regard to domain adaptation. It is mathematically relatively inexpensive and can therefore be computed very quickly even for extensive training corpora, without the need for GPU resources. These factors make it a suitable baseline for our comparisons to neural classification systems.

2.2 CNN Classifier

Convolutional neural networks (CNN) perform very well on tasks like image and sentence classification. In our case, we are classifying sentences in two classes, in-domain and out-of-domain. We applied a plain vanilla system by Yoon Kim Kim (2014), which consists of a simple CNN on top of pretrained word vectors. CNNs consist of layers with convolving filters learning local features. In this architecture one layer of convolution is applied on top of word vectors trained by Mikolov et al. (2013) on Google News. This approach performed well on several sentence classification tasks (Kim, 2014).

Figure 1 shows this simple model architecture. A sentence of length n (shorter sentences are padded) is represented as the concatenation of its word vectors. Similar to computer vision

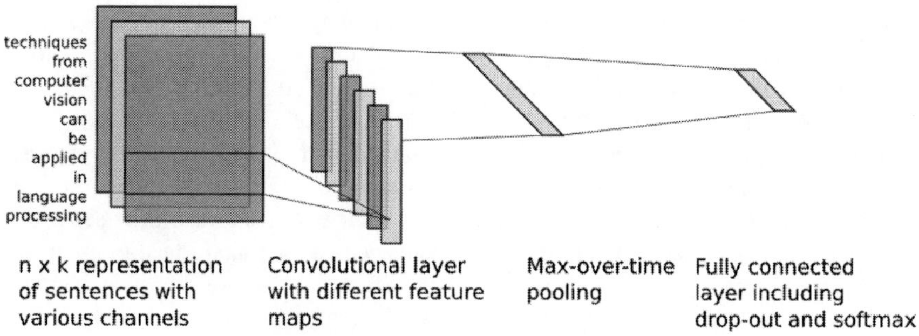

Figure 1: CNN model architecture.

tasks, filters are applied to words in a certain proximity to produce a new feature.

$$c_i = f(\mathbf{w} \cdot \mathbf{x}_{i:i+h-1} + b) \tag{2}$$

b is a bias term and f a non-linear activation function. The filter slides over the input sentence and therefore creates a feature map

$$\mathbf{c} = [c_1, c_2, \ldots, c_{n-h+1}] \tag{3}$$

Then max-over-time pooling is applied, $\hat{c} = max\{c\}$, to capture the most important feature for each feature map. Multiple filters are applied simultaneously and the max-pooling outputs form the penultimate layer. The last layer is a fully connected softmax layer to output the probability distribution over the labels.

For regularization to reduce over-fitting and improve generalization, Dropout and constraining the l_2-norms of weight vectors is applied Krizhevsky et al. (2012). Dropout randomly drops out - i.e. setting to zero - a proportion p of hidden units (in this case in the last layer) during training. Given the output of the max-pooling layer $\mathbf{z} = [\hat{c_1}, \hat{c_2}, \ldots, \hat{c}_m]$, instead of

$$y = \mathbf{w} \cdot \mathbf{z} + b \tag{4}$$

dropout uses

$$y = \mathbf{w} \cdot (\mathbf{z} \circ \mathbf{r}) + b \tag{5}$$

with $\circ$ being element-wise multiplication and $\mathbf{r} \in \mathbb{R}^m$ a "masking" vector of bernoulli distributed random variables with probability p of being 1. Furthermore a threshold s for l_2-norms in introduced, rescaling $\mathbf{w}$ to $||\mathbf{w}||_2 = s$ if $||\mathbf{w}||_2 > s$ after a gradient descent step.

2.3 RNTN Classifier

CNNs work on word vectors and filters, which aggregate local information within a sentence. This is less expressive than richer forms of sentence representation, e.g., parse trees, which take into account the grammatical structure. To deal with parse trees for sentiment classification (Socher et al., 2013) introduced a recursive deep model, the Recursive Neural Tensor Network (RNTN).

The representations of sentences within recursive neural models apply to variable length and syntactic type and is used for classification. First, each sentence is parsed into a binary tree with leaf nodes being single words, represented by a vector. Then the parent vectors will be computed in a bottom-up fashion using compositionality functions g. The parent vectors themselves are recursively given as features to a classifier and their parents respectively.

Each word is represented by a d dimensional word vector. These are fed into activation functions and ultimately used in $softmax$ for classification.

Recursive Neural Network. The simplest approach is the standard recursive neural network (Goller and Küchler, 1996; Socher et al., 2011). First, the parents whose children are already computed (i.e. both children are words) will be evaluated with an activation function $f = tanh$. Following equations are used to evaluate the parent nodes according to Figure 2a:

$$p_1 = f\left(W\begin{bmatrix} b \\ c \end{bmatrix}\right), p_2 = f\left(W\begin{bmatrix} a \\ p_1 \end{bmatrix}\right) \tag{6}$$

where $W \in \mathbb{R}^{dx2d}$ is the main learning parameter.

Matrix-Vector RNN. MV-RNNs are linguistically motivated in a sense that most of the parameters are linked with words and that the composition function depends on the actual words being combined. Each word and subphrase are represented as a vector and a matrix, which are combined in the composition function.

Each word's matrix initially is a dxd identity matrix with Gaussian noise. These matrices will be trained to optimise classification. Each sentence and subphrase is represented by a list of (vector, matrix) pairs and its parse tree. Following the same example from Figure 2a, the computation is as follows:

$$p_1 = f\left(W\begin{bmatrix} Cb \\ Bc \end{bmatrix}\right), P_1 = f\left(W_M\begin{bmatrix} B \\ C \end{bmatrix}\right), \tag{7}$$

while the parent pair (p_2, P_2) is computed using (p_1, P_1) and (a, A). The vectors are fed into the softmax function for classifying each subphrase.

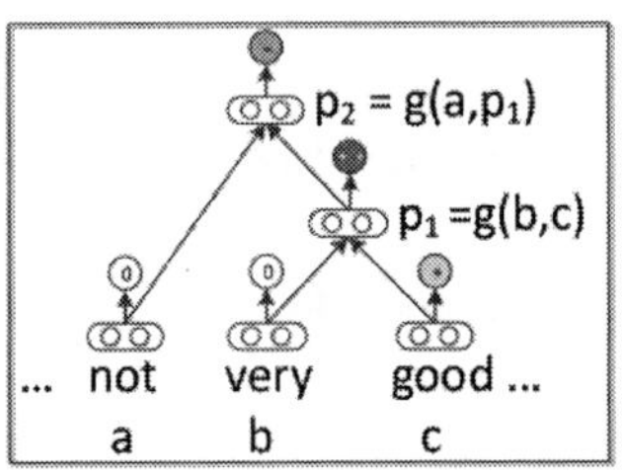

(a) Recursive Neural Network: Parent vectors are computed in a bottom up fashion, with activation function g and node vectors as features for classification. Socher et al. (2013) page 4 (CC BY-NC-SA 3.0 license).

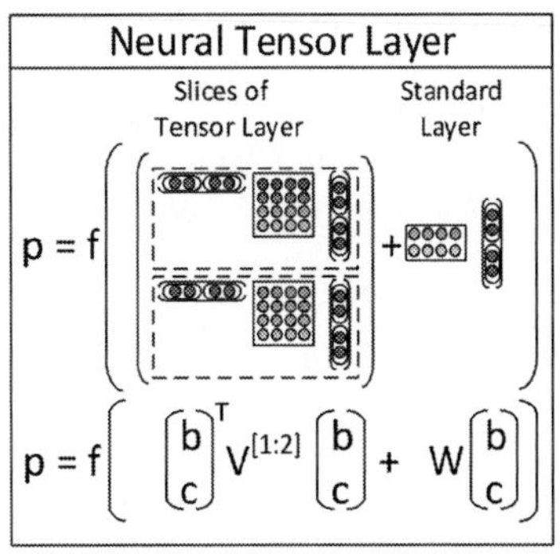

(b) A single layer of an RNTN: Representation of one of d-many slices, that can capture the type of influence a child node can have on its parents. Socher et al. (2013) page 6 (CC BY-NC-SA 3.0 license).

Figure 2: Recursive Neural Network and Recursive Neural Tree Network architecture

Recursive Neural Tensor Network. Since MV-RNNs combine vectors with matrices, the number of parameters becomes very large, also depending on vocabulary size. A fixed number of parameters would be more desirable. The standard recursive neural network has to be extended for this purpose, because there, different from the MV-RNN, the input vectors only interact with each other implicitly.

In search for a single, more powerful composition function to perform better and aggregate meaning from subphrases, they proposed the Recursive Neural Tensor Network. The output for a tensor product $h \in \mathbb{R}^d$ is computed as follows

$$h = \begin{bmatrix} b \\ c \end{bmatrix}^T V^{[1:d]} \begin{bmatrix} b \\ c \end{bmatrix}; h_i = \begin{bmatrix} b \\ c \end{bmatrix}^T V^i \begin{bmatrix} b \\ c \end{bmatrix}, \tag{8}$$

where $V^{[1:d]} \in \mathbb{R}^{2dx2dxd}$ is the tensor that defines multiple bilinear forms.

The RNTN uses a definition very similar to the standard recursive neural network for computing p_1:

$$p_1 = f\left(\begin{bmatrix} b \\ c \end{bmatrix}^T V^{[1:d]} \begin{bmatrix} b \\ c \end{bmatrix} + W \begin{bmatrix} b \\ c \end{bmatrix} \right) \tag{9}$$

The tensor V can directly relate input vectors and its slices can be interpretated as capturing specific types of composition, with a static number of parameters.

3 Intrinsic Evaluation: Domain Classification

3.1 Data

We study the interesting task of translation using limited in-domain monolingual corpora and larger out-of-domain parallel corpora, which is a realistic scenario. All classifiers were trained on 30k medical in-domain and 30k out-domain sentences, selected from the UFAL corpus.[1] This training data was the same for all three classifiers to allow comparison. The RNTN requires a certain input format, so the sentences were pre-processed by the Stanford Parser and brought into the necessary parse tree format.

For intrinsic evaluation, the classifiers were applied to gold standard test data. Newstest 2017 was used as out-of-domain data, whereas the medical HimL test set[2] was used as in-domain data. Both test sets contain about 2k sentences.

The trained classifiers were applied to the test sets, in the next section we analysed the classification errors and compared the respective probability score distribution.

3.2 Evaluation on Test sets

Classifier	Acc. [%]	Out Acc. [%]	In Acc. [%]
CNN	80.4	87.9	72.8
RNTN	76.1	87.3	64.8
XenC	71.1	46.8	95.4

Table 1: Classification results on German out-of-domain and in-domain test data.

Figure 3 and Table 1 show the scoring outputs for in- and out-domain test data. These histograms indicate how many sentences in the test set where assigned a certain score with bins of width 0.05. An output of 1 means high confidence for in-domain data and 0 means high confidence for out-domain data.

When comparing the results for the CNN and the RNTN, the differences are rather small, without obvious difference in shape of their distributions. We see a dominating peak at the correct side of the spectrum, which shows these classifiers have a high degree of confidence in their decisions. This peak diminishes rather quickly to then have a second minor peak around the other end of the spectrum.

This shape looks different for the cross entropy scoring. It resembles a bell curve with its mean slightly skewed towards the correct side of the spectrum. This shows a relatively unclear decision boundary between in- and out-of-domain data, since most of the sentences are scored rather in the middle between the two extremes.

[1]https://ufal.mff.cuni.cz/ufal_medical_corpus
[2]https://www.himl.eu/test-sets

These results should be taken with a grain of salt, as it is difficult to define pure in-domain and out-of-domain data. Discussions in the European Parliament (as found in the Europarl corpus) can revolve around medical topics, while being labeled as out-of-domain. Patient information as found in the data by the Health in my Language (HimL) project can include phrases of a more general nature, while being labeled in-domain. Such effects are not taken into account in our work.

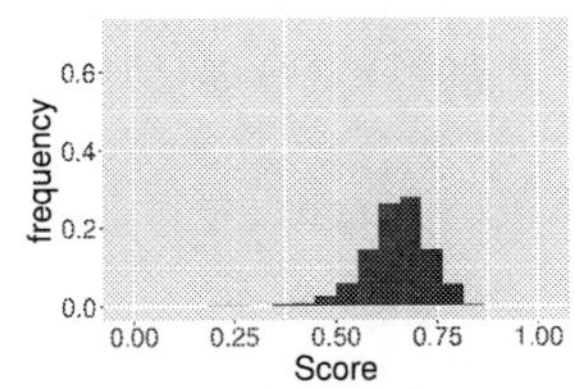

(a) Cross entropy, in-domain test data

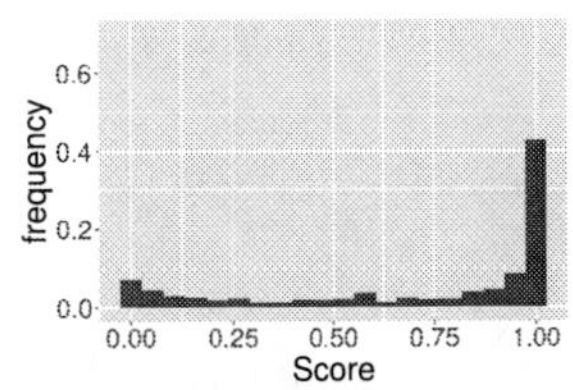

(b) CNN, in-domain test data

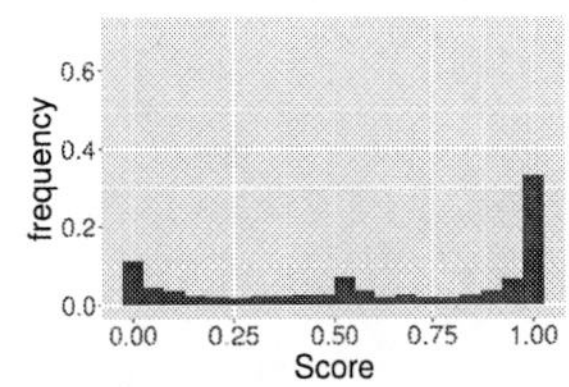

(c) RNTN, in-domain test data

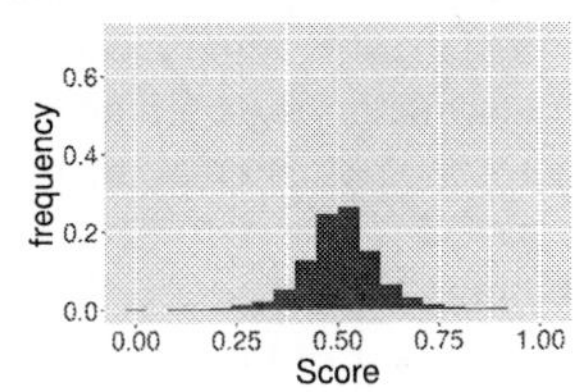

(d) Cross entropy, out-of-domain test data

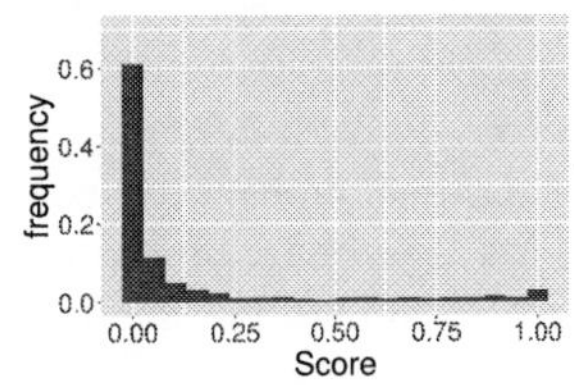

(e) CNN, out-of-domain test data

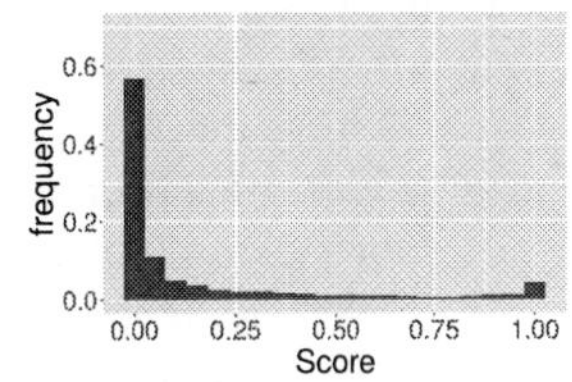

(f) RNTN, out-of-domain test data

Figure 3: Classifier outputs on German test data

3.3 Classifier probability scores on NMT training data

We applied the classifiers to the source (German) side of the NMT training data, leading to scores that can be used as weights during training the NMT system. Figure 4 shows the distribution of the scores for the CNN and the Cross Entropy classifier. Since we do have English data for the same 30K sentences, we also looked at this classification problem, but the graphs are very similar, so they are not presented. The similarity of English and German suggests that our work may apply well to other languages.

The scores by the XenC classifier look similar to a normal distribution, with its mean around 0.5-0.6. Most of the sentences are scored with similar values, indicating an average importance during learning. There are few outliers, overall the distribution is rather narrow with a low standard deviation.

The scores by the CNN classifier look significantly different. Instead of the expected normal distribution, most of the weights are below 0.1 with a few scores above 0.95. This means that the classifier is very confident in it's decisions. This high level of confidence is also visible in Figure 3.

4 Extrinsic Evaluation: Neural Machine Translation

In this section we first present our score transformations, and then we present the experiments and results.

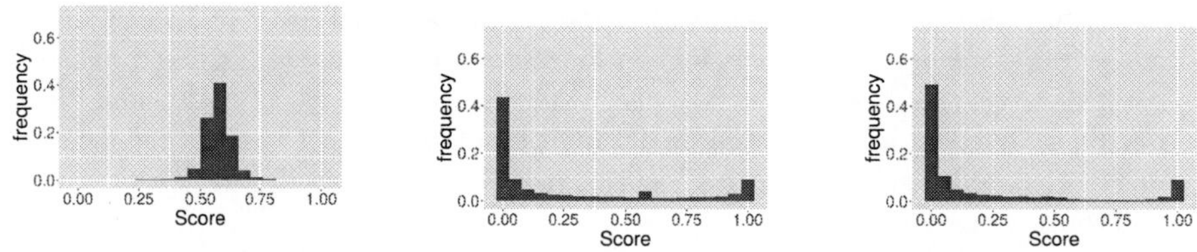

(a) Cross Entropy classifier XenC applied to NMT training data

(b) CNN classifier applied to NMT training data

(c) RNTN classifier applied to NMT training data

Figure 4: Classifier outputs on German NMT training data

4.1 Score Transformations

In initial experiments (which we present in detail later), we found that without applying score transformations instance weighting training of NMT models does not converge. During sentence weighting, the probability score from the classifiers is multiplied with the learning rate. As mentioned previously, the high classification confidence in neural classifiers lead to a vast majority of sentences scored very close to 0, setting the learning rate during training very low. This restricts the Transformer to only learn fully on a small subset of its original training data. We suppose the rather extreme original probability scores let the NMT starve for data.

For the purpose of sentence weighting, the data distributions from the classifier outputs are problematic in a sense that they put most of the mass to the borders of the distribution, i.e., almost all of the scores are very close to 0 or 1. This impacts the sentence weighting techniques significantly, since a score that is almost 0 effectively excludes these sentences from the data set. We therefore applied several score transformations to obtain a normalized score distribution, as we describe next.

Parabolic Transformation. The first approach is to multiply each of the scores with a linear function to increase the very low scores and decrease the very high scores. Here we chose a simple linear function by taking an educated guess without doing further hyperparameter optimisation. For every score x we applied the function

$$f(x) = x * (-4.2 * x + 5) \tag{10}$$

which results in a parabola with its peak around $x = 0.5$. A parabola in this shape increases low scores and decreases high scores. Its parameters were an educated guess, leading to competitive results in preliminary experiments.

Sigmoidal Transformation. The second approach is to limit the scores into a certain interval using a sigmoid function. We tried different hyperparameters indicating different intervals according the following function

$$\alpha * 1/(1 + exp(-6 * (x - 0.5))) + (1 - \alpha)/2 \tag{11}$$

indicating the interval $[0.5 - \alpha/2, 0.5 + \alpha/2]$. These functions are shown in Figure 5a, leading to a normalised distribution on the NMT training data shown in Figure 5b.

Quantile Transformation. The previous approaches lead to narrower and flatter data distributions. As a third approach, we made the distribution completely uniform.

The second attempt was to "normalise" the quantiles by considering the negatively classified (0-0.5) and the positive (0.5-1) sentences separately and then performing the quantile transformation on both subsets individually. Both categories were transformed into quantiles according to their own distribtion and then transformed back into the respective interval.

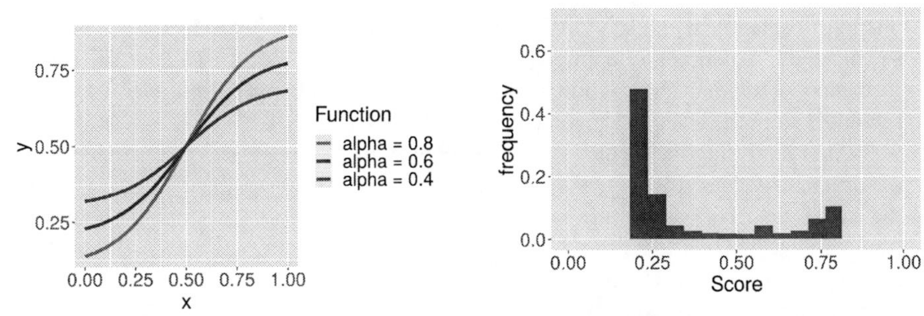

(a) Plot of sigmoidal transformation.

(b) CNN weights for NMT training data after sigmoidal transformation with $\alpha = 0.6$

Figure 5: Sigmoidal transformation and its effects on the probability score distribution

4.2 Experiments and Results

For our translation experiments we applied Marian (Junczys-Dowmunt et al., 2018) because of its ability to incorporate sentence weighting. It offers a transformer (Vaswani et al., 2017) implementation that closely follows the original architecture. This setup is shown to achieve state-of-the-art results. Marian is C++ based, which makes it very time efficient.

We assume a scenario with a sufficient amount of parallel out-of-domain data, but only a small amount of monolingual in-domain data on the source side. We use the classifiers we trained before. 3M out-of-domain sentences (of which 2M are from Europarl, see the UFAL corpus web page) from the UFAL corpus are used for training NMT. We report on two well-known MT test sets (Cochrane and NHS24) which are both from the medical domain.

Table 2 gives an overview of all performed experiments. A baseline transformer model (Table 2, row 1) was trained without any domain specific adaptation.

Since we assume we have 30K of monolingual in-domain data, we wanted to evaluate whether giving the NMT system access to this data could be effective. Since we had a translation of this 30K available, we actually fine-tuned on parallel data (i.e., we assumed perfect translation of the 30K, so this is an upper bound of the gains that could be obtained). The results (row 2) show that this is too little data to make much of a difference in translation quality (0.2 to 0.4 BLEU gains), which is not surprising given the very large out-of-domain corpus. The strong results we present below are qualitatively different from having access to a small amount of in-domain data to train on (even small amounts of in-domain parallel data).

The results for the the XenC classifier (row 3) serve as a stronger baseline for our results with the neural classifiers. We also tried to directly apply the scores from the neural classifiers, but this led to bad or unstable models that did not coverge (not shown in table). Too many sentences are scored too close to 0, letting their impact vanish, not allowing the training to converge. As discussed earlier and shown in Figure 4 for the CNN, most of the probability mass of the CNN's score distribution is concentrated at the extremes, 0 and 1, leading to many sentences having nearly no impact during training (this is similar for the RNTN as well). This is similar to training with too little data, as weighting a sentence very close to 0 skips the sentence.

These effects can be repaired by adding +1 to the classifier scores (rows 4-6), leading to improvements over the baseline for all trained systems, especially for the two neural classifiers. Further experiments focused on the CNN because it outperforms the RNTN and is simpler.

Following this we looked at score transformations. The scores from the CNN were manipulated by various sigmoidal transformations (rows 7-9), as its results in the first experiments looked most promising. As the qualitative analysis already showed in Figure 5b, after the sigmoidal transformation the CNN scores look more natural. The experiment results indicate that this transformation also lead to major improvements (rows 7-9), producing the best result (row 8) among our experiments, an improvement over the baseline of 2.1 BLEU. The sigmoid transformation keeps the CNN's ability to clearly distinguish between in-domain and out-domain sentences from the test sets - much clearer than XenC.

After analysing the results of different values for α on the score distribution for the training data, we restricted our hyperparameter search to three values, covering a reasonably big range, without requiring an excessive number of NMT training runs, which was not possible given our resources. $\alpha = 0.6$ seemed promising as higher values barely change the score distribution and lower values result in very narrow distributions, and indeed leads to better NMT results.

Another possibility of combining the CNN's classifying power and the XenC's natural score distribution, is averaging their scores (rows 10,11). This also lead to improvements over the baseline but could not beat the CNN in combination with the sigmoidal transformation (row 8).

	MT System		BLEU NHS24	BLEU Cochrane
(1)	Baseline		24.2	24.5
(2)	+ Fine-tuning		24.6	24.7
	Weighting	**With Transformation**		
(3)	XenC		23.2	23.8
(4)	XenC	+1	24.2	25.2
(5)	RNTN	+1	24.7	25.2
(6)	CNN	+1	24.9	25.7
(7)	CNN	$\text{Sigmoidal}_{0.8}$	24.7	25.7
(8)	CNN	$\text{Sigmoidal}_{0.6}$	**25.3**	**26.6**
(9)	CNN	$\text{Sigmoidal}_{0.4}$	24.6	25.7
(10)	CNN + XenC		24.9	25.7
(11)	CNN + XenC	+1	25.2	25.5
(12)	CNN	Parabolic +1	24.7	25.2
(13)	CNN	$\text{Sigmoidal}_{0.8}$ +1	24.4	25.8
(14)	CNN	$\text{Sigmoidal}_{0.6}$ +1	24.6	25.7
(15)	CNN	$\text{Sigmoidal}_{0.4}$ +1	24.1	25.8
(16)	CNN	Quantiles 10 +1	24.8	25.7
(17)	CNN	Quantiles NegPos +1	24.5	25.5

Table 2: Machine translation quality. We report case-sensitive BLEU of postprocessed translations.

Finally, as adding +1 to the scores improved the results for all classifiers, we also applied +1 to the previously described transformations (rows 12-17). This still lead to minor improvements over the baseline system, but was harmful to the CNN and its sigmoidal transformation.

In summary we saw that classifier outputs might be too extreme in their distribution, which can be normalised by transformations to even outperform baseline approaches. Neural classifiers show stronger abilities to distinguish between in-domain and out-of-domain data than cross-entropy based classifiers, resulting in higher BLEU scores when applied in sentence weighting.

5 Related Work

Domain adaptation strategies can be separated into four categories: data selection, data generation, instance weighting and model interpolation Chu and Wang (2018). We focus our discussion on data selection and instance weighting, as these are closely related to our approach.

Data-centric methods. Models are trained using in-domain and out-of-domain data to evaluate out-of-domain data and compute a similarity score. Using a cut-off threshold on these scores the training data can be selected. Language Models Moore and Lewis (2010); Axelrod et al. (2011); Duh et al. (2013) or joint models Cuong and Sima'an (2014); Durrani et al. (2015) can traditionally be applied to score corpora. Recently convolutional neural networks (CNN)

Chen et al. (2016) were used. Our work has similarities to this work but uses instance weighting rather than data selection.

In settings where the amount of parallel training corpora is not sufficient, generating pseudo-parallel sentences by information retrieval Utiyama and Isahara (2003), self-enhancing Lambert et al. (2011) or parallel word embeddings Marie and Fujita (2017). Aside from generating sentences, other approaches generate monolingual n-grams Wang et al. (2014) or parallel phrase pairs Chu (2015).

In general, data-centric methods (data selection and data generation) are not SMT specific and can be directly applied to NMT. However, because these methods are not directly related to NMT's training criterion, they only lead to minor improvements Wang et al. (2017a).

Model-centric methods. Instance Weighting is a technique from SMT and was introduced to NMT as well Wang et al. (2017b). An in-domain language model was trained to measure the similarity between sentences and the in-domain data via cross-entropy. The weights are then integrated into the training objective. We improve on their work by using state-of-the-art neural classifiers and showing that they are more effective than cross-entropy.

Two works that are closer to our work are Wang et al. (2018) and Chen et al. (2017). In Wang et al. (2018) they generate sentence embeddings for all in-domain sentences and then measure the distance between every sentence and the in-domain core. The underlying assumption is that the core of all in-domain sentence embeddings is a typical representative and proximity in their sentence embeddings indicates being part of the same domain. This approach is appropriate when we have in-domain parallel text, but we study a different scenario, with no access to in-domain parallel text, which means the encoder has no access to in-domain training examples. In Chen et al. (2017) a domain classifier is incorporated into the NMT system, using features from the encoder to distinguish between in-domain and out-of-domain data. The classifier probabilities are used to weight sentences with regard to their similarity to in-domain data, when training the neural network. Scaling the loss function is similar to multiplying the learning rate with the instance weight. The classifier and NMT are trained at the same time, whereas we chose an approach with pretrained neural classifiers which are trained on a small amount of monolingual data (the scenario we study) with no access to parallel in-domain data.

Finally, while some previous work we have mentioned did look at various ways to use domain classification, such previous work has not focused on how to weight the classifier probabilities for effective use in NMT, which we showed is important for obtaining translation quality improvements, particularly when using neural classifiers which can be overconfident.

6 Conclusion

Neural classifiers have high confidence when separating in-domain from out-of-domain data, leading to a strong decision boundary. Classification results are good, but the boundary was too drastic, resulting in a poor score distribution with most mass near 0 and 1. This can be fixed by adding +1, keeping sentences with a low score as they are and giving a bonus to sentences with a higher score. The scores from, e.g., a CNN, can be transformed by a sigmoid function, making the score distribution more natural while keeping its strong decision boundary. Cross-entropy approaches lead to a poor score distribution. Sigmoid CNN scores performed best.

Our MT experiments showed that neural classifiers can be used to score out-of-domain data effectively. Our work showed that simple transformations of classifier outputs are necessary. The use of the transformed scores by applying sentence weighting on the NMT training data improves translation quality. Our research shows that results from CNNs trained on domain classification achieve significant domain adaptation effects in NMT. It was important to carry out light-weight score transformations. We outperformed baseline experiments by up to 2.1 BLEU points.

Acknowledgments

This project has received funding from the European Research Council under the European Unions Horizon 2020 research and innovation program (grant agreement #640550).

References

Axelrod, A., He, X., and Gao, J. (2011). Domain adaptation via pseudo in-domain data selection. In *Proceedings of the Conference on Empirical Methods in Natural Language Processing*, EMNLP '11, pages 355–362, Stroudsburg, PA, USA.

Chen, B., Cherry, C., Foster, G. F., and Larkin, S. (2017). Cost weighting for neural machine translation domain adaptation. In *NMT@ACL*.

Chen, B., Kuhn, R., Foster, G., Cherry, C., and Huang, F. (2016). Bilingual methods for adaptive training data selection for machine translation. In *AMTA*.

Chu, C. (2015). Integrated parallel data extraction from comparable corpora for statistical machine translation. Doctoral Thesis, Kyoto University.

Chu, C. and Wang, R. (2018). A survey of domain adaptation for neural machine translation. *CoRR*, abs/1806.00258.

Cuong, H. and Sima'an, K. (2014). Latent domain translation models in mix-of-domains haystack. In *Proceedings of COLING 2014, the 25th International Conference on Computational Linguistics: Technical Papers*, pages 1928–1939, Dublin, Ireland.

Duh, K., Neubig, G., Sudoh, K., and Tsukada, H. (2013). Adaptation data selection using neural language models: Experiments in machine translation. In *Proceedings of the 51st Annual Meeting of the Association for Computational Linguistics (Volume 2: Short Papers)*, pages 678–683, Sofia, Bulgaria.

Durrani, N., Sajjad, H., Joty, S., Abdelali, A., and Vogel, S. (2015). Using joint models for domain adaptation in statistical machine translation.

Goller, C. and Küchler, A. (1996). Learning task-dependent distributed representations by backpropagation through structure. In *In Proc. of the ICNN-96*, pages 347–352.

Junczys-Dowmunt, M., Grundkiewicz, R., Dwojak, T., Hoang, H., Heafield, K., Neckermann, T., Seide, F., Germann, U., Fikri Aji, A., Bogoychev, N., Martins, A. F. T., and Birch, A. (2018). Marian: Fast neural machine translation in C++. In *Proceedings of ACL 2018, System Demonstrations*, pages 116–121, Melbourne, Australia.

Kim, Y. (2014). Convolutional neural networks for sentence classification. In *Proceedings of the 2014 Conference on Empirical Methods in Natural Language Processing, EMNLP 2014, October 25-29, 2014, Doha, Qatar, A meeting of SIGDAT, a Special Interest Group of the ACL*, pages 1746–1751.

Krizhevsky, A., Sutskever, I., and Hinton, G. E. (2012). Imagenet classification with deep convolutional neural networks. In Pereira, F., Burges, C. J. C., Bottou, L., and Weinberger, K. Q., editors, *Advances in Neural Information Processing Systems 25*, pages 1097–1105.

Lambert, P., Schwenk, H., Servan, C., and Abdul-Rauf, S. (2011). Investigations on translation model adaptation using monolingual data. In *Proceedings of the Sixth Workshop on Statistical Machine Translation*, WMT '11, pages 284–293, Stroudsburg, PA, USA.

Marie, B. and Fujita, A. (2017). Efficient extraction of pseudo-parallel sentences from raw monolingual data using word embeddings. In *Proceedings of the 55th Annual Meeting of the Association for Computational Linguistics (Volume 2: Short Papers)*, pages 392–398, Vancouver, Canada.

Mikolov, T., Sutskever, I., Chen, K., Corrado, G. S., and Dean, J. (2013). Distributed representations of words and phrases and their compositionality. In Burges, C. J. C., Bottou, L., Welling, M., Ghahramani, Z., and Weinberger, K. Q., editors, *Advances in Neural Information Processing Systems 26*, pages 3111–3119.

Moore, R. C. and Lewis, W. (2010). Intelligent selection of language model training data. In *Proceedings of the ACL 2010 Conference Short Papers*, pages 220–224, Uppsala, Sweden.

Ney, H., Essen, U., and Kneser, R. (1994). On structuring probabilistic dependencies in stochastic language modelling. *Computer Speech and Language*, 8:1–38.

Rousseau, A. (2013). Xenc: An open-source tool for data selection in natural language processing. *The Prague Bulletin of Mathematical Linguistics*, 100:73–82.

Socher, R., Lin, C. C.-Y., Ng, A. Y., and Manning, C. D. (2011). Parsing natural scenes and natural language with recursive neural networks. In *Proceedings of the 28th International Conference on International Conference on Machine Learning*, ICML'11, pages 129–136, USA.

Socher, R., Perelygin, A., Wu, J., Chuang, J., Manning, C. D., Ng, A., and Potts, C. (2013). Recursive deep models for semantic compositionality over a sentiment treebank. In *Proceedings of the 2013 Conference on Empirical Methods in Natural Language Processing*, pages 1631–1642, Seattle, Washington, USA.

Utiyama, M. and Isahara, H. (2003). Reliable measures for aligning japanese-english news articles and sentences. In *Proceedings of the 41st Annual Meeting on Association for Computational Linguistics - Volume 1*, ACL '03, pages 72–79, Stroudsburg, PA, USA.

Vaswani, A., Shazeer, N., Parmar, N., Uszkoreit, J., Jones, L., Gomez, A. N., Kaiser, L. u., and Polosukhin, I. (2017). Attention is all you need. In Guyon, I., Luxburg, U. V., Bengio, S., Wallach, H., Fergus, R., Vishwanathan, S., and Garnett, R., editors, *Advances in Neural Information Processing Systems 30*, pages 5998–6008.

Wang, R., Finch, A., Utiyama, M., and Sumita, E. (2017a). Sentence embedding for neural machine translation domain adaptation. In *Proceedings of the 55th Annual Meeting of the Association for Computational Linguistics (Volume 2: Short Papers)*, pages 560–566, Vancouver, Canada.

Wang, R., Utiyama, M., Finch, A. M., Liu, L., Chen, K., and Sumita, E. (2018). Sentence selection and weighting for neural machine translation domain adaptation. *IEEE/ACM Transactions on Audio, Speech, and Language Processing*, 26:1727–1741.

Wang, R., Utiyama, M., Liu, L., Chen, K., and Sumita, E. (2017b). Instance weighting for neural machine translation domain adaptation. In *EMNLP*.

Wang, R., Zhao, H., Lu, B.-L., Utiyama, M., and Sumita, E. (2014). Neural network based bilingual language model growing for statistical machine translation. In *Proceedings of the 2014 Conference on Empirical Methods in Natural Language Processing (EMNLP)*, pages 189–195, Doha, Qatar.

Sentiment-based Candidate Selection For NMT

Alex Jones alexander.g.jones.23@dartmouth.edu
Dartmouth College, Hanover, NH, 03755, United States

Derry Tanti Wijaya wijaya@bu.edu
Department of Computer Science, Boston University, Boston, MA, 02215, United States

Abstract

The proliferation of user-generated content (UGC)—e.g. social media posts, comments, and reviews—has motivated the development of NLP applications tailored to these types of informal texts. Prevalent among these applications have been sentiment analysis and machine translation (MT). Grounded in the observation that UGC features highly idiomatic, sentiment-charged language, we propose a decoder-side approach that incorporates automatic sentiment scoring into the MT candidate selection process. We train monolingual sentiment classifiers in English and Spanish, in addition to a multilingual sentiment model, by fine-tuning BERT and XLM-RoBERTa. Using n-best candidates generated by a baseline MT model with beam search, we select the candidate that minimizes the absolute difference between the sentiment score of the source sentence and that of the translation, and perform two human evaluations to assess the produced translations. Unlike previous work, we select this minimally divergent translation by considering the sentiment scores of the source sentence and translation on a continuous interval, rather than using e.g. binary classification, allowing for more fine-grained selection of translation candidates. The results of human evaluations show that, in comparison to the open-source MT baseline model on top of which our sentiment-based pipeline is built, our pipeline produces more accurate translations of colloquial, sentiment-charged source texts[1].

1 Introduction

The Web, widespread internet access, and social media have transformed the way people create, consume, and share content, resulting in the proliferation of user-generated content (UGC). UGC—such as social media posts, comments, and reviews—has proven to be of paramount importance both for users and organizations/institutions (Pozzi et al., 2016). As users enjoy the freedoms of sharing their opinions in this relatively unconstrained environment, corporations can analyze user sentiments and extract insights for their decision-making processes, (Timoshenko and Hauser, 2019) or translate UGC to other languages to widen the company's scope and impact. For example, Hale (2016) shows that translating UGC between certain language pairs has beneficial effects on the overall ratings customers gave to attractions and shows on TripAdvisor, while the absence of translation hurts ratings. However, translating UGC comes with its own challenges that differ from those of translating well-formed documents like news articles. UGC is shorter and noisier, characterized by idiomatic and colloquial expressions (Pozzi et al., 2016). Translating idiomatic expressions is hard, as they often convey figurative meaning that cannot be reconstructed from the meaning of their parts (Wasow et al., 1983), and remains one of the open challenges in machine translation (MT) (Fadaee et al., 2018). Idiomatic expressions, however, typically carry an additional property: they imply an affective stance rather

[1]Code and reference materials are available at `https://github.com/AlexJonesNLP/SentimentMT`

than a neutral one (Wasow et al., 1983). The sentiment of an idiomatic expression, therefore, can be a useful signal for translation. In this paper, we hypothesize that a good translation of an idiomatic text, such as those prevalent in UGC, should be one that retains its underlying sentiment, and explore the use of textual sentiment analysis to improve translations.

Our motivation behind adding sentiment analysis model(s) to the NMT pipeline are several. First, with the sorts of texts prevalent in UGC (namely, idiomatic, sentiment-charged ones), the sentiment of a translated text is often arguably as important as the quality of the translation in other respects, such as adequacy, fluency, grammatical correctness, etc. Second, while a sentiment classifier can be trained particularly well to analyze the sentiment of various texts—including idiomatic expressions (Williams et al., 2015)—these idiomatic texts may be difficult for even state-of-the-art (SOTA) MT systems to handle consistently. This can be due to problems such as literal translation of figurative speech, but also to less obvious errors such as truncation (i.e. failing to translate crucial parts of the source sentence). Our assumption however, is that with open-source translation systems such as OPUS MT[2], the correct translation of a sentiment-laden, idiomatic text often lies somewhere lower among the predictions of the MT system, and that the sentiment analysis model can help signal the right translation by re-ranking candidates based on sentiment. Our contributions are as follows:

- We explore the idea of choosing translations that minimize source-target sentiment differences on a continuous scale (0-1). Previous works that addressed the integration of sentiment into the MT process have treated this difference as a simple polarity (i.e., positive, negative, or neutral) difference that does not account for the degree of difference between the source text and translation.
- We focus in particular on idiomatic, sentiment-charged texts sampled from real-world UGC, and show, both through human evaluation and qualitative examples, that our method improves a baseline MT model's ability to select sentiment-preserving *and* accurate translations in notable cases.
- We extend our method of using monolingual English and Spanish sentiment classifiers to aid in MT by substituting the classifiers for a single, multilingual sentiment classifier, and analyze the results of this second MT pipeline on the lower-resource English-Indonesian translation, illustrating the generalizability of our approach.

2 Related Work

Several papers in recent years have addressed the incorporation of sentiment into the MT process. Perhaps the earliest of these is Sennrich et al. (2016), which examined the effects of using honorific marking in training data to help MT systems pick up on the T-V distinction (e.g. informal *tu* vs. formal *vous* in French) that serves to convey formality or familiarity. Si et al. (2019) used sentiment-labeled sentences containing one of a fixed set of sentiment-ambiguous words, as well as valence-sensitive word embeddings for these words, to train models such that users could input the desired sentiment at translation time and receive the translation with the appropriate valence. Lastly, Lohar et al. (2017, 2018) experimented with training sentiment-isolated MT models—that is, MT models trained on only texts that had been pre-categorized into a set number of sentiment classes i.e., positive-only texts or negative-only texts. Our approach is novel in using sentiment to re-rank candidate translations of UGC in an MT pipeline and in using precise sentiment scores rather than simple polarity matching to aid the translation process.

In terms of sentiment analysis models of non-English languages, Can et al. (2018) experimented with using an RNN-based English sentiment model to analyze the sentiment of texts translated into English from other languages, while Balahur and Turchi (2012) used SMT to

[2]`https://github.com/Helsinki-NLP/Opus-MT`

generate sentiment training corpora in non-English languages. Dashtipour et al. (2016) provides an overview and comparison of various techniques used to tackle multilingual sentiment analysis.

As for MT candidate re-ranking, Hadj Ameur et al. (2019) provides an extensive overview of the various features and tools that have been used to aid in the candidate selection process, and also proposes a feature ensemble approach that doesn't rely on external NLP tools. Others who have used candidate selection or re-ranking to improve MT performance include Shen et al. (2004) and Yuan et al. (2016). To the best of our knowledge, however, no previous re-ranking methods have used sentiment for re-ranking despite findings that MT often alters sentiment, especially when ambiguous words or figurative language such as metaphors or idioms are present or when the translation exhibits incorrect word order (Mohammad et al., 2016).

3 Models and Data

3.1 Sentiment Classifiers

For the first portion of our experiments, we train monolingual sentiment classifiers, one for English and another for Spanish. For the English classifier, we fine-tune the BERT Base uncased model (Devlin et al., 2019), as it achieves SOTA or nearly SOTA results on various text classification tasks. We construct our BERT-based sentiment classifier model using BERTForSequenceClassification, following McCormick and Ryan (2019). For our English training and development data, we sample 50K positive and 50K negative tweets from the automatically annotated sentiment corpus described in Go et al. (2009) and use 90K tweets for training and the rest for development. For the English test set, we use the human-annotated sentiment corpus also described in Go et al. (2009), which consists of 359 total tweets after neutral-labeled tweets are removed. We use BertTokenizer with 'bert-base-uncased' as our vocabulary file and fine-tune a BERT model using one NVIDIA V100 GPU to classify the tweets into positive or negative labels for one epoch using the Adam optimizer (Kingma and Ba, 2014) with weight decay (AdamW in PyTorch) and a linear learning rate schedule with warmup. We use a batch size of 32, a learning rate of 2e-5, and an epsilon value of 1e-8 for Adam. We experiment with all hyperparameters manually, but find that the model converges very quickly (i.e. additional training after one epoch improves test accuracy negligibly, or causes overfitting). We achieve an accuracy of 85.2% on the English test set.

For the Spanish sentiment classifier, we fine-tune XLM-RoBERTa Large, a multilingual language model that has been shown to significantly outperform multilingual BERT (mBERT) on a variety of cross-lingual transfer tasks (Conneau et al., 2020), also using one NVIDIA V100 GPU. We construct our XLM-RoBERTa-based sentiment classifier model again following McCormick and Ryan (2019). The Spanish training and development data were collected from Mozetič et al. (2016). After removing neutral tweets, we obtain roughly 27.8K training tweets and 1.5K development tweets. The Spanish test set is a human-annotated sentiment corpus[3] containing 7.8K tweets, of which we use roughly 3K after removing neutral tweets and evening out the number of positive and negative tweets. We use the XLMRobertaTokenizer with vocabulary file 'xlm-roberta-large' and fine-tune the XLM-RoBERTa model to classify the tweets into positive or negative labels. The optimizer, epsilon value, number of epochs, learning rate, and batch size are the same as those of the English model, determined via experimentation (without grid search or a more regimented method). Unlike with the English model, we found that fine-tuning the Spanish model sometimes produced unreliable results, and so employ multiple random restarts and select the best model, a technique used in the original BERT paper (Devlin et al., 2019). The test accuracy on the Spanish model was 77.8%.

[3]https://www.kaggle.com/c/spanish-arilines-tweets-sentiment-analysis

3.2 Baseline MT Models

The baseline MT models we use for both English-Spanish and Spanish-English translation are the publicly available Helsinki-NLP/OPUS MT models released by Hugging Face and based on Marian NMT (Tiedemann and Thottingal, 2020; Junczys-Dowmunt et al., 2018; Wolf et al., 2019). Namely, we use both the en-ROMANCE and ROMANCE-en Transformer-based models, which were both trained using the OPUS dataset (Tiedemann, 2017)[4] with Sentence Piece tokenization and using training procedures and hyperparameters specified on the OPUS MT Github page[5] and in Tiedemann and Thottingal (2020).

4 Method: Sentiment-based Candidate Selection

We propose the use of two language-specific sentiment classifiers (which, as we will describe later in the paper, can be reduced to one multilingual sentiment model)—one applied to the input sentence in the source language and another to the candidate translation in the target language—to help an MT system select the candidate translation that diverges the least, in terms of sentiment, from the source sentence.

Using the baseline MT model described in Section 3.2, we first generate $n = 10$ best candidate translations using a beam size of 10 at decoding time. We decided on 10 as our candidate number based on the fact that one can expect a relatively low drop off in translation quality with this parameter choice (Hasan et al., 2007), while also maintaining a suitably high likelihood of getting variable translations. Additionally, decoding simply becomes too slow in practice beyond a certain beam size.

Once our model generates the 10 candidate translations for a given input sentence, we use the sentiment classifier trained in the appropriate language to score the sentiment of both the input sentence and each of the translations in the interval $[0, 1]$. To compute the sentiment score $S(x)$ for an input sentence x, we first compute a softmax over the array of logits returned by our sentiment model to get a probability distribution over all m possible classes (here, $m = 2$, since we only used positive- and negative-labeled tweets). Representing the negative and positive classes using the values 0 and 1, respectively, we define $S(x)$ to be the expected value of the class conditioned on x, namely $S(x) = \sum_{n=1}^{m} P(c_n \mid x)\, v_n$, where c_i is the ith class and v_i is the value corresponding to that class. In our case, since we have only two classes and the negative class is represented with value 0, $S(x) = P(\text{positive class} \mid x)$. After computing the sentiment scores, we take the absolute difference between the input sentence x's score and the candidate translation t_i's score for $i = 1, 2, ..., 10$ to obtain the *sentiment divergence* of each candidate. We select the candidate translation that minimizes the sentiment divergence, namely $y = \text{argmin}_{t_i} |S(t_i) - S(x)|$. Our method of selecting a translation differs from previous works in our use of the proposed sentiment divergence, which takes into account the degree of the sentiment difference (and not just polarity difference) between the input sentence and the candidate translation.

5 Experiments

5.1 English-Spanish Evaluation Data

The aim of our human evaluation was to discover how Spanish-English bilingual speakers assess both the quality and the degree of sentiment preservation of our proposed sentiment-sensitive MT model's translations in comparison to those of the human (a professional translator), the baseline MT model (Helsinki-NLP/OPUS MT), and a SOTA MT model, namely Google Translate.

[4] http://opus.nlpl.eu

[5] https://github.com/Helsinki-NLP/OPUS-MT-train

The human evaluation data consisted of 30 English (*en*) tweets, each translated using the above four methods to Spanish. We sample 30 English tweets from the English sentiment datasets that we do not use in training (Section 3.1) as well as from another English sentiment corpus (CrowdFlower, 2020)[6]. In assembling this evaluation set, we aimed to find a mix of texts that were highly idiomatic and sentiment-loaded—and thus presumably difficult to translate—but also ones that were more neutral in affect, less idiomatic, or some combination of the two.

5.2 English-Spanish Evaluation Setup

For the English-Spanish evaluation, we hired two fully bilingual professional translators using contracting site Freelancer [7]. Both evaluators were asked to provide proof of competency in both languages beforehand. The evaluation itself consisted of four translations (one generated by each method: human, baseline, sentiment-MT, Google Translate) for each of the 30 English tweets above, totaling 120 texts to be evaluated. For each of these texts, evaluators were asked to:

1. Rate the *accuracy* of the translation on a **0-5** scale, with 0 being the worst quality and 5 being the best
2. Rate the *sentiment divergence* of the translation on a **0-2** scale, with 0 indicating no sentiment change and 2 indicating sentiment reversal
3. Indicate the reasons for which they believe the sentiment changed in translation

5.3 English-Spanish Evaluation Results

As depicted in Table 1, the results of the English-Spanish human evaluation show improvements across the board for our modified pipeline over the vanilla baseline model. For the purposes of analysis, we divide the 30 English sentences (120 translations) into two categories: "all" (consisting of all 120 translations) and "idiomatic," consisting of 13 sentences (52 translations) deemed particularly idiomatic in nature. Although methods exist for identifying idiomatic texts systematically, e.g. Peng et al. (2014), we opt to hand-pick idiomatic texts ourselves. We do this in hopes of curating not only texts that contain idiomatic "multi-word" expressions, but also ones that are idiomatic in less concrete ways, which will enable us to gain more qualitative insights in the evaluation. Examples of such sentences are discussed in Section 7.

In the 'all' subset of the data, we see a +0.12 gain for our modified pipeline over the baseline in terms of accuracy (where higher accuracy is better), as well as a +0.11 reduction in sentiment divergence (where smaller divergence is better). On the idiomatic subset, the differences are more pronounced: we see a +0.80 gain over the baseline for accuracy and a +0.35 reduction in sentiment divergence. While our pipeline lags behind Google Translate in all metrics for English-Spanish—due to the superiority of Google Translate over OPUS MT in multiple regards (training data size, parameters, multilinguality, compute power, etc.)—our modification moves OPUS MT closer to this SOTA system. As a benchmark and to validate the soundness of our evaluation set, we include results for translations performed by a professional human translator, which, as expected, are vastly superior to those for any of the NMT systems used across all metrics and subsets of the data.

We also provide qualitative insights gained from the evaluations, in which evaluators were asked to identify *why* they believe the sentiment of the text *per se* changed in translation. The codes corresponding to these qualitative results are listed in the rightmost column of Table 1, and may be identified as follows:

- "MI" indicates the Mistranslation of Idiomatic/figurative language *per se*

[6]https://data.world/crowdflower/apple-twitter-sentiment

[7]https://www.freelancer.com/

	BLEU (Tatoeba)	BLEU (all tweets)	BLEU (idiom. tweets)	Accuracy (all tweets)	SentiDiff (all tweets)	Accuracy (idiom. tweets)	SentiDiff (idiom. tweets)	Top-3 Qual.
Baseline								
en→es	31.37	38.93	39.28	2.06	0.92	1.37	1.23	MI, O, MO
en→id	31.17	–	–	2.98	0.77	2.50	1.00	MO, O, MI
SentimentMT								
en→es	22.15	39.10	43.47	2.18	0.81	2.17	0.88	MO, IG, MI
en→id	20.85	–	–	3.31	0.65	3.20	0.64	MO, O, MI
Google Transl.								
en→es	51.39	56.76	57.98	3.08	0.43	2.31	0.79	MI, MO, O
en→id	33.93	–	–	3.57	0.55	3.00	0.94	MO, MI, O/IR
Human								
en→es	100	100	100	4.28	0.10	4.44	0.08	MO, O, IR

Table 1: The BLEU scores on the Tatoeba dataset, the accuracy and sentiment divergence scores on Twitter data, and the top 3 reasons given for sentiment divergence for each translation method, language pair, and chosen subset of the Twitter data: all vs. idiomatic. *en→es* represents English-Spanish, and *en→id* represents English-Indonesian. Note that ratings for each language are given by different sets of evaluators, and shouldn't be compared on a cross-lingual basis.

- "MO" indicates the Mistranslation of Other types of language
- "IG" indicates Incorrect Grammatical structure in the translation
- "IR" indicates IRrecoverability of the source text's meaning, i.e. even the gist of the sentence was gone
- "LT" indicates a Lack of Translatability of the source text to the language in question
- "O" indicates some Other reason for sentiment divergence

The top three most frequently cited causes of sentiment divergence for both the baseline and Google Translate were mistranslation of idiomatic language *per se*, mistranslation of other types of language, and other reasons not listed on the evaluation form. For our modified pipeline, the only distinctive top three cause of sentiment divergence was incorrect grammatical structure in the translation; additionally, one human translation was surprisingly flagged as rendering the source text's meaning "irrecoverable." However, the actual *frequency* of these error codes varied among models. For instance, 'MO' was given 5 times to human translations but 13 times to the baseline model's, and 'O' was given 3 times to Google Translate's translations and 7 times to our pipeline's. Some translations flagged with the '**O**ther' category are deemed to be of special interest and are discussed in Section 7.

We also noted strong and statistically significant ($p << 0.05$) negative correlations between accuracy and sentiment divergence for both the whole and idiomatic subsets of the data; the values of Pearson's r (Lewis-Beck et al., 2004) with their corresponding p-values are reported in Table 2.

Additionally, we measure agreement between the two English-Spanish evaluators using Krippendorff's inter-annotator agreement measure α (Krippendorff, 2011), which we choose as a metric in order to compare with previous work examining human agreement on sentiment judgments. In line with Provoost et al. (2019)'s findings of moderate agreement ($\alpha = 0.51$), we see α values ranging from 0.638 to 0.673 for the whole and idiomatic subsets of the data, respectively.

	Pearson's r (p-value) (all)	Pearson's r (p-value) (idiom.)
en→es	-0.764 (3.42e-47)	-0.759 (9.90e-21)
en→id	-0.570 (1.09e-15)	-0.756 (8.67e-14)

Table 2: Pearson's correlation coefficient and corresponding p-value with respect to accuracy and SentiDiff for each of the evaluations, broken down into the full (all) and idiomatic subsets.

In terms of automatic MT evaluation, we note that although our method causes a decrease in BLEU score on the Tatoeba test data for both languages (Table 1: SentimentMT vs. Baseline)—which is to be expected, as Tatoeba consists of "general" texts as opposed to UGC, and we select potentially non-optimal candidates during re-ranking—our method *improves* over the baseline for the Spanish tweets (and more so on the idiomatic tweets) on which the human evaluation was conducted. This result supports the efficacy of our model in the context of highly-idiomatic, affective UGC, and highlights the different challenges that UGC presents in comparison to more "formal" text.

Google Translate still outperforms the baseline and our method in terms of BLEU score on Tatoeba and the tweets. The explanation here is simply that the baseline model is not SOTA, which is to be expected given it's a free, flexible, open-source system. However, as our pipeline is orthogonal to any MT model, including SOTA, it could be used to improve a SOTA MT model for UGC.

6 Method Extension

6.1 Translation with Multilingual Sentiment Classifier

As highlighted in Hadj Ameur et al. (2019), one of the major criticisms of decoder-side re-ranking approaches for MT is their reliance on language-specific external NLP tools, such as the sentiment classifiers described in Section 3.1. To address the issue of language specificity and to develop a sentiment analysis model that can be used in tandem with MT between any two languages, we develop a multilingual sentiment classifier following Misra (2020). Specifically, we fine-tune the XLM-RoBERTa model using the training and development data used to train the English sentiment classifier, and the same tokenizer, vocabulary file, hyperparameters, and compute resources (GPU) used in training the Spanish classifier. We then use this multilingual language model fine-tuned on English sentiment data to perform zero-shot sentiment classification on various languages, and incorporate it into our beam search candidate selection pipeline for MT.

We test the model using the same test data used previously. On the English test data, this multilingual model achieves an accuracy of 83.8%, comparable to the accuracy score achieved using the BERT monolingual model (85.2%). On the Spanish test set, the multilingual model achieves a somewhat lower score of 73.6% (*cf.* 77.8% for the monolingual trained model), perhaps showing the limitations of this massively multilingual model on performing zero-shot downstream tasks.

6.2 English-Indonesian Evaluation Setup

We use the multilingual sentiment classifier in our sentiment-sensitive MT pipeline to perform translations on a handful of languages; examples from this experimentation are displayed in Tables 4 and 5 in the appendix.

We perform another human evaluation, this time involving English→Indonesian translations in place of English→Spanish. We choose Indonesian, as it is a medium-resource language (unlike Spanish, which is high-resource) (Joshi et al., 2020), and because we were able to obtain two truly bilingual annotators for this language pair.

The setup of the evaluation essentially mirrors that of the *en→es* evaluation, except we don't obtain professional human translations as a benchmark for Indonesian, due to the difficulty of obtaining the quality of translation required. Thus, the resulting evaluation set contains only $30 * 3 = 90$ translations instead of 120.

6.3 English-Indonesian Evaluation Results

The accuracy and sentiment divergence averages for different subsets of the *en-id* data are located in Table 1, and we direct readers to Section 5.3 for a qualitative discussion of these results. Quantitatively, we observe that our modified model outperforms the baseline in accuracy and sentiment divergence on every subset of the *en-id* data, while being comparable or better than Google Translate on the "all" and idiomatic subsets, respectively (Table 1). Specifically, on the "all" subset we see reductions of +0.33 and +0.12 over the baseline for accuracy and sentiment divergence, respectively, and on the idiomatic subset we see respective reductions of +0.70 and +0.36. Google Translate achieves slightly better accuracy and sentiment preservation overall (+0.26 and +0.10 over our pipeline for accuracy and sentiment divergence, respectively), but lags behind our pipeline in the idiomatic category (-0.20 and -0.30 for accuracy and sentiment divergence, respectively, compared to our pipeline).

Qualitatively, we see very similar reasons listed for sentiment divergence as we did for English-Spanish: each of the NMT systems we looked at had errors most frequently in the MI, MO, and O categories, denoting mistranslation of idiomatic language, mistranslation of other types of language, and other reasons for sentiment divergence, respectively; with MO being more frequent than MI in English-Indonesian evaluations, potentially due to lower MT performances for this language than Spanish (i.e., BLEU score for English-Indonesian modified model is 20.85 on the Tatoeba dataset compared to 22.15 for English-Spanish). However, as noted in the analysis of the previous evaluation, not all of these errors occurred with equal frequency across systems. For instance, Google Translate and the human translator produced less errors overall than the OPUS MT system, so the error codes should be interpreted as indicating the relative frequency and prevalence of certain translation errors that affect sentiment, not as markers to be compared on a system-to-system basis. As with the English-Spanish evaluation, certain qualitative observations made by our evaluators will be discussed further in Section 7. In line with results on the previous evaluation, accuracy and sentiment divergence are shown to be strongly negatively correlated, with Pearson's r values of -0.570 and -0.756 for the whole and idiomatic subsets of the data, respectively, both of which are statistically significant ($p << 0.05$) and are displayed in Table 2.

	acc. (all)	SentiDiff (all)	acc (idiom.)	SentiDiff (idiom.)
en→es	0.675	0.638	0.767	0.673
en→id	0.661	0.516	0.612	0.541

Table 3: Values of Krippendorff's alpha agreement measure α for both sets of evaluations with respect to accuracy ("acc.") and sentiment divergence ("SentiDiff") across different subsets.

Table 3 shows Krippendorff's alpha agreement measure (Krippendorff, 2011) for accuracy and sentiment divergence across both subsets, indicating moderate agreement, with higher agreement on accuracy. As was found with the English-Spanish evaluation, this is in line with previous findings of moderate human agreement on sentiment judgement (Krippendorff's α=0.51) (Provoost et al., 2019).

7 Discussion

Our experimentation with the various MT models generated a number of interesting example cases concerning the translation of idiomatic language. For example, given the tweet "Time Warner Road Runner customer support here absolutely blows," the baseline MT gives a literal translation of the word "blows" as "pukulan" (literally, "hits") in Indonesian; Google Translate gives a translation "hebat" ("awesome") that is opposite in sentiment to the idiomatic sense of the word "blows" ("sucks") in English; and our model gives a translation closest in meaning and sentiment to "blows," namely "kacau" (approx. "messed up" in Indonesian). There are also cases where our model gives a translation that is closer in degree of sentiment than what Google Translate produces. Given the source text "Yo @Apple fix your shitty iMessage," Google Translate produces "Yo @Apple perbaiki iMessage *buruk* Anda" ("Yo @Apple fix your *bad* iMessage"), which has roughly the same polarity as the source tweet. By contrast, our proposed model produces "Yo @Apple perbaiki imessage *menyebalkan* Anda," using the word "menyebalkan" ("annoying") instead of "buruk," which conveys a closer sentiment to "shitty" than simply "bad".

The evaluators of the English-Spanish translations provided us with rich qualitative commentary as well. For the sentence "Just broke my 3rd charger of the month. Get your shit together @apple," which is translated by the professional translator as "Se acaba de romper mi tercer cargador del mes. Sean más eficientes @apple," one evaluator acutely notes that "The expression 'Get your shit together' was translated in a more formal way (it loses the vulgarism). I would have translated it as 'Poneos las pilas, joder' to keep the same sentiment. We could say that this translation has a different diaphasic variation than the source text." This demonstrates that sentiment preservation is a problem not only for NMT systems, but for human translators as well. There are also problems attributed to challenges in machine translating informal texts. Acronyms such as "tbh" and "smh" made for another interesting case, as they weren't translated by any of the MT models for any language pairing, despite their common occurrence in UGC. The same evaluator also notes that "The acronym 'tbh' was not translated" in the sentence "@Apple tbh annoyed with Apple's shit at the moment," and says "this acronym is important for the sentiment because it expresses the modality of the speaker." In another example, we see our sentiment-sensitive pipeline helping the baseline distinguish between such a semantically fine-grained distinction as that between "hope" and "wish": the baseline translates the sentence "@Iberia Ojalá que encuentres pronto tu equipaje!!" as "@Iberia I *wish* you'd find your luggage soon!!," while our pipeline correctly chooses "@Iberia I *hope* you will find your luggage soon!!." We observe similar issues contribute to sentiment divergence in Spanish and Indonesian despite the fact that these are typologically disparate languages with different amounts of training data in the MT system.

In terms of automatic MT evaluation, our method improves over the baseline for the Spanish tweets on which the human evaluation was conducted. This result supports the efficacy of our model in the context of highly-idiomatic, affective UGC. And while Google Translate still outperforms the baseline and our pipeline in terms of BLEU score on Tatoeba (for both languages) and the tweets (for which only Spanish had a gold-standard benchmark)–given that the baseline model that we built our pipeline on is not SOTA–our pipeline can be added to any MT system and can also improve SOTA MT for UGC.

Furthermore, our approach also lends itself to many practical scenarios, e.g. companies who are interested in producing sentiment-preserving translations of large bodies of UGC but who lack the sufficient funds to use a subscription API like Google Cloud Translation. In these contexts, it may be beneficial—or even necessary—to improve free, open-source software in a way that is tailored to one's particular use case (thus the idea of "customized MT" that many companies now offer), instead of opting for the SOTA but more costly software.

More generally, since our approach shows that we can improve performance of an MT model for a particular use case i.e., UGC translation using signals beyond translation data that is relevant for the task at hand i.e., sentiment, it will be interesting to explore other signals that are relevant for improving MT performance in other use cases. It will also be interesting to explore the addition of these signals in a pipeline (our current method), as implicit feedback such as in Wijaya et al. (2017), or as explicit feedback in an end-to-end MT model for example, as additional loss terms in supervised (Wu et al., 2016), weakly-supervised (Kuwanto et al., 2021), or unsupervised (Artetxe et al., 2017) MT models. Beyond the potential engineering contribution for low-resource, budget-constrained settings, our experiments also offer rich qualitative insights regarding the causes of sentiment change in (machine) translation, opening up avenues to more disciplined efforts in mitigating and exploring these problems.

8 Conclusion

In this paper, we use several distinct sentiment classifiers trained on Twitter data to help machine translation models select sentiment-preserving translations of highly idiomatic source texts. Diverging from previous works, we use continuous (rather than binary or categorical) sentiment scores to select minimally divergent translations, and we test the performance of our pipeline with automated and human evaluations for English-Spanish and English-Indonesian translations.

Furthermore, we implement our sentiment-aware translation pipeline on free, open-source MT models available on Hugging Face[8]. Although many of these models are non-SOTA, our choice to use them represents a real-world scenario: Many users and companies do not have the resources or budget to subscribe to a SOTA translation API or train their own MT model from scratch. Our pipeline poses a lightweight solution for getting more with less, in a somewhat niche yet ubiquitous translation context (social media posts).

In future work, we would like to evaluate the effect of sentiment classifier performance on the downstream MT results, including the effects of classifier architecture, the number of sentiment categories and their distribution in the training data (e.g., UGCs with more informal words may contain more affective texts), etc. We would also like to investigate how continuous sentiment scoring compares with binary or categorical scoring for this task, using a larger evaluation set for idiomatic texts (e.g. in English (Michel and Neubig, 2018) or constructed in other languages (Wibowo et al., 2021)), or from a dataset we create ourselves. Finally, further work should establish benchmarks and put forth improvements for cross-lingual sentiment classification (i.e. the extent to which sentences that are translations of each other are assigned similar sentiments)—including the problem of zero-shot transfer—adding onto recent work in cross-lingual performance benchmarks (Hu et al., 2020; Liang et al., 2020).

References

Artetxe, M., Labaka, G., Agirre, E., and Cho, K. (2017). Unsupervised neural machine translation. *arXiv preprint arXiv:1710.11041.*

[8]https://huggingface.co/Helsinki-NLP

Balahur, A. and Turchi, M. (2012). Multilingual sentiment analysis using machine translation? In *Proceedings of the 3rd Workshop in Computational Approaches to Subjectivity and Sentiment Analysis*, pages 52–60, Jeju, Korea. Association for Computational Linguistics.

Can, E. F., Ezen-Can, A., and Can, F. (2018). Multilingual sentiment analysis: An RNN-based framework for limited data. *CoRR*, abs/1806.04511.

Conneau, A., Khandelwal, K., Goyal, N., Chaudhary, V., Wenzek, G., Guzmán, F., Grave, E., Ott, M., Zettlemoyer, L., and Stoyanov, V. (2020). Unsupervised cross-lingual representation learning at scale. In *Proceedings of the 58th Annual Meeting of the Association for Computational Linguistics*, pages 8440–8451, Online. Association for Computational Linguistics.

CrowdFlower (2020). Apple Twitter sentiment. Online. Data.world dataset. Accessed 21 August 2020.

Dashtipour, K., Poria, S., Hussain, A., Cambria, E., Hawalah, A. Y. A., Gelbukh, A., and Zhou, Q. (2016). Multilingual sentiment analysis: State of the art and independent comparison of techniques. *Cognitive Computation*, 8:757–771.

Devlin, J., Chang, M.-W., Lee, K., and Toutanova, K. (2019). BERT: Pre-training of deep bidirectional transformers for language understanding. In *Proceedings of the 2019 Conference of the North American Chapter of the Association for Computational Linguistics: Human Language Technologies, Volume 1 (Long and Short Papers)*, pages 4171–4186, Minneapolis, Minnesota. Association for Computational Linguistics.

Fadaee, M., Bisazza, A., and Monz, C. (2018). Examining the tip of the iceberg: A data set for idiom translation. *arXiv preprint arXiv:1802.04681*.

Go, A., Bhayani, R., and Huang, L. (2009). Twitter sentiment classification using distant supervision. *Processing*, 150.

Hadj Ameur, M., Guessoum, A., and Meziane, F. (2019). Improving Arabic neural machine translation via n-best list re-ranking. *Machine Translation*, 33:1–36.

Hale, S. A. (2016). User reviews and language: how language influences ratings. In *Proceedings of the 2016 CHI Conference Extended Abstracts on Human Factors in Computing Systems*, pages 1208–1214.

Hasan, S., Zens, R., and Ney, H. (2007). Are very large N-best lists useful for SMT? In *Human Language Technologies 2007: The Conference of the North American Chapter of the Association for Computational Linguistics; Companion Volume, Short Papers*, pages 57–60, Rochester, New York. Association for Computational Linguistics.

Hu, J., Ruder, S., Siddhant, A., Neubig, G., Firat, O., and Johnson, M. (2020). XTREME: A Massively Multilingual Multi-task Benchmark for Evaluating Cross-lingual Generalization. *arXiv e-prints*, page arXiv:2003.11080.

Joshi, P., Santy, S., Budhiraja, A., Bali, K., and Choudhury, M. (2020). The State and Fate of Linguistic Diversity and Inclusion in the NLP World. *arXiv preprint arXiv:2004.09095*.

Junczys-Dowmunt, M., Grundkiewicz, R., Dwojak, T., Hoang, H., Heafield, K., Neckermann, T., Seide, F., Germann, U., Aji, A. F., Bogoychev, N., Martins, A. F. T., and Birch, A. (2018). Marian: Fast neural machine translation in C++. In *Proceedings of ACL 2018, System Demonstrations*, pages 116–121, Melbourne, Australia. Association for Computational Linguistics.

Kingma, D. P. and Ba, J. (2014). Adam: A Method for Stochastic Optimization. *arXiv e-prints*, page arXiv:1412.6980.

Krippendorff, K. (2011). Computing Krippendorff's Alpha-Reliability. *Annenberg School of Communication Scholarly Commons*.

Kuwanto, G., Akyürek, A. F., Tourni, I. C., Li, S., and Wijaya, D. (2021). Low-resource machine translation for low-resource languages: Leveraging comparable data, code-switching and compute resources. *arXiv preprint arXiv:2103.13272*.

Lewis-Beck, M. S., Bryman, A., and Liao, T. F. (2004). Pearson's correlation coefficient. *The SAGE encyclopedia of social science research methods*, 1(0).

Liang, Y., Duan, N., Gong, Y., Wu, N., Guo, F., Qi, W., Gong, M., Shou, L., Jiang, D., Cao, G., Fan, X., Zhang, R., Agrawal, R., Cui, E., Wei, S., Bharti, T., Qiao, Y., Chen, J.-H., Wu, W., Liu, S., Yang, F., Campos, D., Majumder, R., and Zhou, M. (2020). XGLUE: A new benchmark datasetfor cross-lingual pre-training, understanding and generation. In *Proceedings of the 2020 Conference on Empirical Methods in Natural Language Processing (EMNLP)*, pages 6008–6018, Online. Association for Computational Linguistics.

Lohar, P., Afli, H., and Way, A. (2017). Maintaining sentiment polarity in translation of user-generated content. *The Prague Bulletin of Mathematical Linguistics*, 108(1):73–84.

Lohar, P., Afli, H., and Way, A. (2018). Balancing translation quality and sentiment preservation (non-archival extended abstract). In *Proceedings of the 13th Conference of the Association for Machine Translation in the Americas (Volume 1: Research Papers)*, pages 81–88, Boston, MA. Association for Machine Translation in the Americas.

McCormick, C. and Ryan, N. (2019). BERT fine-tuning tutorial with PyTorch. Online. Accessed 21 August 2020.

Michel, P. and Neubig, G. (2018). MTNT: A testbed for machine translation of noisy text. In *Proceedings of the 2018 Conference on Empirical Methods in Natural Language Processing*, pages 543–553, Brussels, Belgium. Association for Computational Linguistics.

Misra, S. (2020). Guessing sentiment in 100 languages. Online. Accessed 21 August 2020. Media type: Blog.

Mohammad, S. M., Salameh, M., and Kiritchenko, S. (2016). How translation alters sentiment. *Journal of Artificial Intelligence Research*, 55:95–130.

Mozetič, I., Grčar, M., and Smailović, J. (2016). Twitter sentiment for 15 european languages. Slovenian language resource repository CLARIN.SI.

Peng, J., Feldman, A., and Vylomova, E. (2014). Classifying idiomatic and literal expressions using topic models and intensity of emotions. In *Proceedings of the 2014 Conference on Empirical Methods in Natural Language Processing (EMNLP)*, pages 2019–2027, Doha, Qatar. Association for Computational Linguistics.

Pozzi, F. A., Fersini, E., Messina, E., and Liu, B. (2016). *Sentiment analysis in social networks*. Morgan Kaufmann.

Provoost, S., Ruwaard, J., van Breda, W., Riper, H., and Bosse, T. (2019). Validating automated sentiment analysis of online cognitive behavioral therapy patient texts: An exploratory study. *Frontiers in Psychology*, 10:1065–1077.

Sennrich, R., Haddow, B., and Birch, A. (2016). Controlling politeness in neural machine translation via side constraints. In *Proceedings of the 2016 Conference of the North American Chapter of the Association for Computational Linguistics: Human Language Technologies*, pages 35–40, San Diego, California. Association for Computational Linguistics.

Shen, L., Sarkar, A., and Och, F. J. (2004). Discriminative reranking for machine translation. In *Proceedings of the Human Language Technology Conference of the North American Chapter of the Association for Computational Linguistics: HLT-NAACL 2004*, pages 177–184, Boston, Massachusetts, USA. Association for Computational Linguistics.

Si, C., Wu, K., Aw, A. T., and Kan, M.-Y. (2019). Sentiment aware neural machine translation. In *Proceedings of the 6th Workshop on Asian Translation*, pages 200–206, Hong Kong, China. Association for Computational Linguistics.

Tiedemann, J. (2017). OPUS. University of Helsinki.

Tiedemann, J. and Thottingal, S. (2020). OPUS-MT – building open translation services for the world. In *Proceedings of the 22nd Annual Conference of the European Association for Machine Translation*, pages 479–480, Lisbon, Portugal. European Association for Machine Translation.

Timoshenko, A. and Hauser, J. R. (2019). Identifying customer needs from user-generated content. *Marketing Science*, 38(1):1–20.

Wasow, T., Sag, I., and Nunberg, G. (1983). Idioms: An interim report. In *Proceedings of the XIIIth International Congress of Linguists*, pages 102–115. CIPL Tokyo.

Wibowo, H. A., Nityasya, M. N., Akyurek, A. F., Fitriany, S., Aji, A. F., Prasojo, R. E., and Wijaya, D. T. (2021). Indocollex: A testbed for morphological transformation of indonesian word colloquialism. In *Proceedings of the 59th Annual Meeting of the Association for Computational Linguistics: Findings*.

Wijaya, D. T., Callahan, B., Hewitt, J., Gao, J., Ling, X., Apidianaki, M., and Callison-Burch, C. (2017). Learning translations via matrix completion. In *Proceedings of the 2017 Conference on Empirical Methods in Natural Language Processing*, pages 1452–1463.

Williams, L., Bannister, C., Arribas-Ayllon, M., Preece, A., and Spasić, I. (2015). The role of idioms in sentiment analysis. *Expert Systems with Applications*, 42(21):7375–7385.

Wolf, T., Debut, L., Sanh, V., Chaumond, J., Delangue, C., Moi, A., Cistac, P., Rault, T., Louf, R., Funtowicz, M., Davison, J., Shleifer, S., von Platen, P., Ma, C., Jernite, Y., Plu, J., Xu, C., Scao, T. L., Gugger, S., Drame, M., Lhoest, Q., and Rush, A. M. (2019). Huggingface's transformers: State-of-the-art natural language processing. *Computing Research Repository*, arXiv: 1910.03771. version 5.

Wu, Y., Schuster, M., Chen, Z., Le, Q. V., Norouzi, M., Macherey, W., Krikun, M., Cao, Y., Gao, Q., Macherey, K., et al. (2016). Google's neural machine translation system: Bridging the gap between human and machine translation. *arXiv preprint arXiv:1609.08144*.

Yuan, Z., Briscoe, T., and Felice, M. (2016). Candidate re-ranking for SMT-based grammatical error correction. In *Proceedings of the 11th Workshop on Innovative Use of NLP for Building Educational Applications*, pages 256–266, San Diego, CA. Association for Computational Linguistics.

A Appendix

A.1 Example Translations

French	
Original	Why are people such wankers these days?
Baseline	Pourquoi les gens sont-ils si branleurs ces jours-ci?
SentimentMT	Pourquoi les gens sont-ils si cons ces jours-ci?
Finnish	
Original	I'm sorry—I'm feeling kinda yucky myself—5am is going to come too quick.
Baseline	Olen pahoillani, olen itsekin aika naljaillen, että aamuviideltä tulee liian nopeasti.
SentimentMT	Olen pahoillani, että olen itse vähän kuvottava, mutta aamuviideltä tulee liian nopea.
Portuguese	
Original	Time Warner Road Runner customer support here absolutely blows.
Baseline	O suporte ao cliente do Time Warner Road Runner é absolutamente insuportável.
SentimentMT	O suporte ao cliente do Time Warner Road Runner aqui é absolutamente estragado.
Indonesian	
Original	Yo @Apple fix your shitty iMessage
Baseline	Yo @Apple perbaiki pesan menyebalkanmu
SentimentMT	Yo @Apple perbaiki imessage menyebalkan Anda

Table 4: Example texts exhibiting our MT pipeline's performance using the multilingual sentiment model fine-tuned with XLM-RoBERTa.

B Evaluation Instructions

The following are excerpts from the instructions given to evaluators for both the English-Spanish and English-Indonesian evaluations:
The document you are now looking at should contain prompts numbered up to 120. For each of these prompts, you will be asked to do three things:

1. Rate the *accuracy* of the translation. Please rate the **accuracy** of the translation on a **0 to 5** scale, where **0** indicates an "awful" translation, **2.5** indicates a "decent" translation, and **5** indicates a "flawless" translation . . .
2. Please rate the sentiment divergence on a **0 to 2** scale, where **0** indicates that the sentiment of the source sentence **perfectly matches** that of the translation and **2** indicates that the sentiment of the source sentence is the **opposite** of that of the translation . . .
3. Indicate the *reasons* for sentiment divergence . . .

C Sample Prompt for Human Evaluations

Below is an excerpt from a translation evaluation prompt that evaluators were asked to respond to:

- *Accuracy:*
- *Sentiment divergence:*
- *Please bold all of the below which had an effect on the sentiment of the translation:*
  1. *The translation contained literal translation(s) of figurative English language*
  2. *The translation contained other types of mistranslated words*
  3. *The original (English) sentence can't be properly translated to Spanish*

  . . .

Studying The Impact Of Document-level Context On Simultaneous Neural Machine Translation

Raj Dabre raj.dabre@nict.go.jp
National Institute of Information and Communications Technology

Aizhan Imankulova aizhan.imankulova@cogsmart-global.com
CogSmart

Masahiro Kaneko masahiro.kaneko@nlp.c.titech.ac.jp
Tokyo Institute of Technology

Abstract

In a real-time simultaneous translation setting, neural machine translation (NMT) models start generating target language tokens from incomplete source language sentences, making them harder to translate, leading to poor translation quality. Previous research has shown that document-level NMT, comprising of sentence and context encoders and a decoder, leverages context from neighbouring sentences and helps improve translation quality. In simultaneous translation settings, the context from previous sentences should be even more critical. To this end, in this paper, we propose `wait-k` simultaneous document-level NMT where we keep the context encoder as it is and replace the source sentence encoder and target language decoder with their `wait-k` equivalents. We experiment with low and high resource settings using the Asian Language Treebank (ALT) and OpenSubtitles2018 corpora, where we observe minor improvements in translation quality. We then perform an analysis of the translations obtained using our models by focusing on sentences that should benefit from the context where we found out that the model does, in fact, benefit from context but is unable to effectively leverage it, especially in a low-resource setting. This shows that there is a need for further innovation in the way useful context is identified and leveraged.

1 Introduction

Neural machine translation (NMT) (Bahdanau et al., 2015; Luong et al., 2016) is an end-to-end approach known to give the state of the art results for a variety of language pairs. In standard NMT, the entire source language sentence is fed to the model, and once the entire target language sentence is generated, it is presented to the user. However, in a real-time translation setting, translation models are expected to present translated words or phrases as they are generated. Furthermore, waiting for the entire source language sentence adds to the latency, and therefore an optimal solution is to have a model that can start generating target language words right after the first few source language words are available for translation. This is known as simultaneous NMT (SNMT) and is known for its poor translation quality, especially in low-resource settings. The concept of waiting for `k` words or tokens before generating target language words or tokens is known as `wait-k` SNMT (Ma et al., 2019). In this paper, we work with the Transformer architecture as the standard NMT model, consisting of a bidirectional encoder and unidirectional decoder. The decoder is able to attend to all source language tokens when generating target language tokens. However, in the case of the `wait-k` SNMT model, the standard encoder and decoder are replaced with their SNMT equivalents, which are a unidirectional encoder and a modified decoder, respectively. The decoder can only look at $i + k - 1$ encoder tokens when predicting the ith token. We are aware of a previous work that has shown that using an image as an additional modality can help improve translation quality in a `wait-k` setting when `k` is a small value around 1 to 4 (Imankulova et al., 2020; Caglayan et al., 2020). The additional image modality provides the model with a form of *context* which helps disambiguate hard-to-translate phenomena, especially when needed information is not available yet during translation. An additional image modality may not always be available, and thus, taking advantage of the context in the form of previously seen sentences is the only viable option.

Research in document-level NMT has already proven that context from neighbouring sentences can help enhance representations and thereby improve translation quality (Tiedemann and Scherrer, 2017; Jean et al., 2017; Wang et al., 2017). The simplest document-level NMT architecture involves using an additional encoder that encodes the context sentences, following which the encoded context is used to augment the representation of the sentence to be translated (Zhang et al., 2018). Just like using an image as a modality helps enrich the encoding of the sentence with additional disambiguation information, the context sentences might also contain such useful information. We already know that in an SNMT setting, due to partial sentences being translated, the amount of context available to the decoder is limited, and thus leveraging the context sentences should significantly boost SNMT translation quality. This motivated us to combine document-level NMT with SNMT leading to document-level SNMT.

Our document-level SNMT architecture is simple, where we have a sentence encoder, context encoder, and a decoder except that the sentence encoder and decoder are `wait-k` SNMT equivalents of the standard encoder and decoder. We experiment with a high-resource OpenSubtitles2018 dataset for English→Russian and Russian→English translation and a low-resource ALT document-level dataset for English→Japanese and Japanese→English translation. Our observations show that document-level context helps improve translation slightly in both settings but not by a large margin. We then perform a statistical and manual analysis of the translations where we observe that while SNMT models definitely benefit from context, they are unable to utilize context effectively and sometimes suffer due to the provided context. This opens up the possibility of research into better mechanisms for leveraging context more effectively.

2 Related Work

For simultaneous translation, it is crucial to predict the words that have not appeared yet. Mainly, SNMT can mostly be implemented with fixed or adaptive policies (Zheng et al., 2019b). Adaptive policy decides whether to READ another source word or WRITE a target word in one model (Grissom II et al., 2014; Matsubara et al., 2000; Oda et al., 2015). Most dynamic models with adaptive policies (Gu et al., 2017; Dalvi et al., 2018; Zheng et al., 2019a,c, 2020a) focus on mechanisms that determine the optimal number of source language tokens to wait for before generating the next target language token. Meanwhile, Ma et al. (2019) proposed a simple `wait-k` method with fixed policy, where the decoder starts generating the target language tokens the moment `k` source language tokens are available. However, their model for simultaneous translation relies only on the source sentence. This research concentrates on the `wait-k` approach leveraging document-level information from previous context sentences.

Document-level NMT leverages context beyond the current sentence in order to improve translation quality (Tiedemann and Scherrer, 2017; Jean et al., 2017; Wang et al., 2017; Voita et al., 2018, 2019; Zheng et al., 2020b; Fernandes et al., 2021). Document-level NMT models can be implemented as a post-processing model or context-aware model. The post-processing models use an additional module to use context on generated translations (Xiong et al., 2019; Voita et al., 2019). However, post-processing generated translations may lead to higher latency, which is counter-intuitive in a simultaneous translation scenario. On the other hand, context-aware models leverage additional context during translation. For example, Tiedemann and Scherrer (2017) proposed to simply concatenate the previous sentences in both the source and target side to the input to the system. Jean et al. (2017); Bawden et al. (2018); Zhang et al. (2018) use separate context encoder for a few previous source sentences. Similarly, we also use a separate context encoder to extract document-level information. However, we incorporate document-level information into SNMT in order to improve translation quality, where only information from the source sentence is insufficient during translation.

3 Methods

3.1 Background: Wait-k Simultaneous NMT

The most straightforward approach for SNMT is the `wait-k` approach (Ma et al., 2019) with a fixed policy. As tokens are fed to the encoder one at a time, we have to rely on a unidirectional encoder that cannot attend to future tokens. Once the encoder has been fed `k` tokens, the decoder starts generating a token at a time. This means that at the ith decoding step, the encoder and decoder can only see the first $\mathtt{k} + i - 1$ encoder token representations. Once the whole input sentence is available, `wait-k` behaves like regular NMT except with a unidirectional encoder. Different from (Ma et al., 2019) we have a unidirectional encoder, so when a new source token arrives, the encoder representations for the previous tokens are not updated. This can have a minor impact on the overall translation quality, but this paper aims to understand how context affects SNMT.

3.2 Background: Document-level NMT

Suppose X, X_c and Y are the source sentence, context sentences, and the target sentence. In this paper, we work with SNMT, and hence X_c only consists of past sentences, which for simplicity we concatenate into a single long context sentence[1]. Document-level NMT involves using X and X_c together for translation. In the case when only X and Y are available, X is fed to an encoder (E), leading to a sentence encoding $E(X)$. This sentence encoding is then attended to by the decoder in order to produce the translation $Y^{'} = D(E(X))$. When X_c is available we encode it using a context encoder (E_c) leading to context encoding $E_c(X_c)$ which is then used for translation along with $E(X)$ as $Y^{'} = D(E(X), E_c(X_c))$. It is a common practice to share the parameters of the sentence and context encoders. A key component of document-level NMT is the incorporation of $E_c(X_c)$ into the framework by combining it with $E(X)$. This paper considers two simple approaches, which we dub as "multi-source" (MS) and "context-attention" (CA).

3.2.1 MS: Multi-Source Based Context Incorporation

This method treats the context as an additional source of information similar to the setting in multi-source NMT (Zoph and Knight, 2016; Dabre et al., 2017). In multi-source NMT, the decoder is modified to attend to multiple source sentences, and this approach should help incorporate context into the decoding process. For vanilla NMT, the cross attention mechanism of the decoder takes in $E(X)$ and produces a weighted representation, the attention, A. Given the context encoding $E_c(X_c)$ we additionally compute the context attention A_c. We combine A and A_c into A_{comb}, the context augmented attention, using a simple gating mechanism as $A_{comb} = \alpha * A + (1 - \alpha) * A_c$ where $\alpha = sigmoid(W_{comb} * [A : A_c])$. [:] indicates concatenation of representations along the hidden layer axis. W_{comb} is the weight matrix of size

[1]This means that the memory requirements will increase, but we believe that this is an acceptable trade-off if translation quality improves. Furthermore, we can use sequence distillation Kim and Rush (2016) to compress these models, which have a smaller memory footprint

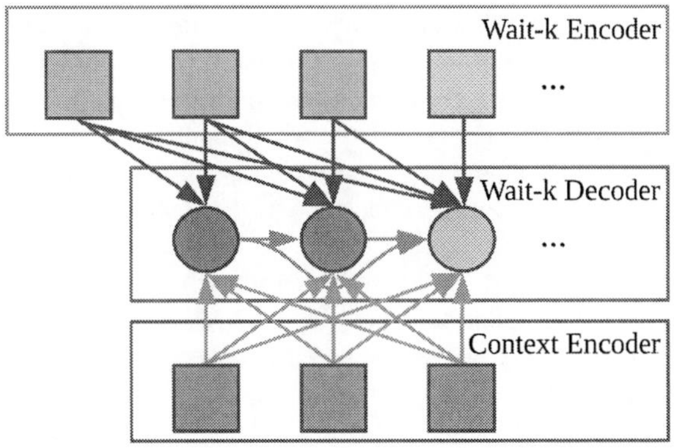

Figure 1: A simplified overview of our simultaneous document level NMT model which uses previous source sentences as context.

$[2h, h]$ where h is the model's hidden size. α is a weight that can help interpolate A and A_c to determine the balance between them.

3.2.2 CA: Context Attention Based Context Incorporation

This method is same as the one in Voita et al. (2018). Where the multi-source approach involves combining $E(X)$ and $E_c(X_c)$ in the decoder by combining the attentions obtained from them (A and A_c), this approach combines $E(X)$ and $E_c(X_c)$ into a single $E_{comb}(X, X_c)$ which is then fed to the decoder. Thus, the decoder sees one encoder representation instead of two.

To combine $E(X)$ and $E_c(X_c)$, $E(X)$ is fed to a self-attention layer which gives $E_{sa}(X)$ and $E_c(X_c)$ is fed to a cross-attention layer where EX is the query and $E_c(X_c)$ is the key/value which gives $E_{ca,c}(X_c)$. By doing so, $E_{sa}(X)$ and $E_{ca,c}(X_c)$ have the same shape and can be combined via the gating mechanism in the previous section into $E_{comb}(X, X_c)$.

Apart from these two combination methods, there are several others (Libovický et al., 2018) which we will explore in the future.

3.3 Our Method: Document-level SNMT

Document-level NMT can be easily extended to document-level SNMT by enforcing the SNMT constraint on the sentence encoder E and the sentence cross-attention mechanism A. No such constraints are placed on the context encoder E_c. Refer to Figure 1 for a simple overview of our method. It shows that at the ith decoding step, the decoder and encoder can access the context representations fully but only $k + i - 1$ source sentence representations.

4 Experimental Settings

We describe experimental settings aimed at helping verify the degree to which document context helps improve translation quality in a simultaneous translation setting.

4.1 Datasets and preprocessing

We experimented with English→Russian and Russian→English translation using a corpus created by (Voita et al., 2018), derived from the OpenSubtitles2018 corpus, consisting of 1.5M training sentences where each sentence has 3 sentences as context. The development and test sets consist of 10,000, 4 sentence documents leading to a total of 40,000 sentences which can have up to 3 context sentences. This dataset belongs to the spoken language domain, where we expect that document context should be very helpful in improving translation quality. Given that Russian has flexible word order, missing information in an incomplete source sentence can be complemented via the context. We also experimented with the low-resource Asian Language Treebank (ALT)dataset (Riza et al., 2016), which contains sentence level aligned document pairs split into training/development/test sets of 18,088/1,000/1,018 lines spanning 1,698/98/97 documents, respectively. We experimented with English→Japanese and Japanese→English translation. Japanese has subject-object-verb word order, whereas English has subject-verb-object, so we expect document context to be helpful whenever the object or verb-related information is missing for incomplete sentences in an SNMT setting.

Regarding preprocessing, we segmented the Japanese source sentences using MeCab, and our NMT implementation handles other preprocessing, such as subword tokenization. When providing document context sentences to our models, we concatenate previous N context sentences to form a single long sentence before feeding it to the model along with the sentence to be translated. Naturally, the first sentence of the document will have no context sentence, which we designate with a special token $< EMPTY >$.

4.2 Implementation and Training Details

We modified the Transformer (Vaswani et al., 2017) implementation in tensor2tensor v1.15.4[2], which has an internal subword segmentation mechanism. We set the separate source and target subword vocabulary sizes of 8,000 for the ALT dataset and 32,000 for the OpenSubtitles2018 dataset. We use hyperparameters of the "transformer_base" model for English→Russian and Russian→English translation whereas for English→Japanese and Japanese→English translation we use the "transformer_base_single_gpu" model hyperparameters. The "transformer_base" models are trained on 8 NVIDIA V100 GPUs, whereas the"transformer_base_single_gpu" models are trained on a single NVIDIA V100 GPU. We save and evaluate our models on the development set every 1000 batches with BLEU (Papineni et al., 2002) as the evaluation metric. We train our models till the BLEU score does not increase for ten consecutive evaluations. We average the last ten saved checkpoints and then decode the model. As we work in a simultaneous translation setting, greedy search makes sense as tokens should be output one at a time [3].

4.3 Models Compared

We train and compare the following types of full sentence and `wait-k` SNMT models for both datasets:

1. Non-contextual models: where the document context is not used

2. Contextual models: which use up to N previous sentences as context. $N = 1$ for English↔Japanese[4] and $N = 1, 2, 3$ for English↔Russian.

5 Results

We describe the results of our experiments in resource-rich and resource-poor settings.

[2]`https://github.com/tensorflow/tensor2tensor/tree/v1.15.4`

[3]It's possible to consider a sophisticated beam search method, but that is beyond the scope of this paper.

[4]In reality, we had experimented with $N = 2$, but found out that the translation quality, measured in BLEU, dropped. We suspect that this is because either the model ends up paying unnecessary attention to the context or that the low-resource setting hinders the model from learning how to utilize context effectively. Ultimately we feel that $N = 1$ is a practical choice for the ALT dataset because it contains sentences with around 20 words on average. The longer the context sentence, the more computations the cross attention mechanism has to make, which slows decoding, which is ultimately what we are trying to avoid via SNMT while incorporating context. We were able to consider all 3 context sentences for English↔Russian because each sentence was substantially smaller, which does not impact decoding time as badly. In the future, we can consider sparse attention mechanisms such as locality sensitive hashing, which is used in the Reformer (Kitaev et al., 2020).

			Russian→English				English→Russian			
Model	`wait-k`	CT	CS=0	CS=1	CS=2	CS=3	CS=0	CS=1	CS=2	CS=3
Full Sentence	-	MS	34.9	35.2	35.5	**35.7**	26.7	27.0	**27.2**	**27.2**
	-	CA	34.9	35.3	**35.8**	35.6	26.7	27.0	27.2	**27.5**
SNMT	1	MS	23.5	23.6	24.0	**24.1**	13.2	13.4	13.4	**13.5**
	1	CA	23.5	23.7	23.8	**24.1**	13.2	13.3	**13.4**	13.3
	2	MS	28.8	28.9	**29.4**	29.3	17.6	17.7	**18.0**	17.9
	2	CA	28.8	29.1	**29.5**	**29.5**	17.6	17.9	18.0	**18.1**
	4	MS	32.9	33.2	33.5	**33.7**	23.7	23.7	23.7	**23.9**
	4	CA	32.9	33.1	**33.6**	**33.6**	23.7	23.6	**23.8**	**23.8**
	6	MS	33.9	34.3	34.5	**34.8**	25.7	25.7	25.8	**26.0**
	6	CA	33.9	34.4	34.6	**34.8**	25.7	25.7	25.9	**26.3**
	8	MS	34.3	34.6	35.0	**35.3**	26.2	26.3	26.5	**26.8**
	8	CA	34.3	34.8	34.9	**35.1**	26.2	26.4	26.5	**26.8**

Table 1: BLEU scores for English→Russian and Russian→English translation using the OpenSubtitles2018 corpus. Results are presented for full sentence and SNMT models using either no context or up to 3 context sentences ($CS = 0, 1, 2, 3$). CT indicates the document context incorporation technique which can be MS (Multi-Source) or CA (Context Attention). As improvements greater than 0.1 BLEU are statistically significant and most cases show improvement over baselines, we do not mark all significantly improved scores to avoid cluttering. For each type of model (full sentence or wait-k) for a language pair, we mark the best scores in bold.

			Japanese→English		English→Japanese	
Model	`wait-k`	CT	CS=0	CS=1	CS=0	CS=1
Full Sentence	-	MS	8.8	**9.0**	13.7	**14.1**
	-	CA	**8.8**	8.6	13.7	**14.2**
SNMT	1	MS	3.1	**3.2**	**9.3**	9.1
	1	CA	3.1	**3.3**	**9.3**	8.7
	2	MS	**3.8**	3.7	**10.4**	9.6
	2	CA	**3.8**	3.7	**10.4**	10.0
	4	MS	**4.8**	4.7	**12.1**	11.7
	4	CA	**4.8**	4.7	**12.1**	11.3
	6	MS	5.5	**5.6**	12.9	**13.0**
	6	CA	5.5	**5.6**	**12.9**	**12.9**
	8	MS	5.9	**6.3**	13.6	**13.7**
	8	CA	5.9	**6.5**	**13.6**	13.2

Table 2: BLEU scores for English→Japanese and Japanese→English translation using the ALT corpus. Results are presented for full sentence and SNMT models using either no context or up to 1 context sentence ($CS = 0, 1$). CT indicates the document context incorporation technique which can be MS (Multi-Source) or CA (Context Attention). For each type of model (full sentence or wait-k) for a language pair, we mark the best scores in bold.

5.1 Resource Rich English↔Russian translation

Table 1 gives the BLEU scores for English↔Russian translation.

5.1.1 Non-contextual: Full Sentence versus SNMT models

Regarding the baselines, it is clear that the SNMT models with small `wait-k`'s give poor translation quality as compared to the full sentence models. Increasing the value of `wait-k` naturally improves the translation quality, where a value of `k` = 8 leads to results that are within 1 BLEU of the results of the full sentence models. Given that the average sentence length for the Russian–English dataset is approximately 8 words, it makes sense that $K = 8$ would give the best results.

5.1.2 Context incorporation technique: Multi-Source (MS) versus Context Attention (CA)

The results show that there is no clear answer as to which of MS or CA is superior, which makes both viable solutions for incorporating context into the NMT model. For the remainder of the results section, the BLEU scores we quote will be for the MS approach. Looking at the results, it will be clear that the trends in the improvement of translation quality by incorporating context are similar regardless of the use of MS or CA.

5.1.3 Non-contextual versus Contextual Full-Sentence models

Next, when context sentences are used for full sentence translation for Russian→English, the quality for when up to 1, 2, and 3 previous sentences as context are used is 35.2, 35.5, and 35.7, respectively. Compared to a baseline score of 34.9, the improvements are 0.3, 0.6, and 0.8 BLEU. Similarly, for English→Russian, compared to a baseline score of 26.7, using up to 1, 2, and 3 previous sentences as context lead to translation quality improvements of 0.3, 0.5, and 0.5, respectively. We performed statistical significance testing (Koehn, 2004) which showed that all improvements are significant[5] at $p < 0.05$. This shows that context certainly helps in a spoken language domain, and as the number of context sentences grows, the translation quality also grows steadily.

5.1.4 Non-contextual versus Contextual SNMT models

Comparing the `wait-k` non-contextual model against contextual models using up to N context sentences shows that, once again, context is helpful in an SNMT setting. When using up to 3 context sentences, for `wait-k` values of 1, 2, 4, 6 and 8, the BLEU score improvements over their non-contextual counterparts are 0.6, 0.5, 0.8, 0.9, 1.0, respectively, for Russian→English translation. Similarly for the reverse direction the improvements are 0.3, 0.3, 0.2, 0.3, 0.6. One important observation is that the improvements are almost proportional to the value of `wait-k`. As we wait for more source language tokens, the impact of the previous sentences as context seems to be higher. This makes sense because the importance of the context is determined using a gating mechanism, and the more information we have about the current sentence, the better the gating mechanism will be at determining what part of the context should be used. Finally note the maximum gain for SNMT models using up to 3 context sentences which is 1.0 for Russian→English and 0.6 for English→Russian. Compared to the full sentence models, the corresponding gains are 0.8 and 0.5. Previously we have seen that a difference of 0.1 BLEU is sufficient for it to be statistically significant, which means that SNMT models experience significantly larger improvements in translation quality when compared to their full sentence counterparts.

[5]Note that the test set contains 40,000 sentences, so even a small improvement of 0.1 BLEU will be significant.

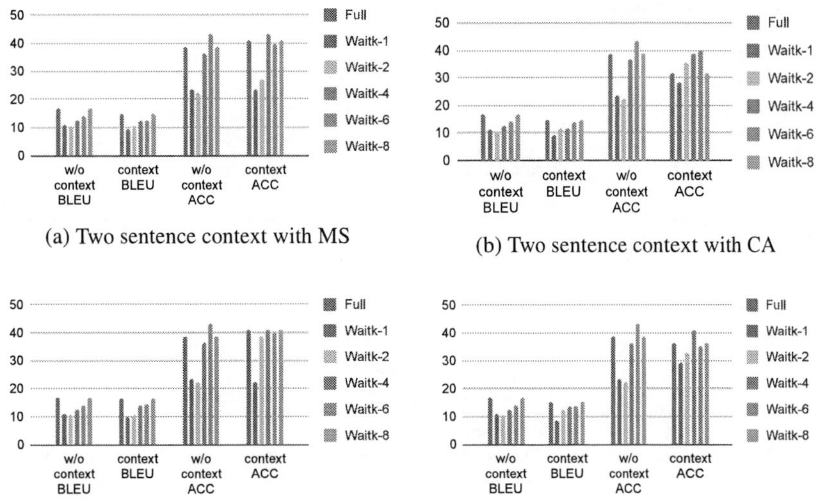

(a) Two sentence context with MS

(b) Two sentence context with CA

(c) One sentence context with MS

(d) One sentence context with CA

Figure 2: BLEU and accuracy (ACC) results for models using one or two previous sentences as context. We perform analyses for the multi-source (MS) and context-attention (CA) based context incorporation mechanisms.

5.2 Resource Poor English↔Japanese translation

Table 2 gives the BLEU scores for English↔Japanese translation. Looking at the absolute BLEU scores shows that context does lead to minor improvements in translation quality regardless of a full sentence or SNMT models. Unfortunately, the improvements are not statistically significant. Although we do not show it here, using additional context sentences led to a drop in translation quality. We suppose that this may be either due to the low-resource nature of the ALT dataset or perhaps there are not many cases where context should be helpful. Note that our context NMT model takes a weighted average of the attentions of the current and the context sentence, and so the translation quality may degrade if there are very few cases where context is needed. To this end, we decided to perform a statistical and manual analysis of the models for English→Japanese translation.

6 Analysis

6.1 Translation of Context-Aware Tokens

We investigate whether SNMT performance is improved by using contextual information. Therefore, we created context-aware parallel data in which the target sentence contains the tokens related to the previous target sentence. For example, given the context source sentence "The 2008 Taipei Game Show, organized by the Taipei Computer Association (TCA), ended on Monday, and was different from shows of past years.", and the source sentence "This could be seen in the gaming population, industry, and exhibition arrangements." in a simultaneous manner, the generated target sentence should be "ゲーム の 人口 、 産業 、 そして 展示 会 の 配列 で 見る こと が でき た 。". Here, "ゲーム" means "game" and it is a token related to the context. The context sentence contains information about the game, and this can help translate "ゲーム" that appears at the beginning of the target sentence, where it is not available yet from the source sentence (e.g., $k < 6$). We randomly investigated such sentence pairs from the

English→Japanese	
Context	Mr. Bush's talks with **Saudi** leaders also are expected to cover arms sales.
Source	Before heading to **Saudi Arabia**, Mr. Bush visited Dubai briefly.
Target	**サウジアラビア** に 向かう 前 に 、 ブッシュ 氏 は ドバイ を 短 期間 訪問 した 。
`wait-2` w/o context	既に 割れ て いる 前 に 、 ブッシュ 氏 は ドバイ について 言及 した 。 (Before it was already cracked, Mr. Bush mentioned Dubai.)
`wait-8` w/o context	**サウジアラビア** の 王室 に 証言 する 前 に 、 ブッシュ 氏 は ドバイ への 説明 を 訪問 した 。 (Before testifying before the **Saudi** royal family, Mr. Bush visited Dubai to explain.)
Full w/o context	**サウジアラビア** の 王室 に 証言 する 前 に 、 ブッシュ 氏 は ドバイ への 説明 を 訪問 した 。 (Before testifying before the **Saudi** royal family, Mr. Bush visited Dubai to explain.)
`wait-2` w/ context	**サウジアラビア** の イスラム 教徒 の 前 に 、 ブッシュ 氏 は 先週 記者 を 訪問 した 。 (Before the **Saudi** Muslims, Mr. Bush visited the press last week.)
`wait-8` w/ context	**サウジアラビア** の 王室 に 向かって 前 に 、 ブッシュ 氏 は ドバイ を 訪問 した 。 (Before heading to the royal family in **Saudi Arabia**, Mr. Bush visited Dubai.)
Full w/ context	**サウジアラビア** の 王室 に 向かって 前 に 、 ブッシュ 氏 は ドバイ を 訪問 した 。 (Before heading to the royal family in **Saudi Arabia**, Mr. Bush visited Dubai.)

Table 3: Translation examples generated by non-contextual models as well as the contextual models using one previous sentence as context and the multi-source (MS) context incorporation method. Sentences in parentheses are the English meanings of the translation results.

test data of WAT data and extracted 50 of them. Using BLEU and accuracy, calculated by the sum of correctly translated sentences that include the token that needs context to be translated, divided by the number of sentences, we evaluate whether the performance of the SNMT model is improved by using the context.

Figure 2 shows that BLEU and accuracy results for contextual models, using up to one or two previous sentences[6] as context, for created context-aware parallel data. In BLEU, it can be seen that the results are almost the same between the non-contextual and the contextual models. On the other hand, the results of accuracy differ between the non-contextual and the contextual models. In particular, accuracy is improved by considering the context at k = 1, 2, and 4. From this result, it can be seen that tokens related to the context can be translated by considering the context in SNMT. Our analysis also leads us to believe that it is difficult for BLEU to evaluate the improvement due to the context because BLEU was not designed in that way. This shows

[6] We have mentioned earlier that using two sentences as context led to a drop in translation quality but our analysis shows that they help provide context that is useful despite lowering the overall translation quality.

that there is a need for context-aware evaluation mechanisms.

6.2 Examples of Translations

In order to understand how the translation quality is improved by using context, we analyze the following translations: Table 3 shows the translation examples generated by non-contextual as well as the contextual models using one previous sentence as context and the multi-source (MS) context incorporation method. The "Saudis" contained in the context sentence is thought to be helpful when translating "サウジアラビア" which means "Saudi Arabia" in the source sentence. If `k` is 4 or less, "Saudi Arabia" will not be seen by the decoder. Since the translation result of `k` = 8 and the full sentence is the same, it can be seen that the effect of the missing words is almost eliminated when `k` is large in `wait-k`. "Saudi Arabia" was not translated with `k` = 2 without context, but it was correctly translated using the contextual model. From this translation example, we can see that the context helps to translate the words related to it. However, given that the overall corpus level BLEU does not show a large amount of improvement, we suspect that the current context incorporation mechanisms are not good at determining when the context should and should not be used. This means that we need to design better context relevance mechanisms.

7 Conclusion

We proposed `wait-k` document-level simultaneous NMT to complement the information of incomplete input during the translation process. Our proposed method is to replace the source encoder and target language decoder with `wait-k` equivalents while keeping the context encoder. The experimental results show that the proposed method slightly improves the translation quality in high-resource settings but not by appreciable amounts in low-resource settings. The analysis showed that `wait-k` models are more context-aware and rely on context whenever it should be helpful. However, the current model is unable to successfully determine when the context should be used, preventing the successful utilization of context. This indicates that we need to investigate further more effective ways to utilize the previous sentences in the document as context. Our human evaluation was also rather limited, and in the future, we plan to conduct a human evaluation to determine which kind of context-aware phenomena (pronoun disambiguation, word sense disambiguation) our approaches can address.

References

Bahdanau, D., Cho, K., and Bengio, Y. (2015). Neural machine translation by jointly learning to align and translate. In *3rd International Conference on Learning Representations, ICLR 2015, San Diego, CA, USA, May 7-9, 2015, Conference Track Proceedings*.

Bawden, R., Sennrich, R., Birch, A., and Haddow, B. (2018). Evaluating discourse phenomena in neural machine translation. In *Proceedings of the 2018 Conference of the North American Chapter of the Association for Computational Linguistics: Human Language Technologies, Volume 1 (Long Papers)*, pages 1304–1313, New Orleans, Louisiana. Association for Computational Linguistics.

Caglayan, O., Ive, J., Haralampieva, V., Madhyastha, P., Barrault, L., and Specia, L. (2020). Simultaneous machine translation with visual context. In *EMNLP*, pages 2350–2361. Association for Computational Linguistics.

Dabre, R., Cromieres, F., and Kurohashi, S. (2017). Enabling multi-source neural machine translation by concatenating source sentences in multiple languages. In *Proceedings of MT Summit XVI, vol.1: Research Track*, pages 96–106, Nagoya, Japan.

Dalvi, F., Durrani, N., Sajjad, H., and Vogel, S. (2018). Incremental decoding and training methods for simultaneous translation in neural machine translation. In *Proceedings of the 2018 Conference of the North American Chapter of the Association for Computational Linguistics: Human Language Technologies, Volume 2 (Short Papers)*, pages 493–499. Association for Computational Linguistics.

Fernandes, P., Yin, K., Neubig, G., and Martins, A. F. (2021). Measuring and increasing context usage in context-aware machine translation. *arXiv preprint arXiv:2105.03482*.

Grissom II, A., He, H., Boyd-Graber, J., Morgan, J., and Daumé III, H. (2014). Don't until the final verb wait: Reinforcement learning for simultaneous machine translation. In *Proceedings of the 2014 Conference on Empirical Methods in Natural Language Processing*, pages 1342–1352.

Gu, J., Neubig, G., Cho, K., and Li, V. O. (2017). Learning to translate in real-time with neural machine translation. In *Proceedings of the 15th Conference of the European Chapter of the Association for Computational Linguistics (Volume 1, Long Papers)*, pages 1053–1062.

Imankulova, A., Kaneko, M., Hirasawa, T., and Komachi, M. (2020). Towards multimodal simultaneous neural machine translation. In *WMT*, pages 594–603. Association for Computational Linguistics.

Jean, S., Lauly, S., Firat, O., and Cho, K. (2017). Does neural machine translation benefit from larger context? *arXiv preprint arXiv:1704.05135*.

Kim, Y. and Rush, A. M. (2016). Sequence-level knowledge distillation. In *Proceedings of the 2016 Conference on Empirical Methods in Natural Language Processing*, pages 1317–1327, Austin, Texas. Association for Computational Linguistics.

Kitaev, N., Kaiser, Ł., and Levskaya, A. (2020). Reformer: The efficient transformer. *arXiv preprint arXiv:2001.04451*.

Koehn, P. (2004). Statistical significance tests for machine translation evaluation. In *Proceedings of the 2004 Conference on Empirical Methods in Natural Language Processing*, pages 388–395, Barcelona, Spain. Association for Computational Linguistics.

Libovický, J., Helcl, J., and Mareček, D. (2018). Input combination strategies for multi-source transformer decoder. In *Proceedings of the Third Conference on Machine Translation: Research Papers*, pages 253–260, Brussels, Belgium. Association for Computational Linguistics.

Luong, M., Le, Q. V., Sutskever, I., Vinyals, O., and Kaiser, L. (2016). Multi-task sequence to sequence learning. In *Proceedings of International Conference on Learning Representations*.

Ma, M., Huang, L., Xiong, H., Zheng, R., Liu, K., Zheng, B., Zhang, C., He, Z., Liu, H., Li, X., Wu, H., and Wang, H. (2019). STACL: Simultaneous translation with implicit anticipation and controllable latency using prefix-to-prefix framework. In *Proceedings of the 57th Annual Meeting of the Association for Computational Linguistics*, pages 3025–3036.

Matsubara, S., Iwashima, K., Kawaguchi, N., Toyama, K., and Inagaki, Y. (2000). Simultaneous Japanese-English interpretation based on early prediction of English verb. In *Proceedings of The Fourth Symposium on Natural Language Processing*, pages 268–273.

Oda, Y., Neubig, G., Sakti, S., Toda, T., and Nakamura, S. (2015). Syntax-based simultaneous translation through prediction of unseen syntactic constituents. In *Proceedings of the 53rd Annual Meeting of the Association for Computational Linguistics and the 7th International Joint Conference on Natural Language Processing (Volume 1: Long Papers)*, pages 198–207.

Papineni, K., Roukos, S., Ward, T., and Zhu, W.-J. (2002). BLEU: a method for automatic evaluation of machine translation. In *Proceedings of the 40th Annual Meeting on Association for Computational Linguistics*, pages 311–318.

Riza, H., Purwoadi, M., Gunarso, Uliniansyah, T., Ti, A. A., Aljunied, S. M., Mai, L. C., Thang, V. T., Thai, N. P., Sun, R., Chea, V., Soe, K. M., Nwet, K. T., Utiyama, M., and Ding, C. (2016). Introduction of the Asian language treebank. In *Proc. of O-COCOSDA*, pages 1–6.

Tiedemann, J. and Scherrer, Y. (2017). Neural machine translation with extended context. In *Proceedings of the Third Workshop on Discourse in Machine Translation*, pages 82–92, Copenhagen, Denmark. Association for Computational Linguistics.

Vaswani, A., Shazeer, N., Parmar, N., Uszkoreit, J., Jones, L., Gomez, A. N., Kaiser, L. u., and Polosukhin, I. (2017). Attention is all you need. In Guyon, I., Luxburg, U. V., Bengio, S., Wallach, H., Fergus, R., Vishwanathan, S., and Garnett, R., editors, *Proceedings of the Advances in Neural Information Processing Systems 30*, pages 5998–6008. Curran Associates, Inc.

Voita, E., Sennrich, R., and Titov, I. (2019). Context-aware monolingual repair for neural machine translation. In *Proceedings of the 2019 Conference on Empirical Methods in Natural Language Processing and the 9th International Joint Conference on Natural Language Processing (EMNLP-IJCNLP)*, pages 877–886, Hong Kong, China. Association for Computational Linguistics.

Voita, E., Serdyukov, P., Sennrich, R., and Titov, I. (2018). Context-aware neural machine translation learns anaphora resolution. In *Proceedings of the 56th Annual Meeting of the Association for Computational Linguistics (Volume 1: Long Papers)*, pages 1264–1274, Melbourne, Australia. Association for Computational Linguistics.

Wang, L., Tu, Z., Way, A., and Liu, Q. (2017). Exploiting cross-sentence context for neural machine translation. In *Proceedings of the 2017 Conference on Empirical Methods in Natural Language Processing*, pages 2826–2831, Copenhagen, Denmark. Association for Computational Linguistics.

Xiong, H., He, Z., Wu, H., and Wang, H. (2019). Modeling coherence for discourse neural machine translation. In *Proceedings of the AAAI Conference on Artificial Intelligence*, volume 33, pages 7338–7345.

Zhang, J., Luan, H., Sun, M., Zhai, F., Xu, J., Zhang, M., and Liu, Y. (2018). Improving the transformer translation model with document-level context. In *Proceedings of the 2018 Conference on Empirical Methods in Natural Language Processing*, pages 533–542, Brussels, Belgium. Association for Computational Linguistics.

Zheng, B., Zheng, R., Ma, M., and Huang, L. (2019a). Simpler and faster learning of adaptive policies for simultaneous translation. In *Proceedings of the 2019 Conference on Empirical Methods in Natural Language Processing and the 9th International Joint Conference on Natural Language Processing (EMNLP-IJCNLP)*, pages 1349–1354.

Zheng, B., Zheng, R., Ma, M., and Huang, L. (2019b). Simultaneous translation with flexible policy via restricted imitation learning. In *Proceedings of the 57th Annual Meeting of the Association for Computational Linguistics*, pages 5816–5822.

Zheng, R., Ma, M., Zheng, B., and Huang, L. (2019c). Speculative beam search for simultaneous translation. In *Proceedings of the 2019 Conference on Empirical Methods in Natural Language Processing and the 9th International Joint Conference on Natural Language Processing (EMNLP-IJCNLP)*, pages 1395–1402.

Zheng, R., Ma, M., Zheng, B., Liu, K., and Huang, L. (2020a). Opportunistic decoding with timely correction for simultaneous translation. In *Proceedings of the 58th Annual Meeting of the Association for Computational Linguistics*, pages 437–442.

Zheng, Z., Yue, X., Huang, S., Chen, J., and Birch, A. (2020b). Towards making the most of context in neural machine translation. In *IJCAI*.

Zoph, B. and Knight, K. (2016). Multi-source neural translation. In *Proceedings of the 2016 Conference of the North American Chapter of the Association for Computational Linguistics: Human Language Technologies*, pages 30–34, San Diego, California. Association for Computational Linguistics.

Attainable Text-to-Text Machine Translation vs. Translation: Issues Beyond Linguistic Processing

Atsushi Fujita atsushi.fujita@nict.go.jp
National Institute of Information and Communications Technology,
3-5 Hikaridai, Seika-cho, Soraku-gun, Kyoto, 619-0289, Japan

Abstract

Existing approaches for machine translation (MT) mostly translate a given text in the source language into the target language, without explicitly referring to information indispensable for producing a proper translation. This includes not only information in the textual elements and non-textual modalities in the same document, but also extra-document and non-linguistic information, such as norms and skopos. To design better translation production workflows, we need to distinguish translation issues that could be resolved by the existing text-to-text approaches from those beyond them. To this end, we conducted an analytic assessment of MT outputs, taking an English-to-Japanese news translation task as a case study. First, examples of translation issues and their revisions were collected by a two-stage post-edit (PE) method: performing a minimal PE to obtain a translation attainable based on the given textual information and further performing a full PE to obtain an acceptable translation referring to any necessary information. The collected revision examples were then manually analyzed. We revealed the dominant issues and information indispensable for resolving them, such as fine-grained style specifications, terminology, domain-specific knowledge, and reference documents, delineating a clear distinction between translation and the translation that text-to-text MT can ultimately attain.

1 Introduction

Translation is not a purely linguistic process (Vermeer, 1992) but also the process of producing a document in the target language that plays the same role (has the same effect) as the given source document written in the source language. When translating a given document, translators refer not only to the textual elements in the document, but also to the role of each textual element (e.g., running text, section title, table element, and caption), other non-linguistic elements (e.g., figures and formulae), and their structure. To produce a translation, we also need some extra-document and non-linguistic information, such as the *norms* specific to the register of the document and corresponding target sub-language (Toury, 1978), the objective and the intended usages of translation, i.e., *skopos* (Vermeer, 2004), and various specifications (Melby, 2012) designated by the translation client if any.

Despite the requirements a (proper) translation must satisfy, techniques for machine translation (MT) have been developed by regarding the task of translation as *text-to-text transfer*. Until very recently, most studies have performed a text-to-text MT for each text *segment*,[1] even though a sequence of perfect segment-level text-to-text translations does not necessarily qualify as a proper translation. Recent studies on neural MT (NMT) have addressed issues beyond

[1] In this paper, we use "segment" for the unit of inputs for MT systems rather than "sentence," because a segment is not necessarily composed of a single sentence, but can often be multiple sentences or non-sentential textual fragments.

this formulation, exploiting further information such as document-level textual context (Voita et al., 2018, 2019; Lopes et al., 2020) and other modalities (Barrault et al., 2018). There are also several focused studies on exploiting extra-document and non-linguistic information. However, such information has not been extensively discussed. As a result, in translation production workflows at translation service providers (TSPs), where MT outputs are treated as draft translations, heavy human labor is necessary to fill the gap between MT outputs and translations in addition to resolving issues at the text-to-text level, for instance, by manual post-editing (PE).

To design and establish more practical ways of exploiting MT systems in translation production workflows as well as to discuss how to make MT systems more useful, we need to understand what lies in the gap between a translation that text-to-text processing can attain and a truly acceptable translation. Moreover, this should be shared among not only translators but also MT researchers and MT users. From this point of view, this paper presents our analytic assessment of MT outputs, taking an English-to-Japanese news translation task as a case study. First, we obtained segment-level text-to-text translation by resolving translation issues in MT outputs. At this stage, a minimal PE was performed referring only to each source segment isolated from any other information, and thus the results represent what segment-level text-to-text MT systems can ultimately attain. Then, the document-level full PE (ISO/TC37, 2017) in the succeeding stage resolved all the remaining issues, i.e., those issues lying in the gap between acceptable segment-level text-to-text translation and proper translation. Finally, the collected revision examples were manually analyzed based on an issue classification scheme. This revealed several dominant issues as well as the information indispensable for resolving them.

The remainder of this paper is organized as follows. Section 2 summarizes related work in translation studies and MT. Section 3 presents the material for our case study. Section 4 describes our workflow, designed for collecting translation issues that cannot be solved by text-to-text processing. Section 5 presents our analytic assessment of translation issues, which relies on an existing issue typology, and explains the dominant issues as well as several types of extra-document and/or non-linguistic information that must be used to solve them. Section 6 describes future research directions and advice for non-expert MT users, and Section 7 concludes the paper.

2 Related Work

In the literature of translation studies, linguistic approaches to translation have been criticized (Kenny, 2001), and the *equivalence* of a source document and a target document has been studied from a diverse range of aspects. In a seminal work, Nida (1964) claimed the necessity of equivalence of recipients' reactions when reading source and target documents. Chesterman (1997) compiled a typology of translation strategies adopted to guarantee the equivalence when producing a translation. His syntactic and semantic strategies can be explained (and potentially realized) referring only to textual information in the source document and linguistic knowledge in general. In contrast, some of his pragmatic strategies, such as cultural filtering and illocutionary changes, require extra-document and/or non-linguistic information.

Some of the kinds of information that must be referred to for producing a proper translation, including terminologies and style specifications, are mentioned in the translation workflow standard, ISO 17100 (ISO/TC37, 2015). Other items are mentioned in existing criteria for quality assurance, such as the Multidimensional Quality Metrics (MQM)[2] and the Dynamic Quality Framework (DQF).[3] Reference sources, such as translation memories and bilingual concordancers, and other access to past translations are valuable assets for improving efficiency in personal practices and workflows in TSPs. However, there is neither a comprehensive inven-

[2]http://www.qt21.eu/launchpad/content/multidimensional-quality-metrics

[3]https://www.taus.net/data-for-ai/dqf

tory of references, nor a common view of the extent of the necessity and availability of each reference depending on the given skopos.

Recent advances in MT go beyond segment-level and/or text-to-text processing. For instance, Voita et al. (2019) focused on several discourse-level issues, i.e., deixis, lexical cohesion, and ellipsis, occurring in segment-level text-to-text MT. Following studies proved that context-aware decoding that refers to several preceding segments better handles these linguistic phenomena (Lopes et al., 2020). There are several focused studies on exploiting extra-document and non-linguistic information, including terminologies (Arthur et al., 2016; Hasler et al., 2018), politeness (Sennrich et al., 2016a), domain (Chu et al., 2017; Kobus et al., 2017; Bapna and Firat, 2019), style (Niu et al., 2017; Michel and Neubig, 2018b), markups (Chatterjee et al., 2017; Hashimoto et al., 2019), and external lexical knowledge (Moussallem et al., 2019). However, the information indispensable for producing a proper translation have not been thoroughly studied. More importantly, no work guarantees to perfectly reflect such information.

The MT community has benefited from manual analyses of translation issues[4] caused by MT systems. Existing methodologies for analyzing translation issues in MT outputs can be two-fold: (a) comparisons of independent products, i.e., MT outputs and human translations (Popović and Ney, 2011; Irvine et al., 2013; Toral, 2020), and (b) annotations of the issues in MT outputs according to pre-determined issue typologies, such as MQM and DQF (Lommel et al., 2015; Ye and Toral, 2020; Freitag et al., 2021). The issues identified in the former approach contain both true errors and preferential differences, i.e., alternative acceptable translations independently selected by MT systems and humans. The latter approach enables us to clearly separate them. For instance, past studies (Hardmeier, 2014; Scarton et al., 2015; Voita et al., 2019) analyzed outputs of segment-level text-to-text MT, showed the limitation of that approach, and encouraged the research on document-level MT. However, they discussed only the differences between two text-to-text approaches. Issues beyond the text-to-text processing, such as those related to extra-document and/or non-linguistic information, have seldom been mentioned (Castilho et al., 2020), and no focused and empirical analysis has been conducted.

3 Subject of Our Case Study

Our focus in this paper is to clarify the types of extra-document and/or non-linguistic information that are indispensable for producing a translation. Among several translation tasks, this paper takes an English-to-Japanese news translation task as a case study and presents our in-depth analysis. We chose it for two reasons. First, despite the high demand for it, the task is still very difficult, since the two languages are linguistically distant and used in substantially different cultures (cf. English-to-German studied by Scarton et al. (2015)). The norms for news texts are also substantially different in these languages, making them more difficult to translate than texts in other domains, such as scientific paper abstracts (Nakazawa et al., 2019) and patent documents (Goto et al., 2013). The second reason is that we wished to conduct an in-depth analytic assessment of translation (see Section 5) by ourselves. We have a linguist who is highly competent in both linguistics and translation and has ample experiences in the analytic assessment of both MT outputs and human translations.

As material for this case study, we used the documents in the Asian Language Treebank (ALT) (Riza et al., 2016).[5] Table 1 gives statistics for the English source documents and Japanese target documents produced by professional human translators, where the numbers of tokens were counted after applying our in-house tokenizers.

[4]As a way of human evaluation, holistic assessment (or scoring) (Barrault et al., 2019; Nakazawa et al., 2019; Läubli et al., 2020; Barrault et al., 2020) is also beneficial, but does not suffice for our needs.

[5]http://www2.nict.go.jp/astrec-att/member/mutiyama/ALT/

Split	#Doc.	#Seg.	#Tok.	
			English	Japanese
Training	1,698	18,088	2,572k	3,743k
Development	98	1,000	139k	202k
Test	97	1,018	143k	208k

Table 1: Statistics for the ALT English–Japanese data (ALT-Standard-Split).

4 Data Collection

To clarify the limitations of the text-to-text approach for MT while acknowledging its status, we began with the outputs of a reasonably strong NMT system and collected examples of translation issues with their revisions through a modified version of the two-stage PE workflow originally proposed by Scarton et al. (2015). Our procedure is as follows.

Stage (1) Segment-level text-to-text NMT: Given source documents are translated by an MT system, which is preferably the one that can produce a translation of exploitable quality. We regard a segment-level text-to-text NMT as the subject.

Stage (2) Segment-level minimal PE: Each segment-level MT output is separately post-edited without referring to any information other than the segment itself, for example, other segments in the same document and other reference documents. To avoid introducing any preferences from human workers, this stage allows only minimal edits.

Stage (3) Document-level full PE: The results of stage (2) are further post-edited at document level to resolve the remaining issues caused by segment-level and/or text-to-text processing, where the human workers are allowed to refer to any necessary information. The resulting data exhibit the limitations of the segment-level text-to-text processing.[6]

Figure 1 compares our workflow (in the right-most path) with conventional human translation ("Non-MT workflow") and the prevalent one in TSPs ("MT+PE"), i.e., segment-level text-to-text MT followed by document-level manual full PE. Our workflow can be seen as an extension of "MT+PE" with an intermediate segment-level minimal PE stage.

The division of segment-level and document-level PE was originally proposed by Scarton et al. (2015) as a means of manually assessing the outputs of statistical MT (SMT) systems. Note that our subject is not the gap between segment-level and document-level text-to-text processing, i.e., MT systems, as in Scarton et al. (2015), but the limitation of such text-to-text processing. We therefore need to collect translation issues that can only be resolved by referring to information other than the given textual information. To exclude issues that can be resolved by referring only to the given textual information as much as possible, we decided to obtain translations that are attainable but closest to the outputs of text-to-text MT through minimal PE; we explicitly constrain the human workers by (i) prohibiting them from referring to any information other than the textual information and (ii) allowing only minimal edits,[7] while also avoiding subjective stylistic changes.[8] Even though document-level text-to-text MT

[6]Translation obtainable through this method is not necessarily of high quality because it is, in the end, *post-editese* (Toral, 2019). We plan to analyze the gap between PE-based translation and high-quality human translation, i.e., the art of translation, in our future work.

[7]This might be comparable with the goal of light PE (ISO/TC37, 2017): "obtain a merely comprehensible text without any attempt to produce a product comparable to a product obtained by human translation."

[8]Scarton et al. (2015) regarded style changes as the translator's choice. However, according to ISO/TC37 (2015), the appropriate style is not determined by the translators, but by the extra-document specifications for translation, for instance in the form of a translation brief that specifies the purpose/usage of the translated documents.

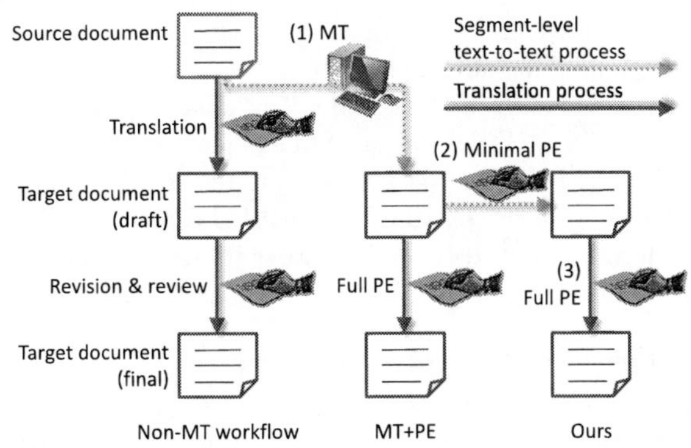

Figure 1: Comparison of translation workflows: the translation process refers to any information other than the given source document (cf. text-to-text process).

has been actively studied (Voita et al., 2018, 2019; Lopes et al., 2020), we decided to begin with segment-level MT and PE because we can ensure the minimality of the edits using segment-level automatic metrics (see Section 4.2).

By performing only minimal PE at segment level, we can leave all the translation issues that can only be resolved by referring to extra-document and/or non-linguistic information for a later stage. These issues are resolved in the succeeding document-level full PE stage, and we distinguish (a) those issues revealing the gap between segment-level and document-level processing and (b) those issues revealing the limitations of the text-to-text processing, through our manual analysis (see Section 5).

Our process for collecting translation issues uses some parameters that differ from those in Scarton et al. (2015), including the MT paradigm (SMT vs. NMT), translation task (English-to-German vs. English-to-Japanese), and worker experiences (students vs. professionals employed by a TSP with ISO certificates (ISO/TC37, 2015, 2017)).

4.1 Stage (1) Segment-level Text-to-Text NMT

To begin with a translation of exploitable quality, we trained a segment-level but reasonably strong[9] English-to-Japanese NMT system on a large-scale in-house English–Japanese parallel corpus (henceforth, *TexTra*)[10] in addition to the ALT training data, using a method for domain adaptation (Chu et al., 2017). First, we trained an English-to-Japanese NMT model on *TexTra* alone, explicitly excluding all the segment pairs in the ALT. For each source and target language, a sub-word vocabulary was also created from the corresponding side of this corpus: we determined 32k sub-words with byte-pair encoding (Sennrich et al., 2016b) after tokenization. Then, we fine-tuned the model parameters on a mixture of *TexTra* and the ALT training data. Following Chu et al. (2017), we used a balanced mixture of the two corpora by inflating the ALT training data K times and randomly sampling the same number of segment pairs from *TexTra*. Finally, we further fine-tuned the NMT model on the ALT training data only.

We used Marian NMT (Junczys-Dowmunt et al., 2018)[11] for all the NMT training and decoding processes, using the Transformer Base model and the hyper-parameters for training as

[9]We are aware that our system would not be state of the art because we do not use synthetic parallel data, a model ensemble, nor re-ranking. However, because these are all the methods for improving segment-level text-to-text MT, we assume that omitting them does not affect the main issues that we identify during the document-level full PE stage.

[10]The size is confidential. The generic model can be used via https://mt-auto-minhon-mlt.ucri.jgn-x.jp.

[11]https://github.com/marian-nmt/marian/, version 1.7.0

used in Vaswani et al. (2017). We terminated the training at each phase by early-stopping with a patience of 5, regarding the model perplexity on the ALT development data, computed after every T iterations, as the evaluation criterion. The value of T was set to 5,000 for the phase 1, and 10 for the phases 2 and 3. For the value of sample size K in phase 2, we selected 32 from the options 1, 2, 4, 8, 16, 32, and 64 according to the BLEU score (Papineni et al., 2002) on the ALT development data, computed by SacreBLEU (Post, 2018).[12] When decoding the ALT test data, the beam size was fixed 10, and the value for the length penalty was tuned on the ALT development data and set to 0.8.

4.2 Stage (2) Segment-level Minimal PE

To perform a segment-level PE, we isolated each segment from the others in the same document by shuffling the pairs of source segment and corresponding segment-level MT output across all the test documents.

We then asked[13] an experienced, ISO-certified TSP with well-designed workflows for translation (ISO/TC37, 2015) and PE (ISO/TC37, 2017) to revise the MT output of each segment independently without referring to any information other than the individual segment. The goal of this stage was to obtain a segment-level translation that fluently and accurately conveys the information in the corresponding source segment. To avoid excessive PE, we imposed a constraint, $hter(m, p) \leq hter(m, r)$, where m, p, and r stand for the MT output, its post-edited version, and reference translation,[14] respectively. $hter(a, b)$ is the Human-targeted Translation Edit Rate (HTER) (Snover et al., 2006), which computes how one segment a is dissimilar from another segment b at surface level, implemented in tercom.[15] We used MeCab[16] to tokenize the Japanese translation, unlike our implementation of NMT, in order to enable the consistent tokenization in both our environment and the workers' environment.

During this process, 95% of the segments (970/1,018) received some revisions. This suggests that our system still seldom generates acceptable segment-level translation in this English-to-Japanese news translation task. Because we allowed only minimal editing operations, the results represent the closest goal of segment-level text-to-text MT.

4.3 Stage (3) Document-level Full PE

After completing segment-level minimal PE for all segments, the documents were reverted by ordering the segments. We then asked[17] another set of workers through the same TSP to further revise the translation referring not only to the entire document but also to any extra-document and/or non-linguistic information, as in the ordinary document-level full PE workflow, i.e., "MT+PE" in Figure 1. Note that we hid the original MT outputs and provided the results of segment-level PE as the draft translation for revision. The workers were asked to make the target documents cohesive, consistent, and appropriate for news articles, also correcting content errors if any. Some examples are presented in Section 5.1.

As a result, 320 segments (31%) in 86 documents (89%) were revised. The total quantity of edits during this stage was much smaller than in the previous stage, but they were indeed necessary to obtain proper translations. This also confirms that a sequence of acceptable segment-level text-to-text translations does not necessarily qualify as translation. It further confirms that,

[12] https://github.com/mjpost/sacreBLEU/, short signature: BLEU+c.mixed+l.en-ja+#.1+s.exp+t.13a+v.1.4.1

[13] The price was based on the number of tokens in the source documents as in an ordinary translation contract. Thus, there was no incentive to increase the amount of PE.

[14] The TSP and workers did not see the ALT reference translation, and were asked to redo the task from the given MT output if we judged that their PE result did not satisfy the constraint.

[15] http://www.cs.umd.edu/~snover/tercom/, version 0.7.25.

[16] https://taku910.github.io/mecab/, version 0.996.

[17] For this task, we paid the same amount as we did for the segment-level PE.

Translation	BLEU (↑)	HTER (↓)
Output of NMT trained only on ALT	14.6	73.9
Output of NMT in phase 1	29.0	55.5
Output of NMT in phase 2	$35.8^{\dagger 1}$	47.6
Output of NMT in phase 3	$36.0^{\dagger 1}$	47.6
Segment-level minimal PE result	$36.8^{\dagger 3}$	47.0
Document-level full PE result	$36.8^{\dagger 3}$	47.0

Table 2: BLEU and HTER scores of different versions of translations with respect to the ALT reference translation (ALT). Note that these results are based on our in-house Japanese tokenizer (cf. MeCab used in the workflow for consistent tokenization). "†1" and "†3" respectively denote the score is significantly better than that for phases 1 and 3 ($p < 0.05$).

as in other well-studied translation tasks (Läubli et al., 2020; Freitag et al., 2021), *human parity* (Hassan et al., 2018) is not yet attainable in this English-to-Japanese news translation task.

4.4 Translation Quality Measured by Automatic Evaluation Metrics

Table 2 summarizes the BLEU and HTER scores of different versions of translations obtained in our workflow. To determine if differences in BLEU scores are significant, we performed statistical significance testing ($p < 0.05$).[18] The BLEU score of our adapted NMT system (phase 3) was significantly better than the non-adapted system (phase 1). We consider that it generated a translation of sufficient quality for this first stage in the process. Whereas the improvement brought by segment-level minimal PE was visible and the BLEU gain was statistically significant, the document-level full PE improved neither BLEU nor HTER scores.

5 Manual Analysis of Translation Issues

Our post-edited translation data contain two separate and different types of translation issues: the remaining issues from the segment-level text-to-text MT, and the issues that require information other than the individual segments to resolve. We manually analyzed the latter translation issues resolved during the document-level full PE in stage (3).

First, using tercom, we automatically identified the corresponding text spans in the two versions of the translations obtained in stages (2) and (3). Then, we manually extracted pairs of text spans: one for an issue in the segment-level PE result, and the other for its revision in the document-level PE result. As a result, we obtained 529 such *revision examples*. Finally, we annotated each revision example with the following three types of labels.

Need for document-level textual information: whether the textual information outside the segment but within the document was necessary to solve the issue.

Need for extra information: whether any extra-document and/or non-linguistic information was necessary to solve the issue. If it was needed, we also noted the information types (more than one if applicable).

Issue type: one of the 16 types in a translation issues typology designed for assessing and learning English-to-Japanese translation (Fujita et al., 2017). We chose this typology because its usefulness for this translation direction had been verified, whereas a widely used MQM had not.

[18] https://github.com/moses-smt/mosesdecoder/blob/master/scripts/analysis/bootstrap-hypothesis-difference-significance.pl

		Extra info.	
		No need	Necessary
Document-level	No need	(a) 196	(c) 168
textual info.	Necessary	(b) 116	(d) 49

Table 3: Revision examples classified according to the types of necessary information.

Issue type		#Examples		
		(a)	(b)	(c),(d)
Lv 1: **Incompleteness**	X4a: Content-untranslated	0	0	16
	X6: Content-indecision	0	1	1
Lv 2: **Semantic errors**	X7: Lexis-incorrect-term	5	6	67
	X1: Content-omission	11	4	2
	X2: Content-addition	3	0	0
	X3: Content-distortion	42	31	25
Lv 3: **Linguistic issues in target document**	X8: Lexis-inappropriate-collocation	5	0	0
	X10: Grammar-preposition/particle	2	0	0
	X11: Grammar-inflection	0	0	0
	X12: Grammar-spelling	0	0	0
	X13: Grammar-punctuation	7	0	0
	X9: Grammar-others	1	0	0
Lv 4: **Felicity issues in target document**	X16: Text-incohesive	31	63	14
	X4b: Content-too-literal	54	0	7
	X15: Text-clumsy	35	3	4
Lv 5: **Register issues in target document**	X14: Text-TD-inappropriate-register	0	8	81
Total		196	116	217

Table 4: Distribution of the revision examples. Refer to Fujita et al. (2017) for the definition of each issue type and the classification procedure, and Table 3 for the classification of (a) to (d).

Tables 3 and 4 show our classification results: whereas Table 3 shows a contingency table based on the first two labels, Table 4 shows the type-wise numbers of revision examples, merging (c) and (d) in Table 3 for the sake of simplicity.

5.1 Issues Beyond Text-to-text MT

Among the four classes shown in Table 3, our main subjects are 217 examples in (c) and (d) that can only be resolved by referring to some extra-document and/or non-linguistic information. Such information is categorized into the following four types.

A) Fine-grained style specifications (121 examples): Texts in Japanese newspapers are written following various specifications, including those for vocabulary, set of characters, usages of symbols including parentheses, degree of formality, and other notational rules. Our source texts themselves might have revealed that they are from the news domain. However, the workers for the segment-level minimal PE task did not perform revisions to fulfill such specifications, leading to translation that is inappropriate for the register (81 X14 issues). Because of a lack of a specification for transliteration at the segment-level PE stage, the workers left some named entities untranslated (16 X4a issues), considering that Latin characters are sometimes used in Japanese documents and that the contents in the source segments are comprehensible.

Source:	Clemens (3-0(#1), 1.90 ERA in seven World Series starts) will make his 33rd career postseason(#6,#7) start(#8) Saturday, at least for a day matching(#5) Pettitte (3-4(#3), 3.90 in 10 World Series starts) for the most ever(#4).
Seg.PE:	クレメンス（ワールドシリーズ７回出場で３対０(#1/3 points vs 0 points)、防御率１．９０）は、少なくとも１日[ ](#2/ϵ)ペティット（ワールドシリーズ１０回出場で３対４(#3/3 points vs 4 points)、３．９０）と[ ](#4/ϵ)組んで(#5/paired)、土曜日に[ ](#6/ϵ)３３回目のポストシーズン(#7/33rd postseason)のスタートを切る(#8/start)。
Doc.PE:	クレメンス（ワールドシリーズ７回出場で３勝０敗(#1/3 wins and 0 losses/(c)/X3)、防御率１．９０）は、少なくとも１日は(#2/topic marker/(a)/X15) ペティット（ワールドシリーズ１０回出場で３勝４敗(#3/3 wins and 4 losses/(c)/X3)、３．９０）と史上最多で(#4/most ever/(a)/X1)並び(#5/ranked same/(c)/X3)、土曜日に生涯で(#6/in ones life/(a)/X1)ポストシーズン３３回目(#7/33rd time in postseason/(c)/X3)の先発登板を行う(#8/to be the first pitcher of the game/(c)/X3)。

Figure 2: An example segment (Doc.ID: 24312, Seg.ID: 15534), where eight issues (numbered in the first element of subscript) were resolved during the document-level full PE. The second elements of the subscript in the translation give phrase-level gloss, and the remaining elements of the subscript for the document-level full PE represent the type of necessary information (see Table 3) and the issue type (see Table 4).

B) Terminology (80 examples): When translating named entities, we must look up the terminologies for authorized translations/transliterations. Consider, for instance, the person name "John Paul." The most likely transliteration for it is "ジョン・ポール" (/dʒ'ɔn p'ɔːl/). However, it must be transliterated into "ヨハネ・パウロ" (/johʌnɛ pʌʊlə/) when it refers to the Pope. Most improper and/or inconsistent term translations (64 X7 issues) and the above untranslated entities (16 X4a issues) were caused due to a lack of a terminology.

C) Domain-specific knowledge (31 examples): Our documents cover diverse topics such as politics, religion, and sports. Some semantic issues required knowledge specific to each of these domains to understand the contents in the source texts and produce appropriate expressions. See, for instance, the example in Figure 2. One must realize that this text is talking about baseball, and have knowledge about that domain, in order to perform the revisions marked (c). Some incohesive issues (five X16 issues) also require such knowledge to resolve.

D) Reference documents (eight examples): When translating ambiguous expressions, we need some clues to disambiguate them. If the document does not contain such information, we must find some reliable information outside the document. Because our text-to-text MT system and our segment-level minimal PE can only access the textual information, some semantic issues (seven X3 issues) and an incomplete translation with multiple options (X6 issue) were left. The X6 issue gives both "兄 (elder brother)" and "弟 (younger brother)" as multiple translation options for "brother." This ambiguity was resolved only when the worker found credible biographical information on the Web. Although we found only eight examples that were resolved in the document-level full PE stage referring to other information sources, we confirmed that our text-to-text MT sometimes correctly disambiguates such expressions by chance.

5.2 Remaining Issues of Text-to-Text MT

The remaining 196 and 116 examples were respectively classified as (a) and (b), i.e., those that had been resolved by referring only to the given textual information. These resolutions could be attainable by algorithmic advancements in the text-to-text approach for MT. Although they are outside the focus of this paper, we make some observations relevant to our study.

Segment-level issues, i.e., (a), lie at the levels 2 to 4 in the issue typology (Table 4). Whereas the ones at levels 2 and 3 should have been resolved through segment-level minimum PE, the ones at level 4 are not considered mandatory as long as the translations are considered comprehensible. We believe that we have successfully excluded much larger number of similar segment-level text-to-text issues by introducing the segment-level minimal PE stage (Section 4.2) and the above remaining issues are not harmful to our study. We could have reduced the examples in this class by removing our constraints for minimal edits. However, this introduces some risks, such as losing examples in our concern, i.e., (c) and (d), and being mislead by some artificial examples, such as combinations of preferential edits in both segment-level PE and document-level PE.

Class (b) examples exhibit revisions made by referring to the textual information in the document, but no more than that. They appeared at all issue levels in the typology except level 3, grammaticality, and the majority were either X16 (incohesive) or X3 (content distortion). To translate the mentions of each entity coherently and cohesively (Voita et al., 2019), we need to identify the correct referent of each mention. In the literature, a matrix called the *entity grid* (Barzilay and Lapata, 2008) is used to represent the appearance of entities and segments in the given source document. Actively studied document-level text-to-text MT might be able to capture such information, for instance, by enhancing the self-attention mechanisms (Vaswani et al., 2017; Maruf et al., 2019; Beltagy et al., 2020). However, as we confirmed in our analysis (Section 5.1), referents are not necessarily given in the source document, and we hence must seek reliable extra-document information.

6 Discussion and Future Directions

Techniques for MT have been advanced thanks to the simplified problem setting, i.e., text-to-text processing, and the advent of automatic evaluation metrics, such as BLEU (Papineni et al., 2002), which are based on comparison with reference translations. However, considering the large gap between what text-to-text MT can ultimately attain and the needs that translation must satisfy, a fully automatic MT approach (Hutchins and Somers, 1992) still looks infeasible. Rather, approaches in machine-aided human translation and human-aided MT, i.e., human–machine interactions, are more promising. Indeed, "MT+PE" in Figure 1, which has been prevalent in the translation production workflow at TSPs for a decade, lies in that direction. In this way, to reduce the cognitive load of PE, we must continue to enhance both wheels, i.e., improving MT systems and determining the best practices in using them.

As confirmed in Section 4.2, segment-level text-to-text MT still has much room for improvement. Yet, as shown in recent studies, textual information within the entire source document is useful. To generate cohesive texts, we should incorporate the latest outcomes in discourse processing and natural language generation, such as discourse parsing (Jia et al., 2018) and generating referential expressions (Paraboni et al., 2007). To assess MT outputs for further improvement while reducing the human labor in PE, we also need to invent document-level automatic evaluation methods, preferably analytic ones rather than holistic ones. Ultimately and ideally, we should also consider going beyond text-to-text processing, seeking better ways for incorporating information indispensable for translation, such as those we described in Section 5.1, rather than indirectly representing them with text data. For instance, to enforce the use of particular expressions specified by pre-compiled terminologies and style specifications, we need to improve the decoding mechanism, such as constrained decoding (Hasler et al., 2018; Post and Vilar, 2018; Zhang et al., 2018). Style specifications and domain-specific knowledge might be learned from text data in a given fine-grained domain, such as the one in Figure 2. We can see related work in adaptive data selection (Chen et al., 2016) and extreme adaptation (Michel and Neubig, 2018a).

In addition to the enhancement of MT systems, we should also establish reliable and effective ways for identifying critical issues in MT outputs as well as determining translation scenarios where MT is promising or hopeless. For instance, word frequency and sentence length affect the segment-level MT quality (Koehn and Knowles, 2017). Such findings motivate the *pre-editing* of segments prior to decoding (Pym, 1990; Miyata and Fujita, 2021).

From a general perspective, we should consider educating people (all people) so that they acquire two types of literacy: *translation literacy* for understanding the norms, skopos, and other specifications in their translation task (Klitgård, 2018), and *MT literacy* for understanding the characteristics of the intended MT service, which helps minimize potential risks (Bowker and Ciro, 2019). We believe that our method for clearly delineating between translation and the translation that text-to-text MT can ultimately attain as well as our case-study findings can be useful resources for such education.

7 Conclusion

To analytically assess issues that cannot be resolved by text-to-text processing, such as text-to-text MT, this paper presented our specific constraints incorporated into the two-stage PE pipeline originally proposed by Scarton et al. (2015). In a case study on the English-to-Japanese news translation task, we found that translation issues beyond text-to-text processing are caused by a lack of extra-document and/or non-linguistic information, such as fine-grained style specifications, terminology, domain-specific knowledge, and reference documents. The resulted parallel data and annotated revision examples are publicly available.[19]

Our method is laborious and requires very high competence in both linguistics and translation. Nevertheless, it is applicable to other translation tasks where we can build an MT system that can produce translation of exploitable quality. We thus hope other researchers use our method to assess the limitations of text-to-text processing and the remaining issues in a wide range of translation tasks. We plan to introduce another document-level minimal PE stage in order to assess the attainable translation by document-level MT.

While clarifying the limitations, we also suggested how we can enable MT systems to explicitly refer to extra-document and/or non-linguistic information. We plan to evaluate the impact of enforcing decoding with external knowledge, such as terminologies and style specifications.

An important issue in present-day society was also illuminated: the need to cultivate translation literacy and MT literacy in people to avoid the risk caused by the innocent use of MT services. To tackle this, we are currently compiling educational materials to help people understand translation, MT, and their differences. We will also analyze various levels of competences required for human translators, following the Competence Framework developed by the European Master's in Translation (Toudic and Krause, 2017).

Acknowledgments

I am deeply grateful to Masao Utiyama for giving me permission to use *TexTra* as well as Kyo Kageura, Masaru Yamada, Rei Miyata, Takuya Miyauchi, and Mayuka Yamamoto for their insightful comments on translation revisions. I would also like to thank Raj Dabre, Hideki Tanaka, and the anonymous reviewers, including those for past submissions, for their valuable comments on earlier versions of this paper. This work was partly supported by JSPS KAKENHI Grant-in-Aid for Scientific Research (S) 19H05660.

[19]https://github.com/akfujita/staged-PE

References

Arthur, P., Neubig, G., and Nakamura, S. (2016). Incorporating discrete translation lexicons into neural machine translation. In *Proceedings of the 2016 Conference on Empirical Methods in Natural Language Processing (EMNLP)*, pages 1557–1567.

Bapna, A. and Firat, O. (2019). Simple, scalable adaptation for neural machine translation. In *Proceedings of the 2019 Conference on Empirical Methods in Natural Language Processing and the 9th International Joint Conference on Natural Language Processing (EMNLP-IJCNLP)*, pages 1538–1548.

Barrault, L., Biesialska, M., Bojar, O., Costa-jussà, M. R., Federmann, C., Graham, Y., Grundkiewicz, R., Haddow, B., Huck, M., Joanis, E., Kocmi, T., Koehn, P., kiu Lo, C., Ljubešić, N., Monz, C., Morishita, M., Nagata, M., Nakazawa, T., Pal, S., Post, M., and Zampieri, M. (2020). Findings of the 2020 Conference on Machine Translation (WMT20). In *Proceedings of the Fifth Conference on Machine Translation*, pages 1–55.

Barrault, L., Bojar, O., Costa-jussà, M. R., Federmann, C., Fishel, M., Graham, Y., Haddow, B., Huck, M., Koehn, P., Malmasi, S., Monz, C., Müller, M., Pal, S., Post, M., and Zampieri, M. (2019). Findings of the 2019 Conference on Machine Translation (WMT19). In *Proceedings of the Fourth Conference on Machine Translation (Volume 2: Shared Task Papers, Day 1)*, pages 1–61.

Barrault, L., Bougares, F., Specia, L., Lala, C., Elliott, D., and Frank, S. (2018). Findings of the third shared task on multimodal machine translation. In *Proceedings of the 3rd Conference on Machine Translation (WMT): Shared Task Papers*, pages 304–323.

Barzilay, R. and Lapata, M. (2008). Modeling local coherence: An entity-based approach. *Computational Linguistics*, 34(1):1–34.

Beltagy, I., Peters, M. E., and Cohan, A. (2020). Longformer: The long-document Transformer. *CoRR*, abs/2004.05150.

Bowker, L. and Ciro, J. B. (2019). *Machine Translation and Global Research: Towards Improved Machine Translation Literacy in the Scholarly Community*. Emerald Group Publishing Ltd.

Castilho, S., Popović, M., and Way, A. (2020). On context span needed for machine translation evaluation. In *Proceedings of the 12th International Conference on Language Resources and Evaluation (LREC)*, pages 3735–3742.

Chatterjee, R., Negri, M., Turchi, M., Federico, M., Specia, L., and Blain, F. (2017). Guiding neural machine translation decoding with external knowledge. In *Proceedings of the 2nd Conference on Machine Translation (WMT)*, pages 157–168.

Chen, B., Kuhn, R., Foster, G., Cherry, C., and Huang, F. (2016). Bilingual methods for adaptive training data selection for machine translation. In *Proceedings of the 12th Biennial Conference of the Association for Machine Translation in the Americas (AMTA)*, pages 93–106.

Chesterman, A. (1997). *Memes of Translation: The Spread of Ideas in Translation Theory*. John Benjamins.

Chu, C., Dabre, R., and Kurohashi, S. (2017). An empirical comparison of domain adaptation methods for neural machine translation. In *Proceedings of the 55th Annual Meeting of the Association for Computational Linguistics (ACL), Short Papers*, pages 385–391.

Freitag, M., Foster, G., Grangier, D., Ratnakar, V., Tan, Q., and Macherey, W. (2021). Experts, errors, and context: A large-scale study of human evaluation for machine translation. *CoRR*, abs/2104.14478.

Fujita, A., Tanabe, K., Toyoshima, C., Yamamoto, M., Kageura, K., and Hartley, A. (2017). Consistent classification of translation revisions: A case study of English–Japanese student translations. In *Proceedings of the 11th Linguistic Annotation Workshop (LAW)*, pages 57–66.

Goto, I., Chow, K. P., Lu, B., Sumita, E., and Tsou, B. K. (2013). Overview of the patent machine translation task at the NTCIR-10 workshop. In *Proceedings of the 10th NTCIR Conference on Evaluation of Information Access Technologies*, pages 260–286.

Hardmeier, C. (2014). *Discourse in Statistical Machine Translation.* PhD thesis, Uppsala University.

Hashimoto, K., Buschiazzo, R., Bradbury, J., Marshall, T., Socher, R., and Xiong, C. (2019). A high-quality multilingual dataset for structured documentation translation. In *Proceedings of the 4th Conference on Machine Translation (WMT) (Volume 1: Research Papers)*, pages 116–127.

Hasler, E., de Gispert, A., Iglesias, G., and Byrne, B. (2018). Neural machine translation decoding with terminology constraints. In *Proceedings of Human Language Technologies: The 2018 Annual Conference of the North American Chapter of the Association for Computational Linguistics (NAACL-HLT)*, pages 506–512.

Hassan, H., Aue, A., Chen, C., Chowdhary, V., Clark, J., Federmann, C., Huang, X., Junczys-Dowmunt, M., Lewis, W., Li, M., Liu, S., Liu, T.-Y., Luo, R., Menezes, A., Qin, T., Seide, F., Tan, X., Tian, F., Wu, L., Wu, S., Xia, Y., Zhang, D., Zhang, Z., and Zhou, M. (2018). Achieving human parity on automatic Chinese to English news translation. *CoRR*, abs/1803.05567.

Hutchins, W. J. and Somers, H. L. (1992). *An Introduction to Machine Translation.* Academic Press.

Irvine, A., Morgan, J., Carpuat, M., III, H. D., and Munteanu, D. (2013). Measuring machine translation errors in new domains. *Transaction of the Association for Computational Linguistics (TACL)*, 1:429–440.

ISO/TC37 (2015). ISO 17100:2015 translation services: Requirements for translation services.

ISO/TC37 (2017). ISO 18587:2017 translation services: Post-editing of machine translation output: Requirements.

Jia, Y., Ye, Y., Feng, Y., Lai, Y., Yan, R., and Zhao, D. (2018). Modeling discourse cohesion for discourse parsing via memory network. In *Proceedings of the 56th Annual Meeting of the Association for Computational Linguistics (ACL), Short Papers*, pages 438–443.

Junczys-Dowmunt, M., Grundkiewicz, R., Dwojak, T., Hoang, H., Heafield, K., Neckermann, T., Seide, F., Germann, U., Aji, A. F., Bogoychev, N., Martins, A. F. T., and Birch, A. (2018). Marian: Fast neural machine translation in C++. In *Proceedings of the 56th Annual Meeting of the Association for Computational Linguistics (ACL), System Demonstrations*, pages 116–121.

Kenny, D. (2001). *Lexis and Creativity in Translation: A Corpus Based Approach.* Routledge.

Klitgård, I. (2018). Calling for translation literacy: The use of covert translation in student academic writing in higher education. *Translation and Translanguaging in Multilingual Contexts*, 4(2):306–323.

Kobus, C., Crego, J., and Senellart, J. (2017). Domain control for neural machine translation. In *Proceedings of the Recent Advances in Natural Language Processing*, pages 372–378.

Koehn, P. and Knowles, R. (2017). Six challenges for neural machine translation. In *Proceedings of the 1st Workshop on Neural Machine Translation*, pages 28–39.

Läubli, S., Castilho, S., Neubig, G., Sennrich, R., Shen, Q., and Toral, A. (2020). A set of recommendations for assessing human–machine parity in language translation. *Journal of Artificial Intelligence Research*, 67:653–672.

Lommel, A., Görög, A., Melby, A., Uszkoreit, H., Burchardt, A., and Popović, M. (2015). QT21 deliverable 3.1: Harmonised metric.

Lopes, A. V., Farajian, M. A., Bawden, R., Zhang, M., and Martins, A. F. T. (2020). Document-level neural MT: A systematic comparison. In *Proceedings of the 22nd Annual Conference of the European Association of Machine Translation (EAMT)*, pages 225–234.

Maruf, S., Martins, A. F. T., and Haffari, G. (2019). Selective attention for context-aware neural machine translation. In *Proceedings of Human Language Technologies: The 2019 Annual Conference of the North American Chapter of the Association for Computational Linguistics (NAACL-HLT)*, pages 3092–3102.

Melby, A. K. (2012). Structured specifications and translation parameters (version 6.0). http://www.ttt.org/specs/.

Michel, P. and Neubig, G. (2018a). Extreme adaptation for personalized neural machine translation. In *Proceedings of the 56th Annual Meeting of the Association for Computational Linguistics (ACL), Short Papers*, pages 312–318.

Michel, P. and Neubig, G. (2018b). MTNT: A testbed for machine translation of noisy text. In *Proceedings of the 2018 Conference on Empirical Methods in Natural Language Processing (EMNLP)*, pages 543–553.

Miyata, R. and Fujita, A. (2021). Understanding pre-editing for black-box neural machine translation. In *Proceedings of the 16th Conference of the European Chapter of the Association for Computational Linguistics (EACL)*, pages 1539–1550.

Moussallem, D., Ngomo, A.-C. N., Buitelaar, P., and Arcan, M. (2019). Utilizing knowledge graphs for neural machine translation augmentation. In *Proceedings of the 10th International Conference on Knowledge Capture (K-CAP)*, page 139–146.

Nakazawa, T., Doi, N., Higashiyama, S., Ding, C., Dabre, R., Mino, H., Goto, I., Pa, W. P., Kunchukuttan, A., Parida, S., Bojar, O., and Kurohashi, S. (2019). Overview of the 6th workshop on Asian translation. In *Proceedings of the 6th Workshop on Asian Translation (WAT)*, pages 1–35.

Nida, E. A. (1964). *Toward a Science of Translating*. Brill.

Niu, X., Martindale, M., and Carpuat, M. (2017). A study of style in machine translation: Controlling the formality of machine translation output. In *Proceedings of the 2017 Conference on Empirical Methods in Natural Language Processing (EMNLP)*, pages 2814–2819.

Papineni, K., Roukos, S., Ward, T., and Zhu, W.-J. (2002). BLEU: A method for automatic evaluation of machine translation. In *Proceedings of the 40th Annual Meeting of the Association for Computational Linguistics (ACL)*, pages 311–318.

Paraboni, I., van Deemter, K., and Masthoff, J. (2007). Generating referring expressions: Making referents easy to identify. *Computational Linguistics*, 33(2):229–254.

Popović, M. and Ney, H. (2011). Towards automatic error analysis of machine translation output. *Computational Linguistics*, 37(4):657–688.

Post, M. (2018). A call for clarity in reporting BLEU scores. In *Proceedings of the 3rd Conference on Machine Translation (WMT): Research Papers*, pages 186–191.

Post, M. and Vilar, D. (2018). Fast lexically constrained decoding with dynamic beam allocation for neural machine translation. In *Proceedings of Human Language Technologies: The 2018 Annual Conference of the North American Chapter of the Association for Computational Linguistics (NAACL-HLT)*, pages 1314–1324.

Pym, P. (1990). Pre-editing and the use of simplified writing for MT. In Mayorcas, P., editor, *Translating and the Computer 10: The Translation Environment 10 Years on*, pages 80–95. Aslib.

Riza, H., Purwoadi, M., Gunarso, Uliniansyah, T., Ti, A. A., Aljunied, S. M., Mai, L. C., Thang, V. T., Thai, N. P., Chea, V., Sun, R., Sam, S., Seng, S., Soe, K. M., Nwet, K. T., Utiyama, M., and Ding, C. (2016). Introduction of the Asian Language Treebank. In *Proceedings of the 2016 Conference of the Oriental Chapter of International Committee for Coordination and Standardization of Speech Databases and Assessment Technique (O-COCOSDA)*, pages 1–6.

Scarton, C., Zampieri, M., Vela, M., van Genabith, J., and Specia, L. (2015). Searching for context: a study on document-level labels for translation quality estimation. In *Proceedings of the 18th Annual Conference of the European Association of Machine Translation (EAMT)*, pages 121–128.

Sennrich, R., Haddow, B., and Birch, A. (2016a). Controlling politeness in neural machine translation via side constraints. In *Proceedings of Human Language Technologies: The 2016 Annual Conference of the North American Chapter of the Association for Computational Linguistics (NAACL-HLT)*, pages 35–40.

Sennrich, R., Haddow, B., and Birch, A. (2016b). Neural machine translation of rare words with subword units. In *Proceedings of the 54th Annual Meeting of the Association for Computational Linguistics (ACL)*, pages 1715–1725.

Snover, M., Dorr, B., Schwartz, R., Micciulla, L., and Makhoul, J. (2006). A study of translation edit rate with targeted human annotation. In *Proceedings of the 7th Biennial Conference of the Association for Machine Translation in the Americas (AMTA)*, pages 223–231.

Toral, A. (2019). Post-editese: an exacerbated translationese. In *Proceedings of the 17th Machine Translation Summit (MT Summit XVII)*, pages 273–281.

Toral, A. (2020). Reassessing claims of human parity and super-human performance in machine translation at WMT 2019. In *Proceedings of the 22nd Annual Conference of the European Association of Machine Translation (EAMT)*, pages 185–194.

Toudic, D. and Krause, A. (2017). European Master's in translation: EMT competence framework.

Toury, G. (1978). The nature and role of norms in literary translation. In Holmes, J., Lambert, J., and van den Broeck, R., editors, *Literature and Translation*, pages 83–100. Levine.

Vaswani, A., Shazeer, N., Parmar, N., Uszkoreit, J., Jones, L., Gomez, A. N., Kaiser, Ł., and Polosukhin, I. (2017). Attention is all you need. In *Proceedings of the 30th Annual Conference on Neural Information Processing Systems (NIPS)*, pages 5998–6008.

Vermeer, H. J. (1992). Is translation a linguistic or a cultural process? *Ilha do Desterro*, 28:37–49.

Vermeer, H. J. (2004). Skopos and commission in translational action. In Venuti, L., editor, *The Translation Studies Reader*, pages 227–238. Routledge.

Voita, E., Sennrich, R., and Titov, I. (2019). When a good translation is wrong in context: Context-aware machine translation improves on deixis, ellipsis, and lexical cohesion. In *Proceedings of the 57th Annual Meeting of the Association for Computational Linguistics (ACL)*, pages 1198–1212.

Voita, E., Serdyukov, P., Sennrich, R., and Titov, I. (2018). Context-aware neural machine translation learns anaphora resolution. In *Proceedings of the 56th Annual Meeting of the Association for Computational Linguistics (ACL)*, pages 1264–1274.

Ye, Y. and Toral, A. (2020). Fine-grained human evaluation of transformer and recurrent approaches to neural machine translation for English-to-Chinese. In *Proceedings of the 22nd Annual Conference of the European Association of Machine Translation (EAMT)*, pages 125–134.

Zhang, J., Utiyama, M., Sumita, E., Neubig, G., and Nakamura, S. (2018). Guiding neural machine translation with retrieved translation pieces. In *Proceedings of Human Language Technologies: The 2018 Annual Conference of the North American Chapter of the Association for Computational Linguistics (NAACL-HLT)*, pages 1325–1335.

Modeling Target-side Inflection in Placeholder Translation

Ryokan Ri li0123@logos.t.u-tokyo.ac.jp
Toshiaki Nakazawa nakazawa@logos.t.u-tokyo.ac.jp
Yoshimasa Tsuruoka tsuruoka@logos.t.u-tokyo.ac.jp
The University of Tokyo, 7-3-1 Hongo, Bunkyo-ku, Tokyo, Japan

Abstract

Placeholder translation systems enable the users to specify how a specific phrase is translated in the output sentence. The system is trained to output special placeholder tokens, and the user-specified term is injected into the output through the context-free replacement of the placeholder token. However, this approach could result in ungrammatical sentences because it is often the case that the specified term needs to be inflected according to the context of the output, which is unknown before the translation. To address this problem, we propose a novel method of placeholder translation that can inflect specified terms according to the grammatical construction of the output sentence. We extend the sequence-to-sequence architecture with a character-level decoder that takes the lemma of a user-specified term and the words generated from the word-level decoder to output the correct inflected form of the lemma. We evaluate our approach with a Japanese-to-English translation task in the scientific writing domain, and show that our model can incorporate specified terms in the correct form more successfully than other comparable models.[1]

1 Introduction

Over the last several years, neural machine translation (NMT) has pushed the quality of machine translation to near-human performance (Sutskever et al., 2014; Vaswani et al., 2017). However, due to its end-to-end nature, this comes with the cost of losing a certain degree of control over the produced translation, which once was explicitly modeled, for example, in the form of phrase table (Koehn et al., 2003) in statistical machine translation (SMT). In practice, users often want to specify how certain words are translated in order to ensure the consistency of document-level translation or to guarantee the model to produce the correct translation for words that may be underrepresented in the training corpus such as proper nouns, technical terms, or novel words.

Given this motivation, a line of previous research has investigated *placeholder translation* (Post et al., 2019). With a source sentence where certain words are replaced with a special placeholder token, the model produces a translation with the special placeholder token in an appropriate position, and then that placeholder token is replaced with a pre-specified term in a post-processing step.

Although this approach ensures that certain words appear in the translation, one limitation is that the user must specify the term that fits in the context surrounding the placeholder token, or specifically, the term should be properly inflected according to the syntactic structure of

[1]Code is available at `https://github.com/Ryou0634/placeholder_translation`.

Specified Translation: 管理 → controlling
Source: フローセンサーの原理は浮遊式流量計のテーパー管内フロートの位置を差動トランスで検出し,これの電圧制御により流量を[VERB]する。
Reference: The sensor controls the flow rate by detecting the position of the float in the tepered tube with a a differential transformer and [VERB] it with the obtained voltage.
System Output: The principle of the flow sensor is that the position of the float in the taper tube of the floating flowmeter is detected by the differential transformer, and the flow rate is [VERB] by this voltage control.

Table 1: A translation example from the ASPEC corpus (Nakazawa et al., 2016) with a placeholder translation model. The specified target term grammatically fits the placeholder in the reference, but not in the system output as it is.

the produced translation. To illustrate the problem, we show an actual output from a normal placeholder translation model in Japanese to English translation in Table 1.

The system is supposed to translate the word 管理 into *controlling* as in the reference, but the output has a different grammatical construction and thus the progressive form *controlling* is invalid in this context; instead, *controlled* should be injected in the placeholder. The appropriate word form is difficult to predict, especially in translation between grammatically distant languages, such as Japanese and English. As manually correcting the inflection in post-editing significantly hurts the convenience of placeholder translation, we need a way to automatically handle inflection.

One possible approach to this problem is the code-switching methods, in which certain words in the source sentence are replaced with the specific target words, and the model is encouraged to include those specific words in the translation. This approach is flexible in that the model can inflect the specified words according to the context (Song et al., 2019), but less faithful to the lexical constraints, often ignoring the specified terms (§5).

To address this problem, we propose a model that automatically inflects a pre-specified term according to the context of the produced translation. We extend the sequence-to-sequence encoder and decoder with an additional character-level decoder that predicts the inflected form of the pre-specified term. Our approach combines the advantages of both the placeholder and the code-switching methods: the faithfulness to lexical constraints and the flexibility of dynamically deciding the word form in the output.

We test our approach with a Japanese-to-English translation task in the scientific-writing domain (Nakazawa et al., 2016), where the translation of technical terms poses a challenge to a vanilla NMT system. The results show that the proposed method can include the specified term in the appropriately inflected form in the translation with higher accuracy than a comparable code-switching method. We also perform a careful error analysis to understand the weaknesses of each system and suggest directions for future work.

2 Related Work

2.1 Placeholder Translation

To ensure that certain words appear in the translated sentence, previous studies have explored the method of replacing certain classes of words with special placeholder tokens and restore the words in a post-processing step, which we call *placeholder translation* in this paper.

Luong et al. (2015) and Long et al. (2016) employed placeholder tokens to improve the translation of rare words or technical terms. However, simply replacing words with a unique placeholder token loses the information on the original words. To alleviate this problem, subsequent studies distinguish different types of placeholders, such as named entity types (Crego et al., 2016; Post et al., 2019) or parts-of-speech (Michon et al., 2020).

Instead of replacing the placeholder token with a dictionary entry, some studies propose generating the content of the placeholder with a character-level sequence-to-sequence model to translate words not covered in the bilingual dictionary. Li et al. (2016) and Wang et al. (2017) incorporated a named entity translator, which is supposed to learn transliteration of named entities. As in their work, our proposed model also uses a character-level decoder to generate the content of placeholders, but our focus is to inflect a lemma to the appropriately inflected form given the context.

2.2 The Code-switching Method

Another way to introduce terminology constraints is the code-switching method (Song et al., 2019; Dinu et al., 2019; Exel et al., 2020). The model is trained with source sentences where some words are replaced or followed by specific target words and expected to copy the words to the translation.

One advantage of the code-switching method is that, unlike the placeholder methods, it preserves the meaning of the original words, which likely leads to better translation quality. Also, the model can incorporate the specified terminology in a flexible way: a model trained with the code-switching method not only copies the pre-specified target words but can inflect the words according to the target-side context (Dinu et al., 2019). In parallel to our work, Niehues (2021) offers a quantitative evaluation of how well the code-switching method handles inflection of a pre-specified terminology when the terminology is given in the lemma form.

Although the code-switching method is flexible, one disadvantage is that it tends to ignore the pre-specified terminology more often than the placeholder method (§5). We propose a placeholder method that handles inflection of pre-specified terms, aiming for both flexibility and faithfulness to terminology constraints.

2.3 Constrained Decoding

Another approach to ensure that a pre-specified term appears in the translation is constrained decoding (Anderson et al., 2017; Hokamp and Liu, 2017; Post and Vilar, 2018). Constrained decoding can be applied to any existing NMT models without modifying its architecture and training regime, but imposes a significant cost on the decoding speed. It is also unclear how to incorporate lexical inflection into constrained decoding. Therefore, we focus on the placeholder and code-switching methods in this study.

2.4 Modeling Morphological Inflection in Neural Machine Translation

Explicitly modeling morphological inflection into NMT models has been studied mainly to enable effective generalization over morphological variation of words. Tamchyna et al. (2017) and Weller-Di Marco and Fraser (2020) propose to decompose certain classes of words into its lemma and morphological tags to reduce data sparsity. At decoding time, the inflected form is restored by a morphological analyzer. Song et al. (2018) proposed a model that only requires a stemmer to alleviate the need for linguistic analyzers. The model decomposes the process of word decoding into stem generation and suffix prediction.

In this work, we propose to model morphological inflection in the process of embedding pre-specified terms into placeholders to improve the flexibility of placeholder translation. Our approach requires no external linguistic analyzer at prediction time; instead, inflection is performed via a neural character-based decoder.

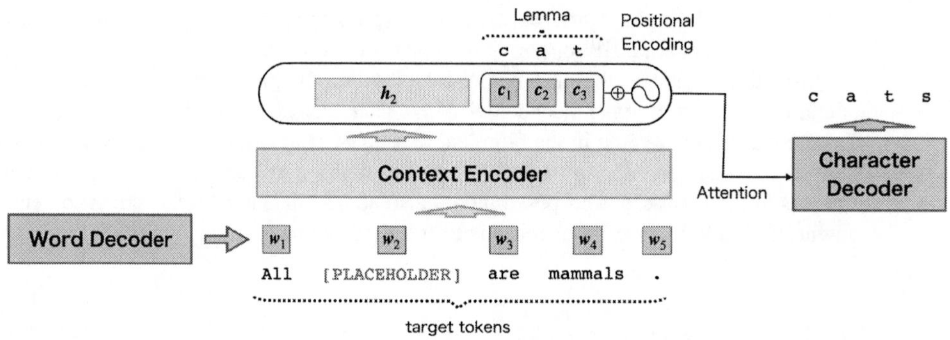

Figure 1: The proposed method: placeholder translation with a character decoder.

3 Approach

The proposed model builds upon a sequence-to-sequence (seq2seq) model with an attention mechanism. Specifically, we use the Transformer model (Vaswani et al., 2017).

In the normal placeholder translation, the model is trained to generate placeholder tokens `[PLACEHOLDER]` when the source sentence includes them. Then the placeholder tokens are replaced with user-provided terms in post-processing.

We extend the model to be able to handle inflection. Specifically, we consider the scenario where lemmas are provided as a specified term. On top of the (sub)word-level decoder, we stack a character-level decoder to generate the content of the placeholder token. The character-level decoder has to predict the correct inflected form of the specified lemma in the surrounding context. Specifically, given the target tokens $\{w_1, ..., w_T\}$ that contain a placeholder token and the specified lemma that consists of L characters $c_{lemma} = \{c_1, .., c_L\}$, the character decoder generates the inflected form $c_{infl} = \{c'_1, .., c'_{L'}\}$.

We model the generation process with a decoder with attention mechanism (Fig. 1). We first summarize the contextual information on the placeholder token by a context encoder. Specifically, we feed the embeddings of the target tokens $\{\boldsymbol{w}_1, ..., \boldsymbol{w}_T\}$ into another Transformer encoder to contextualize the placeholder token (Eq. 1). Then, the contextualized representation of the placeholder token $\boldsymbol{h}_p$ and the character embeddings of the specified lemma $\{\boldsymbol{c}_1, .., \boldsymbol{c}_L\}$ with positional encoding (Vaswani et al., 2017) are concatenated to form key-value vectors for decoder attention (Eq. 2). Finally, the key-value vectors are passed to the character-level Transformer decoder and it generates the inflected form $\{c'_1, .., c'_{L'}\}$ in an auto-regressive manner (Eq. 3).

$$\boldsymbol{h}_1, ..., \boldsymbol{h}_T = \text{ContextEncoder}([\boldsymbol{w}_1, ..., \boldsymbol{w}_T]) \tag{1}$$

$$\boldsymbol{A} = [\boldsymbol{h}_p; \text{Positional}(\boldsymbol{c}_1, .., \boldsymbol{c}_L)] \text{ where } w_p = \texttt{[PLACEHOLDER]} \tag{2}$$

$$c'_t = \text{CharacterDecoder}(\boldsymbol{c}'_{<t}, \boldsymbol{A}) \tag{3}$$

4 Experimental Setups

We evaluate the proposed model with several baselines to show how well the model can produce the appropriately inflected form of a given lemma.

4.1 Corpus

We conduct experiments in a Japanese-to-English translation task with the ASPEC corpus (Nakazawa et al., 2016). This corpus consists of abstracts from scientific articles, which tend to contain many technical terms. Such words are rare and hard for the model to learn the correct translation, and thus this corpus fits the typical use-case of lexically constrained translation. We use the initial 1M sentence pairs from the training split for training.

4.2 Word Dictionary

In this study, lexical constraints in translation are introduced through a source-to-target word dictionary. We construct the dictionary automatically from the ASPEC corpus through the following procedure.

First, we obtain the word alignment by feeding the first 1M sentence pairs of the training split and validation/test splits to `GIZA++`.[2] We tokenize Japanese sentences with `Mecab`[3] and English sentences with `spaCy`.[4] We then construct a phrase table and extract only those with more than 100 occurrences. Then, we split the dictionary into noun and verb entries to facilitate the analysis of the results and remove noise. If both the Japanese and English phrases are noun phrases, the entry is registered in the noun dictionary. If the Japanese phrase is a nominal verb[5] and English is a verb, the entry is registered in the verb dictionary. In this study, we evaluate the model's ability to inflect a provided lemma. Lemmas for the target language (English) are obtained with `spaCy`.

4.3 Models

As the baseline, we implement a Transformer (Vaswani et al., 2017) translation model based on `AllenNLP` (Gardner et al., 2018). We configure the model in the Transformer-base setting and sentences are tokenized using `sentencepiece` (Kudo, 2018), which has a shared source-target vocabulary of about 16k sub-words. The overviews of lexically constrained models are summarized in Fig. 2.

Placeholder (PH). In the placeholder method, the model is trained to translate sentences with a placeholder token and pass that through to the translation. In our experiments, we use different placeholder tokens `[NOUN]` and `[VERB]` for nouns and verbs. Predicted placeholder tokens are replaced by the pre-specified term in the post-processing step. We evaluate three types of placeholder baselines, each of which differs in what inflected form the target placeholder token is replaced with: **PH (oracle)**, where the pre-specified term is embedded in the same form as in the reference; **PH (lemma)**, always the lemma form; **PH (common)**, the most common inflected forms in the training data, which are the singular form for `[NOUN]` and the past tense form for `[VERB]`. The results of PH (lemma) and PH (common) are provided as naive baselines to give a sense of how difficult predicting the correct inflected form is.

We also provide a baseline that performs word inflection through an external resource (**PH (morph)**). As in Tamchyna et al. (2017), words that need inflection are followed by morphological tags, and word formation is realized through an external resource. We use `LemmInflect`[6] to decompose the dictionary entries with their lemma and part-of-speech tags and to recover the inflected word form. As this model uses an external resource to perform inflection, it is not directly comparable with our proposed models but we provide its results as an oracle baseline.

---

[2] https://github.com/moses-smt/giza-pp

[3] https://taku910.github.io/mecab/

[4] https://spacy.io/

[5] The nominal verb (サ変動詞) is the most productive class of verb in Japanese and many new or technical terms fall into this category (*e.g.*, 最適化する-*optimize*, 過学習する-*overfit*).

[6] https://github.com/bjascob/LemmInflect

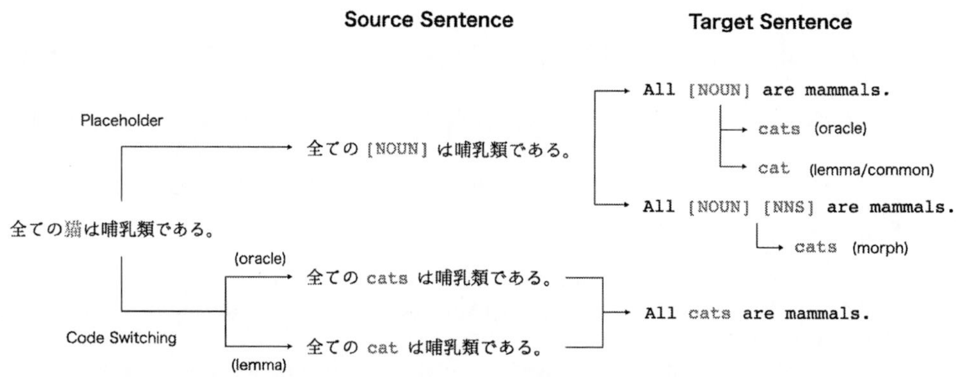

Figure 2: The preprocessing of the lexically constrained baseline models.

Code-switching (CH). The code-switching model replaces a phrase in a source sentence with the corresponding target phrase according to a bilingual dictionary.[7] **CH (oracle)** uses the same target words as in the reference, and **CH (lemma)** uses the lemma form.

Proposed Model. We implement our proposed model described in §3 on top of the placeholder baseline model. Compared to the baseline, our proposed model has three additional modules: the target context encoder, target character embeddings, and character-level decoder. The embedding and hidden sizes are all set to 512, which is the same as in the Transformer-base model. The additional encoder and decoder have two layers, and the feedforward dimension is 1024.

Note that, for all the models, we restrict the number of constraints to at most one in each sentence as an initial investigation. This favors the placeholder-based models as handling more than one placeholder introduces additional complexity in the system and tends to degrade the performance, while the code-switching methods suffer less from multiple constraints (Song et al., 2019). We leave experiments with multiple constraints to future work.

4.4 Training with Lexical Constraints

To apply lexical constraints, the models are trained with data augmentation. Augmented data is created for all sentences that contain any of the source and target phrases found in the dictionary entries. To control the amount of augmented data to around 10% of the original training data, we restrict the dictionary entries to infrequent ones. The restriction to infrequent phrases also simulates real-word use-cases, where user-specified terms are often rare words that typical NMT models struggle with in translation. Specifically, we restrict the noun entries to ones with a count at most 20, and the verb entries to 2000. The threshold is chosen to balance the amount of noun and verb entries in the augmented data.

4.5 Optimization

We optimize the models using Adam (Kingma and Ba, 2015) with the Noam learning rate scheduler with 8000 warmup steps (Vaswani et al., 2017). The training is stopped when the validation BLEU score does not improve for 3 epochs.

For our proposed model, we found that optimizing the word-level modules and character-level modules separately stabilizes the training process and improves the translation quality. We first train a normal placeholder model, use the weights to initialize those of our proposed model,

[7]Dinu et al. (2019) utilize source factors that indicate which tokens are code-switched, but we observe no significant difference by adding source factors. Therefore, we simply report the results from the model with minimal components.

and then only update the parameters of the additional modules. In this second training stage, we use the loss value as validation metric and stop the training when the lowest value is updated for 5 epochs.

5 Results

5.1 Evaluation

For each model, we evaluate the overall translation quality with BLEU (Papineni et al., 2002).[8] We also evaluate the *specified term use rate*, a metric to check if the model correctly includes the specified target term. Note that this is only an approximate measure of what we want to measure: whether the specified term is used in the correct form in the output translation. Since a single source sentence can be translated into different grammatical constructions, it is possible that the inflected form in the system output is different from the one in the reference but still correct in the context. Still, we find a substantial overlap in the inflectional form of the specified term between the reference and the system output, and thus report this metric, followed by a more closely inspected manual evaluation.

Also, we are interested in how well the model generalizes to dictionary entries unseen during training. In typical use cases of lexically constrained translation, the specified terms are new or rare words that are not likely to appear in the training data. We construct two kinds of evaluation dictionaries: *seen* and *unseen*. We first construct a dictionary by aggregating only entries that appear in the dev/test set. Then, we randomly split the entries into *seen* and *unseen* and remove the *unseen* entries from the training dictionary. Thus, the *seen* split contains entries that appear in the training data while the *unseen* not. We evaluate the model separately using the noun and verb dictionary, which results in a total of four kinds of evaluation configurations.

<table>
<tr><th></th><th colspan="2">NOUN</th><th colspan="2">VERB</th></tr>
<tr><th></th><th>seen</th><th>unseen</th><th>seen</th><th>unseen</th></tr>
<tr><td>Baseline</td><td>27.1 / 68.3</td><td>27.1 / 66.5</td><td>27.1 / 63.4</td><td>27.1 / 61.2</td></tr>
<tr><td>CS (oracle)</td><td>27.3 / 86.8</td><td>27.0 / 79.3</td><td>27.5 / 91.9</td><td>27.2 / 43.9</td></tr>
<tr><td>PH (oracle)</td><td>27.2 / 98.8</td><td>27.0 / 99.2</td><td>27.4 / 98.7</td><td>27.5 / 99.4</td></tr>
<tr><td>PH (lemma)</td><td rowspan="2">27.1 / 84.7</td><td rowspan="2">26.9 / 84.0</td><td>26.9 / 9.41</td><td>27.1 / 11.4</td></tr>
<tr><td>PH (common)</td><td>27.3 / 81.8</td><td>27.3 / 68.9</td></tr>
<tr><td>CS (lemma)</td><td>27.4 / 81.7</td><td>27.1 / 74.6</td><td>27.6 / 81.7</td><td>27.3 / 42.1</td></tr>
<tr><td>Proposed</td><td>27.2 / 89.9</td><td>26.9 / 79.1</td><td>27.4 / 88.3</td><td>27.4 / 73.9</td></tr>
<tr><td>PH (morph)</td><td>27.9 / 84.7</td><td>27.8 / 81.2</td><td>28.5 / 91.1</td><td>28.4 / 87.9</td></tr>
</table>

Table 2: BLUE scores and the specified term use rate of the different models over different evaluation dictionaries. CS: Code-switching, PH: placeholder. For NOUN, PH (lemma) and PH (common) are the same model because the most common inflection for nouns is their lemma.

5.2 Main Results

The results are shown in Table 2. For each configuration, we report the average of three models trained with different random seeds.

First, the lexically constrained models show BLEU scores not significantly different from the baseline. The only exception is PH (morph): it consistently improves the BLEU score by

[8] SacreBLEU(Post, 2018) version string:
`case.mixed+numrefs.1812+smooth.exp+tok.13a+version.1.5.1`

	VERB *seen*	VERB *unseen*
CS (lemma)	49 / 0 / 1	26 / 0 / 24
PH with lemmas (proposed)	48 / 2 / 0	39 / 7 / 4
PH (morph)	50 / 0 / 0	47 / 3 / 0

Table 3: The manual evaluation of the 50 sampled sentences. The values in each cell indicate *correct / incorrect / null.*

from 0.7 to 1.4 points from the baseline. This indicates the strength of injecting the NMT model with morphological knowledge for better generalization in translation. In the following discussion, we focus on the comparison of the specified term use rate.

PH (oracle) and CS (oracle) models receive the same inflected form of a specified term as in the reference, and thus offer upper bounds for the specified term use rate. We observe that PH (oracle) exhibits nearly perfect specified term use rates (more than 98% with all dictionaries). Also, it is more successful at incorporating the specified term into translation than CS (oracle) in the setting of one constraint, which is in line with previous observations (Song et al., 2019).

As for the models that need to handle inflection, the results are quite mixed for NOUN. A simple strategy of predicting the most common inflection achieves better specified term use rates than most of the other sophisticated models. We conjecture that some examples allow either singular or plural form and that makes a proper evaluation difficult. Therefore, we turn to the results from VERB for model comparison.

In terms of both *seen* and *unseen* of the VERB dictionary, PH (morph) performs the best. Note, however, that this model is not comparable to our model as it assumes access to a high-quality morphological analyzer at training time to obtain morphological tags and the correct inflectional paradigm of user-specified terms at prediction time.

In a more restricted setting, our proposed model outperforms the comparable code-switching model (CS (lemma)) and the other baselines. In particular, the proposed model is more robust than CS (lemma) to *unseen* specified terms: we observe a consistent tendency that the specified term use rate degrades when the entries are unseen during training especially with CS (lemma) and verb entries (81.7 to 42.1), while this tendency is less pronounced in the placeholder model with lemmas (88.3 to 73.9). Overall, our model exhibits faithfulness to lexical constraints similar to those of the normal placeholder model while having flexibility, which we examine below.

5.3 Fine-grained Analysis

The specified term use rate only checks whether specified terms are used in the same form as in the reference. Now we examine the systems' output more closely by manual inspection. As the problem of inflection matters more in verbs than in nouns in English, here we focus on the translation with the verb dictionary.

We sample from the system's output of the test set 50 sentences with the *seen* and *unseen* lexical constraints respectively. We manually check the sampled sentences and annotate each sentence with one of the three tags: *correct* — the specified term is used in the translation in the correct inflected form (not necessarily the same as in the reference); *incorrect* — the model produces the specified term in some inflected form but that results in an ungrammatical sentence; *null* — the model fails to produce the specified term in any form. The result is shown in Table 3.

Firstly, for the words that are seen in the training data, all the models mostly generate the correct word form in the context. On the other hand, the evaluation with VERB unseen reveals both the advantages and disadvantages of each model, which we discuss with examples below.

The placeholder model with morphological tags can handle inflection well. The model mostly generates the correct inflectional form of the specified terms. The only three exceptions from VERB seen are errors in choosing the transitive or intransitive usage of the term (Table 4).

Source: 特発性肺線維症(IPF)患者14例及びIPF急性増悪で入院した患者8例を対象として,BALF・血漿に関してウィルス検査・免疫血清学的検査を施行した **Reference**: The virus inspection and immunoserologic inspection of BALF and blood plasma were carried out for 14 idiopathic pulmonary fibrosis (IPF) patients and of 8 patients hospitalized for IPF acute aggravation. **System Output**: Wils inspection and immunoserologic inspection were enforced on BALF blood and blood in 14 patients with idiopathic pulmonary fibrosis (IPF) and 8 patients who hospitalized in the IPF acute aggravation.

Table 4: A translation example with the placeholder model with morphological tags. The system output should have generated *were hospitalized* in the red part.

The code-switching method always produces grammatical inflectional forms. We observe no *incorrect* examples from the code-switching model. Since the output is determined solely by the word decoder with no additional post-editing performed, if the word decoder is well trained, we can expect the output sentences to be grammatical.

The code-switching method tends to fail to observe the constraints. However, the code-switching methods fail to produce the specified term in 24 examples out of 50, which is notably higher than the other methods. A typical error is the model ignoring the constraint and producing a synonym, for example, generating *conclude* instead of *judge*, *examine* instead of *study*. This is reasonable given the model architecture. A well-trained NMT model usually assigns similar vector representations to synonyms. Even when the specified term is given in the source sentence, it is given a representation similar to other synonyms inside the model, and thus the decoder can generate any words with similar meaning. We also observe a few character decoding errors: wrongly generating *hot-spitalized* instead of *hospitalized*, *move* instead of *remove*.

The placeholder method almost always produces the specified term, but sometimes fails to inflect it correctly. The placeholder method fails to observe the constraint much less frequently than the code-switching method (only 4 examples out of 50). In most cases (39 examples out of 50), the model can successfully predict the correct form as shown in Table 5.

Source: フローセンサーの原理は浮遊式流量計のテーパー管内フロートの位置を差動トランスで検出し,これの電圧制御により流量を管理する。 **Reference**: The sensor controls the flow rate by detecting the position of the float in the tepered tube with a differential transformer and controlling it with the obtained voltage. **System Output**: The principle of the flow sensor is that the position of the float in the taper tube of the floating flowmeter is detected by the differential transformer, and the flow rate is controlled by this voltage control.

Table 5: A translation example with the placeholder model with a character decoder. The model predicts the correct inflectional form of *control* that fits in the context.

The failures consist of generalization errors of inflectional form: generating *maken* for *make*. It is impossible in principle to correctly predict irregular inflectional forms that are unseen in the training data, but this is usually not much of a problem since the specified term is usually a rare or new word, which tends to have a regular inflectional paradigm. The other kind of error we observe is the model predicting a well-defined word form that is wrong in the

Source: 国立病院機構関門医療センター(国立下関病院)は2002年9月30日に女性総合診療を開設した。
Reference: A National Hospital System Kanmon Medical Center (A National Shimonoseki Hospital) opened the comprehensive woman medical care service on September 30th in 2002.
System Output: National Hospital Mechanism Kanmon Medical Center (the national Shimonoseki Hospital) opening the woman general medical care on September 30th, 2002.

Table 6: A translation example with the placeholder model with a character decoder. The model predicts a wrong inflectional form for *open*.

context (Table 6). We expect that both error types can be addressed by exploiting additional data, either parallel or monolingual, to learn inflection rules in the target language.

6 Conclusion and Future Work

In this study, we point out that the traditional placeholder translation method embeds the specified term into the generated translation without considering the context of the placeholder token, which potentially leads to grammatically incorrect translations. To address this shortcoming, we proposed a flexible placeholder translation model that handles inflection when the specified term is given in the form of a lemma. In the experiment of the Japanese-to-English translation task, we showed that the proposed model can inflect user-specified terms more accurately than the code-switching method.

Future work includes testing the proposed method on morphologically-rich languages or extending the model to handle more than one placeholder in a sentence. Also, the proposed model still has room for improvement to learn inflection. It is possible that we can improve the model by exploiting monolingual corpora in the target language to provide additional training signals for learning the correct inflection in context.

Acknowledgements

The authors would like to thank the anonymous reviewers for their helpful comments. This work was supported by the Research and Development of Deep Learning Technology for Advanced Multilingual Speech Translation, the Commissioned Research of National Institute of Information and Communications Technology (NICT), JAPAN.

References

Anderson, P., Fernando, B., Johnson, M., and Gould, S. (2017). Guided Open Vocabulary Image Captioning with Constrained Beam Search. In *Proceedings of the 2017 Conference on Empirical Methods in Natural Language Processing*.

Crego, J., Kim, J., Klein, G., Rebollo, A., Yang, K., Senellart, J., Akhanov, E., Brunelle, P., Coquard, A., Deng, Y., Enoue, S., Geiss, C., Johanson, J., Khalsa, A., Khiari, R., Ko, B., Kobus, C., Lorieux, J., Martins, L., Nguyen, D.-C., Priori, A., Riccardi, T., Segal, N., Servan, C., Tiquet, C., Wang, B., Yang, J., Zhang, D., Zhou, J., and Zoldan, P. (2016). SYSTRAN's Pure Neural Machine Translation Systems. *arXiv:1610.05540v1 [cs.CL]*.

Dinu, G., Mathur, P., Federico, M., and Al-Onaizan, Y. (2019). Training Neural Machine Translation to Apply Terminology Constraints. In *Proceedings of the 57th Annual Meeting of the Association for Computational Linguistics*.

Exel, M., Buschbeck, B., Brandt, L., and Doneva, S. (2020). Terminology-constrained neural machine translation at SAP. In *Proceedings of the 22nd Annual Conference of the European Association for Machine Translation.*

Gardner, M., Grus, J., Neumann, M., Tafjord, O., Dasigi, P., Liu, N. F., Peters, M., Schmitz, M., and Zettlemoyer, L. (2018). AllenNLP: A Deep Semantic Natural Language Processing Platform. In *Proceedings of Workshop for NLP Open Source Software.*

Hokamp, C. and Liu, Q. (2017). Lexically Constrained Decoding for Sequence Generation Using Grid Beam Search. In *Proceedings of the 55th Annual Meeting of the Association for Computational Linguistics.*

Kingma, D. P. and Ba, J. (2015). Adam: A Method for Stochastic Optimization. In *International Conference on Learning Representations.*

Koehn, P., Och, F. J., and Marcu, D. (2003). Statistical Phrase-Based Translation. In *Proceedings of the 2003 Human Language Technology Conference of the North American Chapter of the Association for Computational Linguistics.*

Kudo, T. (2018). Subword Regularization: Improving Neural Network Translation Models with Multiple Subword Candidates. In *Proceedings of the 56th Annual Meeting of the Association for Computational Linguistics.*

Li, X., Zhang, J., and Zong, C. (2016). Neural Name Translation Improves Neural Machine Translation. *ArXiv*, abs/1607.01856.

Long, Z., Utsuro, T., Mitsuhashi, T., and Yamamoto, M. (2016). Translation of Patent Sentences with a Large Vocabulary of Technical Terms Using Neural Machine Translation. In *Proceedings of the 3rd Workshop on Asian Translation.*

Luong, T., Sutskever, I., Le, Q., Vinyals, O., and Zaremba, W. (2015). Addressing the Rare Word Problem in Neural Machine Translation. In *Proceedings of the 53rd Annual Meeting of the Association for Computational Linguistics and the 7th International Joint Conference on Natural Language Processing.*

Michon, E., Crego, J., and Senellart, J. (2020). Integrating Domain Terminology into Neural Machine Translation. In *Proceedings of the 28th International Conference on Computational Linguistics.*

Nakazawa, T., Yaguchi, M., Uchimoto, K., Utiyama, M., Sumita, E., Kurohashi, S., and Isahara, H. (2016). ASPEC: Asian Scientific Paper Excerpt Corpus. In *Proceedings of the Tenth International Conference on Language Resources and Evaluation.*

Niehues, J. (2021). Continuous learning in neural machine translation using bilingual dictionaries. In *Proceedings of the 16th Conference of the European Chapter of the Association for Computational Linguistics: Main Volume.*

Papineni, K., Roukos, S., Ward, T., and Zhu, W.-J. (2002). Bleu: a Method for Automatic Evaluation of Machine Translation. In *Proceedings of the 40th Annual Meeting of the Association for Computational Linguistics.*

Post, M. (2018). A Call for Clarity in Reporting BLEU Scores. In *Proceedings of the Third Conference on Machine Translation: Research Papers.*

Post, M., Ding, S., Martindale, M., and Wu, W. (2019). An Exploration of Placeholding in Neural Machine Translation. In *Proceedings of Machine Translation Summit XVII Volume 1: Research Track.*

Post, M. and Vilar, D. (2018). Fast Lexically Constrained Decoding with Dynamic Beam Allocation for Neural Machine Translation. In *Proceedings of the 2018 Conference of the North American Chapter of the Association for Computational Linguistics: Human Language Technologies, Volume 1.*

Song, K., Zhang, Y., Yu, H., Luo, W., Wang, K., and Zhang, M. (2019). Code-Switching for Enhancing NMT with Pre-Specified Translation. In *Proceedings of the 2019 Conference of the North American Chapter of the Association for Computational Linguistics: Human Language Technologies, Volume 1.*

Song, K., Zhang, Y., Zhang, M., and Luo, W. (2018). Improved English to Russian Translation by Neural Suffix Prediction. In *Proceedings of the AAAI Conference on Artificial Intelligence*, volume 32.

Sutskever, I., Vinyals, O., and Le, Q. V. (2014). Sequence to Sequence Learning with Neural Networks. In *Advances in Neural Information Processing Systems*, volume 27.

Tamchyna, A., Weller-Di Marco, M., and Fraser, A. (2017). Modeling Target-Side Inflection in Neural Machine Translation. In *Proceedings of the Second Conference on Machine Translation.*

Vaswani, A., Shazeer, N., Parmar, N., Uszkoreit, J., Jones, L., Gomez, A. N., Kaiser, L. u., and Polosukhin, I. (2017). Attention is All you Need. In *Advances in Neural Information Processing Systems*, volume 30.

Wang, Y., Cheng, S., Jiang, L., Yang, J., Chen, W., Li, M., Shi, L., Wang, Y., and Yang, H. (2017). Sogou Neural Machine Translation Systems for WMT17. In *Proceedings of the Second Conference on Machine Translation.*

Weller-Di Marco, M. and Fraser, A. (2020). Modeling Word Formation in English–German Neural Machine Translation. In *Proceedings of the 58th Annual Meeting of the Association for Computational Linguistics.*

Product Review Translation using Phrase Replacement and Attention Guided Noise Augmentation

Kamal Kumar Gupta, Soumya Chennabasavraj,[†] Nikesh Garera,[†] and Asif Ekbal

Department of Computer Science and Engineering, Indian Institute of Technology Patna, Patna, India
[†]Flipkart, India
kamal.pcs17,asif@iitp.ac.in
[†]soumya.cb,nikesh.garera@flipkart.com

Abstract

Product reviews provide valuable feedback of the customers, however, they are available today only in English on most of the e-commerce platforms. The nature of reviews provided by customers in any multilingual country poses unique challenges for machine translation such as code-mixing, ungrammatical sentences, presence of colloquial terms, lack of e-commerce parallel corpus etc. Given that 44% of Indian population speaks and operates in Hindi language, we address the above challenges by presenting an English–to–Hindi neural machine translation (NMT) system to translate the product reviews available on e-commerce websites by creating an in-domain parallel corpora and handling various types of noise in reviews via two data augmentation techniques, *viz.* (i). a novel phrase augmentation technique (PhrRep) where the syntactic noun phrases in the sentences are replaced by the other noun phrases carrying different meanings but in the similar context; and (ii). a novel attention guided noise augmentation (AttnNoise) technique to make our NMT model robust towards various noise. Evaluation shows that using the proposed augmentation techniques we achieve a 6.67 BLEU score improvement over the baseline model. In order to show that our proposed approach is not language-specific, we also perform experiments for two other language pairs, *viz.* En-Fr (MTNT18 corpus) and En-De (IWSLT17) that yield the improvements of 2.55 and 0.91 BLEU points, respectively, over the baselines.

1 Introduction

Product reviews written by the users on e-commerce websites are useful to get the feedback about the products and provide valuable insights to the user for making the buying decision. The product reviews available on different e-commerce websites are mainly in English language. India is a multilingual country with great linguistic and cultural diversities. There are 22 officially spoken languages, and many of them such as Hindi, Bengali, etc. come into the top 10 most spoken languages all over in the world. Since English is not a first language in India and most of the population (approximately, 68.9%)[1] from the rural areas do not have the proper understanding of English language,

[1]http://mohua.gov.in/cms/urban-growth.php

Source (A)	osm product.i really love it. osm camera quality...nice one
Reference	बहुत बढ़िया प्रॉडक्ट. मुझे यह पसंद है. बहुत बढ़िया कैमरा क्वालिटी... अच्छा है
(Transliteration)	bahut badhiya prodakt. mujhe yah pasand hai. bahut badhiya kaim kvaalitee... achchha hai
Gen-NMT	ओसम उत्पाद. मैं वास्तव में इसे प्यार करता हूँ. ओसम कैमरा गुणवत्ता... अच्छा एक
(Transliteration)	osam utpaad. main vaastav mein ise pyaar karata hoon. osam kaimara kvaalitee... achchha hai
Source (B)	NYC product,and cloth quilty is too good
Reference	अच्छा प्रॉडक्ट, और कपड़े की क्वालिटी बहुत बढ़िया है
(Transliteration)	achchha prodakt, aur kapade kee kvaalitee bahut badhiya hai
Gen-NMT	NYC उत्पाद, और कपड़ा रजाई बहुत अच्छा है
(Transliteration)	nyc utpaad, aur kapada rajaee bahut achchha hai
Source (C)	Nice Mobile and value for money 😇😇
Refernce	अच्छा मोबाइल और पैसा वसूल 😇😇
(Transliteration)	achchha mobail aur paisa vasool 😇😇
Gen-NMT	अच्छा मोबाइल और पैसे के लिए मूल्य money
(Transliteration)	achchha mobail aur paise ke lie mooly money

Table 1: Sample outputs for En→Hi translation from sources with various inconsistencies. Here, **Gen-NMT:** Generic NMT **(A)** Abbreviations and colloquial terms, **(B)** Spelling mistake and **(C)** Emojis

it becomes difficult for them to read a review or write a review in English with proper vocabulary and grammar. This makes the availability of product reviews in vernacular languages essential for the vast majority of Indian e-commerce customers. However, building an automated translation system for the large amount of reviews poses unique challenges to the machine translation community.

We illustrate some of the challenges with examples as shown in Table 1. In example A, the word *osm* appears as a short form of the word *awesome*; also there is no *space* between the words *product* and *i*. The model is not able to translate these correctly. Similarly, in example B, *NYC* and *quilty* are the short forms and misspelled versions of the words *nice* and *quality*, respectively. Presence of emojis in example-C also causes translation difficulty.

We address the above challenges with the main contributions or attributes of our work as follows:

- We build an NMT system for product reviews in low-resource scenarios. To the best of our knowledge, this is the very first attempt towards building a machine translation system for English to Indian language review translation.
- We build data resources by crawling reviews from an e-commerce portal, translate them into Hindi using our in-house open domain English-Hindi MT system, and perform manual verification for the correctness (c.f. Section 3.1).
- We introduce novel data augmentation techniques to handle the noise and the scarcity of in-domain training data as follows:
  1. We introduce a novel similar phrase replacement technique (PhrRep) which generates more diverse synthetic parallel samples compared to the word augmentation techniques (c.f. Section 4.3).

2. We use Part-of-Speech (PoS) guided word embedding based and context aware word augmentation techniques for synthetic data creation (c.f. Section 4.1 and Section 4.2), and show that our proposed PhrRep approach significantly outperforms the word based augmentation methods.
3. We introduce a novel attention guided noise augmentation (AttnNoise) technique to make the NMT model robust towards noisy inputs (c.f. Section 5.1). We show that AttnNoise method significantly outperforms the random noise injection (RndNoise) techniques.

2 Related Work

There are two main challenges for translating the product reviews, *viz.* (i). non-availability of parallel corpus; and (ii). noisy sentences in product and/or service reviews. Machine translation with noisy text is, itself, a very challenging task. The typical noises that pose challenges for machine translation include improper grammatical structures, misspellings, punctuation, emojis etc (c.f. Section 3.1) (Michel and Neubig, 2018). In the literature, there are a few works concerning the noise in the text and to increase the robustness of the translation model. Michel and Neubig (2018) presented a noisy dataset and discussed the challenges of noisy contents.

Belinkov and Bisk (2018) and Karpukhin et al. (2019) showed that small noise in the input text can reduce the quality of translation. To improve the robustness of the translation model they introduced synthetic errors like character swapping, deletion and insertion in the corpus. Vaibhav et al. (2019) also inserted synthetic noises and back-translated noise in the original corpus. Apart from the spelling distortion, to make the model immune to the grammatical errors, Anastasopoulos et al. (2019) augmented training data with the grammatical errors. They focused on articles, prepositions, subject-verb agreements etc. Considering the challenges, Berard et al. (2019) analyzed the performance of NMT model over a small French-English corpus of restaurant reviews. Unlike this, we do not inject any random noise, rather we introduce an attention guided noise augmentation (AttnNoise) technique to insert the synthetic noise at the source (English) side.

To address the second challenge related to the availability of training data, we make use of the data augmentation techniques to increase the training samples and noise handling techniques to increase the robustness of the model. Fadaee et al. (2017) replaced the common words by rare words to provide better evidence and contexts for the rare words. Gao et al. (2019) introduced a soft contextual augmentation method where a word's embedding is replaced by a weighted average of its similar words. Kobayashi (2018) used a bi-directional language model to predict the replacement by using the sentence context. Wu et al. (2019) used the BERT (Bidirectional Encoder Representations from Transformers) Devlin et al. (2019) model to predict the randomly masked word. Inspired by Wu et al. (2019), we mask the noun and adjective words in the source sentence and predict the appropriate nouns and adjectives as substitutes based on the sentence context. We introduce a phrase replacement based data augmentation technique (PhrRep) to replace the whole syntactic noun phrase (multiple words in a single attempt) with other diverse but contextually similar noun phrases.

3 Parallel Corpus Creation

In this section we describe the steps followed for parallel corpus creation and the necessary statistics.

3.1 Crawling reviews and challenges in pre-processing

We crawl English product reviews from the e-commerce portal, Flipkart. Product reviews are user generated contents and contain various noises (inconsistencies) as shown in Table 1.

A. Systems	Sentences	%Increase
Baseline (Human translated)	19,457	
Base+BT	122,570	
Base+BT+WDA	297,392	142.6%
Base+BT+CDA	369,765	201.7%
PhrRep	306,475	150%
Development Set (Human trans.)	599	
Testset (Human trans.)	2,539	
B. Systems	**Sentences**	
Base	1,561,840	
PhrRep	1,701,704	8.9%
Development Set	520	
Testset (newstest2014)	2,507	
C. Systems	**Sentences**	
Base	300,000	
PhrRep	488,501	62.83%
Development Set	1,500	
Testset (newstest2015)	1,500	
D. Systems	**Sentences**	
Base	223,021	
PhrRep	312,504	40.12%
Development Set	885	
Testset (IWSLT2017)	1,138	

Table 2: Parallel corpus size. Here, **A:** Product review dataset, **B:** IIT-Bombay English-Hindi dataset Kunchukuttan et al. (2018), **C:** UN-Corpus English-French dataset Ziemski et al. (2016) and **D:** IWSLT2017 English-German dataset.

3.2 Pre-processing

We remove the emojis from the English sentence by providing their unicode range using regular expressions. Any character having repetition of more than two times is trimmed and then checked for its compatible correct word using spell-checker[2] and a list provided by Facebook[3] Edizel et al. (2019). Writing the complete sentence in upper case is also very common in user generated content (i.e. *NICE PHONE IN LOW BUDGET*). Normalization is done to convert all such instances into the lower case. Since we focus on the product reviews data, we make the first character of brand's name[4] (Google, Moto, Nokia etc.) as capital. After the pre-processing steps as mentioned above (emoji removal, character repetition, casing etc.), we found that approximately 62.3% sentences from the total crawled sentences are correct.

3.3 Gold Corpus Creation by Human Post-editing

After pre-processing, we obtain 22,595 standard English sentences as mentioned in Table 2. Instead of translating sentences from scratch, we use our in-house judicial domain system to generate the initial target sentences and post-edit. It is trained for English-Hindi translation using 0.45 million parallel judicial domain samples and additional English-Hindi corpus Kunchukuttan et al. (2018) having 1.6 million parallel samples. It achieves 55.67 BLEU (En-to-Hi) points on our in-house judicial domain testset. After translation into Hindi, manual verification for the correctness of the translation is done by three language experts. The experts are post-graduates in linguistics and have good command in Hindi and English both. The experts read the English sentences and their Hindi translation. They were instructed to make the correction in the sentences, if required. The human post-edited parallel corpus as shown in Table 2 is divided into training, development and test set consisting of 19,457, 599 and 2,539 parallel sentences, respec-

[2]https://pypi.org/project/pyspellchecker/

[3]https://github.com/facebookresearch/moe/tree\\/master/data

[4]https://en.wikipedia.org/wiki/List_of_mobile_phone_brands_by_country

Sentence	There are many **offers** for this smartphone
WDA	There are many provides for this smartphone
CDA	There are many applications/designs/models for this smartphone
PhrRep	There are multiple features in my new smartphone

Table 3: Samples generated using WDA, CDA and PhrRep approaches.

tively. The gold standard corpus, and the parallel corpus created synthetically is made available[5]. We also crawl the Hindi sentences and back-translate them into English. We build a Hindi–to–English NMT model to back-translate the crawled Hindi sentences. We use the IIT Bombay Hindi-English general domain parallel corpus Kunchukuttan et al. (2018) to train a Hindi–to–English NMT model, and then fine-tune it over the human post-edited review domain parallel corpus. The fine-tuned Hindi–to–English NMT model is used to back-translate the crawled monolingual Hindi sentences into English. These back-translated (BT) English-Hindi synthetic parallel sentences are augmented with the human post-edited parallel sentences and referred to as 'Base+BT', shown in Table 2.

4 Data Augmentation

We further enrich the training corpus (in low-resource language) following the data augmentation techniques as discussed below.

4.1 Word Embedding based Data Augmentation (WDA)

Let us take one example: **Original sample:** This ***phone*** is not ***good***. and **New sample:** This ***handset*** is not ***nice***.
In the original sample, the words *'phone'* and *'good'* are replaced by their most semantically close words *'handset'* and *'nice'*, respectively, based on the cosine similarity between their word embeddings. To reduce the alignment complexity, we choose noun and adjective words as the replacement candidates because:

- Hindi is morphologically richer than English. One English verb token may be aligned to more than one Hindi tokens. But nouns and adjectives are most likely to generate only one Hindi token. For example: translation of word '*started* (verb)' (1 token) can be 'शुरू कर दिया' 'shuroo kar diya' (3 tokens) or 'शुरू किया' 'shuroo kiya' (2 tokens). Here, we see that for the word '*started*', more than one translations possible with different token lengths.

To select the noun and adjectives for replacement, we use NLTKLoper and Bird (2002) Part-of-Speech (PoS) tagger for the English sentences. A word2vec skip-gram model[6] Mikolov et al. (2013) is trained using the WMT14 monolingual English dataset and English sentences from the gold corpus. Now for all the noun and adjective words, we find the most similar words using our trained word2vec model. The words having the cosine similarity more than 0.75 will be considered as the substitutes. A mapping dictionary is created with the triplet consisting of the 'original English word', 'its replacement English word' and 'Hindi translation of the replacement word'. Now using the mapping dictionary, the tokens in the original corpus are replaced. Source-target word alignment information using GIZA++ tool (Och and Ney, 2003) is used to replace the aligned Hindi tokens in the Hindi side. But WDA does not guarantee to replace the original word with a similar context word as shown by an example in Table 3.

[5]`https://www.iitp.ac.in/~ai-nlp-ml/resources/data/review-corpus.zip`
[6]`https://code.google.com/archive/p/word2vec/`

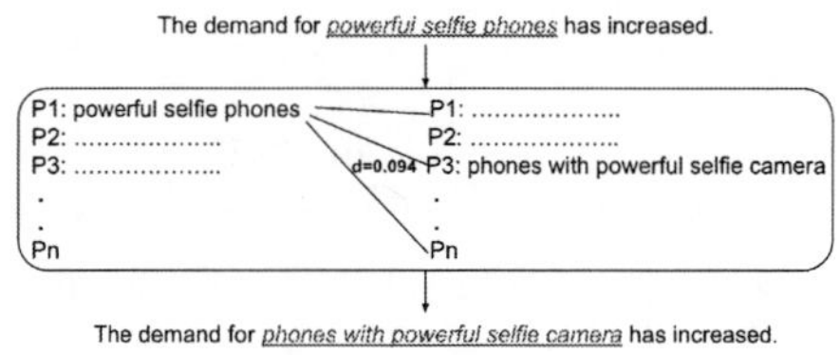

Figure 1: Synthetic sample generation using phrase replacement (PhrRep)

4.2 Context Aware Data Augmentation (CDA)

Wu et al. (2019) used a BERT based method which predicts the substitution for the randomly masked word. Here, we mask only nouns and adjective words. Similar to 4.1, *noun* and *adjective* words in the source sentence are masked, and their appropriate substitutes are predicted based on the sentence context. We use the 'bert-base-uncased' pre-trained model for the prediction which is trained using the default hyper parameters: 12 layers, 728 hidden units and 12 attention heads. Here, we also find the replacements for nouns and adjectives only. A list of noun and adjective tokens is created and in each English sentence, we mask the tokens by replacing the tokens with '[MASK]' which are in the list.

Now, the masked sequence is passed through the trained BERT model. Since BERT contains the bidirectional sequence information, it can predict the most appropriate token for position *'i'* by considering the previous and next context words within the sentence. For generating more augmented samples, we take the top 3 predicted words for position *'i'* and generate different samples. We use Giza++ alignment information to obtain the aligned positions between English and Hindi sentences, and the translated Hindi word of the newly predicted English word is placed at the Hindi side too. A mapping dictionary similar to WDA is needed here to obtain the parallel counterpart of an augmented word. Using CDA, multiple replacements can be found for a single masked token based on the context (because here no fixed mapping dictionary is used). Also, the substitute token suits the syntactic and semantic structure of the sentence. In Table 3, we can see in the example, "There are many **offers** for this smartphone", 'applications', 'designs' and 'models' are predicted at the place of original hidden word 'offers'.

4.3 Data Augmentation using Phrase Replacement (PhrRep)

Here, we introduce a novel approach for data augmentation using similar phrase replacement strategy. The method generates more diverse samples (a phrase of multiple tokens is replaced with similar phrases of different token lengths) in a single attempt. Unlike the previous word augmentation techniques Fadaee et al. (2017); Gao et al. (2019), here we replace a noun phrase (NP) with its semantically similar noun phrase (NP). To extract NP from the English sentences, we use the Stanford parser[7] and obtain the corresponding constituency trees. To reduce the complexity in alignment mapping and trivial replacements, we filter out very large (>8 tokens) and very short (<3 tokens) NPs. Here, we refer to the replacements of very small NPs as trivial replacements since most likely they are already part of larger NPs, and get replaced when larger NPs are replaced. To find the similarity among phrase embeddings, we use a BERT based sentence-transformer[8] Reimers and Gurevych (2019).

For an original phrase P_{oi}, its similar phrase P_{si} is:

$$P_{si} = P_j, [i = (1,....,n) \; and \; j = (1,....,n)] \tag{1}$$

[7]https://nlp.stanford.edu/software/lex-parser.shtml

[8]https://github.com/UKPLab/sentence-transformers

$$P_j = \arg\min_j d(h_i, h_j) \tag{2}$$

n is the number of NPs. h is the hidden representation of the phrases. d represents the Euclidean distance between the two vectors. Equation 2 returns the index j of a phrase having minimum Euclidean distance d with the phrase at index i. As shown in equation 1, the respective phrase P_j at index j is the most similar phrase to the original phrase P_{oi}. Figure 1 shows the mapping of the original phrase *'powerful selfie phones'* with phrase *'phones with powerful selfie camera'* having the Euclidean distance d = 0.094, minimum in the distances with all the other phrases. Further, Hindi counterparts of the English NPs are extracted from the original parallel data itself using the alignment information.

5 Noise Augmentation

We create a noisy copy of the original corpus. To deal with character missing, article missing, punctuation missing and the dropping offs of starting noun-pronouns, we introduce various noise in the original training corpus. In similar ways to the prior works Vaibhav et al. (2019); Anastasopoulos et al. (2019), we also drop the characters randomly from the source (English) side, but with some additional rules.

- It is observed in the reviews that 'vowels' are most likely to be dropped by the users. For example, for a word 'phone', *'phne'* and *"phon'* are most likely to occur compared to the *"pone'* and *"phoe'*. So in each English sentence, along with dropping the random characters we make sure that vowels are also dropped in a few words.
- We randomly drop the articles 'the', 'a' and 'an' from the English side because we observe that in reviews users often drop the articles.
- Users often write reviews without mentioning the starting nouns or pronouns. We drop the starting nouns and pronouns randomly from the sentences. The PoS tagger was used to mark the words to be dropped. For example, "was planning to buy this" or "am happy with the phone".

Here, when we pick the tokens randomly for noise injection (char drop) we call it *random noise* (RndNoise) insertion. All these noises are introduced into a copy of the original corpus. It is then augmented with the original corpus. This provides noisy and correct source versions for a target sentence.

5.1 Attention Guided Noise Augmentation (AttnNoise)

	x_1	x_2	x_{n-1}	x_n
y_1	W11	W12	.	W1n
y_2	W21	W22	.	W2n
y_{m-1}	.	.	.	Wm-1.n
y_m	Wm1	Wm2	.	Wmn
Sum=(W11+..+Wn)	**W1**	**W2**	**Wn-1**	**Wn**
AvgAttn=Sum/m	**AvgW1**	**AvgW2**	**AvgWn-1**	**AvgWn**

Table 4: Attention weight matrix during source-to-target inference. Here, Wij: attention weight between i^{th} target token and j^{th} source token

Most of the existing literature Vaibhav et al. (2019); Anastasopoulos et al. (2019) introduced noise in the training data by randomly dropping characters from the source words. To make our model robust towards misspellings, article missing, punctuation and word missing, we also drop the words or introduce the character inconsistencies in words. Instead of executing these randomly, we follow a guided approach to drop a word or character(s) from these words. To do this, we take the help of attention weights between the source-target pairs. We call this technique as *attention guided noise augmentation* (AttnNoise).

Algorithm 1 Attention guided noise augmentation (AttnNoise)

Notations: $\boldsymbol{s_i}$=$\{x_1, x_2, ..., x_n\}$, i^{th} sequence.
AvgAttn_i: list of avg. attention weights of tokens in s_i
lProb_i: list of probability (occurrence frequency) of tokens in s_i
sN_i: i^{th} noisy source sequence
lMinAttn: indexes of bottom 10% min values in $AvgAttn_i$.
lMaxAttn: indexes of top 25% max values in $AvgAttn_i$.
lMaxProb: indexes of top max 50% values in $lProb_i$.
ind: index of a token in s_i.
$\boldsymbol{x_j}$: token at j^{th} position in s_i.

```
procedure NOISE(s_i, AvgAttn_i, lProb_i)
    for j ∈ 0, ..., len(s_i) do                              ▷ for each token
        if ind[x_j] ∉ lMinAttn then
            if ind[x_j] ∈ lMaxAttn then
                sN_i.append(dropChar(x_j))
            else
                sN_i.append(x_j)
        else if ind[x_j] ∉ lMaxProb then
            dropWord(x_j)
        else
            sN_i.append(dropChar(x_j))
    return (sN_i)
procedure WORD-PROB(s_i, S)
    for k ∈ 0, ..., len(s_i) do                              ▷ for each token
        p = (#x_k in S / #all tokens in S)
        lProb_i.append(p)
    return (lProb_i)
```

We have a corpus D with parallel pairs *[S, T]*, where S and T are the collection of source and target sentences, respectively. s_k and t_k represent a pair of kth source and target sequences in S and T, respectively. Each $s_k = \{x_1,x_2,...,x_n\}$ is a sequence of n source tokens and $t_k = \{y_1,y_2,...,y_m\}$ is a sequence of m target tokens. We calculate the average attention for each source token as shown in Table 4. All the attention heads are considered here. We drop a fraction of tokens from the source sequence having low average attention weight, and introduce noise in a fraction of tokens having high average attention weight. Method *NOISE* in Algorithm 1 describes the steps involved in the AttnNoise. To decide if a token comes under the low or high attention weight category, we choose some *percentage* value as the threshold. For example, we have a list $AvgAttn_i$ of source sequence s_i which has 15 tokens. For our experiments, we empirically decide to drop the bottom 10% of total tokens in s_i having minimum average attention weight (i.e. 10% of 15 = 2 tokens, so we drop 2 tokens having the lowest weights). Similarly, top 25% of tokens in s_i having high weights are made noisy by dropping the characters from them.

We also calculate the occurrence probability of the source tokens of s_i using the method *WORD-PROB* in Algorithm 1 to know whether any token is frequent or rare in the vocabulary. A token with less occurrence probability is said to be rare and we do not drop any rare token even if it has the low average attention weight. The rare

	Systems	BLEU	TER
En→Hi	Base	34.36	46.23
(Review)	Base+BT	35.19	45.10
	+Fadaee et al. (2017)	38.54	41.69
	+WDA	38.67	40.28
	+CDA	39.66	39.65
	+CDA+RndNoise	40.14	40.36
	+PhrRep+RndNoise	**40.61**	**38.79**
	+PhrRep+AttnNoise	**41.03**	**37.92**
En→Fr	Base	20.83	66.74
(MTNT18)	PhrRep	**22.75**	**64.16**
	+AttnNoise	**23.38**	**63.37**

	System	BLEU	TER
1.A	Base	15.42	71.46
	PhrRep	**16.56**	69.62
1.B	Base	22.47	62.84
	PhrRep	**22.69**	61.92
1.C	Base	4.49	89.14
	PhrRep	**6.24**	86.44
En→Fr	Base	19.36	67.15
(newstest2015)	PhrRep	**20.91**	65.83
En→De	Base	18.83	65.91
(IWSLT 2017)	PhrRep	**19.74**	64.38
En→Fr	Base	21.77	63.83
(IWSLT 17)	PhrRep	**22.52**	61.87

Table 5: BLEU and TER scores of different systems for different datasets of English-Hindi, English-French and English-German language pairs. Also for En→Hi translation: **(1.A)** Trained on IITB-Hin-Eng corpus and tested over newstest2014, **(1.B)** Trained on IITB-Hin-Eng corpus and tested over product review testset, **(1.C)** Trained on product review corpus and tested over newstest2014.

tokens correspond to those having high attention weights, and instead of dropping these from the source sequence, we insert noise into it. To prevent the dropping of any rare word having low attention weight, we increase the *percentage* value for the threshold. Here, the top 50% tokens in s_i having low occurrence probabilities are considered as the rare tokens. Since our target is to avoid the rare words to be dropped due to low attention weight, the threshold of 50% is taken with an assumption that the rare tokens would fall in this range only otherwise that token is not rare. After inserting the noise in all the source sentences, we make their pairing with their respective target sentences. Finally, this noisy parallel corpus is augmented to the original parallel corpus for final source–to–target training.

6 Experiment Setup

Our translation model is based on the Transformer architecture Vaswani et al. (2017). We use the Sockeye toolkit[9] Hieber et al. (2018) for our experiments. Table 2 gives the size of the training samples for different systems. We also experiment our proposed method on the IIT Bombay English-Hindi parallel corpus Kunchukuttan et al. (2018). To perform experiments for the English–to–French translation, we use a part (for true resource-poor setting) of the UN-corpus Ziemski et al. (2016) for training and newstest2015 Bojar et al. (2015) as the test set. We also perform experiment for English-German translation and test over the IWSLT 2017 testset[10].

The tokens of the training, test and validation sets are segmented into subword units Sennrich et al. (2016) by applying 4,000 BPE merge operations at the source and target sides. Our training set-up details are given below: No. of layers at the encoder and decoder sides: 6 each; 8-head attention; Hidden layer size: 512; Embedding vector size: 512; Learning rate: 0.0002; Minimum batch size: 4800 tokens; early stopping is used to terminate the training.

7 Results and Analysis

From Table 5, we can see significant BLEU score improvement over the baseline using various data and noise augmentation techniques. Using human translated and back-translated corpus, we train the Base+BT model which yields the BLEU improvement of 0.83. Further, with data augmentation techniques, WDA and CDA, we obtain additional 3.48 and 4.47 BLEU score improvement, respectively. The random noise augmentation

[9] `https://github.com/awslabs/sockeye`
[10] `https://wit3.fbk.eu/2017-01`

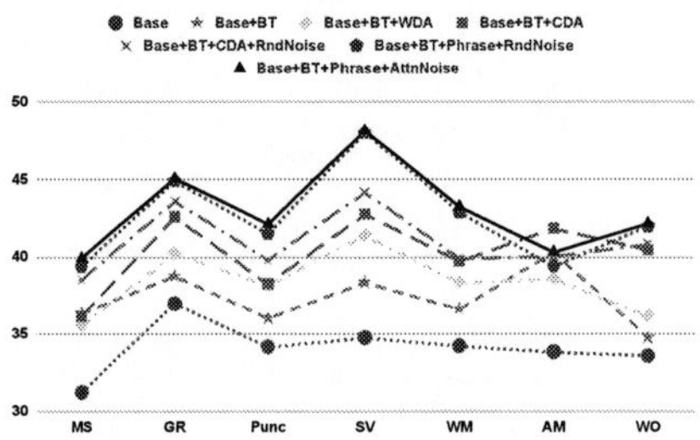

Figure 2: BLEU scores of models in the presence of various kinds of noises in input sentence.

(RndNoise) in CDA model also shows additional improvement of 0.48 BLEU point. In total, with noisy word augmentation methods, we achieve 5.78 BLEU improvement over the base model. After using our proposed phrase replacement (PhrRep) technique, we outperform the word augmentation techniques 'Base+BT+CDA+RndNoise' with 0.47 BLEU score. As mentioned in Table 2, 'PhrRep+RndNoise' model outperforms all the models with comparatively less parallel data. Further adding AttnNoise with 'PhrRep' the model 'Base+BT+PhrRep+AttnNoise' gives 0.42 additional BLEU improvement. In total, with 'Base+BT+PhrRep+AttnNoise' method, we achieve a total of 6.67 BLEU improvement over the 'Base' model. We also perform experiment over the MTNT testset which is a user generated English-French corpus. 'PhrRep' method yields 1.92 BLEU over the baseline score. Further, sing 'AttnNoise' method with 'PhrRep' gives additional 0.63 BLEU improvement.

We also apply our proposed PhrRep technique over the benchmark English-Hindi testset newstest2014 Bojar et al. (2014). As shown in Table 5, we achieve a 1.14 BLEU score improvement over the baseline. We perform statistical significance tests[11] Koehn (2004), and found that the proposed model attains significant performance gain with 95% confidence level (with p=0.013 which is < 0.05). We also apply the PhrRep technique for English–to–French translation. To test the performance in a low-resource scenario, we perform our experiment over a small part of data i.e. 300k parallel sentences. We achieve a gain of 1.55 BLEU (statistically significant) over the baseline. For English–to–German translation task, it also yields significant improvement[12] of 0.91 BLEU over the baseline.

7.1 Analyzing the Robustness

To analyze the models' performance on the product domain testset, we manually tag the test sentences on the basis of major inconsistencies. We divide the testset into the following 7 categories: misspell (MS): 10.09%, wrong Grammar (GR): 6.94%, punctuation mistake (Punc): 7.83%, sub-verb disagreement (SV): 2.56%, word missing (WM): 5.99%, article missing (AM): 1.94% and word order (WO): 3.67%. The distribution in percentage shows how much of the test sentences lie in which noise category. Figure 2 depicts the performance of all the models in presence of different noises. Augmented techniques outperform the 'Base' and 'Base+BT' models in all the major categories. Evaluation results show that 'PhrRep+RndNoise' model outperforms all the other word augmentation models. Further, introducing 'AttnNoise' in 'PhrRep+AttnNoise' improves the performance over 'PhrRep+RndNoise'. It shows that the guided noise augmentation is better than the random noise augmentation based technique. For AM

[11] `https://github.com/moses-smt/mosesdecoder/blob/master/scripts/analysis/bootstrap-hypothesis-difference-significance.pl`

[12] $p<0.005$

	Adequacy	Fluency
Base+BT	2.06	2.74
Base+BT+CDA+RndNoise	**2.49** (+0.43)	**3.28** (+0.54)
Base+BT+PhrRep+RndNoise	**2.63** (+0.57)	**3.35** (+0.61)
Base+BT+PhrRep+AttnNoise	**2.87** (+0.81)	**3.52** (+0.78)

Table 6: Average adequacy and fluency score

error, 'PhrRep+AttnNoise' lags behind the 'CDA'.

7.2 Human Evaluation

We also analyze the translation quality from human perception. Each hypothesis is assigned with adequacy and fluency score from 0–to–4 in the following scale:
0- *Incorrect*, **1-** *Almost incorrect*, **2-** *Moderately incorrect*, **3-** *Almost correct*, **4-** *Correct*. We select 500 random test samples and ask 3 language experts to read and assign the fluency and adequacy scores. Table 6 shows the average rating for different data augmentation models assisted with random noise (RndNoise) and Attention guided noise (AttnNoise). We calculate the inter-annotator-agreement scores (IAA) using Fleiss's Kappa. The scores for "Base+BT" model are found to be 0.874 and 0.891 for adequacy and fluency rating, respectively. The proposed model "Base+BT+PhrRep+AttnNoise" shows the scores of 0.867 and 0.913 for adequacy and fluency, respectively. The 'Choice of output tokens', 'translation of noisy source tokens', 'missing source tokens to translate', 'word order', 'tense preservation', 'punctuation', and 'subject-verb agreement' are some important factors while assigning adequacy and fluency scores. PhrRep and AttnNoise techniques provide incremental improvements as shown in Table 6.

8 Conclusion

In this paper, we have presented an effective NMT model for English–to–Hindi product review translation. As there was no parallel corpus in this domain, we, therefore, crawled English reviews, pre-processed, filtered, translated into Hindi and corrected using professional human translators. Hindi descriptions of electronic gadgets are crawled and back-translated into English using human translated corpus and again augmented with human translated corpus. We make the parallel corpus freely available.

We have introduced a novel phrase replacement based augmentation technique (PhrRep) which replaces the whole noun phrase (multiple tokens at a time) with an alternative noun phrase to generate the new training sample in fewer attempts. For robustness in our model, we use a novel attention guided noise augmentation technique (AttnNoise) which drops the words or makes them noisy on the basis of attention weights. Using phraseRep and AttnNoise, for En→Hi review translation, we achieve an improvement of 6.67 BLEU over the baseline. In order to show the generic behavior of our model, we also evaluate it on the English-French and English-German benchmark datasets, demonstrating the effectiveness of our proposed approach.

In future, we shall focus on the spelling variations and code-mixed challenges in the input and output sentences. A bigger English–to–Indic multilingual product review translation system will be investigated.

9 Acknowledgement

Authors gratefully acknowledge the unrestricted research grant received from the Flipkart Internet Private Limited to carry out the research. Authors thank Muthusamy Chelliah for his continuous feedbacks and suggestions to improve the quality of work; and to Anubhav Tripathee for gold standard parallel corpus creation and translation quality evaluation.

References

Anastasopoulos, A., Lui, A., Nguyen, T. Q., and Chiang, D. (2019). Neural machine translation of text from non-native speakers. In *Proceedings of the 2019 Conference of the North American Chapter of the Association for Computational Linguistics: Human Language Technologies, Volume 1 (Long and Short Papers)*, pages 3070–3080, Minneapolis, Minnesota. Association for Computational Linguistics.

Belinkov, Y. and Bisk, Y. (2018). Synthetic and natural noise both break neural machine translation. In *International Conference on Learning Representations.*

Berard, A., Calapodescu, I., Dymetman, M., Roux, C., Meunier, J.-L., and Nikoulina, V. (2019). Machine translation of restaurant reviews: New corpus for domain adaptation and robustness. In *Proceedings of the 3rd Workshop on Neural Generation and Translation*, pages 168–176, Hong Kong. Association for Computational Linguistics.

Bojar, O., Buck, C., Federmann, C., Haddow, B., Koehn, P., Leveling, J., Monz, C., Pecina, P., Post, M., Saint-Amand, H., et al. (2014). Findings of the 2014 Workshop on Statistical Machine Translation. In *Proceedings of the ninth workshop on statistical machine translation (WMT 2014)*, pages 12–58.

Bojar, O., Chatterjee, R., Federmann, C., Haddow, B., Huck, M., Hokamp, C., Koehn, P., Logacheva, V., Monz, C., Negri, M., Post, M., Scarton, C., Specia, L., and Turchi, M. (2015). Findings of the 2015 workshop on statistical machine translation. pages 1–46, Lisbon, Portugal. Association for Computational Linguistics.

Devlin, J., Chang, M.-W., Lee, K., and Toutanova, K. (2019). BERT: Pre-training of deep bidirectional transformers for language understanding. In *Proceedings of the 2019 Conference of the North American Chapter of the Association for Computational Linguistics: Human Language Technologies, Volume 1 (Long and Short Papers)*, pages 4171–4186, Minneapolis, Minnesota. Association for Computational Linguistics.

Edizel, B., Piktus, A., Bojanowski, P., Ferreira, R., Grave, E., and Silvestri, F. (2019). Misspelling oblivious word embeddings. *ArXiv*, abs/1905.09755.

Fadaee, M., Bisazza, A., and Monz, C. (2017). Data augmentation for low-resource neural machine translation. In *Proceedings of ACL.*

Gao, F., Zhu, J., Wu, L., Xia, Y., Qin, T., Cheng, X., Zhou, W., and Liu, T.-Y. (2019). Soft contextual data augmentation for neural machine translation. In *Proceedings of the 57th Annual Meeting of the Association for Computational Linguistics*, pages 5539–5544, Florence, Italy. Association for Computational Linguistics.

Hieber, F., Domhan, T., Denkowski, M., Vilar, D., Sokolov, A., Clifton, A., and Post, M. (2018). The sockeye neural machine translation toolkit at AMTA 2018. In *Proceedings of the 13th Conference of the Association for Machine Translation in the Americas (Volume 1: Research Papers)*, pages 200–207, Boston, MA.

Karpukhin, V., Levy, O., Eisenstein, J., and Ghazvininejad, M. (2019). Training on synthetic noise improves robustness to natural noise in machine translation. In *Proceedings of the 5th Workshop on Noisy User-generated Text (W-NUT 2019)*, pages 42–47, Hong Kong, China. Association for Computational Linguistics.

Kobayashi, S. (2018). Contextual augmentation: Data augmentation by words with paradigmatic relations. In *Proceedings of the 2018 Conference of the North American Chapter of the Association for Computational Linguistics: Human Language Technologies, Volume 2 (Short Papers)*, pages 452–457, New Orleans, Louisiana. Association for Computational Linguistics.

Koehn, P. (2004). Statistical significance tests for machine translation evaluation. In *Proceedings of the 2004 Conference on Empirical Methods in Natural Language Processing*, pages 388–395, Barcelona, Spain. Association for Computational Linguistics.

Kunchukuttan, A., Mehta, P., and Bhattacharyya, P. (2018). The IIT Bombay English-Hindi parallel corpus. In *Proceedings of the Eleventh International Conference on Language Resources and Evaluation (LREC 2018)*, Miyazaki, Japan.

Loper, E. and Bird, S. (2002). Nltk: The natural language toolkit. In *In Proceedings of the ACL Workshop on Effective Tools and Methodologies for Teaching Natural Language Processing and Computational Linguistics. Philadelphia: Association for Computational Linguistics.*

Michel, P. and Neubig, G. (2018). MTNT: A testbed for machine translation of noisy text. In *Proceedings of the 2018 Conference on Empirical Methods in Natural Language Processing*, pages 543–553, Brussels, Belgium. Association for Computational Linguistics.

Mikolov, T., Le, Q. V., and Sutskever, I. (2013). Exploiting Similarities among Languages for Machine Translation. *arXiv preprint arXiv:1309.4168.*

Och, F. J. and Ney, H. (2003). A systematic comparison of various statistical alignment models. *Computational linguistics*, 29(1):19–51.

Reimers, N. and Gurevych, I. (2019). Sentence-BERT: Sentence embeddings using Siamese BERT-networks. In *Proceedings of the 2019 Conference on Empirical Methods in Natural Language Processing and the 9th International Joint Conference on Natural Language Processing (EMNLP-IJCNLP)*, pages 3982–3992, Hong Kong, China. Association for Computational Linguistics.

Sennrich, R., Haddow, B., and Birch, A. (2016). Neural machine translation of rare words with subword units. In *Proceedings of the 54th Annual Meeting of the Association for Computational Linguistics (Volume 1: Long Papers)*, pages 1715–1725, Berlin, Germany.

Vaibhav, V., Singh, S., Stewart, C., and Neubig, G. (2019). Improving robustness of machine translation with synthetic noise. In *Proceedings of the 2019 Conference of the North American Chapter of the Association for Computational Linguistics: Human Language Technologies, Volume 1 (Long and Short Papers)*, pages 1916–1920, Minneapolis, Minnesota. Association for Computational Linguistics.

Vaswani, A., Shazeer, N., Parmar, N., Uszkoreit, J., Jones, L., Gomez, A. N., Kaiser, Ł., and Polosukhin, I. (2017). Attention is all you need. In *Advances in neural information processing systems*, pages 5998–6008.

Wu, X., Lv, S., Zang, L., Han, J., and Hu, S. (2019). Conditional bert contextual augmentation. In *ICCS*.

Ziemski, M., Junczys-Dowmunt, M., and Pouliquen, B. (2016). The united nations parallel corpus v1. 0. In *Proceedings of the Tenth International Conference on Language Resources and Evaluation (LREC'16)*, pages 3530–3534, Portorož, Slovenia.

Optimizing Word Alignments with Better Subword Tokenization

Anh Khoa Ngo Ho anh-khoa.ngo-ho@limsi.fr
François Yvon francois.yvon@limsi.fr
Université Paris-Saclay, CNRS, LISN
Bât. 508, rue John von Neumann, Campus Universitaire, F-91405 Orsay

Abstract

Word alignment identify translational correspondences between words in a parallel sentence pair and are used, for example, to train statistical machine translation, learn bilingual dictionaries or to perform quality estimation. Subword tokenization has become a standard preprocessing step for a large number of applications, notably for state-of-the-art open vocabulary machine translation systems. In this paper, we thoroughly study how this preprocessing step interacts with the word alignment task and propose several tokenization strategies to obtain well-segmented parallel corpora. Using these new techniques, we were able to improve baseline word-based alignment models for six language pairs.

1 Introduction

Word alignment is a basic task in multilingual Natural Language Processing (NLP) and is used, for instance, to learn bilingual dictionaries, to train statistical machine translation (SMT) systems (Koehn, 2010), to filter out noise from translation memories (Pham et al., 2018) or in quality estimation applications (Specia et al., 2018). Word alignment can also serve to *explain MT decisions* (Stahlberg et al., 2018). Given pairs associating a sentence in a source language and a translation in a target language, word alignment aims to identify translational equivalences at the level of individual word tokens and has been initially approached with generative probabilistic models learning alignment in an unsupervised manner (Och and Ney, 2003; Tiedemann, 2011).

With rapid advances in neural based NLP, word alignment has recently regained some traction (Legrand et al., 2016) and improvements of the state of the art for multiple language pairs have been reported thanks to neuralized generative models (Alkhouli and Ney, 2017; Alkhouli et al., 2018; Ngo-Ho and Yvon, 2019), pre-trained multilingual embeddings (Jalili Sabet et al., 2020; Nagata et al., 2020; Dou and Neubig, 2021) or more powerful architectures based on the Transformer translation model of Vaswani et al. (2017), as reported for instance by Garg et al. (2019); Chen et al. (2020) and Chen et al. (2021).

In addition to using neural architectures, these new models differ from past approaches in that they compute alignments based on a decomposition into subword units (Sennrich et al., 2016; Kudo, 2018), which makes it possible to easily accommodate open-ended vocabularies and mitigate issues related to the alignment of unknown words, which has always been a challenge for discrete models. Another interesting property of subword units in the context of word alignment is that (a) they ease the generation of many-to-one / one-to-many links, which are difficult to handle in standard asymmetric models such as IBM-1 and IBM-4 (Liu et al., 2015; Tomeh et al., 2014; Wang and Lepage, 2016); (b) they also enable to actively manipulate the lengths of the source and target sentences so as to make them more even, arguably a facilitating factor for alignment and translation models (Deguchi et al., 2020).

In this work, we take a closer look at the interaction between alignment and subword tokenization and try to address the following research questions: how much of the reported improvements in alignment performance can be linked to subword splitting? which issue(s) of basic alignment models do they mitigate? is it possible to design more active segmentation strategies that would target the alignment problem for specific language pairs? Our conclusions rests on the analysis of a systematic study of word alignment for 6 language pairs from multiple language families. We notably show that subword tokenization also help discrete alignment models. We also study techniques aimed at optimizing tokenization, which enable us to further improve the alignment accuracy and mitigate the problems cause by rare / unaligned words.

This paper is organized as follows: in § 2 we review the pitfalls of generative word alignment models, and analyse in § 3 how their performance vary with changing subword tokenizations. These analyses help to understand why such preprocessing actually improves word based models. Our main proposals are sketched in § 4, where we show how to optimize subword tokenization for better alignments. In § 5, we then briefly review related work, before concluding in § 6.

2 Pitfalls and limitations of word alignments models

In this section, we experiment with well-known word alignment packages (Fastalign (Dyer et al., 2013), Giza++ (Och and Ney, 2003), Eflomal (Östling and Tiedemann, 2016) as well as `Simalign` (Jalili Sabet et al., 2020)[1]), outlining difficult issues for word alignment models such as the prediction of null links, of many-to-one links, as well as the alignment of rare words. Detailed analyses are in (Ngo Ho, 2021). Asymmetric alignment models associate each source word with exactly one target word; such alignments are denoted as English $\rightarrow$ Foreign, when English is the source language. As a preamble, we start with our data condition.

2.1 Datasets

Our experiments consider multiple language pairs all having English on one side. Our training sets for French and German are made of sentences from Europarl (Koehn, 2005). For Romanian, we use both the NAACL 2003 corpus (Mihalcea and Pedersen, 2003) and the SETIMES corpus used in WMT'16 MT evaluation. For Czech, the parallel data from News Commentary V11 (Tiedemann, 2012) is considered, while we use the preprocessed parallel data for Vietnamese in IWSLT'15 (Luong and Manning, 2015) and the Japanese data from the KFTT (Neubig, 2011).

Our evaluations use standard test sets whenever applicable: for French and Romanian, we use data from the 2003 word alignment challenge (Mihalcea and Pedersen, 2003); the German test data is Europarl;[2] for Czech we use the corpus designed by Mareček (2016); the Japanese test data is from the KFTT and the test corpus for Vietnamese is generated from the EVBCorpus.[3] As is custom when evaluating unsupervised alignments, we append the test set to the training corpus at training time, meaning that there is no unknown word in the reference alignments.

Basic statistics for these corpora are in Table 1.[4] English-French and English-German training data ($\geq$ 1.5M) are much larger than the rest (from 122K to under 400K) and we take them as representative of a "large data" condition. Unsurprisingly, the vocabulary sizes of the German, Romanian and Czech corpora are substantially greater than the corresponding English,

[1] A method of generating alignment links based on the matrix of embedding similarities without parallel data. The options are to use mBert (Devlin et al., 2019) or the multilingual version of Fasttext are used to generate multilingual embeddings from monolingual data. In our experiments, we use the setting: mBert + Argmax.

[2] http://www-i6.informatik.rwth-aachen.de/goldAlignment/

[3] https://code.google.com/archive/p/evbcorpus/

[4] We only use training sentences of length lower than 50.

which contains a smaller number of inflected variants. The opposite pattern is observed for Japanese and Vietnamese, two synthetic languages with less inflectional variability than English.

Corpus	Training data					Test data			
	# sent. pairs	word vocab.		char. vocab.		# sent. pairs	# words		# non-null links
		Eng.	For.	Eng.	For.		Eng.	For.	
En-Fr	~1.7M	~106K	~112K	111	115	447	7 020	7 761	17 438
En-Ge	~1.5M	~96K	~311K	218	235	509	10 413	9 945	10 533
En-Ro	~250K	~74K	~115K	124	131	246	5 455	5 315	5 991
En-Cz	~182K	~62K	~147K	246	157	2 501	59 724	52 881	67 423
En-Ja	~377K	~156K	~126K	~2K	~5K	1 235	30 822	34 403	33 377
En-Vi	~122K	~42K	~19K	133	171	3 447	70 049	94 753	81 748

Table 1: Basic statistics for the training data and test data

2.2 Evaluation protocol

We use the alignment error rate (AER) (Och, 2003), F-score (F1), precision and recall as measures of performance. AER is based on a comparison of predicted alignment links (A) with a human reference including sure (S) and possible (P) links, and is defined as an average of the recall and precision taking into account the sets P and S. AER is defined as:

$$AER = 1 - \frac{|A \cap S| + |A \cap P|}{|A| + |S|} \tag{1}$$

where A is the set of predicted alignments. Note that the English-Romanian, English-Japanese and English-Vietnamese reference data only contain "sure" links, meaning that for these languages pairs, AER and F-measure are deterministically related.

2.3 Main observations

Detailed analyses of automatic word alignments, fully documented in (Ngo Ho, 2021), show that:

- Unaligned words are poorly predicted: we collect correctly/incorrectly unaligned words on the source side for the asymmetrical models. For English→ Czech, there are too few English words aligning with Czech words for `IBM-1` whereas `IBM-4` produces too many unaligned English words (Figure 1).
- Many-to-one/one-to-many links are also poorly predicted, even with symmetrization.[5] This can be seen in Figure 2.
- Larger length differences between parallel sentences yield more errors, as shown in Figure 3. This again hints at the tendency of discrete word models to generate one-to-one alignments.

3 Studying the interaction between alignment and segmentation

3.1 Implementation

In this section, we restrict our analysis to `Fastalign` and `Eflomal` and study how their performance vary when the subword vocabulary changes. We perform the alignment between

[5]We heuristically merge two alignments with opposite directions to produce a symmetric alignment, by using the grow-diag-final (GDF) heuristic proposed in Koehn (2005).

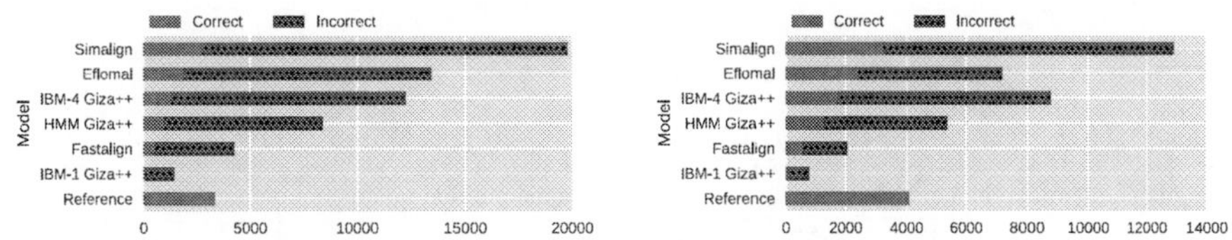

Figure 1: Number of correctly/incorrectly unaligned English and Czech words for English→Czech (left) and Czech→English (right).

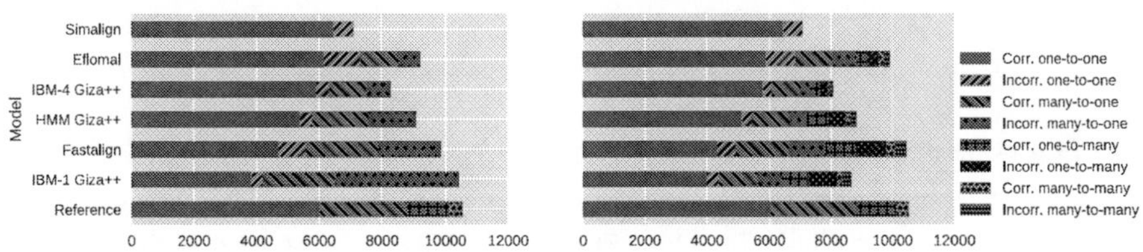

Figure 2: Alignment types for asymmetrical alignments for English→German (left) and symmetrical alignments using Grow-diag-final (right).

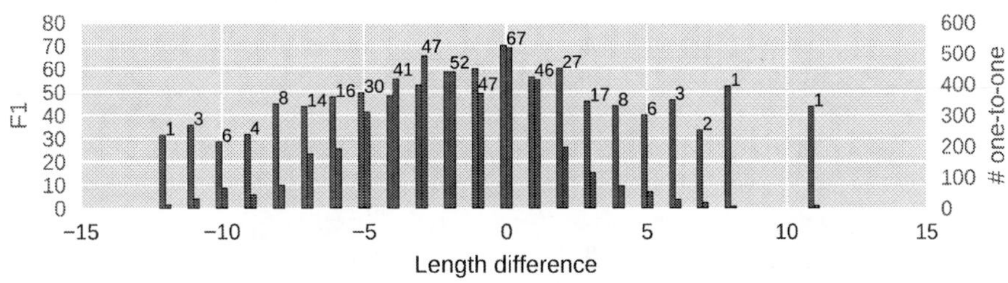

Figure 3: F-score (red) and number of correct one-to-one alignments (blue) as a function of a length difference for the direction English-French, computed by `Fastalign`. The numbers in black are the corresponding number of sentences.

subword units generated by Byte-Pair-Encoding (Sennrich et al., 2016) and the unigram method of (Kudo, 2018), both implemented with the SentencePiece package (Kudo and Richardson, 2018). All parameters of these models are set to their default values. We independently segment sentences in each language with varying vocabulary sizes $V \in \{2K, 4K, 8K, 16K, 32K, 48K\}$. For Japanese, we do not use the vocabulary size of 2K because it is smaller than the character-based vocabulary size. For English-Vietnamese, experiments for English vocabulary size of 48K and Vietnamese vocabulary size larger than 32K were not performed. This is because they would imply larger vocabularies than their word-based counterparts. When using the sampling strategy of SentencePiece, we use $\alpha = 0.1$.

Our results and analyses are however based on *word-level alignments*. Subword-level alignments are thus converted into word-level alignments as follows: a link between a source and a target word exists if there is at least one alignment link between their any of their subwords.

English+ Model	French En-Fr	French Fr-En	German En-De	German De-En	Romanian En-Ro	Romanian Ro-En	Czech En-Cz	Czech Cz-En	Japanese En-Ja	Japanese Ja-En	Vietnamese En-Vi	Vietnamese Vi-En
Fastalign												
Word	15.1	**16.2**	28.9	31.2	33.3	**32.9**	25.7	25.3	50.6	49.3	48.8	32.8
BPE	**14.7** (32K-32K)	16.3 (8K-8K)	**26.7** (4K-32K)	**29.3** (16K, 16K)	**31.4** (16K-8K)	35.0 (16K-2K)	**24.6** (16K-32K)	**24.3** (32K-16K)	**47.5** (8K-8K)	**46.9** (8K-16K)	**45.7** (4K-4K)	**29.5** (4K-8K)
Unigram	18.6 (45K-16K)	20.1 (48K-32K)	31.3 (4K-48K)	33.2 (16K-16K)	36.6 (39K-16K)	40.0 (32K-4K)	30.5 (16K-32K)	31.4 (48K-16K)	49.7 (8K-8K)	48.0 (8K-32K)	49.3 (16K-2K)	35.3 (4K-8K)
Eflomal												
Word	8.0	8.7	22.8	24.8	26.3	25.4	14.1	13.4	46.5	46.7	44.1	27.6
BPE	**6.1** (16K-32K)	**7.7** (32K-16K)	**20.7** (4K-32K)	**21.7** (32K-16K)	**24.4** (16K-48K)	**24.5** (8K-48K)	**12.5** (8K-32K)	**11.9** (48K-16K)	**42.5** (8K-32K)	**41.7** (8K-32K)	**36.1** (2K-8K)	**24.9** (2K-32K)
Unigram	11.3 (45K-48K)	14.4 (32K-32K)	23.9 (32K-32K)	26.7 (48K-32K)	26.9 (32K-48K)	28.7 (48K-16K)	17.5 (32K-32K)	17.5 (48K-16K)	45.3 (16K-8K)	42.7 (30K-16K)	43.5 (16K-8K)	29.7 (2K-16K)

Table 2: AER scores of subword-based models and word-based models. We only report the best result obtained by subword-based models, and the corresponding vocabulary sizes.

3.2 Main results

In order to observe how the alignment accuracy varies with the size of the subword vocabulary, we plot precision and recall as a function of the target vocabulary size for each source vocabulary size. As can be seen in Figure 4, having short units (top-left zones) on both sides yields a better recall but a much worse precision. The opposite trend is found in bottom-right zones where we approach word-based models. Note that however with a proper choice of unit size, BPE-based models are able to outperform their word-based counterparts, with a gain of about 2 AER points. This improvement is not clear for unigram-based models (see Table 2).

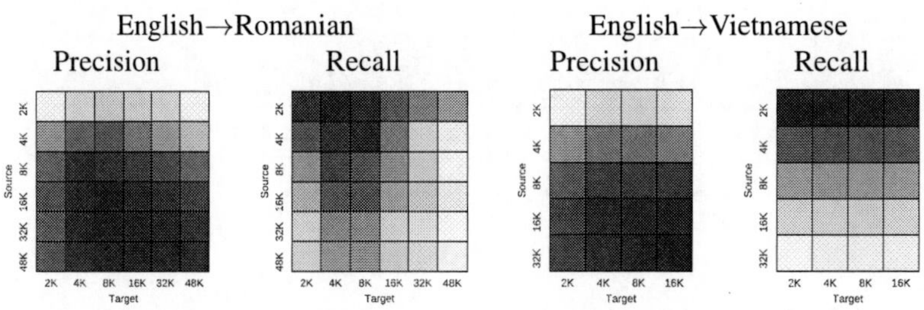

Figure 4: Precision and recall of BPE-based alignments for English→Romanian and English→Vietnamese, computed by Fastalign. The darker the cell, the greater the score.

3.3 Complementary analyses

3.3.1 Unaligned words and alignment types

Figure 5 displays unaligned word patterns generated by several BPE-based models for English-German. Choosing small inventories on the target side yields more fragmented sequences and a reduced number of non-aligned words in the source, as is expected for asymmetrical models. Significantly increasing both recall and precision proves difficult, and we only observe small improvements with respect to the word-based baselines: for instance, with Fastalign, the best BPE-model (4K-32K) removes 40 incorrectly unaligned words and finds 10 correctly unaligned words. Compared with HMM or IBM-4, we also notice that BPE-based models are less prone to over-generate null links. Similar trends were observed for the other language pairs/directions.

We now study how the number of links for each alignment type changes with the vocabulary size (Figure 6). The most noticeable observation is that shorter BPE units (e.g., 2K-2K) generate less one-to-one links and accordingly more of the other alignment types, especially one-to-many

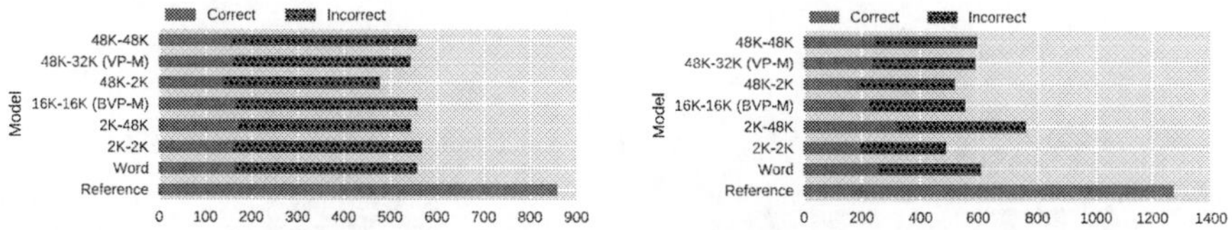

Figure 5: Number of correctly/incorrectly unaligned English (left) and German (right) words generated by `Fastalign` for respectively the directions English-German and German-English. VP-M denotes the vocabulary pair for which the average length difference between source and target sentences is smallest; BVP-M denotes the vocabulary pair yielding the best AER.

and many-to-many links. In other words, tokens that decompose into a sequence of shorter units in the source side have more chance to align with several target tokens. However, this does not result in an increased number of correct one-to-many/many-to-many links. Similar trends were observed for the other language pairs/directions.

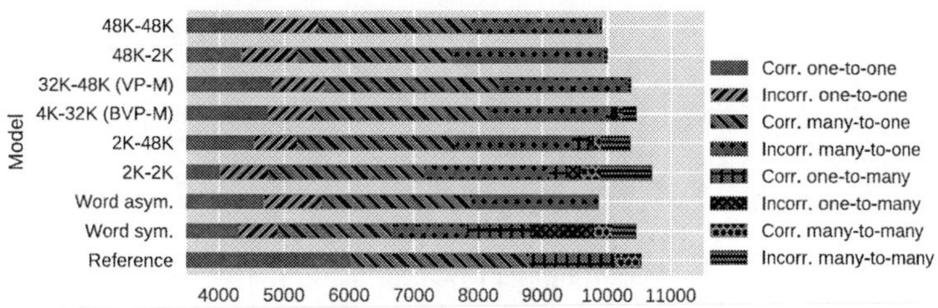

Figure 6: Alignment errors for BPE-based, word-based asymmetrical (Word asym.) and symmetrical alignments (Word sym.) computed by `Fastalign` for English→German.

3.3.2 Aligning rare words

Using subwords affects the overall distribution of units and helps mitigate issues with rare tokens. To measure this effect, we collect rare source words (a word is rare if it occurs once in our training data) and plot their F-scores as a function of target and source vocabulary sizes (see Figure 7). Recall that German has a very large word-based vocabulary size (Table 1). Accordingly, for the German-English direction, we can see a large gain (about +8 points) in F-score when using a reduced German vocabulary size of 32K.

3.4 Improving alignment by voting

As a final experiment, we combine multiple BPE-based alignments using a simple voting procedure.This method is parameterized by the required level of agreement (the percentage of models agreeing on an alignment link). Figure 8 shows that considering the BPE models described above and using an agreement level of 70% improves the F-score by almost 2 points for German→English and Japanese→English. Similar results are obtained for the other language pairs, showing that considering multiple segmentations in alignment can be helpful.

4 Optimizing subword tokenization

In this section, we build on the intuition that pairs of sentences which differ in length are difficult to align (Deguchi et al., 2020), suggesting that subword splitting should be used to make the

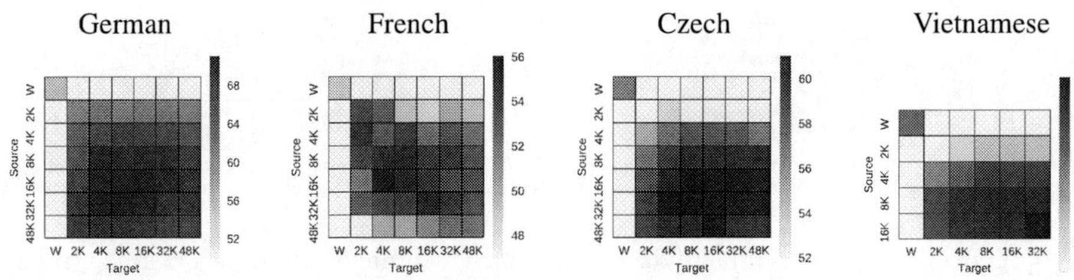

Figure 7: F-scores obtained with `Fastalign` as a function of source and target vocabulary sizes for rare source words in German, French, Czech and Vietnamese, when translating into English. The word-based vocabulary size is denoted W.

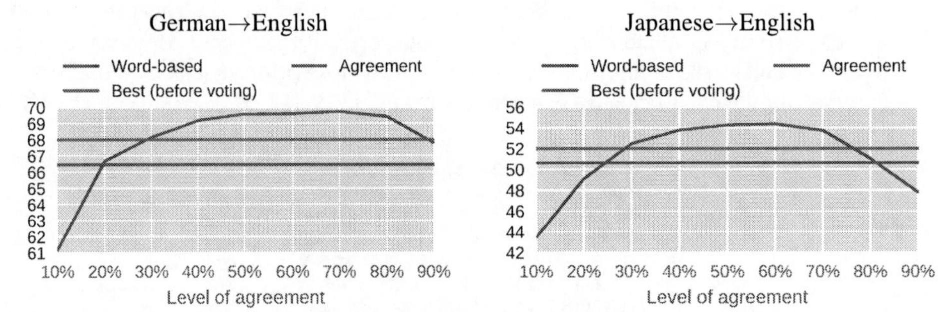

Figure 8: F-score for word-based model (blue line) and for the best BPE-based model (green line). The red curve plots the F-score for each level of agreement for German→English and Japanese→English. For both directions, voting improves the AER of about 2 pts with a 70% level of agreement.

length of parallel sentences more even. We study global and local ways to achieve this goal.

4.1 Global methods for controlling length differences

We first consider two ways to find the vocabulary pair minimizing the average length difference:

- the first one (denoted VP-M) simply picks the vocabulary pair that minimizes this value in the matrix of all vocabulary pairs;
- this solution can be improved using the following greedy search procedure (VP-GS): we compute the average sequence length difference for a vocabulary pair based on a pre-defined search space radius. If we find a new vocabulary pair producing a smaller average than the current pair, we continue to explore the neighbors of this new pair. We reduce the search space radius ε in the case that no new pair is found.[6] Details are in algorithm 1.[7]

We collect the average F-score, length difference and English vocabulary size for all language pairs and directions (see Table 3). For BPE-based models, minimizing length difference between the source and target sentence outperforms word-based models with a gain of at least 1 point in F-score. This performance is close to the best results found from the matrix of vocabulary pair. Unigram-based models fail to match such performance, but we still observe an

[6]The step size ρ remains the same for the whole procedure.

[7]$f(\alpha, \beta)$ returns the average sequence length difference obtained with vocabularies of size α and β.

Method		F-score		Length difference		# English voc.	
		`Fastalign`	`Eflomal`	`Fastalign`	`Eflomal`	`Fastalign`	`Eflomal`
Word		58.7	64.0	4.23		72K	
BPE	BVP-M	**60.4**	**66.3**	5.0	5.5	9K	16.5K
	VP-M	59.6	66.1	3.56		26K	
	VP-GS	59.8	65.5	3.51		~21K	
Unigram	BVP-M	57.1	63.8	5.7	5.5	20K	21.6K
	VP-M	56.2	62.9	4.8		17K	
	VP-GS	**58.4**	**64.4**	4.5		~18K	

Table 3: Average F-score (over language pairs and directions) for global methods of controlling sequence length difference for `Fastalign` and `Eflomal`. We also report the best vocabulary pair found in the vocabulary pair matrix (BVP-M).

improvement for the greedy search, which outperforms the word-based models for `Eflomal` for English-French, English-German, English-Japanese and English-Vietnamese.

Algorithm 1 Finding the vocabulary pair minimizing the average length differences

Require:
α: Source side vocabulary size; β: Target side vocabulary size
ε: search space radius (default = 2000);
ρ: step size (default = 100);
Ensure: $1000 \leq \alpha, \beta \leq 50000$
while $\varepsilon \geq 100$ **do**
  for $\nu \in \{\alpha - \varepsilon, \alpha, \alpha + \varepsilon\}$, $\mu \in \{\beta - \varepsilon, \beta, \beta + \varepsilon\}$ **do**
    if $f(\nu, \mu) < f(\alpha, \beta)$ **then**
      $\alpha = \nu$; $\beta = \mu$; $\epsilon = 2000$
    end if
  end for
  if α and β remain the same **then**
    $\varepsilon = \varepsilon - \rho$
  end if
end while

4.2 Local methods for controlling the length difference

The methods presented above consider ways to optimize the length difference at the corpus level, using one subword vocabulary that is used across the board. We study here four *local* methods that aim to reduce the length differences *separately for each sentence pair* before training the alignment procedure. With the exception of the first method, they all rely on the unigram algorithm, and use a fixed, predefined, vocabulary size for both languages:

- the first (SP-M) simply picks, among all the considered segmentations of each sentence, the one that minimizes the length difference. When there is more than one minimal segmentation, we select the one for which total source and target lengths is smallest;
- the second[8] (SM1-1VP) relies on the idea of Deguchi et al. (2020): (a) we collect the 10 most likely segmentations for each language using the unigram algorithm; (b) we select the highest probability candidate on both sides, and consider the longer of the two as the

[8]This method and next only apply to unigram, which, contrarily to BPE, is based on a sound probabilistic model.

anchor segmentation; (c) we pair this segmentation with the one, in the other language, that is closest in length and maximally likely. We also consider the case SM5-1VP where we include the top five highest probability in the last step for the training data.

- SSM5-1VP extends the previous idea with more candidates: we sample 10 segmentations using the unigram algorithm for each language, then select the 5 pairs of segmentations that have the smallest length difference, and use it as the training data for the word alignment;
- a last idea (SSM5-GS) uses the same strategy as SSM5-1VP, using the "optimal" pair of vocabulary sizes computed by the greedy search algorithm (Algorithm 1).

We always consider one single pair of segmentations for the test data: we chose the highest probability pair for SM5-1VP and one pair producing the smallest length difference for SSM5-*.

For BPE-based models (Figure 9), SP-M only outperforms the word-based model for English-French and English-Vietnamese, and fails to achieve better F-scores than the two global methods. The performance of unigram-baseds method (assuming vocabularies of sizes 16K-16K) is displayed in Figure 10. They all outperform the baseline (a fixed 16K-16K model) and also the word-based models for French, Japanese and Vietnamese. It also seems that including several segmentation samples for each sentence pair in the training data (as in SSM5-1VP) also helps to improve the performance, resulting in a simple scheme based only on length differences, that consistently outperforms all other unigram-based methods. These results open perspectives for further improving these models, especially for German, Czech and Romanian, for which the 16K-16K setting might be suboptimal. The last method (SSM5-GS) does not succeed in improving SSM5-1VP. Similar observations hold for Eflomal, albeit with better baselines.

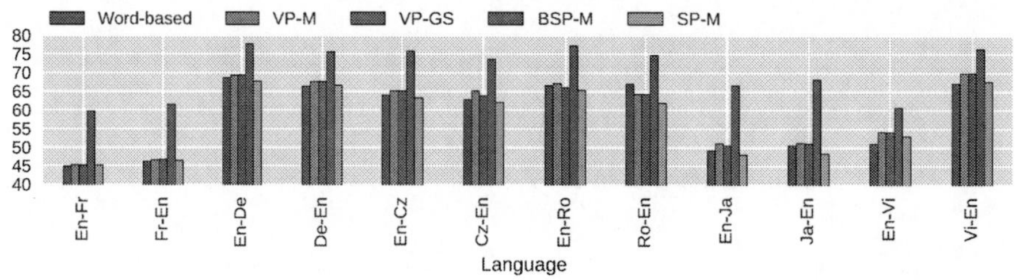

Figure 9: F-scores for BPE-based segmentations. We compare global methods (VP-M and VP-GS) with SP-M and also display scores obtained with best segmentation for each sentence pair (BSP-M), which provides us with an *oracle value*. Alignments are computed by `Fastalign`.

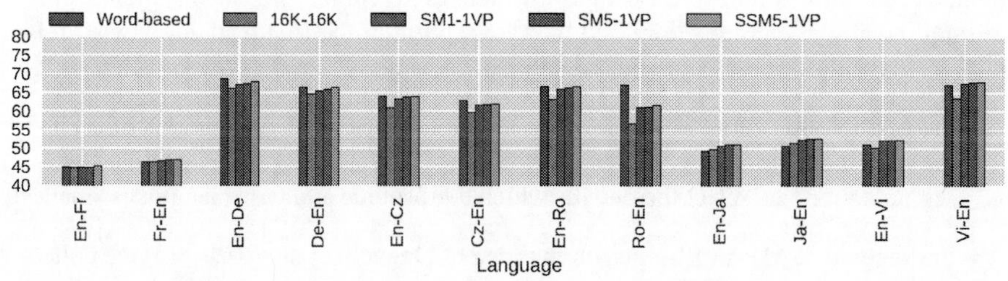

Figure 10: F-scores for unigram-based local strategies; alignments computed by `Fastalign`.

5 Related work

Subword segmentation is introduced in the context of neural translation in (Sennrich et al., 2016), using a reimplementation[9] of the Byte Pair Encoding algorithm of Gage (1994). BPE is a greedy, bottom up algorithm that recursively aggregates frequent bigrams into new symbols, and is thoroughly analyzed in (Gallé, 2019). The main alternative is SentencePiece introduced in (Kudo, 2018; Kudo and Richardson, 2018), which implements a form of variable-length probabilistic unigram model, which can be traced back to (Deligne and Bimbot, 1995).

With BPE/unigram subtokenization becoming a standard for many applications, several studies have started to investigate more closely the impact on these preprocessing decisions on the final performance. The implementation of SentencePiece[10] reports a large number of MT experiments aimed to compare BPE and unigram in multiple conditions, concluding that both yield comparable BLEU scores across the board when used with a fixed tokenization in words.

The shortcomings of BPE/unigram segmentations have been the subject of several studies, reporting comparisons with (a) linguistic segmentations (Huck et al., 2017; Ataman et al., 2017; Banerjee and Bhattacharyya, 2018; Weller-Di Marco and Fraser, 2020) and (b) alternative pre-processing schemes such as character-based models (eg. in Sennrich (2017); Sajjad et al. (2017); Cherry et al. (2018)). Ding et al. (2019) conduct a systematic exploration considering a large numbers of vocabulary sizes to better understand its impact on NMT performance, comparing several NMT architectures such as shallow/deep-transformer, tiny/shallow/deep-LSTM. Bostrom and Durrett (2020) evaluate the impact of tokenization on language model pre-training. They conclude that tokenization encodes a surprising amount of inductive bias and that LM-based tokenization produces subword units that qualitatively align with morphology much better than those produced by BPE, suggesting that the latter is better than the former for pretrained models.

The work of Deguchi et al. (2020) is our main inspiration, and explore ways to optimize the subword segmentation, using, as we do, sampling techniques and length-based heuristics to chose the most appropriate target for each source, and observing gains in translation performance.

6 Conclusion and outlook

In this work, we have studied the interaction between word alignment and word segmentation based on two algorithms (BPE and unigram) and multiple word aligners. Using smaller units notably mitigate issues with rare/unknown words; shorter units also help to retrieve more correct links for non-canonical (one-to-many, many-to-one) alignment links. Based on these observations, we have thoroughly analyzed the variation of alignment scores with respect to vocabulary sizes, showing that the word-based segmentation was less than optimal. We have finally explored various ways to actively optimize the subword tokenization; promising results in this direction have been obtained with the unigram algorithm, owing to its ability to generate multiple high-probability segmentations. We have notably found that adjusting length differences in source and target was a reasonable heuristic to progress towards better joint tokenizations, even though (a) the relationship between length difference and alignment quality was not as clear as one may have wished; (b) inconsistencies have been observed between unigram and BPE. In the future, we will continue to explore inexpensive ways to identify promising joint segmentations and improve the alignment between subword units.

Acknowledgements

This work has been made possible thanks to the Saclay-IA computing platform.

[9]https://github.com/rsennrich/subword-nmt

[10]https://github.com/google/sentencepiece/blob/master/doc/experiments.md

References

Alkhouli, T., Bretschner, G., and Ney, H. (2018). On the alignment problem in multi-head attention-based neural machine translation. In *Proceedings of the Third Conference on Machine Translation: Research Papers*, pages 177–185, Brussels, Belgium. Association for Computational Linguistics.

Alkhouli, T. and Ney, H. (2017). Biasing attention-based recurrent neural networks using external alignment information. In *Proceedings of the Second Conference on Machine Translation*, pages 108–117, Copenhagen, Denmark. Association for Computational Linguistics.

Ataman, D., Negri, M., Turchi, M., and Federico, M. (01 Jun. 2017). Linguistically motivated vocabulary reduction for neural machine translation from turkish to english. *The Prague Bulletin of Mathematical Linguistics*, 108(1):331 – 342.

Banerjee, T. and Bhattacharyya, P. (2018). Meaningless yet meaningful: Morphology grounded subword-level NMT. In *Proceedings of the Second Workshop on Subword/Character LEvel Models*, pages 55–60, New Orleans. Association for Computational Linguistics.

Bostrom, K. and Durrett, G. (2020). Byte pair encoding is suboptimal for language model pretraining. In *Findings of the Association for Computational Linguistics: EMNLP 2020*, pages 4617–4624, Online. Association for Computational Linguistics.

Chen, C., Sun, M., and Liu, Y. (2021). Mask-align: Self-supervised neural word alignment. *CoRR*, abs/2012.07162.

Chen, Y., Liu, Y., Chen, G., Jiang, X., and Liu, Q. (2020). Accurate word alignment induction from neural machine translation. In *Proceedings of the 2020 Conference on Empirical Methods in Natural Language Processing (EMNLP)*, pages 566–576, Online. Association for Computational Linguistics.

Cherry, C., Foster, G., Bapna, A., Firat, O., and Macherey, W. (2018). Revisiting character-based neural machine translation with capacity and compression. In *Proceedings of the 2018 Conference on Empirical Methods in Natural Language Processing*, EMNLP'18, pages 4295–4305, Brussels, Belgium. Association for Computational Linguistics.

Deguchi, H., Utiyama, M., Tamura, A., Ninomiya, T., and Sumita, E. (2020). Bilingual subword segmentation for neural machine translation. In *Proceedings of the 28th International Conference on Computational Linguistics*, pages 4287–4297, Barcelona, Spain (Online). International Committee on Computational Linguistics.

Deligne, S. and Bimbot, F. (1995). Language modeling by variable length sequences: Theoretical formulation and evaluation of multigrams. In *Acoustics, Speech, and Signal Processing, 1995. ICASSP-95., 1995 International Conference on*, volume 1, pages 169–172.

Devlin, J., Chang, M., Lee, K., and Toutanova, K. (2019). BERT: pre-training of deep bidirectional transformers for language understanding. In Burstein, J., Doran, C., and Solorio, T., editors, *Proceedings of the 2019 Conference of the North American Chapter of the Association for Computational Linguistics: Human Language Technologies, NAACL-HLT 2019, Minneapolis, MN, USA, June 2-7, 2019, Volume 1 (Long and Short Papers)*, pages 4171–4186. Association for Computational Linguistics.

Ding, S., Renduchintala, A., and Duh, K. (2019). A call for prudent choice of subword merge operations in neural machine translation. In *Proceedings of Machine Translation Summit XVII Volume 1: Research Track*, pages 204–213, Dublin, Ireland. European Association for Machine Translation.

Dou, Z.-Y. and Neubig, G. (2021). Word alignment by fine-tuning embeddings on parallel corpora. In *Proceedings of the 16th Conference of the European Chapter of the Association for Computational Linguistics: Main Volume*, pages 2112–2128, Online. Association for Computational Linguistics.

Dyer, C., Chahuneau, V., and Smith, N. A. (2013). A simple, fast, and effective reparameterization of ibm model 2. In *Proceedings of the 2013 Conference of the North American Chapter of the Association for Computational Linguistics: Human Language Technologies*, pages 644–648, Atlanta, Georgia. Association for Computational Linguistics.

Gage, P. (1994). A new algorithm for data compression. *Computer Users Journal*, 12(2):23–38.

Gallé, M. (2019). Investigating the effectiveness of BPE: The power of shorter sequences. In *Proceedings of the 2019 Conference on Empirical Methods in Natural Language Processing and the 9th International Joint Conference on Natural Language Processing (EMNLP-IJCNLP)*, pages 1375–1381, Hong Kong, China. Association for Computational Linguistics.

Garg, S., Peitz, S., Nallasamy, U., and Paulik, M. (2019). Jointly learning to align and translate with transformer models. In *Proc. IJCNLP-EMNLP*, Hong Kong, China.

Huck, M., Riess, S., and Fraser, A. (2017). Target-side word segmentation strategies for neural machine translation. In *Proceedings of the Second Conference on Machine Translation*, pages 56–67, Copenhagen, Denmark. Association for Computational Linguistics.

Jalili Sabet, M., Dufter, P., Yvon, F., and Schütze, H. (2020). SimAlign: High quality word alignments without parallel training data using static and contextualized embeddings. In *Findings of the Association for Computational Linguistics: EMNLP 2020*, pages 1627–1643, Online.

Koehn, P. (2005). Europarl: A Parallel Corpus for Statistical Machine Translation. In *Conference Proceedings: the tenth Machine Translation Summit*, pages 79–86, Phuket, Thailand. AAMT, AAMT.

Koehn, P. (2010). *Statistical Machine Translation*. Cambridge University Press, New York, NY, USA, 1st edition.

Kudo, T. (2018). Subword regularization: Improving neural network translation models with multiple subword candidates. In Gurevych, I. and Miyao, Y., editors, *Proceedings of the 56th Annual Meeting of the Association for Computational Linguistics, ACL 2018, Melbourne, Australia, July 15-20, 2018, Volume 1: Long Papers*, pages 66–75. Association for Computational Linguistics.

Kudo, T. and Richardson, J. (2018). SentencePiece: A simple and language independent subword tokenizer and detokenizer for neural text processing. In *Proceedings of the 2018 Conference on Empirical Methods in Natural Language Processing: System Demonstrations*, pages 66–71, Brussels, Belgium. Association for Computational Linguistics.

Legrand, J., Auli, M., and Collobert, R. (2016). Neural network-based word alignment through score aggregation. In *Proceedings of the First Conference on Machine Translation*, pages 66–73, Berlin, Germany. Association for Computational Linguistics.

Liu, C., Liu, Y., Sun, M., Luan, H., and Yu, H. (2015). Generalized agreement for bidirectional word alignment. In *Proceedings of the 2015 Conference on Empirical Methods in Natural Language Processing*, pages 1828–1836, Lisbon, Portugal. Association for Computational Linguistics.

Luong, M.-T. and Manning, C. D. (2015). Stanford neural machine translation systems for spoken language domain. In *International Workshop on Spoken Language Translation*, Da Nang, Vietnam.

Mareček, D. (2016). Czech-English manual word alignment. Technical report, LINDAT/CLARIN digital library at the Institute of Formal and Applied Linguistics (ÚFAL), Faculty of Mathematics and Physics, Charles University.

Mihalcea, R. and Pedersen, T. (2003). An evaluation exercise for word alignment. In *Proceedings of the HLT-NAACL 2003 Workshop on Building and Using Parallel Texts: Data Driven Machine Translation and Beyond - Volume 3*, HLT-NAACL-PARALLEL '03, pages 1–10, Stroudsburg, PA, USA. Association for Computational Linguistics.

Nagata, M., Chousa, K., and Nishino, M. (2020). A supervised word alignment method based on cross-language span prediction using multilingual BERT. In *Proceedings of the 2020 Conference on Empirical Methods in Natural Language Processing (EMNLP)*, pages 555–565, Online. Association for Computational Linguistics.

Neubig, G. (2011). The Kyoto free translation task. http://www.phontron.com/kftt.

Ngo Ho, A. K. (2021). *Generative Probabilistic Alignment Models for Words and Subwords : a Systematic Exploration of the Limits and Potentials of Neural Parametrizations*. PhD thesis, Université Paris-Saclay.

Ngo-Ho, A.-K. and Yvon, F. (2019). Neural Baselines for Word Alignments. In *Proc. IWSLT*, Hong-Kong, China.

Och, F. J. (2003). Minimum error rate training in statistical machine translation. In *Proceedings of the 41st Annual Meeting on Association for Computational Linguistics - Volume 1*, ACL '03, pages 160–167, Stroudsburg, PA, USA. Association for Computational Linguistics.

Och, F. J. and Ney, H. (2003). A systematic comparison of various statistical alignment models. *Comput. Linguistics*, 29(1):19–51.

Östling, R. and Tiedemann, J. (2016). Efficient word alignment with Markov Chain Monte Carlo. *Prague Bulletin of Mathematical Linguistics*, 106:125–146.

Pham, M. Q., Crego, J., Senellart, J., and Yvon, F. (2018). Fixing translation divergences in parallel corpora for neural MT. In *Proceedings of the 2018 Conference on Empirical Methods in Natural Language Processing*, pages 2967–2973, Brussels, Belgium.

Sajjad, H., Dalvi, F., Durrani, N., Abdelali, A., Belinkov, Y., and Vogel, S. (2017). Challenging language-dependent segmentation for Arabic: An application to machine translation and part-of-speech tagging. In *Proceedings of the 55th Annual Meeting of the Association for Computational Linguistics (Volume 2: Short Papers)*, pages 601–607, Vancouver, Canada. Association for Computational Linguistics.

Sennrich, R. (2017). How grammatical is character-level neural machine translation? assessing MT quality with contrastive translation pairs. In *Proceedings of the 15th Conference of the European Chapter of the Association for Computational Linguistics: Volume 2, Short Papers*, pages 376–382. Association for Computational Linguistics.

Sennrich, R., Haddow, B., and Birch, A. (2016). Neural machine translation of rare words with subword units. In *Proceedings of the 54th Annual Meeting of the Association for Computational Linguistics (Volume 1: Long Papers)*, pages 1715–1725, Berlin, Germany. Association for Computational Linguistics.

Specia, L., Scarton, C., Paetzold, G. H., and Hirst, G. (2018). *Quality Estimation for Machine Translation*. Morgan & Claypool Publishers.

Stahlberg, F., Saunders, D., and Byrne, B. (2018). An operation sequence model for explainable neural machine translation. In *Proceedings of the 2018 EMNLP Workshop BlackboxNLP: Analyzing and Interpreting Neural Networks for NLP*, pages 175–186, Brussels, Belgium. Association for Computational Linguistics.

Tiedemann, J. (2011). *Bitext Alignment*. Synthesis Lectures on Human Language Technologies. Morgan & Claypool Publishers.

Tiedemann, J. (2012). Parallel data, tools and interfaces in opus. In Chair), N. C. C., Choukri, K., Declerck, T., Dogan, M. U., Maegaard, B., Mariani, J., Odijk, J., and Piperidis, S., editors, *Proceedings of the Eight International Conference on Language Resources and Evaluation (LREC'12)*, Istanbul, Turkey. European Language Resources Association (ELRA).

Tomeh, N., Allauzen, A., and Yvon, F. (2014). Maximum-entropy word alignment and posterior-based phrase extraction for machine translation. *Machine Translation*, 28(1):19–56.

Vaswani, A., Shazeer, N., Parmar, N., Uszkoreit, J., Jones, L., Gomez, A. N., Kaiser, L., and Polosukhin, I. (2017). Attention is all you need. In Guyon, I., von Luxburg, U., Bengio, S., Wallach, H. M., Fergus, R., Vishwanathan, S. V. N., and Garnett, R., editors, *Advances in Neural Information Processing Systems 30: Annual Conference on Neural Information Processing Systems 2017, 4-9 December 2017, Long Beach, CA, USA*, pages 5998–6008.

Wang, H. and Lepage, Y. (2016). Yet another symmetrical and real-time word alignment method: Hierarchical sub-sentential alignment using f-measure. In Park, J. C. and Chung, J., editors, *Proceedings of the 30th Pacific Asia Conference on Language, Information and Computation, PACLIC 30, Seoul, Korea, October 28 - October 30, 2016*. ACL.

Weller-Di Marco, M. and Fraser, A. (2020). Modeling word formation in English–German neural machine translation. In *Proceedings of the 58th Annual Meeting of the Association for Computational Linguistics*, pages 4227–4232. Association for Computational Linguistics.

Introducing Mouse Actions into Interactive-Predictive Neural Machine Translation

Angel Navarro annamar8@prhlt.upv.es
Francisco Casacuberta fcn@prhlt.upv.es
Patter Recognition and Human Language Technology Research Center, Universitat Politècnica de València - Camino de Vera s/n, 46022 Valencia, Spain

Abstract

The quality of the translations generated by Machine Translation (MT) systems has highly improved through the years, but we are still far away to obtain fully automatic high-quality translations. To generate them, translators use Computer-Assisted Translation (CAT) tools, among which we find the Interactive-Predictive Machine Translation (IPMT) systems. This paper uses bandit feedback as the principal and only information needed to generate new predictions that correct the previous translations. Furthermore, the application of bandit feedback reduces the number of words that the translator needs to type in an IPMT session. In conclusion, this technique saves valuable time, and effort for translators. Moreover, its performance improves improves with the future advances in MT, so we recommend its application in the actuals IPMT systems.

1 Introduction

In recent years there had been a large number of advances in the Machine Translation (MT) field that has led to a significant improvement in the quality of the translations. Currently, even with all the new advances, the MT systems are still not able to generate perfect ready to use translations (Toral, 2020). Indeed, MT systems usually require human post-editing in order to achieve perfect translations.

The Computer-Assisted Translation (CAT) tools aim to generate high-quality translations using the knowledge and experience of professional translators while reducing the effort that they need to do. There is a large variety of CAT tools approaches, among which we focus on the Interactive-Predictive Machine Translation (IPMT) systems.

Some of the recent projects in this field are TransType (Langlais et al., 2000; Esteban et al., 2004; Cubel et al., 2003), Matecat (Federico et al., 2014), CasMacat (Alabau et al., 2014, 2013; Sanchis-Trilles et al., 2014) and MMPE (Herbig et al., 2020). They aim to create a workbench with an array of innovative features that were not available in other tools when they started. IPMT is one of the main paradigms that include these projects, where an expert translator provides feedback to the system, typically using the keyboard and mouse, to generate new predictions that correct previous errors.

There are two main IPMT approaches, both use usually the keyboard and mouse as the main feedback interface, but the validation process changes between prefix (Foster et al., 1997) and segments (Peris et al., 2017; Domingo et al., 2017). In this project, we use the validation by prefix approach. Figure 1 illustrates a conventional IPMT session. Initially, the user is provided with a source sentence x to be translated. At iteration 0, the IPMT system generates the first

SOURCE (x):		Una versión traducida de un texto.
REFERENCE (y):		A translated version of a text.
ITER-0	(**p**)	()
	($\hat{s}_h$)	*A written version of a story.*
ITER-1	(**p**)	A
	(s_t)	*written version of a story.*
	(k)	translated
	($\hat{s}_h$)	*version of a text.*
ITER-2	(**p**)	A translated version of a text.
	(s_t)	( )
	(k)	(#)
	($\hat{s}_h$)	()
FINAL	($p \equiv y$)	A translated version of a text.

Figure 1: Example of a conventional IPMT session to translate a sentence from Spanish to English. Non-validated hypotheses are displayed in italics, and accepted prefixes are printed in normal font.

hypothesis $\hat{s}_h$. At the next iteration, the user moves the cursor to the first error of the sentence, validanting the prefix **p**, and corrects the next word typing k. With this new information, the IPMT system searches the suffix $\hat{s}_h$ with the highest probability for the validated prefix **p**. This process continues until the whole sentence is validated and the user introduces the special token '#'.

IPMT aims to reduce the effort that the experts have to made in their translation sessions while preserving high-quality translations. Indeed, in Figure 1, the user has translated correctly the source sentence performing only three actions. Normally, in a regular post-editing system, the translator would have needed to perform five actions: two mouse movements, two word strokes, and the sentence validation.

In this paper, we reduce the effort done by the user taking into account bandit feedback. The system only needs the error position to correct the sentence, information that can be provided by the user easily with an interface like a mouse. For this reason, and to simplify, we are going to suppose that the feedback is provided with the mouse, although any other interface capable to provide a sentence position or make a click could be useful.

2 Related Work

The reduction of the effort needed in the translation process is a problem that has been thoroughly studied, resulting in a large variety of approaches. Some projects have investigated which information and display are more useful to the users, like showing the word alignment information (Brown et al., 1993), setting a maximum length for the predictions displayed (Alabau et al., 2012) or just using touch-based actions (Wang et al., 2020).

Other approaches reduce the effort that the user has to do more directly: using confidence measures to reduce the number of words to check (González-Rubio et al., 2010), autocompleting the predictions typed by the user (Barrachina et al., 2009), or adding new input information to the system reduces the human effort of generating a new prediction (Sanchis-Trilles et al., 2008a).

There are also projects like Lam et al. (2018, 2019) that investigated how to reduce the human effort in an IPMT system using Reinforcement Learning. This technique lets them use new kinds of feedback to the system that they use as a reward to adjust the parameters of the model and obtain better translations.

In the paper, we take the approach introduced by Sanchis-Trilles et al. (2008a,b), demonstrating that with only the error position, the Interactive-Predictive Statistical Machine Translation (IPSMT) systems are capable of correct their translations. We apply and implement this technique on an Interactive-Predictive Neural Machine Translation (IPNMT) system, obtaining a higher reduction in the human effort.

3 Interactive-Predictive Neural MT

In this section, we see briefly the IPNMT framework. First of all, we have to see the general framework of the Neural Machine Translation (NMT) models that we use to understand how the translations are created and how we later add human feedback to the equation. This framework was introduced by Castaño and Casacuberta (1997) and has demonstrated its power in the last years (Cho et al., 2014; Klein et al., 2017). Given a sentence $x_1^J = x_1, ..., x_J$ from the source language X, to find the sentence $\hat{y}_1^{\hat{I}} = \hat{y}_1, ..., \hat{y}_{\hat{I}}$ from the target language Y, that has the highest probability of being the translation of x_1^J, the fundamental equation of the statistical approach to NMT would be:

$$\hat{y}_1^{\hat{I}} = \underset{I, y_1^I}{\arg\max} \Pr(y_1^I \mid x_1^J) \approx \underset{I, y_1^I}{\arg\max} \prod_{i=1}^{I} \mathrm{p}(y_i \mid y_1^{i-1}, x_1^J; \widehat{\Theta}) \tag{1}$$

where $\Pr(y_i|y_1^{i-1}, x_1^J)$ and $\mathrm{p}(y_i|y_1^{i-1}, x_1^J)$, are the probability distribution and the probability that assigns the neural model to the next word given the source sentence and the previous words so far. $\hat{\Theta}$ are the parameters of the neural model which are obtained from trying to minimize the minus log-likelihood on a set of parallel corpus (Shen et al., 2016).

The IPNMT framework adds the feedback generated by the human to Equation (1) to help with the translation process. When the expert translator finds an error in position p, moves the cursor and types the correct word, producing the feedback $f_1^p = f_1, ..., f_p$ where f_p is the word that the user has typed to correct the error. We add the feedback with the last generated hypothesis to Equation (1):

$$\hat{y}_1^{\hat{I}} = \underset{I, y_1^I}{\arg\max} \Pr(y_1^I \mid x_1^J, \bar{y}_1^{\bar{I}}, f_1^p) = \underset{I, y_1^I}{\arg\max} \prod_{i=1}^{I} \Pr(y_i \mid y_1^{i-1}, x_1^J, \bar{y}_1^{\bar{I}}, f_1^p) \tag{2}$$

subject to

$$\begin{array}{ll} 1 \leq i < p & f_i = y_i = \bar{y}_i \\ & f_p = y_p \neq \bar{y}_p \end{array}$$

where $\bar{y}_1^{\bar{I}} = \bar{y}_1, ..., \bar{y}_{\bar{I}}$ is the previous hypothesis, f_1^p is the feedback provided, and p is the length of the feedback. With the constraints $1 \leq i < p$ $f_i = y_i = \bar{y}_i$ and $f_p = y_p \neq \bar{y}_p$, we assure that the feedback that the expert has provided appears in the hypothesis generated by the system. As the user corrects and validates the translation from left to right, this equation can be seen as obtaining the most probable suffix for the prefix provided.

4 Enriching User-Machine Interaction

Until now, the only interface that we have explored to IPMT is the combination of keyboard and mouse. The IPMT system provides a translation, and the user corrects it by placing the cursor before the first error and typing the correct word.

In this paper, we retake the work introduced by Sanchis-Trilles et al. (2008a). We use the mouse as an interface for the user-machine interaction to provide the IPMT system the information about the position of the first error. First of all, we have to consider the two different classes of actions that can be performed with the mouse, *non-explicit* Mouse Actions (MAs) and *interaction-explicit* MAs.

4.1 Non-Explicit MA

In conventional IPMT systems, before the user types any word, he has to move the cursor to the position where he wants to make the correction. With the cursor movement, the user is already providing valuable information to the system that we can use. He validates all the previous words and tags the next as incorrect. Just with this information, the system can generate a new hypothesis, in which the prefix remains unaltered, and the suffix changes for the following hypothesis with the higher probability that starts by a different word. This action does not suppose an extra cost for the translator, it is automatically performed when the mouse already needs to be moved to perform a correction. This process does not assure that the new suffix is correct but in the worst scenario, the user behaves as in a conventional IPMT system. In Equation (2) we calculate the best hypothesis using the feedback that the user provides to the system $f_1^p = f_1, ..., f_p$ where f_p is the word that the user types to correct the error. In this new situation, the user does not provide the correct word in position p, but we know that it has to be different from the used in the previous hypothesis y_p. This situation can be expressed as follows:

$$\hat{y}_1^{\hat{I}} = \arg\max_{I, y_1^I} \Pr(y_1^I \mid x_1^J, \bar{y}_1^{\bar{I}}, f_1^p) = \arg\max_{I, y_1^I} \prod_{i=1}^{I} \Pr(y_i \mid y_1^{i-1}, x_1^J, \bar{y}_1^{\bar{I}}, f_1^p) \quad (3)$$

subject to

$$1 \leq i < p \qquad f_i = y_i = \bar{y}_i$$

$$y_p : \exists\, y_p \hat{y}_{p+1}^{\hat{I}}$$

$$y_p \hat{y}_{p+1}^{\hat{I}} = \arg\max_{\substack{I', y'_p, {y'}_{p+1}^{I} \\ y'_p \neq \bar{y}_p}} \Pr({y'}_p, {y'}_{p+1}^{I'} \mid x_1^J, y_1^{p-1}) \quad (4)$$

where y_p is the word that the system is trying to correct. To assure that the new word at position p from the suffix is different from the one used in the previous hypothesis y_p we add the constraint $y'_p \neq \bar{y}_p$ to Equation (4) that is responsible for the generation of new suffixes. $y_p \hat{y}_{p+1}^{\hat{I}}$ is the suffix with the highest probability given the source sentence and the prefix that the user has validated.

4.2 Interaction-Explicit MA

The non-explicit MAs does not suppose an extra cost for the translator. In a conventional IPMT system, the user needs to move the cursor to the correct position in order to change a word. Once the user has moved the cursor to the correct position and the system has performed a non-explicit MA, if the translation still has an error in the same position the user can perform an interaction-explicit MA. This kind of MA needs that the user explicitly executes the action of asking for a new suffix, for this reason, the interaction-explicit MAs suppose a little extra cost that can save the user the effort of typing the correct word. In the end, is the user who has to decide which kind of action performs depending on his experience.

In this project, we have used the mouse as an interface to provide to the system the position of the error, and the action of performing an interaction-explicit MA. Note that the interface used could be different, e.g. using a touch screen, or typing some special key such as `F1` or `Tab`. However, it is explained with the mouse because we found it more intuitive and understandable.

SOURCE (x):		Escriba aqu4́ la traducción.
REFERENCE (y):		Write the translation here.
ITER-0	(**p**)	()
	($\hat{s}_h$)	‖ *Write there the translation.*
ITER-1	(**p**)	Write
	(s_t)	‖ *there the translation.*
	($\hat{s}_h$)	*here the translation.*
ITER-2	(**p**)	Write
	(s_t)	‖ *here the translation.*
	($\hat{s}_h$)	*the translation here.*
ITER-3	(**p**)	Write the translation here.
	(s_t)	( )
	(k)	(#)
	($\hat{s}_h$)	()
FINAL	(**p** $\equiv$ **y**)	Write the translation here.

Figure 2: Example of an IPMT session with non-explicit and interaction-explicit MAs. At iteration 0, the user moves the cursor before '*there*', and the system provides a new suffix. At iteration 1, before manually correcting the word, the user performs an interactive-explicit MA. At iteration 3, the user validates the translation. Non-validated hypotheses are displayed in italics, and accepted prefixes are in normal font. The MAs are indicated by the symbol '‖'.

Each time we perform an MA for the same position p, we obtain a new word that we do not want to get in the new suffix. The following equation solves this problem by keeping track of the k previous hypotheses, where k is the number of MAs performed in the same position:

$$\hat{y}_1^{\hat{I}} = \arg\max_{I, y_1^I} \Pr(y_1^I \mid x_1^J, \bar{y}_1^{\bar{I}}, f_1^p, k) = \arg\max_{I, y_1^I} \prod_{i=1}^{I} \Pr(y_i \mid y_1^{i-1}, x_1^J, \bar{y}_1^{\bar{I}}, f_1^p, k) \quad (5)$$

subject to

$$1 \leq i < p \qquad f_i = y_i = \bar{y}_i$$

$$y_p : \exists\, y_p^{(k)} \hat{y}_{p+1}^{\hat{I}}$$

$$y_p^{(k)} \hat{y}_{p+1}^{\hat{I}} = \arg\max_{\substack{I', y'_p, {y'}_{p+1}^{I} \\ y'_p \notin \{\bar{y}_p, y_p^{(1)}, \ldots, y_p^{(k-1)}\}}} \Pr({y'}_p, {y'}_{p+1}^{I'} \mid x_1^J, y_1^{p-1}) \quad (6)$$

where $y_p^{(k)}$ is the word that occupies the position p of the new hypothesis when the user performs the k_{th} MA. $y_p^{(l)}$ $l < k$ are the words that have been generated before the user performs the k_{th} MA, and $\bar{y}$ is the first hypothesis generated before performing any MA in position p.

We can see an example of a conventional IPMT session where the user performs a non-explicit MA and an interactive-explicit MA in Figure 2. At iteration 0 the system provides to the user the translation, and the cursor stays at the start of the sentence. At iteration 1 the user moves the cursor to the first error, validating the prefix (p) and performing a non-explicit MA. The system automatically generates a new suffix $\hat{s}_h$ that the user has to check in the next iterations. At iteration 2, the translation is still incorrect and the user decides to perform an interactive-explicit MA to correct it. The system generates a new suffix that can not start with the words '*there*' or '*here*'. Finally, at iteration 3, the user does not see any error and validates all the sentence.

5 Experimental Setup

5.1 System Evaluation

In this article, we report our results using different metrics to measure the human effort performed in an IPMT session, differentiating between the keystrokes and the mouse actions performed. We report the effort done by the user in Word Stroke Ratio (WSR), Mouse Action Ratio (MAR), character MAR (cMAR), and useful MAR (uMAR) that gives us a reference of the mouse actions performed and the quality of them.

WSR, introduced by Tomás and Casacuberta (2006), is computed as the number of words that the user needs to type to generate the reference translation, normalized by the total number of words in the sentence. In this context, a word stroke is interpreted as a single action. Moreover, it is assumed to have a constant cost.

MAR, cMAR and uMAR were introduced by Sanchis-Trilles et al. (2008b) when they first considered the mouse actions as significant information to IPMT systems. MAR is computed as the number of MAs that the user needs to perform in order to generate the reference translation, normalized by the total number of words in the sentence. The cMAR is calculated normalizing by the total number of characters. Non-explicit and Interaction-explicit MAs have the same cost.

Lastly, uMAR indicates the amount of MAs that are useful to achieve the translation that the user has in mind i.e. the MAs that actually ending changing correctly the first word of the suffix. Formally, uMAR is defined as follows:

$$\text{uMAR} = \frac{\text{MAC} - n\text{WSC}}{\text{MAC}} \tag{7}$$

where Mouse Action Count (MAC) is the total number of MAs performed, Word Stroke Count (WSC) is the number of words typed and n is the maximum amount of MA allowed before the user types in a word. Note that in order to perform a word-stroke the user previously must have performed n MAs, so in Equation (7), we are removing from the total count of MAs those that were not useful and did not help to find the correct word.

5.2 Corpora

We conduct our experiments on the domain Europarl (Koehn, 2005). The Europarl corpus is built from the Proceedings of the European Parliament, which exists in all official languages of the European Union, and is publicly available on the internet. We use the pair of languages Deutch-English (De-En), Spanish-English (Es-En) and French-English (Fr-En) in both directions in all our experiments. Their characteristics are described in Table 1. All the corpora have been cleaned, lower-cased and tokenized using the scripts included in the toolkit Moses, developed by Koehn et al. (2007). Once we have them tokenized, we have applied the subword subdivision BPE, described in Sennrich et al. (2016), with a maximum of 32000 merges.

		De-En		Es-En		Fr-En	
Training	Sentences	751K		730K		688K	
	Avg. Length	20	21	21	20	22	20
	Run. Words	15M	16M	15M	15M	15M	14M
	Vocabulary	195K	65K	102K	64K	80K	61K
Dev.	Sentences	2000		2000		2000	
	Avg. Length	27	29	30	29	33	29
	Run. Words	55K	59K	60K	59K	67K	59K
Test	Sentences	2000		2000		2000	
	Avg. Length	27	29	30	29	33	29
	Run. Words	54K	58K	67K	58K	66K	58K

Table 1: Characteristics of the Europarl corpus. K and M stands for thousands and millions.

5.3 User Simulation

Our experiments have not used real humans to translate the source sentences interactively because it would have been costly and slow. Instead, we have simulated the expected behaviour of professional translators.

When the simulated user receives a new prediction from the IPMT system, they search for the first error of the translation, comparing the words and position from the hypothesis and the reference. Then, when the user has found an error, they perform a non-explicit MA if the mouse is not in the correct position or an interaction-explicit MA. The simulated user performs a maximum of n MAs for the same position, where n is a value set at the start of the experiment. If the error is not corrected once the user performs all the possible actions, they type the correct word looking at the reference. We repeat this process until the simulated user translates all the sentence correctly.

5.4 Model Architecture

We built our NMT models using NMT-Keras (Álvaro Peris and Casacuberta, 2018). We have tested the experiments using a Recurrent Neural Network (RNN) and a Transformer. All the systems used Adam (Kingma and Ba, 2017) as the learning algorithm, with a learning rate of 0.0002. We clipped the L_2 norm of the gradient to 5. The batch size was set to 30 and the beam size to 6.

The RNN-based NMT system used was an encoder-decoder architecture with an attention model (Chorowski et al., 2015) and LSTM cells (Hochreiter and Schmidhuber, 1997). The dimensions of the encoder, decoder, attention model and word embeddings were set to 512. We used a single hidden layer of the encoder and the decoder.

The Transformer (Vaswani et al., 2017) model used a word embedding and dimension size of 512. The hidden and output dimensions of the feed-forward layers were set to 2048 and 512. Each multi-head attention layer had 8 heads, and we stacked 6 layers of encoder and decoder.

Table 2 shows the translation performance in terms of BLEU of RNN-based and Transformer neural models.

	BLEU (↑)	
	RNN	Transformer
De-En	27.8	28.8
En-De	21.8	19.2
Es-En	32.1	32.1
En-Es	31.7	31.4
Fr-En	30.9	31.1
En-Fr	33.0	32.3

Table 2: Translation quality for the Europarl task in terms of BLEU for RNN and Transformer.

5.5 Experimental Results

The results of both models are displayed in Tables 3 and 4. There, we compare the results obtained from a conventional IPMT system, with the addition to the system of the non-explicit MAs, and the interaction-explicit MAs with a maximum of 4 explicit actions per position. By just adding the non-explicit MAs to the system, on average, the user reduces his effort by 27.45%. The models are good enough that the correct word is the second most probably from the error position. And if we take account of the interactive-explicit MAs, the reduction is 55.9%. Note how with the non-explicit MAs the MAR values remains almost identical because the non-explicit MAs does not suppose an extra cost. The differences in values are special cases where the system predicted a correct sentence different to the obtained by typing the correct word.

	baseline		non-explicit			interaction-explicit		
	MAR	WSR	MAR	WSR	WSR rel.	MAR	WSR	WSR rel.
	(↓)	(↓)	(↓)	(↓)	(↑)	(↓)	(↓)	(↑)
De-En	44.2	42.2	46.0	**31.0***	26.5	145.8	**19.2***	54.6
En-De	46.9	45.0	49.0	**34.0***	24.3	162.0	**22.7***	49.6
Es-En	41.0	38.7	42.6	**27.6**	28.6	131.2	**16.9**	56.4
En-Es	41.2	39.3	43.1	**28.8**	26.9	136.2	**17.9**	54.5
Fr-En	42.0	39.6	43.6	**28.7***	27.6	135.9	**17.6***	55.5
En-Fr	38.4	36.5	40.0	**26.2**	28.2	123.1	**15.5**	57.5

Table 3: Experimental results with RNN in the Europarl corpus when considering non-explicit and interaction-explicit MAs. Systems significantly differents from the Transformers systems are indicated with a *.

	baseline		non-explicit			interaction-explicit		
	MAR	WSR	MAR	WSR	WSR rel.	MAR	WSR	WSR rel.
	(↓)	(↓)	(↓)	(↓)	(↑)	(↓)	(↓)	(↑)
De-En	42.5	40.5	44.3	**29.1***	28.2	136.7	**17.5***	56.7
En-De	49.7	47.8	51.8	**36.2***	24.3	173.1	**24.5***	48.8
Es-En	40.5	38.2	42.2	**27.0**	29.3	127.9	**16.3**	57.4
En-Es	41.4	39.6	43.3	**28.7**	27.6	135.9	**17.8**	55.1
Fr-En	41.2	38.9	42.9	**27.3***	29.9	129.6	**16.4***	58.0
En-Fr	38.1	36.2	39.7	**25.7**	29.0	121.2	**15.3**	57.7

Table 4: Experimental results with Transformer in the Europarl corpus when considering non-explicit and interaction-explicit MAs. Systems significantly differents from the RNN systems are indicated with a *.

We have realized an ANOVA (ANalysis Of VAriance) with a confidence of the 95% comparing for each pair of languages the results obtained from the RNN and the Transformer to see if the models are statistically the same or not. The results are displayed in Tables 3 and 4, where we tagged with an asterisk the results that we have statistical significance that they are different.

Figure 3 shows the uMAR results versus the WSR obtainer for each maximum value of MAs up to five with the RNN and Transformer models. Each time that we increase the maximum number of MAs the number of errors fixed without typing the correct word is lower. If we look at the uMAR values obtained at each iteration we can understand how the reduction has worked. The uMAR values do not have a high variance, the value remains more or less the same for both models while increasing the maximum number of MAs, 35. Each time that we have increased the maximum number of MAs the 35% of the errors that were not corrected with the previous maximum are corrected now. Knowing how the uMAR value evolves, helps the human translator to choose between performing an interaction-explicit MA or typing directly the correct word.

5.6 Comparison Results

In the last years, this same approach was explored on Interactive-Predictive Statistical Machine Translation (IPSMT) systems and was tested in the Europarl corpora (Sanchis-Trilles et al., 2008b). In this section, we compare the results obtained in their project with the Statistical Machine Translation (SMT) models versus ours results with NMT models. We compare their results only with the Transformer because both models have obtained very similar results.

In Figure 4, we can see the comparison results obtained in the Europarl corpus with the SMT and NMT models. Taking into account the results obtained with a maximum of 5 MAs, the SMT models get a WSR relative improvement around 24%, while the NMT models obtained a relative improvement around 57%. From the uMAR results, we can see that in the SMT models

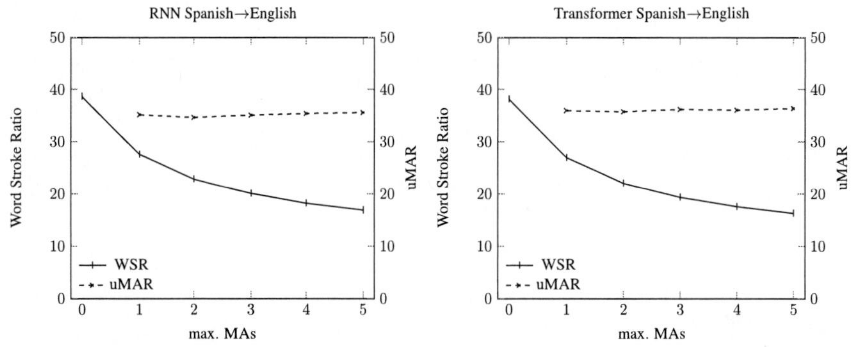

Figure 3: WSR when considering up to five maximum MAs versus uMAR with RNN and Transfromer in the Europarl corpus.

the percentage of uMAR goes from 6% to 12%, causing a lower WSR relative improvement. Meanwhile, the NMT model maintains the percentage of uMAR around 35%.

Looking at these two results we can see how the NMT models are more likely to fix an error correctly than the SMT models. Although the human interaction was simulated the same for both projects, the uMAR score that gives us the percentage of useful MAR is very different, so we can conclude that the NMT models produce better corrections with the information that we are providing.

6 Conclusions and Future Work

6.1 Conclusions

In this paper, we have implemented the use of bandit feedback to generate new predictions preserving the validated prefix. We have tested RNN and Transformer models with the Europarl corpus, and both models obtained very similar results. Both models have improved the baseline, proving that this kind of input information is useful and can reduce drastically the effort needed to correct a translation. Moreover, as the non-explicit MAs do not suppose an extra cost for the translator there are no cons to implement this approach on actual IPMT systems.

Additionally, we have compared our results with a previous work that used this same approach on SMT models, and the WSR relative improvement obtained in our experiments is greater. Proving that the NMT models obtain better results with this kind of interaction and feedback provided than the SMT models.

6.2 Future Work

In all the experiments that we have performed the user has been simulated following some basic rules. As future work, we need to test the use of mouse actions with an application where we can study the results of real humans that need to adapt to this new kind of input.

7 Acknowledgements

This work received funds from the Comunitat Valenciana under project EU-FEDER (*IDIFEDER*/2018/025), Generalitat Valenciana under project ALMAMATER (*PrometeoII*/2014/030), and Ministerio de Ciencia under project MIRANDA-DocTIUM (RTI2018-095645-B-C22).

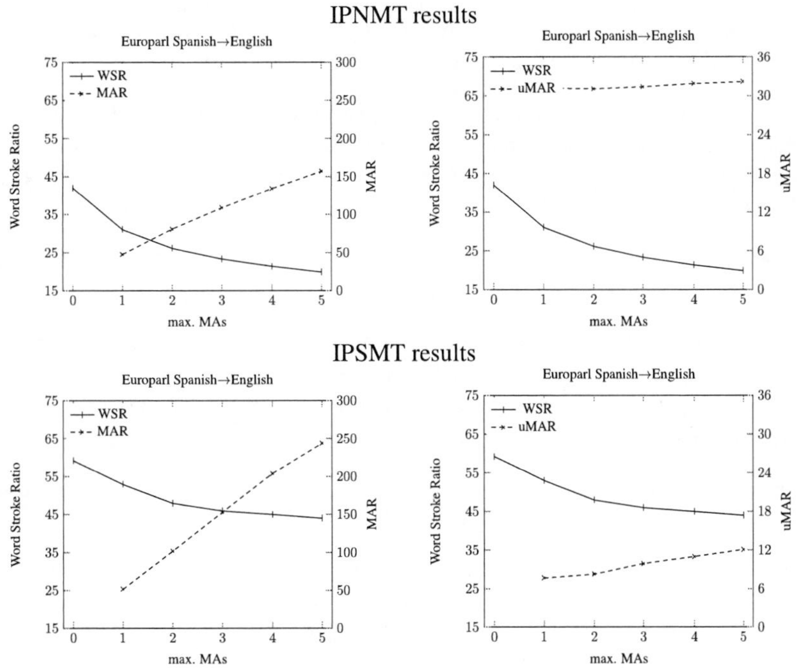

Figure 4: Comparison results with the Europarl Corpus considering up to five maximum MAs. The left column shows WSR versus MAR and in the right column shows WSR versus uMAR. Our results (up) and Sanchis-Trilles et al. (2008b) results (down)

References

Alabau, V., Bonk, R., Buck, C., Carl, M., Casacuberta, F., García-Martínez, M., González, J., Koehn, P., Leiva, L., Mesa-Lao, B., et al. (2013). Casmacat: An open source workbench for advanced computer aided translation. *The Prague Bulletin of Mathematical Linguistics*, 100(1):101–112.

Alabau, V., Buck, C., Carl, M., Casacuberta, F., García-Martínez, M., Germann, U., González-Rubio, J., Hill, R., Koehn, P., Leiva, L., Mesa-Lao, B., Ortiz-Martínez, D., Saint-Amand, H., Sanchis Trilles, G., and Tsoukala, C. (2014). CASMACAT: A computer-assisted translation workbench. In *Proceedings of the Demonstrations at the 14th Conference of the European Chapter of the Association for Computational Linguistics*, pages 25–28, Gothenburg, Sweden. Association for Computational Linguistics.

Alabau, V., Leiva, L. A., Ortiz-Martínez, D., and Casacuberta, F. (2012). User evaluation of interactive machine translation systems. In *Proceedings of the 16th Annual conference of the European Association for Machine Translation*, pages 20–23, Trento, Italy. European Association for Machine Translation.

Álvaro Peris and Casacuberta, F. (2018). NMT-Keras: a Very Flexible Toolkit with a Focus on Interactive NMT and Online Learning. *The Prague Bulletin of Mathematical Linguistics*, 111:113–124.

Barrachina, S., Bender, O., Casacuberta, F., Civera, J., Cubel, E., Khadivi, S., Lagarda, A., Ney, H., Tomás, J., Vidal, E., and Vilar, J.-M. (2009). Statistical approaches to computer-assisted translation. *Computational Linguistics*, 35(1):3–28.

Brown, P. F., Della Pietra, S. A., Della Pietra, V. J., and Mercer, R. L. (1993). The mathematics of statistical machine translation: Parameter estimation. *Computational Linguistics*, 19(2):263–311.

Castaño, A. and Casacuberta, F. (1997). A connectionist approach to machine translation. In *Fifth European Conference on Speech Communication and Technology*, pages 91–94.

Cho, K., van Merriënboer, B., Bahdanau, D., and Bengio, Y. (2014). On the properties of neural machine translation: Encoder–decoder approaches. In *Proceedings of Eighth Workshop on Syntax, Semantics and Structure in Statistical Translation*, pages 103–111, Doha, Qatar. Association for Computational Linguistics.

Chorowski, J. K., Bahdanau, D., Serdyuk, D., Cho, K., and Bengio, Y. (2015). Attention-based models for speech recognition. In *Advances in neural information processing systems*, pages 577–585.

Cubel, E., González, J., Lagarda, A., Casacuberta, F., Juan, A., and Vidal, E. (2003). Adapting finite-state translation to the TransType2 project. In *EAMT Workshop: Improving MT through other language technology tools: resources and tools for building MT*, pages 15–17, Budapest, Hungary. European Association for Machine Translation.

Domingo, M., Peris, A., and Casacuberta, F. (2017). Segment-based interactive-predictive machine translation. *Machine Translation*, 31(4):163–185.

Esteban, J., Lorenzo, J., Valderrábanos, A. S., and Lapalme, G. (2004). TransType2 - an innovative computer-assisted translation system. In *Proceedings of the ACL Interactive Poster and Demonstration Sessions*, pages 94–97, Barcelona, Spain. Association for Computational Linguistics.

Federico, M., Bertoldi, N., Cettolo, M., Negri, M., Turchi, M., Trombetti, M., Cattelan, A., Farina, A., Lupinetti, D., Martines, A., Massidda, A., Schwenk, H., Barrault, L., Blain, F., Koehn, P., Buck, C., and Germann, U. (2014). The MateCat tool. In *Proceedings of the 25th International Conference on Computational Linguistics: System Demonstrations*, pages 129–132, Dublin, Ireland. Dublin City University and Association for Computational Linguistics.

Foster, G., Isabelle, P., and Plamondon, P. (1997). Target-text mediated interactive machine translation. *Machine Translation*, 12(1):175–194.

González-Rubio, J., Ortiz-Martínez, D., and Casacuberta, F. (2010). Balancing user effort and translation error in interactive machine translation via confidence measures. In *Proceedings of the Association for Computational Linguistics 2010 Conference Short Papers*, pages 173–177, Uppsala, Sweden. Association for Computational Linguistics.

Herbig, N., Düwel, T., Pal, S., Meladaki, K., Monshizadeh, M., Krüger, A., and van Genabith, J. (2020). Mmpe: A multi-modal interface for post-editing machine translation. In *Proceedings of the 58th Annual Meeting of the Association for Computational Linguistics*, pages 1691–1702.

Hochreiter, S. and Schmidhuber, J. (1997). Long short-term memory. *Neural computation*, 9(8):1735–1780.

Kingma, D. P. and Ba, J. (2017). Adam: A method for stochastic optimization. *arXiv preprint arXiv:1412.6980.*

Klein, G., Kim, Y., Deng, Y., Senellart, J., and Rush, A. (2017). OpenNMT: Open-source toolkit for neural machine translation. In *Proceedings of the Association for Computational Linguistics 2017, System Demonstrations*, pages 67–72, Vancouver, Canada. Association for Computational Linguistics.

Koehn, P. (2005). Europarl: A parallel corpus for statistical machine translation. In *Machine Translation summit*, volume 5, pages 79–86. Citeseer.

Koehn, P., Hoang, H., Birch, A., Callison-Burch, C., Federico, M., Bertoldi, N., Cowan, B., Shen, W., Moran, C., Zens, R., Dyer, C., Bojar, O., Constantin, A., and Herbst, E. (2007). Moses: Open source toolkit for statistical machine translation. In *Proceedings of the 45th Annual Meeting of the Association for Computational Linguistics Companion Volume Proceedings of the Demo and Poster Sessions*, pages 177–180, Prague, Czech Republic. Association for Computational Linguistics.

Lam, T. K., Kreutzer, J., and Riezler, S. (2018). A reinforcement learning approach to interactive-predictive neural machine translation. *arXiv preprint arXiv:1805.01553*.

Lam, T. K., Schamoni, S., and Riezler, S. (2019). Interactive-predictive neural machine translation through reinforcement and imitation. *arXiv preprint arXiv:1907.02326*.

Langlais, P., Foster, G., and Lapalme, G. (2000). TransType: a computer-aided translation typing system. In *ANLP-NAACL 2000 Workshop: Embedded Machine Translation Systems*, pages 46–51.

Peris, Á., Domingo, M., and Casacuberta, F. (2017). Interactive neural machine translation. *Computer Speech & Language*, 45:201–220.

Sanchis-Trilles, G., Alabau, V., Buck, C., Carl, M., Casacuberta, F., García-Martínez, M., Germann, U., González-Rubio, J., Hill, R. L., Koehn, P., et al. (2014). Interactive translation prediction versus conventional post-editing in practice: a study with the casmacat workbench. *Machine Translation*, 28(3-4):217–235.

Sanchis-Trilles, G., González, M.-T., Casacuberta, F., Vidal, E., and Civera, J. (2008a). Introducing additional input information into interactive machine translation systems. In *Proceedings of International Workshop on Machine Learning for Multimodal Interaction*, pages 284–295. Springer.

Sanchis-Trilles, G., Ortiz-Martínez, D., Civera, J., Casacuberta, F., Vidal, E., and Hoang, H. (2008b). Improving interactive machine translation via mouse actions. In *Proceedings of the 2008 Conference on Empirical Methods in Natural Language Processing*, pages 485–494, Honolulu, Hawaii. Association for Computational Linguistics.

Sennrich, R., Haddow, B., and Birch, A. (2016). Neural machine translation of rare words with subword units. In *Proceedings of the 54th Annual Meeting of the Association for Computational Linguistics (Volume 1: Long Papers)*, pages 1715–1725, Berlin, Germany. Association for Computational Linguistics.

Shen, S., Cheng, Y., He, Z., He, W., Wu, H., Sun, M., and Liu, Y. (2016). Minimum risk training for neural machine translation. In *Proceedings of the 54th Annual Meeting of the Association for Computational Linguistics (Volume 1: Long Papers)*, pages 1683–1692, Berlin, Germany. Association for Computational Linguistics.

Tomás, J. and Casacuberta, F. (2006). Statistical phrase-based models for interactive computer-assisted translation. In *Proceedings of the COLING/ACL 2006 Main Conference Poster Sessions*, pages 835–841, Sydney, Australia. Association for Computational Linguistics.

Toral, A. (2020). Reassessing claims of human parity and super-human performance in machine translation at wmt 2019. *arXiv preprint arXiv:2005.05738*.

Vaswani, A., Shazeer, N., Parmar, N., Uszkoreit, J., Jones, L., Gomez, A. N., Kaiser, L., and Polosukhin, I. (2017). Attention is all you need. *arXiv preprint arXiv:1706.03762*.

Wang, Q., Zhang, J., Liu, L., Huang, G., and Zong, C. (2020). Touch editing: A flexible one-time interaction approach for translation. In *Proceedings of the 1st Conference of the Asia-Pacific Chapter of the Association for Computational Linguistics and the 10th International Joint Conference on Natural Language Processing*, pages 1–11.

Neural Machine Translation with Inflected Lexicon

Nowakowski Artur artur.nowakowski@amu.edu.pl
Faculty of Mathematics and Computer Science, Adam Mickiewicz University, Poznan, 61-614, Poland

Jassem Krzysztof jassem@amu.edu.pl
Faculty of Mathematics and Computer Science, Adam Mickiewicz University, Poznan, 61-614, Poland

Abstract

The paper presents experiments in Neural Machine Translation with lexical constraints into a morphologically rich language. In particular, we introduce a method, based on constrained decoding, which handles the inflected forms of lexical entries and does not require any modification to the training data or model architecture. To evaluate its effectiveness, we carry out experiments in two different scenarios: general and domain-specific. We compare our method with baseline translation, i.e. translation without lexical constraints, in terms of translation speed and translation quality. To evaluate how well the method handles the constraints, we propose new evaluation metrics which take into account the presence, placement, duplication and inflectional correctness of lexical terms in the output sentence.

1 Introduction

The incorporation of an inflected lexicon into Neural Machine Translation (NMT) enables system developers to adapt the translation to specific domains, and users to adjust translations of phrases generated by the translation system.

Phrase-Based Statistical Machine Translation (PB-SMT; Setiawan et al., 2005) provided control over system output, e.g. by using a domain-specific lexicon. The shift from phrase tables in PB-SMT to a continuous-valued representation of text in NMT has made it more difficult to incorporate lexical constraints into the translation process. The task of integrating the lexicon and a neural translator is even more challenging for highly morphological languages, when the lexical items should be correctly inflected in the output text.

We carry out experiments for translation with inflected lexical constraints. As the target language of the translation we choose Polish, whose inflection is typical of the Slavic languages. The number of declination cases is six, and the verbal groups are inflected by tense, number, and person. In terms of correct inflection of the output, translation from English to Polish seems to be a more challenging task than translation in the other direction.

Unlike in some preceding experiments, we require that the lexicon may be modified after the model training has been completed. We believe that in post-editing mode users expect the translation engine to immediately mirror their adjustments to the lexicon.

2 Related Work

One of the first papers that addressed the incorporation of a lexicon into an NMT system was Arthur et al. (2016). The authors noticed that NMT systems tend to produce unexpected output for low-frequency words (such as names of countries). The solution proposed there consisted in designing probability lexicons and combining them with probabilities calculated by an NMT model. Let us note that the motivation for that research was the avoidance of major translation errors, rather than domain adaptation.

Anderson et al. (2017) introduced the concept of a Constrained Beam Search (CBS) in the task of picture captioning. The proposed algorithm forces the inclusion of selected tag words in the output. The solution makes it possible to apply, in the caption, words that were never present in the training data. The method yields the desired results provided that these out-of-vocabulary tags are based on "ground truth", such as labels obtained by reliable object detectors.

The application of CBS for lexical interference in the process of neural text generation was investigated in Hokamp and Liu (2017). In the decoding phase, the beam is limited only to hypotheses, which include predefined phrases or words. The algorithm called the Grid Beam Search (GBS) may be used for various text-generation tasks where auxiliary knowledge is expected to be incorporated into the text output. If applied to translation, the solution searches for lexical items in the source text and, in positive cases, imposes the presence of their equivalents on the beam.

Hasler et al. (2018) pointed out a danger in the CBS method resulting from the lack of correspondence between constraints and the source words they cover – the placement of the constraint translation in the output may not be correct. To avoid this undesirable effect, the authors "employ alignment information between target-side constraints and their corresponding source words."

The downside of the above algorithms is their complexity: exponential (CBS) or linear (GBS) in the number of constraints. Post and Vilar (2018) introduce an improvement of the GBS algorithm, called Dynamic Beam Allocation (DBA), which divides the fixed-size beam into "banks": sets of hypotheses that satisfy the same number of constraints. The algorithm depends only on the sentence length and the beam size, being independent of the number of constraints.

Hu et al. (2019) notice that the use of positive (specific tokens must be present in the output) or negative (specific tokens must not be generated) constraints may be useful in rewriting tasks other than translation. Rewriting (see e.g. Napoles et al., 2016) consists in generating an output sentence in the same language and similar in meaning to the input. Examples of such tasks are paraphrasing, question answering and natural language inference. Hu et al. (2019) regard it as crucial to focus on complexity issues to speed up the process of constrained text generation. They develop a "vectorized DBA algorithm with trie representation", which speeds up the computations fivefold compared with the standard DBA algorithm.

Further complexity improvements to constrained NMT are suggested in Song et al. (2019). They apply the idea of so-called "code-switching", which consists in injecting the target terms to the source side of the training data. The idea is similar to that of using placeholder tags to stand for rare names (Luong et al., 2015) or named entities (Deng et al., 2017). The difference is that the direct translations of terms are placed in the source text instead of tags. The output text is then left untouched. The authors claim that the idea improves translation because it "does not hurt unconstrained words." We believe, however, that in some (not rare) cases the replacement of the constrained word(s) should have an impact on the choice of unconstrained words.

Dinu et al. (2019) apply the idea of "code-switching" in two different scenarios. Depending on the experimental setup the target terms are placed either beside or in place of their source equivalents.

The code-switching method is faster than the previous implementations based on constrained decoding (the presence of constraints need not be verified in the beam). The downside is that it requires interference with the training data.

Exel et al. (2020) verify the efficiency of the code-switching method in an industrial scenario. They inject the terminology of the SAP company into two translation pairs, English–German and English–Russian, and provide both automatic and human evaluation.

From our point of view, the English–Russian case is more interesting because it addresses the problem of inflected forms of lexical constraints. There are two questions of interest to us:

1. How to ensure that the terms are inserted into the target sentence in the correct inflected form?

2. How to evaluate the correctness of term inflection in the translation?

We could not find answers to the above questions in the paper. Therefore, we investigated other solutions, such as the Levenshtein Transformer, introduced in Gu et al. (2019). The method uses "dual policy learning", which consists in using two adversary policies during learning: when training one policy, the output from its adversary at the previous iteration is used as input. In the Levenshtein Transformer the two policies are deletion and insertion of a token in the generated text. The idea is supposed to resemble human intelligence, which sometimes chooses to delete an item from the text intended as output.

In Susanto et al. (2020) the Levenshtein Transformer was used to incorporate lexical constraints in NMT. The idea seemed more appealing to us than code-switching because it does not interfere with the training procedure. However, our initial experiments with the methodology did not succeed – the inflected forms of lexicon entries were not generated correctly. Finally, we decided to carry out our experiments with the base Transformer model, as introduced by Vaswani et al. (2017), and design an algorithm that handles inflected forms of lexical constraints based on the GBS algorithm.

3 Experiments

The purpose of our experiments was to find an efficient solution that applies lexical constraints in interactive-mode translation into a morphologically rich language. To be more specific, we aimed to develop a method that would satisfy the following conditions:

- The translation takes into account inflection of lexical items;
- The training data need not be modified.

3.1 Evaluation metrics

We used the standard BLEU metric for translation quality evaluation on the untokenized reference sentences. We also wanted to verify whether the following conditions are satisfied:

1. The target term is present in the output sentence;
2. The target term is properly placed;
3. The target term is not duplicated;
4. The target term is correctly inflected.

Following Exel et al. (2020), we used the Term Rate (TR) to evaluate condition 1. We define Placement Rate (PR) to evaluate condition 2, Duplication Rate (DR) to evaluate condition 3, and Inflection Rate (IR) to evaluate condition 4.

$$TR = \frac{count(terms\ generated\ in\ output)}{count(terms\ that\ appeared\ in\ input)}$$

$$PR = \frac{count(terms\ placed\ properly\ in\ output)}{count(terms\ generated\ in\ output)}$$

$$DR = \frac{count(terms\ not\ duplicated\ in\ output)}{count(terms\ generated\ in\ output)}$$

$$IR = \frac{count(terms\ inflected\ properly\ )}{count(terms\ generated\ in\ output)}$$

3.2 Lexical constraints

The lexical constraints were extracted from Paterson (2015), a compendium of Polish and English accounting forms, available under a Creative Commons license. The number of extracted term pairs was 1197.

We used the Google search engine to obtain inflected forms of Polish terms. Specifically, we queried the search engine with the base forms of terms and scraped snippets from the first 20 pages of query results. We then limited the number of inflected variants to those that covered 95% of cases (we found out that 5% rare cases were more often than not erroneous). The most frequent number of inflected forms for one term was between two and five.

This language-agnostic approach allowed us to obtain the most widely used inflected forms of multi-word phrases, which are not present in Polish vocabularies such as *SGJP*,[1] which only include inflected forms of single words.

3.3 Data preparation

The direction of translation was from English into Polish. The training corpus consisted of the *Europarl v8*, *EUBookshop v2*, *JRC-Acquis v3.0*, *TildeMODEL v2018* and *Wikipedia v1.0* corpora and most of *DGT v2019*. All corpora were downloaded from the *OPUS*[2] collection (Tiedemann, 2012) and filtered using the *Bicleaner*[3] and *Bifixer*[4] (Ramírez-Sánchez et al., 2020) tools. The size of the training corpus after filtering was 3,103,819 segments.

For the validation set, we used 2000 sentences from the *DGT* corpus, removing them from the training set.

For the test sets, for two experiments, we extracted respectively 1000 and 1104 segment pairs from the *DGT* corpus, making sure that they did not overlap with either the training set or the validation set. The first test set contained randomly selected segments in which at least one lexical term appeared in the source-side segment, regardless of the presence of target lexical equivalents. We further refer to this experiment as the general scenario. The second test set contained all segments from the corpus in which, for each lexical term in the source-side segment, one of the inflected forms of its lexical equivalent appeared in the target-side segment. We refer to this as the domain-specific scenario.

All of the sets were processed by the BPE algorithm (Sennrich et al., 2016) with the SentencePiece tool[5] (Kudo and Richardson, 2018).

3.4 Experimental setup

We carried out our experiments using *fairseq*[6] (Ott et al., 2019), a PyTorch-based open-source sequence modeling toolkit.

We designed a lexicon where for each entry in the source language we provided multiple inflected forms of the corresponding entry in the target language, as described in 3.2. In order to use constrained decoding, we trained the Transformer model with a base configuration of six encoding and decoding layers, as introduced by Vaswani et al. (2017).

[1]http://sgjp.pl
[2]https://opus.nlpl.eu/
[3]https://github.com/bitextor/bicleaner
[4]https://github.com/bitextor/bifixer
[5]https://github.com/google/sentencepiece
[6]https://github.com/pytorch/fairseq

To obtain translations with correct inflected forms of lexical constraints, we introduced the following algorithm, which applies constrained decoding:

1. Translate the input sentence without any lexical constraints; calculate its average log-likelihood score.
2. Use the fuzzy search (see below) to check whether all lexical constraints are satisfied in the translation; end if the answer is positive.
3. For each unsatisfied lexical constraint:
    (a) Take all inflected forms of its lexical equivalent from the lexicon.
    (b) For each inflected form:
    Use lexically constrained decoding to translate the input sentence with the inflected form required to be present in the output.
    (c) Select the inflected form for which the translation has the highest average log-likelihood score.
4. Use lexically constrained decoding to generate the translation with the list of constraints selected in step 3.
5. Mark the translation as "ok" if the score of the selected translation is not worse than half of the score of the unconstrained translation; otherwise mark it as "warning".

Marking translation output as "warning" allowed us to detect potential errors in the constrained translation (mismatched context, a missing morphological form), thus making it possible to revert to the unconstrained translation if an error was detected.

In the fuzzy search (step 2 of the algorithm) we applied the Token Sort Ratio method, as implemented in the *spaczz*[7] library. The Token Sort Ratio algorithm splits the compared strings into tokens, sorts each list of tokens alphabetically and compares the corresponding elements of the lists using the Levenshtein distance on the level of characters. We considered the found term to match the search term if the similarity ratio, calculated by the algorithm, was not lower than 90%.

We used a beam size of 5 for decoding in step 3(b) of the above algorithm. We used a beam size of 12 in steps 1 and 4.

3.5 Evaluation

The baseline for our solution is the translation without lexical constraints. To assess the effectiveness of our method, we compared it with the baseline in the general and domain-specific scenarios and verified the following aspects of its performance:

1. translation quality (BLEU score);
2. translation speed (measured in seconds);
3. Term Rate;
4. Placement Rate;
5. Duplication Rate;
6. Inflection Rate.

[7]https://github.com/gandersen101/spaczz

We performed a manual check to calculate the Term Rate, Placement Rate, Duplication Rate and Inflection Rate. The BLEU scores were calculated using the *SacreBLEU*[8] tool (Post, 2018).

We calculated separate BLEU scores for the entire test sets and for the set of sentences for which the constrained decoding was actually used (i.e. sentences for which the result of unconstrained translation did not satisfy all of the lexical constraints). Additionally, we calculated the BLEU score for the scenario where "warning" translations are reverted to the unconstrained translations. Manual evaluation metrics were calculated for the entire test sets.

The speed tests were performed on a single NVIDIA RTX 2070 GPU and the AMD Ryzen 7 3700X 8-core processor, using the entire test sets. When translating with the lexicon, the first (unconstrained) and last (with all selected inflected forms) translations were performed with a batch size of 1, while the search for the correct inflected forms was performed as a single batch with the size depending on the number of constraints and their inflected forms. The time spent on the search for the appearance of lexicon entries was also included. When translating without a lexicon, we used a batch size of 1.

In the tables of results, we refer to the unconstrained translation as *base*, the translation using the lexicon as *lexicon*, and the translation using the lexicon with reversion to the original in case of "warning" as *lexicon-revert*.

3.5.1 Experiment 1: general scenario

In this scenario the test set consisted of sentences which contained lexical terms in the source text, independently of the presence of their equivalents in the target text.

Constrained decoding was used in the translation of 622 out of 1000 sentences, which corresponds to 62.20% of the entire test set. In these 622 translated sentences, 404 were marked as "ok" and 218 as "warning". In the 378 sentences where constrained decoding was not used, the unconstrained translation satisfied all lexical constraints.

The BLEU results for the experiment are presented in Table 1, the manual evaluation results for the *lexicon* translation type are presented in Table 2, and translation speed results are presented in Table 3.

Table 1: BLEU scores obtained in the general scenario

Translation type	Entire set	Constrained sentences
base	**42.21**	**41.67**
lexicon	39.91	37.59
lexicon-revert	40.97	39.68

Table 2: Results of manual evaluation of *lexicon* translation type in the general scenario

Metric	Result
Term Rate	98.90
Placement Rate	90.79
Duplication Rate	97.00
Inflection Rate	76.48

[8]https://github.com/mjpost/sacrebleu

Table 3: Translation speed in the general scenario

Translation type	Time result (s)
base	**273.88**
lexicon	1200.26

Unsurprisingly, the BLEU results are higher for translation without using the lexicon. This is consistent with the intuition that in the general scenario using the lexicon to correct the neural translation leads to a decrease in the BLEU score. The reversion to the unconstrained translation in situations where the output was marked "warning" may mitigate this effect to some extent. The reversion was particularly helpful in situations where the output from translation with the lexicon was corrupted; for instance, when constraints were placed at the end of the generated sentence or in the wrong inflected form, due to mismatched context or absence of the correct inflected form of the term in the lexicon.

The manual evaluation results indicate that the constraint accuracy in the general scenario is high for three metrics: Term Rate, Placement Rate and Duplicate Rate. Inflection Rate, however, is rather low because of the missing relevant inflected forms of the terms in the lexicon.

Term Rate is lower than 100% because in a few cases the lexical equivalent was generated in a different inflected form than any of the forms present in the lexicon. This is due to the fact that constraints are also divided into subwords (by the BPE algorithm) before the constrained decoding. In some rare cases this may lead to the proper generation of constraint subword units in the output sentence, but to a different constraint form than is required after the sentence is "de-BPEed".

Translation speed results show that constrained decoding significantly slows down the translation process. The decrease in speed is dependent on the number of constraints and the number of inflected forms of target lexical terms.

3.5.2 Experiment 2: domain-specific scenario

In Scenario 2 we evaluated the effectiveness of lexically constrained translation for the sentences where all lexical constraints were satisfied in the reference translation.

Constrained decoding was used in the translation of 150 out of 1104 sentences, which corresponds to 13.59% of the entire test set. In these 150 translated sentences, 143 were marked as "ok" and 7 as "warning". In the 954 sentences where constrained decoding was not used, all lexical constraints were satisfied in the unconstrained translation.

The BLEU results for the experiment are presented in Table 4, the manual evaluation results for the *lexicon* translation type are presented in Table 5, and translation speed results are presented in Table 6.

Table 4: BLEU scores obtained in the domain-specific scenario

Translation type	Entire set	Constrained sentences
base	42.30	36.17
lexicon	**42.76**	**39.80**
lexicon-revert	42.73	39.54

Table 5: Results of manual evaluation of *lexicon* translation type in the domain-specific scenario

Metric	Result
Term Rate	99.37
Placement Rate	98.37
Duplication Rate	99.09
Inflection Rate	97.28

Table 6: Translation speed in the domain-specific scenario

Translation type	Time result (s)
base	**316.79**
lexicon	540.56

The BLEU metric results show that translation with the lexicon leads to an increase in translation quality when the context of the input sentences matches the context of the lexicon and when the relevant inflected forms are present in the lexicon. Reverting to the translation without constraints in situations where the output was marked as "warning" resulted in a very slight decrease in the BLEU score. This is probably due to the fact that such cases were too rare for the results to be reliable.

The manual evaluation results indicate that our method is very effective in selecting a correct inflected form of the constraint in the domain-specific scenario. All of the metrics returned high scores, including the Inflection Rate.

In this scenario, lexical constraints were not satisfied in the unconstrained translation only in 13.59% of cases. This shows that the neural translation model itself is capable of generating translations with the correct terminology given adequate context. It is concluded that the use of lexical constraints in NMT improves translation quality only in scenarios where the lexicon is highly specific for the translation context.

3.6 Examples of translation with inflected lexicon

Table 7 shows two examples of sentences translated with and without the use of inflected lexicon. The lexicon entries consist of a term in English language with the equivalent in Polish language along with its comma-separated list of inflectional forms.

4 Conclusions

We have examined a new approach to terminology translation into a morphologically rich language with the use of lexicons. We verified that our method, based on constrained decoding, enables the selection of accurate inflected forms of lexical constraints. The method yields an increase in the BLEU metric score provided that appropriate lexical variants of terms are present in the lexicon and the input sentence context is consistent with the lexicon entries. The cost of the algorithm is a decrease in the translation speed. We proposed new metrics for the evaluation of terminology translations: Placement Rate, Duplication Rate and Inflection Rate. The manual evaluation results show that our method ensures terminological adequacy and consistency when translating into a morphologically rich language in domain-specific scenarios.

5 Future Work

We believe that there is still much to explore in the field of terminology translation. In future experiments, we plan to compare our solution with the code-switching approach (Dinu et al.,

Table 7: Examples of translation with inflected lexicon

Lexicon entry	audit committee -> komisja rewizyjna, komisji rewizyjnej, komisją rewizyjną, komisję rewizyjną
Source sentence	The **audit committee** should be composed exclusively of non-executive or supervisory directors.
Translation without lexicon	Komitet ds. audytu powinien składać się wyłącznie z dyrektorów niewykonawczych lub będących członkami rady nadzorczej.
Translation with lexicon	W skład **komisji rewizyjnej** powinni wchodzić wyłącznie dyrektorzy niewykonawczy lub będący członkami rady nadzorczej.
Lexicon entry	outlay -> nakład, nakładu, nakłady, nakładów
Source sentence	The statement of the beneficiary's outlay shall be produced in support of any request for a new payment.
Translation without lexicon	Deklarację wydatków beneficjenta przedstawia się na poparcie każdego wniosku o nową płatność.
Translation with lexicon	Deklarację **nakładów** beneficjenta przedstawia się na poparcie każdego wniosku o nową płatność.

2019), (Song et al., 2019) and to investigate methods which do not have such a negative impact on translation speed as constrained decoding. Another potential direction for improvement is to design a method that does not require the presence of multiple inflected forms in the lexicon before translation.

References

Anderson, P., Fernando, B., Johnson, M., and Gould, S. (2017). Guided open vocabulary image captioning with constrained beam search. In *Proceedings of the 2017 Conference on Empirical Methods in Natural Language Processing*, pages 936–945, Copenhagen, Denmark. Association for Computational Linguistics.

Arthur, P., Neubig, G., and Nakamura, S. (2016). Incorporating discrete translation lexicons into neural machine translation. In *Proceedings of the 2016 Conference on Empirical Methods in Natural Language Processing*, pages 1557–1567, Austin, Texas. Association for Computational Linguistics.

Deng, Y., Kim, J., Klein, G., Kobus, C., Segal, N., Servan, C., Wang, B., Zhang, D., Crego, J. M., and Senellart, J. (2017). SYSTRAN purely neural MT engines for WMT2017. In Bojar, O., Buck, C., Chatterjee, R., Federmann, C., Graham, Y., Haddow, B., Huck, M., Jimeno-Yepes, A., Koehn, P., and Kreutzer, J., editors, *Proceedings of the Second Conference on Machine Translation, WMT 2017, Copenhagen, Denmark, September 7-8, 2017*, pages 265–270. Association for Computational Linguistics.

Dinu, G., Mathur, P., Federico, M., and Al-Onaizan, Y. (2019). Training neural machine translation to apply terminology constraints. In *Proceedings of the 57th Annual Meeting of the Association for Computational Linguistics*, pages 3063–3068, Florence, Italy. Association for Computational Linguistics.

Exel, M., Buschbeck, B., Brandt, L., and Doneva, S. (2020). Terminology-constrained neural machine translation at SAP. In *Proceedings of the 22nd Annual Conference of the European Association for Machine Translation*, pages 271–280, Lisboa, Portugal. European Association for Machine Translation.

Gu, J., Wang, C., and Zhao, J. (2019). Levenshtein transformer. In Wallach, H., Larochelle, H., Beygelzimer, A., d'Alché-Buc, F., Fox, E., and Garnett, R., editors, *Advances in Neural Information Processing Systems*, volume 32. Curran Associates, Inc.

Hasler, E., de Gispert, A., Iglesias, G., and Byrne, B. (2018). Neural machine translation decoding with terminology constraints. In *Proceedings of the 2018 Conference of the North American Chapter of the Association for Computational Linguistics: Human Language Technologies, Volume 2 (Short Papers)*, pages 506–512, New Orleans, Louisiana. Association for Computational Linguistics.

Hokamp, C. and Liu, Q. (2017). Lexically constrained decoding for sequence generation using grid beam search. In *Proceedings of the 55th Annual Meeting of the Association for Computational Linguistics (Volume 1: Long Papers)*, pages 1535–1546, Vancouver, Canada. Association for Computational Linguistics.

Hu, J. E., Khayrallah, H., Culkin, R., Xia, P., Chen, T., Post, M., and Van Durme, B. (2019). Improved lexically constrained decoding for translation and monolingual rewriting. In *Proceedings of the 2019 Conference of the North American Chapter of the Association for Computational Linguistics: Human Language Technologies, Volume 1 (Long and Short Papers)*, pages 839–850, Minneapolis, Minnesota. Association for Computational Linguistics.

Kudo, T. and Richardson, J. (2018). SentencePiece: A simple and language independent subword tokenizer and detokenizer for neural text processing. In *Proceedings of the 2018 Conference on Empirical Methods in Natural Language Processing: System Demonstrations*, pages 66–71, Brussels, Belgium. Association for Computational Linguistics.

Luong, T., Sutskever, I., Le, Q., Vinyals, O., and Zaremba, W. (2015). Addressing the rare word problem in neural machine translation. In *Proceedings of the 53rd Annual Meeting of the Association for Computational Linguistics and the 7th International Joint Conference on Natural Language Processing (Volume 1: Long Papers)*, pages 11–19, Beijing, China. Association for Computational Linguistics.

Napoles, C., Callison-Burch, C., and Post, M. (2016). Sentential paraphrasing as black-box machine translation. In *Proceedings of the 2016 Conference of the North American Chapter of the Association for Computational Linguistics: Demonstrations*, pages 62–66, San Diego, California. Association for Computational Linguistics.

Ott, M., Edunov, S., Baevski, A., Fan, A., Gross, S., Ng, N., Grangier, D., and Auli, M. (2019). fairseq: A fast, extensible toolkit for sequence modeling. In *Proceedings of the 2019 Conference of the North American Chapter of the Association for Computational Linguistics (Demonstrations)*, pages 48–53, Minneapolis, Minnesota. Association for Computational Linguistics.

Paterson, R. (2015). In *Compendium of Acounting in Polish & English*. Ministerstwo Finansów by arrangement with the Swiss-Polish Cooperation Program – Financial Reporting Technical Assistance Program (FRTAP).

Post, M. (2018). A call for clarity in reporting BLEU scores. In *Proceedings of the Third Conference on Machine Translation: Research Papers*, pages 186–191, Belgium, Brussels. Association for Computational Linguistics.

Post, M. and Vilar, D. (2018). Fast lexically constrained decoding with dynamic beam allocation for neural machine translation. In *Proceedings of the 2018 Conference of the North American Chapter of the Association for Computational Linguistics: Human Language Technologies, Volume 1 (Long Papers)*, pages 1314–1324, New Orleans, Louisiana. Association for Computational Linguistics.

Ramírez-Sánchez, G., Zaragoza-Bernabeu, J., Bañón, M., and Ortiz-Rojas, S. (2020). Bifixer and bicleaner: two open-source tools to clean your parallel data. In *Proceedings of the 22nd Annual Conference of the European Association for Machine Translation*, pages 291–298, Lisboa, Portugal. European Association for Machine Translation.

Sennrich, R., Haddow, B., and Birch, A. (2016). Neural machine translation of rare words with subword units. In *Proceedings of the 54th Annual Meeting of the Association for Computational Linguistics (Volume 1: Long Papers)*, pages 1715–1725, Berlin, Germany. Association for Computational Linguistics.

Setiawan, H., Li, H., Zhang, M., and Ooi, B. C. (2005). Phrase-based statistical machine translation: A level of detail approach. In *Second International Joint Conference on Natural Language Processing: Full Papers*.

Song, K., Zhang, Y., Yu, H., Luo, W., Wang, K., and Zhang, M. (2019). Code-switching for enhancing NMT with pre-specified translation. In *Proceedings of the 2019 Conference of the North American Chapter of the Association for Computational Linguistics: Human Language Technologies, Volume 1 (Long and Short Papers)*, pages 449–459, Minneapolis, Minnesota. Association for Computational Linguistics.

Susanto, R. H., Chollampatt, S., and Tan, L. (2020). Lexically constrained neural machine translation with Levenshtein transformer. In *Proceedings of the 58th Annual Meeting of the Association for Computational Linguistics*, pages 3536–3543, Online. Association for Computational Linguistics.

Tiedemann, J. (2012). Parallel data, tools and interfaces in OPUS. In Calzolari, N., Choukri, K., Declerck, T., Dogan, M. U., Maegaard, B., Mariani, J., Odijk, J., and Piperidis, S., editors, *Proceedings of the Eighth International Conference on Language Resources and Evaluation (LREC'12)*, Istanbul, Turkey. European Language Resources Association (ELRA).

Vaswani, A., Shazeer, N., Parmar, N., Uszkoreit, J., Jones, L., Gomez, A. N., Kaiser, L., and Polosukhin, I. (2017). Attention is all you need. In Guyon, I., Luxburg, U. V., Bengio, S., Wallach, H., Fergus, R., Vishwanathan, S., and Garnett, R., editors, *Advances in Neural Information Processing Systems*, volume 30. Curran Associates, Inc.

An Alignment-Based Approach to Semi-Supervised Bilingual Lexicon Induction with Small Parallel Corpora

Kelly Marchisio kmarc@jhu.edu
Conghao Xiong cxiong5@jhu.edu
Philipp Koehn phi@jhu.edu
Center for Language and Speech Processing, Johns Hopkins University, Baltimore, MD, 21218, USA

Abstract

Aimed at generating a seed lexicon for use in downstream natural language tasks, unsupervised methods for bilingual lexicon induction have received much attention in the academic literature recently. While interesting, fully unsupervised settings are unrealistic; small amounts of bilingual data are usually available due to the existence of massively multilingual parallel corpora, or linguists can create small amounts of parallel data. In this work, we demonstrate an effective bootstrapping approach for semi-supervised bilingual lexicon induction that capitalizes upon the complementary strengths of two disparate methods for inducing bilingual lexicons. Whereas statistical methods are highly effective at inducing correct translation pairs for words frequently occurring in a parallel corpus, monolingual embedding spaces have the advantage of having been trained on large amounts of data, and therefore may induce accurate translations for words absent from the small corpus. By combining these relative strengths, our method achieves state-of-the-art results on 3 of 4 language pairs in the challenging VecMap test set using minimal amounts of parallel data and without the need for a translation dictionary. We release our implementation at `https://github.com/kellymarchisio/align-semisup-bli`.

1 Introduction

Unsupervised methods for machine translation (MT) and bilingual lexicon induction (BLI) have received considerable attention in recent years, showing impressive performance without bilingual data for supervision. While academically interesting, small amounts of supervised data can almost always help model performance.

The typical use case for unsupervised BLI is to provide initial synthetic training data for a traditional supervised setup where no parallel bitext exists, such as for MT or cross-lingual information retrieval. A starting lexicon is induced in an unsupervised manner, and then serves as initial training data to the supervised model. Practically, however, one struggles to identify a scenario where one would truly fail to have any parallel text whatesoever from which to gain some supervision. The Christian Bible, for instance, is translated into over 1600 world languages, providing multi-way parallel data for many of the world's languages that are typically considered "low-resource" (McCarthy et al., 2020). Human translators can also create a small translation corpus or seed dictionary. The practical necessity of fully unsupervised scenarios for BLI or MT therefore becomes hard to imagine.

Statistical translation/alignment models are very proficient at inducing bilingual lexicons from small amounts of parallel data. Particularly when words occur frequently in the corpus, statistical models easily recover the translation. At the same time, however, the number of seed translation pairs possible to extract is limited by the vocabulary of the parallel corpus.

We address a more realistic scenario: there is ample monolingual data and a small parallel corpus. We combine the strengths of statistical alignment and unsupervised mapping methods and achieve state-of-the-art results on 3 of 4 languages in the challenging VecMap dataset (Dinu et al., 2015; Artetxe et al., 2017, 2018a), trailing by only 0.1 in the 4th language pair.

2 Related Work

Automatic BLI has been a popular task in natural language processing for decades, beginning with statistical decipherment (e.g., Rapp, 1995; Fung, 1995; Koehn and Knight, 2000, 2002; Haghighi et al., 2008). With the advent of the ability to create large monolingual vector spaces from abundant monolingual text, the focus has shifted to finding an optimal linear transformation between such monolingual embedding spaces from which a seed lexicon can be extracted using nearest neighbors search. Practically, this often involves solving variations of the generalized Procrustes problem (e.g., Conneau et al., 2018; Artetxe et al., 2016, 2017; Patra et al., 2019; Artetxe et al., 2018b; Doval et al., 2018; Joulin et al., 2018; Jawanpuria et al., 2019; Alvarez-Melis and Jaakkola, 2018). Differing metrics and heuristics can be used to extract the seed lexicon once the mapping is found. Cross-domain similarity local scaling (CSLS) to mitigate the hubness is popular and effective (Conneau et al., 2018).

While the orthogonal variant of the Procrustes problem has a simple closed-form solution, one must know in advance the pairings of words one wants to be closest after the transformation (i.e., you already know the translations). To adapt to the unsupervised or semi-supervised scenario, such mapping-based BLI procedures must make a "guess" of some correct translation pairs. The solution can then iteratively refined through self-learning. The initial "guess" can come in the form of direct supervision using a bilingual training dictionary, or in an unsupervised manner, such as by identifying the nearest neighbors in a similarity matrix (e.g., Artetxe et al., 2018b) or via adversarial training (e.g., Conneau et al., 2018; Patra et al., 2019).

Like us, Shi et al. (2021) also use statistical alignment within a pipeline for BLI, but unlike our work, they do not use the induced alignments as seeds for monolingual embedding mapping.

3 Background

3.1 The Orthogonal Procrustes Problem

Let A and B be matrices in $\mathbb{R}^{m\times n}$. Let Q be a matrix in $\mathbb{R}^{n\times n}$. The goal of the orthogonal Procrustes problem is to find Q such that:

$$\arg\min_{QQ^T=I} \|AQ - B\|_F$$

The solution to the orthogonal Procrustes problem is $Q = VU^T$, where $U\Sigma V$ is the singular value decomposition of B^TA (Schönemann, 1966).

3.2 IBM Model 2

IBM Model 2 (Brown et al., 1993) is designed to be a noisy channel model for MT, but it is a particularly useful statistical model for word alignment. We view the most likely alignment between a source sentence $\boldsymbol{f}$ and target sentence $\boldsymbol{e}$ as a hidden variable, modeled as the conditional probability

$$\arg\max_{a_1\ldots a_m} p\left(a_1 \ldots a_m \mid f_1 \ldots f_m, e_1 \ldots e_l, m\right)$$

where m is the length of source sentence, l is the length of target sentence, $\{f_1...f_m\}$ and $\{e_1...e_l\}$ are the source words and target words respectively, and a_i is the alignment, indicating that f_i is aligned to e_{a_i}. To compute the alignment, we need two more definitions:

- $p(f|e)$: the lexical translation probabilities. e is a target word, and f is the source word. In addition to the whole vocabulary of target language, the target-side also includes a *NULL* token indicating that a source word aligned to none of the target words.

- $p(j \mid i, l, m)$: the alignment model. The probability of source position j being aligned to target position i.

The IBM models are trained via expectation-maximization. After training, alignments can be determined with:

$$a_i = \arg \max_{j \in \{0...l\}} (p(j \mid i, l, m) \times p(f_i \mid e_j))$$

4 Motivation

Different types of models have different strengths when it comes to determining translations of words. We discuss some contrasting strengths of inducing translations from statistical models versus monolingual embedding space mapping in this section as motivation for our method. We assert that to maximize accuracy, one should induce the translation of common words from statistical models and less frequent words from well-trained monolingual embedding spaces.

Statistical models succeed for common words, struggle for rare words.

In the IBM statistical translation models, word translation probabilities are typically initialized uniformly. In the IBM models, the probability $p(f|e)$ assigned to a given word pair in the translation table is iteratively refined according to the occurrence of f and e in the corpus. While this procedure can capture alignment and translation likelihoods of common words in a large bilingual corpus accurately, the probability can become inaccurate for rare words (not to mention those absent from the corpus). The risk of such inaccuracies of low-frequency words increases as corpus size shrinks.

There are 10,673 unique source tokens in the first 10,000 lowercased lines of the English-side of the Europarl v7 German-English corpus (Koehn, 2005), used later in this work. Of those, 4015 tokens occur just once. Only 5214 — less than half of the vocabulary — occur more than twice. Such a large percentage of rare words is explained by the well-known Zipf's law (Zipf, 1935, 1949; Mandelbrot, 1953, 1961), whereby the *kth* most common word tends to occur with a frequency approaching the below, where $\alpha \sim 1$ and $\beta \sim 2.7$ (Piantadosi, 2014).

$$freq(w) \propto \frac{1}{(rank(w) + \beta)^{\alpha}} \quad (1)$$

Embedding space mapping can take advantage of large amounts of monolingual data.

Just as statistical methods for word translation are more accurate for common words, inducing translations from monolingual word embeddings spaces for common words is also likely more accurate than for rare words, owing to the fact that the word embeddings for more common words are better trained than for rare words. The advantage that monolingual word embedding spaces have over traditional statistical MT methods, however, is that there is typically orders of magnitude more available monolingual text than there is translated parallel bitext for a given language pair. As such, a word that is rare in a bitext may occur frequently enough in a large monolingual corpus for its word embedding to be well-trained and useful.

More correct translation pairs $\rightarrow$ better embedding space mapping.

Empirically, more high-quality seed translation pairs improves the Procrustes mapping of monolingual embedding spaces for BLI. Our method is motivated by the desire to extract a large and accurate seed dictionary to solve Procrustes given only small amounts of parallel bitext from which to extract seeds.

Use the relative strengths of statistical vs. mapping methods to maximize performance.

Using 5000 seeds is common in the supervised BLI literature. In light of the fact that our 10,000-line Europarl bitext only has 5214 tokens that occur more than twice, we are hard-pressed to extract 5000 seed translations that we are confident are correct. We therefore use the relative strengths of IBM Model 2 and mapping-based methods for extracting a seed lexicon from monolingual embedding spaces to extract as many high-quality translation pairs as possible. Because of IBM Model 2's strength in identifying correct translations for high-frequency words, we trust its judgement for high-frequency words in the bitext. Monolingual embedding spaces, however, have the advantage of having a much larger vocabulary (the literature typically uses 200,000) and having been trained on much larger amounts of data. Thus we trust monolingual embedding mapping methods to identify the correct translations for any medium-frequency words, or high-frequency words that happened to not have been present in the parallel bitext given to IBM Model 2. We avoid the very lowest frequency words, but extract bilingual translation pairs for words seen frequently in the parallel corpus from IBM Model 2, and those seen less frequently (or not at all) from the embedding space mapping.

5 Method

5.1 Supervised statistical seed induction from bitext

We first run IBM Model 2 over a small parallel corpus. We rank the resulting word translation table by probability ("confidence"), and retain the top N translation pairs assigned the highest confidence. We discard pairs where either the source or target word occurred less than M times in the bitext, to avoid the problem of the statistical alignment model assigning erroneously high probabilities to rare words. We also discard pairs lower than a chosen confidence threshold.

5.2 Seed set expansion via embedding space mapping

Using the induced translations from the previous step as seeds, we map the monolingual embedding spaces using the public implementation of VecMap[1] in supervised mode (Artetxe et al., 2018a). In this method, word embeddings are length-normalized, mean-centered, and length-normalized again. A whitening transformation is performed, and then VecMap solves the orthogonal Procrustes problem over the known seeds, and the resulting spaces are reweighted and dewhitened. We extract a phrase table from the resulting mapped monolingual embedding spaces using Monoses[2](Artetxe et al., 2019). For a mapped source word e, let its k nearest neighbors in the mapped target embedding space be $N(x,k)$. Here, k=100. We calculate the translation probability for x and each of its k nearest neighbors using the softmax of the cosine similarity. Let $f \in N(x,k)$. Then,

$$p(f|e) = \frac{exp(\cos(e,f)/\tau)}{\sum\limits_{f' \in N(x,k)} exp(\cos(e,f')/\tau)}$$

See Artetxe et al. (2019) for further details.

[1]https://github.com/artetxem/vecmap

[2]https://github.com/artetxem/monoses

We extract the phrase table and rank the translations in descending order by forward translation probability. We again require the potential translation pairs to meet a minimum confidence threshold to be considered for use. We take the highest ranked translation per source word, therefore each source word is only used once.

5.3 Frequency-based seed selection with low-frequency agreement

We select our final seed set based on corpus frequency according to the motivation in Section 4. We retain the top K pairs from the embedding mapping method that are *disjoint* from the N word translations generated by IBM Model 2. In other words, if the source and target word in a potential translation occurred more than a pre-selected minimum number of times in the parallel bitext (M), we trust IBM Model 2 over VecMap. At the same time, we recognize the potential fault that the statistical alignment model could inaccurately guess a translation for a word it only sees once. To compensate for this weakness and allow for the creation of a larger seed dictionary on which to train our second round of VecMap, we turn to VecMap itself to induce the seeds of words rarely or never seen in the training corpus. In doing so, we can induce seed dictionaries larger than the vocabulary of the parallel bitext, but also with higher accuracy than if induced via VecMap alone in a self-learning fashion. Thus for words occurring infrequently (or never) in the parallel bitext, we trust VecMap over IBM Model 2. We merge the two potential seed dictionaries, only retaining low-frequency pairs induced by IBM Model 2 if VecMap can also confirm its desire for the potential pair to be retained.

5.4 Embedding space re-mapping with expanded seed set

Finally, the concatenated list of high-confidence translation pairs are used as seeds to again solve the Procrustes problem and re-map the monolingual embedding spaces. With the expanded joint seed set owing to the complementary strengths of IBM Model 2 and the previous embedding space mapping, this second round of embedding space mapping is expected to be more successful than would have been possible using only seeds from IBM Model 2, or only from self-learning.

6 Experimental Settings

Language	Corpus	# of words
English	WaCky, BNC, Wikipedia	2.8 B
Italian	itWac	1.6 B
German	SdeWaC	0.9 B
Spanish	News Crawl 2007-2012	386 M
Finnish	Common Crawl 2016	2.8 B

Table 1: Corpora used to train the word embeddings for each language in the VecMap dataset, with the number of words in billions (B) or millions (M).

6.1 Pretrained Word Embeddings

The pretrained embeddings from Dinu et al. (2015); Artetxe et al. (2017, 2018a) are 300-dimensional vectors of 200,000 words, trained with CBOW (Mikolov et al., 2013a). Table 1 details the parallel text used to train the embeddings. We conduct experiments on all four available language pairs (English-German, English-Spanish, English-Italian, English-Finnish).

6.2 Data

We use the popular and challenging VecMap data set, which is the original English-Italian data set of Dinu et al. (2015) with the subsequent extensions by Artetxe et al. (2017, 2018a). The dataset was obtained via alignment of the Europarl corpus (Koehn, 2005; Tiedemann, 2012). Test sets contain approximately 1500 source words and 2000 word pairs total. The source words are sampled evenly from frequency bins in the Europarl lexicon: one-fifth from each of frequency ranks [1000-5000], [5000-20,000], [20,000-50,000], [50,000-100,000], and [100,000-200,000]. This makes the test set considerably more challenging than the widely-used MUSE training and test sets (Conneau et al., 2018), where the test set consists of exactly source word frequencies 5,000-6,500 for each language pair. We create a development set for English-German and English-Finnish using the last 2,000 lines of the training seeds provided by Dinu et al. (2015); Artetxe et al. (2017, 2018a), which are disjoint from the test set.

We use Europarl v7 as our parallel bitext, which is a corpus of European Parliamentary proceedings available in 11 languages (Koehn, 2005). We normalize punctuation, tokenize, and clean the corpus to remove sentences with more than 100 tokens or with a source-to-target length ratio above 9. Each of these steps uses scripts from the Moses statistical MT system (Koehn et al., 2007). We then lowercase all bitext. For subsequent experiments varying the data size of the input corpus, we use the first N lines of the bitext, where N ranges from 500 to 50,000. We stop at 50,000 because our focus is on very small corpora. We use the NLTK[3] (Bird et al., 2009) implementation of IBM Model 2, and the public implementation of VecMap.

6.3 Hyperparameter Settings

For the IBM Model 2 step detailed in 5.1, we use N=3000, M=2, and minimum confidence threshold is set to 0.1. Final translations for the test set are retrieved by choosing the nearest neighbor in the target-side mapped space of the source word according to CSLS scaling, to mitigate the hubness problem. These settings are based on early experimentation with en-de using between 10k-100k lines of Europarl, where we observe that the subsequent VecMap stage needed about 3000 seeds extracted from 5,000 lines of Europarl to begin exceeding the unsupervised baseline performance. N=3000 and M=2 were chosen to encourage having 3000+ seeds from IBM2 for data conditions as low as 1k parallel lines. We then apply the chosen hyperparameters to all language pairs.

Seeds	en-de 1K	en-de 10K	en-fi 1K	en-fi 10K
0	38.1	64.1	14.0	44.8
200	48.7	65.0	18.9	46.8
500	55.8	65.5	26.0	47.0
1,000	58.8	65.7	29.8	48.3
3,000	61.2	**66.7**	33.5	48.8
5,000	60.5	**66.7**	33.7	**49.2**
10,000	**61.7**	66.6	**35.6**	48.2
15,000	61.2	65.9	**35.6**	**49.2**
20,000	61.1	65.7	**35.6**	48.3

Table 2: P@1 on en-de and en-fi development sets with increasing number of seeds induced from VecMap. Experiments are performed with models using 1K and 10K lines of parallel bitext input to IBM Model 2.

[3] https://www.nltk.org/

To determine the number of seeds that should be induced from VecMap, we performed experiments using the English-German and English-Finnish development sets. We train systems with N=3000 IBM seeds given 1,000 or 10,000 input sentences to IBM, and vary the amount of VecMap seeds that we extract from the resulting system to be concatenated with the IBM seeds to train the second round of VecMap. The results are presented in Table 2. Note that the vocabulary size is limited for 1,000 input sentences, the number of possible translation pairs is limited by vocabulary size and model confidence. This results in 1058 IBM-induced seeds for en-de and 791 for en-fi, for models using only 1,000 lines of parallel data. We examine all results, and select a number of seeds that appears to work well across all 4 conditions. We decide that this best seed set size is 10,000.

7 Results and Analysis

	en-it	en-de	en-fi	en-es
Unsupervised				
Conneau et al. (2018)* (avg.)	45.2	46.8	0.4	35.4
Artetxe et al. (2018b) (avg.)	48.1	48.2	32.6	37.3
Grave et al. (2019)	45.2	-	-	-
Mohiuddin and Joty (2020)	47.7	48.7	32.6	38.1
Alvarez-Melis and Jaakkola (2018)	49.2	46.5	18.3	37.6
Supervised / Semi-Supervised				
Smith et al. (2017)*	43.1	43.3	29.4	35.1
Patra et al. (2019) BLISS(M)	45.9	48.3	-	-
Patra et al. (2019) BLISS(R)	46.2	48.1	-	-
Mikolov et al. (2013b)*	34.9	35.0	25.9	27.7
Faruqui and Dyer (2014)*	38.4	37.1	27.6	26.8
Artetxe et al. (2016)*	39.3	41.9	30.6	31.4
Artetxe et al. (2017)	39.7	40.9	28.7	-
Artetxe et al. (2018a)	45.3	44.1	32.9	36.6
Jawanpuria et al. (2019) GeoMM	48.3	49.3	36.1	39.3
Mohiuddin et al. (2020)	46.7	47.7	34.1	37.8
Jawanpuria et al. (2019) GeoMMsemi	**50.0**	51.3	36.2	39.7
Ours, N=5,000	49.5	51.2	35.3	**40.0**
Ours, N=10,000	49.9	**51.7**	36.0	**40.1**
Ours, N=20,000	49.7	**51.4**	**36.8**	**40.1**
Ours, N=50,000	49.3	**51.4**	**37.1**	**39.9**

Table 3: Main results. P@1 BLI performance on the VecMap data set, compared with existing literature. *As reported in Artetxe et al. (2018b). "avg" are averaged over 10 runs. For our method, N is the number of sentences in the bitext given to IBM Model 2. Bold is best performance per language pair. We bold all of our models which outperform all previously published results.

Our main results compared with the existing literature are presented in Table 3. We achieve state-of-the-art results in the English-German, English-Finnish, and English-Spanish pairs. For English-Italian, we trail the state-of-the-art semi-supervised system of Jawanpuria et al. (2019) by only 0.1. However, Jawanpuria et al. (2019) use 80% of available training seeds from the VecMap test set (4000 seeds) while ours uses only 3000 seeds induced from a parallel bitext using IBM Model 2. For en-de and en-fi, our models trained on only 10,000 and 20,000 lines of bitext achieve state-of-the-art results, respectively. For en-es, even our model using only 5,000 parallel lines of bitext exceeds the performance of previous literature, achieving state-of-the-art performance.

7.1 Impact of Size of Input Corpus

	500	1000	5000	10000	20000
en-it	40.0	46.7	49.5	**49.9**	49.7
en-de	33.3	46.1	51.2	**51.7**	51.4
en-fi	8.4	24.4	35.3	36.0	**36.8**
en-es	32.7	37.6	40.0	**40.1**	40.1

Table 4: P@1 on VecMap test set varying the number of input parallel sentences. The number of induced seeds from IBM is 3,000 (or less, for lower data sizes with small vocabularies). 10,000 seeds are induced from VecMap. Top row is number of input sentences to IBM Model 2.

In Table 4, we examine the impact of the size of the input corpus to IBM Model 2 on downstream BLI performance. We feed between 500 and 20,000 parallel sentences from Europarl to the statistical translation model. In each experiment, we induce a maximum of 3,000 seeds from IBM Model 2.[4] In line with our intuition, performance generally increases as the size of the input corpus increases, and appears to plateau around 10,000 input sentences.

7.2 Ablation of frequency-based seed selection method

	en-de	en-fi
IBM only	64.1	44.8
VecMap Only	63.9	46.5
50% IBM + 50% VecMap	**64.8**	**47.9**

Table 5: P@1 on the development set of VecMap models trained with 3,000 seeds generated either from (1) IBM Model 2, (2) the previous run of VecMap, or (3) a combination of high-frequency translation pairs from IBM Model 2 and lower-frequency pairs from VecMap. IBM Model 2 was trained on 10,000 parallel sentences.

The size of the seed dictionary used for solving the Procrustes problem is a critically important parameter for success of mapping monolingual embedding spaces. Accordingly, a natural question to ask is whether our improved performance was due to the number of seeds induced alone, or our novel way of combining seeds extracted from both IBM and VecMap. To address this question, we use the en-de and en-fi models which used 10,000 lines of Europarl. In the first condition, we induce 3000 seeds from IBM Model 2 only, and train VecMap using these seeds. In the second condition, we extract 3000 from the first round training of VecMap, and feed only these into VecMap again for embedding space mapping retraining. In the third condition, we induce 1500 frequent words from IBM Model 2 and combine them with 1500 infrequent words induced from the phrase table generated from VecMap, according to our method for frequency-based seed selection with low-frequency agreement. We ensure that the resulting 3000 pair

[4]The number will be less for small vocabulary and if not enough potential translation pairs exceed the minimum confidence threshold.

seed set is split 50/50 between translation pairs induced from IBM Model 2 and those induced from VecMap. The results are presented in Table 5. We observe that when holding the number of induced seeds constant, best performance occurs using our combination method of keeping high-frequency translation pairs from IBM Model 2 and lower-frequency translation pairs from VecMap (according to the words' frequency in the 10,000 line parallel bitext).

Table 6 shows the relative importance of the two steps: induction from IBM 2 and inducing 10,000 additional seeds from VecMap to be fed back to VecMap for the final mapping. We use the first 3,000 seeds from the official VecMap training dictionaries as a baseline ("3k Artetxe Gold"), and show performance these gold seeds plus the additional 10,000 seeds induced from VecMap from the models trained using 10,000 lines of bitext (the models from row "Ours, N=10,000" of Table 3). For comparison, we show performance with the 3,000 pairs mined from IBM 2 only ("3k IBM2") from the same models, and report the development set performance of "Ours, N=10,000" under "3k IBM2 +10K VecMap". We observe that the secondary step of inducing 10,000 pairs from VecMap improves performance over the initial 3,000 seeds across all tested conditions, showing the magnitude of improvement between steps 1 (induction via IBM 2 or a given seed dictionary) and 2 (mining from word embedding space).

	3k Artetxe Gold	+10K VecMap	+3k IBM2	+10k VecMap
en-it	68.5	**70.3** *(+1.7)*	70.0	**70.3** *(+0.3)*
en-de	64.3	**65.3** *(+1.0)*	64.1	**66.6** *(+2.5)*
en-fi	48.9	**50.0** *(+1.1)*	44.8	**48.2** *(+3.4)*
en-es	66.0	**69.2** *(+3.3)*	66.4	**68.5** *(+2.0)*

Table 6: P@1 on the development set of models mapped with 3,000 seeds from the official VecMap Training Dictionary vs. 3,000 seeds induced from IBM2 with 10,000 lines of bitext, with or without an additional 10,000 pairs mined from the monolingual embedding spaces with VecMap.

8 Conclusion

Motivated by the strength of statistical translation and alignment models in inducing accurate word translation pairs from small amounts of data, the breadth of training data used to train monolingual word embedding spaces, we propose a motivated semi-supervised approach for bilingual lexicon induction that demonstrates state-of-the-art results on the challenging VecMap test sets. We capitalize upon the complementary strengths of statistical alignment and embedding space mapping methods for generating translation dictionaries, combining the methods for better downstream bilingual lexicon induction performance than either achieves alone. By taking this middle ground, we achieve state-of-the-art results with as little as 5,000 sentences - an amount readily available in thousands of language pairs. We release our implementation at `https://github.com/kellymarchisio/align-semisup-bli`.

References

Alvarez-Melis, D. and Jaakkola, T. (2018). Gromov-Wasserstein alignment of word embedding spaces. In *Proceedings of the 2018 Conference on Empirical Methods in Natural Language Processing*, pages 1881–1890, Brussels, Belgium. Association for Computational Linguistics.

Artetxe, M., Labaka, G., and Agirre, E. (2016). Learning principled bilingual mappings of word embeddings while preserving monolingual invariance. In *Proceedings of the 2016 Con-*

ference on Empirical Methods in Natural Language Processing, pages 2289–2294, Austin, Texas. Association for Computational Linguistics.

Artetxe, M., Labaka, G., and Agirre, E. (2017). Learning bilingual word embeddings with (almost) no bilingual data. In *Proceedings of the 55th Annual Meeting of the Association for Computational Linguistics (Volume 1: Long Papers)*, pages 451–462, Vancouver, Canada. Association for Computational Linguistics.

Artetxe, M., Labaka, G., and Agirre, E. (2018a). Generalizing and improving bilingual word embedding mappings with a multi-step framework of linear transformations. In *Proceedings of the AAAI Conference on Artificial Intelligence*, volume 32.

Artetxe, M., Labaka, G., and Agirre, E. (2018b). A robust self-learning method for fully unsupervised cross-lingual mappings of word embeddings. In *Proceedings of the 56th Annual Meeting of the Association for Computational Linguistics (Volume 1: Long Papers)*, pages 789–798, Melbourne, Australia. Association for Computational Linguistics.

Artetxe, M., Labaka, G., and Agirre, E. (2019). An effective approach to unsupervised machine translation. In *Proceedings of the 57th Annual Meeting of the Association for Computational Linguistics*, pages 194–203.

Bird, S., Klein, E., and Loper, E. (2009). *Natural language processing with Python: analyzing text with the natural language toolkit.* " O'Reilly Media, Inc.".

Brown, P. F., Della Pietra, S. A., Della Pietra, V. J., and Mercer, R. L. (1993). The mathematics of statistical machine translation: Parameter estimation. *Computational Linguistics*, 19(2):263–311.

Conneau, A., Lample, G., Ranzato, M., Denoyer, L., and Jégou, H. (2018). Word translation without parallel data. In *6th International Conference on Learning Representations, ICLR 2018, Vancouver, BC, Canada, April 30 - May 3, 2018, Conference Track Proceedings*. OpenReview.net.

Dinu, G., Lazaridou, A., and Baroni, M. (2015). Improving zero-shot learning by mitigating the hubness problem.

Doval, Y., Camacho-Collados, J., Anke, L. E., and Schockaert, S. (2018). Improving cross-lingual word embeddings by meeting in the middle. In *Proceedings of the 2018 Conference on Empirical Methods in Natural Language Processing*, pages 294–304.

Faruqui, M. and Dyer, C. (2014). Improving vector space word representations using multilingual correlation. In *Proceedings of the 14th Conference of the European Chapter of the Association for Computational Linguistics*, pages 462–471.

Fung, P. (1995). Compiling bilingual lexicon entries from a non-parallel English-Chinese corpus. In *Third Workshop on Very Large Corpora*.

Grave, E., Joulin, A., and Berthet, Q. (2019). Unsupervised alignment of embeddings with wasserstein procrustes. In *The 22nd International Conference on Artificial Intelligence and Statistics*, pages 1880–1890. PMLR.

Haghighi, A., Liang, P., Berg-Kirkpatrick, T., and Klein, D. (2008). Learning bilingual lexicons from monolingual corpora. In *Proceedings of ACL-08: HLT*, pages 771–779, Columbus, Ohio. Association for Computational Linguistics.

Jawanpuria, P., Balgovind, A., Kunchukuttan, A., and Mishra, B. (2019). Learning multilingual word embeddings in latent metric space: a geometric approach. *Transactions of the Association for Computational Linguistics*, 7:107–120.

Joulin, A., Bojanowski, P., Mikolov, T., Jégou, H., and Grave, É. (2018). Loss in translation: Learning bilingual word mapping with a retrieval criterion. In *Proceedings of the 2018 Conference on Empirical Methods in Natural Language Processing*, pages 2979–2984.

Koehn, P. (2005). Europarl: A parallel corpus for statistical machine translation. In *MT summit*, volume 5, pages 79–86. Citeseer.

Koehn, P., Hoang, H., Birch, A., Callison-Burch, C., Federico, M., Bertoldi, N., Cowan, B., Shen, W., Moran, C., Zens, R., Dyer, C., Bojar, O., Constantin, A., and Herbst, E. (2007). Moses: Open source toolkit for statistical machine translation. In *Proceedings of the 45th Annual Meeting of the Association for Computational Linguistics Companion Volume Proceedings of the Demo and Poster Sessions*, pages 177–180, Prague, Czech Republic. Association for Computational Linguistics.

Koehn, P. and Knight, K. (2000). Estimating word translation probabilities from unrelated monolingual corpora using the em algorithm. In *Proceedings of the Seventeenth National Conference on Artificial Intelligence and Twelfth Conference on Innovative Applications of Artificial Intelligence*, page 711–715. AAAI Press.

Koehn, P. and Knight, K. (2002). Learning a translation lexicon from monolingual corpora. In *Proceedings of the ACL-02 Workshop on Unsupervised Lexical Acquisition*, pages 9–16, Philadelphia, Pennsylvania, USA. Association for Computational Linguistics.

Mandelbrot, B. (1953). An informational theory of the statistical structure of language. *Communication theory*, 84:486–502.

Mandelbrot, B. (1961). On the theory of word frequencies and on related markovian models of discourse. *Structure of language and its mathematical aspects*, 12:190–219.

McCarthy, A. D., Wicks, R., Lewis, D., Mueller, A., Wu, W., Adams, O., Nicolai, G., Post, M., and Yarowsky, D. (2020). The Johns Hopkins University Bible corpus: 1600+ tongues for typological exploration. In *Proceedings of the 12th Language Resources and Evaluation Conference*, pages 2884–2892, Marseille, France. European Language Resources Association.

Mikolov, T., Chen, K., Corrado, G., and Dean, J. (2013a). Efficient estimation of word representations in vector space. *arXiv preprint arXiv:1301.3781*.

Mikolov, T., Le, Q. V., and Sutskever, I. (2013b). Exploiting similarities among languages for machine translation. *arXiv preprint arXiv:1309.4168*.

Mohiuddin, T., Bari, M. S., and Joty, S. (2020). Lnmap: Departures from isomorphic assumption in bilingual lexicon induction through non-linear mapping in latent space. *arXiv preprint arXiv:2004.13889*.

Mohiuddin, T. and Joty, S. (2020). Unsupervised word translation with adversarial autoencoder. *Computational Linguistics*, 46(2):257–288.

Patra, B., Moniz, J. R. A., Garg, S., Gormley, M. R., and Neubig, G. (2019). Bilingual lexicon induction with semi-supervision in non-isometric embedding spaces. In *Proceedings of the 57th Annual Meeting of the Association for Computational Linguistics*, pages 184–193, Florence, Italy. Association for Computational Linguistics.

Piantadosi, S. T. (2014). Zipf's word frequency law in natural language: A critical review and future directions. *Psychonomic bulletin & review*, 21(5):1112–1130.

Rapp, R. (1995). Identifying word translations in non-parallel texts. In *Proceedings of the 33rd Annual Meeting on Association for Computational Linguistics*, ACL '95, page 320–322, USA. Association for Computational Linguistics.

Schönemann, P. H. (1966). A generalized solution of the orthogonal procrustes problem. *Psychometrika*, 31(1):1–10.

Shi, H., Zettlemoyer, L., and Wang, S. I. (2021). Bilingual lexicon induction via unsupervised bitext construction and word alignment. *arXiv preprint arXiv:2101.00148*.

Smith, S. L., Turban, D. H. P., Hamblin, S., and Hammerla, N. Y. (2017). Offline bilingual word vectors, orthogonal transformations and the inverted softmax. In *5th International Conference on Learning Representations, ICLR 2017, Toulon, France, April 24-26, 2017, Conference Track Proceedings*. OpenReview.net.

Tiedemann, J. (2012). Parallel data, tools and interfaces in OPUS. In *Proceedings of the Eighth International Conference on Language Resources and Evaluation (LREC'12)*, pages 2214–2218, Istanbul, Turkey. European Language Resources Association (ELRA).

Zipf, G. K. (1935). *The psycho-biology of language*. Houghton-Mifflin.

Zipf, G. K. (1949). *Human behavior and the principle of least effort*. Addison-Wesley Press.

Association for Computational Linguistics
209 N. Eighth Street
Stroudsburg, Pennsylvania 18360

ISBN 978-1-7138-3919-4
9 781713 839194

CURRAN ASSOCIATES INC.
proceedings.com